THE OXFORD HANDBOOK OF

INTERNET
STUDIES

THE OXFORD HANDBOOK OF

INTERNET STUDIES

Edited by

WILLIAM H. DUTTON

OXFORD
UNIVERSITY PRESS

OXFORD
UNIVERSITY PRESS

Great Clarendon Street, Oxford, OX2 6DP,
United Kingdom

Oxford University Press is a department of the University of Oxford.
It furthers the University's objective of excellence in research, scholarship,
and education by publishing worldwide. Oxford is a registered trade mark of
Oxford University Press in the UK and in certain other countries

First published 2013
First published in paperback 2014

Impression: 1

Published in the United States of America by Oxford University Press
198 Madison Avenue, New York, NY 10016, United States of America

British Library Cataloguing in Publication Data
Data available

ISBN 978-0-19-958907-4 (Hbk.)
ISBN 978-0-19-870884-1 (Pbk.)

PREFACE

Internet Studies is one of the most rapidly developing interdisciplinary fields of the early twenty-first century. With the increasing significance of the Internet, and the range of issues surrounding its use and governance, the field is on a course to continue expanding in its range and diversity through the coming decades. Despite the pace of change, it is a time to take stock of this emerging field, examine current approaches to study of the Internet, and reflect on the field's future. This was the key motivation behind this handbook.

The Oxford Handbook of Internet Studies has been designed to provide a valuable resource for students and scholars of Internet Studies. It brings together leading scholarly perspectives on how the Internet has been studied, coupled with views of how Internet Studies should be pursued over the coming years. These perspectives should help strengthen research and identify the big questions for the field to pursue.

However, the promise of Internet Studies extends beyond the field itself. The development of this field has the potential to shape research, policy, and practice across the allied disciplines and not simply within the field of Internet Studies. It is in this sense that one of the key themes of this handbook is the transformative potential of Internet Studies, not only in establishing a new field of study, but also in changing research across the social sciences and related disciplines, as more social research is driven to consider the role of the Internet and related information and communication technologies within their own orbits of inquiry.

In this spirit, a necessary aim of this handbook has been to focus on 'Internet Studies' as an emerging field, rather than provide a collection of studies of the social implications of the Internet. Each author has been asked to provide a synthesis and critical assessment of research in their particular area of expertise. The assembled chapters cover a broad spectrum of topics, including social science perspectives on the technology of the Internet, the role of the Internet in everyday life and work, implications for communication, power, and influence, and the governance and regulation of the Internet. Taken together, the authors represent the increasingly international range of scholarship that is building in the field, as well as the contribution of young, along with more established scholars. You will find that a number of chapters have senior academics working with their graduate students, many of whom are among the new generation of scholars who have focused on the Internet during their graduate training.

Given the enormous scope of the field, I had to be selective in sampling some of the most critical topics and issues confronting research in this area of inquiry. Taken together, the chapters seek to convey the broad scope of Internet Studies, centered primarily within the social sciences. The chapter authors have not hesitated to span disciplinary boundaries, and together they ensure a multidisciplinary perspective on the study of the Internet.

The scope of Internet Studies is potentially vast and is defined broadly for this volume. As editor, I wanted to keep a broad definition of Internet Studies, and the Internet as a network of networks that includes related media, information, and communication technologies. Of course, the book also seeks to address controversies over the scope of Internet Studies and related fields, such as Web Science and New Media Studies, which propose different boundaries for their own and related fields. However, as editor of this handbook, and a long time researcher within the field, I was convinced that a broad definition of Internet Studies should incorporate many aspects of these related areas of research and teaching.

The Internet and its study are moving at such a rapid pace that many colleagues doubted whether any book could provide a definitive definition of the field. You will find in the chapters of this handbook that the pace of technical and social change is an issue that most authors are grappling with. The field cannot wait for change to slow down, however, before we sketch the developing scope and methods of a field. All students of Internet Studies are doing research on moving objects of analysis. It is nevertheless possible to capture this and other aspects of Internet Studies, and provide a meaningful framework for understanding the scope of the field. In the course of doing so, I hope this book provides a key reference on the nature of 'Internet Studies' of value to contemporary students and scholars that will remain a basis for scholars to judge the progress of the field for years into the future.

This is not the only handbook on Internet Studies; in fact, a number have appeared in the years preceding this collection. In my view, this is one of many signs that this field is maturing and beginning to reflect on its history and future. I hope this book complements other handbooks and helps continue the progress of one of the most vibrant and significant fields of new scholarship in the twenty-first century.

William H. Dutton
Oxford, England
November 2012

ACKNOWLEDGMENTS

I am grateful to many colleagues for their support, advice, and comments on particular chapters and the structure of the book as a whole.

As Professor of Internet Studies at the Oxford Internet Institute (OII), and its founding Director from 2002 to 2011, I benefited greatly from the insights of my students and colleagues, all of whom are pushing forward on the leading edge of Internet Studies. Whether in our Summer Doctoral Programme or Advisory Board meetings, my colleagues have engaged me in a continuing dialogue about the nature and future of Internet Studies, and what we have called the social science of the Internet. OII faculty, students, advisors, and visitors could not know how much I have valued and learned from our day-to-day conversations and debates, and our courses, seminars, and many series of lectures. This extends beyond our department, to my colleagues from other departments and the many colleges across this collegiate University of Oxford. A tremendous virtue of Oxford is an academic culture that resists specialization and nurtures the inter-disciplinary exchange that informs this book. It has been the enthusiasm around the social issues of the Internet, from an interdisciplinary range of Oxford colleagues that has continued to boost my commitment to better understanding the history and future of this field.

As editor, I was fortunate to gain the assistance of a strong international advisory board, which included: Christine Borgman, Presidential Chair in Information Studies, University of California, Los Angeles; Jay Blumler, Emeritus Professor, University of Leeds; Manuel Castells, Wallis Annenberg Chair USC and Open University of Catalonia; Michael Cusamano, Sloan Management Review Distinguished Professor of Management, MIT; Dame Wendy Hall, Professor of Computer Science, Southampton; Guo Liang, Chinese Academy of Social Sciences; Sonia Livingstone, Media and Communications, London School of Economics; Thierry Vedel, The Centre for Political Research at Sciences Po, National Centre for Scientific Research, France; Barry Wellman, Director of Netlab, University of Toronto; and Dorothy Zinberg, Belfer Center for Science and International Affairs, and Program for Science, Technology, and Public Policy, Kennedy School of Government, Harvard.

In addition to members of the Advisory Board, a number of colleagues reviewed and advised me on selected chapters. These colleagues included Professor Charles Ess, University of Aarhus; Dr Mark Graham, University of Oxford; Professor Barrie Gunter, University of Leicester; Professor Steve Jones, University of Illinois, Chicago Circle; Professor David Tewksbury, University of Illinois, Urbana-Champaign; Professor David

Waterman, University of Indiana; Professor Monica Whitty, University of Leicester; and Professor Jonathan Zittrain, Harvard University.

I also gained much from my colleagues in Internet Studies across the globe who have been shaping other volumes on the field, and some of whom worked with me to develop a series of workshops on Internet Studies as one means to help me better understand this rapidly developing field. Charles Ess collaborated with me in setting up a workshop at the University of Aarhus, Denmark, which led to a special issue of *New Media and Society*. This was followed by a workshop focused on consumers and the Internet, at the Interdisciplinary Internet Institute (IN3) at the Open University of Catalonia, which was organized by Inma Rodriguez-Ardura, an Associate Professor of Marketing at IN3 and a Visiting Fellow at the Oxford Internet Institute. Finally, Brian Loader at the University of York, Barry Wellman, at the University of Toronto, and Victoria Nash, at the OII worked with me in organizing 'Ten Years in Internet Time', a symposium held in Oxford in September 2011, which focused on the dynamics of Internet Studies. This symposium led to a special issue of *Information, Communication & Society*. I learned a great deal from both workshops and symposium and their follow-up.

I am, of course, most indebted to the authors who contributed to this volume, not only by writing their respective chapters, but also in reviewing selected chapters, and advising me on issues of scope and coverage. All were exceptionally receptive to guidance on the aims of the handbook and how their chapters could best contribute. I have never worked with such a uniformly strong set of academics.

Robert Bullard provided valuable copy-editing in preparing chapters for the publisher, and indirectly, Malcolm Peltu, my friend and long time editorial consultant, taught me a great deal about editing that advanced my work on this book.

Finally, I wish to thank my editor at Oxford University Press, David Musson, who has been encouraging and supportive of this project from the beginning. His judgment was always valued and contributed much to the completion of this work. His team at Oxford University Press, including Emma Lambert and Rachel Platt, were professional, talented, and responsive at every stage of the book's production.

Contents

List of Figures		xii
List of Tables		xiii
List of Abbreviations		xiv
Notes on the Contributors		xviii

1. Internet Studies: The Foundations of a Transformative Field   1
   WILLIAM H. DUTTON

PART I PERSPECTIVES ON THE INTERNET AND WEB AS OBJECTS OF STUDY

2. The Prehistory of the Internet and its Traces in the Present: Implications for Defining the Field   27
   MARTIN C. J. ELTON AND JOHN CAREY

3. Web Science   48
   KIERON O'HARA AND WENDY HALL

4. Society on the Web   69
   MIKE THELWALL

5. The Internet as Infrastructure   86
   CHRISTIAN SANDVIG

PART II LIVING IN A NETWORK SOCIETY

6. Network Societies and Internet Studies: Rethinking Time, Space, and Class   109
   JACK LINCHUAN QIU

7. Digital Inequality   129
   ESZTER HARGITTAI AND YULI PATRICK HSIEH

8. Sociality through Social Network Sites   151
   NICOLE B. ELLISON AND DANAH M. BOYD

9. The Study of Online Relationships and Dating   173
   BARRIE GUNTER

10. Games, Online and Off   195
    DMITRI WILLIAMS AND ADAM S. KAHN

11. Cross-National Comparative Perspectives from the
    World Internet Project   216
    GUSTAVO CARDOSO, GUO LIANG, AND TIAGO LAPA

PART III CREATING AND WORKING IN A GLOBAL NETWORK ECONOMY

12. New Businesses and New Business Models   239
    MICHAEL A. CUSUMANO AND ANDREAS GOELDI

13. Trust in Commercial and Personal Transactions in the Digital Age   262
    REGINA CONNOLLY

14. Government and the Internet: Evolving Technologies, Enduring
    Research Themes   283
    PAUL HENMAN

15. Digital Transformations of Scholarship and Knowledge   307
    ERIC T. MEYER AND RALPH SCHROEDER

16. Studies of the Internet in Learning and Education: Broadening
    the Disciplinary Landscape of Research   328
    CHRIS DAVIES AND REBECCA EYNON

PART IV COMMUNICATION, POWER, AND INFLUENCE IN A CONVERGING MEDIA WORLD

17. Theoretical Perspectives in the Study of Communication
    and the Internet   353
    RONALD E. RICE AND RYAN P. FULLER

18. Tradition and Transformation in Online News Production and
    Consumption   378
    EUGENIA MITCHELSTEIN AND PABLO J. BOCZKOWSKI

19. The Internet in Campaigns and Elections   401
    DARREN G. LILLEKER AND THIERRY VEDEL

20. The Internet and Democracy 421
HELEN MARGETTS

PART V GOVERNING AND REGULATING THE INTERNET

21. Analyzing Freedom of Expression Online: Theoretical, Empirical, and Normative Contributions 441
VICTORIA NASH

22. Cultural, Legal, Technical, and Economic Perspectives on Copyright Online: The Case of the Music Industry 464
MATTHEW DAVID

23. Privacy and Surveillance: The Multidisciplinary Literature on the Capture, Use, and Disclosure of Personal Information in Cyberspace 486
COLIN J. BENNETT AND CHRISTOPHER PARSONS

24. Digital Infrastructures, Economies, and Public Policies: Contending Rationales and Outcome Assessment Strategies 509
ROBIN MANSELL AND W. EDWARD STEINMUELLER

25. The Internet and Development: A Critical Perspective 531
TIM UNWIN

26. The Emerging Field of Internet Governance 555
LAURA DENARDIS

Index 577

LIST OF FIGURES

4.1 Power law graph of links found by Yahoo! to Live Spaces Blogs
     indexed in Bing (logarithmic scales)   73

4.2 The percentage of blogs mentioning *Japan*, or *Japan* and *nuclear*,
     or *Japan* and *Tsunami* during six months up to the start of April, 2011   80

10.1 Consoles and computers come to the home, 1997–2000
     (% penetration)   199

14.1 UN E-government readiness rankings, 2001–2010   288

14.2 Percentage of availability of government services online and percentage
     of users of online government services in EU(15), 2002–2009   293

17.1 MDS and cluster analysis of inter-relations among the 27 themes   368

25.1 Internet users per 100 inhabitants, 2000–2010   532

25.2 A spectrum of research and practice at the interface between
     development and ICTs   537

LIST OF TABLES

1.1	The multiple foci of Internet Studies	3
6.1	Number of Internet users in world regions, 2000 and 2010	117
6.2	Number of Internet users in top countries, by ranking in 2010 and 2000	118
6.3	The diffusion of mobile phones in world regions, 2000 and 2008	119
6.4	The diffusion of mobile phones in countries by income levels, 2000 and 2010	119
9.1	Demographic profiles of online daters	177
14.1	Top 10 countries by e-Government development	287
17.1	Frequency of Internet, World Wide Web, and Web 2.0 terms in titles and abstracts of social science articles, 2000–2010	354
21.1	Examples illustrating an ecology of freedom of expression on the Internet	456
26.1	Key topics of Internet governance	558

List of Abbreviations

....

A&HCI	Arts and Humanities Citation Index
AfriNIC	African Network Information Centre
AoIR	Association of Internet Researchers
APC	Association for Progressive Communications
API	Application programming interface
APNIC	Asia Pacific Network Information Centre
ARIN	American Registry for Internet Numbers
ARPANET	Advanced Research Projects Agency Network
AS	Autonomous system
ASN	Autonomous System Numbers
BBS	Bulletin board systems
BGP	Border gateway protocol
BRIC	Brazil, Russia, India, and China
ccTLD	Country code top-level domains
CENS	Centre for Embedded Network Sensing
CERN	European Organization for Nuclear Research
CERT	Computer Emergency Response Team
CIR	Critical Internet Resources
CMC	Computer-mediated communication
CNNIC	China Internet Network Information Centre
CPS	Current population survey
CS	Computer Science
CSCW	Computer-supported cooperative work
DARPA	Defense Advanced Research Projects Agency
DBMS	Database management system
DDoS	Distributed denial of service attacks
DE-CIX	Deutscher Commercial Internet Exchange
DMCA	Digital Millenium Copyright Act
DNS	Domain name system
DPI	Deep packet inspection
DRM	Digital rights management
ECHR	European Convention on Human Rights
e-GIFS	Electronic government interoperability frameworks
EMISARI	Emergency Management Information Systems and Reference Index

EoG	Ecology of games
FACT	Federation against Copyright Theft
FAO	Food and Agriculture Organization
FCC	Federal Communications Commission
FIPs	Fair information principles
fMRI	Functional magnetic resonance imaging
FTP	File Transfer Protocol
GAID	Global Alliance for ICTs and Development
GAIN	Genetic Association Information Network
GigaNet	Global Internet Governance Academic Network
GPT	General purpose technology
GUI	Geographical user interface
GWAS	Genome-Wide Association Studies
HTML	Hypertext Markup Language
HTTP	Hypertext Transfer Protocol
IANA	Internet Assigned Numbers Authority
ICA	International Communication Association
ICANN	Internet Corporation for Assigned Names and Numbers
ICT	Information and communications technology
ICT4D	Information and communication technologies for development
IDEA	Institute for Democracy and Electoral Assistance
IETF	Internet Engineering Taskforce
IGF	Internet Governanace Forum
IMPACT	International Multilateral Partnership against Cyberthreats
IN3	Interdisciplinary Internet Institute
IP	Internet protocol
IPR	Intellectual property rights
ISDN	Integrated Services Digital Networks
ISO	International Organization for Standardization
ISP	Internet Service Provider
IT	Information technology
ITU	International Telecommunication Union
IWB	Interactive whiteboard
IWF	Internet Watch Foundation
IXPs	Internet Exchange Points
JISC	Joint Information Systems Committee
JPEG	Joint Photographic Experts Group
LACNIC	Latin America and Caribbean Network Information Centre
LAN	Local area networks
LHC	Large Hadron Collider
LP	Learning platform

LTS	Large technical systems
LTT	Libyan Telecom and Technology
MDG	Millenium Development Goals
MDS	Multidimensional scaling
MENA	Middle East and North Africa
MMO RPG	Massively multiplayer online role-playing games
MOO	Multi-user object-oriented technology
MPAA	Motion Picture Association of America
MUD	Multi-user dungeon
NCSA	National Center for Supercomputer Applications
NGA	Next generation access
NGO	Non-governmental organization
NIE	Newly industrialized economies
NII	National Information Infrastructure
NSA	National Security Agency
NSF	National Science Foundation
NTIA	National Telecommunication and Information Administration
OECD	Organization for Economic Co-operation and Development
OER	Open educational resource
OII	Oxford Internet Institute
PET	Privacy enhancing technologies
PII	Personally identifiable information
PIU	Problematic Internet use
R&D	Research and development
RBOC	Regional Bell Operating Companies
RDF	Resource Description Framework
RIM	Research in Motion
RIPE NCC	Regional Internet Registry Network Coordination Centre
RIR	Regional Internet Registries
SES	Socioeconomic status
SIDE	Social identity model of deindividuation effects
SMTP	Simple Mail Transfer Protocol
SND	Swedish National Data Service
SNS	Social networking sites
SPLASH	Structure of Populations, Levels of Abundance, and Status of Humpbacks
SaaS	Software as a Service
SSCI	Social Sciences Citation Index
SSL	Secure Socket Layers
STS	Science and Technology Studies
SwiNG	Swiss National Grid Association
TCP	Transmission Control Protocol
TLD	Top-level domains

TPB	The Pirate Bay
TRIPS	Trade-Related Intellectual Property and Services Treaty
U&G	Uses and gratification
UCC	User created content
UDRP	Uniform Domain Name Dispute Resolution Policy
UNESCO	United Nations Education, Scientific and Cultural Organization
URI	Uniform Resource Identifier
VoIP	Voice over Internet Protocol
VOSON	Virtual Observatory for the Study of Online Networks
VPNS	Virtual property network servers
W3C	World Wide Web Consortium
WAP	Wireless Application Protocol
WELL	Whole Earth 'Lectronic Link
WGIG	Working Group on Internet Governance
WIP	World Internet Project
WIPO	World Intellectual Property Organization
WSIS	World Summit on the Information Society
XML	Extensible Markup Language

Notes on the Contributors

Colin J. Bennett researches on privacy and surveillance and teaches in the Department of Political Science at the University of Victoria, Victoria, British Columbia, Canada.

Pablo J. Boczkowski is a Professor and Director of the Program in Media, Technology and Society in the Department of Communication Studies, Northwestern University, Evanston, Illinois, USA.

Danah M. Boyd is Senior Researcher at Microsoft Research, a Research Assistant Professor in Media, Culture, and Communication at New York University, a Fellow at Harvard's Berkman Center for Internet and Society, and an Adjunct Associate Professor at the University of New South Wales, Australia.

Gustavo Cardoso is an associate researcher at CIES, ISCTE-IUL, and Professor of Technology and Society at ISCTE—Lisbon University Institute, Lisbon, Portugal.

John Carey is Professor of Communications and Media Management in the Fordham University Schools of Business, New York City, USA.

Regina Connolly is a Senior Lecturer at Dublin City University, Ireland, and Editor-in-Chief of the *Journal of Internet Commerce*.

Michael A. Cusumano is the Sloan Management Review Distinguished Professor of Management at the Massachusetts Institute of Technology's Sloan School of Management, Massachusetts, USA, with a joint appointment in the MIT Engineering Systems Division.

Matthew David is a Senior Lecturer in Sociology at Durham University's School of Applied Social Sciences, Durham, UK.

Chris Davies leads the Learning and New Technologies Research Group at the Department of Education, and is Vice President of Kellogg College, University of Oxford, UK.

Laura DeNardis is an Associate Professor in the School of Communication at American University and a Fellow of the Yale Information Society Project at Yale Law School, USA.

William H. Dutton is the Quello Professor in the Department of Media and Information at Michigan State University, where he is Director of the Quello Center. He was founding Director of the Oxford Internet Institute, University of Oxford, UK, and an Emeritus Professor at the University of Southern California, USA.

Nicole B. Ellison is an Associate Professor in the School of Information at the University of Michigan, USA.

Martin C. J. Elton, was a Professor and Chair in the Interactive Telecommunications Program at New York University's Tisch School of the Arts, and Director of the Columbia Institute for Tele-Information while a Visiting Professor of Business at the Columbia Business School, New York City, USA.

Rebecca Eynon is a Research Fellow in the Oxford Internet Institute, and Lecturer in the Department of Education at the University of Oxford, UK.

Ryan P. Fuller is an Assistant Professor in the Department of Speech Communication, University of Arkansas at Little Rock, USA, and a researcher for the Carsey-Wolf Center.

Andreas Goeldi is the Chief Technology Officer of online video marketing company Pixability Inc. in Cambridge, MA. He co-founded several successful start-ups in Internet technology and online marketing.

Barrie Gunter is Professor of Mass Communication, Department of Media and Communication, University of Leicester, UK.

Wendy Hall, DBE, FRS, FREng is Professor of Computer Science at the University of Southampton, UK, and Dean of the Faculty of Physical and Applied Sciences. She was Head of the School of Electronics and Computer Science from 2002–07.

Eszter Hargittai is the Delaney Family Professor of Communication Studies in the Department of Communication Studies, Northwestern University, Illinois, USA.

Paul Henman is Associate Professor of Social Policy, University of Queensland, Australia.

Yuli Patrick Hsieh is a Doctoral Candidate in the Media, Technology & Society Program, Department of Communication Studies, Northwestern University, Illinois, USA.

Adam S. Kahn is a doctoral candidate at the Annenberg School for Communication and Journalism at the University of Southern California, USA.

Tiago Lapa is a researcher at CIES, ISCTE-IUL, Portugal. He has an Mphil degree from Cambridge University, UK, and is a doctoral candidate in the School of Sociology and Public Policy, ISCTE-Lisbon University Institute.

Guo Liang is an Associate Professor in the Institute of Philosophy, and Director of the China Internet Project, Chinese Academy of Social Sciences, Beijing, China.

Darren G. Lilleker is Senior Lecturer and Director of the Centre for Public Communication Research at Bournemouth University, UK.

Robin Mansell is Professor of New Media and the Internet in the Department of Media and Communications of the London School of Economics and Political Science, London, UK.

Helen Margetts is Director, Oxford Internet Institute, Professor of Society and the Internet, and Professorial Fellow of Mansfield College, all at the University of Oxford, UK.

Eric T. Meyer is a Research Fellow in the Oxford Internet Institute, University of Oxford, UK.

Eugenia Mitchelstein is a doctoral candidate in the Department of Communication Studies, Northwestern University, Evanston, Illinois, USA.

Victoria Nash is Deputy Director and Policy and Research Fellow at the Oxford Internet Institute, University of Oxford, UK.

Kieron O'Hara is a senior research fellow in Electronics and Computer Science at the University of Southampton, UK.

Christopher Parsons is a Postdoctoral Fellow at the Citizen Lab, Munk School of Global Affairs at the University of Toronto, Canada.

Jack Linchuan Qiu is an Associate Professor in the School of Journalism and Communication, the Chinese University of Hong Kong.

Ronald E. Rice is the Arthur N. Rupe Professor in the Social Effects of Mass Communication, and Co-Director of the Carsey-Wolf Center, in the Department of Communication at the University of California, Santa Barbara, California, USA.

Christian Sandvig is an Associate Professor in the Department of Communication Studies at the University of Michigan, USA.

Ralph Schroeder is Professor and Director of Research in the Oxford Internet Institute, University of Oxford, UK.

W. Edward Steinmueller is Professor at SPRU—Science and Technology Policy Research, University of Sussex, UK.

Mike Thelwall is Professor of Information Science, School of Technology, University of Wolverhampton, UK.

Tim Unwin is Chief Executive Officer of the Commonwealth Telecommunications Organisation, and Emeritus Professor of Geography and UNESCO Chair in ICT4D at Royal Holloway, University of London, Surrey, UK.

Thierry Vedel is a senior researcher of the Center for Political Research at Sciences Po (CEVIPOF), Sciences Polytechnic, Paris, France.

Dmitri Williams is an Associate Professor at the Annenberg School for Communication and Journalism, University of Southern California, USA, where he is a part of the Annenberg Program on Online Communities (APOC).

CHAPTER 1

··

INTERNET STUDIES: THE FOUNDATIONS OF A TRANSFORMATIVE FIELD

··

WILLIAM H. DUTTON

THE RISE OF INTERNET STUDIES
AS A NEW FIELD OF GLOBAL SIGNIFICANCE

ACROSS the world, people from almost all sectors of society are using the Internet for a variety of purposes, from everyday life and work to local, strategic, and global issues.[1] The diverse sets of practices, beliefs, and attitudes evolving around these uses have brought to prominence a mounting number of key related issues, such as the future of privacy, freedom of expression, the quality of the news and entertainment, and the nature and distribution of employment. This has driven the growth of "Internet Studies" as an important new field of research and teaching.

Internet Studies draws on multiple disciplines covering political, economic, cultural, psychological, and other social factors as well as computer studies, information sciences, and engineering. The emergence of this field has given a focus to theory and research on questions concerning social and cultural implications of the widespread diffusion and diverse uses of the Internet, the Web, and related information and communication technologies (ICTs). The field has grown in step with the rising significance of the technology for its expanding global user community. It has offered a framework within which academics from the many related disciplines have joined with interdisciplinary scholars to form growing communities of researchers. These are building new foundations and reshaping some traditional disciplines to address the rapidly changing dynamics of networked societies and the institutions and individuals within them.

---

[1] The Internet had over 2 billion users, nearly one-third of the world's population, by 2012 according to <http://www.internetworldstats.com/stats.htm>. Accessed February 8, 2012.

Meta-research on academic publications provides strong indicators of this burgeoning field. For instance, Tai-Quan (Winson) Peng and others (2011) found that academic output on the Internet in refereed journals increased dramatically over the first decade of the twenty-first century.[2] In this period, Internet-related studies became more prominent than work on such topics as culture, the economy, politics, or globalization, albeit less prominent than research on the environment or society.

However, the field is so diverse that it is difficult to define its scope. This is exacerbated by the pace of change in research, which mirrors the rapidly evolving technologies of the Internet. It is reasonably concentrated around key topics, such as societal implications, but more specializations are continuously being formed, such as around social networking (Peng et al. 2011; Rice and Fuller Chapter 17).

The increasing status of this new field is reflected also in the emergence of efforts to pull the field together and to define its scope, such as through the development of a number of compendiums and handbooks (Hunsinger et al. 2010; and Consalvo and Ess 2011), including the present volume, and an increasing number of academic symposia and special issues of journals,[3] as well as a growing number of research centers and programs.[4] This handbook builds on these foundations to provide authoritative perspectives on key areas of Internet Studies and to offer direction on the further development of research areas within this rapidly advancing field.

The broad scope of the field

Internet researchers draw from a wide array of theoretical and empirical perspectives to explore the ways in which people have shaped the Internet and its growing array of social implications in a wide variety of contexts. Studies range across three distinguishable but closely interrelated objects of study—the central focus of what research seeks to explain. These can be loosely categorized as:

- technology, including its design and development;
- use, including patterns of use and non-use across different kinds of users and producers in various contexts; and
- policy, referring to law and policy in such areas as privacy and freedom of expression that shape the design or use of the Internet, as well as emerging institutions and processes of Internet governance (Table 1.1).

---

[2] Peng et al. (2011) based their statistical analysis on the use on selected words, such as Internet and Web, in the abstracts or keywords of scholarly journal articles published in English from 2000 to 2009 listed in the Social Science Citation Index (SSCI) and Arts & Humanities Citation Index of ISI Web of Science.

[3] As this chapter was being written, two journals key to the field (*Information Communication and Society* and *New Media and Society*) have forthcoming issues devoted to Internet Studies. An early symposium of *The Information Society*, 21 (2005) provides a discussion of the scope and methods of this field.

[4] Hunsinger et al. (2010: 549–604) have compiled a useful list.

Table 1.1 The multiple foci of Internet Studies

	Technology	Use (in Context)	Policy
Who?	Who shapes the design and implementation of the Internet?	Who uses (does not use) the Internet and in what ways?	Who shapes law and policy of relevance to the Internet?
Why?	What goals and objectives are driving choices in design and development?	Why do individuals, groups, communities, regions (not) use the Internet in particular ways in specific contexts?	What are the goals and objectives shaping relevant legal and policy choices governing the Internet?
With what implications for whom?	Do technical designs bias patterns of use and impacts?	Do patterns of use support different political, economic, or social aims or groups?	How is the evolving ecology of law and policy shaping the design and use of the Internet?

With respect to each category, Internet Studies raises three main types of question:[5]

- Who shapes the Internet?
- Why? What structures, cultures, aims, and objectives are shaping choices?
- With what implications for whom?

Table 1.1 provides a more systematic framework relating objects of Internet Studies to these general issues in order to help capture the broad scope of the field.[6]

Technology as an object of study

The design and implementation of the underlying technology of the Internet, including the personal computer, Web, browsers, wireless networks, social networking sites, applications, and infrastructure, is a common object of study. The promise tied to the Internet as a technical innovation, which would have systematic implications for who gets access to what information, people, services, and technologies, has been one of the enduring aspects of this field. This "futures" dimension of the literature can engender much hyperbole, but also inform expectations about the implications of technological change. Visionary forecasts were prominent even before the Internet was launched, and they continue with each new stage of the Internet's design and diffusion, including developing visions of an "Internet of things," "big data," and other emerging technologies.

---

[5] These are Lasswellian questions that mimic Harold Lasswell's (1971: 84) famous definition of the field of communication as the study of "Who Says What In Which Channel To Whom With What Effect?"

[6] Maria Bakardjieva (2011: 61) links these different research areas to specific epistemologies. However, it is arguable that each of these questions can be approached from multiple approaches to research.

Students of Internet Studies most often assume that the Internet is distinctly different from earlier technologies for communication and information access and that the technology matters, making a difference that merits particular attention in theory and research (Jones 1998; Schroeder 2007). This is most often tied to the Internet and Web-enabling networks that move beyond one-to-many broadcasting, or person-to-person telecommunication, to enable users and producers to create these and other networks of access to resources, such as many-to-one and many-to-many.

For example, Ithiel de Sola Pool (1983) conceived of computer-mediated communication as inherently a "technology of freedom." Jonathan Zittrain (2008) argued that appliances, such as tablets, would undermine the "generativity" of the PC-based Internet. These expectations of technical designs making a difference do not imply a blind acceptance of a technologically deterministic stance within the field, although theoretical perspectives that emphasize technological rather than social aspects often provide baselines for researchers who challenge assumptions about the Internet and its societal implications. Social researchers generally reject technologically deterministic notions, questioning rational forecasts of impacts that are based on extrapolations tied to features of the technology, such as its global reach or democratic implications.

The central challenge of Internet Studies research revolves around the discovery of concepts, models, theories, and related frameworks that provide a more empirically valid understanding of the factors shaping the Internet and its societal implications. These include frameworks based on the social shaping of technology—such as social informatics, the ecology of games, and network theories, but also science and technology studies, such as within the social construction of technology, actor network theory, and infrastructure studies, as well as broad conceptions of the cultures of the Internet (Castells 2001: 36–61), such as the "hacker ethic" (Himanen 2001)—as one illustration of a growing community of scholars interested in cultural attitudes about technology,[7] and the rise of computerization, open source, and other social movements shaping the Internet (Elliott and Kraemer 2008).

Use as the object of study

Another common object of study is use, focusing on the patterns of (non)use across different ICTs, social, and institutional contexts, such as households, schools, businesses, and cyber cafes, as well as on the move (Howard and Jones 2004). Much of the empirical work on the Internet does not assume that features of the technology will provide an adequate basis for understanding how it will be used and with what effect. On the contrary, studies of Internet use most often assume that users will employ—and tend to "domesticate"—technologies in some unanticipated and unintended ways that could have major societal consequences (Haddon 2006). However, these patterns of use could

---

[7] A series of conferences have been organized by scholars associated with "Cultural Attitudes towards Technology and Communication" (CATaC).

vary across different institutional contexts and across different local and national legal and cultural contexts. This book is structured around three general categories of use contexts: everyday life, work, and use in a converging media world.

Use in everyday life: living in a network society

Since the household has been one of the primary social contexts of use, a great deal of empirical research focuses on how individuals and households use the Internet, much in the tradition of mass media research around newspapers, radio, and television. A number of key empirical studies in the field are based on studies of the Internet in everyday life (Wellman and Haythornthwaite 2002; Rainie and Wellman 2012), including work on the World Internet Project that also takes a comparative, cross-national perspective (Cardoso et al. Chapter 11). And use studies can focus on many different technologies, from email to blogs to social networking sites. Unlike the study of mass media, the study of Internet users also considers them not only as consumers, but also as producers of content. The potential for users to strategically "reconfigure access" to information, people, services, and technologies, and to produce as well as consume content are the defining aspects of the Internet and related ICTs (Dutton 1999, 2005).

Studies of patterns of access and use of the Internet and related ICTs often extend to study of skills (Hargittai and Hsieh Chapter 7) and the values, attitudes, and beliefs of users, such as acceptance and trust (Connolly Chapter 13). Social issues that arise in this context include (in)equality in access, creating digital divides to infrastructures and information resources, as well as implications for social relationships, community, participation, identity, and popular culture. Users can choose to open themselves to a greater plurality of messages, or create an "echo chamber" to reinforce their preconceived views (Sunstein 2009). They can create content, be more passive consumers, or create in a diverse range of activities that fall short of the full potential that the Internet enables (van Dijck 2009). Competing expectations over such patterns of choices, constraints on these choices, and their social implications, are among the big questions driving Internet Studies.

Use in work and organizations: creating and working in a network economy

Another varied range of social contexts includes the many activities and institutions involved with creating and working in a network economy. This would include studies of the Internet in the workplace, and in business and commerce, including implications for employment, online commerce, and new business models, but also government, including public services, productivity, responsiveness, e-regulation, and structural change tied to governments on the Web. Other more specific institutional contexts include studies of the Internet in science and research, and in education and learning more generally, such as related to informal and formal patterns of learning. Many empirical studies of the implications of computing and telecommunications began in organizational settings, where computing was most intensively applied before the personal computer, but researchers focused on work, and the management and cultures of organizations have been quick to reorient research around the Internet and such related issues as e-commerce and new business models that extend beyond the formal boundaries of the organization (Sproull et al. 2007).

Media use: (dis)empowering communication and influence

Across households and other institutional settings, such as in politics and society at large, the Internet raises issues over communication, power, and influence in a converging media world. This involves processes explicitly tied to communication and the media, including the press, online news, and new media, but also communication in other arenas, such as campaigns and elections, including remote Internet voting, use by parties and candidates, with implications for such issues as turnout in elections and the effectiveness of campaign messages. Likewise, democracy and democratic processes are an issue within government, including the use of networks by institutions, such as for online consultation, but also the Internet's use by networked individuals, such as in grassroots movements or in the potential for more democratic social accountability across many institutional arenas (Dutton 2009).

Policy as the object of study

A third major object of study has been on law and policies governing the design and use of the Internet, as well as the institutions and processes shaping Internet governance. One of the most influential works in this area was Lawrence Lessig's (1999) discussion of how copyright law has shaped code, the design of technologies, in ways that further enforce the law. That said, the area of copyright has illuminated the many ways in which neither law nor technology necessarily determine user behavior (David Chapter 22).

Early in the study of the Internet, policy research was not as prominent as it has become, in part because the future of the Internet was uncertain. Early work was more focused on policy around national and global infrastructures aimed at stimulating development (Gore 1991; Kubicek et al. 1997). As the Internet has become far more central to everyday life and work, and perceived to be critical in a variety of major events, such as the Arab Springs, the study of Internet policy and regulation has become increasingly in focus, such as on issues of freedom of expression and privacy, but also on "Internet governance," examining the institutions and processes of governing key attributes of the Internet.

Outside the field of Internet Studies and society

Many people interested in aspects of the Internet are not necessarily engaged in Internet Studies within the social and behavioral sciences as defined by this handbook. For example, a computer scientist might primarily be interested in the design of particular technical aspects of this network of networks, such as the design of an integrated electronic circuit (chip), without an academic interest in how this technical artifact has been influenced by an array of social and economic considerations, or how it might influence larger technical systems and their societal implications. Also, social scientists from many disciplinary perspectives might feel that those matters of interest to them can be explained by factors other than the Internet or technology more broadly, such as through their particular social, economic, or political perspective. These are entirely legitimate disciplinary positions that help to define the boundaries, identity, and future of the field.

The scope of this handbook

These are some of the most central areas of Internet Studies in the social and behavioral sciences, and they have provided the basis for organizing the contributions to this handbook. Most closely related to the present volume are two previous handbooks devoted to Internet research (Hunsinger et al. 2010) or Internet Studies (Consalvo and Ess 2011). The Oxford Handbook seeks to complement and update these volumes, most of whose constituting chapters are centrally concerned with presenting research on a wide range of specific topics by leading Internet researchers. The Oxford Handbook's authors have focused on how research in their particular area of interest has been pursued, and have provided direction for future research. They deal primarily with Internet Studies rather than the findings of research on the Internet, although key findings and themes of the research are an inescapable added value of this volume.

This handbook does not focus on work largely outside the social and behavioral sciences, such as work purely within the computer sciences and engineering or the health and medical sciences. Moreover, this book does not give equal weight to the full range of Internet-related studies, in order to avoid duplication with other published work. For instance, there have been collections on closely related topics, such as new media (Lievrouw and Livingstone 2006), psychological aspects of the Internet (Joinson et al. 2007), on information and communication technologies (Mansell et al. 2007), and on the Internet and politics (Chadwick and Howard 2008), all of which are topics covered in this handbook to a lesser extent than they might otherwise merit. Likewise, other collections have focused on online research methods (Jones 1999; Fielding et al. 2008) and digital research innovations (Dutton and Jeffreys 2010), permitting this handbook to be primarily tied to studies of the Internet and its implications.

Competing perspectives on the field

Over the years, Internet Studies has been variously referred to as a fashionable topic, a multidisciplinary field, subfield of other disciplines, or a discipline in its own right (McLemee 2001; Baym 2005). Talk of the field as a fad has virtually disappeared with the Internet's global diffusion. Likewise, discussion within the Internet research community generally avoids any claim that Internet Studies is a discipline, in favor of defining it as an "interdisciplinary" or "multidisciplinary" field, particularly in light of its fragmentation across so many existing departments, disciplines, and newly formed journals (Baym 2005).

Interdisciplinary entails a recognition that research is focused most often on addressing problems, such as understanding the social implications of the Internet, like narrowing digital divides, rather than advancing a particular theory. Studies often draw from more than one disciplinary perspective, and are often anchored in multidisciplinary teams. In fact, many problems in Internet Studies require an interdisciplinary approach. For example, it would be difficult to study anonymity online without a strong background in technology as well as in the social sciences, law, and policy. Even here, some prefer to speak of "multidisciplinary" research to emphasize the degree to which studies are anchored in a variety of theories and research methods in particular disciplines, although these inter- and multidisciplinary distinctions are seldom fundamental, and the terms are used almost interchangeably.

There are other developing areas of consensus within this field, such as a move away from any strict duality between the old and the new or the real and the virtual (Consalvo and Ess 2011: 4; Woolgar 2002), as well as an evolving set of major questions, such as defined in Table 1.1 (Consalvo and Ess 2011: 4–5). Likewise, there is a general agreement that research should question taken-for-granted assumptions about the Internet and its societal implications.

Nevertheless, a lack of consensus characterizes the field on a number of issues (Schrum 2005). It is not due to major cleavages within the field, as much as to the youth, rapid development, and diversity of Internet Studies. One of the more pivotal differences of perspective surrounds the very definition of the Internet. The next section briefly discusses this issue and how its resolution is related to how narrowly or broadly people draw the history of the Internet as well as the boundaries of the field.

Defining the Internet—narrow and broad conceptions

As an interdisciplinary field, Internet Studies does not have an orthodox approach. Moreover, the culture of this developing field is highly individualistic, as reflected in its evolution as a horizontal network of individuals working across geographical and institutional boundaries, as opposed to a more highly ordered institutional structure, such as a Royal Society. For example, ambiguity surrounds many terms across Internet studies, with scholars offering various specific definitions.

This includes the very definition of the "Internet," as well as rather trivial debates like whether or not to have an initial capital letter for "Internet" and "Web." You will see variation within this volume on how narrowly or broadly the Internet and technology are defined. Some authors, such as Tim Unwin (Chapter 25) endorse a narrow, technical definition of the Internet as a specific set of artifacts, protocols, or standards that enable computers to be networked—Transmission Control Protocol/Internet

Protocol (TCP/IP),[8] while others, such as Christian Sandvig (Chapter 5) endorse a growing ecology of related technical and social innovations within their conception of the Internet.

A focus on the underlying technical infrastructure is correct up to a point, as these protocols have been central to the development of the Internet. However, from a social scientific perspective, they can be too limited to define the Internet. At the broadest level, even in the earliest years of the ARPANET, the Internet was conceptualized as a "network of networks" (Craven and Wellman 1973). This broad definition captures the central role of this technology in linking networks of computers in ways that they can share resources, such as information. Also it is compatible with broadly accepted definitions of technology as encompassing not just specific technological artifacts, but also the people who use and are affected by it, as well as other equipment, techniques, and skills. All these elements are critical resources in this network of networks. Moreover, it is a definition that is open to the Internet's constant state of being reinvented through a cascading array of innovations in technologies and uses.

The Internet's history

There is much debate about the history of the Internet in terms of the relative contributions of different innovations, individuals, groups, organizations, and technical advances (Abbate 1999; Castells 2001; Leiner et al. 2005). This history is likely to grow in importance and become more textured as the Internet becomes an even more central resource. No serious student of the Internet's history would subscribe to the notion of a single inventor jump-starting a predetermined trajectory of development. The reality is far more complex, as the Internet emerged through the interaction of multiple advances across different sectors, made by a variety of individuals, groups, and organizations with different objectives (Dutton et al. 2012).

Many technical developments have shaped the Internet of the twenty-first century. For example, the social role of the Internet has been dramatically affected in the earliest years by enabling email, and later by the emergence of the Web. Tim Berners-Lee and colleagues at the European Laboratory for Particle Physics (CERN) in Switzerland, invented the World Wide Web from a set of networking projects (Berners-Lee 1999). As important as this development was, the Web's design and cultural ethos was strongly influenced by the open innovation principles at CERN and an earlier conception of "hypertext" inspired by Ted Nelson's (1987) visionary work on the Xanadu project, which in turn drew on Douglas Engelhard's "oN-Line System" (NLS) at Stanford Research Institute that aimed to make computers a more useful tool to help people think and work.

---

[8] TCP/IP standards were developed by Robert Kahn and Vent Cerf in 1973 through research supported by the Advanced Research Project Agency of the US Department of Defense, leading to the ARPANET adopting new protocols based on the notion that the Internet should provide a very limited role—transmitting and routing traffic through a packet switched network—with key functions being based at the nodes or ends of the network.

In turn, the significance of the Internet and Web owed much to the development of browsers, such as the Mosaic browser, commercialized as Netscape Navigator, and joined in competition from Windows Explorer and other browsers, which enabled personal computer users to more easily access websites through a graphical user interface (GUI). The later development of the semantic (linked data) Web promises to further enhance the role of the Web, yet the development of mobile applications, for example on smart phones and tablet computers, bypass the Web in some respects, for example by providing more direct links to Internet applications. Similarly, social networking sites, such as Twitter and Facebook, are creating new spaces for interaction that are distinct from the Web and not searchable from outside, and thus revise the structure and function of the Internet. Further emerging developments around face and posture recognition over webcams, voice search, and brain–machine interfaces could transform human computer interaction in ways that could enable a step jump in access to the Internet, for example by older people, or usher in a truly Orwellian future of surveillance.

These are just some of the many ways in which a cascading array of innovations in search, video, voice, social networking, and more, are constantly evolving the ecology of the Internet, the Web, and related ICTs, and their implications for society. Throughout their history, the Internet and the Web continued to be shaped by contributions from a vast and growing number of users around the world, pursuing a multiplicity of aims and objectives, ranging from the commercial to the public-spirited, many of which are only indirectly tied to the Internet but which nevertheless shape its uses and implications. In such ways the Internet, as defined by the TCP/IP standards, has had a rich pre- and post-history of developments and visions in computing and telecommunications. It unfolded from the choices of a large number of players in intertwined academic, commercial, technical, industrial, and other arenas making decisions about how specific aspects of the Internet should be designed, developed, used, or governed (Dutton 2008; Dutton et al. 2012). Each decision met goals and made sense within different arenas, and the interaction between choices combined to create this continually evolving twenty-first-century phenomenon represented by the Internet and a growing array of related ICTs.

Particularistic and synoptic conceptions of Internet Studies

Definitions of the Internet filter down into disagreement between the "lumpers" and the "splitters." A developing orthodoxy around the origins of Internet Studies, which I will refer to as a particularistic perspective of the splitters, can be juxtaposed with a broader synoptic perspective of the lumpers, which anchors this handbook and places Internet Studies into a more comprehensive view of the study of ICTs.

The particularistic view sees Internet Studies as a development that arose at a specific time, most often pinned to the first conference of the Association of Internet Researchers (AoIR) in 2000 entitled "The State of the Discipline." This conference was organized through a mailing list that was begun in 1998, and became a landmark for attracting over two hundred participants to Lawrence, Kansas, a college town in the American Midwest (Baym 2005).

This particularistic view was most influentially articulated by Wellman (2004, 2011), who defined three stages of the development of Internet Studies, the third stage of which was marked by this meeting. He argued that the field progressed from an early period of Utopian-dystopian visions that were uninformed by social research, to a second stage characterized by systematic descriptive work, to a final stage of more theoretically informed research.

However, as Wesley Shrum (2005: 273) put it, the idea that the field began or consolidated with the 2000 AoIR Conference is more of an accepted myth, than a reality. Many were conducting research on the Internet and closely related ICTs well prior to this time. The Internet itself predated definition of the field of Internet Studies by decades, and much significant social research on the Internet and related ICTs came well before 2000 (Elton and Carey Chapter 2). In fact, before and throughout the stages described by Wellman, there has been a continuation of Utopian-dystopian punditry, descriptive surveys, and more theoretically driven research. As parsimonious as the particularistic stage theory might be, it is riddled with contradictions and exceptions.

More importantly, by not highlighting its foundations, the particularistic definition can isolate Internet Studies from other research traditions that provide continuity and cumulativeness to a broader field of study. The risk is that a particularistic conception of this field can disconnect Internet Studies from its past, related present, and future, leading a number of leading scholars, such as Rob Kling, to object to the concept of "Internet Studies" on the grounds that it was too narrow (Baym 2005: 231).

This has been answered by the lumpers, who take a more synoptic perspective and link Internet Studies to multidisciplinary streams of research on ICTs that predated the first discussions of Internet Studies. Since conceptualizing information technology in the 1950s, academics have been studying the implications of computing and telecommunications from multiple disciplinary perspectives in ways that feed directly into contemporary studies of the Internet.

Foundations in early research on Information and Communication Technologies

The conceptualization of information technology (IT) can be traced to the 1950s (e.g. Leavitt and Whisler 1958), and visions of a public information utility were prominent in the late 1960s (e.g. Sackman and Nie 1970). Daniel Bell's (1973) work on the information society has been complemented and advanced by Manuel Castells (1996) in conceptualizing a network society, which provides a foundation for Internet studies. Some of the earliest studies of computers and privacy, such as Westin and Baker's (1972) *Databanks in a Free Society*, remain relevant to ongoing debate over the implications of the Internet for privacy and surveillance (Bennett and Parsons Chapter 23). Howard Rheingold's (1993) seminal work on virtual communities continues to influence Internet research and its frequent focus on communities. Sherry Turkle's (1995) conceptions of the psychological implications of computing, built on the work of Seymour Papert (1980) and Joseph Weizenbaum (1976), and continue to inform work on such issues as identity. These and many other parallel streams of multidisciplinary work have provided foundations for study of the Internet from a synoptic perspective.

In addition, since the early 1970s, a number of interdisciplinary research efforts helped create foundations for Internet Studies. Jacques Vallee and others at the Institute for the Future pioneered behavioral studies of computer-mediated communication,[9] as did Murray Turoff and his colleagues, who developed the Emergency Management Information Systems and Reference Index (EMISARI) in 1971, using teletype terminals that linked to a central computer over telephone lines for real time chat, polling, and threaded discussion. These projects enabled some of the first interdisciplinary studies of how social and psychological factors shape the use of computer-mediated communication (Vallee et al. 1974; Hiltz and Turoff 1978). From the mid-1970s, the Irvine Group's study of computers in government, led by Kenneth Kraemer at UC Irvine, developed theoretical perspectives such as "reinforcement politics" (Danziger et al. 1982)—a perspective that remains central to later views on the Internet in politics (van Dijk 2012).

In 1985, the UK's Economic and Social Research Council launched the "Programme on Information and Communication Technologies" (Dutton 1999), which concluded in 1995, but fed into follow-up programs, such as the "Virtual Society?" (Woolgar 2002). Similar efforts to organize the field in the US were led by Lee Sproull and Sara Kiesler who pioneered studies of computer-mediated communication from an organizational studies perspective (Sproull and Kiesler 1991). With support from the Social Science Research Council, they organized colleagues around the concept of "social informatics"—a topic championed by the late Rob Kling (Kling 1991; Kling et al. 2000), a member of the Irvine group.

In parallel, academic institutions began to reconfigure themselves in response to technical and social innovations. In the early 1970s, the Annenberg School of Communication at the University of Southern California was among the first communication departments to organize around the new media driven by the prospect of the convergence of computing, telecommunications, and the media (Williams 1982). A similar logic led the library school at Syracuse University to be renamed the School of Information Studies, and was followed by other information schools, such as the University of Michigan in 1996. In 1998, as AoIR was being organized, Harvard University supported funding of the Berkman Center for Internet and Society. While based in a law school, it had a broader mission, and was soon followed by the founding of the Oxford Internet Institute (OII) in 2001 as a multidisciplinary department at the University of Oxford with a mission to focus on the societal implications of the Internet. These and related initiatives stimulated the establishment of Internet research centers around the world.

---

[9] The US National Science Foundation (NSF) supported Vallee and others to design a computer conferencing system called FORUM and explore its implications. Volume 2 of their report looks at social effects (Vallee et al. 1974).

THE TRANSFORMATIVE ROLE OF INTERNET STUDIES

From a more synoptic perspective, it is arguable that the Internet's development and convergence, creating a broader IP environment for media and related ICTs, and fostering the field of Internet Studies, has helped transform the study of ICTs and their societal implications. Increasingly, the study of computing, telecommunication, cable and satellite, mobile, and other ICTs are falling under the umbrella of Internet Studies. Increasingly, any study of the Internet is aware of the larger and often interrelated if not convergent ecology of media and ICTs within which the Internet is embedded. You will see throughout this handbook that studies of politics, relationships, news, and other phenomena are examining the Internet within a larger ecology of ICTs.

The emergence of Internet Studies, such as around AoIR, initially created a new subfield, but eventually provided an umbrella under which an increasing number of scholars could bring their work. Will Internet Studies become a more specialized niche within the study of ICTs, or continue to grow and help integrate or network this larger field?

THE FUTURE OF INTERNET STUDIES

The future of this field is wide open, but there are three among many general scenarios that are useful to develop as alternative normative forecasts on how scholars within this field should and could align themselves.

Networking an interdisciplinary status quo

The most likely scenario is for Internet researchers to continue to collaborate within and across the existing academic disciplines and structures of universities. Naomi Baron (2005) argued that this was a desirable approach given the existence of collaborative spaces, such as the AoIR conference, and the growing popularity of interdisciplinary studies across universities. This is also a pragmatic scenario, given that the disciplinary landscape of most universities is heavily populated with multiple disciplines each of which have a claim to particular aspects of Internet Studies, including media, communication, information studies, sociology, and more. One of the only departments of Internet Studies at a major university, the Oxford Internet Institute, was founded in a virtual disciplinary green field, since Oxford University did not have a department of media studies, communication, or information at the time of founding the OII in 2001. Networking across the disciplinary divides might continue to enable the growth of Internet Studies with a firm footing in multiple disciplines.

Specialization and fragmentation

Another feasible scenario is that the field peaks and disassembles as it becomes increasingly fragmented by technical and disciplinary specializations. This could undermine the strength of this field by separating pieces of the same ecology of technologies, use, and policy issues.

However, specialization can be constructive. Social informatics was an effort to broaden informatics and ensure that social aspects of technical change would be explicitly incorporated.[10] Web Science (O'Hara and Hall Chapter 3) and Internet Science are both somewhat distinct from Internet Studies, founded primarily within the computer sciences. They could enable more computer scientists to pursue Internet research, and share many features, such as a commitment to including the social sciences. Nevertheless, they could further fragment Internet Studies. Likewise, efforts to focus on mobile communication have split some scholars studying this technical and social development from Internet Studies, when convergence of mobile and the Internet is defining the next generation Internet user (Blank and Dutton 2012).

Specialization can also be defined around the implications of the Internet, such as creating communities of scholars focused on geography or politics, and in specific issue-based communities of researchers, such a privacy or freedom of expression. This push toward specialization is easily supported by new journals and associations and this is one way of inventing new fields that become more significant with time, such as when mass media researchers moved away from sociology to form the communication field.

Integrative: creating a derivative discipline

A third perspective is that Internet Studies becomes a derivative discipline—an increasingly integrated multidisciplinary field with an increasingly variegated range of specialized topics. Other strong fields of research were derived from the combination of multiple disciplines. For example, political science focused on power and government as objects of study, with work in political philosophy, psychology, sociology, and economics, among other disciplines, being pulled together to form a field that has over the decades became widely recognized as a discipline. Likewise, communication has been derived from academics within sociology, social psychology, political science, and other disciplines to focus on media and the problems they raise, such as the influence of mass communication.

This might be the most promising direction for Internet Studies, but it faces resistance to strengthening Internet Studies as a field for practical and philosophical reasons tied to the individualist culture of the field. Practically, the institutional difficulties in developing new disciplines and departments have diverted many Internet researchers

[10] Baron argues that new disciplines arise due to new problems or questions, or for political reasons, such as to insure adequate resources.

from such a pursuit. It requires dramatic change in how top academics in the major institutions think about the Internet and the mainstream disciplines. Culturally, many within the field of Internet Studies resist "institutionalization," fearing that an increasingly well-agreed definition of the field will undermine the eclectic, creative individualism of this ever emerging field (Baym 2005)—what Wesley Shrum (2005) called "Internet Indiscipline."

When students of Internet Studies got together in Lawrence, Kansas, in 2000, the dotcom bubble was bursting and many social scientists continued to consider the Internet a fad. By 2012 there was almost unquestioned acknowledgement that this network of networks had become not simply significant, but increasingly essential to more and more aspects of life and work (Blank and Dutton 2012). The most compelling driving force behind Internet Studies is the worldwide diffusion and increasing significance of the Internet. Globally, there is clearly the development of a "new Internet world" shaped by the global diffusion of the Internet (Dutta et al. 2011). The center of gravity of the Internet has already moved from North America and Western Europe, where it was rooted in 2000, to East Asia and the rapidly developing nations, such as Brazil, India, and China, where the greatest number of Internet users reside.

This global significance is likely to increase further in the coming years. This is because convergence across media and ICTs is actually developing in key areas, such as in mobile communications with the rise of Internet enabled "smart phones" and everyone living in an IP-environment, where television, voice, and other services are increasingly Internet applications. In addition, the Internet is becoming more embedded within the wider ecology of other media, information, and communication technologies, such as in the provision and consumption of news, which is tied to search, social media, online journalism as well as more traditional media (Newman et al. 2011; Mitchelstein and Boczkowski Chapter 18).

Across the contributions to this handbook, you will see evidence of the global significance of the Internet and related ICTs, which is a major factor shaping the future of this field. This trend is supported by the chapters of this handbook, in related research across over 30 nations of the World Internet Project (Cardoso et al. Chapter 11), as well as by other systematic empirical research in the US and worldwide. Generally, in line with the power shifts identified by Castells (2009), and my own work on the Fifth Estate (Dutton 2009), Lee Rainie and Barry Wellman (2012) write of the transformative nature of the Internet, where search, the rise of social networking, and the always-on connectivity of mobile devices are combining to empower users in ways that are making this network of networks increasingly central to social and economic development. And yet, a growing body of critical scholarship questions the empowerment thesis, seeing more reinforcement of enduring patterns of communication (Lilleker and Vedel Chapter 19; van Dijk 2012). This division between transformations of empowerment or disempowerment characterizes the debate surrounding the societal implications of the Internet that has driven the rise of Internet Studies before and since 2000 and will continue to do so well into the future.

OUTLINE OF THIS HANDBOOK

The chapters of this handbook follow the structure outlined in Table 1.1. The chapters in Part I convey selected perspectives on the Internet, World Wide Web, and related ICTs as the principle object of study. These include perspectives from the study of the history of new media, Web Science, the information sciences of Webmetrics, and conceptions of the Internet as an "infrastructure." These contributions demonstrate the multiplicity of approaches to conceptualizing the Internet, and the changing roles of different technologies, actors, and social issues shaping its design and development.

Martin Elton and John Carey (Chapter 2) show how relevant the study of new media and telecommunication innovations, such as videotex,[11] has been to research on developments around the Internet and the Web. Their chapter clarifies the distinctions between the Internet and the Web, which is the object of study in a new field of Web Science. Fostered by one of its key inventors, Tim Berners-Lee, the central motivations behind the development of a "discipline" of Web Science is the subject of Kieron O'Hara and Wendy Hall (Chapter 3), who see this research agenda as critical to shaping the future development of the Web. Internet Studies does not encompass all of what the authors define as Web Science, and is more anchored in the social than computer sciences, but these two fields assume that macro-level societal implications can flow from the micro-level decisions made about the Web's protocols, such as in creating the Web of Linked Data.

Mike Thelwall (Chapter 4) continues a discussion of the Web, but targeted on its hyperlinked structure. This structure emerges from patterns of use, but shapes the social role of the Web, such as the types of websites that people find through search engines and the degree that popular sites become even more privileged in a winner-take-all process facilitated by the technology. This chapter also argues that the structure of the Web reflects the offline world, making it a valuable lens for studying society—not just technology. In the last chapter of this section, Christian Sandvig (Chapter 5) describes how useful it can be to view the Internet as an infrastructure, a perspective emerging from science and technology studies. The argument of this chapter reinforces all the contributions to this section, showing how technical changes of the infrastructure can have unanticipated and unintended societal consequences.

Parts II–IV move away from a focus on the Internet as the object of study to its use in a variety of social contexts. Part II focuses on how choices about the (non)use of the Internet and related ICTs in everyday life can reshape access to information and people in ways that influence what people know; whom they know; how and from where they obtain services, from information to entertainment; and what individuals and households need to know to function well in a digital society. The section begins with a broad macro-level focus on the "network society," to which Jack Linchuan Qiu (Chapter 6) brings a new perspective, anchored in his research in China. By addressing within- and cross-national differences in the nature of network societies, he provides a convincing

---

[11] "Videotex" is accepted internationally; videotext is used in the UK.

case for the need for a global perspective on the social role of the Internet that will counter the potential for ethnocentric universal claims.

Jack Linchuan Qiu's research has emphasized the different role that networks can play across different social strata, a focus of Eszter Hargittai and Yuli Patrick Hsieh (Chapter 7), who examine research on inequalities in society driven by such factors as the distribution of the skills to use it effectively. Their use of stratification theory to refine research on digital divides, an enduring issue of Internet Studies, leads them to direct work on digital inequality beyond overly simplistic conceptions of access to technologies to consider related issues of skills and media literacy.

A key social implication tied to the Internet has been its role in shaping interpersonal interaction and the development of communities. Nicole Ellison and danah boyd (Chapter 8) provide authoritative insights into one of the most significant developments related to social interaction: social network sites. They provide an analytic framework for studying these new sites, while underscoring the centrality of social interaction since the Internet's earliest days, such as through email.

Interpersonal relationships carry into Barrie Gunter's (Chapter 9) synthesis of research on the many dimensions of the Internet and dating. He shows how the circumstances surrounding how people meet online provides an arena for exploring key issues, ranging from deception to reconfiguring once-in-a-lifetime decisions. Just as the Internet becomes embedded in routine practices, so online dating is becoming part of the normal repertoire, and even more important as a subject of research.

The Internet is becoming more central to entertainment, and games are one of the most central aspects of an increasingly wide range of entertaining activities, even if often used for serious purposes. Dmitri Williams and Adam Kahn (Chapter 10) describe the evolution of innovative research on game playing in the household and online, such as in studies of massive multiplayer, three-dimensional Internet game environments. This chapter illustrates the need for Internet Studies to deal with the ebbs and flows of the market and the rapid pace of technical change.

The final chapter of this section moves back to a cross-national comparative focus on the role of the Internet in society by describing the development and findings of the World Internet Project (WIP). Gustavo Cardoso, Guo Liang, and Tiago Lapa (Chapter 11) have been leaders of this work in Europe and Asia, helping to track the diffusion, uses, and impacts of the Internet worldwide and over time. Their perspective points out the challenges of this research as well as the need for complementary studies with a more global reach.

In Part III, the focus on use turns to research on creating and working in a global network economy, focusing on the Internet in key aspects of work, from business and commerce to the public sector, including academic research and education.

Michael Cusumano and Andreas Goeldi (Chapter 12) lead this part by illuminating one of the most significant issues facing old and new businesses in the digital age, the development of new business models. They identify a wide range of business models enabled by new platforms for computing and communications over the Internet. They show how these "platforms" can lead to winner-take-all scenarios or enhance established businesses, or enable the provision of new products and services, or create completely new types of businesses.

Most business, as well as many personal transactions online, depend on a level of trust. Regina Connolly (Chapter 13) focuses on how trust has been conceptualized and studied, providing a refined understanding of many trust-related issues that influence commerce but arguably also other online transactions in the digital age, such as in the public services.

Compared to the commercial sector, the public sector has been more challenged in adapting to the digital age. Paul Henman (Chapter 14) takes up some of these challenges in his overview of e-Government or digital government. His treatment is remarkable in the degree to which the topics of digital government incorporate nearly all of the issues tied to society and the Internet more generally, from digital divides to the impact of social networking.

While Internet researchers have explored many institutional settings, few researchers have examined the impact of the Internet and related ICTs on their own academic institutions. Eric Meyer and Ralph Schroeder (Chapter 15) have done leading research into the ways in which digital technologies could be transforming academic research across the disciplines. They convey the significance, but also highlight the conceptual challenges, of advancing work in this area.

The academy is also the subject of Chris Davies and Rebecca Eynon (Chapter 16), who take an interdisciplinary approach to examine the role of the Internet in reshaping learning and education. They draw valuable distinctions between formal education, such as in classrooms, where the Internet has made few inroads, and informal learning, where the Internet seems to have excelled. Their chapter helps guide research towards the task of disentangling and explaining the role of the Internet in these different contexts of use and impact in order to draw conclusions for policy and practice.

Part IV is the final section on patterns of use, exploring stability and change in communication, media, and politics linked to the Internet. In these contexts of Internet use, questions arise over whether the Internet is enabling a radical decentralization of control over communication and the media, such as by undermining broadcasting and the concept of the audience—while empowering individuals and networks, such as in political arenas. Despite popular conceptions of this promise, the research is mixed in its findings, but also struggling to find methods for examining these issues in complex, fast-paced, and contentious events, such as in campaigns and elections.

The first chapter in this section presents the findings of a systematic and detailed meta-analysis of research on the Internet within the field of communication. Ronald Rice and Ryan Fuller (Chapter 17), focusing on the first decade of the twenty-first century, use content analysis to uncover the prominence of different theoretical perspectives on the Internet. Although much of the early Internet research has been criticized as being atheoretical, they find that a wide range of primary and secondary theories have been increasingly applied to understanding social and communicative aspects of the Internet and the increasingly specialized areas being developed by Internet researchers, such as around social media.

This review of communication research is followed by a focus on one of the most critical of the media in liberal democratic societies: the news. Eugenia Mitchelstein and Pablo Boczkowski (Chapter 18) are particularly concerned with stability and change in patterns of news production and consumption with the advent of online news. The directions they provide for future research are novel and challenging.

Darren Lilleker and Thierry Vedel (Chapter 19) critically assess a number of positive claims surrounding the role of the Internet in campaigns and elections, and, in the process, examine high-profile campaigns in North America and Europe. While they are skeptical of claims about the Internet empowering citizens, they find the Internet becoming increasingly embedded within campaigns and elections, moving the study of the Internet into mainstream studies of politics—one illustration of the way in which Internet Studies is transforming other disciplines.

Communication, the media, and campaigns are all linked to aspects of democratic governance and accountability; but in the final chapter in this section, Helen Margetts (Chapter 20) deals directly and broadly with the Internet and democracy, a topic that the Arab Springs have brought to the forefront of Internet Studies. Her chapter is particularly valuable in clarifying the many ways and levels in which there are links between the Internet and different models of democracy and the institutions that support them.

Part V concludes this handbook by addressing policy and focusing on issues around governing and regulating the Internet. Early proponents of the Internet often argued that the Internet was ungovernable, but far from the proverbial "Wild West," many laws and regulations apply to the Internet and its use around the world. Nevertheless, post Arab Springs, and England riots, even more efforts have been launched to control a technology that some politicians see to be enabling anarchy or autocracy, rather than democracy.

Major policy issues are at stake in how policy-makers respond to these uncertainties, including freedom of expression, which Victoria Nash (Chapter 21) engages through a normative and empirical overview of debate and research. Proponents of new communications tools as technologies of freedom are finding increasing pressures to control and filter online communication across an increasing number of jurisdictions. This chapter suggests that a broader theoretical framework is needed to capture the full range of law and policies shaping expression online, and develop responses for policy and practice.

Closely related to freedom of expression are efforts to stop illegal file sharing through the application of copyright and intellectual property rights in the online world. Matthew David (Chapter 22) reviews cultural, legal, technical, and economic approaches to enforcing copyright, concluding that rights holders need to rethink their business models in the digital age, such as by concentrating on live performances, rather than simply trying to shore up old business models by criminalizing copyright infringement.

Another key set of policy issues concerns privacy and surveillance, which many regard as under threat from social networks and other new Internet developments, such as the mining of big data sets created through the use of Internet services and networks. Colin Bennett and Christopher Parsons (Chapter 23) review the multidisciplinary literature on the protection of personal information in the online world, which extends back to the origins of social research on computing. Bennett is among the leading scholars of privacy, making this chapter an informative overview but also a valuable guide to the most promising directions for research on privacy as well as related issues of security and identity online.

Many countries are pursuing the development of digital infrastructures as a proactive approach to technology-led economic and industrial policy, such as faster broadband infrastructure initiatives. Robin Mansell and Edward Steinmueller (Chapter 24) provide a critical synthesis of research tied to such policy initiatives, focusing on Europe and North America, highlighting the complexity of the research questions, as well as the responsibility to balance economic with other cultural and societal implications.

Tim Unwin (Chapter 25) extends a critical perspective on the economic impact of the Internet to study of ICT for development. He questions taken-for-granted assumptions about the Internet as a tool for development. Focusing on the least developed nations, his observations and synthesis identify unanticipated consequences, such as the widening of inequalities, which underpin his directions for future research.

The final chapter by Laura DeNardis (Chapter 26) illuminates the significance of the emerging field of Internet governance, highlighting issues over standards, names and numbers, and net neutrality, which are unfolding in a variety of contexts around the world, including the Internet Governance Forum. She combines an engineering background with insightful social analysis of technical design issues to show how technology could bias outcomes across policy arenas, such as privacy or freedom of expression. She shows how engineering and standards are not just technical matters, but also issues of governance.

Conclusion

This introductory chapter has provided a broad overview of Internet Studies, seeking to place subsequent chapters in the context of one of the most dynamic fields of academic research in the early twenty-first century. In the course of editing this handbook, my view of the field has been sharpened and lifted even further by the quality of work that is being conducted across such a wide range of areas. It will be apparent from a close reading of this handbook that the field is being built on increasingly strong foundations, and that the pace of innovation in this field will not slow down. This progress will be enhanced by the work brought together in this volume and the directions the authors point to in the further development of this interdisciplinary field.

Acknowledgments

My thanks to Rebecca Eynon, Charles Ess, and Malcolm Peltu for comments on this chapter.

References

Abbate, J. (1999). *Inventing the Internet*, Cambridge: MIT Press.

Bakardjieva, M. (2011). "The Internet in Everyday Life: Exploring the Tenets and Contributions of Diverse Approaches," in Consalvo and Ess (2011), pp. 59–82.

Baron, N. S. (2005). "Who Wants to Be a Discipline?," *The Information Society*, 21: 269–71.

Baym, N. K. (2005). "Internet Research as It Isn't, Is, Could Be, and Should Be," *The Information Society*, 21(4): 229–32.

Bell, D. (1973). *The Coming of Post-Industrial Society: A Venture in Social Forecasting*, New York: Basic Books.

Berners-Lee, T. (1999). *Weaving the Web: The Origins and Future of the World Wide Web*, London: Orion Books.

Blank, G. and Dutton, W. H. (2012 forthcoming). "The Emergence of Next Generation Internet Users," in J. Hartley, J. Burgess, and A. Bruns (eds). *Blackwell Companion to New Media Dynamics*, London: Wiley-Blackwell.

Castells, M. (1996). *The Rise of the Network Society*, Oxford: Blackwell Publishers.

—— (2001). *The Internet Galaxy: Reflections on the Internet, Business, and Society*, Oxford: Oxford University Press.

—— (2009). *Communication Power*, Oxford: Oxford University Press.

Chadwick, A. and Howard, P. N. (eds) (2008). *The Routledge Handbook of Internet Politics*, London: Routledge.

Consalvo, M. and Ess, C. (eds) (2011). *The Handbook of Internet Studies*, Oxford: Wiley-Blackwell.

Craven, P. and Barry Wellman, B. (1973). "The Network City," *Sociological Inquiry* 43(1): 57–88.

Danziger, J. N., Dutton, W. H., Kling, R., and Kraemer, K. L. (1982). *Computers and Politics*, New York: Columbia University Press.

De Sola Pool, I. (1983). *Technologies of Freedom*, Cambridge, MA: Belknap Press.

Dutta, S., Dutton, W. H., and Law, G. (2011). "The New Internet World: A Global Perspective on Freedom of Expression, Privacy, Trust and Security Online," New York: World Economic Forum.

Dutton, W. H. (1999). *Society on the Line: Information Politics in the Digital Age*, Oxford and New York: Oxford University Press.

—— (2005). "The Internet and Social Transformation: Reconfiguring Access," in W. H. Dutton, B. Kahin, R. O'Callaghan, and A. W. Wyckoff (eds). *Transforming Enterprise*, Cambridge, MA: MIT Press, pp. 375–97.

—— (2008). "Social Movements Shaping the Internet: The Outcome of an Ecology of Games," in M. Elliott and K. L. Kraemer (eds). *Computerization Movements and Technology Diffusion*, Medford, NJ: Information Today, Inc., pp. 499–517.

—— (2009). "The Fifth Estate Emerging through the Network of Networks," *Prometheus*, 27(1), March: 1–15.

—— and Jeffreys, P. (eds) (2010). *World Wide Research: Reshaping the Sciences and Humanities*, Cambridge, MA: The MIT Press.

Dutton, W. H., Schneider, V., and Vedel, T. (2012). "Large Technical Systems as Ecologies of Games: Cases from Telecommunications to the Internet," in J. M. Bauer, A. Lang, and V. Schneider (eds), *Innovation Policy and Governance in High-Tech Industries*. Berlin: Springer-Verlag, pp. 49–75.

Elliott, M. and Kraemer, K. L. (eds) (2008). *Computerization Movements and Technology Diffusion: From Mainframes to Ubiquitous Computing*, Medford, NJ: Information Today, Inc.

Fielding, N., Lee, R. M., and Blank, G. (eds) (2008). *The Sage Handbook of Online Research Methods*, London: Sage.

Gore, A. (1991). "Infrastructure for a Global Village," *Scientific American*, 265(3), September: 108–11.

Haddon, L. (2006). "The Contribution of Domestication Research to In-Home Computing and Media Consumption," *The Information Society*. 22(4): 195–205.

Hiltz, S. R. and Turoff, M. (1978). *The Network Nation: Human Communication via Computer*, Reading, MA: Addison-Wesley Publishing Company, Inc.

Himanen, P. (2001). *The Hacker Ethic and the Spirit of the Information Age*, New York: Random House.

Howard, P. N. and Jones, S. (eds) (2004). *Society Online*, Thousand Oaks, CA: Sage.

Hunsinger, J., Klastrup, L., and Allen, M. (eds) (2010). *International Handbook of Internet Research*, London and New York: Springer.

Joinson, A., Mckenna, K. Y. A., Postmes, T., and Reips, U.-D. (eds) (2007). *The Oxford Handbook of Internet Psychology*, Oxford: Oxford University Press.

Jones, S. (1998). *Cybersociety 2.0: Revisiting Computer-Mediated Communication in Cyberspace*, London and Thousand Oaks, CA: Sage Publications.

—— (1999) (ed.). *Doing Internet Research*, London: Sage Publications.

Kling, R. (1991). "Computerization and Social Transformations," *Science, Technology, and Human Values*, 16(3): 342–67.

—— Crawford, H., Rosebaum, H., Sawyer, S., and Weisband, S. (2000). *Learning from Social Informatics: Information and Communication Technologies in Human Contexts*, Bloomington, IN: Indiana University Press.

Kubicek, H., Dutton, W., and Williams, R. (eds) (1997). *The Social Shaping of the Information Superhighway: European and American Roads to the Information Society*, Frankfurt: Campus Verlag and New York: St. Martin's Press.

Lasswell, H. D. (1971). "The Strucure and Function of Mass Communication in Society," in W. Schramm and D. F. Roberts (eds). *The Process and Effects of Mass Communication*, Revised Edition, Urbana, IL: University of Illinois Press, pp. 84–99.

Leavitt, H. J. and Whisler, T. L. (1958). "Management in the 1980s," *Harvard Business Review*, 36(6): 41–8.

Leiner, B. M., Cerf, V. G., Clark, D. D., Kahn, R. E., Kleinrock, L., Lynch, D. C., J. Postel, Roberts, L. G., and Wolff, S. (2005). "A Brief History of the Internet." Available at <http://www.internetsociety.org/internet/internet-51/history-internet/brief-history-internet>. Accessed January 1, 2012.

Lessig, L. (1999). *Code and Other Laws of Cyberspace*, New York: Basic Books.

Lievrouw, L. and Livingstone, S. (2006). *Handbook of New Media: Social Shaping and Social Consequences of ICTs*, London: Sage.

Mansell, R., Avgerou, C., Quah, D., and Silverstone, R. (eds) (2007). *The Oxford Handbook of Information and Communication Technologies*, Oxford: Oxford University Press.

McLemee, S. (2001). "Internet Studies 1.0: A Discipline is Born," *The Chronicle of Higher Education*, 47(29): A24.

Nelson, T. (1987). *Literary Machines*, Swathmore, PA: Mindful.

Newman, N., Dutton, W. H., and Blank, G. (2011). "Social Media in the Changing Ecology of News Production and Consumption: The Case in Britain." Paper presented at the Annual Conference of the International Communication Association (ICA), Boston, MA.

Papert, S. (1980). *Mind-Storms*, New York: Basic Books.

Peng, T. Q., Zhu, J. J. H., Zhang, L., and Zhong, Z. J. (2011). "Mapping the Landscape of Internet Research: Text Mining of Social Science Journal Articles 2000–2009." Joint Working Paper of the Faculty of Humanities and Arts, Macau University of Science and Technology, and the Web Mining Lab, Department of Media & Communication, City University of Hong Kong.

Rainie, L. and Wellman, B. (2012). *Networked: The New Social Operating System*, Cambridge, MA: MIT Press.

Rheingold, H. (1993). *The Virtual Community: Homesteading on the Electronic Frontier*, New York: Addison-Wesley [revised for MIT Press 2000].

Sackman, H. and Nie, N. (eds) (1970). *The Information Utility and Social Choice*, Montvale, NJ: AFIPS Press.

Schroeder, R. (2007). *Rethinking Science, Technology and Social Change*, Stanford: Stanford University Press.

Shrum, W. (2005). "Internet Indiscipline: Two Approaches to Making a Field," *The Information Society*, 21(4): 273–5.

Sproull, L., Dutton, W. H., and Kiesler, S. (eds) (2007). "Online Communities," a special issue of *Organization Studies*, 28(3), March: 277–408.

Sproull, L. and Kiesler, S. (1991). *Connections*, Cambridge, MA: MIT Press.

Sunstein, C. R. (2009). *Republic.com 2.0*, Princeton, NJ: Princeton University Press.

Turkle, S. (1995). *Life on the Screen: Identity in the Age of the Internet*, New York: Simon & Schuster.

Vallee, J., Johansen, R., Randolph, R. H., and Hastings, A. C. (1974). *Group Communication Through Computers. Volume 2: A Study of Social Effects*, Menlo Park, CA: Institute for the Future.

van Dijck, J. (2009). "Users Like You? Theorizing Agency in User-Generated Content," *Media, Culture & Society*, 31(1): 41–58.

—— (2012). *The Network Society: Social Aspects of New Media*, London: Sage.

Weizenbaum, J. (1976). *Computer Power and Human Reason*, San Francisco: W. H. Freeman & Company.

Wellman, B. (2004). "The Three Ages of Internet Studies: Ten, Five and Zero Years Ago," *New Media and Society*, 6(1): 123–9.

—— (2011). "Studying the Internet through the Ages," in Consalvo and Ess (2011), pp. 17–23.

—— and Haythornthwaite, C. (eds) (2002). *The Internet in Everyday Life*, Oxford: Blackwell Publishing.

Westin, A. F. and Baker, M. A. (1972). *Databanks in a Free Society: Computers, Record-Keeping and Privacy*, New York: Quadrangle Books.

Williams, F. (1982). *The Communications Revolution*, Beverly Hills, CA: Sage Publications.

Woolgar, S. (ed.) (2002). *Virtual Society? Technology, Cyberbole, Reality*, Oxford: Oxford University Press.

Zittrain, J. (2008). *The Future of the Internet and How to Stop It*, New Haven, CT: Yale University Press.

PART I

PERSPECTIVES ON THE INTERNET AND WEB AS OBJECTS OF STUDY

THE PREHISTORY OF THE INTERNET AND ITS TRACES IN THE PRESENT: IMPLICATIONS FOR DEFINING THE FIELD

MARTIN C. J. ELTON AND JOHN CAREY

INTRODUCTION

ACCOUNTS of the creation and early years of the Internet nearly always confine themselves to early research in packet-switching and to projects funded by the US Defense Department. Starting in the late 1960s, these led to the ARPANET, which evolved into the Internet, the infrastructure that allowed the Web to emerge (e.g. Hafner 1998; Leiner et al. n.d.). With an almost exclusive focus on how the infrastructure and its technology came to be developed, such accounts fail to recognize the significance of the online services that preceded the World Wide Web and the roles these services played in the Internet's dramatically fast early diffusion. The omission results in an incomplete and overly US-centric perspective.

   To provide a more complete understanding of how the Web came into being, this chapter offers only a very brief summary of the, by now, well-known development of the Internet's early technology, so that it can focus on often overlooked developments in email, computer conferencing, electronic banking, online databases, bulletin boards, and, in particular, videotex—a platform dating back to the early 1970s in the UK that supported a wide variety of online services for business and consumers, generally provided by third parties and accessed via the regular telephone network. Collectively, these online applications contributed in a major way to the understanding of user interfaces, advertising, content, shopping, online games, graphics, communications, and the needs and wants of ordinary people—key elements in the array of web services that emerged in the late 1990s and early 2000s. They also provided the early Web with substantial numbers of users who were already familiar with online services. There is a considerable body of research on these earlier online applications that can inform today's community of scholars in its studies of the modern Web.

Some of the prehistory and early history of the Web is relevant to important issues of today—for example, the degree to which the Internet will remain an open system via which anyone can provide applications, and the role of governments in supporting infrastructure. The last part of the chapter identifies some of the more interesting connections between research issues from long ago (in Internet time!) and those of significance today.

The development of the Internet and the Web—The well-known version

The early impetus for the development of computer networks is often attributed to the Soviet Union's launching of the first artificial satellite, Sputnik, in 1957. This shocked Americans into a realization that, contrary to their widespread belief, the US was not ahead in developing real-world applications of scientific knowledge. The US government's reactions included substantial increases in its investment in applied science and the creation of the Advanced Research Projects Agency (ARPA, now DARPA) in the US Defense Department. ARPA was charged with supporting research and development projects that went beyond purely military applications. In the late 1960s, it funded the planning of a network that could link computers—ARPANET—based on the new technology of packet-switching. The motivation was simple: timesharing (Roberts 1966). In those days, a computer was a large, expensive mainframe, either accessed from terminals in the same building that were hard-wired to it or, generally, using stacks of punched cards or punched tape to receive input. Given the high cost and relative scarcity of these computers, significant benefits were expected from distributed computing, whereby users could access a computer (a "host" computer) at one location from a computer or terminal elsewhere and, for example, use programs running on the host to make calculations.

There were a number of major developments that led from ARPANET to the Internet and, subsequently, the Web. One occurred in the early 1970s when Vinton Cerf, Bob Kahn, and colleagues developed the suite of protocols that came to be named TCP/IP (for Transmission Control Protocol/Internet Protocol) to allow computers with different operating systems to communicate with each other over packet-switched networks. In another key development, Tim Berners-Lee and colleagues at CERN (European Organization for Nuclear Research) in Geneva, Switzerland, created the World Wide Web: a system of interlinked hypertext documents accessible via the Internet that is the core component of the modern-day Web. Hypermedia, which allow users to click on a word, phrase, or image and be transferred to another location, and DNS (Domain Name System), which allows users to type a URL such as Whitehouse.gov instead of a long string of numbers, were crucial developments enabling ordinary people to use the Internet. The World Wide Web was first demonstrated in 1991 and released by CERN for general use in 1993.

In 1993, a group working at the National Center for Supercomputing Applications at the University of Illinois-Urbana created the Mosaic browser (Berners-Lee and colleagues had developed a browser in 1991). This introduced a graphical user interface (GUI) that made it much easier to access websites—a development that was further advanced with the commercial release of Netscape. Perhaps the most important contribution by this group collectively was the development of a highly effective decentralized model for sharing information across computers, with no need for a single, large hub storing all the information.

With minor exceptions, ARPANET was used initially by the military and computer scientists at several major universities, primarily ones which were Defense Department contractors. User groups increased over time, but never included the public or general businesses. ARPANET was a network for sophisticated technologists, principally computer scientists, that enabled them to share computer resources in their research. Further, it was funded by the government—no one paid to use it—and no content (in a mass media sense), let alone advertising, was produced for it. Indeed, commercial use was banned. Advertising and marketing were so frowned upon that someone who created a forum entry that even hinted at promotion or marketing was likely to receive a barrage of angry emails. ARPANET was used for calculations, testing programs, accessing data and, soon afterwards, electronic mail, computer conferencing, and information exchange forums called Usenets, which collectively came to dominate usage. Person-to-person email was not in the original ARPANET plan but, having quickly proved more popular than expected, it was incorporated a few years later.

In the mid-1980s, NSFNET was created with funding from the National Science Foundation, eventually replacing ARPANET in 1990. It is not clear when the word "Internet" was first employed (in the sense it has today) but, by the early 1990s, it was in widespread use for what was created from this internetworking of computer networks—the Internet was a network of networks owned by entities in many different countries. It was a remarkable achievement and a sterling example of the benefits of the federal government's sustained commitment to investing in information infrastructure (Leiner et al. n.d.).

This version of the emergence of online services is largely a story of outstanding technical achievements within a universe of users who were for the most part sophisticated technologists. Important as these advances were, however, they did not include development of content, graphics, online games, shopping, search, advertising, direct marketing, business models, or understanding the needs of non-technologists who would have to pay for the online services they received. Knowledge in these areas came from another set of applications that has since been relegated to the dustbin of history, except by some academics who have preserved the story.

TURNING OVER THE DUSTBIN

By the mid-1970s ARPANET, and subsequently NSFNET, were two among many online networks with a wide range of users and uses. The end-user services provided over either the other online networks or regular telephone networks fell into seven groups: database services for businesses, later offered to consumers; computer conferencing; electronic mail services; electronic banking; computer bulletin boards; online services for education and non-profit groups; and videotex services which provided platforms for many different types of services and were intended for many different types of users, especially consumers. Although these services were researched extensively (see, e.g., Aumente (1987) and Fidler (1997)), today they are largely forgotten (AOL being the exception), having been overtaken by the enormous success of email and the Web from the mid-1990s on. Nevertheless, they contributed significantly to the base of knowledge and experience that so quickly made email and the Web successful. The context for their development is informative as well, especially in the case of videotex, which involved government policies to support development in furtherance of trade and international prestige; corporate investment for fear of being left out; existing technologies in homes to access new services; and the skill levels of the general public in using new media.

The context for the development of online media: the mid-1970s through the 1980s

In the late 1970s and throughout the 1980s, the context for developing online services was very different from today's. Very few households in Asia, Europe, or North America had computers, much less ones with modems for communicating over the telephone network. The large mainframe computers and minicomputers (still fairly large and expensive) prevalent in organizations were the domain of specialists: office workers and most students had no direct access to them. While there was considerable interest in the potential of smaller computers for a variety of applications, it would take time for them to be widely adopted.

Also part of the context were the telephone companies. In almost all European countries and, until 1985, Japan, national telephone companies were monopolies owned and managed by governments or newly formed, state-owned corporations. Their networks tended to be underutilized, especially outside the working day; online services were viewed as a way to remedy this. Governments, as well as telephone companies, also viewed online services as a catalyst for national economic development and leadership in international telecommunications.

In the US, most of the public network was owned and managed by the Bell System (i.e. AT&T), a large and very powerful monopoly that was under pressure from the US Justice Department to break into smaller units. To settle the federal government's anti-trust suit,

AT&T itself proposed divestiture in 1984, and the government agreed. AT&T became a long-distance company, with the right to enter the computer business; seven regional Bell operating companies (RBOCs) were formed to own and manage the local telephone networks in seven regions of the US. Old and new, these telephone companies saw electronic publishing as a potential source of new revenue. Since they were still very powerful, some publishing groups feared their entry into the field.

Government policies were another important component of the context. There was much debate about the potential impact of information technologies. Would videotex (described below) and related technologies have as much impact on economies as the telephone itself had earlier in the twentieth century? Videotex seemed attractive for three reasons: it could potentially drive economic development; an early entrant into this new field might come to dominate it and sell its technology to the rest of the world; and success in videotex would be a feather in the cap of the country that led the way.

Not surprisingly, governments became actively involved. It was natural for those of France and Japan, longtime devotees of industrial policy, to support the development of potentially flag-carrying videotex systems. More noteworthy, in Canada, where the national telephone company was in the private sector, the government followed a similar approach. The British government provided some financial support for Prestel, though at a very much more modest level. Even in the United States, the government supported exploratory projects: for example, the US Department of Agriculture's sponsorship of the development and test of the Green Thumb videotex service, with a purpose-designed terminal, for farmers; and the state of Minnesota's provision of a videotex service called Datanet for the citizens of that state.

Within the publishing industries, especially the US newspaper industry, there was apprehension about the potential for these new information technologies and considerable fear that someone else (most obviously telephone companies) would take the lead, leaving publishing companies behind, if not out of business. Some publishers saw opportunity in electronic publishing; others were motivated to enter it by fear.

There was much disagreement about models for services. Was videotex a database service adapted for homes, a newspaper of the future, or a hybrid of several models? Should each videotex service stand alone or should they be aggregated in a large mall of services?

For consumers, all this was new. They were not well prepared to adopt videotex or related services. They lacked computers, skill in using interactive terminals, and a willingness to pay high fees for unfamiliar services. Further, they were not in the habit of seeking out information or corresponding electronically with others (Dordick 1985).

Major developments in stand-alone online services

Some early online services were offered on a stand-alone basis, others as options on a videotex platform (Arlen multiple years; Tydeman et al. 1982; Carey and Elton 2010). In this section, we focus on the more important stand-alone services and lessons they provided for later web applications. Following it, we will turn to the more prominent videotex services.

Online databases can be traced to the early 1960s (Williams 1985). The earliest of these contained scientific and technical information, as well as bibliographic information and journal articles in science and medicine. They grew to include law cases, journal articles in other fields, newspaper articles, and airline guides, among much else. In some ways they mirrored today's web information services, but the means to access them and the way data were presented was different. Access was generally by purpose-designed terminals connected to international data networks; from the 1970s, the latter were usually commercial packet-switching networks such as Tymnet and Telenet. Data were retrieved through often complex logical combinations of search terms (Boolean searches) and information was typically presented as a series of records. Because of the complexity and high cost of searches (typically US$100 per hour plus communication costs), they were usually conducted by specialists familiar with the associated techniques and able to minimize charges. Over time, the search process was simplified and many non-specialists were able to conduct searches. By the mid-1980s, there were more than 2,500 databases worldwide provided by more than 1,300 organizations, and more than a million users, mostly in businesses, universities, and government (Aumente 1987). In the 1980s, a number of database operators decided to offer their service to consumers and small businesses by linking them to mainstream videotex services. They correctly anticipated consumer interest in locating old newspaper articles, current stock quotes, or airline schedules—common web information services today. However, they misjudged what consumers were willing to pay. In their minds, if businesses were willing to pay US$100 per hour to access this information, consumers would view US$12 per hour as a bargain. There was, however, little consumer interest at this price level. Nonetheless, online databases in this era created the initial designs for information services that would later appear on the Web.

The services pioneered in computer conferencing are very much present on today's Web as email, forums, person-to-person and group chat, blogs, RSS feeds, newsletters, and shared documents. Terminology was different in the early days of computer conferencing: for example, today's "chat" was called "synchronous conferencing." Computer conferencing grew out of an initiative by the then Office of Emergency Preparedness in the late 1960s and subsequently developed along several paths (Vallée 1984). The core concept was to harness the economical transmission of timeshare networks, along with the processing capability and storage of computers, for the purpose of person-to-person communication that went well beyond simple email. Though taken for granted nowadays, this was far from obvious in the early 1970s. Computer conferencing was used by academics, members of research organizations, corporate employees, and government workers. Today's online web courses evolved, in part, from distance education services utilizing computer conferencing.

A great deal of research has been published about computer conferencing, much of it relevant to the development of web services (Hiltz and Turoff 1993; Johansen 1984). Researchers found that many people read the content in computer conferences but rarely or never posted any messages; they came to be called "lurkers." Email was very popular. A number of systems allowed users to create anonymous pen names to hide their identity and, in some, to develop an *alter ego*, a feature that has become so important on the Web (Nisenholtz 1981). Early obstacles included its high cost and, since computer conferencing predated personal computers, lack of terminals in many businesses, schools, and especially homes. Over time, however, prices fell and personal computers became the ubiquitous terminal of choice. Computer conferencing continued to evolve, becoming lost as a recognizable entity only as its functionality became woven into the fabric of Internet services.

Email and electronic banking were core components in many general videotex services, but they were also stand-alone, proprietary services. The first email system using a computer was probably the MIT Mailbox, developed in 1965 by Noel Morris and Tom Van Vleck. By the early 1970s, there was already a literature about email (Day 1972). In 1983, there were more than seventy commercial email providers in North America and many more corporate systems. Commercial email was growing in Europe as well. Some of the larger public email services included Western Union Easy Link, ITT Dialcom, MCI Mail, and Sprint Telemail. A serious limitation of early services was lack of interconnection. Only by the late 1980s did the proprietary email services interconnect with each other, as well as with email services on videotex platforms and NSFNET. Junk email was not as prevalent as today, but some spam was being sent by the early 1980s. Eventually, these public email services declined as people moved over to the Internet.

Electronic banking was an extension of the computerization of banking in the 1960s and 1970s. Home banking trials began in the late 1970s in both the US and Britain (Prestel, e.g., provided limited home banking). Some banks chose to join one of the general videotex services; others set up their own proprietary services. With low penetration of personal computers, banks tried two other approaches as well. One was to use a TV set to display banking information sent over a telephone line. This was unsuccessful, probably because of the perceived lack of security and privacy. The other approach was a "screen phone" that could send and receive data, displaying it on a four-inch screen built into the telephone. It was simple to use, but expensive and not widely adopted. Banks had to wait for households to adopt personal computers; till then, home banking grew slowly. Besides the low penetration of computers in households, there were a number of other early obstacles to growth. One was the concern about privacy on the part of some potential users. Another was the popularity of audiotex banking in the 1980s. Many banks had set up automated systems to let people inquire about their balance or transfer funds between accounts over the telephone. Millions of customers used this audiotex banking and felt it was sufficient for their needs.

Banks believed that electronic banking could become a profit center, so they charged a fee of US$10 to US$15 per month for the service. However, the households most likely to become early adopters of home banking were generally wealthy, had significant assets in their banking accounts, and did not pay anything for bank services, so they balked at paying for electronic banking.

The uptake of proprietary electronic banking services grew only modestly through the mid-1990s. At that point, Citibank dropped its fee for home banking, viewing it not as a source of direct revenue, but as a key strategy for attracting and retaining upscale customers; other banks followed suit. The pace of adoption picked up significantly; by 1998, more than seven million households were conducting some form of banking online. Although many banks were watching activities on the Web, they were not yet ready to offer electronic banking on it because of fears about security. Instead, they set up modest websites with information but no transactional banking services. Electronic banking on the Web would emerge over the next few years, as banks and their customers gained greater confidence in security on the Web.

Throughout the early years of online media, non-profit organizations played a prominent role in developing content and communication services. They employed a range of systems to deliver these services including mainframes or minicomputers, existing videotex services, and small bulletin-board systems on personal computers. Many applications were related to education; others provided access to public records, help in learning how to use computers, specialized content such as health information, and community forums (Hafner 2001). Online services from "non-profits" demonstrated that many groups previously lacking access to online media could benefit from them. They also provided important clues for the development of future web services: for example, services that provide medical information and government information services for citizens.

Bulletin Board Systems (BBS) were poor people's computer conferencing. In most cases, they resided on a single personal computer equipped with special software and a modem. Most were free and operated by an individual who kept the computer on twenty-four hours a day and let others dial in to read and post messages. Limitations included users having to dial a BBS directly, which sometimes involved a long-distance call, and each system operator having to dedicate a personal computer and a telephone line to the system.

Typically, they were dedicated to a single topic. Many provided discussion about particular brands of computer, but the range of topics was very wide and included religion, hobbies, sports, and education. BBS were a craze in the late 1980s and early 1990s, much like citizens' band radio a decade earlier. In the late 1980s, there were at least 5,000 BBS operating in the US (*BBS Bible* 1989). They were also popular in Britain and Australia. Most users were computer hobbyists or people who shared a strong interest in a topic. In addition, many systems allowed users to create "handles" and post anonymously, which encouraged some uninhibited (and, on occasion, unwanted) behavior. When successful, a BBS fostered a community among its users, rather like modern social networking sites on the Web. Much of the content on BBS foreshadowed the contemporary blog.

Videotex: a platform for online services

During the 1960s, the British Post Office, then the country's national provider of both postal and telecommunications services, initiated the development of videotex. The idea was to provide homes and businesses with on-demand access to a centralized database through which anyone (it was an open system) could provide information or services (Reid 1980). Since very few households had PCs, the Post Office designed a special terminal to access videotex over regular telephone lines and display pages on TV sets. Initially called Viewdata (and subsequently Prestel), the service was intended to provide access to a broad range of information presented as pages of alphanumeric characters and very simple graphics. Communication was not part of the original concept, though the early service did allow users to transmit simple preformatted messages. Transactional services and email were added at an early stage, and the term "service provider" took over from "information provider."

Prestel faced many difficulties on the consumer front. The residential terminal was expensive and it took several seconds for a page to "paint" on a TV screen. Pricing was complex and expensive. Furthermore, Prestel tied up two key residential services: telephone and television. Given these obstacles, early use was overwhelmingly by businesses. Although a few component services were successful, notably one for smaller travel agents enabling them to book tickets for their clients, overall usage did not grow to a sufficient scale, and the service was phased out in the mid-1990s.

Prestel provided many lessons for videotex services that started later and for the development of web services. It was clear that consumers would not buy or rent a terminal that could only access videotex. Also, they wanted a flat-rate subscription and were unwilling to pay long-distance charges to reach the host computer (Hooper 1985). People also wanted to communicate and have fun more than to access significant amounts of serious information, and the navigational architecture for reaching information had to be improved (Sutherland 1980).

Videotex developments in Britain were followed closely in France. The French were in the process of upgrading their telephone network and wanted applications that would boost its use. They were also seeking an alternative to the paper telephone directory. The hope of creating a technology that could be exported and enhance France's image in telecommunications technology provided further incentive to develop videotex. Their Minitel service was rolled out in 1983. It utilized a small, stand-alone terminal with a 9-inch black-and-white screen, which had the advantage of not requiring the use of the television set.

The French government decided to subsidize millions of terminals, distributing them free of charge to households who agreed to forego paper directories. It believed free terminals would overcome the resistance to videotex encountered elsewhere (Aumente 1987). The online telephone directory was free; other services cost approximately $10 per hour. By the early 1990s, five million free terminals had been distributed to French homes. Businesses could rent terminals, and many did.

Qualitatively, usage of Minitel mirrored that of Prestel in many ways. Communication services and professional applications were popular. There was a wide range of additional services, including news, banking, mail order, and booking travel. Particularly popular on Minitel were "messageries roses"—sexually oriented chat areas.

Minitel proved that videotex could reach a critical mass, but it did not prove that it could do so in the absence of a significant government subsidy. Some compared it to the supersonic Concorde: a widely admired technology but one requiring government sub-sidy throughout its useful life. By the late 1990s, as many users migrated to the Internet, usage of Minitel started to decline, and it was eventually phased out.

Videotex trials and services were launched in more than a dozen countries, other examples being the Captain service in Japan and Bildschirmtext in Germany. In North America, Canada and the US were very active in videotex and related online technolo-gies. Canada ran a series of trials using its government-developed Telidon videotex sys-tem and deployed public access terminals with its Teleguide service. Videotex services launched in the US could be divided into two groups: ASCII services, which used simple text with no graphics and were generally monochrome; and graphical services, which had both color and graphics. The former provided unformatted text which scrolled down the screen; the latter provided formatted text that filled one screen of information at a time.

The best known ASCII videotex services were CompuServe and The Source, both launched in the US during the late 1970s. Each consisted of news, games, email, a dating service, forums, and chat. Early users were predominantly male and came from both businesses and households. The primary service (25 percent of all usage) was email (Tydeman et al. 1982).

CompuServe acquired The Source in 1989 and absorbed its user base. By 1990, the combined service had nearly 600,000 subscribers. The early obstacles to rapid growth for both CompuServe and The Source were price, speed, and scarcity of terminals in homes. Over time, prices for both services were reduced, transmission speed increased, and terminal problems eased as millions of homes acquired personal computers. In the mid-1990s, CompuServe was one of three major videotex operators (AOL and Prodigy being the others) that opened up its service to the Web. In combination, these videotex services placed several million people on the Web. This was a crucial step that enabled the Web to reach critical mass so quickly.

Viewtron and Gateway were two prominent graphical videotex services in the early and mid-1980s. They were similar in their technologies, services, and outcomes. Both were partnerships between a telephone company (AT&T) and a newspaper publisher (Knight Ridder and Times Mirror, respectively), with dozens of additional information providers. They offered high-end graphics (which slowed the services significantly) and provided a robust range of services including news, banking, travel, games, email, chat, and forums. Both became laboratories for advertising. One agency, Ogilvy and Mather, formed an interactive marketing group that created advertisements for multiple clients on both services. It developed banner ads and advertising "sites" a decade before the Web.

Research on Viewtron and Gateway revealed that consumers were more interested in communication than information: email and chat were the most heavily used services, as had already been discovered in Europe. Both started with an electronic newspaper supplemented by other services and finished with a communication and games service that included news and shopping. It was also clear that the PC, now starting to enter homes, was the preferred access terminal. There were some tantalizing clues in the

Viewtron research about what would work in a future web environment. For example, an eBay-style auction, "Bidquick," was surprisingly popular. Viewtron also made significant advances in online advertising by mixing content and banner advertising on the same screen—a model taken for granted on today's Web.

The Prodigy videotex service was launched in 1988, having started as a trial in 1982. It was not an electronic newspaper, but an entertainment, communication, transaction, and information service for consumers. It had a friendly graphical user interface and employed caching to reduce access time. The innovations it introduced included services for young children; "Fast Track" access to services (the equivalent of today's "Favorites"); customized information (e.g. personalized stock portfolios); information about "best prices"; local community information; and opinion polls. It developed local access nodes, allowing access by a local telephone call from most major markets.

Prodigy opened an email gateway to the Internet, and in 1995 it created its own web browser, becoming the first of the large videotex services to offer web access. Though it reached a few million subscribers at its peak, it was far outpaced by its rival, AOL, and failed to turn a profit. The business model was correct for the long term but inadequate in the short term. The company was sold and resold, eventually being absorbed by telecommunications giant SBC (now AT&T).

America Online (AOL) came late to the videotex arena and was, by some standards, unremarkable compared to rivals such as Prodigy. Yet, it far outpaced its competitors, and at one point had more than 30 million subscribers worldwide. In the mid-2000s it lost considerable ground as subscribers migrated to broadband Internet service providers, but it had been a remarkable success story through the early 2000s. In the early 1990s, as millions of people bought their first computers, the company positioned itself as a service for computer neophytes. Its service was simple to use and had content categories that appealed to the mass public. Emphasis was on communication, not information; it provided an email service for the masses. When the Web arrived, AOL hesitated initially to make it available to their subscribers, but soon opened the doors to selected websites (a "walled garden" approach) and subsequently to the entire Web. They also changed their pricing to a flat US$19.95 per month for unlimited access. By 1996, AOL had five million subscribers in the US. It was both a proprietary videotex service, with content and services controlled by AOL, and, at the same time, the largest Internet service provider in the US.

With a few exceptions, these US videotex systems were closed—an information or service provider needed the operator's permission to offer a service. To be sure, the videotex system operators were soliciting companies to offer services and, in some cases, paying them. However, the system operator remained in control and could deny access to any service provider. There were understandable concerns: information providers might offer salacious content that would drive users away; third parties might sue the system operator because of erroneous or slanderous content distributed by information providers; and the reputation of the system operator (especially in the case of telephone companies and newspaper publishers) might be damaged if content did not meet certain standards. Users, too, were expected to abide by a set of policies about appropriate behavior, and they could be (and sometimes were) thrown off a service.

THE RELEVANCE OF EARLIER
ONLINE ACTIVITIES

Both the number of users of the Internet and the number of sites on the Web grew at stunning rates from 1995 when the Internet was opened to commercial use and the videotex community of consumers and businesses began to merge with the Internet's preexisting community comprising, for the most part, academics, students, and others from outside the corporate world. If a comparison is made with the lackluster adoption of videotex over the preceding ten to twenty years, there are several factors besides the quality and cost of infrastructure that need to be borne in mind. First, by the mid-1990s, there were far more computers in households and far more people who had learned to use computers at school. Second, communication was the force driving use of the Internet, and the existence of a large number of people already communicating online made it attractive for others to sign on, minimally for email. As a result, there was no chicken-and-egg problem of the kind that occurs when network services start from scratch. Third, in the years that followed the opening of the Internet to commercial use, operators of videotex services—some sooner, others later—came to provide their subscribers with connection to the Internet, thus contributing a substantial number of established users of online services. Finally, experience with videotex and other online services had contributed much valuable understanding about what people did and did not want in the online world and about factors that were important in the design of services. We turn now to which of those lessons were learnt and which were not.

Lessons learned, lessons ignored

Many successful web applications in the transition period of the mid-1990s to early 2000s had roots in earlier online services that had either worked well or provided clues for successful implementation (Dutton and Blumler 1989). For example, it was very clear from earlier research that many forms of communication would be attractive to Internet users: email, forums, and chat. Communication could also be added to information or transaction services and boost usage, as in consumers' product reviews. Experience with earlier online services had indicated that user-generated content could successfully compete with or, as in readers' comments about newspaper articles, complement professional content. Popular content on earlier online services also proved popular on the Web, for example weather, sports, news, and games. Earlier research indicated that consumers would accept advertising, especially if it helped to reduce the price of services, but that advertisements should not be so graphically intense that they slowed down the user experience. Private sections of online systems such as The Source or CompuServe, which met the needs of companies for internal information and communication services, also provided links to other organizations with which the companies did business.

These private sections evolved into intranets and extranets. It was very clear from earlier online services that flat-rate pricing was preferred to metered pricing.

Earlier online research provided many clues about what could be attractive to users if improvements were made. Auctions on The Source and Viewtron were moderately successful, hinting that a more robust and better-designed auction service could be very successful. eBay filled this gap. Early online databases were used to search for information, but they were too complicated for ordinary users; Prodigy had three forms of search, all of them primitive. Portals (e.g. Yahoo) and search engines advanced the search process significantly. There were also clues in earlier research that multiple forms of online commerce could be successful, provided transactions met consumer requirements for security, trusted brands, transparency in the transaction, quality merchandize, fulfillment, and favorable return policies. Over time, many web commerce applications met these goals; price comparisons and user reviews were an added benefit. Experience from the early Prestel service through Prodigy indicated that online travel and brokerage services were likely to be popular—and they were.

Much of what did not work in web applications through the early 2000s had not worked in earlier online services. But the lessons from failure were not learned, and mistakes were repeated (Noll 1985). A frequent error was to create websites from company brochures or printed marketing materials, with no adaptation to the online environment and its users' expectations. Brochureware, as this was called, represented a fundamental misunderstanding of online services as a distinctive medium. Another such mistake was failure to update web content or to remove abandoned sites—deadly mistakes in the videotex era, repeated on the early Web.

Newspapers and magazines struggled with how to adapt their print products to the Web. Initially, many simply published the same print content on the Web—in the same format and after publication of the print product. This did not work well for videotex, nor did it work well during the web transition period. Newspapers and magazines needed to redesign the electronic versions of their products in accordance with how people read online, their expectations of timeliness, and their desire to communicate about news stories.

Subscription revenue featured prominently in business plans for web services during this period. Seemingly ignorant of the history of earlier online services, many publishers believed that new groups of consumers coming onto the Web would pay for content through subscriptions, much as they paid for newspapers and magazines. Like earlier online users, however, new web users were unwilling to do so, exceptions being some businesses that had paid for access to online databases and now paid for specialized online newsletters. Only a few publications, for example, *The Wall Street Journal Interactive Edition* and *Consumer Reports Online*, succeeded in generating significant subscription revenue. Many newspapers and magazines offered the bulk of their online content at no cost; when they charged for special sections or tiers of content above the free level, this produced only modest revenue.

User experience with online content was another area where earlier mistakes were repeated. A key issue was designing content to work within the limits of modem speeds.

Many videotex applications had been heavy on graphics at a time when modem speeds were very slow, so the user experience suffered. Many early websites repeated the mistake and had long access times, for example taking more than one minute for access to their home page (generating jokes about the "World Wide Wait").

Research as early as the late 1970s indicated that, when people had to make choices from menus on successive screens in a tree-and-branch architecture, they made many errors and often abandoned the search through frustration (Sutherland 1980). This common problem in the videotex era recurred in the transition to the Web. Some sites even had a "Welcome" page that merely provided an entrance to the site. Users wanted information to be brought up from the basement of extra screens and presented as close as possible to the initial web page.

Then and now

Today, some of the research and policy issues that were raised in connection with videotex are of importance in shaping the future of the Internet: questions about openness provide an obvious example. But an understanding of the period of transition from pre-Internet online services to the early Internet is valuable for a rather different reason, too: it causes a number of issues of continuing importance to stand out in sharp relief—examples being the provision of financial support by government, how well industry insiders actually understand what is going on around them, the value of the Internet in providing a continually improving infrastructure which is so incredibly open to service innovation, and how changing user context will be of importance in shaping the future of the Internet. We now provide a brief discussion of these examples.

Visions and understanding

Though videotex fell by the wayside, its underlying vision was sound in some important respects. Among the general public, there was indeed an enormous latent demand for online access to a wide variety of information and communication services. It was correct that a broad-based online industry would be a powerful engine for national economic development. And the British Post Office team was right in foreseeing the eventual advantages of an open platform, rather than one or a number of walled gardens. Videotex, however, was not sufficiently in sync with the technological context of its time. For its realization, it needed a far more suitable transmission and switching infrastructure than the public telephone network could provide, and it needed to make use of home terminals much less awkward than the initial television-telephone combinations and with lower incremental costs than subsequent purpose-designed devices.

It is noteworthy that ARPANET was being developed and extended in the United States at the same time as European countries and Japan were formulating and trying out their visions of videotex. ARPANET, however, was not guided by any such vision; it did not have an ambitious concrete goal similar to the man-on-the-moon target of the US space program. (From 1971, the concept of the "wired city" with its electronic highway had attracted attention in the US, and to a lesser extent in Europe and Japan, but it was associated with an infrastructure provided by cable television systems (Dutton et al. 1986), not by ARPANET; different research communities centered on the "wired city" and on ARAPANET.) Technology push was strong enough to succeed in the US, while demand pull could not overcome technology constraints in Europe and Japan. Far from it being disrespectful to state that the Internet "grew like Topsy," this is to recognize the essence of its success: it is inconceivable that a major telephone company would have implemented a system over which it would quickly come to have so little control and which would come to cause such a decline in its core business, or that a government, let alone one subject to corporate lobbying, would have fostered a technology so disruptive of vested interests.

Telephone companies were strikingly slow to understand the Internet: in the parlance of the time, they just didn't "get it." (Isenberg (1997) provided a trenchant critique of the US telephone companies in this regard.) Microsoft was one of many others who were also slow to recognize the potential of the Internet (Auletta 1997).

As NSFNET emerged, the prevailing value system of what was soon to become the Internet was one of sharing: it went beyond being non-commercial to being positively anti-commercial. At the time when the network was opened up to commercial transactions, many insiders predicted that its then value system was so strongly entrenched that commercial applications could never become a significant part of the whole. How quickly they were proved wrong! John Perry Barlow (1998) captured the feelings of many in his celebrated manifesto, "A Declaration of the Independence of Cyberspace." Six years later, he remarked about his earlier optimism, saying "We all get older and smarter" (Doherty 2004).

Well-placed members of the Internet community have frequently been seriously mistaken in their broad predictions about what would happen with the Internet only a very few years ahead. These errors were not limited to the Internet's start-up years, caused mainly by the astonishing rate of its expansion; as the dotcom crash showed, gross errors in prediction continued to at least the year 2000. One can also look at the past to find multi-billion dollar blunders in a greatly calmer telecommunications field when new applications came mainly from those who controlled networks rather than from unpredictable users at their periphery: AT&T's Picturephone, Craig McCaw's (and Bill Gates's) Teledesic satellite project, and AT&T's withdrawal from the cellular telephone market in the early 1980s are a few among the better known examples.

One of many factors making the Internet such a treacherous domain for prediction is the role of serendipity or, more generally, luck. Some applications succeed because they become fashionable, but how well can one expect to predict fashion?

The Internet has a vast number of disparate users, some of them highly creative. A new service may be introduced with one purpose in mind and enjoy enormous success after users have discovered a different use for it. Twitter appears to have been started as a service for providing very short messages with the information, "Here is where I am and this is what I'm doing" provided by ordinary people. But its success appears to be bound up with providing information such as "This is what I am thinking" or "This is what people should know" by ordinary people, celebrities, news organizations, and companies promoting themselves. There may be a logic that explains why the service has been such a success, but maybe the logic can be understood only in hindsight. As Jonathan Zittrain commented: "The qualities that make Twitter seem inane and half-baked are what make it so powerful" (Cohen 2009).

For both videotex and the Internet, fear has been a powerful factor propelling firms to take the plunge into the online world. It showed up, for example, in US videotex trials when newspapers allied themselves with a telephone company. It showed up in the "clicks versus bricks" issue in Internet-based e-commerce. When drawing lessons from experience with Prestel in the UK, Richard Hooper (1985), one of its former directors, noted that companies that had entered the online world primarily for defensive reasons had not done so successfully. This has probably remained the case since then.

Fears about the impact of online services on established industries—in particular, newspapers and postal services—did prove to be well founded, but the timing of the projected impacts was incorrect because it was necessary to wait for the Internet, rather than videotex, to wreak its havoc (Kyrish 1996). The time when it is most important to assess the impact of a new technology is before it has become established, but unfortunately there is no acceptable methodology for doing so (Carey and Elton 2010).

Provision of financial support by government

While governments in Europe, Japan, and Canada provided financial support for their national videotex projects, only the French government subsidized its system to any significant extent. By contrast, the US government nurtured ARPANET and NSFNET over the long term, and this was essential to the Internet's coming into existence. The success of the Internet is a tribute to farsighted government involvement and investment, just as much as it is to the subsequent entrepreneurial energy unleashed upon it.

Notwithstanding that nowadays the Internet is certainly a proven technology well able to stand firmly on its own feet, the issue of financial support from different national governments has certainly not disappeared. The most obvious example lies in governments' contributions to the costs of building infrastructure that will enormously improve speeds of access to the Internet: South Korea provides an example. Investments of this kind became all the more attractive to some governments as a means of stimulating economies in the wake of the devastating banking collapse of 2008.

As the United States shows, governments' financial support of the Internet and activities that ride on it need not come wholly from their own tax revenues. In the US, some of the money to be invested in broadband networks in rural areas is to come from the Universal Service Fund, which is financed by a levy on vendors (hence users) of telecommunications (as opposed to Internet) services. More curiously, by its failure to enact legislation to remove obstacles to states' collection of sales tax on Internet purchases from out-of-state vendors, the federal government still causes state governments to be unwilling subsidizers of e-commerce. While understandable as a means of incentivizing e-commerce when it was a "fledgling industry," it seems somewhat strange today.

Infrastructure and the openness of platforms

By the first half of the 1970s, commercial packet-switched networks had become available. Their coverage was international, and they could be accessed either by private lines or by dial-up gateways connected to the public telephone network. The other early online services, however, were severely hampered by inadequacy of infrastructure: they were totally or heavily reliant on the public telephone network, which was far less suitable and, generally, far more expensive for data transmission than the packet-switched networks. As a result, compared with what we enjoy on the Web today, videotex services were extremely slow and expensive, and interconnectivity was severely constrained. In the case of market trials, especially those of interactive cable television systems (many of which provided online services), it was often necessary to install purpose-designed infrastructure at very high cost (Carey and Elton 2010).

Initially, the Internet was an infrastructure which transmitted data (including text and graphics) efficiently and at very low cost; fairly soon, it also became able to transmit asynchronous and real-time voice and video. It is not controlled by a central authority whose permission is necessary before would-be providers of information and services can open for business. Storage and intelligence are under the control of users (including providers of information and services) at the edge of the network. A particularly important result of the Internet's openness is that it has greatly reduced the costs of failure for an enormous variety of innovative services—especially those for which home computers and multipurpose mobile devices can preclude the need for purpose-designed terminals—and vastly expanded the universe of those around the globe who can introduce them. The former makes it possible to adopt a "try it and see" approach to the marketing of some new service, rather than a more measured, research-based approach; the latter provides pressure to "get it out the door" as soon as possible, before some competitive service is introduced, thus also weakening the case for research.

Those in charge of the British videotex system decided from the start that it should be open: any traders prepared to pay the rent would be permitted to set up their stalls in its electronic marketplace and, subject to minimal restrictions, charge whatever they wanted for their wares. This was all the more noteworthy because the concept of a "common carrier" did not have a place in British telecommunications; later, in the United States, where the concept did have a central role, the operators of graphics videotex services decided against creating truly open systems. According to Hooper (1984):

> The common carrier policy was justified by British Telecom on three main grounds.
> It was politically wise for the telephone company to avoid getting involved in editorial

content. . . . It was administratively wise since the supervision of hundreds of thousands of different pages would be difficult. It was commercially wise because market forces and competition would ensure that low-priced Prestel sets would be produced, and that good pages on the database would drive out bad.

After Prestel's disappointing progress in its early years, British Telecom moved away from its common carrier approach. In discussing the reasons, Hooper explained that:

> It did not solve the problems of building subscribers from a zero base. It would probably be an excellent policy when Prestel has 200,000 subscribers, but it did not help Prestel get from 0 to 200,000! . . . Subscribers will only subscribe when there are good information and transaction services. But [information providers] cannot afford to invest in good services until there is a good population of subscribers.

He also pointed to the horrendous problem of central indexing because of the incomplete and variable nature of the services offered. Another of the reasons he offered was the lack of evidence that, in a competitive environment, a videotex operator could make sufficient revenue from "pure bit transport." Finally, he noted that since Prestel was perceived by customers and politicians as belonging to and endorsed by British Telecom, the corporation could not sidestep the problem of "legal but distasteful pages" by means of a common carrier policy.

Though Prestel was an open system, initially, those who used its platform to provide information or services had to store their pages in a Prestel computer, use its operating system, and be subject to its indexing system. The Web is open in ways that Prestel in its common carrier days was not.

The openness of the Web is an issue to which increasing attention is being paid today. Threats to it range from impediments imposed by non-democratic governments to the proliferation of "apps" which bypass web browsers; Apple's exercise of control over which apps are allowed onto its mobile platform has been seen as a possible portent for the future. Additionally, in the US and elsewhere, controversies about net neutrality involve concerns about openness.

The user context

Between the mid-1970s and today there have been massive changes in what may be termed the user context: users' prior experience with interactive technologies, their skills, their expectations, and the technologies available to them. With hindsight, it is clear just how high a hurdle to the uptake of videotex services these were. In the earliest days of videotex, many potential users did not even know the purpose of an "Enter" key—there was no such key on telephones or the remote controls of TV sets (Carey 1985). As noted above, by the mid-1980s the diffusion of home computers (and, gradually, modems) meant that the hurdle was appreciably lower for ASCII videotex in North America. Today, skill levels of the general public are very much higher, but technology and software continue to push the envelope past the skill levels of many, for example when a functionality appears on a web page only as a user moves a mouse over an otherwise empty space on the screen.

Broadly speaking, videotex started by using television sets and touchtone telephones as primary components of a consumer terminal; next it moved to purpose-designed devices and then on to personal computers. For consumers on the Internet, new kinds of terminals have generally come to complement previous kinds, rather than replace them, and the direction of change has been reversed: starting with home computers then progressing through cell phones, other mobiles, videogame consoles, and television sets (with some purpose-specific devices, such as Internet radios, along the way). In some parts of the world, notably in developing countries, it is clear that web access for many will bypass the computer completely and the mobile phone will become the access terminal of choice or necessity.

The future significance of access to the Internet by mobile phones was foreshadowed by the success of DoCoMo's mobile Internet service, i-mode, in Japan, where, starting in 1999, it provided access to the Internet for the many young Japanese without a computer at home. Outside Japan, however, i-mode was not a success; the first generation of WAP (Wireless Application Protocol) services in Europe was a failure; and a subsequent generation of mobile web browsers received a lukewarm reception from users. Only with the development of apps, accessed by symbols on a smartphone screen, did usage take off. What had been slow, cumbersome, and boring then became fast, fun, and convenient.

The videotex era started with many problems associated with ease of use. In the modern web era, navigating to reach content is much easier, but there are some forces pushing back in the other direction. Examples are the proliferation of requirements for passwords, especially complex passwords, and for other forms of authentication, as when in order to see a live video of a sports event on the Web one must prove that one is a paying subscriber to a cable, telephone company, or satellite service that is carrying the event.

CONCLUSION

Online services for the general public did not start with the Web. In a dozen or more countries, they started earlier, and they certainly helped drive the remarkably vigorous early diffusion of the Internet. The history of the Internet can be made richer and more complete by drawing on past studies of these earlier services—failures as well as successes—both in their in stand-alone days and as new immigrants to the Internet.

The Internet community solved the problem of interconnecting disparate computer systems so as to create new and synergistic wholes. Studies of the Web and, more generally, the Internet have not, however, been interconnected well with studies of earlier online services and, more generally, new media. To provide a more complete appreciation of the history of the Internet, the research community—really, disparate communities— needs to solidify the field. Moreover, the benefits of more joined-up approaches would, in our view, provide benefits far transcending better historical studies.

Acknowledgment

Parts of this chapter draw from Carey and Elton (2010).

References

Arlen, G. (multiple years). *Interactivity Report*, Bethesda, MD: Arlen Communications.

Auletta, K. (1997). *The Highwaymen*, New York: Random House.

Aumente, J. (1987). *New Electronic Pathways: Videotex, Teletext and Online Databases*, Newbury Park, CA: Sage Publications.

Barlow, J. (1998). "A Declaration of the Independence of Cyberspace." Available at <https://projects.eff.org/~barlow/Declaration-Final.html>. Accessed September 11, 2010.

BBS Bible (1989). Collegeville, PA: No listed publisher.

Carey, J. (1985). "Terminals in Public Locations," in M. Greenberger (ed.), *Electronic Publishing Plus*. White Plains, NY: Knowledge Industries Publications, pp. 13–25.

—— and Elton, M. C. J. (2010). *When Media Are New: Understanding the Dynamics of New Media Adoption and Use*, Ann Arbor: University of Michigan Press.

Cohen, N. (2009). "Twitter on the Barricades: Six Lessons Learned," *New York Times*, June 20. Available at <http://www.nytimes.com/2009/06/21/weekinreview/21cohenweb.html>. Accessed July 5, 2012.

Day, L. (1972). "Electronic Mail Services in the Information Age." Bell Canada Business Planning Paper 1.

Doherty, B. (2004). "John Perry Barlow 2.0: The Thomas Jefferson of Cyberspace Reinvents his Body—and his Politics." *Reason*, August/September. Available at <http://reason.com/archives/2004/08/01/john-perry-barlow-20>. Accessed July 5, 2012.

Dordick, H. (1985). "The Search for the Electronic Publishing Business," in M. Greenberger (ed.), *Electronic Publishing Plus*, White Plains, NY: Knowledge Industries Publications, pp. 205–7.

Dutton, W., Blumer, J., and Kraemer, K. (eds) (1986). *Wired Cities: Shaping the Future of Communications*, Boston: G.K. Hall & Company.

Dutton, W. and Blumler, J. (1989). "A Comparative Perspective on Information Societies," in J. Salvaggio (ed.), *The Information Society: Economic, Social and Structural Issues*, Hillsdale, NJ: Lawrence Erlbaum Associates, pp. 63–88.

Fidler, R. (1997). *Mediamorphosis: Understanding New Media*, Thousand Oaks, CA: Pine Forge Press.

Hafner, K. (1998). *Where Wizards Stay Up Late: The Origins of the Internet*, New York: Simon & Schuster.

—— (2001). *The WELL: A Story of Love, Death and Real Life in the Seminal Online Community*, New York: Carroll and Graf Publishers.

Hiltz, S. and Turoff, M. (1993). *The Network Nation: Human Communication via Computer*, Cambridge: The MIT Press.

Hooper, R. (1984). "Prestel, Escher, Bach: Changes within Changes," Cambridge, MA: Harvard University (Program on Information Resources Policy, Center for Information Policy Research). Available at <http://pirp.harvard.edu/pubs_pdf/hooper/hooper-i84-1.pdf>. Accessed September 13, 2010.

—— (1985). "Lessons From Overseas: The British Experience," in Greenberger, M. (ed.), *Electronic Publishing Plus*, White Plains, NY: Knowledge Industries Publications, pp. 181–99.

Isenberg, D. (1997). "The Rise of the Stupid Network," *Computer Telephony*, 5(8), August: 16–26.

Johansen, R. (1984). *Teleconferencing and Beyond: Communication in the Office of the Future*, New York: McGraw-Hill.

Kyrish, S. (1996). *From Videotex to the Internet: Lessons from Online Services, 1981–1996*, Melbourne: La Trobe University Online Media Program.

Leiner, B., Cerf, V., Clark, D., Kahn, R., Kleinrock, L., Lynch, D., Postel, J., Roberts, L., and Wolff, S. (n.d.). *A Brief History of the Internet*, Geneva: The Internet Society. Available at <www.isoc.org/internet/history/brief.shtml>. Accessed September 15, 2010.

Nisenholtz, M. (1981). "Information Technology and New Forms of Collective Participation in the Narrative." Paper presented at the Ninth World Computer Congress.

Noll, A. M. (1985). "Videotex: Anatomy of a Failure," *Information and Management*, 9(2): 99–109.

Reid, A. A. L. (ed.) (1980). *Prestel 1980*, London: Post Office Telecommunications.

Roberts, L. (1966). "Towards a Cooperative Network of Time-Shared Computers." MIT Working Paper.

Sutherland, S. (1980). *Prestel and the User*, Brighton: University of Sussex Centre for Research on Perception and Cognition.

Tydeman, J., Lipinski, H., Adler, R., Nyhan, M., and Zwimpfer, L. (1982). *Teletext and Videotext in the United States*, New York: McGraw Hill.

Vallée, J. (1984). *Computer Message Systems*, New York: McGraw Hill.

Williams, M. (1985). "Electronic Databases," *Science*, 299(4): 450–5.

CHAPTER 3

....

WEB SCIENCE

....

KIERON O'HARA AND WENDY HALL

INTRODUCTION: THE RATIONALE
FOR WEB SCIENCE

....

THE World Wide Web is an extraordinarily transformative technology. Claims for its significance range from hype to skepticism, but most agree that its capacity for supporting communication and access to documents is several orders of magnitude greater than previous technologies, bringing great changes, not only to the Internet and information and communications technology (ICT), but also to the offline world, affecting the media, entertainment, politics and government, science and research, administration, and commerce. Whole new areas of activity such as social networking and e-crime have flourished using its protocols. The number of users is vast and growing, and its decentralized structure—there is no editor of content, no quality control, and anyone can link to anything—has democratized communication in all sorts of ways.

Yet for all that, the Web is remarkably under-studied and under-theorized. There seem to be three principal reasons for this. First, it is a dauntingly large and complex structure. Understanding the Web in its context requires working at a number of scales from the micro-level of the detail of individual protocols like HTTP (Hypertext Transfer Protocol) or HTML (Hypertext Markup Language), to the macro-level of emergent behavior such as blogging, spamming, or e-commerce. Second, it evolves very quickly, so data soon become outdated. Third, it is a curious amalgam of technologies (hardware, software protocols, and programming environments such as Java and AJAX [Asynchronous JavaScript and XML]), and human activities (the Web links not only documents and data, but people as well).

Hence a comprehensive overview demands multidisciplinary skills relevant to computing, law, economics, sociology, management and organization studies, media studies, semiotics, mathematics, and innumerable subdisciplines (Berners-Lee et al. 2006a). Too often the Web is studied as an example of a particular phenomenon—a network, a set of computer languages, or a platform for commerce. It is all those, but taken as a whole it is so much more.

In particular, we must not fall into the error of thinking that the proper study of the Web is within computer science (CS). In CS, Web-related research focuses on technical issues, such as information retrieval algorithms or the algorithms for routing information through the underlying Internet. Yet these properties, important as they are, cannot be the whole story. Google's PageRank link analysis algorithm, for instance, is a brilliant piece of work, but its significance to the Web depends not only on the algorithmic structure, but also on the *context* of its use, which is outside the province of CS. Nothing about the algorithm per se explains how the eigenvectors that it computes map miraculously onto the conversations that web users have, nor about how it is constantly adapted to avoid spoofing.

Many research memes within CS are positively hostile to the Web's governing principles. For example, consider the famous letter written by the formalist Edsger Dijkstra entitled "GOTO Statement Considered Harmful" (Dijkstra 1968). In it he argued (correctly) that the sudden and arbitrary leaps that the GOTO command made possible, render the formalization of programs extremely difficult, and therefore the use of the command should be avoided in programming for critical systems. Yet, in effect, hyperlinks mean the Web is *constituted* by the wretched GOTOs!

How is the Web likely to develop? Sensemaking, reuse, and retrieval are vital. It is currently largely made up of linked documents, often text documents, so Natural Language Processing techniques add value by extracting some form of meaning from the human-readable text of the pages based on heuristics or statistics (Wilks and Brewster 2009). But an increasingly important extension, the *Semantic Web*, envisages linking *data* resources enriched by ontologies that give interpretations of terms used, to allow machine processing of the Web's content (Shadbolt et al. 2006). This development is exciting yet challenging. How can we allow independent consistent data systems to be connected locally without requiring an implausible and totalitarian *global* consistency? How do we query an unbounded Web of linked information repositories? How should we align different data models, and visualize and navigate the huge connected graph of information that results? Who should bear liability for shared data resources?

To answer such questions and understand the basic issues underlying them, researchers are fostering the new discipline of Web Science (Berners-Lee et al. 2006a, 2006b; Shneiderman 2007; Shadbolt and Berners-Lee 2008) to develop methods and curricula to understand the Web and provide foundations for engineering methodologies. Web Science is not just modeling the Web. It includes engineering infrastructure protocols using tools from many disciplines which may involve radical thinking about technology and society, while still respecting the Web's invariants: decentralization to avoid bottlenecks and facilitate scalability; serendipitous reuse of information; fairness, openness, and trust (Berners-Lee et al. 2006a). If Web Science delivers a greater understanding of the Web, threats can be identified and addressed, opportunities pursued, and the Web itself can be adapted to social change.

This chapter explores the agenda of Web Science for the development of the future Web. We begin with a definition of the object of study, the architecture and conventions of the World Wide Web itself. The next section explores the foundational assumptions of Web Science, looking in the abstract at how the Web's development can be influenced. The following section takes as an example the role of Web Science in the development of a Web of Linked Data, before rounding off with a concluding discussion.

What exactly is the Web?

The distinction between the Internet and the Web is not widely understood: the Web is certainly the most visible Internet application, and most Internet users are also web users, so the two are often confused. In this section, we will briefly set out the simple technologies which make the Web a flexible, usable information space which, most importantly, scales when the number of users increases (see Jacobs and Walsh 2004 for more detail). Our task in this section is, therefore, to set out the essential technologies and protocols that make up the Web, and the social regularities that have helped it flourish.

Web architecture

The Web is a space in which *resources* are identified by *Uniform Resource Identifiers* (URIs—Berners-Lee et al. 2005). *Protocols* support *interaction* and *information transfer* between computers, while *formats* are used to *represent* the information resources. These are the basic ingredients of the Web, upon whose designs depends the utility and efficiency of web interaction.

Identification of resources is essential for sharing information about them, reasoning about them, modifying or exchanging them. Resources may be anything that can be linked to or spoken of. Not all resources are on the Web. Even if they are *identifiable* from the Web, they may not be *retrievable* from it. Those resources which are essentially information, and which can therefore be rendered without abstraction and characterized completely in a digital artifact (for example, a text file or a video) are called *information resources*.

For reasoning and referencing to happen on a global scale, an identification system is required to provide a single global standard: URIs provide that system. It would be possible to develop alternatives to URIs, but a *single* universal system of identifiers facilitates linking, bookmarking, and other value-adding functions across heterogeneous applications. Ideally, each URI identifies a single resource in a context-independent manner (this is desirable, but not enforceable). Accessing a resource via a URI is called *dereferencing* the URI.

URIs fall under particular defined *schemes*, of which the most commonly used are *HTTP*, *FTP* (File Transfer Protocol), and *mailto:*. If we take HTTP as an example, an HTTP URI should ideally refer to a single resource, and be allocated to a single owner. What accessing a resource entails varies from context to context, but a common experience is receiving a representation of the (state of the) resource on a browser. It need not be this way: it may be that no representation of the resource is available, or that access is limited (e.g. password-controlled). Not all types of URI are intended to provide access to representations of the resources they identify. For instance, the mailto: scheme identifies resources that are reached using Internet mail (e.g. mailto:romeo@example.edu identifies a particular mailbox), but those resources aren't *recoverable* from the URI in the same way as a web page is. Rather, the URI is used to *direct* mail to that particular mailbox, or alternatively to find mail from it.

The development of the Web as a space for *interaction* follows from the ability of agents to alter the states of resources and to incur obligations and responsibilities. Retrieving a representation is an example of a so-called *safe* interaction where no alteration occurs, while posting to a list, is an *unsafe* interaction where resources' states may be altered. Note that the universal nature of URIs helps identification and tracking of obligations incurred online through unsafe interactions.

The power of the Web in enabling communication, free expression, querying, and interaction stems from the linking it makes possible. A resource can contain a reference to another resource in the form of an embedded URI that can be used to access the second resource, thereby allowing associative navigation of the Web. To facilitate linking, a format should include ways to create and identify links to other resources, should allow links to any resources anywhere over the Web, and should not constrain authors to particular URI schemes. Although a stable reference system will reduce ambiguities, allow consistent reference to resources of whatever type across heterogeneous applications, and facilitate the automation of information-retrieval tasks, URI schemes cannot be enforced. For a name in a public language to be successful, it must be adopted by a community that has some tacit agreement on its use (Halpin 2009). It is not essential to have a well-ordered set of names—advances in statistically based search techniques mean that much information can be retrieved relatively efficiently—but the value of the best current search techniques is proportional to the quality of links.

Finally, it is an essential principle of web architecture that errors should be handled simply and flexibly. Errors are inevitable in an information space of thousands of terabytes, whose users number in the billions. If dangling links (URIs with no resource at the end of them), ill-formed content, or other predictable errors caused the system to crash, it would never have functioned in the first place. Furthermore, interoperability requires that agents should be able to recover from errors without compromising awareness that the error has occurred. Hence a dangling link, for example, will merely return the irritating but hardly fatal "404 error."

Conventional aspects of web use

It would be incorrect to see web architecture as a core topic, and social and ethical questions as "bolt-ons" to be addressed after the fact. These latter are fundamental. The Web is a deliberately decentralized structure, which means that there is no authority to enforce good behavior. Many types of behavior essential for the Web to work (meaning, convention, commitment) are understandable from the point of view of rational self-interest (Skyrms 1996), but there are pay-offs to bad behavior, commission (opportunities to gain by cheating), and omission (failure to maintain a website satisfactorily). Hence self-interested rationality cannot *entirely* explain how such cooperative behaviour gets off the ground (Hollis 1998; Seabright 2004); for the Web's existence requires *social norms* as well as technical protocols. These social norms have doubtless evolved partly in the context of previous mass telecommunications technologies, which will therefore have an indirect effect upon the development of the Web (Perkins and Neumayer 2011).

Web Science can help determine which practices and conventions are essential and how they relate to people's willingness to behave in a cooperative fashion. Such analysis can lead to codes of behavior that may not be enforceable but which in a sense define "desirable" or even "moral" online behavior. Social norms and engineering turn out to be linked, and may have profound consequences for the Web's future (O'Hara 2009). Some have even suggested that value be embedded in design (Baken et al. 2010), although the Web's decentralization will make that hard, and probably undesirable, to enforce.

Let's consider the example of the connection between a URI and a resource in more detail. As anyone who has had to maintain a website will know, pressure to change URIs builds up. One diachronic study of 150m web pages found that after nine weeks, access was lost to over 10 percent of them (Fetterly et al. 2004). Some degradation is caused by genuine engineering difficulties, some is merely sloth, but the Web will function better if URIs don't change and always point to the same document (or its latest version).

Avoiding changing URIs is easier said than done. For instance, when a website is reorganized, the temptation is to provide a neat new rationalized structure, expressed as a new set of URIs, expressing the new organizational philosophy. It is tempting, but unwise, to create directories called "latest" or "current" which will become outdated. Dangling links are frustrating and do a lot to undermine trust in websites and companies (Grabner-Kräuter and Kaluscha 2003). Any record of a URI by an interested party, whether a bookmark, a link from another site, or a scribbled note on paper, records the URI of a page at a moment in time and cannot easily be automatically updated (Berners-Lee 1998).

Hence convention collides with web engineering. One incurs obligations and duties when online because of the cooperative nature of the Web, and sustaining the Web's important invariants depends on them being taken seriously. Lessig (1999) has correctly argued that behavior can be constrained online by architecture, regulation, and market-based incentives, but he is careful to emphasize that social norms play a vital part as well. One of the goals of Web Science is to be able to provide models of behavior and architecture that allow different types of constraint to be virtually explored and experimented with. We are a long way from achieving a unified view, but investigations of these problematic cases are important early steps.

The science of the Web

One common misconception about engineering is that it is the application of scientific theory to achieve desired ends, given prior agreement on framing a problem and on the ends. Yet because of the *sui generis* nature of many engineering problems—this, of course, certainly applies to the Web—much of the essential knowledge needed for a solution must be derived in practice, often in response to unforeseen challenges perceived during a project itself. This has led to the development of a theory of design and engineering called *reflective practice* (Schön 1983).

In this methodology, the problem as initially set is not fixed, as practitioners must change their perceptions and strategies in response to uncertainty, instability, and unique features of the problem. They proceed experimentally, to create and discover new solutions that need be neither unique nor optimal. Controlled, reversible experiments are out of the question: the Web (as with other major engineering projects) is not a closed system, and any large-scale intervention will tend to change the object of study itself. Hence each experiment that the engineer tries must as far as possible be sensitive to the needs of the context, and take into account understanding of the social and psychological context: theoretical knowledge about complex systems cannot be tested in isolated, closed subsystems.

Web Science as reflective practice

Web Science is a type of reflective practice (O'Hara and Hall 2010). Given the complexity of the problem space, it will be essential to develop engineering methods that use the insights of reflective practice, dynamically and recursively reconfiguring the problem specification as knowledge is gained during the design and engineering processes.

Engineering the Web requires sensitivity to both technical and social concerns. The designer has an idea for an innovation and develops protocols, formalisms, software, and hardware to realize the vision, which may or may not be formally or precisely specified. However, no digital system exists in a vacuum, and its use will depend on a number of assumptions about social context implicit in the design. Note that the designer cannot specify every aspect of the system's behavior: at some point, assumptions about context will have to carry some functional weight. For instance, the email system SMTP (simple mail transfer protocol) was developed on the basis of assumptions about what people would want communications to carry, about organizational context, and about the motives of senders (specifically that messages would be sent in good faith by a homogeneous academic community, all of whose members would be concerned with the same group of problems, so messages would be relevant to the receiver, generated in response to a genuine requirement, with a transparent meaning).

On the Web, however, unintended consequences at the macro-level can emerge from changes at the micro-level. For example, as more users take up a system, there might be a marked and noticeable change in social behavior. Analysis of these macro-level effects is likely to uncover new social issues, which need to be addressed in their turn—and one way of doing this is to design and build new technology, leading to another cycle of design and social change.

To continue the example of SMTP, when it became a macro phenomenon used by people beyond the target community, the unintended consequences of free and simple communication became clear. Problems such as spam and phishing began to emerge. Social changes also accompanied the technology. Emails leave a semi-permanent record, so it became harder for companies to hide their internal decision-making, for scientists their suppression of data, and for errant spouses their infidelities. New technical solutions, such as spam filtering, were now needed to solve the problems created by the emergent phenomena. These developments have been accompanied by parallel adjustments in the law, corporate best practice, and our intuitive understanding of privacy (McArthur 2001) which themselves raise more issues (e.g. O'Hara and Shadbolt 2008), and so the cycle continues.

The dynamics and topography of the Web

The characterization of web engineering as a cyclical conversation between scientists and engineers, users and techies, fits neatly into Schön's (1983) ideas about reflective practice. However, the position is not as simple as this makes it appear (O'Hara and Hall 2010). Although the Web shares some of its developmental characteristics with other telecommunications technologies (Perkins and Neumayer 2011), the *singularities* of the Web as a piece of designed technology demand its intensive study as a first order object as envisaged by the Web Science program.

Consider the zone of time in which an action may make a difference, what Schön calls the *action-present* (1983: 62), which depends on the pace of activity and the boundaries of potential action. For the Web, this is both tiny and vast, depending on the point of view. The cycles of web development are measured in years. Blogging, for instance, took a number of years to develop from small beginnings, and then "suddenly" took off at the beginning of the century. "Suddenly" in this case takes us from the appearance of the first blogging tools and guides and the first major political issues influenced by bloggers in 2001 and 2002, to the exponential growth characteristic of the years after 2004. But we also need to factor in the timescale of an effective intervention. What seems imperative in year zero of a research project may be completely out of date by year three when a product appears.

New types of online behavior can become very popular very quickly. At the time of writing, Facebook and Twitter dominate thinking about cutting-edge large-scale web phenomena (e.g. Gaffney 2010), but by, say, 2015 it is quite likely that the landscape will be very different and those giants will appear hopelessly out of date. As each new star application comes along, new users (who may have been children during the previous cycle) arrive with it, rendering older assumptions void. In short, what might seem a relatively long action-present for Web Science is in reality very attenuated. By the time data are gathered, models created, and simulations run, the opportunity to influence events may already be past.

Hence Web Science must be concerned not only with topography but also the dynamics of the Web. There are a number of technologies and methods for mapping the Web (see Thelwall Chapter 4). What do such maps tell us (e.g. Donato et al. 2004)? The visualizations are often impressive, with three-dimensional interpretations and color-coded links between nodes. But how verifiable are such maps? In what sense do they tell us "how the Web is"? What are the limitations? Furthermore, the Web is not a static information space, but rather is dynamic and evolving (O'Neill et al. 2003), and models should ideally have built into them the growth of the system (in terms of constant addition of new vertices and edges into the graph), together with a link structure that is not invariant over time and hierarchical domain relationships that are perpetually prone to revision (e.g. Barabási et al. 2000).

The rapid growth of the Web made a complete survey out of the question years ago. In such circumstances, representative sampling is important, but how should a sample be gathered in order to be properly called representative (Leung et al. 2001)? To be properly useful, a sample should be *random*; but what does "random" mean here? Are we concerned, for instance, with websites or web pages? Furthermore, so cheap are operations on the Web that a small number of operators can skew results however carefully the sample is chosen. One survey (Fetterly et al. 2004) discovered that 27 percent of pages in Germany's .de domain changed every week, as compared with three percent for the Web as a whole. The explanation turned out not to be the peculiar industriousness of users in Germany, but rather that over a million URIs, most but not all on servers registered in the German domain, resolved to a single IP address, an automatically generated and constantly changing pornography site.

The Web has lots of unusual properties that make sampling trickier; how can a sampling method respect what seem prima facie significant properties such as, for example, the percentage of pages updated daily, weekly, etc? How can we factor in such issues as the independence of underlying data sources? Do we have much of a grasp of the distribution of languages across the Web (and of terms within languages—Kilgarrif and Grefenstette 2003), and how does increasing cleverness in rendering affect things (Henzinger 2004)? Even if we were happy with our sampling methodology, how—amid all the noise—could we discover interesting structures efficiently (López-Ortiz 2005)?

Web Science needs to take into account the variance of scale between intervention and outcome. Any experimental change will be relatively small scale: a new type of software, a new type of communications protocol, a small social network. The consequences of the change *relative to the intention of the innovation* can be described and studied in small-scale experiments in the lab or with a small set of pioneer users. Such intentions are usually focused on the experience of a single type of user or organization. The problem, of course, is that few if any of the *global* consequences of web technologies are of this tractable type, because they affect very large groups of people and organizations, so that most consequences at the scale of the Web are unintended. What experiment could have predicted the phenomenal growth of Facebook? Early experiments among small social groups for particular purposes gave Mark Zuckerberg and colleagues early impetus, although "Thefacebook's [*sic*] Palo Alto geeks [including Zuckerberg] lacked confidence in their own judgments about how people would respond to the product" (Kirkpatrick 2010: 64). The geeks were shrewd: there was clearly no empirical basis for saying that (a) Facebook would have 600 million active users, (b) it would outperform apparently stronger rivals such as MySpace, (c) it would challenge and even change very basic social norms and concepts such as privacy and friendship, or (d) that Zuckerberg would be able to wield political influence with politicians such as Barack Obama and David Cameron seeking airtime with him.

THE DEVELOPMENT OF THE WEB AND THE ROLE OF WEB SCIENCE: SEMANTICS AND LINKED DATA

Berners-Lee's original Semantic Web vision argued that there is too little machine-readable information on the WWW as it was then constituted:

> The meaning of the documents is clear to those with a grasp of (normally) English, and the significance of the links is only evident from the context around the anchor. To a computer, [on the other hand], the Web is a flat, boring world devoid of meaning. This is a pity, as in fact documents on the Web describe real objects and imaginary concepts, and give particular relationships between them.... Adding semantics to the Web involves two things: allowing documents which have information in machine-readable forms, and allowing links to be created with relationship values. Only when we have this extra level of semantics will we be able to use computer power to help us exploit the information to a greater extent than our own reading. (Berners-Lee 1994)

This vision of automation and machine-processability came to be dubbed the *Semantic Web*, but an important preliminary stage, the *Linked Data Web*, was the release of linked and linkable data (Bizer et al. 2009). Early adopters of linked data include e-science and e-social science, which depend on the integration and automatic interrogation of large quantities of distributed data (O'Hara et al. 2010). Governments, such as the UK government in its data.gov.uk program, have also shown interest in the Linked Data Web as the medium for representing and releasing public data (Shadbolt et al. 2011, 2012). In this section, we will discuss the potential of the Linked Data Web and the role of Web Science in facilitating it.

How does the Linked Data Web work?

The Linked Data Web relies on a series of formalisms and technologies. URIs provide a global naming convention for resources, as described above. The *Resource Description Framework* (RDF; Manola and Miller 2004) is a knowledge representation language that was designed with the Semantic Web in mind. Its basic format is a simple subject–predicate–object structure ("<u>Brian</u> is the <u>child</u> of <u>Albert</u>"); and because it has three elements, an RDF statement is therefore called a *triple*. RDF assigns URIs to the subjects, predicates, and objects that it links, allowing representation of data in such a way that anything referred to in the data (whether an object or a relation) can be linked to. Ideally, dereferencing the URIs should provide access to useful information about the resources, as well as useful links to other data.

Links can be made using various mechanisms, the simplest of which is a URI that points to another. For example (taken from Berners-Lee 2006–09), someone might describe some relationships (that Albert is the father of Brian and Carol) in RDF as follows:

```
<rdf:Description about="#albert">
<fam:child rdf:Resource="#brian">
<fam:child rdf:Resource="#carol">
</rdf:Description>
```

This RDF is about three resources which have local identifiers "#albert," "#brian," and "#carol," and might be obtained from a file called "<http://example.org/smith>." HTTP can be used to generate a globally invariant identifier for the three resources; for instance "http://example.org/smith#albert" refers to #albert as defined in the named file, and so on. Now that there is a global identifier, links can be made by anyone without ambiguity. For instance, a document "<http://example.org/jones>" might contain the following RDF:

```
<rdf:Description about="#denise">
<fam:child rdf:Resource="#edwin">
<fam:child rdf:Resource="http://example.org/smith#carol">
</rdf:Description>
```

Here a series of relationships between resources #denise, #edwin, and #carol have been asserted, but the datum about #carol links it to the data in the other file. Someone following the link can dereference the URI by decomposing "http://example.org/smith#carol" into two parts: the part before the "#" which gives the name and location of the file and "#carol" which is the local identifier in that file. Hence the information about #carol in the first file can be accessed thanks to the link included in the second file. This is the simplest way of linking data, though of course there are more complex methods (Berners-Lee 2006–09).

In 2010, the Linked Open Data project counted 13 billion triples of linked data on the Web (Möller et al. 2010). The ability to move between data linked in such a way opens up the possibility of exposing data on the Web and being able to access them from any application. The advantage of this is that when data from other sources are accessed, following the links gives the information user access to a contextualization of the data, or to more information that can be exploited about the subject. If the data retrieved is also linked, then following *those* links gives access to more information, and so on. Linking data therefore allows the creation of an extremely rich context for an inquiry, which furthermore can be interrogated automatically.

The value of Linked Data

The Web of Linked Data will change our model of the value of information. Currently, the value of information stems from its *scarcity*—people and organizations gain value from information they have gathered and exploit monopoly rights via legal contrivances such as copyright, intellectual property rights, licensing, and so on. Even when organizations do not resort to the law, they make great investments in protecting trade secrets. However, this scarcity-based model seems inadequate for the digital age.

In the first place, the social benefits from unlicensed use of "protected" knowledge and innovation, were already large in the pre-digital economy, and indeed account for much of our wealth today: "some 80 percent of the benefits [from innovation] may plausibly have gone to persons who made no direct contribution to innovation. The rather startling implication of all this is that the spillovers of innovation, both direct and indirect, can be estimated to constitute well over half of current GDP—and it can even be argued that this is a very conservative figure" (Baumol 2002: 135). And second, the Web has made it harder to preserve monopoly rights to information as copying and distribution reduces the marginal cost to copiers to close to zero. Although many media companies have taken rearguard action to protect their intellectual property, so simple is the distribution model on the Web that the basis of the value of information is rapidly switching from scarcity to *abundance*. It is the large quantity of data that can be placed in novel and unintended contexts with little cost that gives it value in the age of digital technologies—and the Linked Data Web is designed to foster such abundance.

Trust

The technical means to support the linking of data are necessary but insufficient for Web-scale adoption to realize the potential value. Many social mechanisms are required, including incentives for individuals, and legal frameworks and protections, but *trust* is perhaps key to the spread of linked data. If information is to be drawn routinely from heterogeneous sources, then it is important that users are able to trust it in order to be able to act on the wider set of inferences they can make. Trust, which mediates risk, will depend on the criticality of the inferences and the risk-aversion of the trustor (O'Hara et al. 2004; Bonatti et al. 2006; Creese and Lamberts 2009). Measuring trust, however, is a complex problem (Golbeck and Hendler 2004). An important parameter is the provenance of data (including statements about the methods of production and the organization that carried them out). Methods are appearing to describe provenance in open systems (Moreau 2010), but more needs to be discovered about how information spreads across the Web, and therefore how it can be tracked and understood (Berners-Lee et al. 2006a).

Online trust in general

Ideally, trust and trustworthiness would be linked causally so that all and only trustworthy people/systems/data are trusted. This presents us with another set of Web Science research challenges (O'Hara and Hall 2008). How can we maintain the causal link using web technology? What incentives and economic models are available to promote trust and trustworthiness together?

Offline and online trust have somewhat different properties, with con-men and masqueraders able to exploit different properties of the interactive context to undermine interlocutors' expectations. Online, the user labors under two important disadvantages. First, he or she is deprived of the complexity of signal available in the offline world. Online, the signals are basically the visual ones specified by the HTML source file of the page, augmented possibly by the roles played by the parties in the transaction (e.g. the website is that of one's bank). However, role-based trust is not a very secure foundation, as people often fail to verify roles (Dhamija et al. 2006). Second, the designer of the website is in total control of the signals that it gives out: the user has little or no opportunity to engage the website in "conversation," to see how it "performs," to "size it up," as we do offline when we are judging people.

This presents us with a second set of research challenges. How should trust be represented, maintained, and repaired on the Web? What variables are important? Will these change as we move from human to artificial agents? What sort of institutions and methods will help online trust? Can information from social networks inject some objectivity (Szomszor et al. 2007; Breslin et al. 2009; Victor et al. 2009)?

The social dynamic of online trust is an area requiring far more research, but one review focused on three *perceptual* factors that were particularly relevant. *Perception of credibility* has to do with honesty, expertise, predictability, and reputation. *Ease of use* relates to the simplicity and design of the website. *Risk* is the perceived likelihood of an undesirable outcome (Corritore et al. 2003). The first two factors in particular are strongly connected to the gathering and evaluation of signals of trustworthiness. This confirms the findings of an earlier study which found six major features that encouraged trust in e-commerce sites—the site's brand, seals of approval, ease of navigation, a fulfilling ordering experience, the site's presentation, and the technologies used to create the website—again strongly connected with the signaling systems characteristic of local trust (Cheskin Research 1999; and see Connolly Chapter 13).

However, web users are not particularly efficient at picking up the right signals that provide the causal connection between trust and trustworthiness. Dhamija and colleagues (2006) investigated the reasons why bogus sites work, and discovered that existing anti-phishing browser cues are ineffective. A participant group in that experiment made mistakes 40 percent of the time (even though primed to look out for phishing sites), and surprisingly neither age, gender, nor computing experience were significant variables. The study showed that people are unaware of the sorts of signaling systems that have been developed to ensure trustworthiness (e.g. the padlock symbol to show that the page was delivered securely by SSL), or of the typical strategies of counterfeiters (e.g. using images to mask underlying text, or placing an SSL-padlock in the body of a web page). Furthermore, users often failed to notice the *lack* of expected signals of trustworthiness. Attention to the needs of actual web users leads to a further set of Web Science research challenges. How can secure systems be made usable and effective for consumers, given the limited knowledge and bounded rationality of web users? Indeed, as Halpin et al. (2010) argue, this is a vital question, given the increasingly strong bonds between extended human cognition and online information representation, where people outsource much of their model of the world and their memory to digital resources.

Trusting data

Trusting data requires understanding the way it was created and the principles underlying its representational format. Information about these issues can be associated with data by *annotation* with *metadata*. Metadata are descriptive data about data, including basic elements as the author name, title, or abstract of a document, and administrative information such as file type, access rights, intellectual property rights, date, version number, and so on.

In general, metadata are important for effective search (they allow resources to be discovered by a wide range of criteria and are helpful in adding searchable structure to non-text resources), organizing resources (e.g. allowing portals to assemble composite web pages automatically from a variety of suitably annotated resources), archiving guidance (Day 2002), and identifying information (such as a unique reference number). Perhaps the most important use is to promote interoperability, allowing the combination of heterogeneous resources across platforms without loss of content. Schemata facilitate the creation of metadata in standardized formats for maximizing interoperability, and there are a number of such schemes, including the Dublin Core (<http://dublincore.org/> accessed July 5, 2012) and the Text Encoding Initiative (TEI, <http://www.tei-c.org/> accessed July 5, 2012). RDF provides mechanisms for integrating these.

As to what metadata are required, much depends on the reasons for annotation and the demands of data users. For many purposes—for example, sharing digital photos—the metadata can be curated by volunteer communities, as the success of Web 2.0 sites like Flickr shows (Breslin et al. 2009). More generally, interesting possibilities for metadata include time-stamping, provenance, uncertainty, and licensing restrictions.

Another key factor in assessing the trustworthiness of a document is the reliability or otherwise of the claims expressed within it; metadata about provenance will help in such judgments though need not necessarily resolve them. Representing confidence in reliability has always been difficult in epistemic logic. Approaches include subjective logic, which represents an opinion as a real-valued triple (belief, disbelief, uncertainty) where the three items add up to 1 (Jøsang 2001; Jøsang and McAnally 2004; Ceolin et al. 2010); grading based on qualitative judgments, although such qualitative grades can be given numerical interpretations and then reasoned about mathematically (Gil and Ratnakar 2002; Golbeck et al. 2003); fuzzy logic (Sanchez 2006); and probability (Huang and Fox 2004).

There are two main problems with annotation on the Web. The first is the difficulty of reasoning with metadata: the formalisms listed in the previous paragraph exhibit the common trade-off that the most expressive are the most difficult to use. Second, the task of annotating legacy data is an enormous, if not a Sisyphean, one. It has been argued that annotating the Web will require large-scale automatic methods, which will in turn require strong knowledge-modeling commitments (Kiryakov et al. 2005); whether this will contravene the decentralized spirit of the Web is as yet unclear. Much will depend on creative approaches such as annotating on the fly, or automatically annotating legacy resources such as databases underlying the deep Web (Volz et al. 2004).

The role of governments and the political effects of the Web

Politics will inevitably loom large in Web Science, for a number of reasons. First, although governments were generally somewhat slow in adopting the Web as a tool for communication and administration (Accenture 2004; Homburg 2008; and Nixon et al. 2010, sum up developments and challenges), they have been taking the lead in the population of the Web of data, particularly linked data. Various trends in governance have promoted this development (Dunleavy et al. 2006; Hood and Margetts 2007). In the United States, the need for transparency in the 2009 stimulus of the economy led to the creation of the data.gov site to host open government data. In the United Kingdom, a more ideological drive toward transparency was adopted by the government of Prime Minister Gordon Brown, and has been accelerated by the Coalition government of Prime Minister David Cameron, elected in 2010, in order to improve the efficiency and accountability of public services, as well as to facilitate the use of information by activists and entrepreneurs (O'Hara 2011). The data.gov.uk site hosts thousands of government datasets, many of which are available under the Open Government Licence (which is very non-prescriptive and modeled on Creative Commons). These third-generation transparency initiatives (see Fung et al. 2007: 169, who place this in the context of the history of transparency government) have been prominent in the push towards linked data, partly by the publication of data in linkable form, and partly by the efforts of a developer community to convert government open data to linked data (Dickinson 2010). Meanwhile, in the wider EU, attempts have been made to implement Semantic Web technologies in e-Government (Vitvar et al. 2010), but there has been a shift towards an open-data agenda here as well.

The effects of these initiatives, which have a momentum of their own, have yet to be fully felt, and may not have been completely anticipated by governments. Nevertheless, they have been vital in increasing the amount of linked data on the Web. However, there is an important role for Web Science in the risk analysis and management of potentially sweeping changes in governmental models to ones more appropriate to the digital era (Dunleavy et al. 2006).

Second, it is already becoming clear that new means of communication can be used by people to circumvent official channels of information and to organize and spread messages beyond narrow local circles; open data and transparency are part of that, but they are not the whole story. These tendencies of modern ICT were already evident when the Falun Gong began using email to organize itself in China, and text messaging helped coordinate protesters against President Estrada of the Philippines. Web 2.0 methods of communication have proved important in challenging entrenched governments, and some early commentaries on the Arab Uprisings that spread in 2011 have drawn attention to the protesters' use of Twitter (at the time of writing, there has been relatively little academic work on this, and some skepticism about how much microblogging had helped, as opposed merely to drawing the attention of the Western world to the protests; see Papic and Noonan 2011). Certainly the early use of microblogging in the protests against the reelection of President Ahmadinejad of Iran in 2009 turned out to be counterproductive. The government was able to paint the tech-savvy protesters as an unrepresentative elite. Furthermore, once the rest of the world learned of the situation in Tehran, the protesters' Tweets were drowned out by the sheer volume of supportive Tweets from the United States and elsewhere, thereby neutralizing the effect of the use of microblogging (*The Economist* 2009).

Such Web Science analyses are important to ensure reasoned debate; for example in the wake of the riots in England in August 2011, many commentators rushed to the conclusion that microblogging had been an important tool to coordinate the rioting, and some politicians and law enforcement officers even considered banning or suppressing Twitter and BlackBerries. However, early analysis of Twitter traffic showed that it was mainly used to pass on news, police advice, and eye witness reports, and to coordinate clean-up efforts (Ball and Lewis 2011).

And, third, to paraphrase a recent argument by Evgeny Morozov, although the Web has traditionally been seen as a tool for spreading liberalism and conversation (Berners-Lee et al. 2006a) and as a counterhegemonic medium (Warf and Grimes 1997), it may also provide a means of repression (Morozov 2011). Maybe that will influence its development too. The resolution of arguments about both the revolutionary and the repressive aspects of the Web will demand input from Web Science, which could act as an authoritative voice in a field currently driven from journalism and the blogosphere.

Conclusions

The Web is currently under-theorized, despite being the core of the world's information infrastructure. Most approaches see it as an instance of a particular type of structure, whether a mathematical network, a social network, a medium of communication, a set of computing languages and protocols, a medium of exchange, an ecology, an unpoliced domain for rugged individualists, an anarchist's paradise, a locus of cultural hegemony, or even a Great Pulsating Brain At The Centre Of The Multiverse. No doubt most or all of these are valid in many ways, but one is reminded very much of the parable of the blind men creating mutually exclusive theories of an elephant's anatomy purely by touch. Without disparaging the work of investigators working within a single disciplinary perspective, it is the contention of this chapter that transcending these individual per-spectives will yield important results.

The Web is not an exogenous entity. As Marx's 11th Thesis on Feuerbach has it, "philosophers have hitherto only interpreted the world in various ways: the point is to change it." Surprisingly, many have studied the Web without considering that they could influence its development. It is an engineered technology, and so can be altered. Conversely, many engineers have succeeded in changing the Web, but if those changes are uninformed by an understanding of the wider consequences, this creates the risk of causing harm either to the Web itself or wider society.

This chapter has discussed the discipline of Web Science, investigating the World Wide Web as a first order object of study using a catholic variety of methods. It has argued that the hybrid analysis/engineering nature of Web Science allies it with the design/engineering methodology of reflective practice, although the variety of scales at which the Web can be studied makes it peculiarly problematic. Nevertheless, Web scientists can play a part in developing the future Web. In this chapter, we looked at the idea of developing the Linked Data Web in some detail; other developments of interest, which could not be covered in this space, include the mobile Web; the dis-semination of the Web in the developing world; the Policy Aware Web; the Web as a trusted, secure, and private space; the Semantic Grid as an e-science tool, mechanisms for governance, standards development, and the design of new standards. All these areas have been the focus of Web Science study, and it is the hope of the community that research will ultimately deliver a more socially conscious and socially sensitive World Wide Web.

It is, of course, an important challenge for Web Science that studying the Web as a first order object does not result in the neglect of its technical, social, economic, and political context. Arguments about, say, net neutrality or walled gardens are highly ideologically charged, but the acceptability or otherwise of innovation will evolve alongside social attitudes, the social demands made on the Web (e.g. the increased demand for video), and the capacity of the technical infrastructure. No Web scientist can afford to remain ignorant of issues such as the growth of social networking sites as a means of managing users' identities, or the failure of American network operators to deliver sufficient bandwidth in one of the most mature web domains. Neither can the Web's intimate contribution to human psychology be neglected (Halpin et al. 2010, which uses the philosophy of extended cognition to argue that the Web helps constitute human minds—a striking conclusion, even if, like Turkle 2011 or Lanier 2010, one is appalled by the prospect). When the web scientist examines what a future would be like in which all data is "stored in the cloud," he or she cannot ignore the carbon emissions of those data warehouses, with their insatiable appetite for air conditioning (in 2007, the carbon emissions of the ICT industry as a whole were actually equivalent to those of the airline industry, i.e. about two percent of the world's emissions; see Climate Group 2008: 17).

The Web is an important system, highly contested between different interests, whose development can only be partially steered by invested authority, and which has been an object of ideological dispute almost as long as it has been in existence. The amalgamation of many disciplines is essential for understanding it (a) in full, and (b) in context. Ultimately, the aim of Web Science is to create, by education, training, and practice, a research and engineering community within which diverse methods of analysis and synthesis are routinely integrated. Rather than a multidisciplinary approach to a single complex object, a measure of its success will be its acceptance as a discipline in its own right.

Acknowledgements

The work reported in this chapter was partly supported by the projects LiveMemories (Active Digital Memories of Collective Life), Bando Grandi Progetti 2006, Provincia Autonoma di Trento, and the EU FET project Living Knowledge (http://livingknowledge -project.eu/), contract no. 231126. Some of the text has been derived from Tim Berners-Lee, Wendy Hall, James A. Hendler, Kieron O'Hara, Nigel Shadbolt, and Daniel J. Weitzner, "A Framework for Web Science."

References

Accenture (2004). *eGovernment Leadership: High Performance, Maximum Value*, Accenture. Available at <http://www.accenture.com/Global/Research_and_Insights/By_Industry/ Government/HighValue.htm"?>. Accessed May 6, 2012.

Baken, N. H. G., Wiegel, V. and van Oortmerssen, G. (2010). "The Value (Driven) Web," in *2nd Web Science Conference*, Raleigh, NC. Available at <http://journal.webscience.org/309/2/ websci10_submission_50.pdf> Accessed May 6, 2012.

Ball, J. and Lewis, P. (2011). "Riots Database of 2.5m Tweets Reveals Complex Picture of Interaction," *The Guardian*, August 24.

Barabási, A.-L., Albert, R., and Jeong, H. (2000). "Scale-Free Characteristics of Random Networks: The Topology of the World Wide Web," *Physica A*, 281: 69–77.

Baumol, W. J. (2002). *The Free-Market Innovation Machine: Analyzing the Growth Miracle of Capitalism*, Princeton: Princeton University Press.

Berners-Lee, T. (1994). Plenary at WWW Geneva 94. Available at <http://www.w3.org/Talks/WWW94Tim/>. Accessed May 6, 2012.

—— (1998). *Cool URIs Don't Change*. Available at <http://www.w3.org/Provider/Style/URI>. Accessed May 6, 2012.

—— (2006/2009). *Linked Data*. Available at <http://www.w3.org/DesignIssues/LinkedData.html>. Accessed May 6, 2012.

—— Fielding, R. T., and Masinter, L. (2005). *Uniform Resource Identifier (URI): Generic Syntax*. Available at <http://www.ietf.org/rfc/rfc3986.txt>. Accessed May 6, 2012.

—— Hall, W., Hendler, J. A., O'Hara, K., Shadbolt, N., and Weitzner, D. J. (2006a). "A Framework for Web Science," *Foundations and Trends in Web Science*, 1(1): 1–130.

—— Hall, W., Hendler, J. A., Shadbolt, N., and Weitzner, D. J. (2006b). "Creating a Science of the Web," *Science*, 313(5788): 769–71.

Bizer, C., Heath, T., and Berners-Lee, T. (2009). "Linked Data—The Story so Far," *International Journal on Semantic Web and Information Systems*, 5(3): 1–22.

Bonatti, P. A., Duma, C., Fuchs, N., Nejdl, W., Olmedilla, D., Peer, J., and Shahmehri, N. (2006). "Semantic Web Policies—A Discussion of Requirements and Research Issues," in Y. Sure and J. Domingue (eds). *The Semantic Web: Research and Applications, 3rd European Semantic Web Conference 2006 (ESWC-06)*, Springer: Berlin.

Breslin, J. G., Passant, A., and Decker, S. (2009). *The Social Semantic Web*, Berlin: Springer.

Ceolin, D., van Hage, W. R., and Fokkink, Wan (2010). "A Trust Model to Estimate the Quality of Annotations Using the Web," in *2nd Web Science Conference*, Raleigh, N.C. Available at <http://journal.webscience.org/315/2/websci10_submission_81.pdf>. Accessed May 6, 2012.

Cheskin Research and Studio Archetype/Sapient (1999). *eCommerce Trust Study*. Available at <http://www.added-value.com/source/wp-content/uploads/2012/01/17__report-eComm-Trust1999.pdf>. Accessed May 6, 2012.

The Climate Group (2008). *Smart2020: Enabling the Low Carbon Economy in the Information Age*. Available at <http://www.theclimategroup.org/_assets/files/Smart2020Report.pdf>. Accessed May 6, 2012.

Corritore, C. L., Kracher, B., and Weidenbeck, S. (2003). "On-line Trust: Concepts, Evolving Themes, a Model," *International Journal of Human-Computer Studies*, 58(6): 737–58.

Creese, S. and Lamberts, K. (2009). "Can Cognitive Science Help Us Make Information Risk More Tangible Online?," in *1st Web Science Conference*, Athens, Greece. Available at <http://journal.webscience.org/142/2/tangibility_of_risk_websci09_FINAL.pdf> Accessed May 6, 2012.

Day, M. (2002). *Cedars Guide to Preservation Metadata*. Available at <http://www.ukoln.ac.uk/metadata/cedars/guidance/metadata.html>. Accessed May 6, 2012.

Dhamija, R., Tygar, J. D., and Hearst, M. (2006). "Why Phishing Works." In *Conference on Human Factors in Computing Systems (CHI 2006)*. Available at <http://people.seas.harvard.edu/~rachna/papers/why_phishing_works.pdf> .

Dickinson, I. (2010). "COINS as Linked Data." Available at <http://data.gov.uk/resources/coins>. Accessed May 6, 2012.

Dijkstra, E. (1968). "Go To Statement Considered Harmful," *Communications of the ACM*, 11(3): 147–8.

Donato, D., Laura, L., Leonardi, S., and Millozzi, S. (2004). "Large Scale Properties of the Webgraph," *European Physical Journal B*, 38(2): 239–43.

Dunleavy, P., Margetts, H., Bastow, S., and Tinkler, J. (2006). *Digital Era Governance: IT Corporations, the State, and E-Government*, Oxford: Oxford University Press.

The Economist (2009). "Twitter 1, CNN 0," *The Economist*, June 18.

Fetterly, D., Manasse, M., Najork, M., and Wiener, J. (2004). "A Large-Scale Study of the Evolution of Web Pages," *Software: Practice and Experience*, 34(2): 213–37. Available at <http://research.microsoft.com/research/sv/sv-pubs/p97-fetterly/p97-fetterly.html>. Accessed May 6, 2012.

Fung, A., Graham, M., and Weil, D. (2007). *Full Disclosure: The Perils and Promise of Transparency*, New York: Cambridge University Press.

Gaffney, D. (2010). "#iranElection: Quantifying Online Activism." In *2nd Web Science Conference*, Raleigh, NC. Available at <http://journal.webscience.org/295/2/websci10_submission_6.pdf>. Accessed May 6, 2012.

Gil, Y. and Ratnakar, V. (2002). "Trusting Information Sources One Citizen at a Time," in *Proceedings of the 1st International Semantic Web Conference (ISWC)*, Sardinia, Italy. Available at <http://www.isi.edu/~gil/papers/GilRatnakarISWC2002.pdf> Accessed July 5, 2012.

Golbeck, J. and Hendler, J. (2004). "Accuracy of Metrics for Inferring Trust and Reputation in Semantic Web-Based Social Networks," in E. Motta, N. Shadbolt, A. Stutt, and N. Gibbins (eds). *Engineering Knowledge in the Age of the Semantic Web, Proceedings of 14th International Conference, EKAW*, Berlin: Springer, pp. 116–31.

Golbeck, J., Parsia, B., and Hendler, J. (2003). "Trust Networks on the Semantic Web," in M. Klusch, S. Ossowski, A. Omicini, and H. Laamanen (eds). *Proceedings of the 7th International Workshop on Cooperative Intelligent Agents*, Berlin: Springer-Verlag, pp. 238–49. Available at <http://www.mindswap.org/papers/CIA03.pdf>. Accessed May 6, 2012.

Grabner-Kräuter, S. and Kaluscha, E. A. (2003). "Empirical Research in On-line Trust: A Review and Critical Assessment," *International Journal of Human-Computer Studies*, 58(6): 783–812.

Halpin, H. (2009). "Social Meaning on the Web: from Wittgenstein to Search Engines," in *1st Web Science Conference*, Athens, Greece. Available at <http://journal.webscience.org/190/3/halpin-websci09.pdf>. Accessed May 6, 2012.

—— Clark, A. and Wheeler, M. (2010). "Towards a Philosophy of the Web: Representation, Enaction, Collective Intelligence," in *2nd Web Science Conference*, Raleigh, NC. Available at <http://journal.webscience.org/324/>. Accessed May 6, 2012.

Henzinger, M. R. (2004). "Algorithmic Challenges in Web Search Engines," *Internet Mathematics* 1(1): 115–26.

Hollis, M. (1998). *Trust Within Reason*, Cambridge: Cambridge University Press.

Homburg, V. (2008). *Understanding E-Government: Information Systems in Public Administration*, Abingdon: Routledge.

Hood, C. C. and Margetts, H. Z. (2007). *The Tools of Government in the Digital Age*, Basingstoke: Palgrave Macmillan.

Huang, J. and Fox, M. S. (2004). "Uncertainty in Knowledge Provenance," in *Proceedings of 1st European Semantic Web Symposium*. Available at <http://www.eil.utoronto.ca/km/papers/EuroSemWeb04-online.pdf>. Accessed May 6, 2012.

Jacobs, I. and Walsh, N. (eds) (2004). *Architecture of the World Wide Web Volume One*. Available at <http://www.w3.org/TR/webarch/>. Accessed May 6, 2012.

Jøsang, A. (2001). "A Logic for Uncertain Probabilities." *International Journal of Uncertainty, Fuzziness and Knowledge-Based Systems*, 9(3): 279–311. Available at <http://eprints.qut.edu.au/7204/>. Accessed May 6, 2012.

—— and McAnally, D. (2004). "Multiplication and Comultiplication of Beliefs," *International Journal of Approximate Reasoning*, 38(1): 19–51. Available at <http://folk.uio.no/josang/papers/JM2004-IJAR.pdf>. Accessed May 6, 2012.

Kilgarrif, A. and Grefenstette, G. (2003). "Introduction to the Special Issue on the Web as Corpus," *Computational Linguistics*, 29(3): 333–48. Available at <http://www.kilgarriff.co.uk/Publications/2003-KilgGrefenstette-WACIntro.pdf>. Accessed May 6, 2012.

Kirkpatrick, D. (2010). *The Facebook Effect: The Inside Story of the Company that is Connecting the World*, London: Virgin.

Kiryakov, A., Popov, B., Terziev, I., Manov, D., and Ognyanoff, D. (2005). "Semantic Annotation, Indexing and Retrieval," *Journal of Web Semantics*, 2(1). Available at <http://citeseerx.ist.psu.edu/viewdoc/summary?doi=10.1.1.122.2996>. Accessed May 6, 2012.

Lanier, J. (2010). *You Are Not a Gadget: A Manifesto*, London: Allen Lane.

Lessig, L. (1999). *Code and Other Laws of Cyberspace*, New York: Basic Books.

Leung, S.-T. A., Perl, S. E., Stata, R., and Wiener, J. L. (2001). *Towards Web-Scale Web Archaeology*, Compaq Systems Research Center Report #174.

López-Ortiz, A. (2005). "Algorithmic Foundations of the Internet," *ACM SIGACT News*, 36(2): 45–62.

McArthur, R. L. (2001). "Reasonable Expectations of Privacy," *Ethics and Information Technology*, 3(2): 123–8.

Manola, F. and Miller, E. (2004). *RDF Primer*. Available at <http://www.w3.org/TR/2004/REC-rdf-primer-20040210/>. Accessed May 6, 2012.

Möller, K., Hausenblas, M., Cyganiak, R., Handschuh, S., and Grimnes, G. A. (2010). "Learning From Linked Open Data Usage: Patterns and Metrics," in *2nd Web Science Conference*, Raleigh, NC. Available at <http://journal.webscience.org/302/2/websci10_submission_36.pdf>. Accessed May 6, 2012.

Moreau, L. (2010). "The Foundations for Provenance on the Web," *Foundations and Trends in Web Science*, 2(2–3): 99–241.

Morozov, E. (2011). *The Net Delusion: How Not to Liberate the World*, London: Allen Lane.

Nixon, P. G., Koutrakou, V. N., and Rawal, R. (eds) (2010). *Understanding E-Government in Europe: Issues and Challenges*, Abingdon: Routledge.

O'Hara, K. (2009). "Let a Hundred Flowers Bloom, a Hundred Schools of Thought Contend: Web Engineering in the Chinese Context," in X. Zhang and Y. Zheng (eds). *China's Information and Communications Technology Revolution: Social Changes and State Responses*, London: Routledge.

—— (2011). *Transparent Government, Not Transparent Citizens: A Report on Privacy and Transparency for the Cabinet Office*, London: Cabinet Office Available at <http://eprints.soton.ac.uk/272769/>. Accessed July 20, 2012.

—— Alani, H., Kalfoglou, Y., and Shadbolt, N. (2004). "Trust Strategies for the Semantic Web," in *Workshop on trust, security and reputation on the Semantic Web, 3rd international Semantic Web conference (ISWC 04)*, Hiroshima, Japan. Available at <http://eprints.ecs.soton.ac.uk/10029/>. Accessed May 6, 2012.

—— Berners-Lee, T., Hall, W., and Shadbolt, N. (2010). "Use of the Semantic Web in e-Research," in W. H. Dutton and P. W. Jeffreys (eds). *World Wide Research: Reshaping the Sciences and Humanities*, Cambridge, MA: MIT Press, pp. 130–4.

—— and Hall, W. (2008). "Trust on the Web: Some Web Science Research Challenges," *University of Catalonia Papers: e-Journal on the Knowledge Society*, 7. Available at <http://www.eprints.ecs.soton.ac.uk/16686/>. Accessed May 6, 2012.

—— and Hall, W. (2010). "Web Science as Reflective Practice," in M. Cockell, J. Billotte, F. Darbellay, and F. Waldvogel (eds). *Common Knowledge: Rising to the Challenge of Transdisciplinarity*, Lausanne: EPFL Press, pp. 205–18.

O'Hara, K. and Shadbolt, N. (2008). *The Spy in the Coffee Machine: The End of Privacy As We Know It*, Oxford: Oneworld.

O'Neill, E. T., Lavoie, B. F., and Bennett, R. (2003). "Trends in the Evolution of the Public Web 1998–2002," *D-Lib Magazine*, 9(4). Available at <http://www.dlib.org/dlib/april03/lavoie/04lavoie.html>. Accessed May 6, 2012.

Papic, M. and Noonan, S. (2011). "Social Media as a Tool for Protest," *Stratfor Global Intelligence*. Available at <http://www.stratfor.com/weekly/20110202-social-media-tool-protest>. Accessed May 6, 2012.

Perkins, R. and Neumayer, E. (2011). "Is the Internet Really New After All? The Deteminants of Telecommunications Diffusion in Historical Perspective," *The Professional Geographer*, 63(1): 55–72.

Sanchez, E. (ed.) (2006). *Fuzzy Logic and the Semantic Web*, Amsterdam: Elsevier.

Schön, D. A. (1983). *The Reflective Practitioner: How Professionals Think In Action*, London: Maurice Temple Smith.

Seabright, P. (2004). *The Company of Strangers: A Natural History of Economic Life*, Princeton, NJ: Princeton University Press.

Shadbolt, N. and Berners-Lee, T. (2008). "Web Science Emerges," *Scientific American*, October 2008, 299(4): 60–5.

——Hall, W., and Berners-Lee, T. (2006). "The Semantic Web Revisited," *IEEE Intelligent Systems*, 21(3): 96–101.

——O'Hara, K., Berners-Lee, T., Gibbins, N., Glaser, H., Hall, W., and schraefel, m.c. (2012). "Linked Open Government Data: Lessons From data.gov.uk," *IEEE Intelligent Systems*, 27(3): 16–24.

——O'Hara, K., Salvadores, M., and Alani, H. (2011). "E-government," in J. Domingue, D. Fensel, and J. Hendler (eds). *Handbook of Semantic Web Technologies*, Berlin: Springer , pp. 849–910.

Shneiderman, B. (2007). "Web Science: A Provocative Invitation to Computer Science," *Communications of the ACM*, 50(6): 25–7.

Skyrms, B. (1996). *Evolution of the Social Contract*, Cambridge: Cambridge University Press.

Szomszor, M., Alani, H., Cantador, I., O'Hara, K., and Shadbolt, N. (2007). "Semantic Modelling of User Interests Based on Cross-Folksonomy Analysis," in A. Sheth, S. Staab, M. Dean, M. Paolucci, D. Maynard, T. Finin, and K. Thirunarayan (eds). *The Semantic Web—ISWC 2008, 7th International Semantic Web Conference*, Berlin: Springer, pp. 632–48.

Turkle, S. (2011). *Alone Together*, New York: Basic Books.

Victor, P., Cornelis, C., De Cock, M., and Teredesai, A. M. (2009). "Trust- and Distrust-Based Recommendations for Controversial Reviews," in *1st Web Science Conference*, Athens, Greece. Available at <http://journal.webscience.org/161/2/websci09_submission_65.pdf>. Accessed May 6, 2012.

Vitvar, T., Peristeras, V., and Tarabanis, K. (eds) (2010). *Semantic Technologies for E-Government*, Berlin: Springer-Verlag.

Volz, R., Handschuh, S., Staab, S., Stojanovic, L., and Stojanovic, N. (2004). "Unveiling the Hidden Bride: Deep Annotation for Mapping and Migrating Legacy Data to the Semantic Web," *Journal of Web Semantics*, 1–2. Available at <http://citeseerx.ist.psu.edu/viewdoc/summary?doi=10.1.1.9.5682>. Accessed May 6, 2012.

Warf, B. and Grimes, J. (1997). "Counterhegemonic Discourses and the Internet," *Geographical Review*, 87(2): 259–74.

Wilks, Y. and Brewster, C. (2009). "Natural Language Processing as a Foundation of the Semantic Web," *Foundations and Trends in Web Science*, 1(3–4): 199–327.

CHAPTER 4

··

SOCIETY ON THE WEB

··

MIKE THELWALL

INTRODUCTION

THE Web supports increasingly many of the daily activities of an expanding fraction of the world's population. During a single day we may go online to catch up with friends and family via social network sites (SNSs), shop, play a game, seek information such as TV schedules, or study. As collectives, we may organize into web discussion groups, debate the elections in the blogosphere, or argue about news stories via BBC website comments. From a social science perspective this has raised many research questions about each new web phenomenon such as:

- *How is it similar to and different from offline phenomena?* How do interactions in SNSs, chatrooms, and blogs differ from face-to-face communication?
- *How does it work—what are the key characteristics and what makes it attractive or useful?* Why have SNSs become so successful? How can they spread so quickly and why do so many people join? Why did Facebook overtake MySpace?
- *What are its threats and potentials?* Can blog-based discussions open up democracy to mass participation and create an inclusive public sphere for political debate? Are SNSs undermining privacy? Do anarchic environments like 4chan promote antisocial behavior?
- *How does it change existing activities and relationships?* Do people expect more from a life partner met via the large databases of online dating agencies? Are distant relationships easier to maintain over time with Facebook? Do migrants retain closer connections with their birth country if they share family videos on YouTube?

In terms of social research about the Web there have been two important trends. First, there has been a move away from generalization and towards detailed analyses of the differences between phenomena. It is widely recognized now that cyberspace is not homogenous but is highly varied. Second, the early dichotomy between the online and "real" world has been replaced by recognition that the Web plays a role in many offline activities. Moreover, even purely online activities, such as anonymous chatrooms and online fantasy gaming, influence and are influenced by offline activities (e.g. Nardi 2010; also Williams and Kahn Chapter 10). In consequence, there is a need for social research not only to understand new Web technologies, but also to aid pre-existing social science research issues. For the Web or any particular web phenomenon, surely many social scientists could reasonably ask one of the following questions:

- *How does it impact on my topic?* Democracy: does blogging encourage democratic participation? Public health: does the widespread availability of online health information increase awareness of public health issues or spread misconceptions? Social psychology: what impact do SNSs have on the quality of face-to-face friendship?
- *Can I use it to gain insights into my topic?* Youth cultures: can a virtual ethnography (Hine 2000) gain insights into the attractions of particular subcultures? Education: are online questionnaires an easy and appropriate way to ascertain student attitudes on any topic? Research evaluation: can Web-based measurements give cheap and quick insights into the communication patterns or research performances of universities or departments?

This chapter gives an introduction to one aspect of web social science: studies of all or part of the Web. It is concerned only with the public Web: web pages that could, in theory, be accessed by anyone with a web browser. This excludes private communication, such as closed discussion groups and private SNS messaging, and is mostly concerned with the Web itself as a collection of content. In consequence, this chapter discusses research that observes aspects of the Web and its uses rather than research that primarily uses the Web as a medium through which to interact with others online (e.g. questionnaires, interviews). The chapter starts with theories and issues that make general observations about the Web and then gives examples of investigations into particular topics, such as academic web use. The objectives are to give insights into how the Web works from a social perspective as well as giving a very general overview of methods for studying it, and how this approach to research can be developed further in the coming years.

THEORIZING THE WEB

This section describes a selection of prominent socially relevant web issues. This is far from an exhaustive list but includes three widely relevant and influential issues and one less well-known group of related issues and theories that are particularly relevant to web researchers. The first two relate to social factors underlying the link structure of the Web, the third discusses mass participation, and the last is concerned with the social implications of the permanence of web content.

Rich get richer and search engine dominance

The Web has been widely heralded for its potential to democratize access to, and the provision of, information. Unlike many previous information systems, which had commercial owners, the Web was designed to be a universal and free "pool of human knowledge" (Berners-Lee et al. 1993). Today, overseen by the non-profit World Wide Web Consortium (w3.org), anyone can view the Web for the price of access at an Internet café. At the same time, they can post information visible to the billion web users, for example in a blog or free website, making it far more open than the mass media, at least in theory. This gives anyone who wants to publish on the Web an unparalleled ability to (theoretically) disseminate information and gives web users access to an unparalleled variety of information, dwarfing libraries.

This theoretical equality in information provision does not occur in practice. Most bloggers must realize that while their news blog post is equal to a BBC online news story in theory since both are web pages and are given equal treatment by the Internet infrastructure and web browsers, in practice few people will look for their post and it is very unlikely that many will find it by accident. Anyone searching for a news story and not going to a major news portal directly is likely to find the Google search results page populated by well-known news brands rather than amateur blogs. Why is this? Why has the democratizing Web become dominated by powerful organizations, at least in terms of news content?

One key reason is that search engines, the key web information portals, favor content that is popular over unknown content. As part of a competitive commercial operation, search engine designers strive to give results that users are most likely to find useful (Van Couvering 2004, 2007). This is generally useful but also gives a highly conservative bias and means that sites like BBC News and CNN.com, which are widely recognized and valued, are likely to appear in everybody's search results (at least for relevant countries), and individual blogs with little or no following are unlikely to appear in anybody's results. Popular sites are not as popular as mathematical models of bias predict, however, perhaps because users do not just submit general searches that will predominantly return major sites, but also submit more specific queries that may lead them to niche sites or specific pages (Fortunato et al. 2006). This argument connects to the long tail concept, discussed below. Also related to bias, search engines have started to investigate clever ways of predicting the type of person that searchers are likely to be based upon their IP address, including their age, gender, income group, and ethnicity (Weber and Castillo 2010; see also: http://clues.yahoo.com). This gives them the possibility to tailor searches to likely interests. For instance, the top ranked result for a US female searching for Wagner could be a page about the composer, whereas the top ranked result for a male could be Wagner-branded male grooming products (Weber and Castillo 2010). This creates additional ethical problems, however, as it is essentially stereotyping users by delivering them content that people "like them" typically prefer. One solution may be to allow people to select the profile of the person that they want to "search like," allowing them to effectively opt in to stereotyping.

Search engines repeatedly claim that they do not manipulate their results for money, so how do they decide which sites to prioritize? The primary data that they use to identify popular websites is the structure of the Web itself in the form of hyperlinks: the more links point to a website, the more likely it is to have a large audience (Brin and Page 1998). This creates a rich-get-richer effect, because popular websites attract more visitors from commercial search engines, making them even more popular and likely to attract even more links. This should be called the "popular get more popular" effect except that the term has been borrowed from similar phenomena that have been noticed elsewhere in terms of wealth (rich get richer/Paretto law) and scientific prestige (the Matthew effect (Merton 1968): that well-known scientists tend to receive most of the credit for joint work, and their work is more highly regarded than that of junior researchers) among others. Many researchers have confirmed that a tiny minority of web pages attract a huge number of links and that the majority of pages attract few, if any (Adamic and Huberman 2000; Barabási 2002).

At the micro-level the *process* leading to the huge disparity in numbers of links pointing to websites has been termed "preferential attachment": when new web pages are created and hyperlinks embedded within them, they are much more likely to point to popular sites than little-known sites simply because the authors are more likely to know about the popular sites. Offline knowledge can help to overturn this to a limited extent, however (Pennock et al. 2002), as searchers may look for organizations or people known offline rather than just those previously found online.

The end result of this hyperlinks-mediated popularity dynamic is that for any type of information a few sites tend to develop a search engine results dominance that is hard for newcomers to displace. Hence the mass of bloggers go virtually unnoticed, while a few news websites dominate the online news audience. This still leaves room for news organizations with known brand names to be searched for and found online, such as regional newspapers, and even for a few individual bloggers to attract mass audiences. Moreover, there is still space for amateur blogs to find small audiences, especially in niche markets or in groups of like-minded individuals, but they will find it difficult to attract significant numbers of readers. It is important to realize, however, that the Web differs from other mass media, for example, in supporting very specialized topics that do not have a large following. This is perhaps one of the most democratic features of the Internet and Web.

The same dynamic occurs with searches for all types of information. For instance, when searching online for products, well-known sites are likely to dominate the Google results and small shops may be ranked so low as to be effectively invisible. Similarly, when searching for academic information, Wikipedia and pages at large universities are likely to be at the top of the results pages. Hence, with some exceptions mentioned below, it is difficult to break the dominance of major websites and reach an audience. Wikipedia is a partial exception because its content is produced by its readers and volunteer editors, making it easy in theory for anyone to join and make contributions that would automatically be highly ranked in Google, although there are concerns about inappropriate influence from governments and large corporations on topics sensitive to them (Hafner 2007).

The long tail, power laws, and specialist interests

A consequence of the rich-get-richer effect on the Web is that when graphs are plotted of the popularity of (or links to) websites, they are highly skewed, with a few sites having high popularity (i.e. many links to them) and the vast majority of sites having little or no popularity (i.e. few links). Mathematically, these graphs approximately follow a model known as the power law, which is generated by the rich-get-richer process discussed above (Adamic and Huberman 2000). Figure 4.1 shows data on the popularity (as estimated by hyperlinks) of a selection of blogs. The figure is a double logarithmic graph, revealing the characteristic power law "broomstick" shape. Most website or web page popularity graphs are not perfect power law broomsticks, however, reflecting that other factors affect popularity such as offline brand awareness or natural audience size limitations for particular websites (Pennock et al. 2002). Many types of web phenomena give rise to this type of shape and this is particularly true of links. The graph shows that while two blogs have attracted thousands of links, most blogs attract very few. This huge disparity can be partly explained by the rich-get-richer, power law phenomenon.

The bottom right-hand side of the power law graphs is sometimes called the "long tail" and, despite the relative obscurity of the sites in this area, the long tail has an important impact on the ecology of the Web. The reason is that there are enough web users to give viable audiences for many specialist sites. For example, few people build their own personal hovercraft and so it may not be viable to have hovercraft enthusiast clubs or shops even in major cities, but Internet forums can cheaply and conveniently connect enthusiasts from around the world, and the Web might be able to support specialist mail-order shops. In summary, the sheer size of the global web user-base makes it

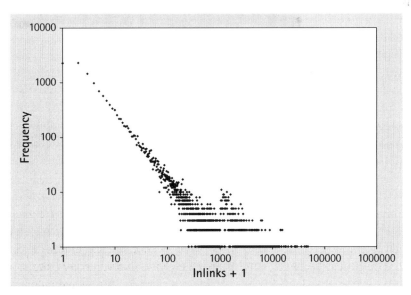

FIGURE 4.1: Power law graph of links found by Yahoo! to Live Spaces blogs indexed in Bing. The data has logarithmic scales on the axes.

possible for those with niche interests to connect and for viable economic activity around much smaller niche groups than ever before (Andersen 2006, 2009). In terms of finding sites through search engines, this is possible for niche interests simply because there will be fewer matches for specialist topic searches, and the reduced competition will allow sites to appear that would not be highly ranked in more general searches with many matches.

The wisdom of crowds, tagging, and trust

With Web 2.0 it can be possible to identify solutions to problems or develop useful systems using a mass approach rather than individual experts. The basic idea is that a large collective may know more in total than a few experts and in certain contexts its average opinion or overall behavior may out-perform the experts (Surowiecki 2005). The power of numbers on the Web also has a related benefit: access to someone who knows the answer to a specialist question. It seems that many questions can be answered on the Web by posting them to a relatively open relevant forum where a few interested people may attempt to answer and a consensus answer may emerge. A well-organized example of this is the computer science problem-solving site ExpertsExchange.com. Anyone can post questions to relevant topics (organized by technology type) and wait for another contributor to post an answer.

Like ExpertsExchange.com, many websites work primarily through mass contributions and the news-sharing website Digg.com is an important example. Contributors post links to stories of interest and others vote on whether these stories are good or bad. The recent stories attracting most votes (diggs) are prominently displayed, generating a user-created meta-newspaper (Lerman 2006). A criticism of using this kind of crowd wisdom, however, is that site owners may generate profits from the unpaid labor of users (see also Ritzer 1996).

The Digg approach of user voting is also used elsewhere, such as Facebook and YouTube "like" votes. In fact, the idea is more widespread because implicit votes are also used by search engines and automatic recommender systems. For instance, Google will "learn" which web pages are frequently selected from search results pages and promote them in their rankings. Similarly, Amazon recommends books based upon comparing purchase histories and browsing patterns in the site (e.g. people who bought X also bought Y).

Another important example of crowd wisdom is the *folksonomy* (= folk taxonomy): the tagging of web content by the owner or others. For example, those who post pictures in Flickr or videos in YouTube can input a set of words as tags that can help other users find the pictures with keyword searches or by navigating tag names. Other systems, such as Viddler.com and Steve.Museum (Chun et al. 2006), encourage non-owners to tag resources. From a traditional librarianship perspective, this is horrible: tags are like keywords assigned by librarians to books and other resources. Thus they should be assigned by experts after careful consideration and possibly also using a controlled vocabulary: a pre-constructed list of approved terms (but see also Rafferty and Hidderley 2007).

Nevertheless, the folksonomy approach seems to work well for several reasons. First, there are not enough experts to categorize web content so the real choice is between a folksonomy and nothing. Second, the uses of web content are so varied that experts' tags may be no better than amateur tags. Finally, if enough people tag resources then the resulting tag set will be large and hence potentially rich (Golder and Huberman 2006). In fact, librarians recognize the value of folksonomy tagging and are its most enthusiastic researchers (e.g. Bar-Ilan et al. 2008).

Permanence, privacy, and deleting

The Web contains a huge amount of personal information and interpersonal communications in SNSs, blogs, personal websites, and elsewhere. This content seems to be ephemeral because owners can delete web pages or entire sites at any time and the content of popular sites tends to change frequently, especially in the case of news sites. Nevertheless, much web content is effectively permanent because, even after deletion or changes, copies may be stored in the Internet Archive (archive.org) or other archives, and in some cases the information may be retained by the website owner in accordance with their terms and conditions. As an example of the latter, Facebook may retain deleted profiles for marketing or other purposes. This permanence can be a benefit for researchers to track changes over time, or for retrospective analyses, as discussed below.

There are many problems for individuals that can derive from undeletable information, in addition to the well-known issue of potential employers finding unprofessional content in SNSs (Mayer-Schonberger 2009). A simple example is personal relationship information. It may be distressing to see information about previous relationships when with a new partner. Offline, such information may be tactfully not referred to by others, giving new couples the privacy to build relationships. On the Web, however, the information may be available to the curious (and perhaps slightly paranoid) new partners, and this lack of privacy may cause problems (Nissenbaum 2009). Mayer-Schonberger (2009) proposes giving digital information an expiry date unless there is a good reason to keep it. This is effectively what data protection legislation often does: requiring organizations to delete personal information about others after a specific time period. This approach does not seem to have been taken up by any creators of digital devices or web authoring software, however, suggesting that people may prefer the risks of permanence to the fear of losing important information or the extra work to decide what to keep and for how long. In the context of sites like Facebook that use members' personal information for marketing purposes, permanence may be a price that users are (currently) willing to pay for the benefits of the service.

In terms of implicit information, an important aspect of privacy is related to the provision of free information and services. The Web gives unparalleled access to free information from Wikipedia to news websites and from government information portals to search engines. The hidden cost of much commercially provided free content is increased commercial surveillance leading to more targeted marketing (Zimmer 2008). While this may be a small price to pay it is nevertheless a tangible cost in terms of loss of privacy (Nissenbaum 2009: p. 83). This financial model also seems to benefit larger organizations that can develop the computing infrastructure to monetize user information.

STUDYING THE WEB

The above theories and issues are among the few that have general relevance to the Web or web structure. In contrast, most social science web research seems to operate within a much more restricted context: often with a particular genre, such as blogs, SNSs, or chatrooms, and for a particular issue, such as elections, crises, or scientific publishing. The goal of such research is sometimes to understand an important web phenomenon or to investigate the role of the Web for an offline issue, such as elections. Moreover, the Web is also used as a convenient data source for investigating offline phenomena. As an example of the latter, blogs have been advocated as a substitute for diaries in diary research (Hookway 2008). Nevertheless, a key limitation is that the Web is unlikely to be a perfect mirror for society but is likely to introduce its own set of biases for any study, such as towards more educated, more computer-literate, and younger members of society.

The following subsections sample two broad approaches to studying society on the Web, based around link analysis and Web 2.0 investigations. While some of the topics discussed have overlaps with other chapters in the book, the emphasis here is on whether and how the Web reflects society, particularly in terms of informal social organization.

Link structures, academia, and authority

The Web was originally conceived of as an interconnected collection of documents with users navigating between documents by clicking on hyperlinks (Berners-Lee et al. 1993). Today, users can also navigate via bookmarks/favorites and search engines. Moreover, much of the Web, including SNSs and search engine results pages, is dynamically generated by visitor actions, rather than being relatively static and permanent. Nevertheless, the links between (static) web pages are a valuable source of evidence about the relatedness of web pages and can yield emergent structural information. In other words, analyzing the Web as a network structure where the nodes are individual web pages (or sites) and the connections between nodes correspond to hyperlinks is a way to extract new information that allows researchers to make inferences about social phenomena. For instance, the most important documents or websites may be identified as those with the most links pointing to them, as discussed below.

The information science research field of webometrics has developed a number of methods for gathering and quantitatively analyzing web data, and particularly hyperlinks

(Björneborn and Ingwersen 2004). It has partly focused on identifying hyperlinking patterns in academic web spaces but has also researched other topics and developed more generally useful methods and software (Thelwall 2009).

Early computer science and information science research using hyperlinks was motivated by academic citations (Brin and Page 1998; Ingwersen 1998). Citations, like hyperlinks, are inter-document connections, but are studied in the field of scientometrics. Two key scientometric ideas are particularly pertinent: first, the network formed by documents and inter-document citations is highly clustered because articles tend to cite papers from the same field. Hence it is even possible to map science as a network using citation data alone (Small 1999). In such maps, disciplines loosely cluster together, and fields or specialisms cluster together more tightly. It is also possible to identify interrelated fields or disciplines from the density of citations between them.

A second property of citations is that they can be used to help identify influential work. This is well known to many scientists in the form of journal Impact Factors, which assess the average rate of citation of a journal's published articles, and in citation counts to the work of individual scholars, such as used in the h-index. The theory behind citation analysis is that science is a cumulative enterprise and if work is useful and influential then it is likely to be cited often. Hence the most frequently cited articles/authors/journals are likely to be among the most influential. In consequence, citation-based metrics are frequently used for academic promotion and evaluation purposes.

On the Web, hyperlinks can also be used to identify pages with similar topics and important pages/sites (Kleinberg 1999). Unlike science, however, the Web is not a cumulative knowledge-building process and web pages are not peer-reviewed, and so hyperlink patterns are much weaker than citation patterns. In particular, many hyperlinks are for navigation, advertising, or acknowledgment. Nevertheless, web pages/sites attracting many hyperlinks tend to be more important and popular than those attracting fewer. This is exploited by Google's hyperlink-based algorithm PageRank that helps Google to return highly linked sites at the top of its results.

Pre-Web, search engines tended to return the best text matches for a search rather than the most important matches. Computer scientist Kleinberg (1999) described pages that were linked to by many topic-relevant pages as "authorities" and those that linked to many topic-relevant pages as "hubs." Surprisingly, little research has investigated the most linked-to web pages, but in academic web spaces it seems that content is not king: the most linked-to pages are university home pages and pages containing widely useful resources (Thelwall 2002b). This suggests that the Web is more of a functional information navigation system than a knowledge-building enterprise in the sense of Wikipedia. Nevertheless, there is a connection between hyperlinks and citations at the level of university websites: the number of academic links received by a university is approximately proportional to its research productivity, at least for the case of the UK (Thelwall and Harries 2004).

Patterns in the link structure of the Web have also been investigated in various contexts. For instance, hyperlinks between political bloggers have been shown to closely follow party lines in the US (Adamic and Glance 2005), and similar results have been found for US political candidate websites (Foot et al. 2003) and Korean politicians' blogs (Park and Thelwall 2008). In academia, pairs of pages connected by links tend to be about the same topic (Thelwall and Wilkinson 2004), with links between computer science and other disciplines being common among cross-disciplinary hyperlinks (Björneborn 2004). This last pattern may be partly due to computer scientists publishing more content on the Web, rather than only due to computing being particularly frequently of value in other disciplines.

In terms of geography, physical distance is also important in cyberspace despite its international nature (Dodge and Kitchin 2001). In the UK, universities link to neighbors about twice as much as to distant UK universities (Thelwall 2002a). Internationally, universities link disproportionately to neighbors and those sharing a common language, at least in the EU (Thelwall et al. 2003). Globally, English-speaking countries seem to be an exception in terms of hosting and attracting disproportionately many academic links (Thelwall and Zuccala 2008). This may be due to English being the dominant current academic language of science, English being the standard international language of communication, or much Web and computer science documentation being in English. Hence this phenomenon partly reflects society (academia in this case) and partly reflects the Web itself.

Hyperlinks are not the only possible type of web citation and several studies have shown that it is possible to conduct online citation analyses for academic journal articles by counting how many web documents (e.g. pages, course syllabuses, word documents) cite them in the traditional sense—using advanced web search engine searches to collect the data (Kousha et al. 2010). Indirect links can also be useful to identify implicit web structures when direct links are rarely used. For this, two web pages/sites are said to be co-inlinked if there exists a third web page/site that contains a hyperlink to both (Björneborn and Ingwersen 2004). Co-inlinks have been used to identify clusters of similar businesses on the Web (Vaughan et al. 2009), even though companies rarely link directly to their competitors, to map relationships between academics (Zuccala 2006) or academic websites (Ortega and Aguillo 2008), and between local government organizations (Holmberg 2010).

Web 2.0, public opinion, and language

The term Web 2.0 grew to prominence from about 2004 for a variety of technologies, such as blogs, SNSs, and YouTube, that allowed individuals to post text, pictures, videos, or other content to the Web with relative ease. Driven by the O'Reilly publishing organization, it was widely heralded as a revolutionary shift from a fairly static organization-centred Web to a dynamic people-centred version (e.g. Vossen and Hagemann 2007). Paradoxically, this people shift was underpinned by technological development: the creation of software that could manage the steps necessary for web publishing, reducing significantly the technical competence needed to publish.

An early example was the Open Diary software that made it easy to maintain regularly updated diary-like websites: a format that became known as the blog. Today, in a few minutes web users can start publishing their own content in free popular blog sites, SNSs, or image/video-sharing sites. This has fundamentally changed the shape of the Web. According to Alexa (2011), many of the world's most visited websites connect friends or share content, including Facebook (#2), YouTube (#3), Blogger.com (#5), and Wikipedia (#8). For many people, the Internet has always been a means of communication, with email being popular since the early days of the Internet. However, the Web is moving in this direction as well, as Web 2.0 is making it more of a place to interact with friends and others, rather than a place to access information (e.g. news, celebrity gossip, pornography). For example, friendship interaction in SNSs has directly replaced accessing pornography for many users (Trancer 2008); and in the US, according to measurements company comScore, Internet users started to spend more time on Facebook than on Google in about September 2010 (CNN 2010).

Of course, traditional information-centred web uses continue despite Web 2.0, but have not expanded as rapidly. Moreover, sites are now frequently hybrid in the sense that they combine traditional and user-generated content. A prominent example is readers' comments sections in online newspapers. Musicians' MySpace profiles are another case: they combine music and video releases with band news but allow fans' comments to be posted on the home page.

Web 2.0 has spawned extensive research to investigate its impact on various aspects of society. For instance, amateur blogs have been shown to be occasionally influential in political news (Bond and Abtahi 2005), and blogs have been widely adopted by politicians as a mechanism to communicate with the electorate. In terms of democracy, blogging seems to have the potential to create a public sphere where issues can be debated (Thompson 2003) but the reality seems to be that like-minded bloggers tend to find each other and avoid debate (Adamic and Glance 2005). Indeed, some argue that the wide variety of choices that are available in the digital world makes it easier for individuals to avoid unwanted opinions, potentially undermining the normal democratic process rather than strengthening it (Sunstein 2004).

Social SNSs have overtaken blogs in popularity but typically seem to revolve around interpersonal communication and friendship rather than discussions of the public good. Although most blogs are online personal diaries rather than debating platforms, discussing general or specialist news and politics occupies a significant minority, perhaps 20 percent (Herring et al. 2004). Conversely, although a few people use SNSs to discuss the news, and SNSs often contain embedded blogs, their purpose is typically personal, and communication seems to rarely contain any information in the sense of non-gossip facts (Thelwall and Wilkinson 2010).

One interesting outcome of Web 2.0 is that a significant minority of the planet have now posted personal information or other content into the Web, where it is exploited by marketers on an unprecedented scale and, to a far lesser extent, by researchers. For example, Google's knowledge of people from their searches, SNS profiles, and Gmail allows it to target advertisements to individuals (Zimmer 2008), and software exists that can scan online forums and deliver companies summaries of the aspects of their products (e.g. cars) that customers like or dislike (Pang and Lee 2008). It may even be possible to predict future sales from online chatter (Gruhl et al. 2005). Similar potential exists for researchers, some of it being simple to discover, as is the case for public opinion.

In terms of public opinion, it is particularly easy to assess the intensity of online interest in topics over time. This can be estimated by using a tool like trend.icerocket .com to assess the proportion of blogs that mention a topic every day for the past six months. The graph below (Figure 4.2) shows the approximate volume of blog postings mentioning Japan, or the Japanese tsunami and related nuclear incident in Japan, using keyword matching. Clicking on the graph online would reveal why the topic was mentioned by listing relevant blog posting from the selected date. Researchers wishing to gain additional insights into attitudes towards a topic over time can also use date-specific blog searches to find and analyze relevant blog posts. These capabilities reflect that the Web is partly an archive of old content. When this content is reliably dated, as is the case for blogs, it can be mined to explore public opinion about recent events.

Another aspect of the Web as a repository of informal content is that it is also a repository of the language used to express that content (Meyer et al. 2003). Linguists can therefore easily examine language in blogs, SNSs, and online forums to identify online communication language genres. For instance, there have been many interesting studies of abbreviations and emotions used in many languages (e.g. Katsuno and Yano 2007).

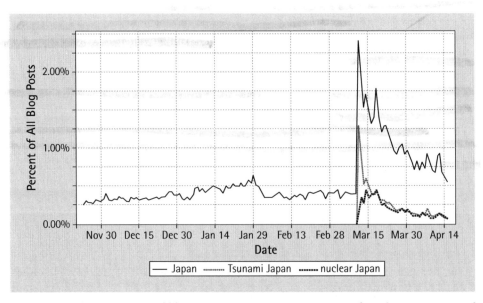

FIGURE 4.2: The percentage of blogs mentioning *Japan*, or *Japan* and *nuclear*, or *Japan* and *Tsunami* during six months up to the start of April, 2011.

Source: Generated by BlogPulse Copyright 2011 the Nielson Company.

Summary

The above examples show that while in some sense the Web is an anarchic mass of varied content there are still many things that can be said about it in general and many ways to analyze particular phenomena and issues on the Web. From the perspective of studying society, Web 2.0 is particularly important (and currently more relevant than the semantic Web/Web 3.0, which adds metadata to web pages to systematically prepare the information contained in them for automatic data processing to enable machines to help individual users). Web 2.0 is important for the new phenomena of mass informal publishing in many guises, as well as for the new uses of the Web and interpersonal communication affordances that it gives. From a researcher's perspective this sets out a range of challenges to understand the new phenomena as well as opportunities to use the Web as a lens through which to study old phenomena.

The Web can be meaningfully studied at both a micro and macro level. At the micro level, studies using qualitative or content analyses of small sets of blogs, SNS profiles, or YouTube videos are a logical type of research. Complementing this, larger scale studies abstract the Web to a collection of pages/sites and links (link analysis) or collections of words (e.g. for the blog trend graphs). Ideally, future research should routinely combine the two since the Web is at each researcher's desktop and easy to access for study. This should help to generate a new generation of powerful mixed methods for Web-based social science research.

An important consideration for researching society on the Web is that Web-based methods have many limitations. They typically involve making assumptions at some level about user actions or opinions from the web content created by them, which is problematic. When mining the Web for evidence about offline issues, sample bias is also a key concern. In practice, these issues can be solved or ameliorated by method or data source triangulation, but the general problems associated with this type of web investigation have not been well researched.

Future research is also needed to explore the limitations of using web data to investigate society on the web, especially in terms of the contexts in which it makes sense to use it. As the above discussion shows, there is some evidence that webometric data is useful to study academic, political, and media topics, but there are many other social research topics for which its usefulness is unknown. Research is also needed to explore the extent to which conclusions from online data are valid, for example by triangulating with offline data. It will be particularly helpful to have guidelines about the extent to which web data can be trusted in different situations. A key aspect of the future of researching society on the Web is that studies will become more powerful through a combination of the development of new types of software and the publishing of increasingly personal information online. In terms of new software, sentiment analysis programs have already shown that it is possible to tap into the emotions of the public and gain insights into patterns of emotion on a global scale (Kramer 2010) or with regard to particular events

(Thelwall et al. 2011). Another example is the development of increasingly powerful data mining and visualization software. The publishing of personal information on the Web, particularly on the social web, seems likely to continue and expand. This is because privacy can be traded for increasingly powerful (and normally fun) communication capabilities. While SNSs encourage users to report personal information to a limited or wide audience, Twitter's use via mobile phone allows more frequent public updates in a public way, encouraging posts about relatively trivial aspects of life. This can be combined with geotagging, which users can optionally switch on to reveal their exact location. Unusually for web data, this gives researchers the ability to geolocate authors, allowing more powerful and more fine-grained research. This is an example of a facility that gives away personal information in exchange for benefits, such as the features available on foursquare.com for interacting with friends via handheld devices on the basis of geographical location. It seems likely that many future applications will exploit ubiquitous computing to deliver fun experiences to users prepared to share some personal information, such as location, and current desires or goals.

References

Adamic, L. A. and Glance, N. (2005). "The Political Blogosphere and the 2004 US Election: Divided they Blog." *WWW2005 blog workshop*. Available at <http://citeseerx.ist.psu.edu/viewdoc/summary?doi=10.1.1.59.9009>. Accessed May 5, 2006.

Adamic, L. A. and Huberman, B. A. (2000). "Power-Law Distribution of the World Wide Web," *Science*, 287(5461): 2115a.

Alexa (2011). Alexa top 500 global sites. Available at <http://www.alexa.com/topsites> (Accessed April 12, 2011).

Andersen, C. (2006). *The long Tail: Why the Future of Business is Selling Less of More*, New York, NY: Hyperion Books.

——(2009). *The Longer Long Tail: How Endless Choice is Creating Unlimited Demand*, London: Random House.

Bar-Ilan, J., Shoham, S., Idan, A., Miller, Y. and Shachak, A. (2008). "Structured Versus Unstructured Tagging: A Case Study," *Online Information Review*, 32: 635–47.

Barabási, A. L. (2002). *Linked: The New Science of Networks*, Cambridge, Massachusetts: Perseus Publishing.

Berners-Lee, T., Cailliau, R., Luotonen, A., Nielsen, H. and Secret, A. (1993). "The World Wide Web," *Communications of the ACM*, 37(8): 76–82.

Björneborn, L. (2004). *Small-World Link Structures across an Academic Web Space—A Library and Information Science Approach*, Department of Information Studies, Copenhagen, Denmark: Royal School of Library and Information Science.

——and Ingwersen, P. (2004). "Toward a Basic Framework for Webometrics," *Journal of the American Society for Information Science and Technology*, 55(14): 1216–27.

Bond, M. and Abtahi, M. A. (2005). "The Blogger of Tehran," *New Scientist*, 188(2521): 48–9.

Brin, S. and Page, L. (1998). "The Anatomy of a Large Scale Hypertextual Web Search Engine," *Computer Networks and ISDN Systems*, 30(1–7): 107–17.

Chun, S., Cherry, R., Hiwiller, D., Trant, J., and Wyman, B. (2006). "Steve.museum: An Ongoing Experiment in Social Tagging, Folksonomy, and Museums," *Museums and the Web 2006*.

Available at <http://www.archimuse.com/mw2006/papers/wyman/wyman.html>. Accessed July 1, 2010.

CNN (2010). "Web Users now on Facebook Longer than Google." Available at <http://articles.cnn.com/2010-09-10/tech/facebook.google.time_1_mark-zuckerberg-facebook-web-users?_s=PM:TECH>. Accessed April 10, 2011.

Dodge, M. and Kitchin, D. R. (2001). *Mapping Cyberspace*, London: Routledge.

Foot, K. A., Schneider, S. M., Dougherty, M., Xenos, M., and Larsen, E. (2003). "Analyzing Linking Practices: Candidate Sites in the 2002 US Electoral Web Sphere," *Journal of Computer Mediated Communication*, 8. Available at <http://jcmc.indiana.edu/vol8/issue4/foot.html>.

Fortunato, S., Flammini, A., Menczer, F., and Vespignani, A. (2006). "Topical Interests and the Mitigation of Search Engine Bias." Proceedings of the National Academy of Sciences of the USA, 103(34): 12684–9.

Golder, S. A. and Huberman, B. A. (2006). "The Structure of Collaborative Tagging Systems," *Journal of Information Science*, 32(2): 198–208.

Gruhl, D., Guha, R., Kumar, R., Novak, J., and Tomkins, A. (2005). "The Predictive Power of Online Chatter", in R. L. Grossman, R. Bayardo, K. Bennett, and J. Vaidya (eds) *KDD '05: Proceeding of the eleventh ACM SIGKDD international conference on Knowledge discovery in data mining*, New York, NY: ACM Press.

Hafner, K. (2007). "Seeing Corporate Fingerprints in Wikipedia Edits," *New York Times*, August 17, A1. Available at <http://www.nytimes.com/2007/08/19/technology/19wikipedia.html> (Accessed September 7, 2010).

Herring, S. C., Scheidt, L. A., Bonus, S., and Wright, E. (2004). "Bridging the Gap: A Genre Analysis of Weblogs." *Proceedings of the Thirty-seventh Hawaii International Conference on System Sciences (HICSS-37)*, Los Alamitos: IEEE Press.

Hine, C. (2000). *Virtual Ethnography*, London: Sage.

Holmberg, K. (2010). "Co-inlinking to a Municipal Web Space: A Webometric and Content Analysis," *Scientometrics*, 83(3): 851–62.

Hookway, N. (2008). "Entering the 'Logosphere': Some Strategies for Using Blogs in Social Research," *Qualitative Research*, 8(1): 91–113.

Ingwersen, P. (1998). "The Calculation of Web Impact Factors," *Journal of Documentation*, 54(2): 236–43.

Katsuno, H. and Yano, C. (2007). "Kaomoji and Expressivity in a Japanese Housewives' Chat Room," in B. Danet and S. C. Herring (eds). *The Multilingual Internet: Language, Culture, and Communication Online*, Oxford: Oxford University Press, pp. 278–300.

Kleinberg, J. M. (1999). "Authoritative Sources in a Hyperlinked Environment," *Journal of the ACM*, 46(5): 604–32.

Kousha, K., Thelwall, M., and Rezaie, S. (2010). "Using the Web for Research Evaluation: The Integrated Online Impact Indicator," *Journal of Informetrics*, 4(1): 124–35.

Kramer, A. D. I. (2010). "An Unobtrusive Behavioral Model of "Gross National Happiness." *Proceedings of CHI 2010*, New York: ACM, pp. 287–90.

Lerman, K. (2006). "Social Networks and Social Information Filtering on Digg. *ArXiv.org (Also a poster at International Conference on Weblogs and Social Media)*. Available at <http://arxiv.org/abs/cs.HC/0612046>. Accessed 20 July 2012.

Mayer-Schonberger, V. (2009). *Delete: The Virtue of Forgetting in the Digital Age*, Princeton, NJ: Princeton University Press.

Merton, R. K. (1968). "The Matthew Effect in Science," *Science*, 159(3810): 56–3.

Meyer, C., Grabowski, R., Han, H.-Y., Mantzouranis, K., and Moses, S. (2003). "The World Wide Web as Linguistic Corpus," *Language and Computers*, 46(1): 241–254.

Nardi, B. A. (2010). *My Life as a Night Elf Priest: An Anthropological Account of World of Warcraft*, Ann Arbor: University of Michigan Press.

Nissenbaum, H. (2009). *Privacy in Context: Technology, Policy and the Integrity of Social Life*, Stanford, CA: Stanford University Press.

Ortega, J. L. and Aguillo, I. F. (2008). "Visualization of the Nordic Academic Web: Link Analysis Using Social Network Tools," *Information Processing & Management*, 44(4): 1624–33.

Pang, B. and Lee, L. (2008). "Opinion Mining and Sentiment Analysis," *Foundations and Trends in Information Retrieval*, 1(1–2): 1–135.

Park, H. W. and Thelwall, M. (2008). "Web Linkage Pattern and Social Structure Using Politicians' Websites in South Korea," *Quality & Quantity*, 4(6): 687–97.

Pennock, D., Flake, G. W., Lawrence, S., Glover, E. J., and Giles, C. L. (2002). "Winners Don't Take All: Characterizing the Competition for Links on the Web," *Proceedings of the National Academy of Sciences*, 99(8): 5207–11.

Rafferty, P. and Hidderley, R. (2007). "Flickr and Democratic Indexing: Dialogic Approaches to Indexing," *Aslib Proceedings: New Information Perspectives*, 59(4/5) 397–410.

Ritzer, G. (1996). *The McDonaldization of Society: An Investigation into the Changing Character of Contemporary Social Life*, London: Sage.

Small, H. (1999). "Visualising Science through Citation Mapping," *Journal of American Society for Information Science*, 5(9): 799–813.

Sunstein, C. R. (2004). "Democracy and Filtering," *Communications of the ACM*, 47(12): 57–9.

Surowiecki, J. (2005). *The Wisdom of Crowds: Why the Many are Smarter than the Few*, New York, NY: Abacus.

Thelwall, M. (2002a). "Evidence for the Existence of Geographic Trends in University Web Site Interlinking," *Journal of Documentation*, 58(5): 563–74.

—— (2002b). "The Top 100 Linked Pages on UK University Web Sites: High Inlink Counts are not Usually Directly Associated with Quality Scholarly Content," *Journal of Information Science*, 28(6): 485–93.

—— (2009). *Introduction to Webometrics: Quantitative Web Research for the Social Sciences*, San Rafael, CA: Morgan & Claypool.

—— Buckley, K., and Paltoglou, G. (2011). "Sentiment in Twitter Events," *Journal of the American Society for Information Science and Technology*, 62(2): 406–18.

—— and Harries, G. (2004). "Do the Web Sites of Higher Rated Scholars Have Significantly More Online Impact?," *Journal of American Society for Information Science and Technology*, 55(2): 149–59.

—— Tang, R., and Price, E. (2003). "Linguistic Patterns of Academic Web Use in Western Europe," *Scientometrics*, 56(3): 417–32.

—— and Wilkinson, D. (2004). "Finding Similar Academic Web Sites with Links, Bibliometric Couplings and Colinks," *Information Processing & Management*, 40(3): 515–26.

—— and Wilkinson, D. (2010). "Public Dialogs in Social Network Sites: What is their Purpose?," *Journal of the American Society for Information Science & Technology*, 61(2): 392–404.

—— and Zuccala, A. (2008). "A University-Centred European Union Link Analysis," *Scientometrics*, 75(3): 407–20.

Thompson, G. (2003). "Weblogs, Warblogs, the Public Sphere, and Bubbles," *Transformations*, 7. Available at <http://transformations.cqu.edu.au/journal/issue_07/article_02.shtml>. Accessed July 20, 2012.

Trancer, B. (2008). *Click: What Millions of People Are Doing Online and Why it Matters*, London: Hyperion.

Van Couvering, E. (2004). "New Media? The Political Economy of Internet Search Engines." *Annual Conference of the International Association of Media & Communications Researchers*, Porto Alegre, Brazil.

—— (2007). "Is Relevance Relevant? Market, Science, and War: Discourses of Search Engine Quality," *Journal of Computer-Mediated Communication*, 12(3): article 6. Available at <http://jcmc.indiana.edu/vol12/issue3/vancouvering.html>. Accessed July 20, 2012.

Vaughan, L., Tang, J., and Du, J. (2009). "Examining the Robustness of Web Co-Link Analysis," *Online Information Review*, 33(5): 956–72.

Vossen, G. and Hagemann, S. (2007). *Unleashing Web 2.0: From Concepts to Creativity*, New York: Morgan Kaufmann.

Weber, I. and Castillo, C. (2010). "The Demographics of Web Search," SIGIR, New York: ACM Press. Available at: <http://research.yahoo.com/files/fp485-weber.pdf>. (Accessed April 10, 2011).

Zimmer, M. (2008). "The Gaze of the Perfect Search Engine: Google as an Infrastructure of Dataveillance," in A. Spink and M. Zimmer (eds), *Web Search: Multidisciplinary Perspectives*, Berlin: Springer.

Zuccala, A. (2006). "Author Cocitation Analysis is to Intellectual Structure as Web Colink Analysis is to …?," *Journal of the American Society for Information Science & Technology*, 57(11): 1487–502.

CHAPTER 5

....

THE INTERNET AS
INFRASTRUCTURE

....

CHRISTIAN SANDVIG

IN October 2010 the international web development community was thrown into disarray when it suddenly appeared that millions of common websites across the world would be required to satisfy the decency standards of Sharia, the religious law of Islam.[1] To understand how this unlikely situation came about requires that we know about the infrastructure of the Internet; it is a story about the collision of what is ultimately a variety of seemingly unrelated actors and actions, and this instance is comprehensible only after assembling all of them. Beginning with this example, this chapter will argue for the value of investigating the details of Internet infrastructure as a method of studying the Internet and society more generally. It will argue for the study of Internet Infrastructure and also for the value of considering the Internet infrastructurally, as a system foundational to other activities.

AN INFRASTRUCTURE EXAMPLE: FROM
THE GET METHOD TO A WOMAN'S BARE ARMS

....

The first factors in this particular story about Sharia and the Web are technical. Over fifteen years earlier, web server programmers on the www-talk mailing list anticipated that the Web would become more than just static web pages: they proposed a method for adding the information required for interactive web applications to the right side of a web page's address or URL (this was called the "GET" method; see Robinson and Coar 2004: 33). By 2010, the increasing dynamism of the Web had confirmed their vision, causing the URLs

---

[1] The original blog post that started this controversy is Ben Metcalfe's "The .ly domain space to be considered unsafe" (Metcalfe 2010).

for web services to become lengthy with codes, id numbers, and ephemera that made them ungainly to remember, type, and share. Eventually, these ever-longer addresses in turn created a demand for what became known as "URL shortening services": applications that would produce a short synonym that could be used to represent the ever-longer and harder-to-share URL.

The next factors in this story are financial. The first such service, TinyURL.com, created in 2002 as a not-for-profit organization, was quickly joined by hundreds of commercial firms: bit.ly, is.gd, ow.ly, tiny.cc, go2.me, and so on. Governments joined in (go.usa.gov). Major web companies developed their own shorteners: goo.gl (Google), nyti.ms (The New York Times), fb.me (Facebook), and bbc.in (BBC). Nine years later, millions of dollars had been invested in a variety of URL shortening start-ups (Johnson et al. 2010) as it became clearer that shortening URLs was about more than convenience: every click on a shortened URL generated data that could be captured, and this data about who clicked on which links could have considerable commercial value. It could also be re-sold. The leading URL shortening company, bit.ly, served over 4.7 billion clicks every month (Siegler 2010).

The flash point where Sharia intersected web hosting came from a site hosted by the URL shortener vb.ly. It contained a picture of San Francisco Chronicle sex columnist Violet Blue in a sleeveless top, drinking a beer.[2] The service hosting the image (vb.ly) was ordered closed by Libyan Telecom & Technology (LTT), Tripoli. The LTT representative involved in the case commented that "a scantily clad lady with some bottle in her hand isn't exactly what most would consider decent" (Johnson 2010).

To know how Libya gained the power to take down this website and potentially billions of others requires some history. In the quest for shorter and shorter web addresses, URL shortening services had turned away from three-letter addresses ending in .com and .net and toward two-letter domain name suffixes (.ly, .gd, .cc, .me, .in, and so on)—after all, every character that could be saved would produce a faster-to-type URL. Two-letter Internet addresses are called "country codes," and they were added to the Internet's naming and addressing system in the 1980s in order to provide an alternative way of naming websites that would be linked to nationality (e.g. the United Kingom's is .uk). Yet the original engineers of the Internet were wary of "the business of deciding what is and what is not a country" (Postel 1994: 5), so they decided that the system of names would be based on a recognized international standard dating from 1974 that establishes two-letter abbreviations for countries (arcanely known as ISO #3166; see ISO 2011).

The next part of the story depends on peculiarities of the English language and the process of standardization, with a dash of geopolitics. This ISO standard decrees that the nation of Libya shall be represented in English with the two-letter code "LY." An English-speaker will recognize the -ly suffix and its synonym -y as a way to transform nouns, adjectives, and verbs into adverbs (from "quick" to "quickly"). The suffixes can also have a cute sound as a diminutive ("kitty"). Adding -ly to "bit" to produce "bit-ly" could thus

---

[2] A discussion of the controversy and a screen shot of the original picture can be found in the blog post, "I, For One, Welcome our New TLD Overlords With Bare Arms" (Blue 2010).

mean "just like a bit" or "a little bit." Since the Internet is made of bits, this is a promising name for an Internet company. Other countries like Latvia (LV), Liechtenstein (LI), and Liberia (LR) didn't happen to have ISO standard abbreviations that are also cute English suffixes. Unlike ".ly" (for Libya), other handy English two-letter words were in the hands of pro-Western allies, but these were politically unstable—like the Kingdom of Tonga (TO). Safer suffixes existed, such as the British overseas territory of South Georgia and the South Sandwich Islands (GS), but quirky addresses like "blo.gs" didn't catch on (for more examples, see Steinberg and Mcdowell 2003).

The assignment of these two-letter address codes to national administrators that would parcel them out was yet another step, and it was fraught with politics. The engineers weren't at all successful in avoiding controversy and they found they couldn't simply implement the ISO standard. They were forced to tackle knotty problems like: "Does a sovereign abo-riginal nation receive a 'national' two-letter country code?" (No, according to the stand-ard.) "Should Catalonia have an independent country code, or is it part of Spain?" (No, it is part of Spain, according to the standard.) "Should Hong Kong have an independent coun-try code, or is it part of China?" (Yes, it should have a code [.hk], according to the stand-ard.) "Is Antarctica a country?" (No, but it gets a code anyway [.aq], according to the standard.) "What happens to nations that disappear, like the USSR?" (Their domain names remain anyway [.su], even though that violates the standard). "Everyone already calls Great Britain 'the UK' and not 'GB,' what should we do?" (Give it the address [.uk] even though that violates the standard.) "Who should control the country code for Iraq [.iq] while it is at war in 2003?" (Instead of a country, give it to the InfoCom Corporation of Richardson, Texas, USA, even though that violates the standard.[3]) Libya, the sovereign nation, at that time governed by Moammar Gadhafi, was delegated control of .ly.

The remaining elements of this story are legal, cultural, familial, and religious. Gadhafi gave the job of running .ly to LTT, a company owned and nominally run by his eldest son, Muhammad. LTT sold the rights to use some .ly domains to American URL short-ening services, such as bit.ly and ow.ly. LTT's contracts included clause 3.5, requiring that "the domain name is not being registered for any activities/purpose not permitted under Libyan law." Libya is one of a handful of countries whose legal system is based on Sharia (Islamic Law). The Qur'an asks women to "guard their modesty" (24:31), and Violet Blue's bare arms were taken to be a violation.

The Libyan decision caused significant consternation in the Internet industry. The suffix .ly had become the most popular suffix for URL-shortening, and a significant frac-tion of the English-speaking world's URLs were therefore reliant on a symbolic resource that was controlled by the dictator of an Arabic-speaking country who was traditionally hostile to the English-speaking world. Indeed, it now appeared that he might invoke religious law to redirect traffic away from popular websites. An almost immediate, major substantive reaction was an investor panic around URL shortening companies—surely encouraged by Islamophobia. Details emerged later that LTT had formed a plan to

---

[3] This is an Internet Service Provider dedicated to hosting websites for Muslim organizations in the United States.

re-issue the extremely valuable .ly domains it seized from the West to Libyan nationals, presenting an economic motive instead of a religious one (Horn 2010).

LTT backed down from these threats after an international controversy in the technical community, but this still resulted in a significant reorganization of capital and Internet addressing. For example, if you tried to reach the popular URL shortener bit.ly in 2011 you would have been redirected to the ungainly URL "bitly.com." By February 2011 a revolution was in progress in Libya, and LTT cut off Internet links with the outside world (Google 2011).[4] By October, the Libyan government had fallen and was replaced by a transitional council of revolutionaries. LTT finally declared itself through with the confusing situation, and it ordered that no future .ly domain names, three characters or less, would be registered without a local presence in Libya.[5]

For the purposes of this chapter, Violet's bare arms are useful because they represent a baffling network of relationships producing significant outcomes that no single actor seems particularly able to foresee (and, in this case, that no actor is really that happy about). The case of Violet Blue implicates technical decisions about the design of interactive software (via URLs and the GET method), usability, culture, religion, history, politics, and economics.

Approaching the case from only one perspective is doomed to fail: if we considered this is simply an instance of Libyan censorship, for example, this would beg the question of how on earth a legendarily capricious dictator came to acquire veto power over an important part of the Internet's functionality. As it unfolded, the situation put the sex columnist for the San Francisco Chronicle in a public conversation with the eldest son of the ruler of Libya—a bizarre pairing.

This episode led to the financial ruin of some investors in URL shortening firms, the loss of millions of dollars, and at the time it appeared that LTT's actions could have affected millions of English-speaking Internet users. Despite all this, the story is an obscure one, receiving only minor press coverage. The full arc of the story is available only for those technical insiders involved in Internet addressing who follow specialized fora, dedicated mailing lists, and blogs.

Messy, holistic investigations that cross social and technical boundaries like this brief example have lately come to be called "infrastructure studies."[6] As both a label and, increasingly, a research method, infrastructure studies has a growing scholarly currency and relevance to the study of the Internet. This chapter will trace the evolution of this field of work and outline two major constituent intellectual components. It argues that "infrastructure" is the new "network." That is, although infrastructure is at times inchoate as a concept and it holds many, sometimes inconsistent meanings for different researchers, nevertheless the term is now galvanizing a newly vibrant pool of Internet-related scholarship in the same way that equally diffuse and inconsistently applied concepts like "network" have in the past (Watts 2004).

---

[4] *.ly domain names mostly continued to work, however.
[5] See <www.nic.ly/lyregistrars.php>. Accessed July 7, 2011.
[6] This phrasing of the approach owes a debt to Actor-Network Theory (Latour 2007).

Linking structure and symbol:
defining infrastructure

The word infrastructure doesn't usually sound exciting, and infrastructure studies is "a call to study boring things" and to vitalize them—to make them exciting (Star 1999: 337). Studying the Internet as infrastructure involves turning away from the topics that motivate a great deal of writing about the Internet. For example, Silver boldly asserted that "the twin pillars of cyberculture studies are virtual communities and online identities" (Silver 2006: 3). Studying the infrastructure, as described below, implies turning away from the symbolic and investigating the structural—this is the Internet not as "what people say with it" but as "how it works."

The following excerpt from Vanderbilt's journalistic account of his online life demonstrates how one might describe Internet use infrastructurally:

> I have photos on Flickr (which is owned by Yahoo, so they reside in a Yahoo data center, probably the one in Wenatchee, Wash.); the Wikipedia entry about me dwells on a database in Tampa, Fla.; the video on YouTube of a talk I delivered…might dwell in any one of Google's data centers, from The Dalles in Oregon to Lenoir, N.C.; my LinkedIn profile most likely sits in an Equinix-run data center in Elk Grove Village, Ill.; and my blog lives at Modwest's headquarters in Missoula, Mont. If one of these sites happened to be down, I might have Twittered a complaint, my tweet paying a virtual visit to (most likely) NTT America's data center in Sterling, Va. (Vanderbilt 2009)

In this story about the Internet, otherwise obscure features such as ownership and network topology (here, the geography of data centers) are pushed to the forefront. This chapter will describe which researchers are doing this inversion, how it is done, and why it is useful and important.

Infrastructure refers to "the subordinate parts of an undertaking" or its "foundation," and it is a modern coinage, dating to 1927 (Oxford English Dictionary), but really finding traction in the 1970s. In common usage it is often used in a similar sense to "utility," or "public utility," meaning "a service regarded as essential." We commonly think of utilities as involving a public purpose and as including electricity, gas, and water, and sometimes roads and telecommunications, although there is no exact legal definition of the set, and no ironclad rule across political systems as to whether these should be public or private undertakings.

It is obvious, after a moment's thought, that these examples of infrastructures and utilities must be quite context-specific. Both piped, clean water and the wired telephone were once considered a luxury fit only for the rich and not at all an essential (de Sola Pool 1983). This view is still held in some places. As Edwards writes, "Given the heterogeneous character of systems and institutions referenced by the term, perhaps 'infrastructure' is best defined negatively, as those systems without which contemporary societies cannot function" (2003: 187).

Germane to this chapter's purpose, the Internet is in the process of becoming foundational. In the last twenty years it has become an emergent essential—a new infra-structure—across the globe and in a wide range of human activity. Certain components of the Internet have also been notably singled out for "meta-infrastructural" status as essential components of the Internet without which the Internet itself would not func-tion: most notably search engines (Bracha and Pasquale 2008) and the Internet's addressing and naming system introduced in the example at the beginning of this chapter (Mueller 2002).

Infrastructure studies, for the purposes of this handbook, refers to the multidisciplinary body of scholarship that is increasingly directed toward understanding the co-evolution of the Internet and society, and it does so by considering the Internet as infrastructure. Definitionally, in this phrasing it is helpful to distinguish the study of infrastructure and "infrastructure studies." Many disciplines and scholars from electrical engineers to specialists in human development (see Unwin Chapter 25) follow the dictionary defini-tions just given above and are concerned about infrastructures. Yet there is a more dis-tinct group that considers infrastructure not as a member of some definable group of objects, networks, or companies like "the providers of water, communication, heat, light ..." but rather as an analytic and even a research method in itself. This chapter will emphasize the latter—those who employ the idea of infrastructure as an analytic and a research method.

The chapter will thus review infrastructure studies of the Internet as two complementary approaches: it will call the first grouping "the relationists," a group of scholars exempli-fied by Bowker, Star, and Edwards (see below), closely aligned intellectually with the science and technology studies movement, and sometimes found in information science programs or called "information infrastructure studies."[7] The second, smaller grouping will be termed "the new materialists," a group exemplified by Sterne and Parks (see below) that often identifies itself as media studies, cultural studies, or cultural history. These groupings are artificially imposed and non-exclusive, and are proposed merely as an aid to traversing the research in this area.

THE RELATIONISTS, THE INTERNET, AND THEIR TURTLES

An origin story of one strain of the relationist approach begins with a series of disasters. In its first decades, computing appeared to be a new kind of engineering drastically unlike other kinds of engineering, like building bridges or buildings. In the hybrid social and technical area of research then called "systems analysis" (and later "computer-supported

---

[7] This use of the word "relationism" is meant to imply that these thinkers see infrastructure as relational. It is not meant to evoke Mannheim's philosophical relationism or any other use of the term (Tsekeris 2010).

cooperative work," CSCW), social researchers who turned to computing and socially minded computer scientists both continually faced the problem that when new large-scale computing projects were planned, designed, or introduced, things almost never happened as expected (Kling 1992).

It is true that most complicated projects of any kind have unforeseen consequences, yet computing projects seemed especially likely to be doomed. Initiatives involving new computers and (later) computer networking were often costly fiascoes that failed totally, with multi-million dollar systems abandoned before completion, never able to perform the tasks written in their specifications, and abandoned (or at least hated) by the users they were intended to serve (Brooks 1995). For example, as strange as it may seem, large-scale computing projects were portrayed in the normally staid technical computing literature of the 1980s with the image of a monstrous, unkillable werewolf (Brooks 1995: ch. 16; cf. also Law 1991) certainly beyond the control of mere human programmers and analysts. These computing werewolves continue to haunt the industry (Wright 2011).

In the late 1980s and early 1990s, influenced by the newly vibrant science and technology studies movement (Bijker et al. 1987), CSCW researchers began to argue that understanding this situation required systematic reconsideration of "the scope of the boundaries that [we] draw around the computer system" (Kling 1992: 5). At the time it was normal to consider computer systems to be a kind of infrastructure, but this word referred only to the computer boxes themselves and maybe to the wires connecting them.

Kling, and others, found that when trying to understand what was happening in a particular computing project, they needed to ignore the material objects and foreground the previously hidden or background activities that made the system possible—they needed to examine the infrastructure for the computing infrastructure (Jewett and Kling 1991). They initially framed this distinction as "hard" vs "soft" infrastructure, where soft infrastructure denoted things like the everyday habits of the human operators.

Infrastructure as relational

Star, Bowker, and collaborators took this inspiration to develop a theoretical and methodological apparatus for the study of infrastructure (e.g. Star and Ruhleder 1996). For them, infrastructure is a relation and not a set of things. The study of infrastructure is a change in perception like the figure-ground shift explored by Gestalt psychology—when we change the way that we look at something, the background becomes the foreground and vice-versa (Bowker 1994, cited in Star and Ruhleder 1996: 112). Infrastructure is then not a thing but a question: what does this activity depend on?

Crucially, this means that since different actors are differentially positioned as to what goals they want to achieve, one person's background is already another person's foreground, and one person's infrastructure is another's obstacle (Star 1991). Thinking about infrastructure as a relation sensitizes the scholar to these multiple perspectives by asking to whom an infrastructure is addressed and, therefore, who is left out. To the person in a wheelchair, stairs to the second floor are not "seamless subtenders of use, but barriers" (Star 1999: 380). In Internet terms, to the network engineer, the Internet's everyday traffic in bits is not a substrate or a foundation to other work but instead the major topic of their working life. An Internet blocking and filtering system is one person's infrastructure to maintain important public values, while this same system is another person's threat to the freedom of expression, while it is yet a third person's irritating check on their ability to easily obtain pornography (see Nash Chapter 21).

Finally, a key implication of this relational framing of infrastructure is that it represents "an infinite regress of relationships" (Bateson 1978: 279). This means that there is no particular point in the sequence of infrastructure where things stop being social and become purely technical (or vice-versa), or where infrastructure itself stops—any thing that one points to has "subordinate parts" (therefore, it has an infrastructure), and this infrastructure must also have an infrastructure, and so on. In philosophy and cosmology, untangling this recursion is known as the problem of first cause (from Aristotle's *primum movens*). Stephen Hawking popularized the anecdote that one cosmology holds that the earth is supported on the back of a tortoise. In this cosmology, when asked, what supports the tortoise? the answer given is, "it's turtles all the way down" (Hawking 1988: 1).[8] Infrastructure theorists hold that "it's infrastructure all the way down" (e.g. Star 2000).

Selecting a topic: infrastructure studies as an applied art

Since every infrastructure (turtle) has an infrastructure (turtle) that supports it, the task of the infrastructure scholar is to find a useful point of entry into this infinite series: to choose an infrastructure that raises to consciousness some unstudied background detail, but not just for the sake of its curation and preservation. Instead, infrastructure studies is practiced as an applied art—it diverges from the mainstream fields of history and anthropology because in each study its practitioners usually try to find a lens that reflects insight onto a present-day problem. The methods used may still be historical, but the goal is unlikely to be preservation. Pioneers like Star demanded that in choosing a topic the focus should be on those who are left out (Star 1999): who is harmed, who is forgotten, who is unserved, and how research might rectify the situation. For instance, a book-length history of computing could fall within this framing, but only one that argues that the military origins of computing and the precursor technologies for the Internet still constrain the shape of these technologies today and the way that we think about them (e.g. Edwards 1996). In contrast, a purely descriptive or curatorial history of computing might discuss infrastructure (and focus on the technical—"how it works") but it would still have little in common with the group of scholars identified here as belonging to "infrastructure studies."

---

[8] In the anecdote, the speaker does not appear to realize that turtles and tortoises are different animals. This anecdote is sometimes linked to Native American or Hindu mythology (as an elephant).

To drive this point home, recall that some early work in the then-emerging domain of "technology studies" had been castigated as bloodless and overly theoretical. It was charged and found guilty of "disdain for anything resembling an evaluative stance or any particular moral or political principles" (Winner 1993: 371). In contrast to these critics, the researchers aligning themselves with the study of infrastructure refused to participate in scholarship that showed such a separation from human experience. It is this repeated orientation toward societal problems, social justice, and applied knowledge, when combined with a comparative urge and a present-focus that distinguishes the relationists from other infrastructure researchers or from other fields. They argue: "Understanding the nature of infrastructural work involves unfolding the political, ethical, and social choices that have been made throughout its development" (Bowker et al. 2010: 99). The CSCW literature seems an unlikely location for these developments. CSCW can otherwise be quite restrained—according to its acronym it was devoted, after all, to the suspiciously Taylorist task of "supporting" people's "work." Yet affiliating with infrastructure studies by following the voice of writers like Star (1999) can feel like manning the barricades.[9]

Infrastructure, urbanism, and history

Major intellectual allies in this endeavor have come from urban planning and the history of technology—these thinkers are so closely allied as to be at times indistinguishable as an intellectual tradition. In the historical work sometimes known as "large technical systems" (LTS) research (a term of art), Thomas Parke Hughes provided groundbreaking, detailed and compelling treatments of infrastructure where a major theoretical drive was to explain difference and possibility in technological systems (see Hughes 1983, 1998). Rather than "straight" history, Hughes's comparative approach outlined the political and social choices in arenas that had previously seemed only technical and mundane—such as the early electrical power systems of the world. Hughes also advocated for theorizing system development across time and space rather than studying devices or people in isolation, and he promoted the value of research across specific instances of infrastructure (most notably, transport, computing, power, and communications). He proposed that all infrastructures, the Internet included (Hughes 1998: ch. 6), passed through loose and overlapping but recognizable phases of development. These can be roughly summarized as (1) invention and early development, (2) transfer across space and context, (3) growth in scale, and (4) momentum or inertia (Hughes 1983).

---

[9] For example, see Star (2010: 614–15), or consider that Star writes "there are millions of tiny bridges built into large-scale information infrastructures and millions of (literal and metaphoric) public buses that cannot pass through them" (1999: 389). For more on this controversial bus example, see Winner (1986) and Woolgar and Cooper (1999).

As another example, at nearly the same moment but proceeding independently, Sawhney, writing as a historian of the telephone system, advocated that the evolution of transport and communications networks were often parallel, and proposed an eight-stage model of infrastructure development that explained the gradual replacement of one technological network by a complement (Sawhney 1992, 1993). He later demonstrated the value of this framework for understanding the evolution of the Internet (2003). Today, the relationists agree that historical knowledge like this is a requirement for any study of infrastructure—even if it is not meant to be a historical study. As infrastructures are always complex networks that change relatively slowly they can only be appreciated with a historian's sense of time (Edwards et al. 2007: 8). As they often follow parallel trajectories they must be understood via comparisons to other infrastructures across history.

Theorists of the built environment represent a separate group of close allies, as they often choose their object of study to be "the city," they have in parallel developed infrastructurally-comparative historical approaches and theories. Most notably, writers like Castells (1989) and Graham and Marvin (1996) demonstrated forcefully that telecommunications' infrastructures like the Internet had been left out of urban planning, and argued for the integration of telecommunications and the Internet into thinking about urbanism, space, and place (for an overview of this work, see Graham 2003). Later, they developed an important periodization of infrastructure itself, writing in *Splintering Urbanism* (Graham and Marvin 2001) that infrastructures generally had been conceptualized in the early twentieth century and earlier as a "modernist infrastructural ideal" of homogenization, utopian integration, and master planning under one provider. For example, consider Haussmann's famous boulevards for nineteenth century Paris: a master plan for transportation that was also meant to regularize and distribute gas lighting, water mains, sewers, drainage, and even security (54). Graham and Marvin argued that by 1975 this ideal had broken down. Coincident with the rise of the Internet, infrastructures of all kinds became "splintered" and unbundled, relying on competition, market mechanisms, and segmentation of users into the privileged and the less privileged who were offered different services (or no service at all). While from 1975 to the present the Internet itself was splintering (Bar et al. 1995; Kesan and Shah 2001), in Graham and Marvin's view, the Internet (and telecommunications) was the single most important infrastructure "leading [the] shift towards the splintering of mass markets under forces of global capitalism and privatization" (2001: 233–4) by providing a model of a privately managed, transnationally funded distributed system apparently free from the old-fashioned meddling of government planning. Under the regime of splintering urbanism, the organization of the Internet has now become the mental model used to think about the future of other systems like transport (e.g. smart roads, dynamic road pricing, the driverless car) or electrical power (e.g. the smart grid). The Internet, the newest infrastructure, has become an infrastructural primitive or template for its parents: a model privately organized system of distributed computation—the *ur*-infrastructure.

Methods: The heuristics of infrastructure

For method, the relationists draw broadly from the humanities and interpretive social sciences, with a special affinity for both history and ethnography. They explicitly hope to address scholars in the fields of sociology, history, systems engineering, science and technology studies (STS), communication, urban planning, and cultural geography (e.g. see the list of fields in Graham and Marvin 2001: 33). Atop these more general methods and disciplines sits a common toolbox of analytics. As seen above, a prerequisite for the relationist's work is to stipulate that infrastructure is relative and context-specific, but that all infrastructures share features such that its proper study must be comparative and historically informed. These starting points lead inevitably to infrastructure as the proper object of theory. That is, a relationist may give you an article about the telephone system, a book about the infrastructure for climate science, or a book about the classification of diseases. Yet in each of these cases the ultimate goal will be to theorize "systems" and never just the instance of one. Infrastructure studies are about "a growing body of evidence pointing to patterns or dynamics common to the development of many infrastructures over many times and places" (Jackson et al. 2007). Studies of computing and information technology are best undertaken in a broadly comparative fashion, linking (for instance) seemingly separate areas like bioinformatics and architecture (Lenoir and Alt 2003). This means that the pinnacle of infrastructural thinking consists of precepts like: "Infrastructure creates systemic vulnerabilities to nature" (Edwards 2003: 221). This very high level of abstraction has opponents, who argue that such broad comparisons across contexts and technologies should be considered invalid prima facie (Fischer 1985).

Nonetheless, defining a set of overarching "dynamics," "tensions," or "heuristics" (see Jackson et al. 2007) common to all infrastructure is a major contribution of this strain of work, and the ability to use these as analytics to relate disparate technologies to each other gives the relationists their name in this chapter. Five attributes of infrastructure have been found by many authors and will be explained below by way of example. They are: invisibility, dependence on human practices, modularity, standardization, and momentum. Other common attributes exist, but these five provide an introduction (for a review, see Jackson et al. 2007). These attributes are meant as features that all infrastructures are claimed to possess, but also as guides that researchers should use to target their investigations.

The first such attribute of infrastructure states that it is normally invisible, becoming apparent only when it breaks (Star 1999: 382). Breakdowns have become a key investigative tool for the infrastructure analyst because they illustrate dependencies (Nye 2010). Visibility can itself be a site of struggle around infrastructure: for instance, cities exist politically in order to provide shared services, therefore cities often actively work toward infrastructural visibility to try to prove their value. As Mitchell puts it, cities celebrate their infrastructure (Mitchell 2005)—but with a few exceptions like this or that brightly lit, iconic bridge, cities are mostly not successful in making these systems stand out. Infrastructure is taken for granted. Nowhere is this rule of invisibility more true than the

Internet, whose major physical parts are often literally invisible: they include wireless signals, buried wires (e.g. fiber optic lines), or machines hidden in nondescript, locked office buildings (e.g. data centers and Internet traffic exchange points). Yet beyond its material components, the idea of the Internet is also invisible, with web pages arriving as if by magic, relying on processes that are totally unknown and unquestioned by most Internet users.

The second common attribute of infrastructure is perhaps derived from Kling's original distinction between "hard" and "soft" (discussed above). Recent work on infrastructure always emphasizes the importance of the "soft" (non-technical) practices and routines to the system. The successful infrastructure investigator must, in this view, guard against being distracted by the shiny material parts and uncover the tacit labor that must always be present. Infrastructures are arrangements of practices. Star (2010) gives the example of the QWERTY computer keyboard, which was originally one arrangement of keys on a typewriter among many competing arrangements. Over time, most typists learned the QWERTY layout, and it has endured to the present day from its origin in 1873 (David 1985). It eventually appeared on the keyboard for devices of all kinds, and the widespread practice of typing this way was re-integrated into the physical and material parts of infrastructure: even the designers of office furniture meant for working with computers now take the orientation of the QWERTY layout into account (Becker, cited in Star 2010: 611). Yet it has been argued that the QWERTY layout is a very inefficient way to type (David 1985). In this example a human practice, such as learning to type one way vs another, can be powerful and important, even though it is also intangible.

One specific focus within the study of routines and practices of infrastructure has lately emerged surrounding maintenance and upkeep (Graham and Thrift 2007). When our stories about technologies like the Internet do focus on human practices, these are usually practices of development and invention. This ignores the fact that the bulk of a system's work and expense is actually maintenance (see also Ribes and Finholt 2009). Graham and Thrift go so far as to urge a focus on "decay" and "entropy" to understand the true scope and life cycle of infrastructure and infrastructural work (2007: 5).

When analyzing Internet infrastructure, uncovering important practices and routines is particularly difficult because the world of computing presents itself with a mythology that insists, ideally, that computers do not need to be learned at all: they are "intuitive" or "user friendly" (for a critique, see Bardini 2000: 226). We are also told that simple exposure to the Internet at an early age produces impressive skills without a need for formal education about the Internet—these "digital natives" already know it all (Palfrey and Gasser 2008). On the producer side, the Internet industry promotes back-end products with sales jargon like "turn-key." Calling a product like an Internet router "turn-key" means that the device requires no labor; as with starting a car, you only need to "turn the key" and the engine will run. This is clearly a romanticized vision of both routers and automobiles. The Internet is likewise composed of "user friendly" systems that require a great deal of skill to learn, while "turn-key" computing devices are actually maintained by an army of shadowy laborers. For instance, in 2009, a video surreptitiously taken at a Google engineering talk revealed how failed computers are replaced inside Google's top secret Internet data centers.

A technician—a young man with a ponytail and headphones—was shown riding his official Google-provided two-wheeled scooter back and forth between shipping containers that are filled wall-to-wall with servers (DataCenterVideos 2009). He keeps the spare computers in a messenger bag.

As the third attribute of infrastructure, Star (1999) also emphasized that infrastructure is modular and incremental. Even when a billion-dollar apparently top-down effort is made to rationalize and standardize an infrastructure, this proceeds in a process that takes years (Hughes 1998) and is more akin to negotiation between many disparate parts and actors (Latour 2007). Infrastructure itself could be described as an achievement of negotiation, as its interconnectedness means that modifying one part requires adjustments in another—and these adjustments are both social and technical. This precept of infrastructure is a strike back at older theories of technological systems like Ogburn's "culture lag" (1957) that presuppose a technology can be a monolith or exogenous, understood as separate from culture. The Internet is an excellent example of this precept because it is officially leaderless and decentralized: it is no longer a project of any particular country or person (Mueller 2002). Infrastructure studies would hold that this is also true of infrastructures that *seem* to be projects of a particular institution, place, or person (such as Google or the Great Firewall of China). In that case, observers simply overlook the full complexity of the system, and falsely ascribe a single human will to a network of decentralized actors. The task of the analyst, in this view, is to find and make comprehensible the invisible negotiations that are producing the infrastructure.

Fourth, standardization is a critical point of inquiry to learn more about infrastructure. "[H]owever much standards appear to be neutral, benign, merely technical, obscure, and removed from daily life . . . they are largely an unrecognized but extremely important and growing source of social, political, and economic relations of power" (Busch 2011: 28). Standardization allows seamless interconnection with other systems and processes, and it also promotes the normalcy and invisibility of the system itself (Star 1999). But standardization is both a technical and business tactic—it is an aid to consolidation in a diverse system. Standardization proceeds via "strategic intermediaries" (Jackson et al. 2007) that many scholars have labeled gateways (Egyedi 2001). Like the Internet's gateways, these are intermediaries that provide a translation from one system (or network) to another. But in the parlance of Egyedi, and others, the gateway can be a device or it can be a written agreement—or even an organizational practice. The significance of the gateway is that by focusing our attention on the boundaries of an infrastructure we can better comprehend its form and its limits. The advice that follows from this precept is: to understand a system, study its boundaries and the gateways that allow it to work with other systems.

Fifth, as large-scale systems of great complexity, infrastructures all suffer or benefit from what Hughes called "momentum" (1983). "[O]nce established, systems tend to continue in particular directions, making reversals or wholesale leaps to alternative approaches costly, difficult, and in some cases impossible" (Jackson et al. 2007). In this, the relationists embrace the economics of path dependence, a form of network externality (e.g. David 1985) and they often refer to a technological system's "interia" or "trajectory." In terms of research method, the existence of system momentum argues for an attention to the early days of any infrastructure, as "early technical choices (including some relatively casual or arbitrary ones) have a tendency to get reinforced as subsequent system elements are built around or on top of them" (Jackson et al. 2007). For example, almost all of the URLs on the Internet begin with "http://www" although most of this prefix is no longer necessary—it was originally meant to differentiate web traffic from other protocols that are now defunct (e.g. nntp:, gopher:), and the prefix refers to an era where individual computers were named by their services (www, news, mail). Sir Tim Berners-Lee, inventor of the World Wide Web, recently admitted that some of the characters in URLs never served a useful purpose, and "were a mistake." These characters now simply make URLs longer and harder to type—Berners-Lee once publicly apologized for wasting everyone's ink and effort with them (Firth 2009). While these redundancies are now slowly disappearing from URLs, despite efforts to stamp them out after twenty-three years most URLs still have the "http://www" prefix. This is an example of infrastructural inertia.

Returning to Libya for the lessons of relationism

It should be clear by now that our introductory example for this chapter can easily be adapted to fit the relationist mold. The threatened censorship of the .ly domain name suffix under the Libyan interpretation of Sharia law demonstrates all of the heuristics mentioned above. The apparatus behind the operation of Internet domain names is obscure and was invisible until it threatened breakdown. Libya acquired power over a large number of foreign websites because of human practices (the preference for some "cute" suffixes like "ly" over others like "gs"), amplified by inertia as more and more users gravitated to the most popular domain name shortening services (which ended in .ly). Libya's claim on the .ly suffix also came from a formal standardization process that was both organizational (at the ISO) and technical (in the domain name software of the Internet). Throughout the whole story there was no central fulcrum that controlled the infrastructure or the narrative. Instead, a wide variety of actors were in a constant tug-of-war or negotiation for the future of the system. However, to make this truly a relationist account we would need to add a cross-system understanding of addressing as a persistent feature of infrastructure, and theorize the act of addressing in a way that would allow it to shed light on other infrastructures (e.g. Sandvig 2008).

THE NEW MATERIALISTS: TECHNOLOGY, ARTIFACTS, AND PLACE

Unlike the relationists, this chapter will spend only a small amount of space discussing the new materialists. As there is a great deal of overlap between the two groups, it may be that in some circumstances it is not productive to distinguish them from each other.

However, a major difference worthy of note is that for relationists like Star, the use of the word "infrastructure" is usually a semantic move intended to take a social process and make it seem more material, concrete, or foundational. These relationist writers often started their careers with the history of technology or with computer science, which can both be quite material and quite technical to begin with. The relationists wanted to break away and brand intangible social practices so that they appeared just as important and solid as technical practices and objects. Following in the traditions of STS, they tended to start with a technology and gently or roughly lead their readers to exclaim, "Oh, look: it's actually cultural!" (or political, or social, or economic). Much of the writing in the relationist tradition of infrastructure studies doesn't use the word "infrastructure" in the way a common English speaker might—the average person would expect roads, power systems, and communications networks, but the relationists use infrastructure analytically as a way to materialize the ephemera of norms and organizations. They claim to do this in the service of understanding material systems, to be sure, but the material parts of these objects are de-emphasized. Turner, for instance, asks if the Burning Man festival is an "infrastructure" that provides cultural forms, ideas, and labor practices to the Internet industry in Silicon Valley (Turner 2009).

The new materialists, in contrast, are a group of scholars who are making the opposite transit. Starting in media studies and communication, they have long been concerned with the airy expanse of culture, but they want to lead the reader through an analysis of a communicative experience to eventually exclaim, "Oh, look: It's actually material!" (or technical, or spatial). The turn toward infrastructure is, for them, an attempt to ground their earlier cultural passions, focusing new attention on what the everyday dictionary-reading person would think about the word "infrastructure:" that is, roads, power systems, and communication networks; wires, signals, and dirt. Even though the backlash against the high theory of the 1980s is now decades old, it still may be the cause that impelled some postmodernists to decamp for the earthier environs of materialism. This turn is then comprehensible as their move away from earlier writing about production, reception, and texts.

The focus on "how it works" is still very much in play: A good example is the recent turn toward environmental ethics in media studies. These new materialists ask: Where do the components in media infrastructures come from? Where do server farms and media devices get their power? While a decade ago the cultural text of a TV-sitcom would be considered in cultural terms, today it is also queried as to its carbon footprint. The Internet is introduced with statistics like: approximately 1.5 percent of the electricity supply of the US is consumed by centralized server farms (Maxwell and Miller 2008); or with shocking slogans like: your old laptop is killing people in China (Slade 2007). This turn toward the environment is overdue in media studies, as communication systems are responsible for consequences like massive deposits of toxic lead (from cathode ray tubes). The communication industry holds the dubious honor of producing the consumer product with the single shortest product life cycle of any product—the mobile phone. It is almost instantly obsolete and toxic, and is typically not recycled.

Admittedly, these connections to the substrate of power grids and waste dumps are topics that other authors have explored before. However, the new materialists are of note as an intellectual movement in part because of their origin point: they are moving from the theoretical to the empirical. Phillips, writing in *Social Text* (2005), uses the work of Judith Butler and queer theory to theorize privacy as visibility in the context of ubiquitous computing environments. A few years later, Phillips and Clement (2008) focus on discovering the likely routes taken by network traffic and the locations of "carrier hotels" (points where data are exchanged between two carriers) traversed along the way. Indeed, the spatialization of formerly placeless media-related practices is a hallmark of the emerging tradition. Neff interrogates the production processes in new media organizations and argues that their physical location in space is one of the most important ways to understand their development (Neff 2005). Starosielski (2010) argues that to understand film culture in Fiji it is important to know that most people obtain their movies by picking up pirated DVDs from the car wash. Still, the new materialists do not intend to wholly release their past focus on culture or content. New materialists ask questions like: how do specific undersea cable routes "contort and deform" digital film culture (Starosielski 2011). For them, to do infrastructure studies is to try to heal the dialectic between structure and form. It is to consider "the mechanics of transduction, storage, [and] transmission alongside creation, distribution, and reception" (Sterne 2003: 8).

This tradition has a longer history in the study of the media. Materialism itself usually refers to the Marxist conception of history, which informed cultural materialists like Raymond Williams (1974), but it is also possible to find a genealogy of materialism in the "Toronto School" of communication theory (Katz et al. 2003), specifically in the work of Harold Innis (e.g. 1951). Just as Williams (1974) wanted to explain cultural formats like TV variety shows but devoted pages and pages of prose to the technical minutae of the television apparatus, Innis (1950) sought to link the loftiest themes of history—such as the rise of Empire in ancient Rome—to the prevalence and characteristics of ancient papyrus and to particular techniques for rolling it up. Although these early accounts could be very technologically determined (Innis argued that the shift from papyrus to parchment led to the decentralization of religion), they still pushed their readers to a fresh consideration of the objects and technologies that underpin communications.

The urge for comparison between systems that is the hallmark of the relationists takes a different form among the new materialists, where communication systems are almost always central and are therefore the object of the theory that results. A book-length history of sound is a history of sound, not an attempt to theorize transportation or electricity as well (Sterne 2003). Nonetheless, these scholars build on a tradition of cross-infrastructure comparison of their own, quite often involving transport. In a classic essay that remains a touchstone in the field of communications, Carey argued that the technology of the telegraph marked a crucial break in the way that scholars should reason about communication technologies because it separated communication and transport for the first time (Carey 1989: esp. ch. 8). Indeed communication in its original meaning was transportation, a box of goods was said to be "communicated" when it was delivered (Peters 1999).

The new materialists are a less coherent grouping than the relationists. So far, although they call for the study of format (Sterne 2012) and a "populist" approach (Parks 2011), they lack an overarching manifesto or a checklists of heuristics. Methodologically, they are much more varied. They endorse experimental partnerships between artists, historians, and geographers, and advocate research methods like art exhibitions, media archaeology, photo essays (Parks 2009), and interactive visualization (Sandvig 2007). There are probably more similarities than differences between the two groups, including a new focus on decay (Acland 2006) and alliances with urban theory. Yet each grouping has a different inflection, as Star's (1999) directive to emphasize hidden social practices aligns imprecisely with Parks's (2011) call for a "populist approach to infrastructure."

Conclusion: get into the guts

To sum up, the emerging area of "infrastructure studies" can be thought of as two largely compatible research streams: the relationists and the new materialists. A rough alliance of multidisciplinary work spanning media studies, art, geography, history, sociology, and more, both streams provide advice for the scholar of the Internet, and they are both engaged in an intellectual struggle that seeks to overcome the "mind-body dichotomy" that in the past separated content from infrastructure (Star and Ruhleder 1996: 118). The relationists start with the material parts of systems then run toward the social, while the new materialists pass them heading in the opposite direction. From either perspective, the Internet demands our attention as a foundation for modern life. The flowering of this research under the heading of "infrastructure studies" is poised to contribute new ways to unpack the Internet's complexity and to enroll the guts of its operation in future scholarly arguments about the Internet and society.

References

Acland, C. R. (ed.) (2006). *Residual Media*, Minneapolis: University of Minnesota Press.

Bar, F., Borrus, M., and Steinberg, R. (1995). "Islands in the Bit-stream: Mapping the NII Interoperability Debate." BRIE Working Paper #79, Berkeley, CA: Berkeley Roundtable on the International Economy (BRIE).

Bardini, T. (2000). *Bootstrapping: Douglas Engelbart, Coevolution, and the Origins of Personal Computing*, Stanford: Stanford University Press.

Bateson, G. (1978). *Steps to an Ecology of Mind*, New York: Ballantine.

Bijker, W., Hughes, T., and Pinch, T. (eds.) (1987). *The Social Construction of Technological Systems: New Directions in the Sociology and History of Technology*, Cambridge, MA: MIT Press.

Blue, V. (2010). "I, For One, Welcome Our New TLD Overlords With Bare Arms," *Tinynibbles*, October 6. Available at <http://www.tinynibbles.com/blogarchives/2010/10/i-for-one-welcome-our-new-tld-overlords-with-bare-arms.html>. Accessed July 7, 2011.

Bowker, G. (1994). "Information Mythology and Infrastructure," in L. Bud-Frierman (ed.). *Information Acumen: The Understanding and Use of Knowledge in Modern Business*, London: Routledge, pp. 231–47.

—— Baker, K., Millerand, F., and Ribes, D. (2010). "Towards Information Infrastructure Studies: Ways of Knowing in a Networked Environment," in J. Hunsinger, I. Klastrup, and M. Allen (eds). *International Handbook of Internet Research*, New York: Springer, pp. 97–118.

Bracha, O. and Pasquale, F. (2008). "Federal Search Commission? Access, Fairness, and Accountability in the Law of Search," *Cornell Law Review*, 93(6): 1149.

Brooks, F. (1995). *The Mythical Man-Month: Essays on Software Engineering*, anniv. edn., New York: Addison-Wesley.

Busch, L. (2011). *Standards: Recipes for Reality*, Cambridge: MIT Press.

Carey, J. (1989). *Communication as Culture: Essays on Media and Society*, New York: Routledge.

Castells, M. (1989). *The Informational City: Information Technology, Economic Restructuring, and the Urban Regional Process*, Oxford: Blackwell.

DataCenterVideos. (2009). "Inside a Google Data Center." Available at <www.youtube.com/watch?v=bs3Et540-_s>. Accessed September 20, 2011.

David, P. (1985). "Clio and the Economics of QWERTY," *American Economic Review* 75(2): 332–7.

de Sola Pool, I. (1983). *Forecasting the Telephone: A Retrospective Technology Assessment*, Norwood, NJ: Ablex.

Edwards, P. N. (1996). *The Closed World: The Computers and Politics of Discourse in Cold War America*, Cambridge, MA: MIT Press.

—— (2003). "Infrastructure and Modernity: Force, Time, and Social Organization in the History of Sociotechnical Systems," in T. Misa, P. Bray, and A. Feenberg A. (eds). *Modernity and Technology*, Cambridge, MA: MIT Press, pp. 185–225.

—— Jackson, S. J., Bowker, G. C., and Knobel, C. P. (2007). "Understanding Infrastructure: Dynamics, Tensions, and Design, Final Report of a Workshop on 'History and Theory of Infrastructure: Lessons for New Scientific Cyberinfrastructures,'" Final report of the workshop, *History and Theory of Infrastructure: Lessons for New Scientific Cyberinfrastructures*, University of Michigan, Ann Arbor, January. Available at <http://hdl.handle.net/2027.42/49353>. Accessed July 7, 2011.

Egyedi, T. (2001). "Infrastructure Flexibility Created by Standardized Gateways: The Cases of XML and the ISO Container," *Knowledge, Technology, and Policy*, 14(3): 41–54.

Firth, N. (2009). "Sir Tim Berners-Lee admits the forward slashes in every web address 'were a mistake,'" *Daily Mail*, October 14. Available at <www.dailymail.co.uk/sciencetech/article-1220286/Sir-Tim-Berners-Lee-admits-forward-slashes-web-address-mistake.html>. Accessed September 20, 2011.

Fischer, C. S. (1985). "Studying Technology in Social Life," in M. Castells (ed.). *High Technology, Space, and Society*, Beverly Hills, CA: Sage.

Google (2011). "Google Transparency Report: Libya, February 2011–October 2011." Available at <http://www.google.com/transparencyreport/traffic/>. Accessed May 17, 2012.

Graham, S. (ed.) (2003). *The Cybercities Reader*, New York: Routledge.

—— and Marvin, S. (1996). *Telecommunications and the City: Electronic Spaces, Urban Places*, New York: Routledge.

—— and Marvin, S.(2001). *Splintering Urbanism: Networked Infrastructures, Technological Mobilities, and the Urban Condition*, New York: Routledge.

Graham, S. and Thrift, N. (2007). "Out of Order: Understanding Repair and Maintenance," *Theory, Culture, & Society*, 24(3): 1–25.

Hawking, S. (1988). *A Brief History of Time*, New York: Bantam-Dell.

Horn, L. (2010). "Libya Siezes URL Shortener Vb.ly," *PC Magazine*, October 6. Available at <www.pcmag.com/article2/0,2817,2370354,00.asp>. Accessed July 8, 2011.

Hughes, T. P. (1983). *Networks of Power: Electrification in Western Society, 1880–1930*, Baltimore: Johns Hopkins University Press.

—— (1998). *Rescuing Prometheus*, New York: Pantheon.

Innis, H. (1950). *Empire and Communications*, Oxford: Oxford University Press.

—— (1951). *The Bias of Communication*, Toronto: University of Toronto Press.

ISO (2011). "Codes for the Representation of Names of Countries and Their Subdivisions," *International Organization for Standardization*, Standard 3166. Available at <http://www.iso.org/iso/country_codes.htm>. Accessed July 7, 2011.

Jackson, S. J., Edwards, P. N., Bowker, G. C., and Knobel, C. P. (2007). "Understanding Infrastructure: History, Heuristics, and Cyberinfrastructure Policy," *First Monday* 12(6). Available at <http://firstmonday.org/htbin/cgiwrap/bin/ojs/index.php/fm/article/view/1904/1786>. Accessed July 8, 2011.

Jewett, T. and Kling, R. (1991). "The Dynamics of Computerization in a Social Science Research Team: A Case Study of Infrastructure, Strategies, and Skills," *Social Science Computer Review*, 9(2): 246–75.

Johnson, B., Arthur, C., and Halliday, J. (2010). "Libyan Domain Shutdown No Threat, Says bit.ly," *The Guardian*, October 9. Available at <http://www.guardian.co.uk/technology/2010/oct/08/bitly-libya>. Accessed July 8, 2011.

Katz, E., Peters, J. D., Liebes, T., and Orloff, A. (eds) (2003). *Canonic Texts in Media Research*, Cambridge: Polity.

Kesan, J. P. and Shah, R. C. (2001). "Fool Us Once Shame on You—Fool Us Twice Shame on Us: What We Can Learn from the Privatizations of the Internet Backbone Network and the Domain Name System," *Washington University Law Quarterly*, 79(1): 89–220.

Kling, R. (1992). "Behind the Terminal: The Critical Role of Computing Infrastructure in Effective Information Systems' Development and Use," in W. Cotterman and J. Senn (eds). *Challenges and Strategies for Research in System Development*, New York: Wiley, pp. 153–201.

Latour, B. (2007). *Reassembling the Social: An Introduction to Actor-Network Theory*, Oxford: Oxford University Press.

Law, J. (1991). "Introduction: Monsters, Machines and Sociotechnical Relations," in J. Law (ed.). *A Sociology of Monsters? Essays on Power, Technology and Domination*, London: Routledge, pp. 1–23.

Lenoir, T. and Alt, C. (2003). "Flow, Process, Fold: Intersections in Bioinformatics and Contemporary Architecture," in A. Picon and A. Ponte (eds). *Science, Metaphor, & Architecture*, Princeton: Princeton University Press, pp. 314–53.

Maxwell, R. and Miller, T. (2008). "Ecological Ethics and Media Technology," *International Journal of Communication*, 8: 331–53. Available at <http://ijoc.org/ojs/index.php/ijoc/article/view/320/151>. Accessed September 20, 2011.

Metcalfe, B. (2010). *The .ly Domain Space to be Considered Unsafe*. Available at <http://benmetcalfe.com/blog/2010/10/the-ly-domain-space-to-be-considered-unsafe/>. Accessed July 7, 2011

Mitchell, W. J. (2005, May), Personal communication.

Mueller, M. (2002). *Ruling the Root: Internet Governance and the Taming of Cyberspace*, Cambridge, MA: MIT Press.

Neff, G. (2005). "The Changing Place of Cultural Production: Locating Social Networks in a Digital Media Industry," *The Annals of the American Academy of Political and Social Science*, 597(1): 134–52.

Nye, D. E. (2010). *When the Lights Went Out: A History of Blackouts in America*, Cambridge: MIT Press.

Ogburn, W. F. (1957). "Cultural Lag as Theory," *Sociology & Social Research* 41(3): 167–74.

Palfrey, J. and Gasser, U. (2008). *Born Digital: Understanding the First Generation of Digital Natives*, New York: Basic Books.

Parks, L. (2009). "Around the Antenna Tree: The Politics of Infrastructural Visibility," *Flow TV* 9(8). Available at <http://flowtv.org/2009/03/around-the-antenna-tree-the-politics-of-infrastructural-visibilitylisa-parks-uc-santa-barbara/>. Accessed July 8, 2011.

—— (2011). "Spotting the Satellite Dish: Populist Approaches to Infrastructure," in *Satellites, Border, Footprint*, Dortmund, Germany: Hartware MedienKunstVerein, pp. 7–25.

Peters, J. D. (1999). *Speaking Into the Air: A History of the Idea of Communication*, Chicago: University of Chicago Press.

Phillips, D. (2005). "From Privacy to Visibility: Context, Identity, and Power in Ubiquitous Computing Environments," *Social Text* 23(2): 95–108.

—— and Clement, A. (2008). "Carrier Hotels: Mapping Internet Interconnection," Information Policy Research Program. Available at <http://iprp.ischool.utoronto.ca/system/files/CHmappingITSTproposal.pdf>. Accessed July 7, 2011.

Postel, J. (1994, March). "Domain Name System Structure and Delegation," RFC 1591, Internet Engineering Task Force. Available at <http://tools.ietf.org/html/rfc1591>. Accessed September 20, 2011.

Qur'an. (n.d.). Translated by Yusuf Ali and Marmaduke Mohammad. Center for Muslim-Jewish Engagement, Los Angeles: University of Southern California. Available at <www.usc.edu/schools/college/crcc/engagement/resources/texts/muslim/quran/> Accessed September 20, 2011.

Ribes, D. and Finholt, T. A. (2009). "The Long Now of Technology Infrastructure: Articulating Tensions in Development," *Journal of the Association for Information Systems*, 10(5): 2.

Robinson, D. and Coar, K. (2004). "The Common Gateway Interface (CGI) Version 1.1," RFC 3875, Internet Engineering Task Force. Available at <http://tools.ietf.org/html/rfc3875>. Accessed September 20, 2011.

Sandvig, C. (2007). "The RED Project: Rendering Electromagnetic Distributions," *Vectors: Journal of Culture and Technology in a Dynamic Vernacular*, 3(1). Available at <http://vectors.usc.edu/projects/index.php?project=87>. Accessed September 12, 2011.

—— (2008). "Addressing Internet Infrastructure." Paper presented to the Wharton Colloquium on Media and Communications Law, Wharton School of Business, University of Pennsylvania, December 5.

Sawhney, H. (1992). The Public Telephone Network: Stages in Infrastructure Development, *Telecommunications Policy*, 16(7): 538–52.

—— (1993). "Circumventing the Center: The Realities of Creating a Telecommunications Infrastructure in the USA," *Telecommunications Policy*, 17(7): 504–16.

—— (2003). "Wi-Fi Networks and the Rerun of the Cycle," *Info: The Journal of Policy, Regulation, and Strategy for Telecommunications*, 5(6): 25–33.

Siegler, M. G. (June 3, 2010). "Bitly Links Now at 4.7 Billion Clicks a Month," *TechCrunch*. Available at <http://techcrunch.com/2010/06/03/bitly-pro-data/>. Accessed September 20, 2011.

Silver, D. (2006). "Introduction: Where is Internet Studies?," in Silver, D. and Massanari, A. (eds.), *Critical Cyberculture Studies*, New York: New York University Press, pp. 1–14.

Slade, G. (2007). *Made to Break: Technology and Obsolescence in America*, Cambridge, MA: Harvard University Press.

Star, S. L. (1991). Power, Technologies, and the Phenomenology of Conventions: On Being Allergic to Onions, in J. Law (ed.). *A Sociology of Monsters: Essays on Power, Technology, and Domination*, London: Routledge, pp. 26–56.

—— (1999). "The Ethnography of Infrastructure," *American Behavioral Scientist* 43(3): 377–91.

—— (2000). "It's Infrastructure All the Way Down." Keynote Address given to the 5th ACM Conference on Digital Libraries, San Antonio, TX, June 4.

—— (2010). "This is not a Boundary Object: Reflections on the Origin of a Concept," *Science, Technology, & Human Values*, 35(5): 601–17.

Star, S. L. and Ruhleder, K. (1996). "Steps Towards an Ecology of Infrastructure: Design and Access for Large Information Spaces," *Information Systems Research*, 7(1): 111–34.

Starosielski, N. (2010). "Things and Movies: DVD Store Culture in Fiji," *Media Fields Journal*, 1: 1–10.

—— (2011). "Underwater Flow," *Flow TV*, 15(1). Available at <http://flowtv.org/2011/10/underwaterflow/>. Accessed October 20, 2011.

Steinberg, P. E. and Mcdowell, S. D. (2003). "Mutiny on the Bandwidth: The Semiotics of Statehood in the Internet Domain Name Registries of Pitcairn Island and Niue," *New Media & Society*, 5(1): 47–67.

Sterne, J. (2003). *The Audible Past: Cultural Origins of Sound Reproduction*, Durham: Duke University Press.

—— (2012). *MP3: The Meaning of a Format*, Durham: Duke University Press.

Tsekeris, C. (2010). "Relationalism in Sociology: Theoretical and Methodological Elaborations," *Facta Universitatis*, Series: Philosophy, Sociology, Psychology and History, 9 (1): 139–48.

Turner, F. (2009). "Burning Man at Google: A Cultural Infrastructure for New Media Production," *New Media & Society* 11(1/2): 73–94.

Vanderbilt, T. (2009). "Data Center Overload," *The New York Times Magazine*, June 8. Available at <http://www.nytimes.com/2009/06/14/magazine/14search-t.html>. Accessed May 17, 2012.

Watts, D. (2004). "The 'New' Science of Networks", *Annual Review of Sociology*, 30: 243–70.

Williams, R. (1974). *Television: Technology and Cultural Form*, London: Collins.

Winner, L. (1986). *The Whale and the Reactor: A Search for Limits in an Age of High Technology*, Chicago: University of Chicago Press.

—— (1993). "Upon Opening the Black Box and Finding It Empty: Social Constructivism and the Philosophy of Technology," *Science, Technology, & Human Values*, 18(3): 362–78.

Woolgar, S. and Cooper, G. (1999). "Do Artifacts Have Ambivalence? Moses' Bridges, Winner's Bridges, and Other Urban Legends in STS," *Social Studies of Science*, 29(3): 433–49.

Wright, O. (2011). "NHS Pulls the Plug on its £11bn IT system: After Nine Years and with Billions Already Spent, Doomed Computer System is Abandoned," *The Independent*, August 3. Available at <http://www.independent.co.uk/life-style/health-and-families/health-news/nhs-pulls-the-plug-on-its-11bn-it-system-2330906.html>. Accessed October 14, 2011.

PART II

LIVING IN A NETWORK SOCIETY

NETWORK SOCIETIES AND INTERNET STUDIES: RETHINKING TIME, SPACE, AND CLASS

JACK LINCHUAN QIU

INTRODUCTION

SINCE Umesao (1963) proposed the concept of "joho sangyo," that is, the information or intelligent society, a sustained multidisciplinary effort has been focused on building a general framework for conceptualizing the relationship between society on the one hand and information and communication technologies (ICTs) on the other. This larger endeavor frames—and constrains—Internet Studies as a burgeoning academic field, whose rise coincided with the end of the Cold War, hence the "end of history" (Fukuyama 1992) and the "end of geography" (O'Brien 1992). One risk of such universalistic visions is a renewed form of ahistorical ethnocentrism, epitomized by the imagination of a single, seamless global web of connection that is Western, contemporary, and post-industrial.

Such an oversimplification has been criticized, however, both theoretically and empirically by scholars drawing from an abundance of evidence from around the world and from disconnected corners at the very core of the Western-centric world system. For example, Internet solutions appear to be pointless in the face of the 2008 global financial crisis, surging religious fundamentalism, and increasing ethnic diversity in cyberspace itself. The trend towards "network societies," rather than a single unified information society, is accelerated by a host of factors. These include: the rise of China as home to the world's largest national Internet user population (CNNIC 2010), the tremendous yet uneven diffusion of mobile services in rural areas of the Global South (ITU 2010), the role of territorial authorities in the "war against terrorism," the continuation of private businesses making decisions for Internet publics (Gibson 2010), the predominance of online micro-cosmoses and their "echo chamber effect" (Sunstein 2007) exacerbated by popular social-networking services (SNS).

Is it sensible to think about Internet Studies as a scholarly field with a sufficient degree of coherence that reflects key general patterns of increased interconnectedness in a global network society? The overall argument of this chapter is a cautious support for Internet Studies as a field of research. That is, it remains possible to achieve unity in diversity if we revisit and rethink the most fundamental dimensions of society—along the dimensions of time, space, class—in relation to Internet developments around the world and historically, as major theorists like Daniel Bell and Manuel Castells have done from their own distinct viewpoints.

This chapter begins with a brief review of the concepts of an information/knowledge/post-industrial society, and the later notion of a network society, and the challenges posed to these ideas. It then moves this discussion forward by taking the plurality of network societies as a basic condition in considering Internet Studies since the 1990s. It does not claim to invent another single unified framework, but tries to synthesize relevant research issues and results using time, space, and class as the three, key connective tissues. In so doing, it discusses how Internet studies in a plethora of contexts have led to the re-framing of questions for network society as a general theory. The goal is to provide a review of key concepts and then look critically at numerous schools of research by considering historical, geographical, and class and labor issues. These dimensions are central to current global transformations taking place through diverse institutional pathways towards new social contracts and new social theories, in which the Internet and Internet Studies are embedded.

THE INFORMATION AND NETWORK SOCIETY

In sociological literature, the idea of an information society can be traced back to Daniel Bell's coining of the term "post-industrialism" in the late 1950s (Webster 2002: 30). Later he also used "information society" and "knowledge society" to refer to this new stage of social development, that is, the "post-industrial society" as explicated in his classic, *The Coming of Post-Industrial Society: A Venture in Social Forecasting* (Bell 1973). In this monumental piece of work, he describes three structural transformations:

> in the economic sector, it is a shift from manufacturing to services; in technology, it is the centrality of the new science-based industries; in sociological terms, it is the rise of new technical elites and the advent of a new principle of stratification. (1973: 487)

These characterizations are essential to later conceptions of information society by the more popularly oriented futurologists (Toffler 1980, 1990; Naisbitt 1984) or more serious scholars including Manuel Castells. Fundamental to this set of truly innovative, indeed revolutionary, ideas at the time, was a linear mode of thinking that divides human history into three periods: (1) the pre-industrial era characterized mostly by agriculture, (2) the industrial era dominated by manufacture, and (3) the post-industrial era in which services and information industries predominate. Thirty years later, this has become a common evolutionary framework of thinking that corresponds roughly with the primary, secondary, and tertiary sectors in a progressive manner.

Yet, in his 1973 book, Bell had already demonstrated a level of intellectual sophistication that is rare among all his futurology followers. For one thing, he emphasized over and again that the transformations towards post-industrialism is not equivalent to the total restructuring of society at large. Yes, the most strategic resource is changing from energy to information. Yes, the rise of meritocracy marks a most important change in class structure. However, Bell maintains that these are mainly changes in the economic system and stratification structure that may or may not lead to equally fundamental ruptures in the cultural and political spheres of society. Quite likely, the pace and nature of development may be inconsistent, even contradictory, as argued in his 1976 book, *The Cultural Contradictions of Capitalism*.

By the post-industrial society Bell therefore understands, not a straightforward techno-deterministic change, but a sectoral transformation characterized by internal conflicts; not a complete social revolution but a partial structural realignment resulting in the re-structuring of occupation and stratification. Recent developments in North America, Western Europe, Japan, and the NIEs (newly industrialized economies) of the Asian Pacific (that is, South Korea, Taiwan, Hong Kong, and Singapore) have basically confirmed Bell's insightful forecasts. Yet, critics such as Krishan Kumar disagree on the historical novelty of all these sectoral, occupational, and cultural shifts, calling them "extrapolations, intensifications, and clarifications of tendencies which were apparent from the very birth of industrialism" (1978: 232). Whether the rise of post-industrialism and the information society marks the beginning of a brand new era is, in this sense, still a controversial argument.

Another crucial element in Bell's conception of the post-industrial society is the "axial" importance of theoretical knowledge. As he points out, "what is radically new today is the codification of theoretical knowledge and its centrality for innovation, both of new knowledge and for economic goods and services" (1979: 189). In other words, unlike main actors in pre-industrial and industrial times whose creative activities are inseparable from concrete, practical experiences, key innovators of the post-industrial era rely, first and foremost, on abstract knowledge—"theories"—which is codified, generalizable, and more easily communicable through such venues as classroom teaching, mathematical modeling, and patents. For critics like Frank Webster, the centrality of theoretical knowledge is the most "persuasive argument for our inhabiting an 'information society' today," although he still maintains that in Bell's writings the idea of theoretical knowledge remains "underdeveloped" and "too vague" (Webster 2002: 58).

The greatest flaw in Bell's theorization is its ethnocentrism. It depicts post-industrialism after "the image of a god-like society" (Touraine 1977: 472), based on a particular set of observations in the United States that ignore, not only counter trends in other advanced capitalist societies such as France, Germany, and Japan, but also alternative and grassroots movements in the US itself, for example those involving women, ethnic minorities, and the unemployed. Moreover, if examined at a truly global level, the geographical scope of post-industrialism remains limited to the Global North, including the NIEs, but excluding most countries of the Global South, from Asia to Africa to Latin America, even Oceania. Yet, it is these Southern societies that constitute the bulk of humanity. As I have argued elsewhere, "industrialization in the Third World...is in fact a mirror process of post-industrialization in First World countries" (Qiu 2009: 91). The rise of BRIC countries (i.e. Brazil, Russia, India, China) as motors of global economic growth at the beginning of the new century has cast serious doubt on Bell's ethnocentric views, both of US-style capitalism as the destination of linear progression and of post-industrialism as historically inevitable for global economy at large.

In contrast, Manuel Castells' proposal for the network society is much more global, cross-cultural, sensitive to national, regional, and local traditions—and much less ethnocentric—as another way to conceptualize information/knowledge society. His trilogy of the Information Age (1996, 1997, 1998) is widely considered as a *tour de force* that synthesizes interdisciplinary debates about the information society. Unlike Bell, Castells deliberately avoids the language of *post*-industrialism. Instead, he talks about the "informational mode of development" or "informationalism," which is "the techno-logical paradigm that constitutes the material basis of early twenty-first century societies", and "a technological paradigm based on the augmentation of the human capacity of information processing and communication made possible by the revolu-tions in microelectronics, software, and genetic engineering" (2004: 8–9). Such theori-zation allows Castells to avoid declaring the end of industrialism, economically and technologically, and the irrelevance of existing political institutions and cultural tradi-tions in non-Western contexts. As a result, he offers a more diverse, and truly global, framework of understanding that serves as a milestone for the updating of social theory, including theories for Internet Studies, since mid-1990s.

Judging from conventional disciplinary perspectives within the social sciences, Castells' framework may appear to be too broad and eclectic (Webster 2002: 123). Yet for Castells, it is unified by the epochal contradiction between "the Net and the Self" which cuts across cultural and institutional boundaries (1996: 1–25). "Our societies are increas-ingly structured around the bipolar opposition of the Net and the Self," wrote Castells (1996: 3). Here, "the Net" is a technological metaphor that refers to all kinds of social networks among people, organizations, and symbols, mediated or unmediated, of which the Internet is the latest embodiment. The Net is expanding, connecting some previ-ously unconnected nodes, and resulting in a much higher degree of consolidation glo-bally, and more rapid interaction among cities, companies, and institutions of global capitalism with their regional variations.

However, "[t]he network society works on the basis of a binary logic of inclusion/ exclusion, whose boundaries change over time, both with the changes in the network's programs and with the conditions of performance of these programs" (Castells 2004: 23). While the global network society expands and accelerates, it also exacerbates social exclusion and threatens "losers" of globalization, digitization, and capitalization with complete historical annihilation. These threats do not just silence and marginalize people, jeopardizing entire cultures and nations. Rather, they stimulate strong counter movements centered on the Self, or identify projects and efforts to defend traditional culture while creating new meanings through such programs as the Zapatistas in Southern Mexico, religious fundamentalism from the Middle East to the US, economic nationalism in East Asia, and the "global justice" demonstrations at various World Trade Organization meetings (Castells 1997, 1998).

In examining specific manifestations of the contradiction between the Net and the Self in various regional contexts, especially the "distinctive feature of being globally connected and locally disconnected" in the world's key urban areas (1996: 436), Castells presents a theoretical framework that is at once more holistic, more geographical, and more culturally diverse than Bell's conception of the post-industrial/information society. However, like Bell, Castells maintains that the technological revolution signified by latest ICT breakthroughs marks a fundamental change in economy, history, and social structure. Many debates concerning Bell's post-industrial society therefore persist with Castells' conception of the network society: how new is this development to call it a brand new era? If human beings always exist in networks, like they always rely on information, why is it necessary to label contemporary society as a network/information society? If there is really something qualitatively different between the present and the past, how do we measure it? What is a network? What is information? (Webster 2002: 121–2).

Despite these lingering questions, the idea of the information/network society has proven to be enormously fruitful in stimulating inter-disciplinary interests in, and preparing fertile ground for, the growth of Internet Studies since the 1990s. Because this chapter aims at providing a global and critical reflection on Internet Studies across the world, the following discussions shall focus on research results in Internet Studies along three basic dimensions of the network society theory: time, space, and class. In so doing, we shall explore Castells' concepts in more depth while entertaining the idea of "network societies" in the plural.

TIME, HISTORY, AND IDENTITY

According to Castells (1996), the network society is one of the three fundamental modes of social organization along with the state—"statism," and the market—"capitalism." Humans have always organized themselves in networks. But it was only after the spread of microelectonics-based ICTs in the late twentieth century when networks started to prevail over the other two basic modes of social organization, producing the "network state" and "network enterprise." The rise of the network society is, in this sense, a major historical transformation.

This fundamental transformation over time not only changes the way the state and the market organize themselves institutionally, it also alters people's perception of history and life cycles. It destroys traditional temporal structures with linear sequences, biological, mechanistic, or bureaucratic. It is argued that the network society establishes "timeless time" as a dominant cultural framework in a seemingly perpetual movement of digital exchange that attempts to eliminate the linear sequencing of events and practices, as best exemplified by hyperlinked communication, on what Castells calls "the edge of forever" (1996: 460).

This certainly is not an entirely new argument. Political economists have been talking about "just-in-time" production, flexible accumulation, and flexible capitalism for decades (Harvey 1991). Sociologists have been discussing "time-space distanciation" and the compression of time (Giddens 1991). Postmodernists have also contributed observations to notions of temporal non-linearity, including the bricolage of signs from uncertain historical periods (Lash and Urry 1993). Yet, the notion of "timeless time" as a basic characteristic of network societies emphasizes several particular dimensions of research, some new, some already existing. Important here is to go back to Castells' understanding of the global network society as, above all, a structure of nodes that is interconnected but not determined by any "center" of exchange. On one level, it is more transhistorical and more modern than ever, operating 24/7, non-stop, at the speed of light (Hassan and Purser 2007), such as in the global financial market. Hence, it is "timeless." But on another level, it is also more chaotic, ready to be dominated by the current moment and then quickly move on to the next big event, created unforeseeably through network effects.

In other words, although the sequencing of moments can be rearranged in apparently arbitrary ways, it is still "time," just with a less stable temporal structure. Indeed, time never really disappears if we look at the development of the Internet more closely. One contribution by Internet Studies overall is precisely about the sequence of Internet "periods": from the early days of the APARNET in 1960s, to the virtual communities of LAMDA MOO in 1990s, to emerging Web 2.0 services of the 2000s.

Meanwhile, because older people around the world have gone online after the initial Internet boom as a mostly youth phenomenon in the 1990s, these older users have brought with them their past experiences, collective memories, and current biological timing as well. This trend became particularly obvious with the growing popularity of user-created content (UCC). Since the early days of the Internet, it has become a tremendously rich archive for people at different stages of their life cycles: not only youth but also middle-aged and senior citizens; and not only students progressing from elementary and secondary schools to college but also mothers at different stages of pregnancy, retirees writing memoirs or genealogies, and patients in online mutual-support networks providing company to each other in different phases of their ailments. Seen from afar, all these may look like a chaotic cloud, more "timeless" than a decade ago. But from the perspective of individual-user experiences and UCC service provision businesses, one can certainly see a much closer matching between biological time and Internet time.

A revealing case observed in China is the online "re-envisioning" of the Cultural Revolution that lasted from 1966 to 1976 and affected an entire generation of Chinese "sent-down youth (*zhiqing*)" (Yang 2003, 2007). These were millions of teenagers sent from cities to the countryside under radical Maoist policy. Collectively, they went through a period of extreme idealism, material difficulty, and emotional helplessness. Yet, when most of them returned home in late 1970s and early 1980s, the Maoist era was over. The space of collective memory was initially very limited, and later nearly non-existent after the rapid commercialization of mass media in the 1990s. But with the spread of the Internet, members of "sent-down youth," now in their 40s and 50s, found the most important way to reconstruct their generational culture beyond official-sanctioned depictions of the political turmoil and beyond the stereotypes of the Red Guards.

Such a re-emergence of historical accounts and collective memories in tandem with Internet diffusion is certainly not unique to this particular group of middle-aged Chinese. Online communication facilitates the connection of temporal "nodes" into sizeable "clusters," especially those of minority identities and marginalized groups whose voices are silenced (Brinkerhoff 2009). Indeed, the annihilation of history (or more precisely, alternative histories) is not a business confined to cyberspace. Governments, especially the most powerful nation-states, have been in this business for long, so have markets and enterprises, especially the most resourceful ones. In this sense, the "timeless" feature of Internet time can be seen as initially destructive but ultimately liberating as it allows for more diverse routes of historical rediscovery and reconstruction of tradition.

The revival of such non-mainstream histories on the Internet is not automatic. The persistence of digital divides means that certain minority groups are still absent or under-represented. Moreover, it is not uncommon that such alternative histories may provoke traditional defenders of what Castells calls "bureaucratic time" (2009: 34) back into their offensive mode. The expansion of the Chinese sent-down youth online network, for example, has been quite limited, especially within Mainland China—due to less than supportive government measures. As a result, several key nodes of it exist overseas involving members of the Chinese diaspora who are part of the sent-down youth generation. This pattern can be seen in collective memories about the Cultural Revolution as a whole (Lee and Yang 2007). And it won't be too surprising to see similar patterns in other contexts when the history-making authorities of particularly intrusive governments or corporate players are challenged (Brinkerhoff 2009; Yang 2007).

Even though traditional state or business actors can react to new online histories and try to continue promoting their preferred sequencing as the only possible temporal structure, they can no longer fully predict or control the outcome as they could in the past with print or broadcast media. From time to time, efforts of top-down control may also backfire, which is another fundamental change toward non-linear time in network society. It has to do both with the sequencing of practices and with the definition of the "event" itself, which leads to the rise of the so-called "new media events" (Qiu 2009; Qiu and Chan 2009).

According to Dayan and Katz (1992), "media events" represent a mode of consensual communication when the live broadcast of significant "events"—orchestrated by powerful political and/or economic players—leads to a shared sense of history. This is most clearly seen in such cases as the Apollo moon landing, the Olympics, and ceremonies like the funeral of a famous public figure, that are usually broadcast via communication satellites to millions, sometimes billions, of viewers globally. However, since the turn of the century, especially since September 11, 2001—when the terrorist attacks could be seen as a "media event"—there have been more incidents when event organizers could no longer expect to control the interpretations and consequences of the broadcast content. Consensual "media events" have therefore become often "disenchanted, derailed, and disrupted" (Dayan 2008).

While Dayan and Katz's seminal work (1992) already stressed the uneasiness to orchestrate media events, the general movement away from consensual "media events" is greatly accelerated by the spread of the Internet as a key alternative channel for collective memory. In many occasions, the top-down logic of consensus making is completely subverted, resulting in "new media events" not only due to the new ICT platforms of the Internet and mobile phone but also the fundamental shift of discursive power away from the center of a broadcast network (Qiu and Chan 2009). This can be seen repeatedly in the contexts of authoritarian regimes like China and Iran, as well as more democratic countries. Consider, for example, Abu Ghraib in 2004, Wikileaks in 2010, and the Arab Spring of 2011.

In sum, what we have learned from Internet studies in comparison with findings from traditional mass media is that the sequencing of events has become less stable, more pluralistic, and, in a way, closer to the complexity of social reality (if the construction of alternative online histories is not pure performance). This may sound very different from the original idea of "timeless time." Call it "multiple times" if you will. But it echoes another key dimension in Castells' conceptualization of the network society: "the power of identity" and the persistence of traditions, be they minority cultures or suppressed memories (1997).

Moreover, industrial "bureaucratic" time has not completely gone. From call centers in India to electronic factories in China, the work time of employees is governed as tightly as it used to be in the West or Japan decades ago, if not more, due in part to the application of more sophisticated surveillance technologies in organizational settings (Lyon 2002). Meanwhile, ICT policy-makers and advertising agencies keep on repeating narratives of the "digital sublime" (Mosco 2004): that the Internet is bringing us a flat world free of serious social problems and that history no longer matters. New media technologies are, in this way, more than platforms for the construction of collective memories. They are battlegrounds for the imagination of alternative futures, as well.

SPACE OF FLOWS AND PLACES

The fundamental shift towards a network society also creates a "space of flows" that supersedes traditional places and territorial structures, be they nation-states or local communities (Castells 1996, 1998). This spatial transformation is exemplified by the non-stop operation of global financial markets and the worldwide network of airports (a typical "non-place"). Both tend to be concentrated unevenly in key urban centers or mega-cities. In the aftermath of the 2008 financial crisis, there have been initial signs for territorial authorities—national, regional, and intergovernmental—to exert more control over global networks of neoliberal capitalism. However, the measures have not brought an end to the space of flows.

It is still too early to predict whether the neoliberal spatial project in eliminating traditional places and imposing abstract space globally is going to be reversed or per-petuated. But Internet and related ICT developments are of little doubt part of the story. Besides government action, market forces are also powerful in bringing along a decisive spatial reconfiguration, shifting from the Western-centric mode of Internet develop-ment to a much more diffused pattern of Internet geography around the world (Samarajiva and Zainudeen 2008).

Table 6.1 and Table 6.2 demonstrate the remarkable change in the global distribution of the Internet user population. Africa, Middle East, and Asia are the world's fastest growing Internet markets, especially the BRIC. As of July 2010, China became home to the world's largest Internet user population, boasting 425 million users; and it led the US, whose Internet population stood at 240 million, by a wide margin. The collective share of Africa, Asia, the Middle East, and Latin America in the world's total Internet user population was merely 38.8 percent by the end of 2000. But in mid-2010, its share increased to 55.6 percent. Most of the world's Internet users now live in non-Western societies.

It was against such a background that Goggin and McLelland thought "rethinking the Internet as international" (2009: 4) is an imperative task. For one thing, the classic models of a global network society came first from experiences accumulated in key Western contexts, most importantly the entrepreneurial culture of Silicon Valley and the tradition of sharing in the Finnish information economy (Castells and Himanen 2004). The spread of Internet in the Global South—developing countries of Asia, Africa, Latin America—is in this sense a truly historic process of de-Westernizing the world's

Table 6.1 Number of Internet users in world regions, 2000 and 2010

World Regions	Million Internet Users (2000)	Million Internet Users (2010)	Penetration (% Population in 2010)	Growth 2000–2010
Africa	4.5	110.9	10.9	2,357.3
Asia	114.3	825.1	21.5	621.8
Europe	105.1	475.1	58.4	352.0
Latin America/Caribbean	18.0	204.7	34.5	146.3
Middle East	3.3	63.2	29.8	1,825.3
North America	108.1	266.2	77.4	146.3
Oceania/Australia	7.6	21.2	61.3	179.0
WORLD TOTAL	361.0	1,966.5	28.7	444.8

Source: www.internetworldstats.com

Table 6.2 Number of Internet users in top countries, by ranking in 2010 and 2000

Country	Million Internet Users (2010)	Rank (2010)	Rank (2000)
China	425.0	1	4
US	240.0	2	1
Japan	99.2	3	2
India	81.0	4	12
Brazil	76.0	5	15
Mexico	68.4	6	14
Germany	65.2	7	3
Russia	59.9	8	20
UK	51.5	9	6
France	44.6	10	10

Source: ITU World Telecommunication/ICT Indicators Data

ICT landscape. The pattern is even more impressive when it comes to the diffusion of mobile communication in Southern societies.

As late as 2000, most of the world's population had never even made a phone call. But by the end of 2008, there were an average 61 mobile phones for each 100 people. The change is most vividly seen in South Asia, Sub-Saharan Africa, and the Middle East and North Africa (MENA) regions where mobile phone penetration per 100 people jumped from 0–2 in 2000 to 33–58 in 2008 (Tables 6.3 and 6.4). This change is more than just the spread of telephones, but also the availability of a host of new digital content and services, including mobile Internet access. Although urban areas of the Global South still tend to be more connected, the recent wave of mobile phone dissemination has also made significant inroads into rural communities (Aker and Mbiti 2010; Akter et al. 2010).

However, in what ways does the availability of ICT tools lead to spatial formations beyond the "space of flows"? Do they create a new space of places, revive traditional communities, or transform existing geographical networks? The answer is not pre-determined. Indeed, wider connectivity for rural populations may not mean that farmers using computer kiosks and migrant workers using mobile Internet are necessarily empowered to gain more spatial autonomy. Rather, the further diffusion of Internet and mobile communication merely opens up opportunities for change. Whether the promise of a more equitable landscape of global communication can materialize depends very much on contextual factors as well as the political will of the people themselves in either protecting their local/national/regional communities offline or creating new ones online.

Even within Western societies, the promise of the Internet as a decentralizing and flattening force does not hold up to empirical examination. As Matthew Zook's (2005: 32) ground-breaking study of Internet geography shows, the spatial distribution of commercial domain names in the US is highly uneven both nationally, concentrating in the northeast and south-west regions, and city-wise, focusing on a few selected areas of downtown

Table 6.3 The diffusion of mobile phones in world regions, 2000 and 2008

World Regions	Mobile Phone per 100 Population (2000)	Mobile Phone per 100 Population (2008)
South Asia	0	33
Sub-Saharan Africa	2	33
Middle East & North Africa	2	58
East Asia & Pacific	6	53
Euro area	60	122
Latin America & Caribbean	12	80

Source: Compilation based on the World Bank's Development Data Platform.

Table 6.4 The diffusion of mobile phones in countries by income levels, 2000 and 2010

Countries by income levels	Mobile Phones per 100 Population (2000)	Mobile Phones per 100 Population (2010)
High income	51	106
Middle income	5	57
Low income	0	28

Source: Compilation based on the World Bank's Development Data Platform.

San Francisco and downtown New York. Although the registration of domain names only gives a rough estimation for the origins of online content, this pattern of Internet geography contradicts the widely held view of "distance no longer matters" as the Internet spreads globally.

Since the initial boom of "space of flows" in the 1990s after the fall of Berlin Wall and since the years of the dot-come bubble, there have been at least five ways in which the emergence and/or resurfacing of "space of places" has added key functional or cultural nodes to the enlarged network society. First is the continued centrality of certain urban areas in the global Internet industry as found by Zook (2005), which are essentially also what Florida (2005: 48) sees as the few "spikes" of creative industry worldwide.

Second, while territorial boundaries between the national cyberspaces persist—like in China, Cuba, and Saudi Arabia due to state censorship and filtering policies (Deibert et al. 2008)—similar spatial boundaries emerge due to linguistic and cultural factors. This is quite akin to what is known in international and global communication studies as the "geo-linguistic regions" (Sinclair et al. 2002; Thussu 2006). For example, while Facebook remains the world's leading global SNS, several notable SNS spheres exist in key regional or national markets, appealing to their users' cultural and linguistic characteristics: QQ and Baidu Space in China, MIXI in Japan, MXit in South Africa, Vkontakte and VK and Odnoklassniki in Russia, Wer-Kennt-Wen and

Studivz sites in Germany, and Orkut in Brazil and India. For instance, as of October 2009, Orkut, one of Google's SNS websites, had 54 million subscribers, whose overwhelming majority came from Brazil and India (Sperry 2010). It is by far the most popular SNS in Brazil, more so compared to Facebook, Twitter, and Windows Live Profile, whose users originate mostly from English and French-speaking countries.

Third, the rapid diffusion of ICTs gives rise to ICT-related places such as electronics malls, bazaars, Internet cafés, computer kiosks, and street-corner stands selling used handsets or prepaid mobile phone cards, which widely exist throughout the Global South. Many such places are renewed traditional centers of trade and service in the small towns or villages of developing counties, meeting the needs of local and regional markets (Ilahiane and Sherry 2008; Akter et al. 2010).

Fourth is the place of manufacture and communities of workers who produce hardware, software, and provide services, often for consumers far away. Most typically this includes working-class communities of IT factory workers such as Foxconn, the main manufacturer of Apple products (Qiu 2009; Chan and Pun 2010), and communities of call center employees in India, Kenya, or the Philippines (Taylor and Bain 2004; Holman et al. 2007; Russell 2008). While the third type is a renewal of traditional places of trade, this fourth type is predominantly the development of industrial places of Fordist and post-Fordist production and reproduction.

The last type of "space of places" is at the new frontier of cyberspace, that is, the formation of virtual communities. Immaterial co-presence, most recently seen through popular SNS, like Facebook, is giving rise to a new kind of locale where social meaning and collective memory can be created. This is even more manifest in online gaming, where online spatial landscapes of Second Life and Worlds of Warcraft have become concrete structures of collective social experience. In some cases, collective actions like strikes have also taken place to reassert gamers' rights as part of online citizenship (Chew and Fung 2007).

Two profound dynamics are underlying each of these five kinds of spatial formation in major metropolitan areas or small towns and countrysides. On the one hand, the growth of a space of flows necessitates the creation of new places and the renewal of some traditional places. On the other hand, the new and renewed places are highly heterogeneous. While some of them still belong to the traditional structures of nation-state or global capitalism, most others are local, translocal, and regional. There is not a single "space of places" but many "*spaces* of places," reflecting and reproducing a mosaic of human spatial structures on- and offline.

CLASS AND LABOR

Time and space are two of the most fundamental dimensions of social organization. Another dimension, harder to conceive but arguably more decisive for the cohesion or disintegration of society, is the transformation of social class. Before Daniel Bell (1972) proposed the idea of post-industrial society, the knowledge-possessing class of meritocracy was already central to his conceptualization of a new social order. In an age of shrinking middle class, Manuel Castells (1989) also used the binary opposition of "self-programmable labor" and "generic labor" to capture the polarization of work and employment conditions within the labor force in the network society. That is, on the one hand, higher-class employees need to keep learning and upgrading their knowledge and skills in order to keep creating value for their employers in whatever form as demanded, while, on the other hand, employees at the bottom of the employment hierarchy can only sell their physical labor that is seen as dispensable and easily replaceable in order to earn subsistence level wages. Self-programmable labor refers to those included in the global networks of service provision and knowledge creation; generic labor refers to those being excluded (Castells 1996).

However, with the spread of ICTs and the rise of emerging economies of the Global South since the turn of century, more interesting patterns of class formation have been observed, especially the new stratum of "the information have-less" straddled between the digital divide of the haves and the have-nots (Cartier et al. 2005). In China, these "have-less" populations include migrant workers, laid-off workers, students, and retirees in low-income families, all having become low-end ICT users and thus begun to take part in network society formations, through either formal- or informal-economy activities.

On the surface, the information have-less can be seen as a lower class of ICT users because, compared to the "haves," they usually spend less and have less influence over telecom providers. However, go slightly deeper into the worlds of working-class ICTs, and you can see a whole new range of technical functions, social uses, and collective creativity that are unimaginable to members of the upper classes.

A most revealing case in point is Shipai Village in Guangzhou of South China. This is a working-class community of 0.6 square-kilometers, in which we identified 481 commercial informational services that belong to 46 categories (Qiu 2009: 169–182). Most of them relate to computer, Internet, and mobile phone services; many are rental and second-hand businesses beyond the imagination of those who are not familiar with working-class communities. For example, many stores offer content downloading services that help customers download ringtones or MP3 music for a modest fee. Others allow migrant workers in the neighborhood to rent digital cameras on a daily basis, or computers and ADSL broadband service on a monthly basis.

Another key indicator for class-based differentiation within China's cyberspace is the stratification of SNS. While most of China's middle-class Internet users adopt Microsoft's portal (MSN), which they use through computers, the overwhelming proportion of have-less users adopt QQ, China's most important instant messaging tool (Koch et al. 2009), which is particularly popular among migrant workers in the coastal regions, where Mobile QQ delivered through handsets has become an integral part of working-class life. To many, Mobile QQ has become synonymous to the mobile Internet. The richness of content and community-building functions—for example, in QQ clusters (QQ qun, a virtual-community function equivalent to Facebook groups)—are far beyond the imaginations of those who only know about MSN. Not only is QQ popular among China's information have-less, it is also more stable compared to other SNS communities of the upper classes. In recent years, a series of SNS websites have been in vogue, resulting in upper- and middle-class Internet users moving constantly among Xiaonei (aka Renren), Kaixin, Fanfou, and Sina Weibo, sometimes because of pure fashion and peer pressure, sometimes due to sudden change in regulation. Yet, working-class users of QQ tend to be fairly stable. For instance, it is not uncommon for an older factory worker to maintain the same QQ account for seven or eight years without shifting to other services. This is because he or she uses QQ for the instrumental purposes of contacting people to meet existential needs such as job seeking and being informed about what happens back home. Changing accounts would mean losing these invaluable contacts, just as Internet users tend to keep the same email address. In SNS, stability matters more to working-class SNS users.

Besides working-class entrepreneurialism and working-class SNS, the most decisive process of class formation happens in the workplace. A growing army of the Chinese labor force, for instance, is the so-called "gray collars," who are situated in between the white collar and the blue collar workers. The gray collars usually perform repetitive work procedures but in front of computers or using telephones, like in quality control or basic-level graphic design. These low-end skilled or semi-skilled employees who constitute a new stratum of non-elite knowledge workers are also referred to as "programmable labor," that is, those in between self-programmable labor and generic labor (Qiu 2009, 2010).

This overall pattern is not unique to the Chinese context. In India, similar developments of the information have-less are recorded in Delhi's grassroots' media practices that collectively construct a "pirate kingdom" of non-legal digital urban life that is extremely rich in post-colonial social networks (Sundaram 2010: 105). It is also observed in the "global body shopping" of software engineers from Hyderabad (Xiang 2006), in which case the supposedly high-status "intelligent" jobs created by the IT industry, both in India and for Indian software engineers in countries as far flung as Australia, the US, and the UK, turn out to be no better than traditional labor-intensive sectors in terms of work conditions and employment benefits. Sometimes they are even worse due to the unpredictable nature of the globally networked industrial regime.

These findings apply to a large degree in key industries of the West as well. As demonstrated in Saskia Sassen's (2001) classic study on New York, London, and Tokyo, the financial sector, a pillar of the global network society, produces as many low-end jobs (especially in the service sector such as office cleaning and delivery) as high-end ones. Meanwhile, in the back alleys of bank towers, the "survival circuits" persist among countless nannies and sex workers (Sassen 2001).

Indeed, the expansion of network societies globally has to depend on the enlargement of the industrial systems in manufacturing computers and mobile phones and in providing content and services to these new devices. More important, people involved in these new industrial systems are not always passive under the pressure of management that tends to atomize the labor force. In May–June 2010, large-scale labor unrest took place in Honda and Toyota factories located in the Guangdong Province of China, where thousands of workers used mobile phones to organize and mobilize protests (Barboza and Bradsher 2010). These were not entirely new to the manifestation of labor power through Internet and mobile phone because, at least since Debember 2004, Chinese workers have been using Weblogs to reach the rest of the world and create mass-media pressure (French 2004). This follows a model not too different from what Castells calls "mass self-communication," by which he understands ICT diffusion prompting "the development of horizontal networks of interactive communication that connect local and global in chosen time" (2007: 246). This process occurs among not only the upper- and middle-classes but also members of the working class as well.

The substance of the working class—its membership, social scope, and identity—is of course also different in the new time-space of the network society. The notion of "network labor" is therefore proposed to fill in the gap between new forms of capitalism (the network enterprise) and new forms of statism (the network state). Not all members of the information have-less belong to network labor. The former is merely a techno-social basis, a necessary but insufficient condition, for the latter. One has to actually take part in working-class formations, be they formal trade unions or informal online support groups or offline flash mobilizations, to become a member of the network labor force, whose internal structuration is still under way. Nonetheless, the appearance and consolidation of such network labor formations, in urban China and beyond, are per-haps the single most decisive change in global network society in the first decade of the twenty-first century (Qiu 2009).

This trend towards the formation of network labor is still in a formative stage. But it is important to note that, facilitated by ICTs and always interacting with network enter-prise on the one hand and network state on the other, this new class formation process is no longer confined to traditional parameters of class formation. That is, they do not always happen within the institutional frameworks of political parties or the profession-based industrial work centered on the full-time "organizational man." This gendered transformation from the "organizational man" to "flexible woman" has long been under way (Castells 1996). It reflects a fundamental shift towards more outsourcing, self-employment, and overall unpredictability of work that characterizes contemporary capitalism as a whole (Sennett 1998). Hence, the notion of network labor stresses that, due to all these structural changes at societal and organizational levels, and the spread of working-class ICTs at individual level, the locale of class making has diffused beyond the confines of twentieth-century politics, be they formal trade unions or political parties. The labor movement itself has also become a network structure in which the nodes matter more than the center(s) (Qiu 2010).

From the perspective of class formation, an optimistic interpretation of this profound change is that it creates a new condition of "membership unlimited" (Thompson 1966), in which much larger proportions of society can now identify themselves with the new working class in the making. ICT-for-development projects have brought billions of formerly unconnected populations of the Global South into the process, while the growth of global civil society, the open source movement, and the World Summit on Information Society (WSIS) all help bring down old barriers against the formation of network labor. A radical take on this trend is Hardt and Negri's "multitude" that is theorized as the global challenge to the dominant neoliberal "empire" (2004).

When Hardt and Negri explored the bold idea of the multitude as an alternative to the capitalistic world-system, they also discussed the relevance of "immaterial labor" as another key realm of expansion for labor formations to go beyond materialistic constraints (2004: 290–3). Yet if we trace the origins of "immaterial labor" to either Fortunati (2007) or Lazzarato (1996), the concept was meant to be a critique and a problematizing device more than anything else. No matter from a feminist perspective focusing on affective labor and care-work (Fortunati 2007) or from a more classic Gramscian perspective seeing media and public relation workers as prototypical immaterial labor (Lazzarato 1996), both traditions of Italian scholarship criticize "immaterial labor" as a new tool of exploitation. This critique can find a more updated expression in the "playbor" phenomenon of the online gaming industry, when players of computer games volunteer their time to "modding," that is, the creation of computer game modifications, often free of charge because of unfair intellectual property right arrangements (Kücklich 2005).

The contrasting views may look impossible to reconcile. But this dilemma echoes again profound internal contradictions of post-industrialism that Daniel Bell had identified as a dangerous state of "disjunction" between technological rationality and emotional impulses, and between economic efficiency and cultural hedonism, "from the protestant ethic to the psychedelic bazaar" (1976: 54).

Most importantly, old challenges to class formation persist at the beginning of the new century when manipulated identity politics—of gender, race, ethnicity, nationality, and religious belief—are used to undermine class politics; when memories of deeply dividing, and divided, labor movements in the past blind us from seeing opportunities of a better democracy in the future, that reunites all material and immaterial workers of the world. After all, class formation is a relational process through which collective identities are discovered, constructed, and shared across traditional social and cultural boundaries. The ideas of network labor and this new ICT-based working class are helpful precisely because they highlight not only the class-making process but also the rare chance of social change: that this new class-making process may indeed be bottom-up and horizontal rather than imposed from top down.

Concluding remarks

The network society, as a general theory developed by Manuel Castells, has been widely used in Internet studies. Yet, as the title "network socie*ties*" suggests, this chapter focuses more on the multiplicity of various theorizations about the information/knowledge/post-industrial society, ICTs, and social change based on cultural, institutional, and power transformations on the ground. Some of these are formulated by Castells and his colleagues; others by scholars from a wide variety of backgrounds including Daniel Bell and his critics. As a result, this chapter does not present a single unified framework. Rather, it takes the plurality of information and network societies as a basic condition in considering macro social change since the mid-1990s when Internet Studies began to take shape. This plurality reflects diverse developmental trajectories of the Internet and mobile ICTs around the world, especially in non-Western societies and among working-class communities.

Such a pluralistic overview is in order because the spread of ICTs has gone far beyond the very elite "core" of the world system, thus creating many local and regional patterns of Internet usage; because rising giants like China and India often refuse to adopt past models of development, thus breaking the norm of "modernization" as a one-way ticket toward Westernization; and because the lines are shifting between the public and the private, with all its diverse ways of systemic configuration, including the trends toward "mass self-communication" (Castells 2007), connect agentic action, and structural change in very different contexts with very different characteristics.

In sum, as a basic theoretical framework, the network society and its many insights and critiques about the contemporary world—including "timeless time" and "space of flows," "self-programmable labor" and "generic labor"—have remained central since the publication of Castells' triology in 1996–98. But the world has also changed quite fundamentally, for example in terms of post-9/11 geopolitics, post-2008 global economy, and the rise of BRIC countries. In these new global and regional contexts we have also begun to see signs of new class politics starting to resemble networks and adopt network logic, as highlighted by developments of "network labor." Hence, while the threats continue with regard to even more ephemeral "timeless time" and even faster "space of flows," we have seen the persistence, revival, and/or renewal of histories, places, and class structures around the world. This is why we need to conceptualize multiple network societies: because the human experiences of network-based social organization have been so much enlarged, deepened, and diversified, not only technologically and institutionally, but also culturally and epistemologically.

However, compared to Bell's futurology followers, who have popularized oversimplified versions of the post-industrial society throughout the world, there is still only a limited amount of literature that examines the development of the Internet from rigorous sectoral, occupational, and social class perspectives, especially when it comes to the analysis of network societies in non-Western contexts. It will therefore be fruitful if ideas of network societies can be brought into constant dialogue with empirical observations on the ground, fostering more systematic comparisons, not only between advanced capitalist societies and developing countries, but also South–South comparisons among developing countries, especially emerging Internet powers like China, India, and Brazil. In so doing, more attention needs to be paid to contexts, institutions, and grassroots-level usage patterns centered increasingly on mobile rather than PC-based Internet services, which may lead to structural change. The task of Internet Studies in a truly global sense is not only descriptive but also explanatory—of the network societies in connection with each other.

Acknowlegment

This chapter draws in part from an ongoing project "Constructing Working-Class Networks: A Study of QQ and Tencent" funded by the South China Program, Hong-Kong Institute of Asia-Pacific Studies (principal investigator: Jack Linchuan Qiu, co-investigators: Wei Ding, Larissa Hjorth, Baohua Zhou).

References

Aker, J. C. and Mbiti, I. M. (2010). "Mobile Phones and Economic Development in Africa," *The Journal of Economic Perspective*, 24(3): 207–32.

Akter, M. S., Rajasekera, J., and Rahman, M. M. (2010). "Serving the Poor by Marketing Information: Developing a Sustainable Village Phone Model in Bangladesh," *International Journal of Economics and Business Research*, 2(3–4): 288–309.

Barboza, D. and Bradsher, K. (2010). "In China, Labor Movement Enabled by Technology," *The New York Times*, June 16, B1.

Bell, D. (1972). "On Meritocracy and Equality," *The Public Interest*, 29: 29–68.

—— (1973). *The Coming of Post-Industrial Society*, New York: Basic Books.

—— (1976). *The Cultural Contradictions of Capitalism*, New York: Basic Books.

—— (1979). "The Social Framework of the Information Society," in M. L. Dertouzous and J. Moses (eds). *The Computer Age: The Next Twenty Years*, Cambridge, MA: MIT Press, pp. 163–211.

Brinkerhoff, J. (2009). *Digital Diasporas: Identity and Transnational Engagement*, Cambridge: Cambridge University Press.

Cartier, C., Castells, M., and Qiu, J. L. (2005). "The Information Have-Less: Inequaltiy, Mobility and Translocal Networks in Chinese Cities," *Studies in Comparative International Development*, 40(2): 9–34.

Castells, M. (1989). *The Informational City: Information Technology, Economic Restructuring, and the Urban-Regional Process*, Oxford: Blackwell.

—— (1996). *The Rise of the Network Society*, Oxford: Blackwell.

—— (1997). *The Power of Identity*, Oxford: Blackwell.

—— (1998). *The End of Millennium*, Oxford: Blackwell.

—— (2004). "Informationalism, Networks, and the Network Society: A Theoretical Blueprint," in M. Castells (ed.). *The Network Society: A Cross-Cultural Perspective*. Cheltenham: Edward Elgar, pp. 3–47.

—— (2007). "Communication, Power and Counter-Power in the Network Society," *International Journal of Communication*, 1: 238–66.

—— (2009). *Communication Power*, Oxford: Oxford University Press.

——, Fernandez-Ardevol, M., Qiu, J. L., and Sey, A. (2006). *Mobile Communication and Society: A Global Perspective*, Cambridge, MA: MIT Press.

Castells, M. and Himanen, P. (2004). "Institutional Models of the Network Society: Silicon Valley and Finland," in M. Castells (ed.). *The Network Society: A Cross-Cultural Perspective*, Cheltenham: Edward Elgar, pp. 49–83.

Chan, J. and Pun, N. (2010). "Suicide as Protest for the New Generation of Chinese Migrant Workers: Foxconn, Global Capital, and the State," *The Asia-Pacific Journal: Japan Focus*. Available at <http://japanfocus.org/-Jenny-Chan/3408>. Accessed October 28, 2010.

Chew, M. and Fung, A. (2007). "Virtual Property Problems in China." Paper presented at the Information Technology and Social Responsibility conference, Hong Kong, December 17–18.

CNNIC (China Internet Network Information Center) (2010). *The 26th Statistical Report on the Development of Internet in China*, Beijing: CNNIC.

Dayan, D. (2008). "Beyond Media Events: Disenchantment, Derailment, Disruption," in M. Price and D. Dayan (eds.). *Owning the Olympics: Narratives of the New China*, Ann Arbor, MI: The University of Michigan Press, 391–402.

—— and Katz, E. (1992). *Media Events: The Live Broadcasting of History*, Cambridge, MA: Harvard University Press.

Deibert, R. J., Palfrey, J. G., Rohozinski, R., and Zittrain, J. (2008). *Access Denied: The Practice and Policy of Global Internet Filtering*, Cambridge, MA: MIT Press.

Florida, R. (2005). "The World is Spiky," *The Atlantic Monthly*, (10): 48–51.

Fortunati, L. (2007). "Immaterial Labor and its Machinization," *Ephemera*, 7(1): 139–57.

French, F. W. (2004). "Workers Demand Union at Wal-Mart Supplier in China," *The New York Times*, December 16: A3.

Fukuyama, F. (1992). *The End of History and the Last Man*, New York: Free Press.

Gibson, W. (2010). "Google's Earth," *The New York Times*, September 1: A23.

Giddens, A. (1991). *Modernity and Self-Identity: Self and Society in the Late Modern Age*, Stanford: Stanford University Press.

Goggin, A. and M. McLelland (eds) (2009). *Internationalizing Internet Studies: Beyond Anglophone Paradigms*, New York: Routledge.

Hardt, M. and Negri, A. (2004). *Multitude: War and Democracy in the Age of Empire*, New York: Penguin Press.

Harvey, D. (1991). *The Conditions of Postmodernity: An Inquiry into the Origins of Cultural Change*, Oxford: Blackwell.

Hassan, R. and Purser, R. E. (eds) (2007). *Time and Temporality in the Network Society*, Stanford: Stanford University Press.

Holman, D., Batt, R., and Holtgrewe, U. (2007). *The Global Call Center Report*, The Global Call Center Network. Available at <http://www.globalcallcenter.org>. Accessed May 18, 2012.

Ilahiane, H. and Sherry, J. (2008). "Joutia: Street Vendor Entrepreneurship and the Informal Economy of Information and Communication Technologies in Morocco," *The Journal of North African Studies*, 13(2): 243–55.

ITU (International Telecommunications Union) (2010). *World Telecommuniation/ICT Development Report 2010*, Geneva: ITU.

Koch, P. T., Koch, B. J., Huang, K., and Chen, W. (2009). "Beauty is in the Eye of the QQ User: Instant Messaging in China," in G. Goggin and M. McLelland (eds) *Internationalizing Internet Studies: Beyond Anglophone Paradigms*, New York: Routledge, pp. 265–84.

Kücklich, J. (2005). "Precarious Playbor: Modders and the Digital Games Industry," *Fibre Culture*, 5. Available at <http://www.journal.fibreculture.org/issue5/kucklich.html>. Accessed October 19, 2010.

Kumar, K. (1978). *Prophecy and Progress: The Sociology of Industrial and Post-Industrial Society*, London: Allen Lane.

Lash, S. and Urry, J. (1993). *Economies of Signs and Space*, London: Sage.

Lazzarato, M. (1996). "Immaterial Labor," in P. Virno and M. Hardt (eds). *Radical Thought in Italy: A Potential Politics*, Minneapolis: University of Minnesota Press, pp. 132–46.

Lee, C. K. and Yang, G. (eds) (2007). *Re-envisioning the Chinese Revolution: The Politics and Poetics of Collective Memories in Reform China*, Stanford: Stanford University Press.

Lyon, D. (2002). *Surveillance as Social Sorting: Privacy, Risk and Digital Discrimination*, London: Routledge.

Mosco, V. (2004). *The Digital Sublime: Myth, Power, and Cyberspace*, Cambridge, MA: MIT Press.

Naisbitt, J. (1984). *Megatrends: Ten New Directions Transforming our Lives*, London: Futura.

O'Brien, R. (1992). *Global Financial Integration: The End of Geography*, New York: Council on Foreign Relations Press.

Qiu, J. L. (2009). *Working-Class Network Society: Communication Technology and the Information Have-Less in Urban China*, Cambridge, MA: MIT Press.

—— (2010). "Network Labor and Non-Elite Knowledge Workers in China," *Work, Organization, Labor and Globalization*, 4(2): 80–95.

—— and Chan, J. M. (2009). "Approaching New Media Events Research," *The Chinese Journal of Communication and Society*, 9: 19–37 (in Chinese).

Russell, B. (2008). "Call Centers: A Decade of Research," *International Journal of Management Reviews*, 10(3): 195–219.

Samarajiva, R. and Zainudeen, A. (eds) (2008). *ICT Infrastructure in Emerging Asia: Policy and Regulatory Roadblocks*, Ottawa: IDRC/Los Angeles: Sage.

Sassen, S. (2001). *The Global City: New York, London, Tokyo*, Princeton, NJ: Princeton University Press.

Sennett, R. (1998). *The Corrosion of Character: The Personal Consequences of Work in the New Capitalism*, New York: W.W. Norton & Company.

Sinclair, J., Jacka, E., and Cunningham, S. (2002). "Peripheral Visio," in J. Sinclair, E. Jacka, and S. Cunningham (eds). *New Patterns in Global Television: Peripheral Vision*, Oxford: Oxford University Press, pp. 1–32.

Sperry, S. (2010). "World Wide Friends," *National Geographic Magazine Blog*, March 13. Available at <http://blogs.ngm.com/blog_central/2010/03/world-wide-friends.html>. Accessed July 19, 2011.

Sundaram, R. (2010). *Pirate Modernity: Delhi's Media Urbanism*, London: Routledge.

Sunstein, C. R. (2007). *Republic.com 2.0*, Princeton, NJ: Princeton University Press.

Taylor, P. and Bain, P. M. (2004). "Call Center Offshoring to India: The Revenge of History?," *Labour and Industry*, 14(3): 15–38.

Thompson, E. P. (1966). *The Making of the English Working Class*, New York: Vintage Books.

Thussu, D. (2006). *International Communication: Continuity and Change*, London: Hodder Arnold Publications.

Toffler, A. (1980). *The Third Wave*, London: Pan Books.

—— (1990). *Power Shift: Knowledge, Wealth, and Violence at the Edge of the Twenty-first Century*. New York: Bantam.

Touraine, A. (1977). *The Self-Production of Society*, D. Coltman, trans., Chicago: University of Chicago Press.

Umesao, T. (1963). "On Information Industry," *Chuo-kohron*, March: 46–58 (in Japanese).

Webster, F. (2002). *Theories of the Information Society*, 2nd edn., London: Routledge.

Xiang, B. (2006). *Global "Body Shopping: An Indian Labor System in the Information Technology Industry,"* Princeton: Princeton University Press.

Yang, G. (2003). "China's Zhiqing Generation: Nostalgia, Identity and Cultural Resistance in the 1990s," *Modern China*, 29(3): 267–96.

—— (2007). "A Portrait of Martyr Jiang Qing: The Chinese Cultural Revolution on the Internet," in C. K. Lee and G. Yang (eds). *Re-envisioning the Chinese Revolution: The Politics and Poetics of Collective Memories in Reform China*, Stanford: Stanford University Press, pp. 267–96.

Zook, M. (2005). *The Geography of the Internet Industry: Venture Capital, Dot-coms, and Local Knowledge*, Oxford: Blackwell.

CHAPTER 7

....

DIGITAL INEQUALITY

....

ESZTER HARGITTAI AND YULI PATRICK HSIEH

INTRODUCTION

....

HERALDED at first as the great potential equalizer (Barlow 1996; Compaine 2001a; Reuters 1997), research on the Internet's unequal spread and uses over the years has suggested a more complicated picture about who is most likely to benefit from the medium's diffusion. As the Internet has become increasingly integrated into people's everyday lives, it is important to consider the implications of differentiated uses for people's social status and mobility. Given the myriad of opportunities they make available, digital media have the potential to alleviate existing societal inequalities. Depending on the pattern of uptake, however, they also have the potential to contribute to increased stratification. In this chapter, we review literature about the relationship of people's background and their digital media uses with particular focus on how demographic and socioeconomic factors relate to Internet use.

Rather than simply thinking about the so-called digital divide in binary terms—a person either has access to the Internet or not, is either a user or not—it is better to recognize that individuals, organizations, and countries may be differentiated by online experiences and abilities beyond core technical access (e.g. Barzilai-Nahon 2006; DiMaggio et al. 2004, 2001; Guillén and Suárez 2005; Hargittai 2002; van Dijk 2005; Warschauer 2003; Zillien and Hargittai 2009). Given the potential implications of digital inequality for people's life chances in particular, we focus primarily on individual-level differences rather than issues concerning digital divides at the level of organizations and institutions, while recognizing that inequalities in those realms exist as well (e.g. Forman 2005; Forman et al. 2005; Guillén and Suárez 2005; Kirschenbaum and Kunamneni 2001). We first review theoretical perspectives on the topic, followed by an examination of the core access divide both within and across nations. Next, we consider how people's background characteristics relate to their web-use skills and what they do online. Then we look at the social implications of differentiated Internet uses. Finally, we offer suggestions for next steps in this domain of inquiry.

THEORETICAL APPROACHES TO DIGITAL INEQUALITY

Social inequality has long been an important research inquiry for scholars and policy-makers alike (e.g. Grusky 2008). The main focus of such scholarship concerns the forms, sources, and structure of social inequality, mechanisms of mobility, consequences of social stratification, and the severe gaps in people's life chances across different societal groups (Grusky and Ku 2008: 3–4.). Linking to this domain of inquiry, scholars of digital inequality have suggested various theoretical approaches for studying the implications of the Internet for social stratification (Bonfadelli 2002; DiMaggio et al. 2004; Halford and Savage 2010; Hargittai 2008; van Dijk 2005). A consistent aspect of these theoretical approaches is that physical access to and ownership of information and communication technologies (ICTs) is only one of several important resource inequalities that need to be considered in the domain of digital inequality. Accordingly, it is problematic to constrain discussions and investigations to whether or not a core digital divide exists—that is, differences between haves and have nots when it comes to basic hardware and connectivity—given that the unequal distribution of other types of Internet-related resources such as digital skills are also very important to understanding the contours of inequality in the digital age (Hargittai 2002; DiMaggio et al. 2004).

DiMaggio and colleagues (2004) were among the first to offer a theoretical framework that accounts for the factors and outcomes related to digital inequality. Their approach highlights five aspects of inequality related to information and communication technologies: (1) the quality of hardware, software, and network connection; (2) autonomy of use; (3) skill; (4) availability of social support; and (5) extent and quality of use. Regarding the underlying mechanisms that explain digital inequality, the authors proposed that demographic and socioeconomic factors influence the level and quality of the first four factors, which in turn influence the types of uses, which then result in differentiated benefits and opportunities, and thus divergent life outcomes. Some of this work (DiMaggio and Hargittai 2001; Hargittai and Hinnant 2008; Zillien and Hargittai 2009) has suggested that certain Internet uses qualify as specifically "capital-enhancing" activities and should be especially of interest to scholars of social stratification. For example, web users who look for jobs online may become more informed jobseekers with respect to job market opportunities, which might in turn help them find a job more quickly, perhaps help identify better employment options, or assist in negotiating better terms or a higher salary (DiMaggio and Bonikowski 2008). Undoubtedly, one may consider such outcomes as opportunities for social mobility, and thus ICT uses may help reduce inequalities. However, given that such opportunities are likely to be unequally distributed along existing stratification lines, differentiated uses may be more prone to reinforcing existing inequalities rather than alleviating them (Bonfadelli 2002; Chen and Wellman 2005; Hargittai 2008).

Another related approach to digital inequality came from van Dijk (2005) who focused on the unequal distribution of four types of digital resources: (1) motivational access; (2) material access; (3) skill access; (4) and usage access. This approach suggests that there is a positive relationship between these resources whereby greater motivation to use ICTs may lead to more possession of technological equipment resulting in better material access that encourages the development of higher-level skills, which in turn leads to more intense and diverse ICT uses. Similar to Hargittai (Hargittai 2002, 2003, 2008), van Dijk (2005) also argues that the relationship between socioeconomic status (SES) and the possession of digital resources is reciprocal, indicating that digital inequality and existing forms of social inequality may reinforce one another.

Although differences in Internet usage rates have only been of concern since that medium's mass diffusion in the 1990s, earlier research had already focused on differences in other media consumption across population segments, finding variation by background characteristics (e.g. Greenberg and Dervin 1970; Tichenor et al. 1970). Greenberg and Dervin (1970), for example, found that low-income adults tended to spend more time watching television and less time reading newspapers regularly. Tichenor and his colleagues (1970) proposed the "knowledge gap" hypothesis, which suggested that people from higher socioeconomic status may become more informed and acquire more knowledge from their media consumption than those from lower SES backgrounds, widening existing inequalities between different population segments. Subsequent research also revealed that knowledge gaps between status groups were due to various factors such as variation in people's motivation to acquire information, prior know-how and selective use, as well as the utility of information for one's daily life (e.g. Ettema and Kline 1977; Gaziano 1983). Cook and colleagues (1975) looked at the viewership of the educational program *Sesame Street* and found that children from households with more educated parents were more likely to watch the show, suggesting that youth already in a more privileged position were more likely to benefit from it.

In the realm of early research on the adoption of personal computers, studies showed that socioeconomic factors such as income, education, and occupation of the head of household were important predictors of having this resource in the home (Attewell 2001; Dutton et al. 1987; Dutton et al. 1989). Overall, research on the relationship between social status and uses of media predating the Internet has found a systematic relationship between the two.

Linking Internet usage to the knowledge gap hypothesis, Bonfadelli (2002) argued that knowledge gaps in the domain of digital media uses may be more severe than gaps in uses of traditional media (a point also made by van Dijk (2005)), given that meaningful Internet use requires new skill sets such as refined searching strategies (e.g. Hargittai 2003; Rothbaum et al. 2008; Van Deursen 2010) and critical approaches to evaluating content credibility (e.g. Hargittai et al. 2010; Menchen-Trevino and Hargittai 2011; Metzger 2007) that are less associated with using traditional media. Bonfadelli (2002) empirically tested these propositions and found that there were clear gaps in computer skills as well as Internet access, usage, and attitudes towards the Internet among different

Swiss population groups, with those in more privileged positions using the Internet more than those from lower SES backgrounds.

Overall, the main contributions of the aforementioned theoretical perspectives are that they call attention to various forms of inequality related to ICT uses and they look at both the causes and consequences of digital inequalities from various research fields and traditions. Next, we discuss in more detail the so-called "first-level digital divide" or differences in access at both the individual as well as the nation-state level. Then, we review the literature on the "second-level digital divide" or differences in usage (Hargittai 2002), followed by an examination of differentiated Internet uses' social implications.

THE FIRST-LEVEL DIGITAL DIVIDE: DIFFERENCES IN ACCESS

ICT access divides among different population segments

Differences in Internet access rates started to attract public and scholarly attention beginning with the publication of the US National Telecommunication and Information Administration's (NTIA) "Falling Through the Net" report in the mid-1990s, which documented differential rates of adoption across different population segments (NTIA 1995). In the subsequent decade several other reports showed an increase in adoption rates but a persistent gap across population groups (NTIA 1995, 1998, 1999, 2000, 2002, 2004). Overall, findings from the reports suggested that despite a gradual increase in the proportion of Americans who had access to the Internet at home and who were going online, certain groups were much more likely to be in the "connected" category than others, namely, men, younger people, non-Hispanic white people, urban residents, the higher educated and those with higher income were more likely to use the Internet (e.g. Hoffman and Novak 1998). Using a diverse set of national and regional samples, scholars have also found varying inequalities in ICT access over the years (Bimber 2000; Dutton et al. 2009; Mesch and Talmud 2011; Raban 2007; Wilson et al. 2003; Zhang et al. 2008).

Over time, focus has shifted to identifying gaps in broadband access rather than simply looking at basic Internet access (NTIA 2010). Divides persist among population groups with different levels of education and income as well as metropolitan status when it comes to broadband diffusion (Horrigan 2009; LaRose et al. 2007; Smith 2010; Stern et al. 2009). And while gender differences in broadband access no longer exist in the US (Ono and Zavodny 2003; Smith 2010) nor in several other countries (Dutton et al. 2009; Ono and Zavodny 2007), as we note in subsequent sections, this should not be interpreted as a disappearance of all types of gender variation in Internet use (as opposed to basic infrastructural access), given that differences in types of uses persist.

A more nuanced look at the access question considers the number of locations where people can go online. DiMaggio and Hargittai (2001) argued that autonomy of use—or the freedom to use the technology when and where one wants to—is an important aspect of differentiated opportunities regarding digital media. Indeed, research has found that autonomy of use is related to using the Internet for capital-enhancing activities (Hargittai and Hinnant 2008) and is itself dependent on users' socioeconomic status (Hassani 2006) with tangible beneficial outcomes (DiMaggio and Bonikowski 2008).

Global divide in ICT access

While the diffusion of the Internet to increasing segments of the population in certain countries prompted much enthusiasm for its potential globally (e.g. Barlow 1996; Press 1996; Reuters 1997; Rheingold 1993), researchers started noting its unequal international spread already in the 1990s (Goodman et al. 1994; Hargittai 1999), finding that more developed nations were achieving higher rates of diffusion than lesser-developed countries (e.g. Guillén and Suárez 2005; Norris 2001).

The International Telecommunication Union's (ITU) report "Measuring the Information Society" documents worldwide Internet diffusion trends, showing that a global-level digital divide remains significant as the overall magnitude of the gap among countries has continued to persist over time despite increases in connectivity across nations (ITU 2010). According to the report, more than 80 percent of households have computer and Internet access in certain European countries (i.e. Norway, Sweden, Luxembourg, and the Netherlands) and certain Asian countries (i.e. South Korea and Japan). In stark contrast, this figure drops to lower than 5 percent in many African, South Asian, and Latin American nations. The report also shows that, despite the rapid diffusion of broadband in certain countries during the end of the twenty-first century's first decade, this technology's spread also exhibits notable gaps among countries, ranging from 41 broadband subscribers per 100 inhabitants in Sweden to less than 1 broadband subscriber per 100 inhabitants in lesser-developed countries such as Swaziland, Guatemala, and Laos.

An extensive literature has developed trying to explain these persisting inequalities across nations (e.g. Drori and Jang 2003; Guillén and Suárez 2005; Wilson 2004). The above-cited ITU report (2010) points to disparities in the cost of subscriptions as an important impediment to larger levels of uptake in certain countries. While broadband connectivity is affordable in many more-developed nations, in other parts of the world such as many African countries, the monthly broadband subscription fee can amount to large portions of people's earnings (ITU 2010: 74), making the service prohibitive to a considerable segment of the population. Academic scholarship has identified factors such as a country's wealth, its inhabitants' literacy and education levels, its political system, and telecommunications policies as causes of the variations observed (Andrés et al. 2007; Billon et al. 2009; Crenshaw and Robison 2006; Drori and Jang 2003; Drori 2010; Guillén and Suárez 2005; Hargittai 1999; Wilson 2004).

THE SECOND-LEVEL DIGITAL DIVIDE:
DIFFERENTIATED SKILLS AND USES

Differentiated ICT skills and uses among different demographic groups

Beyond examining differences in core access to the Internet, a growing body of research has focused on differences in how people use and incorporate digital media into their everyday lives, including their abilities with using them (e.g. Eynon 2009; Hargittai 2010; Howard et al. 2001; Livingstone and Helsper 2007; Mossberger et al. 2003). Applying cluster analysis to data from five European countries (Austria, Norway, Spain, Sweden, UK), Brandtzæg and colleagues (Brandtzæg et al. 2011) defined five user typologies (Non-Users, Sporadic Users, Instrumental Users, Entertainment Users, and Advanced Users), examining how gender, age, household size, and Internet access type related to types of usage, finding that in some cases these factors explain where a user falls on the typology.

While the gender gap in basic Internet access has disappeared in some countries such as the US, Sweden, Japan, South Korea, Singapore (Ono and Zavodny 2007), and the United Kingdom (Dutton et al. 2009), gender differences in skills and usage have persisted over time (Boneva et al. 2001; Hargittai 2010; Hargittai and Walejko 2008; Helsper 2010; Wasserman and Richmond-Abbott 2005; Weiser 2000). Women tend to engage in communicative ICT uses more (Boneva et al. 2001) and differently than men (Herring 1996), and tend to do more health information seeking online (Helsper 2010), while men are more likely to get financial information (Howard et al. 2001) and engage in leisure activities (Helsper 2010) online than their female counterparts, suggesting that gender differences in ICT uses may be associated with existing gender variation in social activities (Dholakia 2006). Helsper (2010) noted, however, that level of variation was partly dependent on life stage (i.e. marital and employment status). Additionally, men and women differ in their perception of their online abilities (Hargittai and Shafer 2006), which in turn influences the extent to which they contribute to online content (Hargittai and Walejko 2008; Schradie 2011).

Examining differences in Internet use by age has been a topic of inquiry ever since the first reports identified age as an important correlate of ICT diffusion (e.g. Charness and Holley 2004; Livingstone and Helsper 2007; Loges and Jung 2001; NTIA 1995; Selwyn et al. 2003). A survey of UK residents 14 years of age and older found persisting age-group differences in ICT access and use over the years, showing older adults continue to utilize new digital technologies at lower rates than their younger counterparts (Dutton et al. 2009). When it comes to the digital media uses of elderly adults, of particular interest has been a focus on cognitive abilities across generations. One study observed that the negative relationship between age and ICT use is mediated by cognitive abilities as well as computer self-efficacy and computer anxiety (Czaja et al. 2006). In a similar vein, by analyzing longitudinal data about older adults' Internet uses matched with their adolescent cognitive abilities measured several decades earlier, Freese and colleagues (2006) found that higher cognitive ability in adolescence was associated with higher likelihood of having Internet access and use of the Web (as opposed to email only) later in life. The authors argued that cognitive ability may play an important role in explaining the differences in older adults' Internet uses due to the high literacy demands and text-based informational content of the Internet at the time of data collection (2003–04). As multimedia content has become increasingly common and accessible online, it will be important to track whether such relationships between cognitive ability and usage persist.

While some have argued that young adults who grow up with digital media are inherently better at using the medium (Prensky 2001), there is little empirical evidence to support such a claim (Bennett et al. 2008; Hargittai 2010). Rather, studies looking at youth find considerable variation in ICT uses and skills, indicating that growing up with technology in and of itself does not lead to a uniformly skilled population (Correa 2010; Hargittai 2010; Livingstone and Helsper 2007).

Differentiated ICT skills and uses by socioeconomic status

As noted earlier, socioeconomic status such as educational background and income are strongly related to disparities in ICT access. A similar relationship has also been found with levels of online skill and types of uses to which people put digital media. Additionally, autonomy of use relates to online behavior. One of the most consistent findings in the study mentioned above by Brandtzæg and colleagues (2011) about user typologies was the importance of Internet access type for whether a user was only sporadically or more actively engaged with the Web.

A growing body of work has examined differences in people's skills with using the Internet, finding that online abilities are related to people's socioeconomic status (Gui and Argentin 2011; Hargittai 2002, 2010; Hargittai and Hinnant 2008; Page and Uncles 2004; Van Deursen 2010). This is especially of interest as some scholarship has also found that difference in web-use skills are related to differentiated online behavior, whereby more skilled Internet users are more likely to engage in more types of online activities than those less knowledgeable about and comfortable with the Web (Correa 2010; Hargittai 2010; Hargittai and Hinnant 2008; Hargittai and Walejko 2008; Livingstone and Helsper 2010; Zillien and Hargittai 2009). Relying on face-to-face interviews of 120 American parents representing different socioeconomic backgrounds, researchers found a relationship between SES and web search sophistication as well as the ability to evaluate content credibility (Rothbaum et al. 2008).

How people spend their time online is also related to their socioeconomic status. Data about German adults' Internet experiences from 2004 showed that social status was very much related to capital-enhancing uses of the Web even after controlling for demographic characteristics, technical equipment, digital experiences, and topical interest (Zillien and Hargittai 2009). Analysis of a national sample of 18–26-year-old American adults' Internet uses in 2004 also found a similar relationship between socioeconomic status and capital-enhancing uses of the Web, such as seeking out news, information about health, finance, and government services (Hargittai and Hinnant 2008). Other research has also highlighted a relationship between SES and certain types of web uses (Anderson 2008; Buente and Robbin 2008; Eynon 2009; Hale et al. 2010) including the use of social media such as social network sites in particular (boyd 2011; Chou et al. 2009; Hargittai 2011).

Global divide in ICT uses

International examinations of digital inequality have largely focused on access differences, rarely venturing into the domain of differentiated uses among population groups across nations. This may well be due to the dearth of available data sets containing information about people's Internet uses for several countries. A notable exception is a series of reports from the Statistical Office of the European Communities (Eurostat) that is based on data about people's Internet uses among the member states of the European Union (Eurostat 2008, 2009). These reports point out considerable variation in how people in different countries are using the medium. For example, in 2008, Denmark, Finland, Luxembourg, the Netherlands, and Sweden had the highest proportion of individuals engaging in various online activities such as using banking and travel services, as well as seeking health information, while considerably lower proportions of Internet users in countries like Bulgaria, Poland, Portugal, and Romania had done so. Additionally, more than 60 percent of individuals in Denmark, the Netherlands, Sweden, and the United Kingdom had shopped online in 2009, compared to less than 10 percent in Bulgaria, Lithuania, and Romania in that year.

Another source for looking at differentiated Internet uses across countries is the World Internet Project (WIP), a global collaborative survey project. Reports from WIP (2010) show that there are notable differences in web users' online activities and experiences across countries. For example, in 2008 only the United Kingdom (47 percent), the United States (46 percent), New Zealand (40 percent), and Australia (38 percent) had high proportions of Internet users buying products online at least monthly. In sharp contrast, less than 10 percent of users in Colombia, Hungary, Macao, and Singapore reported engaging in online purchasing activities. These patterns have remained consistent over time.

However, when it comes to multimedia consumption on the Web, the findings from WIP suggest a different picture. Results show that, in 2008, more than 30 percent of users in urban China, the Czech Republic, Hungary, Israel, and Macao claimed to have downloaded or watched videos online at least monthly and 40 percent reported going online to download or listen to music and songs at least monthly. By comparison, less than a quarter of users in Sweden (19 percent), Colombia (19 percent), and the United

States (24 percent) had engaged in online video watching and downloading at least monthly in the same period.

While the Internet access divide may be highly consistent with global inequality in economic development, the aforementioned variation in web use across different countries does not always mirror economic circumstances. Findings about differences in multimedia consumption pose interesting questions for future work in this area as it seems that in addition to economic and infrastructural factors, variations in social, cultural, and legal contexts across borders may well account for how users in different countries are incorporating the Internet into their everyday lives (Wu 2008).

IMPLICATIONS OF DIFFERENTIATED
ICT ACCESS, SKILLS, AND USES

Current investigations of digital inequality mainly focus on issues regarding disparities in possessions and uses of various digital resources. An essential next step for the digital inequality research agenda is to figure out what outcomes are associated with differentiated access, skills, and uses. After all, if variations have no implications for people's life chances then such differentiation may not be of much concern to scholars of social stratification. However, if the benefits people can and do reap from their Internet uses vary, and do so systematically by user background and Internet experiences, then the overall social implications of digital media may be an exacerbation of inequalities rather than a leveling of the playing field (Chen and Wellman 2005). Do those who have more and better ICT access, who are more skilled with digital media, and those who engage in certain types and a more diverse set of ICT uses, see higher gains in human, financial, cultural, and social capital? While much remains to be done in this domain, some work has explored such questions in particular. Most initial investigations have tended to look at the implications of basic access and use, with very little work focusing on how specific types of Internet uses link to various outcomes. Undoubtedly, this is likely due to the lack of appropriate data sets that would allow the necessary more nuanced, and ideally longitudinal, analyses (Brynin et al. 2007).

The implications of Internet uses for human and financial capital

Digital media have the potential to help people acquire skills and information that may improve their academic achievement and labor market success. However, they also may serve as distractions resulting in decreased productivity and may lead to exposure of information that can jeopardize people's job prospects. While limited research has addressed these questions specifically about the Internet, research on related phenomena such as computer use in the classroom and at the workplace suggests what trends may emerge in this domain.

Using data from the 1997 National Longitudinal Survey of Youth and the 2000–3 Current Population Survey, Fairlie and his colleagues (2010) identified a positive relationship between students' home computer ownership and their educational outcomes. Analyzing data from the 1988 National Educational Longitudinal Study, Attewell and Battle (1999) also found that home computer use was positively related to adolescents' academic achievement. Moreover, they showed that boys, white people, and those from higher socioeconomic background were more likely than others to reap the benefits.

In contrast, some researchers have challenged the positive link between computer use and educational outcomes (Fuchs and Woessmann 2004), finding that once family background and school characteristics are taken into account, computer use exhibits an inverted U-shaped relationship with students' test scores. These results suggest that students who do not use a computer at all or use it at the extremes may perform lower academically. Additionally, work has also found that introducing computers in less-privileged households to children who would otherwise not have these resources in the home may have negative implications for educational outcomes (Vigdor and Ladd 2010), echoing concerns about the distraction effects of such devices. A serious shortcoming of such studies, however, is that they disregard the important social processes through which the introduction of a computer or Internet access to the home may influence academic outcomes. In particular, they do not consider how social processes of learning and skill development may affect the uses to which new hardware is put. These studies have no measures of students', their peers', their parents', or their teachers' Internet skills, or any training or support that may be available to students either before or after the intervention. As earlier sections of this chapter point out, skills are not randomly distributed across the population, and social context of use matters to how people incorporate digital media into their lives. Accordingly, examining the effects of hardware intervention without contextual variables may miss a crucial part of the puzzle.

While some attempts have been made at linking various types of Internet uses with academic outcomes (Hargittai and Hsieh 2010; Junco and Cotten 2011; Pasek et al. 2009), these studies suffer from the limitations of cross-sectional data. Other studies in this realm look at student perceptions of how Internet use may influence academic outcomes, rather than looking at more objective measures of academic performance (Kubey et al. 2001), making it unclear whether findings are about perceived or actual outcomes.

In education research, scholars have argued that digital media have important implications for learning and the changing nature of literacy in particular (e.g. Barron 2006; Buckingham 2007; Eshet-Alkalai 2004; Eynon and Helsper 2011). Researchers have noted that, as the volume and variety of information and sources accessible online continue to expand, the ability to search, process, and use information critically will become an increasingly important skill (van Dijk 2005; Warschauer 2003). Again, however, lack of longitudinal data makes it difficult to test these propositions empirically.

In the realm of labor-market outcomes, considerable work has examined how computer use may affect the wage structure (Allen 2001; Autor et al. 1998; Krueger 1993; Stevenson 2009). Using nationally representative data from 1984 and 1989, Krueger (1993) found that American workers who used computers on the job earned higher wages than their counterparts. In response, however, other researchers (DiNardo and Pischke 1997; Entorf et al. 1999) cast doubt on this relationship between computer use and wages, arguing that the earnings advantages observed were due to higher worker quality rather than use of computers on the job per se.

Autor (2001) suggested three possible consequences of increasing Internet diffusion for the labor market, arguing that it may change (a) people's job search strategies, (b) how work gets done (i.e. that less work may be done on-site), and (c) dependence on local labor markets; and he warned against possible new inequalities emerging due to these changes. DiMaggio and Bonikowski (2008) empirically examined whether Internet use is related to Americans' earnings, finding that Internet use at work and at home—independent of computer use—was associated with higher earnings when controlling for a host of demographic and socioeconomic factors including prior year earnings. Looking at a similar question, but using a different unit of analysis, Forman and colleagues (2009) found that at the regional level, between 1995 and 2000, only the US counties with the most wealthy, highly educated workforce, and most IT-intensive industry, saw substantial wage growth. Similar analyses of more recent data are not available, leaving questions about what the Internet's effects may be for the wage structure in years when digital media had reached more considerable mass diffusion having been integrated into more people's everyday lives.

Some studies have focused on how Internet use may influence the job search process (Fountain 2005; Stevenson 2009). Using longitudinal panel data of unemployed job-seekers constructed from the 1998 and 2000 Current Population Survey (CPS), Fountain (2005) showed that people who searched for jobs online were more likely to get a job sooner than those who did not perform such searches. Another study looked at longitudinal panel data matched from the 2001 and 2002 CPS data sets, finding a positive relationship between Internet access and jobseekers' engagement in online job search and their job turnover rate (Stevenson 2009). The author argued that the positive relationship was likely due to the fact that employees who are better informed about their options (i.e. through accessing the Internet and looking for job information online) are more likely to assess and match their labor market opportunities better.

The implications of Internet uses for social capital and civic engagement

The potential of using ICTs for maintaining one's social relationships and engaging in political processes is enormous, as people not only connect with others in social networks but also in online networks (Wellman et al. 1996). The implications of ICT uses for social capital as measured by social connectivity or civic participation have seen numerous investigations with sometimes conflicting results (see Haythornthwaite and Rice 2006 for a further review of this literature). Some have suggested that online social interactions and ICT uses are likely to undermine social bonds as well as decrease people's social capital at both individual and societal levels, arguing that the more time one spends online, the less one can spend socializing with others (e.g. Kraut et al. 1998; McPherson et al. 2006; Nie et al. 2002; Putnam 2001). In contrast, others have found that digital media uses are associated with an increase in interpersonal communication and community participation, and in turn may provide both bridging and bonding social capital (e.g. Ellison et al. 2007; Katz and Rice 2002; Kraut et al. 2002; Norris 2004).

Several other scholars have also suggested that the Internet mostly enhances users' existing social relationships and their social engagement with communities and society at large (Boase et al. 2006; Hampton et al. 2009; Hampton and Wellman 2003; Quan-Haase et al. 2002; Rainie and Wellman 2012). For example, in the study of a high-speed wired neighborhood near Toronto, Canada, researchers (Hampton and Wellman 2003) found some evidence of a positive relationship between web use and social connectivity. Internet use was associated with having larger neighborhood networks, being able to recognize more neighbors, as well as having greater frequency of both on- and off-line communication and participation in the public and private realms. Supporting such claims, a more recent analysis of a representative US adult sample (Hampton et al. 2009) suggested that the ownership of a mobile phone and engagement in various online activities were associated with larger and more diverse core discussion networks, and that Internet use facilitated communication with both local and distant social contacts.

A growing body of research has also investigated whether certain types of ICT uses may link to increases in social connectivity and civic participation. For example, an analysis of college students at a large US public university showed that more intense Facebook users are more likely to experience an increase in their bridging social capital over time, and such an increase is greater for students with lower self-esteem than those with higher self-esteem (Steinfield et al. 2008). Another study of a nationally representative sample of US youth showed that individuals who seek information online more frequently are more likely to engage in civic activities and possess more political knowledge (Pasek et al. 2009). This study also found that while frequency of young people's use of online social network sites is positively related to their offline civic engagement (e.g. participating in a club or other extra-curricular activities), it is negatively related to their trust in others, suggesting that online activities may have different implications for different aspects of social capital. Analyzing data about Americans' Internet uses and civic engagement in 1999 and 2000, Shah and his colleagues (2005) found a relationship between seeking news and politics-related information online as well as engaging in civic discussion online and general civic participation (e.g. doing volunteer work, participating in community meetings). Such findings suggest that the Internet may have somewhat distinct affordances regarding civic and political participation: it may serve as a source of political information while also offering a venue for actively engaging in civic and political activities.

As suggested by the above-cited literature, there is no consensus on whether digital media usage enhances or decreases people's social capital. One possible source of conflicting results may be the ambiguity and complexity of the definition of social capital (Kadushin 2004). As reviewed above, from personal network size and perceptions of interpersonal trust to levels of civic engagement and political participation, work in this area has relied on a wide variety of measures. Also, given that the mechanisms connecting ICT uses and social capital are likely multidimensional, different types of online activities may have divergent implications for varying aspects of social capital.

An additional challenge to work in this area concerns the direction of causality between ICT usage and social capital. Traditionally, research in this domain has tended to treat social capital as a result of ICT uses, overlooking the possibility that level of social capital may be an important predictor of how people use ICTs in the first place. Hsieh and Hargittai (2010) proposed a complementary framework for examining whether people's social capital is related to their digital skills and subsequently how individuals' social capital and digital skills may explain variations in how they stay in touch with those in their networks using multiple media. Such an attempt at rethinking the causal link between digital media and social capital highlights a continued need for thinking carefully and critically about the reinforcing relationship between ICT uses and various types of capital.

Conclusion

As demonstrated by the literature reviewed above, digital inequality can refer both to how existing social inequalities influence the adoption and use of digital technologies as well as how differential uses of the Internet itself may influence social stratification. While considerable research exists to address the first question, much less evidence is available to interrogate the second. Part of the reason for the lack of evidence is the continued challenge of appropriate data and measurement. The field of Internet research requires the ongoing development of refined measures that capture the nuances of long-time existing services and activities as well as measures of newly emerging opportunities and options.

Overall, there are three possible outcomes of widespread digital media uses when it comes to social inequality. Even if we assume that everybody will benefit to some extent from digital media uses—itself an assumption that has yet to see the kind of empirical investigation necessary to be warranted—the implications are divergent depending on the relative level of benefit by different groups across society. If those in already more privileged positions are more likely to use ICTs in ways that enhance their human, financial, social, and cultural capital than those from less privileged backgrounds then the Internet will have exacerbated rather than alleviated social inequality. If people from all backgrounds are benefiting from digital media at similar levels then we will see little change in social status and thus would conclude that the Internet has no implica tions for social inequality. The third possibility is that those in less privileged positions are taking advantage of digital media more than those of higher socioeconomic status, resulting in decreased inequality. Given that ample research has now shown how Internet access, skills, and uses are in many ways related to people's demographic background and socioeconomic status, there is a good chance that these inequalities will be perpetuated when it comes to outcomes of digital media uses rather than resulting in an ameliorating effect.

Making matters more complicated, it may not be correct to assume universally positive outcomes from digital media uses. That is, it may be that some people not only do not benefit from using digital media, but may even be harmed by their uses. Considerably less scholarly work has focused on the negative implications of ICT uses than on the positive ones, but such potential outcomes do exist. From the possible negative psychological effects of cyberbullying to negative consequences for people's labor market success due to problematic uses of social media, and to the loss of financial resources due to online scams, there are many instances that may lead to a decrease in various forms of capital as a result of online behavior. Examining whether such consequences are systematically related to user background has yet to be addressed in detail by scholarly investigations.

As information and communication technologies diffuse to an increasing portion of the population, some have argued that digital inequality ceases to be a concern (Compaine 2001b). However, while older technologies do diffuse to more and more people, new technologies, tools, and services continue to emerge consistently, privileging those in already more advantageous positions. For example, socioeconomic status predicts ownership of smart phones, just as it predicted basic Internet connectivity, broadband connectivity, and access to other resources (Smith 2011). Similarly, while people may learn more about how to use digital media over time, as new tools emerge with new features, the additional know-how required to navigate these services likely will not be randomly distributed either, again privileging those in already advantageous positions.

While we have learned much about the contours of digital inequality since the mid-1990s, much work remains. We know especially little about the consequences of differentiated Internet uses for people's social status. Longitudinal data would go especially far in addressing questions of how use of digital media may shape people's life chances (Anderson 2005; Brynin et al. 2007). Also, having established that inequality exists in the realm of Internet skills and usage, developing and testing interventions that may improve people's web-use skills and thereby expand their online activities could be especially beneficial for ensuring that the many opportunities of digital media are within the reach of people from across the societal spectrum and not just those already in advantageous positions.

REFERENCES

Allen, S. G. (2001). "Technology and the Wage Structure," *Journal of Labor Economics*, 19(2): 440–83.

Anderson, B. (2005). "The Value of Mixed-Method Longitudinal Panel Studies in ICT Eesearch," *Information, Communication & Society*, 8(3): 343–67.

—— (2008). "The Social Impact of Broadband Household Internet Access," *Information, Communication & Society*, 11(1): 5–24.

Andrés, L., Cuberes, D., Diouf, M. A., and Serebrisky, T. (2007). "Diffusion of the Internet: A Cross-Country Analysis," World Bank Policy Research Working Paper Series. Available at <http://www-wds.worldbank.org/external/default/WDSContentServer/IW3P/IB/2007/12/03/000158349_20071203114216/Rendered/PDF/wps4420.pdf>. Accessed May 6, 2012.

Attewell, P. (2001). "The First and Second Digital Divides," *Sociology of Education*, 74(3): 252–9.

—— and Battle, J. (1999). "Home Computers and School Performance," *Information Society*, 15(1): 1–10.

Autor, D. H. (2001). "Wiring the Labor Market," *Journal of Economic Perspectives*, 15(1): 25–40.

—— Katz, L. F., and Krueger, A. B. (1998). "Computing Inequality: Have Computers Changed the Labor Market?," *The Quarterly Journal of Economics*, 113(4): 1169–213.

Barlow, J. P. (1996). "A Declaration of the Independence of Cyberspace," *Humanist*, 56(3): 18–19.

Barron, B. (2006). "Interest and Self-Sustained Learning as Catalysts of Development: A Learning Ecology Perspective," *Human Development*, 49(4): 193–224.

Barzilai-Nahon, K. (2006). "Gaps and Bits: Conceptualizing Measurements for Digital Divide/s," *Information Society*, 22(5): 269–78.

Bennett, S., Maton, K., and Kervin, L. (2008). "The 'Digital Natives' Debate: A Critical Review of the Evidence," *British Journal of Educational Technology*, 39(5): 775–86.

Billon, M., Marco, R., and Lera-Lopez, F. (2009). "Disparities in ICT Adoption: A Multidimensional Approach to Study the Cross-Country Digital Divide," *Telecommunications Policy*, 33(10–11): 596–610.

Bimber, B. (2000). "Measuring the Gender Gap on the Internet," *Social Science Quarterly*, 81(3): 868–76.

Boase, J., Horrigan, J., Wellman, B., and Rainie, L. (2006). "The Strength of Internet Ties," Pew Internet and American Life Project, January 25. Available at <http://www.pewinternet.org/Reports/2006/The-Strength-of-Internet-Ties.aspx>. Accessed June 20, 2012.

Boneva, B. S., Kraut, R., and Frohlich, D. (2001). "Using E-Mail for Personal Relationships: The Difference Gender Makes," *American Behavioral Scientist*, 45(3): 530–49.

Bonfadelli, H. (2002). "The Internet and Knowldege Gaps: A Theoretical and Empirical Investigation," *European Journal of Communication*, 17(1): 65–84.

boyd, d. (2011). "White Flight in Networked Publics: How Race and Class Shaped American Teen Engagement with MySpace and Facebook," in L. Nakamura and P. Chow-White (eds). *Race After the Internet*, New York: Routledge.

Brandtzæg, P. B., Heim, J., and Karahasanović, A. (2011). "Understanding the New Digital Divide—A Typology of Internet Users in Europe," *International Journal of Human-Computer Studies*, 69(3): 123–38.

Brynin, M., Anderson, B., and Raban, Y. (2007). "Introduction," in B. Anderson, M. Brynin, J. Gershung, and Y. Raban (eds). *Information and Communication Technologies in Society: E-living in a Digital Europe*, London: Routledge.

Buckingham, D. (2007). "Digital Media Literacies: Rethinking Media Education in the Age of the Internet," *Research in Comparative and International Education*, 2(1): 43–55.

Buente, W. and Robbin, A. (2008). "Trends in Internet information Behavior, 2000–2004," *Journal of the American Society for Information Science and Technology*, 59(11): 1743–60.

Charness, N. and Holley, P. (2004). "The New Media and Older Adults: Usable and Useful?," *American Behavioral Scientist*, 48(4): 416–33.

Chen, W. and Wellman, B. (2005). *Minding the Cyber-Gap: The Internet and Social Inequality*, Malden, MA: Blackwell Publishing Ltd.

Chou, W. S., Hunt, Y., M., Beckjord, E. B., Moser, R. P., and Hesse, B. W. (2009). "Social Media Use in the United States: Implications for Health Communication," *Journal of Medical Internet Research*, 11(4): e48.

Compaine, B. M. (2001a). "Information Gaps," in B. Compaine (ed.). *The Digital Divide: Facing a Crisis or Creating a Myth?*, Cambridge, MA: The MIT Press.

——(ed.) (2001b). *The Digital Divide: Facing a Crisis or Creating a Myth?* Cambridge, MA: MIT Press.

Cook, T. D., Appleton, H., Conner, R. F., Shaffer, A., Tamkin, G. and Weber, S. J. (1975). *"Sesame Street" Revisited*, New York: Russel Sage Foundation.

Correa, T. (2010). "The Participation Divide Among 'Online Experts': Experience, Skills and Psychological Factors as Predictors of College Students' Web Content Creation," *Journal of Computer-Mediated Communication*, 16(1): 71–92.

Crenshaw, E. M. and Robison, K. K. (2006). "Globalization and the Digital Divide: The Roles of Structural Conduciveness and Global Connection in Internet Diffusion," *Social Science Quarterly (Blackwell Publishing Limited)*, 87(1): 190–207.

Czaja, S. J., Charness, Neil, Fisk, Arthur D., Hertzog, Christopher, Nair, Sankaran N., Rogers, Wendy A. and Sharit, J. (2006). "Factors Predicting the Use of Technology: Findings from the Center for Research and Education on Aging and Technology Enhancement (create)," *Psychology and Aging*, 21(2): 333–52.

Dholakia, R. R. (2006). "Gender and IT in the Household: Evolving Patterns of Internet Use in the United States," *Information Society*, 22(4): 231–40.

DiMaggio, P. and Bonikowski, B. (2008). "Make Money Surfing the Web? The Impact of Internet Use on the Earnings of US Workers," *American Sociological Review*, 73(2): 227–50.

——and Hargittai, E. (2001). "From the 'Digital Divide' to 'Digital Inequality': Studying Internet Use As Penetration Increases," Working Paper 15, Princeton, NJ: Center for Arts and Cultural Policy Studies at Princeton University.

——, Hargittai, E., Celeste, C., and Shafer, S. (2004). "Digital Inequality: From Unequal Access to Differentiated Use," in Kathryn Neckerman (ed.). *Social Inequality*, New York: Russell Sage, pp. 355–400.

——, Hargittai, E., Neuman, W. R., and Robinson, J. P. (2001). "Social Implications of the Internet," *Annual Review of Sociology*, 27: 307–36.

DiNardo, J. E. and Pischke, J. S. (1997). "The Returns to Computer Use Revisited: Have Pencils Changed the Wage Structure Too?," *Quarterly Journal of Economics*, 112(1): 291–303.

Drori, G. S. (2010). "Globalization and Technology Divides: Bifurcation of Policy between the 'Digital Divide' and the 'Innovation Divide'," *Sociological Inquiry*, 80(1): 63–91.

—— and Jang, Y. S. (2003). "The Global Digital Divide: A Sociological Assessment of Trends and Causes," *Social Science Computer Review*, 21(2): 144–61.

Dutton, W. H., Helsper, E. J., and Gerber, M. M. (2009). "The Internet in Britain 2009," Oxford Internet Institute, University of Oxford. Available at <http://www.oii.ox.ac.uk/research/oxis/OxIS2009_Report.pdf>. Accessed May 6, 2012.

——, Rogers, E. M., and Jun, S.-H. (1987). "Diffusion and Social Impacts of Personal Computers," *Communication Research*, 14(2): 219–50.

——, Sweet, P. L., and Rogers, E. M. (1989). "Socioeconomic Status and the Early Diffusion of Personal Computing in the United States," *Social Science Computer Review*, 7(3): 259–71.

Ellison, N. B., Steinfeld, C., and Lampe, C. (2007). "The Benefits of Facebook 'Friends': Social Capital and College Students' Use of Online Social Network Sites," *Journal of Computer-Mediated Communication*, 12(4): article 1.

Entorf, H., Gollac, M., and Kramarz, F. (1999). "New Technologies, Wages, and Worker Selection," *Journal of Labor Economics*, 17(3): 464–91.

Eshet-Alkalai, Y. (2004). "Digital Literacy: A Conceptual Framework for Survival Skills in the Digital Era," *Journal of Educational Multimedia and Hypermedia*, 13(1): 93–106.

Ettema, J. S., and Kline, F. G. (1977). "Deficits, Differences, and Ceilings: Contingent Conditions for Understanding the Knowledge Gap," *Communication Research*, 4(2): 179–202.

Eurostat. (2008). "Nearly 30 percent of Individuals Use Internet Banking," Eurostat.

—— (2009). "One Person in Two in the EU27 Uses the Internet Daily," Eurostat.

Eynon, R. (2009). "Mapping the Digital Divide in Britain: Implications for Learning and Education," *Learning, Media and Technology*, 34(4): 277–90.

—— and Helsper, E. (2011). "Adults Learning Online: Digital Choice and/or Digital Exclusion?" *New Media & Society*, 13(4): 534–51.

Fairlie, R. W., Beltran, D. O., and Das, K. K. (2010). "Home Computers and Educational Outcomes: Evidence from the NLSY97 and CPS," *Economic Inquiry*, 48(3): 771–92.

Forman, C. (2005). "The Corporate Digital Divide: Determinants of Internet Adoption," *Management Science*, 51(4): 641–54.

——, Goldfarb, A., and Greenstein, S. (2005). "The Geographic Dispersion of Commercial Internet Use," in L. F. Cranor and S. S. Wildman (eds). *Rethinking Rights and Regulations Institutional Responses to New Communications Technologies*, Cambridge, MA: MIT Press, pp. 113–45.

——, Goldfarb, A., and Greenstein, S. (2009). "The Internet and Local Wages: Convergence or Divergence?," National Bureau of Economic Research Working Paper Series No. 14750. Available at <http://www.nber.org/papers/w14750>. Accessed June 20, 2012.

Fountain, C. (2005). "Finding a Job in the Internet Age," *Social Forces*, 83(3): 1235–62.

Freese, J., Rivas, S., and Hargittai, E. (2006). "Cognitive Ability and Internet Use among Older Adults," *Poetics*, 34(4–5): 236–49.

Fuchs, T. and Woessmann, L. (2004). "Computers and Student Learning: Bivariate and Multivariate Evidence on the Availability and Use of Computers at Home and at School," CESifo Working Paper Series No. 1321. Available at <http://ideas.repec.org/p/ces/ceswps/_1321.html>. Accessed June 20, 2012.

Gaziano, C. (1983). "The Knowledge Gap: An Analytical Review of Media Effects," *Communication Research*, 10(4): 447–86.

Goodman, S. E., Press, L. I., Ruth, S. R., and Rutkowski, A. M. (1994). "The Global Diffusion of the Internet: Patterns and Problems," *Communications of the ACM*, 37(8): 27–31.

Greenberg, B. and Dervin, B. (1970). "Mass Communication among the Urban Poor," *Public Opinion Quarterly*, 34(2): 224–35.

Grusky, D. (ed.) (2008). *Social Stratification: Class, Race, and Gender in Sociological Perspective*, Boulder, CO: Westview Press.

——and Ku, M. (2008). "Gloom, Doom, and Inequality," in D. B. Grusky (ed.). *Social Stratification: Class, Race, and Gender in Sociological Perspective*, Boulder, CO: Westview Press.

Gui, M. and Argentin, G. (2011). "Digital Skills of Internet Natives: Different Forms of Digital Literacy in a Random Sample of Northern Italian High School Students," *New Media & Society*, 13(6): 963–80.

Guillén, M. F. and Suárez, S. L. (2005). "Explaining the Global Digital Divide: Economic, Political and Sociological Drivers of Cross-National Internet Use," *Social Forces*, 84(2): 681–708.

Hale, T. M., Cotten, S. R., Dremtea, P., and Goldner, M. (2010). "Rural-Urban Differences in General and Health-Related Internet Use," *American Behavioral Scientist* 53(9): 1304–25.

Halford, S. and Savage, M. (2010). "Reconceptualizing Digital Social Inequality," *Information, Communication & Society*, 13(7): 937–955.

Hampton, K. N., Sessions, L. F., Her, E. J., and Rainie, L. (2009). "Social Isolation and New Technology: How the Internet and Mobile Phones Impact Americans' Social Networks," Pew Internet and American Life Project, November 4. Available at <http://pewresearch.org/pubs/1398/internet-mobile-phones-impact-american-social-networks>. Accessed June 20, 2012.

Hampton, K. N. and Wellman, B. (2003). "Neighboring in Netville: How the Internet Supports Community and Social Capital in a Wired Suburb," *City and Community*, 2(4): 277–311.

Hargittai, E. (1999). "Weaving the Western Web: Explaining Differences in Internet Connectivity among OECD Countries," *Telecommunications Policy*, 23(10–11): 701–18.

——(2002). "Second-Level Digital Divide: Differences in People's Online Skills," in *First Monday*, 7(4). Available at <http://firstmonday.org/htbin/cgiwrap/bin/ojs/index.php/fm/article/view/942/864/>. Accessed 6 May 2012.

——(2003). *How Wide a Web? Inequalities in Accessing Information Online*, Unpublished dissertation, Sociology Department, Princeton University, Princeton, NJ.

——(2008). "The Digital Reproduction of Inequality," in D. B. Grusky, M. C. Ku, and S. Szelényi (eds). *Social Stratification: Class, Race, and Gender in Sociological Perspective*, Boulder, CO: Westview Press, pp. 936–44.

——(2010). "Digital Na(t)ives? Variation in Internet Skills and Uses among Members of the 'Net Generation'," *Sociological Inquiry*, 80(1): 92–113.

——(2011). "Open Doors, Closed Spaces? Differentiated Adoption of Social Network Sites by User Background," in P. Chow-White and L. Nakamura (eds). *Race after the Internet*, New York: Routledge.

——, Fullerton, L., Menchen-Trevino, E., and Yates Thomas, K. (2010). "Trust Online: Young Adults' Evaluation of Web Content," *International Journal of Communication*, 4: 468–94.

——and Hinnant, A. (2008). "Digital Inequality: Differences in Young Adults' Use of the Internet," *Communication Research*, 35(5): 602–21.

——and Hsieh, Y. P. (2010). "Predictors and Consequences of Differentiated Practices on Social Network Sites," *Information, Communication & Society*, 13(4): 515–36.

——and Shafer, S. (2006). "Differences in Actual and Perceived Online Skills: The Role of Gender," *Social Science Quarterly*, 87(2): 432–48.

——and Walejko, G. (2008). "The Participation Divide: Content Creation and Sharing in the Digital Age," *Information, Communication & Society*, 11(2): 239–56.

Hassani, S. N. (2006). "Locating Digital Divides at Home, Work, and Everywhere Else." *Poetics*. 34(4–5): 250–72.

Haythornthwaite, C. and Rice, R. E. (2006). "Perspectives on Internet Use: Access, Involvement and Interaction," in L. A. Lievrouw and S. Livingstone (eds). *The Handbook of New Media: Social Shaping and Social Consequences of ICTs*, Thousand Oaks, CA: SAGE Publication, pp. 92–113.

Helsper, E. J. (2010). "Gendered Internet Use across Generations and Life Stages," *Communication Research*, 37(3): 352–74.

Herring, S. (1996). "Bringing Familiar Baggage to the New Frontier: Gender Differences in Computer-Mediated Communication," in V. Vitanza (ed.). *CyberReader*, Boston, MA: Allyn & Bacon, pp. 144–54.

Hoffman, D. L. and Novak, T. P. (1998). "Bridging the Racial Divide on the Internet," *Science*, 280(5362): 390–1.

Horrigan, John B. (2009). "Home Broadband Adoption (2009)," Pew Internet and American Life Project, June 17. Available at <http://www.pewinternet.org/Reports/2009/10-Home-Broadband-Adoption-2009.aspx>. Accessed June 20, 2012.

Howard, P. E. N., Rainie, L. E. E., and Jones, S. (2001). "Days and Nights on the Internet: The Impact of a Diffusing Technology," *American Behavioral Scientist*, 45(3): 383–404.

Hsieh, Y. P. and Hargittai, E. (2010). "Social Capital and Communication Multiplexity in Social Relationship Maintenance: An Alternative Theoretical Approach," Paper presented at the annual meeting of the American Sociological Association Annual, August 14. Atlanta GA.

ITU (International Telecommunication Union) (2010). "Measuring the Information Society 2010." Available at <http://www.itu.int/ITU-D/ict/publications/idi/index.html>. Accessed June 20, 2012.

Junco, R. and Cotten, S. R. (2011). "Perceived Academic Effects of Instant Messaging Use," *Computers and Education*, 56(2): 370–8.

Kadushin, C. (2004). "Too Much Investment in Social Capital?," *Social Networks*, 26(1): 75–90.

Katz, J. E. and Rice, R. E. (2002). "Syntopia: Access, Civic Involvement and Social Interaction on the Internet," in B. Wellman and C. Haythornthwaite (eds). *The Internet in Everyday Life*, Oxford, UK: Blackwell, pp. 114–38.

Kirschenbaum, J. and Kunamneni, R. (2001). "Bridging the Organizational Divide: Toward a Comprehensive Approach to the Digital Divide." A PolicyLink Report. Available at <http://www.policylink.org/atf/cf/%7B97C6D565-BB43-406D-A6D5-ECA3BBF35AF0%7D/BridgingtheOrgDivide_final.pdf>. Accessed June 20, 2012.

Kraut, R., Kiesler, S., Boneva, B., Cummings, J., Helgeson, V., and Crawford, A. (2002). "Internet Paradox Revisited," *Journal of Social Issues*, 58(1): 49–74.

Kraut, R., Patterson, M., Lundmark, V., Kiesler, S., Tridas, M., and Scherlis, W. (1998). "Internet Paradox: A Social Technology that Reduces Social Involvement and Psychological Well-being?," *American Psychologist*, 53(9): 1017–31.

Krueger, A. B. (1993). "How Computers Have Changed the Wage Structure: Evidence from Microdata, 1984–1989," *The Quarterly Journal of Economics*, 108(1): 33–60.

Kubey, R. W., Lavin, M. J., and Barrows, J. R. (2001). "Internet Use and Collegiate Academic Performance Decrements: Early Findings," *Journal of Communication*, 51(2): 366–382.

LaRose, R., Gregg, J. L., Strover, S., Straubhaar, J., and Carpenter, S. (2007). "Closing the Rural Broadband Gap: Promoting Adoption of the Internet in Rural America," *Telecommunications Policy*, 31(6–7): 359–73.

Livingstone, S. and Helsper, E. (2007). "Gradations in Digital Inclusion: Children, Young People and the Digital Divide," *New Media & Society*, 9(4): 671–96.

Livingstone, S. and Helsper, E. (2010). "Balancing Opportunities and Risks in Teenagers' Use of the Internet: The Role of Online Skills and Internet Self-Efficacy," *New Media & Society*, 12(2): 309–29.

Loges, W. E. and Jung, J.-Y. (2001). "Exploring the Digital Divide: Internet Connectedness and Age," *Communication Research*, 28(4): 536–62.

McPherson, M., Smith-Lovin, L., and Brashears, M. E. (2006). "Social Isolation in America: Changes in Core Discussion Networks over Two Decades," *American Sociological Review*, 71(3): 353–75.

Menchen-Trevino, E. and Hargittai, E. (2011). "Young Adults' Credibility Assessment of Wikipedia," *Information, Communication & Society*, 14(1): 24–51.

Metzger, M. J. (2007). "Making Sense of Credibility on the Web: Models for Evaluating Online Information and Recommendations for Future Research," *Journal of the American Society for Information Science and Technology*, 58(13): 2078–91.

Mesch, G. and Talmud, I. (2011). "Ethnic Differences in Internet Access", *Information, Communication and Society*, 14(4), 445–71.

Mossberger, K., Tolbert, C. J., and Stansbury, M. (2003). *Virtual Inequality: Beyond the Digital Divide*, Washington, DC: Georgetown University Press.

Nie, N., Hillygus, S., and Erbring, L. (2002). "Internet Use, Interpersonal Relations and Sociability: A Time Diary Study," in B. Wellman and C. Haythornthwaite (eds). *The Internet in Everyday Life*, Oxford: Blackwell, pp. 244–62.

Norris, P. (2001). *Digital Divide? Civic Engagement, Information Poverty & the Internet Worldwide*, New York: Cambridge University Press.

—— (2004). "The Bridging and Bonding Role of Online Communities," in P. N. Howard and S. G. Jones (eds). *Society Online: The Interaction in Context*, Thousand Oaks, CA: SAGE Publication, pp. 31–42.

NTIA (National Telecommunications and Information Administration) (1995). "Falling through the Net: A Survey of the "Have Nots" in Rural and Urban America," Washington, DC: US Department of Commerce.

—— (1998). "Falling Through the Net II: New Data on the Digital Divide," Washington, DC: US Department of Commerce.

—— (1999). "Falling Through the Net: Defining the Digital Divide," Washington, DC: US Department of Commerce.

—— (2000). "Falling Through the Net: Toward Digital Inclusion," Washington, DC: US Department of Commerce.

—— (2002). "A Nation Online: Internet Use in America," Washington, DC: US Department of Commerce.

—— (2004). "A Nation Online: Entering the Broadband Age," Washington, DC: US Department of Commerce.

—— (2010). "Digital Nation: 21st Century America's Progress Towards Universal Broadband Internet Access," Washington, DC: US Department of Commerce.

Ono, H. and Zavodny, M. (2003). "Gender and the Internet," *Social Science Quarterly*, 84: 111–21.

—— and Zavodny, M. (2007). "Digital Inequality: A Five Country Comparison Using Nicrodata," *Social Science Research*, 36(3): 1135–55.

Page, K. and Uncles, M. (2004). "Consumer Knowledge of the World Wide Web: Conceptualization and Measurement," *Psychology & Marketing*, 21(8): 573–91.

Pasek, J., more, e., and Hargittai, E. (2009). "Facebook and Academic Performance: Reconciling a Media Sensation with Data," *First Monday* 14(5). Available at: <http://firstmonday.org/htbin/cgiwrap/bin/ojs/index.php/fm/article/view/2498/2181/>. Accessed June 20, 2012.

——, More, E., and Romer, D. (2009). "Realizing the Social Internet? Online Social Networking Meets Offline Civic Engagement," *Journal of Information Technology & Politics*, 6(3–4): 197–215.

Prensky, M. (2001). "Digital Natives, Digital Immigrants," *On the Horizon* 9(5): 1–6.

Press, L. (1996). "The Role of Computer Networks in Development," *Communications of the ACM*, 39(2): 23–30.

Putnam, R. D. (2001). *Bowling Alone: The Collapse and Revival of American Community*, New York: Simon and Schuster.

Quan-Haase, A., Wellman, B., Witte, J. C., and Hampton, K. N. (2002). "Capitalizing on the Internet: Network Capital, Participatory Capital, and Sense of Community," in B. Wellman and C. Haythornthwaite (eds). *The Internet in Everyday Life*, Oxford: Blackwell, pp. 291–324.

Raban, Y. (2007). "Trends in ICTs," in B. Anderson, M. Brynin, J. Gershung, and Y. Raban, *Information and Communication Technologies in Society: E-living in a Digital Europe*, London: Routledge, pp. 18–30.

Rainie, L. and Wellman, B. (2012). *Networked: The New Social Operating System*, Cambridge, MA: MIT Press.

Reuters. (1997). "Negroponte: Internet is Way to World Peace," *CNN Interactive*, November 25. Available at <http://www.cnn.com/TECH/9711/25/internet.peace.reut/>. Accessed May 6, 2012.

Rheingold, H. (1993). *The Virtual Community: Homestanding on the Electronic Frontier*, Reading, MA: Addison-Wesley.

Rothbaum, F., Martland, N., and Jannsen, J. B. (2008). "Parents' Reliance on the Web to find Information about Children and Families: Socio-Economic Differences in Use, Skills and Satisfaction," *Journal of Applied Developmental Psychology*, 29(2): 118–28.

Schradie, J. (2011). "The Digital Production Gap: The Digital Divide and Web 2.0 Collide," *Poetics*, 39(2): 145–68.

Selwyn, N., Gorard, S., Furlong, J., and Madden, L. (2003). "Older Adults' Use of Information and Communications Technology in Everyday Life," *Ageing & Society*, 23(5): 561–82.

Shah, D. V., Cho, J., Eveland, W. P. J. R., and Kwak, N. (2005). "Information and Expression in a Digital Age: Modeling Internet Effects on Civic Participation," *Communication Research*, 32(5): 531–65.

Smith, A. (2010). "Home Broadband 2010," Pew Internet and American Life Project, August 11. Available at <http://pewinternet.org/Reports/2010/Home-Broadband-2010.aspx>. Accessed June 20, 2012.

—— (2011). "Smartphone Adoption and Usage," Pew Internet and American Life Project, July 11. Available at <http://pewinternet.org/Reports/2011/Smartphones.aspx>. Accessed June 20, 2012.

Steinfield, C., Ellison, N. B., and Lampe, C. (2008). "Social Capital, Self-Esteem, and Use of Online Social Network Sites: A Longitudinal Analysis," *Journal of Applied Developmental Psychology*, 29(6): 434–45.

Stern, M. J., Adams, A. E., and Elsasser, S. (2009). "Digital Inequality and Place: The Effects of Technological Diffusion on Internet Proficiency and Usage across Rural, Suburban, and Urban Counties," *Sociological Inquiry*, 79(4): 391–417.

Stevenson, B. (2009). "The Internet and Job Search," in D. H. Autor (ed.). *Studies of Labor Market Intermediation*, Chicago: University of Chicago Press, pp. 67–86.

Tichenor, P. J., Donohue, G. A., and Olien, C. N. (1970). "Mass Media Flow and Differential Growth in Knowledge," *Public Opinion Quarterly*, 34(2): 159–70.

Van Deursen, A. J. A. M. (2010). "Internet Skills: Vital Assets in an Information Society," Thesis, Department of Communication, University of Twente: Enscheded, Netherlands. Available at <http://doc.utwente.nl/75133/1/thesis_van_Deursen.pdf>. Accessed June 20, 2012.

van Dijk, Jan A. G. M. (2005). *The Deepening Divide: Inequality in the Information Society.* London: Sage Publications.

Vigdor, Jacob L., and Ladd, Helen F. (2010). "Scaling the Digital Divide: Home Computer Technology and Student Achievement," in *NBER Working Paper Series.*

Warschauer, Mark (2003). *Technology and Social Inclusion: Rethinking the Digital Divide,* Cambridge, MA: MIT Press.

Wasserman, Ira M., and Richmond-Abbott, Marie (2005). "Gender and the Internet: Causes of Variation in Access, Level, and Scope of Use*," *Social Science Quarterly* 86(1): 252–70.

Weiser, Eric B. (2000). "Gender Differences in Internet Use Patterns and Internet Application Preferences: A Two-Sample Comparison," *CyberPsychology & Behavior,* 3(2):167–78.

Wellman, Barry, Salaff, Janet, Dimitrova, Dimitrina, Garton, Laura, Gulia, Milena, and Haythornthwaite, Caroline (1996). "Computer Networks as Social Networks: Collaborative Work, Telework and Virtual Community," *Annual Review of Sociology* 22: 211–38.

Wilson, Ernest J., III. (2004). *The Information Revolution and Developing Countries,* Cambridge, MA: MIT Press.

Wilson, Kenneth R., Wallin, Jennifer S., and Reiser, Christa (2003). "Social Stratification and the Digital Divide," *Social Science Computer Review* 21(2): 133–43.

World Internet Project. (2010). "World Internet Project: International Report 2010," Los Angeles, CA: USC Annenberg School Center for the Digital Future. Press release about the report available from <http://www.worldinternetproject.net/_files/_Published/_oldis/wip2010_long_press_release.pdf>. Accessed May 6, 2012.

Wu, X. (2008). "When Pirated Films Met the Internet: The Chinese Cultural Public Sphere of Movies in an Unorthodox Globalization." Paper presented at the 2008 Annual Conference of the International Association of Media and Communication Research. Stockholm, Sweden. July.

Zhang, Chan, Callegaro, Mario and Thomas, Melanie (2008). "More than the Digital Divide? Investigating the Differences between Internet and Non-Internet Users," in *Annual Conference of the Midwest Association for Public Opinion Research*, Chicago, IL.

Zillien, Nicole, and Hargittai, Eszter (2009). "Digital Distinction: Status-Specific Types of Internet Uses," *Social Science Quarterly* 90(2): 274–91.

CHAPTER 8

SOCIALITY THROUGH SOCIAL NETWORK SITES

NICOLE B. ELLISON AND DANAH M. BOYD

INTRODUCTION

THE global system of networked computers, servers, and routers known as the Internet has transformed many aspects of modern society and social interaction. The online distribution of goods and services, for instance, has influenced almost every industry and has radically transformed many. Alongside commerce-oriented technological development has been a rise in what has been termed "social media." One of the most significant developments connected to social media is the rise of social network sites (SNSs) such as Facebook, LinkedIn, MySpace, Cyworld, and Google Plus. Although sites of this nature first emerged around 1997, they rose to cultural significance as a phenomenon in 2003, when Friendster first attracted mass media attention. Less than a decade later, millions of people of all ages across the globe have joined SNSs (Anderson and Bernoff 2010). In the US, 65 percent of Internet-using US adults report using social network sites such as Facebook, MySpace, or LinkedIn (Madden and Zickuhr 2011).

In the early stages of this phenomenon, terminology varied widely with the inter-changeable use of "social networking sites," "online social networks," or even simply, "social networks" to refer to a diffuse—and sometimes improbable—range of sites and services. In boyd and Ellison (2007), we attempted to stabilize the discussion by offering a definition of social network sites:

> web-based services that allow individuals to (1) construct a public or semi-public profile within a bounded system, (2) articulate a list of other users with whom they share a connection, and (3) view and traverse their list of connections and those made by others within the system.

This definition served a need, but the social and technical landscape of these sites has changed dramatically since then. In this chapter, we document some of the ways

SNSs have evolved since 2007, place their evolution within a context of Web 2.0 and scholarship on computer-mediated communication, and discuss some of the opportunities and challenges embedded in the study of social media and social network sites.

As SNSs proliferate and evolve, defining what constitutes a social network site becomes increasingly challenging. Some of the features that initially distinguished them have faded in significance, while others have been reproduced by other genres of social media. Media-sharing websites, gaming sites, and locative media all encourage participants to list contacts and "Friends," making this affordance a poor criterion for distinguishing between social network sites and other genres. Meanwhile, other features, such as media streams like Facebook's "News Feed," have emerged as more salient components of the SNS user experience. Blurring things further, open application programming interfaces (APIs) and other platform technologies have enabled countless third-party websites to develop on top of social network sites or to integrate the social graph from popular social network sites into other tools and sites. Search engines and news sites surface Facebook and Twitter content, while MySpace allows people to use their Facebook credentials on MySpace, blurring the distinction between the two sites. In short, the technical affordances that define a social network site have become increasingly fluid. Of course, people's practices, expectations, and social norms have also co-evolved alongside the technical features and social interaction opportunities.

Scholars face a unique challenge in trying to investigate this rapidly moving phenomenon, as they struggle to understand people's practices while the very systems through which they are enacted shift. Even efforts to describe social network sites themselves are challenged by the ongoing evolution of the phenomenon. While scholars conscientiously describe *who* they are studying, they are less likely to describe the state of the technology at the particular moment in which they are studying it. As we will argue later, this compromises scholars' ability to synthesize different studies and discern higher order patterns.

In this chapter, we begin by reconsidering how to define a social network site given the shifts in technology and practice. We examine the three primary features—profiles, connection lists, and traversing—and offer an alternate definition that we believe will provide a more useful analytic framework for interpreting and understanding social network sites as they have evolved, fully recognizing that things may continue to shift in unexpected ways. To more properly contextualize social network sites, we situate them within the broader landscapes of the entrepreneurial tech scene of "Web 2.0" and the evolution of computer-mediated communication (CMC) scholarship. We conclude by discussing the opportunities and challenges associated with research on social network sites, arguing that researchers must attend to both the technical and the social components of these socio-technical systems when they design and report their work. In sum, this chapter examines how the genre of social network sites has evolved over time and offers thoughts on how scholarship might adapt to the rapid rate of innovation inherent in this space.

THE ORIGINS AND RAPID EVOLUTION
OF SOCIAL NETWORK SITES

In 2007, the three defining features of a social network site appeared to be the profile, the connections lists, and the functional ability to traverse those connections. As social network sites have evolved, the salience of these features has shifted. Most notably, the role of the profile has changed, as media streams have increasingly taken a more prominent role and the activity of "updating" has become less burdensome. Meanwhile, the articulation of contacts has become more central, both because of the rise of media streams and because of third-party technologies that incorporate the "social graph" as a way of organizing content. In contrast, the act of traversing did not change from a technical perspective, but became less central over time.

A public or semi-public profile

Lacking visible bodies, self-representation in online spaces offers participants many possibilities to actively construct a representation of how they would like to be identified. In some contexts, an online identity is explicitly linked to an offline presence—for instance, online dating profiles represent a person who is, presumably, available for future offline interactions (Ellison et al. 2012). In other contexts, the linkage to an offline presence is less salient. For instance, the reputation associated with a particular pseudonym on an online discussion site may exist independently of the offline identity (Donath 1998). Yet, in all cases, making oneself visible to others requires the enactment of a digital identity. Most CMC services encourage participants to create a screen name or use another identifier—such as an email address—to uniquely identify themselves. Early on, chatrooms and bulletin boards introduced the notion of a profile, linking personal information provided by individuals to their screen name. Profiles grew out of earlier UNIX-based protocols where users entered information into .project and .plan files that were displayed when others ran a "finger" command on them. With the rise of the World Wide Web, homepages became an important site of identification, as early web users posted biographies, photos, and entertaining links for viewers who surfed to their page (Döring 2002). Online communities and related genres of CMC began incorporating profiles into their services. Profiles were especially important for sites that were designed to broker offline relationships among members, such as online dating sites; users of these sites were typically invited to upload photos and fill out detailed questionnaires that included demographic information, interests, and open-ended spaces for self-description.

Early social network sites like Friendster were designed with dating in mind and were thus profile-centric in nature, organized explicitly around a set of profiles that represented individuals within the system. Friendster's profiles closely resembled those typically found in online dating sites and included options for uploading a profile photograph and fields for self-descriptive text. Early social network sites generally adopted this same profile format, with two notable differences. Unlike online dating profiles, SNS profiles included a Friends list, consisting of names and photos representing a subset of the user's connections (e.g. MySpace's "Top 8") and a public space for visitor-supplied comments (e.g. "Testimonials" on Friendster or the "Wall" on Facebook).

The first SNS profiles were primarily designed to be relatively static portraits, explicitly constructed through text and other media provided by the profile owner, and only updated when the individual felt the need to do so. Yet, because of the Friends list and comments section, SNS profiles were often updated simply through the actions of others—a change in a Friend's photograph or a new "Testimonial" would alter the content on that individual's profile. Because social network site profiles are located within a web of relationships and those relationships are made visible on profiles, social network site profiles are *co-constructed*. Current SNS profiles increasingly include multiple channels through which individuals can contribute to and shape the profiles of their Friends.

In 2007, two types of SNSs were dominant: profile-centric sites, like LinkedIn and MySpace, and media-centric sites like LiveJournal, Flickr, and YouTube. A third type of SNS—location-focused services like Dodgeball—were still primarily the domain of early adopters in urban centers. While media-centric sites also included profiles, profiles were de-emphasized as destinations; rather, the structure of these sites highlighted the most recently updated content. While many contemporary location-based services like Foursquare and Gowalla technically have profiles, they are very rarely accessed. As social network sites matured as a genre, profiles simultaneously lost their centrality and also became the product of aggregated media, personal updates, and system-generated content based on user activity.

Over time, SNSs introduced various features that made it possible for individuals to easily update their profiles. Although present in the beginning, commenting became more central with the rise of media sharing and the popularization of updating. Facebook's "status updates," Twitter's "tweets," and MySpace's "status and mood" are all examples of opportunities that SNSs provide to encourage users to create content to share with their contacts in response to prompts like "[username] is …," "Tell your friends what you are doing right now", or "What are you doing right now?" As the cost of storing photos and videos declined, SNSs also began to support large-scale media sharing; mobile applications made posting photographs and videos easy. Features that made it easier for users to post lightweight content to their profiles while simultaneously sharing it with Friends enhanced profiles by making them more dynamic, but in the process made the basic profile increasingly irrelevant as a destination.

Over time, the profile has shifted from a self-presentational message created by the individual to a portrait of an individual as an expression of action, a node in a series of groups, and a repository of self- and other-provided data. This combats one of the central problems that emerged with social network site profiles—they grew stale and, as such, started to resemble an abandoned space. In some ways, by 2011 sites like Friendster felt like a dormant snapshot of 2003, a collection of portraits that had been left unaltered since users abandoned the site for more vibrant spaces. Streams of quotidian, ephemeral content encourage people to participate more in that they provide an initial artifact around which others can engage. Features that support actions associated with status updates—the ability to post comments to, share, or register interest in an update—also encourage a stream of activity that is prompted by an update but often takes on a life of its own in the central stream. Today's SNSs are more like news aggregators than they are like profile-based contexts, even if the algorithm for displaying content is quite obfuscated. On some SNSs, a user's "profile" might consist solely of their activities on the site (such as media they have contributed) and list of contacts, with none of the user-supplied biographical data associated with traditional profiles.

Today's profiles are not simply self-descriptive, static text, but rather a dynamic combination of content provided by the user (such as status updates), activity reports (such as groups they've joined), content provided by others (such as virtual gifts that are displayed on the profile or "tagged" photographs uploaded by others), and/or system-provided content (such as a subset of one's Friend network and activities on third-party sites.)

The "Friends" list

The ability to delineate someone as a public contact—or "Friend"[1]—and thus create an aggregated list that constitutes one's network on the site is the key differentiating feature of SNSs. Earlier communication tools enabled individuals to create a private list of contacts (for instance a buddy list on instant messaging), to establish a group of contacts that were shared by others (such as a listserv membership list), or to publish a list of related links (such as a blogroll), but SNSs extended the practice of creating a publicly visible, personally curated list of contacts and made it a mainstream practice.

The connections between people—and, thus, profiles—serve multiple purposes on a social network site. They are employed to mark and display relationships, delineate who can access what content, and serve as a filter through which viewers can browse profiles and discover friends in common. For users, these connections represent what sociologists refer to as a person's *social network*—the collection of social relations of varying strengths and importance that a person maintains.

Friending practices are at the core of SNS activity, but are often misunderstood by popular press narratives that assume that because these sites use a global term, users are unable to distinguish among kinds of relationships in their circle. An early study noted that the global label of "Friends" may have introduced confusion among users: "it is often difficult for two users who both call each other a friend to know if they are talking about the same thing" (Fono and Raynes-Goldie 2006). Yet, there is no evidence that SNS users are unable to distinguish different kinds of relationships within their SNS

[1] We capitalize Friends when we are referring to the connections on a SNS in order to differentiate these connections from the colloquial reference to friendship. When people use SNSs, they often identify friends, acquaintances, celebrities, and many others as "Friends" (Parks 2010).

network. When asked, users report about 25–30 percent of their total Facebook Friends are "actual" friends (Ellison et al. 2011a; Ellison et al. 2011b), suggesting that users are in fact able to discern between these relationships although they all use the same label on the SNS.

Initially, SNS "Friends lists" were predominantly reciprocal, meaning that a link between two people was only instantiated when both parties agreed. As Twitter grew popular, so did the notion that relationships could be uni-directional, with people following others who did not reciprocate. Google Plus launched with directed connections and, in 2011, Facebook began to allow people to "subscribe" to others. Even for systems in which reciprocal friendship links are necessary, the ability to "hide" updates from a Friend or to limit the ability of some Friends to see updates allows for more asymmetrical disclosure of information. These more flexible arrangements may give users more freedom to express complex connections, but the tools to negotiate these relationships are often too complicated to be truly usable.

In offline contexts, we maintain many different kinds of relationships, ranging from weak ties to strong connections, which exist in multiple contexts such as work, family, and hobby or school-based groups. Having to simultaneously present oneself to different groups in the same social encounter can be challenging and predates the Internet (Meyrowitz 1985; Leary 1995). As SNSs became more popular with a wider range of individuals, many individuals' contact lists became more diverse as these users Friended people representing a range of contexts (family, professional contacts, church members, etc.). This growing diversity has contributed to cases of "context collapse," which describes the ways in which individuals that we know from different social contexts come together in SNSs in potentially uncomfortable ways (Marwick and boyd 2011). Over time, the size of users' Friends lists has grown, in part because SNS users don't tend to delete old connections, even if they lose touch with those people.

Social network site designers have developed different approaches to help people manage large networks. MySpace introduced the "Top 8" (eventually relabeled "Top Friends") to allow participants to choose eight contacts that would be highlighted on their profile page; MySpace assumed that people would list the people whose profiles they visited the most often, but this feature was often used to publicly display important connections. Facebook took a more algorithmic approach, attempting to assess the importance of a user's Friends in order to prioritize updates, but allowing users to tweak these formulae by "hiding" certain kinds of content in their news stream. Some SNSs— including Facebook, Twitter, Google Plus, and YouTube—have allowed people to create different types of lists to organize their connections privately so that participants can consume only content from or limit content to people on those lists. Google Plus allows users to place others into "circles" as a way of organizing incoming and outgoing content and does not require symmetrical linking.

The rise of open APIs and developer platforms meant that these collections of articulated contacts became valuable in contexts outside that particular SNS. Engineers and entrepreneurs alike began talking about the "social graph"—the global network of linkages between all individuals within a system (Fitzpatrick and Recordon 2007). This language emerged at a time when commercial entities began to believe that the social graph had value beyond the individual's relationship with a given social network site. Marketers started recognizing the economic potential of using the social graph for advertising purposes, while media companies realized that they could leverage the social graph to shape the flow of information. From an engineering perspective, user experience designers recognized that the more accurately a system could discern the relationship between two users, the more valuable its recommendations would be and the more relevant the content displayed to the user.

As the social graph has risen in significance, companies have begun leveraging it to do more complex algorithmic work, such as suggest relevant content, offer recommended contacts, and provide targeted advertisements. At a broader industry level, SNSs are metamorphosing from a destination site to a platform that enables third-party developers to build software on top of the social graph. Companies have begun exposing the social graph through APIs and negotiating deals to help connect information with people through their relationships.[2] For example, technologies like "Facebook Connect" allow other websites to suggest unique content based on a person's Facebook Friends list. In this way, the social graph of SNSs is increasingly used beyond the bounded space of the SNS itself.

View and traverse connections

When people first flocked to SNSs, the ability to traverse one's own connections and those of others was a critical and defining component of SNSs. Yet, as profiles faded, media streams emerged, Friends lists became more infrastructural; traversing connections has lost its salience as the core participation activity. The ability to see—and traverse—others' contact lists was innovative and important in several ways. From an adoption perspective, it enabled users to find shared contacts easily, thus lowering the barriers to initiating contact with other users and enabling users to harness network effects more easily. From a social perspective, it allowed people to easily see the relationships between others, to reconnect with old friends and acquaintances, and to travel through the network in a way that enhanced social interactions. Although some SNSs may enable users to hide portions of their network, the critical point here is that the design of the site makes it possible to display one's articulated network and that this is the default and typical setting.

Prior to social network sites, the closest analog to the traversable Friends list was the construction of blogrolls on blogs. Individual bloggers often listed other sites that they respected, providing an HTML link pointing to them. This allowed visitors on Blog A to surf to Blog B. The flow of information was unilateral, though, so visitors who stumbled upon Blog B were unable to see that Blog A recommended Blog B. This was because blogrolls were, by and large, manually inserted and maintained, and the structure of many blog platforms did not support display of this information. Services like LiveJournal and

---

[2] Google, Facebook, and Twitter all provide APIs that allow third parties to leverage the social graph. Conferences like O'Reilly's Strata connect people who are working with the kinds of data provided by these APIs, and books like Russell (2011) provide technical guidance for engineers.

Xanga—retrospectively viewable as a cross between blog platforms and SNSs—were some of the first services to make traversing the network possible.

The visibility and traversability of connections through articulated tie lists of "Friends" or "Followers" is still common on SNSs, and has become an assumed property of publicly accessible Friends lists. Yet, one significant shift has unfolded: the traversability of connections has become more important for machines than users. As APIs make the social graph available to broader audiences, algorithms are being designed to traverse the graph and learn about the individual nodes' relationship to one another. Such machine learning is the backbone of search engine technology, but it is increasingly central to the development of social network sites.

As social network sites have become mainstream, traversing the connections between people to view profiles is no longer the sole—or, even primary—way of participation. Content is surfaced through streams, and each piece of content is embedded with numerous links to other content nuggets. While early iterations of sites like Friendster allowed users to browse interests to find other people, more recent SNSs have evolved to make nearly everything traversable. Features like Twitter's "hashtags" allow people to pivot off of topics: clicking on a hashtag will reveal all other posts referencing that term. On Facebook, the vast majority of profile content has become clickable, allowing people to traverse everything from alma mater to tagged content. Although early social network sites provided numerous points of navigation, Friends lists were the most notable; today, they have faded into the background as sites increasingly offer countless alternate discovery pathways.

DEFINITION 2.0

Given the evolution of social network sites—and the importance of these sites in popular culture—it is important to reconsider how to define them. The definition that we offered in 2007, while useful, does not accurately describe the landscape of SNSs today. As of this writing, we believe the following is a more accurate and nuanced definition:

> A social network site is a *networked communication platform* in which participants 1) have *uniquely identifiable profiles* that consist of user-supplied content, content provided by other users, and/or system-level data; 2) can *publicly articulate connections* that can be viewed and traversed by others; and 3) can consume, produce, and/or interact with *streams of user-generated content* provided by their connections on the site.

We still believe the term "social network sites" is more accurate than "social networks" (which is a sociological term for one's social relationships), "social networking" (which evokes a practice of actively seeking connections and also happens offline), "online social networks" (one's online connections more generally), or "social networking sites" (which emphasizes connecting to new people). The term "social network site" rightfully emphasizes that these are sites that enable individuals to articulate public lists of connections—to present a social network and to view others' networks. This ability is what differentiates social network sites from earlier forms of online interaction spaces and the term "social network site" highlights the role of the network (as a noun) as opposed to the practice of networking (as a verb).

The desire to communicate and share content is a primary driver of SNS use. These interactions are supported through a variety of communication-oriented features. Almost every aspect of SNS user activity is fundamentally enhanced by the ability of SNSs to lower the barriers to communication and sharing and thus reshape the kinds of networks that people are able to build and support. Many of the weak tie relationships articulated on SNSs would fade away were it not for the ease with which people can communicate, share, and maintain simple connections. For this reason, this new definition positions social network sites first and foremost as a communication platform, while also highlighting the importance of sharing content, typically consumed through a stream.

All SNSs support multiple modes of communication: one-to-many and one-to-one, synchronous and asynchronous, textual and media-based. On most social network sites, these features can be public or more private. Features like comments on Facebook, @ replies on Twitter, and shouts on Foursquare allow people to communicate with their network of Friends in ways that are visible to broad audiences. Meanwhile, many SNSs have private messaging or chat features that allow for more intimate dialogue. Importantly, through features such as the ability to comment on Friends' content or social gaming, users are able to communicate with the networks of their Friends. These Friends of Friends may be useful sources of novel information and diverse perspectives. The context of the SNS—such as the fact that these users share a Friend in common and are communicating in a semi-public forum—may support more productive exchanges than those that take place in other online fora such as anonymous chat rooms where accountability and motivation are lower.

As part of a broader shift echoed in other social media, SNSs have become more media-centric and less profile-centric. By 2011, most social network sites were organized around a stream of recently updated content, whether in the form of Facebook's News Feed or as the landing page on Twitter and Tumblr. Naaman, Boase, and Lai (2010) refer to these streams as "social awareness streams." On most social network sites, each person's stream is populated with content provided by those whom they've chosen to Friend or follow. Spaces for media sharing—whether text, video, or photos—are also nearly universal on popular social network sites; the availability of this content is often announced in the stream of updates. On some sites, automated messages about people's actions on the site are also posted in the stream. The aggregated collection of media and text from one's Friends serves as the point of departure for other activities on the site or the Web, replacing the act of surfing from profile to profile to discover updated content.

Social network sites have evolved, but their foundational activities—sharing content with a bounded group of users—are fundamentally the same. The significance of profiles in the user experience has declined, but profiles as spaces for self-presentation and content distribution are still the anchor of social network sites. Friends lists are still the core organizing principle, but have gone from being a way of knitting together profiles to becoming the "social graph" backbone. Most importantly, the implicit role of communication and information sharing has become the driving motivator for participation.

SITUATING SOCIAL NETWORK SITES IN CONTEXT

In essence, social network sites are a computer-mediated communication (CMC) genre that emerged during an industry-wide innovation boom referred to as the "Web 2.0" phenomenon, and thus is part of a category of tools referred to as "social media." In order to understand the significance of SNSs and the practices that unfolded around them, it is important to contextualize them against the backdrop of Web 2.0 and situate them within the framework of CMC scholarship more generally.

The Web 2.0 phenomenon

When Friendster first gained widespread attention in 2003—prompting numerous imitators—social network sites were quickly labeled as one type of "social software" in what would be later described as the "Web 2.0" phenomenon. While many scholars have eschewed these labels, arguing that there's nothing about "social software" that couldn't be addressed through existing academic frames such as "virtual communities" or "computer-supported cooperative work," many in Silicon Valley were enamored by the potential of this new wave of innovation.

Functionally speaking, there was very little new about social software—or, as the technologies would later be called, "social media." Many of the prominent features, such as the ability to host photographs online or the ability to update a web page, had existed for years. What makes "social media" significant as a category is not the technology, but rather the socio-technical dynamics that unfolded as millions of people embraced the technology and used it to collaborate, share information, and socialize. Popular genres of social media integrated the public nature of interest-driven CMC with the more intimate dynamics of interpersonal CMC. For instance, news aggregator sites like Reddit and Digg enable individuals to post links to news stories online as well as comment and vote on them, reshaping the economics of attention in a way that enabled bottom-up filtering of online content. Meanwhile, SNSs have become a genre of social media that lowers barriers to communication, facilitates the display of identity information, and enables like-minded individuals to easily discern their common ground, thus helping users cultivate socially relevant interactions (Ellison et al. 2011a).

Web 2.0 means different things to different people. Tim O'Reilly is usually credited with popularizing the term, although the moniker dates back to the 1990s. In organizing the first Web 2.0 conference, O'Reilly and John Battelle sought to discuss how the Web could serve as a platform (O'Reilly 2005). Their approach paralleled how technologists and entrepreneurs generally viewed Web 2.0.

At a technical level, Web 2.0 signaled a shift from server-driven back-end websites to front-end centric ones powered by Javascript, Ruby on Rails, and other web development packages. Procedurally, Web 2.0 meant moving from a model of "design, develop, and deploy" to an iterative development process known as the "perpetual beta." MySpace's approach to development illustrates this mindset. In the early years of the site, MySpace launched new features frequently based on watching what people did with the service, eschewing traditional in-house quality control and instead relying on users to indicate what was working and what wasn't, what they liked and what they didn't.

For the business community, Web 2.0 represented a potential return to the irrational exuberance of the dot com boom. In many ways, the "2.0" moniker refers to the potential for Silicon Valley to recover from the collapse of the first Web-related boom. As such, Web 2.0 signaled a return of venture capitalists, entrepreneurs, and a new battle over power and status in the technology scene (Marwick 2010).

While the technical and business aspects of Web 2.0 are significant in and of themselves, more germane to this discussion are the cultural shifts that came with Web 2.0. In short, Web 2.0 brought online communities into the mainstream. Although online communities have been in existence since the earliest days of the internet—and services like AOL made online communities accessible to more mainstream internet users—they have not been the central focus of most internet users. Prior to Web 2.0, people spent the bulk of their time online browsing websites and engaging with email, instant messaging, and casual gaming; actively participating in online communities was still considered geeky. Social network sites reconfigured people's engagement with online communities because they signaled a shift from interest-driven to friendship-driven spaces. Rather than going to an online community to meet others who were interested in a particular topic or hobby, people primarily turned to social network sites like Facebook to publicly engage with people they already knew (Ellison et al. 2007, 2011a). The focus on one's personal network and the familiarity between participants made social media feel very different than previous varieties of online communities.

The concept of "Web 2.0" was an industry-driven phenomenon, hyped by the news media and by business analysts alike. Many of the technologies that were eventually labeled Web 2.0 were developed years earlier. For example, the structural foundations of blogging were first created during the dot com bubble with services like LiveJournal and Blogger, both founded in 1999. Still, blogging started rising out of the post-crash ashes circa 2003 and, in 2004, the US presidential election took blogging mainstream and news agencies began critiquing the role that "web diarists" could play as amateur journalists (Lee 2004). Likewise, the functional components of social network sites date back to at least 1997, but Friendster got people excited in part because it was seen as a new type of online dating site, and online dating sites were one of the few profitable services in 2001, after the economic downturn.

Web 1.0 veterans—bored, out of work, and still enamored by the Internet, which, at the time, was being described as a "fad" by analysts—began developing new applications for communicating and sharing information. People were exploring blogging, tagging, social bookmarking, podcasting, photo sharing, video sharing, and social gaming. Old CMC tools were being revisited and reconsidered while the industry itself began making claims about innovation that excited investors. For example, buzzwords like "user-generated content" became widespread in order to signal a shift from commercially edited or curated content to content provided by individuals. Social network sites emerged out of the Web 2.0 and social media phenomena, mixing new technologies and older CMC practices infused by tech industry ideals.

Genres of computer-mediated communication

SNS-enabled communication patterns both differ from and incorporate aspects of earlier forms of online communication, including email, instant messaging, and MUDs. While SNSs emerged at a moment in the Internet's history where mediated interactions were increasingly widespread, in part because the Internet was being broadly embraced, they owe a lot to earlier CMC genres. In fact, many SNS features were incorporated from earlier tools. Although the true historical origins of CMC are found in the introduction of print, which enabled communication to span temporal and geographical boundaries for the first time, the first instances of *computer*-mediated communication are located in the exchange of text messages over the Internet which occurred soon after the first file transfers over ARPANET and quickly constituted the majority of the system's traffic. Since these early exchanges, the ability of the Internet to support social interaction has played a central role in its adoption.

Early CMC genres can typically be understood across two axes: synchronous versus asynchronous, one-to-one versus one-to-many. One-to-one CMC channels were primarily for connecting people directly in more intimate fashions, while one-to-many channels connected strangers, typically around shared interests. For instance, motorcycles aficionados went to Usenet's rec.motorcycles to find like-minded communication partners, while close friends often communicated via IM or email. The tools for interpersonal group communication and the tools for topically-oriented gatherings often blurred, with mailing lists serving both as a forum for groups of people who knew each other and as places where strangers could gather around a topic. Likewise, some channels blurred synchronous and asynchronous communication, such as MUDs—environments where users created fantastical representations of self and communicated with others in text-based environments.

While groups of friends often met at collectively agreed-upon online spaces—and online communities like the Whole Earth 'Lectronic Link (WELL) initially formed through networks of friends—many online communities in the 90s were not designed to support pre-existing friend groups. Rather, they served as interest-focused conversational hubs that brought together people based on shared interests—not just shared geography—and enabled them to "form webs of personal relationships in cyberspace" (Rheingold 1993). This first generation of virtual communities was, for the most part, built upon people encountering one another for the first time in an online context that grouped people by interest, not geography. Some of these relationships moved to other communication channels, including face-to-face (Parks and Floyd 1996), especially when they were associated with a particular geographical nexus (such as the WELL in the Bay Area of California). Later work found similar patterns: DiGennaro and Dutton (2007) find that 20 percent of their sample of Internet users report meeting new friends online and Tufekci (2010) reports that people who are looking to make friends online often do.

Early research on virtual communities explored how these collections of individuals transformed into communities with distinctive cultures, norms, and a sense of connection. For instance, Nancy Baym's (2000) ethnographic account of a newsgroup devoted to soap operas highlights the shared norms that developed among participants as they created a space for communication and community. Rheingold (1993) documented the development of the WELL and coined the phrase "virtual community." Sherry Turkle's (1995) analysis of MUDs described a space where interactions that occurred outside of traditional embodied experiences were heady and liberating. As one of Turkle's participants explains, "[real life] is just one more window, and it's not usually my best one" (Turkle 1995: 13).

The notion that individuals could develop intimate friendships and emotional connections with people they had never met "in real life" was surprising to those who didn't use these tools, and some of the early laboratory studies reinforced the notion that CMC was less effective than face-to-face for group communication processes (e.g. Kiesler et al. 1984). Although the hundreds of listservs and newsgroups that flourished during this time reflected a diverse set of interests, the user base powering them was far less diverse. During this period, the typical Internet user was more likely to be white, male, tech-savvy, older, and wealthier than those who were not online. And most of them spoke English and were passionate about geeky topics. Thus, even as strangers encountered each other online, they often had quite a lot in common.

Many of the features underlying early CMC tools have been incorporated into SNSs. Being able to group users by interest, describe oneself textually, and engage in both synchronous and asynchronous communication are key aspects of the SNS user experience today. As with these earlier communication forums, individuals are using SNSs to achieve a multitude of personal and professional goals.

Early research on the topic suggested that SNS users were more likely to articulate existing relationships on social network sites than meet new people (see boyd and Ellison 2007, for a review). Recent research on Facebook suggests that connecting with close friends is more common than using the site to meet new people, but that using the site to find out more information about peripheral others, such as casual acquaintances or someone one has met socially, is also a strategy employed by users (Ellison et al. 2011a; Joinson 2008). On other sites, different practices have evolved. Early research on the topic found that MySpace users appeared more likely than Facebook users to meet new people (Dwyer et al. 2007). On Twitter, which allows asymmetrical relationships, it is more common to follow accounts of those whom one does not know personally (Marwick and boyd 2011), reconfiguring how connection and intimacy are managed (Crawford 2009).

The infrastructure behind social network sites—particularly the articulation and navigation of preexisting relationships—also complicates how "community" can be conceptualized. While online forums that are organized around topic or interests can be reasonably understood as a discrete group, networks of people connected to disparate others are not as easy to categorize. Similar to the way in which early users might belong to multiple discussion forums—each with its own culture, norms, and history—SNS users may interact with different groups that they see as communities on SNSs. For instance, a college student may have Friends that include fraternity brothers, chemistry major friends, high school friends and family members. While there are tools for segmenting these individuals into lists for the purposes of sharing and restricting content, these features are often challenging to use.[3] Instead, individuals are recreating their communities on an individual basis as opposed to accessing a commonly held distribution list, as is typical in many other forms of online interaction. Rainie and Wellman (2012) point out that, in networked societies, we are likely to connect with multiple shifting networks that meet our informational or other needs at that moment, as opposed to a smaller number of static groups that serve all our needs.

SNSs incorporate features from earlier forms of CMC, but they do so in a way that amplifies the power of these features because they are placed in a social context. For instance, consider the profile. Profiles that are linked to a group of contacts are often more accurate than those that exist in a social vacuum; the presence of these contacts implicitly vets presentational claims, and third-party comments are perceived as more credible than self-reported information (Walther et al. 2008). In this way, people's self-presentations on social network sites may be less highly embellished when compared to sites without visible social connections, such as online dating sites. Earlier forms of mediated communication allow for identity information to be shared, but SNSs do this in different and potentially more powerful ways due to the presence of the third-party Friends network. Other features are similarly amplified through the Friends list. One reason SNSs are a compelling focus for the field of CMC is that they are well-designed to support interaction and are adopted by so many diverse kinds of individuals who are connecting with one another in novel ways, leveraging existing tools to do unexpected things, and reconfiguring CMC technologies to meet their needs. Much of what is novel stems from how participants incorporate an articulated list of connections—or Friends—into their online practices.

---

[3] Google Plus attempts to address this design issue with its "Circles" but, at the time of publication, patterns of use have not yet stabilized.

RESEARCH CHALLENGES

SNS scholarship offers scholars in a diverse range of fields the opportunity to study empirical questions as wide-ranging as how the number of Friends one accumulates on an SNS affects impressions (Tong et al. 2008), how participants leverage SNSs to get their questions answered (Morris et al. 2010a, 2010b), how social media connects journalists and citizens during political uprisings (Lotan et al. 2011), or how constructing one's profile can affect one's view of self (Gonzales and Hancock 2008).[4] Arguably, the range of activities and goals that users are employing SNSs to meet, and the diversity of the user base, make social network sites a relevant context for scholarship in almost every discipline.

However, studying SNSs also poses unique challenges. By far the most pressing challenge for SNS scholars lies in the rapid pace at which innovations and technical changes are implemented in this space. For scholarship in this arena to develop, SNS researchers need to be mindful of the ways in which these sites evolve over time and the effects this may have on the interpersonal, psychological, and sociological processes they are studying.

The networked nature of SNS interactions provides an additional layer of complexity not experienced by earlier media scholars examining the role of television or radio. What one experiences on SNSs and the content to which one is exposed differs depending on the structure of one's network, a user's individual preferences and history, and her activities at that moment. This is quite unlike previous media like television, where the program does not change depending on who can see it. Although interpretations of media have always varied, mere access varies widely with SNSs, complicating what constitutes the object of content analysis.

Much like research on the effects of Internet use have evolved to measure granular activities as opposed to global measures of use such as time online, SNS researchers are also moving towards a consideration of specific activities on the site. Because of how people's position within the SNS shapes their experiences of it, activity-centric analyses require contextualization and translation, not unlike what social scientists studying differing cultural practices have had to do for decades.

Documenting socio-technical changes

One key challenge of studying social media is that designers of these tools are innovating at a very rapid timeframe and often with little advance notice. Given the rapidly changing infrastructure and the timeframe of academic publishing, the site at the time of data collection is likely to be very different from its incarnation at the point of publication. Furthermore, features that one scholar examines one year may simply disappear the next.

---

[4] For a broader sampling of research into SNSs, visit the following bibliography: <http://www.danah.org/researchBibs/sns.php>. Accessed June 2, 2011.

Thus, two studies of a particular site that produce different findings may not be "contradictory"—they may actually have examined what are in essence two different socio-technical contexts.

We believe it is critical that SNS scholars consider the implications of technological change more explicitly in their work. As systems change, so will the practices they enable and constrain. Unless researchers attend to technology-based features, and are more careful about describing and considering the impact of the technology itself, scholarship on SNSs may become a landscape of individual, niche studies that preclude synthesis across them—a connect-the-dots canvas of points with no organizing framework that reveals the connections between them and allows the larger picture to emerge.

All technologies evolve over time (see Pinch and Bijker 1987). As feature sets change, so too do user practices, expectations, and norms. Unlike many previous technologies— like the television or telephone—social media applications evolve far more quickly, often without warning and in ways that may have significant implications for users and their practices. Social media researchers may be halfway through data collection when they discover that an important feature has been redesigned or removed altogether. Or they may find their analysis assumes an old set of norms and features. For example, a study of manual retweeting practices on Twitter (boyd et al. 2010) quickly became outdated when Twitter launched its retweet functionality. In order to study phenomena as they are unfolding, researchers must flexibly negotiate the shifting toolset, but they must also be careful about how they document their findings.

In order to produce scholarship that will be enduring, the onus is on social media researchers to describe the technological artifact that they are analyzing with as much care as survey researchers take in describing the population sampled, and with as much detail as ethnographers use when describing their field site. This is not to say that researchers must continue to describe technologies as if no one knows what they are— we are beyond the point where researchers must explain how electronic mail or "email" is like or unlike postal mail. But, rather, researchers must clearly describe the socio-technical context of the particular site, service, or application their scholarship is addressing. In addition to attending to the technology itself, and the interchange between technical and social processes, we believe SNS researchers should make a concerted effort to include the date of data collection and to describe the site at the moment of data collection and the relevant practices of its users. These descriptions will enable later researchers to synthesize across studies to identify patterns, much in the same way reporting exact effect sizes allows for future meta-analyses.

For those of us who believe that social network sites are socio-technical systems, in which social and technical factors shape one another, failing to describe the site under study ignores the fact that the technological constraints and affordances of a site will shape user practices and that social norms will emerge over time. Not including information about what the feature set was at the time of data collection forecloses the possibility of identifying patterns that emerge over time and through the accumulated scholarship across a range of sites and user samples. Unfortunately, because they have no knowledge about how things will continue to evolve and which features will become important to track, researchers may not be able to identify the salient features to report and may struggle with devoting scarce publication space to these details, but this doesn't undermine the importance of conscientious consideration towards describing the artifact being analyzed.

Even minute technical changes can have meaningful effects on human behavior. For instance, changing the default ages that show up on the front page of major online dating sites for suggested searches might influence how searches are conducted and how individuals choose to present themselves. Online daters report shaving off a year or two from their age so as to not be "filtered out" by people searching for typical age brackets such as 35 or 40 (Ellison et al. 2006).

These issues are more magnified when addressing larger socio-technical issues, like privacy and the shifting nature of social network site privacy settings. Unlike face-to-face contexts, where the audience for a particular utterance is usually visible (e.g. the other people in the room), content that's visible to a limited audience can be confusing to those who see them but do not know who else can, and thus may not be able to discern the extent to which the information is truly "public." For example, scholars who were analyzing privacy settings and privacy practices on Facebook in 2005 (Gross and Acquisti 2005) document very different practices than those who study privacy later (e.g. boyd and Marwick 2011; Lampinen et al. 2011; Stutzman and Kramer-Duffield 2010). Seeing how the default privacy settings on Facebook have changed over time highlights the rapid and meaningful nature of change on SNSs (McKeon 2010). The introduction of features that enable users to target content to certain people, such as Facebook's "lists" feature and, more recently, Google Plus's "circles," are examples of technical changes that could reshape how users engage with others on the site, and potentially force users to negotiate a new level of social complexity. Knowing whether users had access to these advanced features or just early simplistic structures for making content "public", "private," or "Friends-only" is important to know when interpreting findings from a study of SNS privacy issues.

SNS scholars should aim to produce work that contributes insights and develops theory in a way that transcends the particular site at a moment in time, but rather is useful and informative even after the site design shifts. This requires historically locating the technology alongside descriptions of the population and practices.

The challenges and opportunities of large datasets

Because of both the content that people upload and the behavioral traces that they leave behind, social network sites have unprecedented quantities of data concerning human interaction. This presents unique opportunities and challenges. On one hand, SNSs offer a vibrant "living lab" and access to behavioral data at a scale inconceivable to many social scientists. On the other, the data that are available present serious research ethics questions and introduce new types of biases that must be examined (boyd and Crawford 2012).

A lot of the core challenges stem from the opportunities, problems, and limitations to accessing server-level data. Harnessing server-level data—the data captured by the site, not just the traces made visible through the public-facing screens—provides an opportunity to study and track user behavior without the issues posed by self-report data or privacy settings, although it introduces other complications. Server-level data often provide activity data at a granular level not possible through other methods. For instance, using Facebook server-level data, Burke and colleagues are able to identify the social capital outcomes of different kinds of activities on the site, such as passively consuming others' content or broadcasting messages (Burke et al. 2011). The cognitive load required of users to answer detailed questions about their micro-activities often precludes survey questions about these kinds of usage details, even assuming users could accurately report them.

Server-level data provide a unique opportunity to access detailed behavioral data about what people are doing on SNSs. Yet, it's not clear that those who participate on SNSs want to be observed in this way. Nor is it clear that researchers can always correctly interpret these data. Furthermore, only some researchers have access to server-level data, which limits the kinds of research questions that are explored. Interpretation requires accounting for all of the reasons behind why content may have been produced. It's easy to misinterpret data when researchers can't directly ask users about their motivations, perceptions, or attitudes. Similarly, self-reported user characteristics in profile fields are susceptible to self-presentational tendencies and response biases, so just as with survey questions, researchers need to be careful to articulate the biases in their samples. Meanwhile, access to these data is difficult to procure, often requiring collaboration with a commercial organization or requiring researchers to create social media systems in order to access data. For example, while some researchers have easy access to the Twitter "firehose," many others do not. As Lev Manovich (2011) has argued, limited access to data may reproduce significant inequalities among researchers and limits what kinds of questions are asked. While the research challenges surrounding server-level data are not yet well understood or articulated, it is important that scholars begin interrogating this aspect of studying SNSs.

As more and more attention is given to the large datasets associated with social media applications, it is also important for researchers to recognize that many powerful inquiries about SNS practices do not require server-level access or technical analyses. Indeed, there is critical research value in understanding how individuals interpret the technological artifacts of SNSs or how individuals work to challenge expectations about how they are supposed to engage with the systems. Just because a system is designed to do something in particular does not mean that users will engage with it in that way. For example, Facebook gives users the ability to "deactivate" (as opposed to delete) their accounts so that users who regret their decision could reactivate their account without suffering data loss. Yet, boyd and Marwick (2011) interviewed a teenage girl who repurposed this feature to make Facebook a real-time experience for privacy reasons. Every day, she logged into Facebook and reactivated her account; when she was done, she deactivated her account. Her regular de/re-acti-vation strategy may have been visible as a glitch in the server logs, but the rationale for her behavior would be impossible to discern without direct interrogation of some kind. It is important not to lose sight of the kinds of questions that cannot be answered by server-level datasets alone.

CONCLUSION

In this chapter, we've attempted to highlight changes in social network sites over time and to introduce a definition of SNSs that more accurately articulates the features and frameworks that are salient to users. We have attempted to outline some of the ways in which SNSs have changed since their popularization, drawing attention to the ways in which technical and social changes are dependent upon one another. As a genre, SNSs are still in their adolescent stage and we expect that they will continue to evolve. By con-textualizing them in light of the Web 2.0 phenomenon and revealing how they build on previous genres of CMC, we have grounded their history so that future developments can better be understood in terms of the past.

Our definition of social network sites is deeply connected to these sites' features and affordances. Yet, as we have found in our own work, focusing primarily on the technical features of a particular tool might be less useful than highlighting how the tools are used in practice. Although the feature set is the most visible characteristic—as is the case of many technologies—many of the more interesting insights emerge when we consider user practices and social implications, although it is far more chal-lenging to measure, articulate, and theorize about these kinds of changes. Thus, we acknowledge the way in which technical and social factors mutually shape one another and call for SNS researchers to attend to and describe the technical system in which they are collecting data.

Although studying SNSs introduces new challenges, this area also provides great oppor-tunities. As a rapidly moving phenomenon, SNSs complicate researchers' traditional modes of analysis, but this also introduces new methodological opportunities. The vast amounts of behavioral and server-level data they contain is seductive, but it is important that researchers do not lose sight of the value of inquiries that do not rely on large datasets. Social network sites have opened up new venues and possibilities for analyzing human interactions, but it is essential that researchers do not become too enamored with these new systems. Scholars have the potential to—and, indeed, the responsibility to—interrogate emergent phenomena with a critical eye. Thus, we invite researchers to clearly articulate the assumptions and biases of their methods, attend to the wide array of research possibilities presented by social network sites, and embrace the possibilities these contexts offer for refining existing theories and developing new ones.

REFERENCES

Anderson, J. and Bernoff, J. (2010). "A Global Update of Social Technographics," Forrester Research Report, September 28.

Baym, N. K. (2000). *Tune In, Log On: Soaps, Fandom, and Online Community*, Thousand Oaks, CA: Sage.

boyd, d. and Crawford, K. (2012). "Critical Questions for Big Data: Provocations for a Cultural, Technological, and Scholarly Phenomenon," *Information, Communication, & Society* 15(5): 662–79.

boyd, d. and Ellison, N. B. (2007). "Social Network Sites: Definition, History, and Scholarship," *Journal of Computer-Mediated Communication*, 13(1): 210–30.

boyd, d., Golder, S., and Lotan, G. (2010). "Tweet Tweet Retweet: Conversational Aspects of Retweeting on Twitter." Proceedings of HICSS-42, Persistent Conversation Track. Kauai, HI: IEEE Computer Society. January 5–8, 2010.

boyd, d. and Marwick, A. (2011). "Social Privacy in Networked Publics: Teens' Attitudes, Practices, and Strategies," Paper presented at Oxford Internet Institute's Decade in Time Symposium, September 22.

Burke, M., Kraut, R., and Marlow, C. (2011). "Social Capital on Facebook: Differentiating Uses and Users." ACM CHI 2011: Conference on Human Factors in Computing Systems.

Crawford, K. (2009). "These Foolish Things: On Intimacy and Insignificance in Mobile Media," in G. Goggin and L. Hjorth (eds). *Mobile Technologies: From Telecommunications to Media*, New York: Routledge, pp. 252–265.

Di Gennaro, C. and Dutton, W. (2007). "Reconfiguring Friendships: Social Relationships and the Internet," *Information Communication & Society*, 10(5): 591–618.

Donath, J. (1998). "Identity and Deception in the Virtual Community," in M. Smith and P. Kollock (eds). *Communities in Cyberspace*, London: Routledge.

Döring, N. (2002). "Personal Home Pages on the Web: A Review of Research," *Journal of Computer-Mediated Communication*, 7(3). Available at <http://jcmc.indiana.edu/vol7/issue3/doering.html>. Accessed May 6, 2012.

Dwyer, C., Hiltz, S. R., and Passerini, K. (2007). "Trust and Privacy Concern within Social Networking Sites: A Comparison of Facebook and MySpace." Proceedings of the Thirteenth Americas Conference on Information Systems (AMCIS).

Ellison, N., Hancock, J. T., and Toma, C. L. (2012). "Profile as Promise: A Framework for Conceptualizing Veracity in Online Dating Self-Presentations," *New Media & Society*, 14(1): 45–62.

—— Heino, R., and Gibbs, J. (2006). "Managing Impressions Online: Self-Presentation Processes in the Online Dating Environment," *Journal of Computer-Mediated Communication*, 11(2): article 2. Available at <http://jcmc.indiana.edu/vol11/issue2/ellison.html>.

—— Steinfield, C., and Lampe, C. (2007). "The Benefits of Facebook 'Friends': Exploring the Relationship between College Students' Use of Online Social Networks and Social Capital," *Journal of Computer-Mediated Communication*, 12(3): 1143–68.

——, Steinfield, C., and Lampe, C. (2011a). "Connection Strategies: Social Capital Implications of Facebook-Enabled Communication Practices," *New Media & Society* 13(6): 873–92.

—— Vitak, J., Gray, R., Lampe, C., and Brooks, B. (2011b). "Cultivating Social Resources on Facebook: Signals of Relational Investment and their Role in Social Capital Processes," Paper presented at the iCS-OII 2011 "A Decade in Internet Time," Symposium, Oxford, UK.

Fitzpatrick, B. and Recordon, D. (2007). "Thoughts on the Social Graph." *Brad Fitz.com,* August 17. Available at <http://bradfitz.com/social-graph-problem/>.

Fono, D. and Raynes-Goldie, K. (2006). "Hyperfriends and Beyond: Friendship and Social Norms on LiveJournal," in M. Consalvo and C. Haythornthwaite (eds). *Internet Research Annual. Vol. 4: Selected Papers from the Association of Internet Researchers Conference,* New York: Peter Lang.

Gonzales, A. L. and Hancock, J. T. (2008). "Identity Shift in Computer-Mediated Environments," *Media Psychology,* April–June: 11(2): 167–85.

Gross, R. and Acquisti, A. (2005). "Information Revelation and Privacy in Online Social Networks," Paper presented at proceedings of WPES'05, Alexandria, VA: Association of Computing Machinery, pp. 71–80.

Joinson, A. N. (2008). "Looking at, Looking up or Keeping up with People?: Motives and Use of Facebook," Proceedings of the twenty-sixth annual SIGCHI conference on Human factors in computing systems, New York: ACM, pp. 1027–36.

Kiesler, S., Siegel, J., and McGuire, T. W. (1984). "Social Psychological Aspects of Computer-Mediated Communication," *American Psychologist,* 39(10): 1123–34.

Lampinen, A., Lehtinen, V., Lehmuskallio, A., and Tamminen, S. (2011). "We're in it Together: Interpersonal Management of Disclosure in Social Network Services," CHI'11 ACM.

Leary, M. R. (1995). *Self-Presentation: Impression Management and Interpersonal Behavior,* Dubuque, IA: Brown and Benchmark Publishers.

Lee, J. 8. (2004). "Year of the Blog? Web Diarists Are Now Official Members of Convention Press Corps," *New York Times,* July 26. Available at <http://www.nytimes.com/2004/07/26/us/eyes-nation-internet-year-blog-web-diarists-are-now-official-members-convention.html>. Accessed June 2, 2011.

Lotan, G., Graeff, E., Ananny, M., Gaffney, D., Pearce, I., and boyd, d. (2011). "The Revolutions Were Tweeted: Information Flows during the 2011 Tunisian and Egyptian Revolutions," *International Journal of Communications,* 5: Feature 1375–405.

McKeon, M. (2010). "The Evolution of Privacy on Facebook," *MattMcKeon.com,* May 19. Available at <http://www.mattmckeon.com/facebook-privacy/>. Accessed October 4, 2011.

Madden, M. and Zickuhr, K. (2011). "65% of Online Adults Use Social Networking Sites," Pew Internet & American Life Project, August 26. Available at <http://pewinternet.org/Reports/2011/Social-Networking-Sites.aspx>. Accessed June 20, 2012.

Manovich, L. (2011). "Trending: The Promises and the Challenges of Big Social Data," in M. K. Gold, (ed.). *Debates in the Digital Humanities,* Minneapolis, MN: The University of Minnesota Press. Available at <http://www.manovich.net/DOCS/Manovich_trending_paper.pdf>. Accessed July 15, 2011.

Marwick, A. (2010). "Status Update: Celebrity, Publicity, and Self-Branding in Web 2.0," Dissertation, New York University.

—— and Boyd, D. (2011). "I Tweet Honestly, I Tweet Passionately: Twitter Users, Context Collapse, and the Imagined Audience," *New Media and Society,* 13: 96–113.

Meyrowitz, J. (1985). *No Sense of Place: The Impact of Electronic Media on Social Behaviour,* NewYork: Oxford University Press.

Morris, M. R., Teevan, J., and Panovich, K. (2010a). "What Do People Ask Their Social Networks, and Why? A Survey Study of Status Message QandA Behavior," Proceedings of CHI 2010, New York: ACM, pp. 1739–48.

——, Teevan, J., and Panovich, K. (2010b). "Comparison of Information Seeking Using Search Engines and Social Networks." Proceedings of ICWSM. Available at <http://www.aaai.org/Press/Proceedings/proceedings.php>. Accessed May 6, 2012.

Naaman, M., Boase, J., and Lai, C.-H. (2010). Is it really about me? Message content in social awareness streams. CSCW. Proceedings of the 2010 ACM Conference on Computer Supported Cooperative Work (pp. 189–92). New York, NY, USA: ACM. doi:http://doi.acm.org/10.1145/1718918.1718953

O'Reilly, T. (2005). "What is Web 2.0?," *O'Reilly Blog*, September 30. Available at <http://oreilly.com/Web%202/archive/what-is-web-20.html>. Accessed May 6, 2012.

Parks, M. (2010). "Who are Facebook Friends?," Paper presented at the International Communication Association annual meeting, Singapore.

—— and Floyd, K. (1996). "Making Friends in Cyberspace," *Journal of Computer-Mediated Communication*, 1(4). Available at <http://jcmc.indiana.edu/vol1/issue4/parks.html>. Accessed May 6, 2012.

Pinch, T. J. and Bijker, W. E. (1987). "The Social Construction of Facts and Artefacts: or How the Sociology of Science and the Sociology of Technology might Benefit Each Other," *Social Studies of Science*, 14(3): 399–441.

Rainie, L. and Wellman, B. (2012). *Networked: The New Social Operating System*, Cambridge, MA: MIT Press.

Rheingold, H. (1993). *The Virtual Community: Homesteading on the Electronic Frontier*, Cambridge, MA: MIT Press.

Russell, M. A. (2011). *Mining the Social Web: Analyzing Data from Facebook, Twitter, LinkedIn, and Other Social Media Sites*, Sebastapol: O'Reilly.

Stutzman, F. and Kramer-Duffield, J. (2010). *Friends Only: Examining a Privacy-Enhancing Behavior in Facebook*, CHI 2010: Atlanta, GA.

Tong, S. T., Van Der Heide, B., Langwell, L., and Walther, J. B. (2008). "Too Much of a Good Thing? The Relationship Between Number of Friends and Interpersonal Impressions on Facebook," *Journal of Computer-Mediated Communication*, 13(3): 531–49.

Tufekci, Z. (2010). "Who Acquires Friends Through Social Media and Why? 'Rich Get Richer' versus 'Seek and Ye Shall Find,'" Proceedings of the 4th International AAAI Conference on Weblogs and Social Media. AAAI Press.

Turkle, S. (1995). *Life on the Screen: Identity in the Age of the Internet*, New York: Simon & Schuster.

Walther, J. B., Van Der Heide, B., Kim, S.-Y., Westerman, D., Tom Yong, S., and Langwell, L. (2008). "The Role of Friends' Appearance and Behavior on Evaluations of Individuals on Facebook: Are we Known by the Company we Keep?," *Human Communication Research*, 34(1): 28–49.

CHAPTER 9

....

THE STUDY OF ONLINE RELATIONSHIPS AND DATING

....

BARRIE GUNTER

INTRODUCTION

....

THE Internet has long been a social medium that is used to facilitate communication with others through a number of different modalities. The early centrality of email has been augmented by new modes of text, audio, and video for interpersonal communication. It has therefore opened up multiple opportunities for people to make new social contacts through generic online tools that can be adapted to idiosyncratic applications, such as social networking sites, and via more closed online services that are designed to provide specialist functions, such as online dating sites. In this context, online dating has emerged as one of the most widely used applications on the Internet. It has also developed into a highly profitable business with growing numbers of people worldwide being prepared to pay for access to services that will find them a romantic or sexual partner, or enhance their relationship prospects.

This chapter examines a range of evidence about online dating behavior, as well as a synthesis of approaches to research in this area. It examines the nature of the market and the experiences of those who have engaged in online dating. The market for online dating is both a "mass" and fragmented: that is, there are services that promote themselves to all comers and others that target specific sub-groups in society defined by demographics, socio-cultural factors, or special interests (The Internet Dating Guide 2007; Matchmaking Institute 2009). Questions about the motives that users display for online dating are examined. Further issues associated with patterns of online self-disclosure and self-presentation and concerns about deception in online dating are also examined. Online dating is also considered within a broader context of the "social" Internet.

EMERGENCE OF ONLINE DATING

The use of advertising to find a romantic partner dates back to the nineteenth century with the phenomenon of mail-order brides and the matchmaker services found among certain communities—particularly those transplanted via migration to locations far distant from their original homelands (Jagger 1998; Steinfirst and Moran 1989). These services had restricted impact, however, and it was not until much later in the final quarter of the twentieth century that personal advertising for romantic or social partners became widely established (Bolig et al. 1984).

The potential for using the Internet as a method for finding a romantic or sexual partner has increased as the prevalence of Internet use has grown dramatically within a fairly short period of time. By June 2010, for instance, Internet penetration had almost reached two billion worldwide, or 29 percent of the world's population, and most people in developed nations and increasingly in developing countries now go online for a variety of purposes (Internet World Stats 2010).

In the twenty-first century, the adoption of the Internet has been driven increasingly by its use as a social communications medium. Online communication, most especially the use of email, was always one of the most widespread applications among Internet users (Horrigan 2001; Cole et al. 2004; Gunter et al. 2004). As web technology developed, more dynamic, real-time forms of communications evolved enabling online conversations to occur on a one-to-one or one-to-many basis. Social networking on the Internet quickly became widespread after 2003 with major brands such as Bebo, Facebook, and MySpace evolving dramatically from small-scale use among localized communities to global applications and millions of regular users. These tools became especially popular among young people (Lenhart 2007). These sites are also used in the context of romantic relationships, both to find new companions and to report upon the status of existing relationships.

Another factor associated with online dating is the growth, in many countries, of the proportion of the population that is single and therefore may potentially be in the market to find a partner. There is greater population mobility resulting in local community networks becoming diluted. In addition, career and time pressures are increasing for many people and make it more difficult for growing numbers of singles to find romantic partners (Barraket and Henry-Waring 2004; Hardey 2002). Online dating represents a more convenient search tool where external support is available to provide singles with a shop window of choice of potential partners brought straight to their computer screen. A further factor of relevance in this context is the decline of workplace romances in the face of sexual harassment concerns (see Brym and Lenton 2001).

Given the scale of the online dating phenomenon and the significance of the issues with which it is concerned, it is important that we develop a comprehensive understanding of why people engage with it and with what desired outcomes. Any online activity that involves some degree of self-disclosure in a public arena in which unseen and unknown observers are present and whose motives may not always be transparent or truthfully expressed, carries a degree of risk. The significance of this "risk assessment" is underlined by observations that people can develop deep emotional attachments to others they meet online that are every bit as powerful as offline relationships (McKenna et al. 2002; Walther and Parks 2002). Furthermore, such online connections can lead to short-term or sometimes lasting intimate relationships in real physical life (Joinson 2001, 2003; McKenna 2007).

WHAT IS THE PREVALENCE OF INTERNET DATING?

Online dating estimates derive from a number of sources. These include self-report estimates made by respondents in ad hoc surveys, online digital log measures of website hit rates, and corporate data released by major online dating companies about their customer bases.

Corporate evidence

Internet dating companies provide some data about use of their sites and this can vary in quantity and quality, ranging from generalized statistical information about memberships or customer bases to more detailed market or social scientific research on specific aspects of dating behavior. Corporate research is impressive in terms of its scale, but less so in respect of the insights it can provide into the subtleties of online dating behavior that enhance our understanding of it. Even as measures of market size, corporate data need validation from independent sources of market analysis because user data, as reported on corporate websites, are an integral part of corporate promotions, where a key agenda is to attract yet more users.

Corporate data have indicated that the online dating business is mostly on an upward trajectory. The economic recession in 2007–09 did not seem to affect this growth. Many online dating agencies reported significant increases in both membership lists and revenues during this period (Dawley 2008; Espinoza 2009).

Self-report evidence

Questionnaire-based surveys in which respondents provide self-reports about their online dating activities derive from a number of different sources, including academics, commercial pollsters, and the industry itself. American research has found that although bars and clubs remain important meeting places, growing numbers of people report going online explicitly to find people to date (Fallows 2004; Madden and Lenhart 2006; Netimperative 2005). Similar evidence has emerged from the UK (Gunter et al. 2003; Gunter et al. 2004). Online dating is now widely seen as socially acceptable and not the behavior of desperate, lonely people (Madden and Lenhart 2006; Response Source 2008).

Online measurement

Continuous measurement of Internet use has also yielded data on the prevalence of online dating. A number of specialist marketing research agencies routinely monitor and measure Internet traffic. Among the leading data suppliers in this field are ComScore, Hitwise, and Nielsen.

ComScore (2006) reported that nearly one in five European Internet users (18 percent) visited online personals sites during the month of July 2006, which slightly exceeded the equivalent figure for North America (17 percent). This meant there were 38.2 million online dating site users in Europe and 29.1 million in North America. More recently, research by Nielsen, reported that American online dating sites attracted 27.5 million unique visitors in June 2009 (Comstock 2009).

WHAT KINDS OF PEOPLE USE ONLINE DATING?

Evidence has emerged from some markets, that the demographic profile of online daters does not match that of the general Internet-using population. Online dating was initially embraced by younger Internet users, but eventually spread to other age groups. It remains more popular among young adults in their 20s and 30s than any other age group (Brym and Lenton 2001; Madden and Lenhart 2006; Marketing Vox 2007; Gunter 2008). Evidence from academic and industry research has indicated only small degrees of user variance based on gender (Madden and Lenhart 2006; Hitwise 2007; Marketing Vox 2007).

Table 9.1 summarizes key findings from prominent studies of the demographics of online daters in different parts of the world. Men adopted this form of dating more extensively than did women early on, but over time both genders have come to make widespread use of such services. Online dating has also been popular among young people, mostly aged under 40 years, but again over time, old age-groups have increasingly used these services. Of particular significance is the extent to which people already in relationships, and not just those who are single, use online dating services. The findings reveal the varied motivations that can underpin online dating behavior.

It might be expected that most users of online dating sites would be individuals who are romantically unattached. There is mounting evidence, however, that this is not always true. Canadian research found that nearly one in five online dating site users (18 percent) were either married or in a live-in relationship (Brym and Lenton 2001).

Table 9.1 Demographic profiles of online daters

Study	Sample	Gender	Age	Marital status
Brym & Lenton (2001)	Canada Telephone Survey N = 1,200 17 +	68% of Online Daters Male 32% of Online Daters Female	Online daters 26%—18–29 30%—30s/40s 10% 50s +	18% of Online Daters are Married
Madden & Lenhart (2006)	USA Telephone Survey N = 3,215	Use Online Dating 12% Male Internet Users 9% Female Internet Users	Use online dating 18% 18–29 11% 30–49 6% 50–64 3% 65 +	23% of Online Daters are Married 31% of Online Daters are Divorced/Separated/Widowed
Marketing Vox (2007)	In-home Interviews by Mediamark Research Inc N = 26,000 18 +	52% Online Daters are Men [in last 30 days]	Use online dating 18% 18–29s 11% 30–49s 6% 50–64s 3% 65 +	
Dutton et al. (2008)	Online Surveys—All Respondents were Married Australia: N = 1,496 Spain: N = 2,186 UK: N = 2,401 USA: N = 10,675	Male = 50% Female = 50%	Mean age: Australia = 42 Years Spain = 41 Years UK = 49 Years USA = 32 Years	Proportion of Married Couples Who Met Online Australia = 9% Spain = 5% UK = 4% USA = 19%
Gunter (2008)	UK Online Survey N = 3,844 16 +	Used Online Dating 40% Male Internet Users 24% Female Internet Users		

In the US the proportion of online dating site members who were married or in a relationship was even higher (30 percent) (PRWeb 2005). This evidence suggests a different kind of motive for using these sites, driven more by risqué excitement than a genuine desire for romance. It might also be regarded by some users, who feel trapped in unhappy marital relationships, as an escape route. More evidence is needed on these questions.

The idea that online daters are desperate individuals who are socially isolated or inadequate has received equivocal support from empirical research. This perception was prevalent in the earliest days of online dating and may have reflected opinions that prevailed about use of the personals columns in magazines and newspapers (see Klement 1997). Online daters have been found to have active offline social lives and see themselves as self-confident. Dating websites represent one avenue of social contact among many (Brym and Lenton 2001; Gunter 2008)

There is interesting evidence concerning the age differences of online daters who go on to form lasting partnerships (Dutton et al. 2008). In more than six in ten cases (61 percent) online daters formed long-term relationships with someone with whom the age difference was less than six years. There was more likely to be an age difference of six or more years, however, between couples meeting online (39 percent) than between those meeting offline (24 percent). In a later report by the same researchers, the tolerance for age differences among online daters was found to vary somewhat between countries. While online daters in Spain and the UK were similarly likely to display an age difference of greater than six years, this proportion was markedly lower in Australia (Dutton et al. 2009).

These findings may reveal greater age difference tolerance of online daters and a willingness to embrace a wider choice of partners compared with offline-only daters. This in turn increases the likelihood that lasting partnerships will develop between people of varying characteristics. As we see later, there are also differences between genders in what they seek from a partner that can mediate the success of different forms of self-disclosure that occur in online social contact settings.

What motivates online daters?

People visit or use online dating sites for a variety of reasons. There are two aspects to motivation: the nature of the motive and the strength of motivation. Strength of motivation can be indicated through the degree of persistence that online-dating-site users exhibit in sticking with the task. Once they get started, many online daters use Internet services repeatedly (Gunter 2008).

Gender differences in expectations and outcomes have been found. Women were more likely to go online seeking friendships, while men sought a relationship. Men were four times as likely as women to say they sought a "no-strings" fling. Men were also more likely to instigate contact on the basis of an attractive photograph whereas women responded to an interesting description (Netimperative 2005). These findings are consistent with evolutionary theory explanations of male versus female sexual-partner-seeking behavior. According to this theory, women tend to be more selective than men (Feingold 1992). Consistent with this theory, female Internet daters tend to specify more attributes than do males in relation to determining the right partner for themselves (Bartling et al. 2005).

Further evidence has emerged that male online daters are most influenced by the apparent age and physical attractiveness of potential female partners, whereas female online daters look more closely at social status indicators such as education and occupation (Lance 1998). Other research, discussed later, reinforces the position of this theory that men and women seek different characteristics in potential mates within the context of Internet dating that reflects differences in the way they are "hard-wired." Their distinctive socio-biological orientations may also underpin their propensity to emphasize or distort specific features about themselves that they believe will enhance their attractiveness to potential mates.

ARE ONLINE DATERS SATISFIED WITH ONLINE DATING?

Research has shown that most online daters agreed that it is an effective way of meeting people (Brym and Lenton 2001). Most users of these sites express broad satisfaction with the service received, though this was less prevalent in terms of the numbers of contacts provided and dates achieved (Gunter 2008).

One common source of concern was retention of anonymity while online. Thus, while online daters seek face-to-face contact opportunities, this must be done in secure locations from which they can walk away. While actual dates would provide an opportunity to engage in more direct contact with a potential new friend or romantic partner, many online daters would like to remain in shopping-around mode, perhaps, but in a more socially rich online situation (Gunter 2008). The perceived advantages of online dating include the provision of a large pool of potential dates that increases the chances of finding a suitable match (Madden and Lenhart 2006).

If the explanations of gender differences in mating habits of evolutionary theory are to be accepted as relevant here, this expanded choice is likely to be utilized differently by men and women Internet daters. We would expect women to do more window shopping before committing to a purchase, while men might be more likely to try out multiple goods.

It was noted earlier that online daters seem to be willing to accept bigger differences between themselves and their partners than is often found among offline daters (Dutton et al. 2008). This observation has been reinforced by other evidence obtained from active or recent online daters that they cast the net wider in terms of the character range of potential companions they are willing consider compared with the usual choice profiles that are prevalent in the offline world. Thus, men are no more likely than women to be influenced by the physical attractiveness of potential online dates and women in the online world are not as strongly motivated to find a male partner with high socio-economic status (Whitty 2008).

The degree of satisfaction (or dissatisfaction) experienced by online daters has been directly linked to the formats adopted by online dating sites. Online dating site interfaces that offer standard profile-based information about potential companions can be off-putting. Research has indicated that many online dating sites users increasingly fail to be fully engaged by sites that offer search opportunities for partner matches using check-box profiling. One study found that Internet daters reported spending more time searching through profiles than engaging in the kinds of interactions usually associated with dating. It therefore tested new formats in which participants could send instant messages to each other and post images as conversation points. This approach created greater immediacy in otherwise remote interactions, which modeled more closely exchanges that might take place in initial real-time, face-to-face encounters. Participants preferred others with whom they had initially interacted rather than those whose profiles they had read during face-to-face meetings (Frost et al. 2008).

HOW SUCCESSFUL IS ONLINE DATING FOR MAKING SOCIAL CONTACTS?

The success of online dating is difficult to determine in any absolute sense as it is dependent upon users' expectations associated with their reasons for doing it. Casual users and seekers of life-long partners have different motives. In between these two extremes, however, there are many other potential measures of success calculated in terms of dates achieved, dates with potentially good matches, and so on.

A number of independent studies in different countries have confirmed that most users make multiple contacts with potential dates, either through self-initiated actions or by responding to the actions of others (Brym and Lenton 2001; Trueman 2005; Gunter 2008). One meeting often led to others although relationships surviving more than one year occurred for fewer than one in five (Trueman 2005).

Criteria of success may differ for online dating simply because dating is conducted remotely, whereas in the offline world the establishment of a relationship requires physical proximity between romantic partners (Levine 2000; Wildermuth 2001). Studies of online dating have found, however, that one central criterion of success was whether it led to offline meetings (Brym and Lenton 2001; Parks and Roberts 1998). Ultimately then even for online daters for a relationship to flourish, it must be feasible for them actually to meet someone face to face. Hence geographical proximity for online daters remains an issue just as in the offline dating world.

WHAT ARE THE CONSEQUENCES
OF ONLINE DATING?

Making initial contacts from which face-to-face encounters are arranged are the first steps in realizing what might be a more involved objective of engaging in a full-blown relationship that might be purely sexual in nature or entail a longer-term commitment. A majority of Canadian online daters (63 percent) said they had had a sexual relationship with at least one person they met online. This outcome was slightly more likely among men (66 percent) than among women (58 percent) and was especially high among gay men (79 percent). Many (60 percent) reportedly enjoyed at least one long-term relationship from meeting with someone they initially contacted via one of these sites. Far fewer (27 percent), said they met someone they came to consider as their "partner." Only a tiny proportion (3 percent) married someone they met online. This outcome generally followed a protracted courtship online in the form of exchanges of emails and photographs (Brym and Lenton 2001).

In the US, more than four in ten (43 percent) online daters said they had gone on dates with people they met through Internet dating sites, with far fewer (17 percent) entering long-term relationships or marrying people they met this way. Across US Internet users, 3 percent who were married or in a long-term relationship said they met their partners online (Madden and Lenhart 2006).

In the UK, more than four in ten users of online dating services claimed to have experienced at least one sexual relationship as a result, while only around three in ten enjoyed a lasting relationship and just under one in ten found a marriage partner (Gunter 2008). A major study of online daters in the UK and Australia revealed that 6 percent of responding Internet users in the UK and 9 percent in Australia said they had met their current partner online (Dutton et al. 2008).

HOW IMPORTANT IS SELF-DISCLOSURE STYLE?

Online dating, as with any other form of dating, requires participants to disclose details about themselves as part of the process of building a rapport and then a relationship with another person. In the online dating world, face-to-face contact is delayed and may never occur. Instead, other channels of communication are used. These include email, online real-time chat, exchanges of photographs and even audio or video links. Contacts initially begin with the preservation of anonymity through text-only communication. Other channels that reveal more about participants can subsequently be introduced when participants wish to take the initial contacts further (Couch and Liamputtong 2008).

The ways that people represent themselves can vary between different online settings. Thus, self-disclosures and virtual "courtship" behaviors have been observed to differ between online dating sites and other virtual communities such as chat rooms and discussion boards. The real-world geographical distance between participants in these sites can also vary. In online virtual communities not established explicitly for dating purposes, users may be more tolerant of large geographical distances because memberships of these communities may typically be international. In respect of online dating sites, where the primary intention may be to find a new romantic partner, there will be an expectation that eventually an online friendship will evolve into an offline relationship. In this case, geographical proximity will become an important factor underpinning how easy and convenient it will be for both partners to arrange a face–to–face meeting. Consequently, online friends are more likely to meet in person when they live relatively close to each other and will be more likely to meet sooner to test the offline dating potential of someone contacted online (Baker 2005). In general, those who meet via dating sites are more likely to meet at all compared with those who meet on other online virtual communities (McKenna 2007).

Research with online daters has revealed that they use a number of different communications channels. In Australia, for example, a small qualitative study with fifteen online daters found that they used email, online chat, and webcams to interact with potential romantic partners. They also used an array of filtering mechanisms to help them decide whether to take any of these remote contacts through to face-to-face meetings. These filters again took advantage of text, audio, and video channels to inform impressions of others with whom remote interactions were taking place (Couch and Liamputtong 2008).

Self-presentation has emerged as a critically important variable that can influence success in Internet dating. There should be no surprises about this because developing intimate, romantic relationships, whatever the context, generally involves an unveiling of the self to another. In the offline world, during face-to-face meetings, a person's anonymity is forfeited and first impressions based on judgments about appearance and initial disclosure of personality can be critical. In the online world, the individual is afforded some protection through invisibility when initial disclosures occur in text message form. This can lead to individuals adopting a more strategic approach to self-disclosure that entails being carefully selective in the information they present about what they are and what they are like (Bargh et al. 2002; McKenna et al. 2002). At the same time, in an online setting, individuals may disclose specific details about themselves sooner than they might ordinarily do in offline settings and develop a closeness with another even sight unseen (Walther et al. 2001). Despite these differences between the offline and online worlds, relationships in both spheres have been observed to display a gradual development from exploration of surface level characteristics to disclosures of deeper-seated values and attributes, a psychological process articulated by social penetration theory (Altman and Taylor 1973; Whitty and Carr 2006).

Whitty (2008) has explained how past theories of the "self" have routinely distinguished between different levels of personal representation, usually embracing a concept of the "real self," some other "idealized self," and possibly an "externalized self" that may reveal parts of the real self, but not all of it. It is therefore only to be expected that these offline processes and habits should migrate into the online world. Whitty (2008) also noted that in the context of relationship formation in the offline world, the self is revealed a bit at a time. Such exchanges between those who are dating represent an intricate part of relationship formation. Disclosure of intimate details occurs gradually as trust is built up between daters, and as more of each other's true selves are revealed judgments can be reviewed about whether there is a good match. This ritualized pattern of self-disclosure may be followed in the online world though the pace at which it proceeds can be more rapid, in some respects, than in the offline world.

There is evidence, for example, that online daters use their online dating experiences as opportunities to try out new identities. The intention here may be as much about self-exploration as giving misleading impression of who they really are. Thus, online daters may post idealized selves characterized by attributes they do not actually possess, but would like to. Feedback is then received on these alternative self-images from other users, enabling posters to judge which attributes are most highly valued by others. One possible outcome of this exploratory behavior is identity re-creation on the part of the individual (Yurchisin et al. 2005).

Another aspect of online behavior that has emerged as important to progression of a relationship beyond initial stages of online contact is the use of emotional words in early text exchanges. Emails with strong emotional terms in which the correspondent indicates their excitement at the opportunity to find someone new can lead to more favorable first impressions and a greater likelihood that the recipient of such messages will choose to pursue the relationship further (Rosen et al. 2008).

Internet daters may try out different representations of themselves. This process can include deciding on different ways of verbally describing what they are like as well as carefully selecting photographs of themselves that they post on dating websites or send to potential offline dates. Online daters may seek to put forward the best of themselves (Heino et al. 2005). This is understandable in that they wish to present themselves as possessing attributes potential partners will find attractive. This motivation can result in distorted, exaggerated, or misleading self-portrayals emerging (Toma et al. 2008). Such behavior can also create a tension among some online daters who feel under pressure to be more open and honest about themselves because they ultimately want their dating experience to be successful (Ellison et al. 2006).

The repercussions from telling lies about oneself online are that eventually someone might find out. Furthermore, in the online dating context, if the real persona as revealed in an offline meeting is totally different from the image projected online, potential partners may be put off. Totally exposing one's true self can place an online dater at a disadvantage, however, so some degree of mild deception in the form of selective disclosure could prove the most effective strategy (Whitty 2008). While such mild deceit may be ethically acceptable and justifiable in terms of safeguarding both personal privacy and security and self-regard in settings of personal disclosure to unseen strangers, more serious forms of malicious deceptive behaviour has also been recorded online, sometimes in dating contexts, that can result in real harm to victims in the offline world (Whitty and Joinson 2009).

The concept of "warrants" has been invoked in this context which is related to the closeness of contact between a person's real world and online identity (see Walther et al. 2009).

Warrants comprise disclosures that permit another to authenticate or verify any personal claims an individual might make about their character. The reduction in degree to which offline and online lives and identities are divorced from each other can control the level of deception likely to occur in online self-disclosures (Warkentin et al. 2010).

Even though online daters may be aware of the risks they run in respect of the success of subsequent face-to-face meetings with potential romantic partners initially courted online, they may still fall into the temptation of telling minor untruths or "white lies" about themselves. Validation tests of online self-descriptions in the form of direct observations and measurements of online daters have indicated that both men and women lie about some of their personal attributes. Deceptions included details disclosed about height, weight, and age, with claims made of being taller, less heavy and younger than was the truth. In most cases, however, the deception was mild rather than severe (Toma et al. 2008).

Conflicting evidence has emerged that men and women distort different attributes. Men seek women who are physically attractive and youthful, leading women to exaggerate these attributes in themselves in their self-disclosures. Women seek men who can offer them comfort, status, and security and therefore look for these attributes in the self-disclosures of male online daters. In terms of evolutionary theory, to which reference has already been made, men seek women with reproductive fitness and therefore focus on physical and biological characteristics of potential mates. Women, in contrast, seek not simply a mate with whom they can procreate but also one who will provide longer-term security both for herself and her offspring (Buss 1988; Buss and Schmitt 1993).

The "screen names" that online daters use can shape the impressions others form of them in terms of their personality or physical attractiveness (Whitty and Buchanan 2009). Online daters have openly admitted posting profiles that misrepresent them. Once again, though, it seems that this is not done through malicious intent but simply to find out which self-images work best in that environment (Whitty 2008).

The open text descriptions that Internet daters provide of themselves can also vary in their truthfulness. As a form of self-protection, online daters who lie on their personal profiles tend to use fewer self-references and fewer emotionally negative words, both to enhance the self-impression they hope to create while at the same time psychologically distancing themselves from any distortions their self-descriptions might contain. Despite these findings, most online daters in this research were found on independent validation to tell the truth about themselves (Toma and Hancock 2010).

ARE THERE OTHER ONLINE AVENUES TO FINDING A PARTNER?

The Internet offers users a variety of different options for meeting people for social and romantic purposes. There is mounting evidence to show that that there are other online opportunities for finding romantic partners in addition to specialist dating sites. Internet users adopt these alternatives sometimes instead of or in addition to dating websites (Mintel 2009).

The dramatic rise of social networking sites has enabled millions of people world-wide to expand their lists of social contacts (Lenhart 2009). Social networks have always represented a critical aspect of the fabric of our lives. They underline family and community ties that define self-identity and can provide us with social, emotional, and economic support (Wellman and Gulia 1999; Wellman and Potter 1999). Offline social networks have migrated into cyberspace and online social networks represent both a reinforcement and an extension of offline networks (Donath and boyd 2004). While people present their identity through their physical selves in the offline world, in online settings they must create a screen profile dependent on self-report. In such contexts, there is often less richness of personal information available in online profiles for others to form an impression of an online actor as compared with a face-to-face meeting in the physical world (Postmes et al. 1998; Walther and Tidwell 2002). Nevertheless, such computer-mediated communication environments can promote the development of new relationships and the maintenance of existing relationships that can be socially as powerful as offline interactions (Walther 1997; Wang et al. 2009).

Within computer-mediated settings, however, the rules governing interpersonal engagement and impression formation can differ from those found in face-to-face encounters. Social identity effects that arise from situations in which anonymity of communicants places group-level cues centre stage enhances impressions of group cohesiveness and common identity where broad group membership attributes are shared. SIDE (social identity of deindividuation effects) theory has posited that computer-mediated relationships can be strengthened through this process even in the absence of many of the cues that underpin interpersonal attraction in the physical world (Postmes et al. 1999). The common sense of group identity can be so strong, that subsequent exposure to more personalized information about participants in a computer-mediated communication task can reduce interpersonal attraction responses (Lee 2004; Postmes et al. 1998; Walther 1997).

At the individual level, Walther (1995) offered an alternative theoretical interpretation of how online interpersonal relationships can emerge and develop. His social information processing theory posited that even online individuals will draw upon many of the cues they might use offline in assessing others, but the pace at which a relationship develops online is slower. Early tests of this theory, however, found that it may have underestimated the extent to which computer-mediated communication can facilitate relationship formation.

In an extension, called hyperpersonal theory, it was argued that the capacity afforded by computer-mediated communication to modify self-disclosures and to modify the self-identity that is projected can create a setting in which extremely powerful interpersonal relationships develop (Walther 1996, 1997). In computer-mediated settings, individuals may take great care over self-presentation by carefully drafting and re-drafting personal profiles to control the tone, complexity, and emotionality of the language used (Walther 2007). Although synchronous online communications can be littered with anonymous and deceptive self-descriptions, in asynchronous online environments, users can take greater care over the impressions they create of themselves, responding to the reactions of others and modifying their profiles strategically to maximize their attractiveness while not straying too far from the truth. In such contexts, powerful interpersonal relationships can emerge (Tidwell and Walther 2002).

US research with teenage social networkers indicated that while most used their profiles to maintain contact with established friends, around half used them to make new friends, and in some cases social networks were used to flirt with others (Lenhart and Madden 2007). UK research found that nearly one in four Internet users had made new social contacts online and about half of these individuals had gone online with the intention of meeting new friends (DiGennaro and Dutton 2007; Dutton and Helsper 2007).

Research in Australia, Spain, and the UK among Internet users who met their spouses online reported that although online dating sites were named more often than any other online site among UK respondents, this was not true in Australia or Spain (Dutton et al. 2008, 2009). In the UK, online chat rooms and instant messaging provided contact points as well as dating sites. In Spain and Australia, chat rooms were the most popular sites of first social contact (Dutton et al., 2009).

We saw earlier, in the context of using Internet dating sites, that the issues of deception and trust in relation to personal profiles were regarded as problematic factors that could cause tension among online daters. Trust in personalized information is relevant in other online social interaction settings, including those that involve highly popular social network sites such as Facebook (Walther et al. 2009). In this context, the concept of warrants can be significant in that they can serve to constrain the inclination to stray too far from the truth when constructing online self-descriptions. In particular, any personal claims are more likely to command the trust of others when they are authenticated by independent sources. Thus, in the context of Facebook, for example, remarks generated by others tended to be trusted more than those generated by self in relation to judgments made about personal profiles (Walther et al. 2009).

Further evidence has emerged however that the propensity to tell lies—even if only mildly deceptive in nature—varied between online social interaction platforms. Deceptions were less likely to occur in emails and social network sites than in live chat rooms, Internet forums, or instant messaging. Warrants, or self disclosures that revealed information about self that others could check out, were least likely to be deployed in those areas where lies were most prevalent—chat rooms, forums, and instant messages. If warrants suppress deception, as has been hypothesized, then social network sites would appear to offer potentially the most trustworthy personal profiles (Warkentin et al. 2010).

Whether social networking sites designed primarily to enhance general social contacts and (non-romantic) friendships represent significant competition for specialist dating sites remains to be seen. It is likely that they will at least represent one more tool in the dating toolbox for those who seek convenient and economical routes to making new romantic contacts. Certainly, on the basis of recent evidence, they may are more likely than other online disclosure to provide the most authentic personal profiles.

WHAT DOES THE FUTURE HOLD?

From the end of the twenty-first century, online dating emerged as one of the most widely used applications of the Internet. In the space of less than a decade, this market has evolved rapidly. It has grown in terms of overall market size. The phenomenon of online dating is global in reach. The number of suppliers of these services has also increased over time at an accelerating pace. The immaturity of the market in many countries is an important contributory factor in the rapid growth in numbers of different suppliers. As the market matures and consolidates with a few dominant suppliers capturing the greatest market share, market entry for smaller suppliers could become more difficult because of the costs involved in establishing a viable market presence (Mintel 2009).

Although online social networking services that are not branded specifically in relation to dating have surfaced as competition to specialist online dating agencies, most of the biggest online dating agencies have a distinct selling proposition based on the detailed profiling they carry out with their clients to ensure that contacts represent good romantic matches. Given that most online daters do not simply want to gain contacts, but contacts with a specific type of relationship potential, the more sophisticated matching services should always find a market.

Empirical research has indicated that deception in personal profiling online is regarded as a problem (Toma et al. 2008). There are factors that can be introduced to suppress the propensity to lie online (Lucid 2009). Moreover, deception seems less likely to occur in asynchronous online communication settings, such as Internet dating sites, than in synchronous online communication environments (Warkentin et al. 2010). Signals of authentication of personal profiles are likely to enhance the reputation of online dating sites among users, even in the face of growing competition within the market and from social network sites.

Within the specialist online dating supply chain, however, market changes are occurring that will pose business challenges to market leaders. Even the specialist market is becoming increasingly crowded. There are two significant phenomena that have affected market dynamics. The first of these is the emergence of free dating sites that do not charge users any fees directly. Instead, their business models depend upon the generation of revenue via advertising on their sites. The second change is market fragmentation.

Parts of the pay market for online dating have responded to "free" sites by launching free sites of their own. Some major companies have merged to capture bigger market shares in specific national markets. It is also important to note that online daters do not always remain loyal to one site or restrict their search to one supplier at a time. Even free sites, such as PlentyofFish, have acknowledged that up to 15 percent of its users also sign up to pay sites (Mintel 2009). As in other service markets, quality of service is a critical factor that drives customers' choices. Online daters still use paid-for sites because many free sites offer limited customer service.

Another positive factor for pay sites is that few "free" sites make enough money from advertising to sustain their businesses (Mintel 2009). There remains scope for further analysis of business models likely to prove successful in the future. Given the significance of factors such as deception and trust, that may be linked in turn to privacy and security issues on the part of online daters, fee-based dating services could remain competitive if they offer greater value in terms of profile authenticity checking, which is likely to demand additional resources on the part of service suppliers.

The online dating market is fragmenting. There are growing numbers of online dating services within national markets that are targeting niche sub-markets defined by sexual orientation, ethnicity, religion, age group, lifestyle preferences, and a range of special interests or needs. Perhaps one of the most intriguing aspects of market fragmentation has been manifest in the growth of dating sites that cater for members with unusual distinguishing attributes or interests (Scott and Martin 2009).

A further dynamic that is influencing the shape of the online dating market is the entry into the market of other well-known brands, in particular media companies. Media organizations that publish outlets that have traditionally carried personal ads or that run dating competitions have sought to extend their reach in the dating arena via online dating. Media companies have achieved this objective via partnerships with established online dating companies, through take-overs of such companies or by setting up new online dating services themselves. In the UK, a number of major newspapers have established or bought into online dating sites. Many of these have enjoyed business growth, although they have yet to penetrate the top ten (Mintel 2009). Hence, although such mergers that combine powerful brands could be seen as having strong and widespread appeal, their success will depend upon which partner dominates the business decision-making and upon whether for consumers the partnership seems like a good fit.

FINAL REMARKS

There is a steadily expanding body of research about online dating that derives from industry market monitoring, commercial ad hoc studies of users' experiences by online dating agencies and opinion pollsters, and research by academics. Online dating has become socially accepted and in many countries and demographic strata has long passed the stage of early adoption and become a mass participation activity.

There remain important questions on which more research is needed. How will online dating continue to evolve? Will the online dating market become more fragmented, with agencies targeting smaller and more tightly defined groups or communities? Will the major dating companies need to diversify more in the future to embrace communities that are defined by more than standard demographics?

To be successful, online dating services may need to become more literate in terms of their understanding of the rules of social interaction that apply in computer-mediated environments (see Walther 1996; Walther et al. 2001). As online dating expands, will it experience problems that have been linked to the wider social networking phenomenon of site misuse, invasion of privacy, personal security threats, and identity theft? Most users have been found to exhibit sensitivity to dishonesty in online dating, but few perceived it as a real risk (Brym and Lenton 2001; Madden and Lenhart 2006).

Market analysts have provided macro-level data that are helpful in tracking global and national market movements in this sector. Their methods, as they stand, are inappropriate for understanding the key drivers of online dating behavior. More theory-based research is required that determines the degree to which offline norms and rules relating to interpersonal communication, impression, and relationship formation can be migrated into the online world is essential.

More studies that combine linguistic analysis of the texts of personal profiles with analysis of discourses used by online daters to describe their intentions and expectations could provide valuable insights. In addition, interventionist designs that manipulate specific features of online personal profiles to evaluate the responses elicited by specific features in the presence of controls over other features could reveal micro-level attributes. The latter could then be utilized in macro-level analyses of online dating site texts using data mining software permitting systematic and subtle levels of evaluation of massive quantities of online content (e.g. Thelwall 2008; Feizy et al. 2009). In view of cross-national differences in online dating habits (e.g. Dutton et al. 2009), such triangulated analyses should also be conducted cross-culturally.

Finally, in light of growing concerns about deviant practices on the Internet, some of which are manifest in the context of ostensibly genuine online relationship formation (Whitty and Carr 2006), there is a need for greater understanding of the types of people who utilize the Internet in search of friends and partners, beyond the standard market demographics. This need is underlined by emergent evidence that individuals who lack confidence in terms of self-presentation may be more likely than others to prefer social interaction online. This syndrome has been described under the broad heading of Problematic Internet Use (PIU) (Caplan 2002, 2003, 2005).

Socially responsible online dating services might seek to profile their clients psychologically so that value-added advisory services can be provided to guide potentially more vulnerable Internet users, for example, those who might be taken in by the phenomenon of so-called "romance scams" whereby criminals infiltrate online dating sites with fake profiles in order to construct bogus romantic relationships with susceptible victims, often culminating in attempts to extort money from them. Researchers have begun to study the linguistic styles of these fake profiles to develop algorithms for their detection to provide support to law enforcement agencies that are often called in to such cases (see Whitty and Buchanan 2011).

References

Altman, L. and Taylor, D. A. (1973). *Social Penetration: The Development of Interpersonal Relationships*, New York: Holt, Rinehart and Winstone.

Baker, A. J. (2005). *Double Click: Romance and Commitment among Online Couples*, Cresskill, NJ: Hampton Press.

Bargh, J. A., McKenna, K. Y. A., and Fitzsimons, G. M. (2002). "Can you See the Real Me? Activation and Expression of the 'True Self' on the Internet," *Journal of Social Issues*, 58(1): 33–48.

Barraket, J. and Henry-Waring, M. (2004). "'Everybody's Doing it'": Examining the Impacts of Online Dating." Available at <http://www.tasa.org.au/conferencepapers04/docs/COMMUNCATION/BARRAKET>. Accessed November 5, 2009.

Bartling, C. A., LeDoux, J. A., and Thrasher, D. J. (2005). "Internet Dating Ads: Sex, Ethnicity, Age-Related Differences and Support for Evolutionary Theory," *American Journal of Psychological Research*, 1(1): 21–31.

Bolig, R., Stein, P. J., and McKenry, P. C. (1984). "The Self-Advertisement Approach to Dating: Male-Female Differences," *Family Relations: Journal of Applied Family & Child Studies*, 33(1): 587–92.

Brym, R. J. and Lenton, R. L. (2001). *Love Online: A Report on Digital Dating in Canada*, A Report of Surveys Funded by MSN.CA, Toronto.

Buss, D. M. (1988). "The Evolution of Human Intrasexual Competition: Tactics of Mate Attraction," *Journal of Personality and Social Psychology*, 54(4): 616–28.

—— and Schmitt, D. P. (1993). "Social Strategies Theory: An Evolutionary Perspective on Human Mating," *Psychological Review*, 100(2), 204–32.

Caplan, S. E. (2002). "Problematic Internet Use and Psychosocial Well-Being: Development of a Theory-Based Cognitive-Behavioural Measurement Instrument," *Computers in Human Behaviour*, 18(5): 553–75.

—— (2003). "Preference for Online Social Interaction: A Theory of Problematic Internet Use and Psychosocial Well-Being," *Communication Research*, 30(6): 625–48.

—— (2005). "A Social Skill Account of Problematic Internet Use," *Journal of Communication*, 55(4): 721–36.

Cole, J. I., Suman, M., Schramm, P., Lunn, R., and Aquino, J. S. (2004). *Ten Years, Ten Trends: The Digital Future Report—Surveying the Digital Future, Year 4*, USC Annenberg School, Centre for the Digital Future, Los Angeles.

ComScore (2006). "Europeans Nearly Fifty Percent More 'Engaged' in Online Dating Compared to North Americans," ComScore Press Releases, September 25. Available at <http://www.comscore.com/Press_Events/Press_Releases/2006/09/European_Online_Dating_Habits>. Accessed September 3, 2009.

Comstock, C. (2009). "The Top Online Meat Markets," August 25th. Available at <http://www.forbes.com/2009/08/25/popular-online-dating>. Accessed August 27, 2009.

Couch, D. and Liamputtong, P. (2008). "Online Dating and Mating: The Use of the Internet to Meet Sexual Partners," *Qualitative Health Research*, 18(2): 268–79.

Dawley, H. (2008). "In These Tight Times, Lovelorn Go Online," *Media Life Magazine*, December 1. Available at <http://www.medialifemagazine.com/in-these-tight-times-lovelorn-go-online/>. Accessed October 17, 2009.

DiGennaro, C. and Dutton, W. H. (2007). "Reconfiguring Friendships: Social Relationships and the Internet," *Information, Communication and Society*, 10(5): 591–618.

Donath, J. and boyd, d. (2004). "Public Displays of Connection," *BT Technology Journal*, 22(4): 71–82.

Dutton, W. H. and Helsper, E. (2007). *The Internet in Britain*, Oxford, UK: Oxford Internet Institute, University of Oxford.

——, Helsper, E., Li, N., and Whitty, M. (2008). "Me, My Spouse and the Internet: Meeting, Dating and Marriage in the Digital Age," Oxford Internet Institute, January. Available at <http://www.oii.ox.ac.uk/research/projects/?id=47>. Accessed August 20, 2010.

Dutton, W. H., Helsper, E., Whitty, M. T., Nai, L., Buckwalter, J. G., and Lee, E. (2009). "The Role of the Internet in Reconfiguring Marriages: A Cross-National Study," *Interpersona*, 3 (Suppl. 2): 3–18.

Ellison, N., Heino, R., and Gibbs, R. (2006). "Managing Impressions Online: Self-Presentation Processes in the Online Dating Environment," *Journal of Computer-Mediated Communication*, 11(2). Available at <http://www.jcmc.indiana.edu/vol11/issue2/ellison>. Accessed August 20, 2010.

Espinoza, J. (2009). "Online Dating Sites Flirt with Record Growth," *Forbes*, June 1. Available at <http://www.forbes.com/2009/01/06/online-dating-industry-face-markets-cx_je_0105autofacescan01.html>. Accessed October 17, 2009.

Fallows, D. (2004). "The Internet and Daily Life," Pew Internet and American Life Project, August 11. Available at <http://www.pewinternet.org/Reports/2004/The-Internet-and-Daily-Life.aspx>. Accessed November 4, 2004.

Feingold, A. (1992). "Gender Differences in Mate Selection Preferences: A Test of the Parental Investment Model," *Psychological Bulletin*, 112(1): 125–39.

Feizy, R., Wakeman, I., and Chalmers, D. (2009). "Distinguishing Fact and Fiction: Data Mining Online Identities," Informatics Department, University of Brighton. Available at <http://www.informatics.sussex.ac.uk/research/groups/FoSS/news/STM_Roya%20Feizy.pdf>. Accessed January 20, 2010.

Frost, J. H., Chance, Z., Norton, M. I., and Ariely, D. (2008). "People are Experience Goods: Improving Online Dating with Virtual Dates," *Journal of Interactive Marketing*, 22(1): 51–61.

Gunter, B. (2008). Internet Dating: A British Survey, *Aslib Proceedings*, 60(2): 88–97.

——, Russell, C., Withey, R., and Nicholas, D. (2003). "The British Life and Internet Project: Inaugural Survey Findings," *Aslib Proceedings*, 55(4): 203–16.

—— Russell, C., Withey, R., and Nicholas, D. (2004). "Broadband in Britain: How Does it Compare with Narrowband?," *Aslib Proceedings*, 56(2): 89–98.

Hardey, M. (2002). "Life beyond the Screen: Embodiment and Identity through the Internet," *The Sociological Review*, 50(4): 570–85.

Heino, R. D., Ellison, N. B., and Gibbs, J. L. (2005). "Are we a 'match'? Choosing partners in the online dating market." Paper presented at the International Communication Association Convention, in New York, NY, May.

Hitwise (2007). "Male and Female Disconnect in Preferred Online Dating Websites," Hitwise Press Releases, February 14. Available at <http://www.hitwise.com/ca/press-center/press-releases/archived-press-releases/valentinesday2007/>. Accessed November 5, 2009.

Horrigan, J. B., Rainie, L., and Fox, S. (2001). Online communities: Networks that nurture long-distance relationships and local ties. Pew Internet & American Life Project, October 31. Available at <http://www.pewinternet.org/Reports/2001/Online-Communities.aspx>. Accessed June 20, 2012.

Internet World Stats (2010). "Internet Usage Statistics: The Internet Big Picture." Available at
<http://www.internetworldstats.com/stats.htm>. Accessed August 1, 2010.

Jagger, E. (1998). "Marketing the Self, Buying an Other: Dating in a Post-Modern Consumer
Society," *Sociology*, 32(4): 795–814.

Joinson, A. (2001). "Self-Disclosure in Computer-Mediated Communication: The Role of
Self-Awareness and Visual Anonymity," *European Journal of Social Psychology*, 31(2): 177–92.

—— (2003). *Understanding the Psychology of Internet Behaviour: Virtual Worlds, Real Lives*,
Basingstoke: Palgrave Macmillan.

Klement, J. A. (1997). "Love at First Byte: Internet Romance is Cheaper, Less Stressful than a
Blind Date," *The Salt Lake Tribune*, September 8: B1.

Lance, L. (1998). "Gender Differences in Heterosexual Dating: A Content Analysis of Personal
Ads," *Journal of Men's Studies*, 6(3): 297–305.

Lee, E.-J. (2004). "Effects of Visual Representation on Social Influence in Computer-Mediated
Communication: Experimental Tests of the Social Identity Model of Deindividuation
Effects," *Human Communication Research*, 30(2): 234–59.

Lenhart, A. (2009). "Adults and Social Network Websites," Pew Internet Project Data Memo.
Available at <http://www.pewInternet.org>. Accessed September 3, 2009.

—— and Madden, M. (2007). "Social Networking Websites and Teens: An Overview," Pew
Internet Project Data Memo, January 7. Available at <http://www.pewInternet.org>.
Accessed September 3, 2009.

Levine, D. (2000). "Virtual Attraction: What Rocks Your Boat?," *Cyberpsychology and
Behaviour*, 3(4): 565–73.

Lucid, L. (2009). "(Mis)Representrating the Self in Online Dating," *Mind Mattera: The
Wesleyan Journal of Psychology*, 4: 37–49.

McKenna, K. Y. A. (2007). "A Progressive Affair: Online Dating to Real World Mating," in
M. Whitty, A. Baker, and J. Inman (eds) *Online Matchmaking*, Basingstoke, UK: Palgrave
MacMillan, pp. 112–124.

—— Green, A. S., and Gleason, M. E. J. (2002). "Relationship Formation on the Internet:
What's the Big Attraction?," *Journal of Social Issues*, 58(1): 9–31.

Madden, M. and Lenhart, A. (2006). "Online Dating." Pew Internet and American Life Project,
March 5. Available at <http://pewinternet.org/Reports/2006/Online-Dating.aspx>. Accessed
August 20, 2010.

Marketing Vox (2007, September). "US Adults Increasingly Erode Stigma of Seeking Cyber
Love." Available at <http://www.marketingcharts.com/interactive/nearly-25mm-us-adults
-took-part-in-online-dating-in-past-30-days-1788/>. Accessed September 3, 2009.

Matchmaking Institute (2009). *2009 Matchmakers Survey*, October 17th. Available at <http://
www.matchmakinginstitute.com/2009_matchmakers_survey>. Accessed October 17, 2009.

Mintel (2009). "Love in a Cold Climate," Mintel Press Release, May. Available at <http://www
.mintel.com/press-centre/press-releases/353/love-in-a-cold-climate>. Accessed August 20, 2009.

Netimperative (2005). "Internet Now Third Most Popular Way to Get a Date," Netimperative,
August 3, 2005. <http://www.netimperative.com/news/2005/08/03/Internet_dating_
popular/>. Accessed August 9, 2005.

Parks, M. and Roberts, L. (1998). '"Making Moosic"': The Development of Personal
Relationships On-line and a Comparison to their Off-line Counterparts," *Journal of Social
and Personal Relationships*, 75 (4): 517–537.

Postmes, T., Spears, R., and Lea, M. (1998). "Breaches or Building Social Boundaries,"
Communication Research, 25(6): 689–715.

——, Spears, R., and Lea, M. (1999). "Social Identity, Group Norms, and "Deindividuation": Lessons from Computer-Mediated Communication for Social Influence in the Group," in N. Ellemers, R. Spears, and M. Lea (eds). *Social Identity: Context, Commitment, Content,* Oxford: Blackwell, pp. 164–83.

PRWeb (2005). "Study Shows 30% of Internet Dating Site Users are Married." September 28. Available at <http://www.prweb.com/releases/2005/09/prweb290988.htm>. Accessed March 10, 2010.

Response source (2008). "Internet Dating Statistics: 7.8 Million UK Singles Logged on to Find Love in 2007," January 18. Available at <http://www.responsesource.com/releases/rel_display.php?relid=36263>. Accessed October 17, 2009.

Rosen, L. D., Cheever, N. A., Cummings, C., and Fell, J. (2008). "The Impact of Emotionality and Self-Disclosure on Online Dating Versus Traditional Dating," *Computers in Human Berhavior,* 24(5): 2124–57.

Scott, C. and Martin, K. (2009). "There's a Date for Everyone," *Metro,* November 2: pp. 20–1.

Steinfirst, S. and Moran, B. B. (1989). "The New Mating Game: Matchmaking via the Personal Columns in the 1980s," *Journal of Popular Culture,* 22(4): 129–39.

The Internet Dating Guide (2007). <http://www.theInternetdatingguide.com>. Accessed September 3, 2009.

Thelwall, M. (2008). "Social Networks, Gender and Friending: An Analysis of MySpace Member Profiles," *Journal of the American Society for Information Science and Technology,* 59(9): 1523–7.

Tidwell, L. C. and Walther, J. B. (2002). "Computer-Generated Communication Effects on Disclosure, Impressions, and Interpersonal Evaluations: Getting to Know One Another a Bit at a Time," *Human Communication Research,* 28(3): 317–48.

Toma, C. L. and Hancock, J. T. (2010). "Reading Between the Lines: Linguistic Cues to Deception in Online Dating Profiles," *Computer Supported Cooperative Work,* February 6–10: 5–8.

——, Hancock, J. T., and Ellison, N. B. (2008). Separating Fact from Fiction: An Examination of Deceptive Self-Presentation in Online Dating Profiles," *Personality and Social Psychology Bulletin,* 34(8): 1023–36.

Trueman, T. (2005). "Internet Dating Much More Successful Than Thought," Eurekalert!, February 13. Available at <http://www.eurekalert.org/pub_releases/2005-02/uob-idm021305.php>. Accessed August 27, 2009.

Walther, J. B. (1995). "Relational Aspects of Computer-Mediated Communication: Experimental Observations Over Time," *Organization Science,* 6(2): 186–203.

—— (1996). "Computer-Mediated Communication: Impersonal, Interpersonal, and Hyperpersonal," *Human Communication Research,* 23(1): 3–43.

—— (1997). "Group and Interpersonal Effects in International Computer-Mediated Collaboration," *Human Communication Research,* 23(3): 342–69.

—— (2007). "Selective Self-Presentation in Computer-Mediated Communication: Hyperpersonal Dimensions of Technology, Language and Cognition," *Computers in Human Behaviour,* 23(5): 2539–57.

—— and Parks, M. R. (2002). "Cues Filtered Out, Cues Filtered in: Computer-Mediated Communication and Relationships," in M. L. Kemp and J. A. Daly (eds). *Handbook of Interpersonal Communication,* 3rd edn., Thousand Oaks, CA: Sage, pp. 529–63.

—— and Tidwell, L. (2002). "Computer-Mediated Communication Effects on Disclosure, Impressions and Interpersonal Evaluations: Getting To Know One Another A Bit At A Time," *Human Communication Research,* 28(3): 317–48.

Walther, J. B., Slovacek, C., and Tidwell, L. (2001). "Is a Picture Worth a Thousand Words? Photographic Images in Long-Term and Short-Term Computer-Mediated Communication," *Communication Research*, 28(1): 105–34.

—— Van Der Heide, B., Hamel, L. M., and Schulman, H. C. (2009). "Self-Generated Versus Other-Generated Statements and Impressions in Computer-Mediated Communication: A Test of Warranting Theory Using Facebook," *Communication Research*, 36(2): 229–53.

Wang, Z., Walther, J. B., and Hancock, J. T. (2009). "Social Identification and Interpersonal Communication in Computer-Mediated Communication: What You Do Versus Who You Are In Virtual Groups," *Human Communication Research*, 35(1): 59–85.

Warkentin, D., Woodwirth, M., Hancock, J. T., and Cormier, N. (2010). "Warrants and Deception in Computer Mediated Communication," *Computer Supported Cooperative Work*, February 6–10, 9–12.

Wellman, B. and Gulia, M. (1999). "The Network Basis of Social Support: A Network is More than the Sum of Its Parts," in B. Wellman (ed.) *Networks in the Global Village*, Boulder, CO: Westview Press, pp. 83–118.

—— and Potter, S. (1999). "The Elements of Personal Community," in B. Wellman (ed.) *Networks in the Global Village*, Boulder, CO: Westview Press, pp. 1–35.

Whitty, M. (2008). "Revealing the 'Real Me,' Searching for the 'Actual' You: Presentations of Self on an Internet Dating Site," *Computers in Human Behavior*, 24(1): 1707–23.

—— and Buchanan, T. (2009). "Looking for Love in so many Different Places: Characteristics of Online Daters and Speed Daters," *Interpersonal: An International Journal on Personal Relationships*, 3(2): 63–86. Available at <http://abpri.files.wordpress.com/2010/12/interpersona-3-suppl-2_4.pdf>. Accessed June 20, 2012.

—— and Buchanan, T. (2011). "Online Dating Romance Scam Project. Project," Department of Media and Communication, University of Leicester. Available at <http://www2.le.ac.uk/departments/media/documents>. Accessed August 20, 2010.

—— and Carr, A. N. (2006). *Cyberspace Romance: The Psychology of Online Relationships*, Basingstoke: Palgrave Macmillan.

—— and Joinson, A. N. (2009). *Truth, Lies and Trust on the Internet*. New York, NY: Psychology Press.

Wildermuth, S. (2001). "Love on the Line: Participants' Descriptions of Computer-Mediated Close Relationships," *Communication Quarterly*, 49(2): 89–95.

Yurchisin, J., Watchravesrigkan, K., and McCabe, D. B. (2005). "An Exploration of Identity Re-Creation in the Context of Internet Dating," *Advances in Consumer Research*, 32(1): 193–4.

CHAPTER 10

GAMES, ONLINE AND OFF

DMITRI WILLIAMS AND ADAM S. KAHN

By any benchmark—economic, mind-share, cultural impact, etc.—video games are now a ubiquitous and important element of modern culture. After decades in the social and commercial wilderness, games are taken as seriously as anything "fun" can be in an industrial society. Yet this very sense of frivolity is a major reason why few people understand the medium, and why research is often more focused on what evils lurk below the surface than on a fundamental understanding of what is going on above it. Accordingly, this chapter will serve as a primer to anyone looking for basic background knowledge about games, gamers, and the expanding online world they inhabit. The first half offers a historical perspective, tracing the industry's origins and the social diffusion of games, while the second half offers a closer look at several trends and important differences across the medium, and concludes with a brief note on research traditions. We focus on the so-called "casual" explosion, the continuing importance of console-based games, the boom of virtual worlds, the migration of children into online spaces, and finally, the oddly named "serious games" movement. We offer this second set of perspectives because games are often mistakenly assumed to be as uniform as other media. But unlike books, film, magazines, or television, the formats, uses, and types of video games are dizzyingly complex and varied. Similarly, our understanding of the cognitive processes and social spaces surrounding games tends to lag behind the more nuanced and larger body of literature studying more established media. We know a great deal about television's effects, culture, and how people use it, but we often have a hard time understanding why a solo *Bejeweled* player is on an entirely different planet than a raiding team in *World of Warcraft*. But to begin, it's best to take the long view and see where video games came from.

A BRIEF HISTORY OF VIDEO GAMES

The video game industry—largely based in the United States—is one of the most profitable and dynamic industries in entertainment. Games featuring the humble plumber Mario have made twice as much money as all five *Star Wars* films combined

(Borrow 2003). It is also an industry that nearly wasn't—one that survived technological upheaval, a rapidly changing consumer base, and a host of leaders known as much for their personal excesses and luck as for their insight and technical brilliance.

Origins: games and players, 1951–2003

The game industry is marked by rapid and dynamic change, owing to seismic shifts in both technology and in the user base. From its earliest origins as a hobby and into its modern form of a fully corporatized mainstream entertainment medium, the games business has endured wild swings and shocks. The economist Joseph Schumpeter (1943) has written of such "gales of creative destruction" in business—changes that shift paradigms and transform the market. A savvy consumer base thriving on interactive, networked technologies turns out to be a gale of creative destruction just as powerful as any new technology (Cowan 1999).

In the early 1960s, game development took place in university basements, with young and enthusiastic programmers working long hours for their own gratification. In contrast, today's industry structure is marked by vertical integration, professional management, and a fiercely competitive marketplace driven by the non-interoperability of the major game systems. For example, although DVDs made by Sony will work on DVD players made by another firm, game consoles do not feature such compatibility. Games are actually five overlapping markets: console systems, handheld games, arcades units, PC games, and mobile devices (Williams 2002). How did we get from there to here?

The initial era began with computer enthusiasts in the 1960s, moving eventually to a corporate model that collapsed in the early 1980s with the failure of Atari. This collapse can be considered the end of the first game era, and a time when the industry was essentially given up for dead. The second, and we might say modern, era began when the Nintendo corporation started to rebuild the industry in the late 1980s. From its efforts, the game industry as a whole rebounded to surpass the first game era. This story is recounted in detail in several journalistic accounts (Herman 1997; Herz 1997; Kent 2000; Kline et al. 2003; Sheff 1999), and is briefly outlined here.

Much like the invention of radio (Douglas 1987), the home video game industry began with hobbyists and enthusiasts before eventually transitioning to a corporate structure. These original tinkerers were nearly all male, young, white, middle class, and engaged in computer programming or engineering as part fun and part learning. They built and adapted out of insatiable curiosity, to amuse themselves, and to advance the endless holy quest to discover How Things Work.

The first known video game dates back to 1951, when a Cambridge University computer science graduate student named A. S. Douglas created a "naughts and crosses" (more popularly known in the US as Tic-Tac-Toe) game, followed a few years later by a US government nuclear research scientist named Wally Higginbotham, who invented a tennis game using the ballistics programs from the military (Herman 1997). The first team programmers emerged from MIT in the late 1950s and early 1960s, populated by science-fiction loving young men who programmed the aptly titled *Spacewar!*, which in later iterations pioneered multiplayer modes and even networking (Levy 1994; Montfort 2001). One of *Spacewar!*'s original enthusiasts, Nolan Bushnell, saw the commercial potential and eventually founded the first large-scale gaming corporate success, Atari. Bushnell, however, clashed with another inventor, Ralph Baer, who is generally credited with the title "father of video games" for his work on the first home console, the Magnavox Odyssey, which was released, without much fanfare or success, in 1972 (Kent 2000). Bushnell's simpler tennis game *Pong* was the medium's true breakout hit, and inspired a wave of innovation, copycats, trade disputes, and corporate interest, plus the transformation of public arcades into video game hotspots (Herz 1997).

Atari's corporate culture was a fraternity of engineers fueled by sex, drugs, and rock 'n' roll (Kent 2000). The hothouse atmosphere led to a continuous stream of innovation, often at the expense of any sense of professionalism. There were few schedules, no marketing plans, and little long-term strategy. It was as if the MIT hacker ethic had been given a fantastic toolbox of gadgets, encouragement, and narcotics (Levy 1994). This culture would lead to many of the industry's milestones, including the Atari 2600 home console, which was its first widespread success. It also led to spectacular corporate skullduggery and the single largest corporate collapse (to that time) in US history, when Time Warner acquired, and then largely destroyed Atari by focusing on mass production over quality. By 1983, Atari was losing $500 million per year and had collapsed Warner's stock. The following year, Warner sold Atari assets to cut its losses. By 1986, total home game sales had dropped from $3 billion to $100 million, and the industry was seemingly left for dead.

Unsurprisingly, pundits of the time were quick to label video games a passing fad. The industry's collapse was easy to explain as just another example of short attention-span American tastes: first disco, then Pet Rocks, and Pac-Man. However, a closer look at the demographics and demand shows that video games helped usher in a new kind of consumer who was increasingly aware of new tools and new possibilities. Having played video games, this consumer was not going to go back to wooden blocks and dice. The change was of course more global than just video games. Consumers were beginning to embrace home computers, compact discs, and the concept of digital systems as convenient and powerful entertainment tools. Analysts assumed that Atari's collapse meant a return to more simple one-way broadcast consumption patterns, but the resurgence of the industry in the late 1980s and the explosion of network culture in the late 1990s suggests that those early game players were exposed to a world of challenge, interactivity, and community, and the genie was permanently released from the bottle.

This pattern is reinforced by data on free time and disposable income. For Americans, the former has steadily dropped, while the latter has steadily risen, meaning that consumers spend more to enjoy less time. Consider a board game. It is slower, if cheaper, than its video game counterpart. Someone with more money, and less time, is likely to adopt the video version. From 1970 to 1994, Americans went from spending 4.3 percent of their incomes on recreation and entertainment to 8.6 percent, while working more hours and having less free time (Vogel 2001). Demographic cohorts played a role as well. The group coming of age in this era, popularly known as Generation X, has continued to be a source of game players while new cohorts of young people have added to the total audience. A casual observer of the industry was typically quick to assume that games were a child-only phenomenon, but this incorrect (but still widely held) view is in fact driven largely by the extremely successful marketing efforts of the Nintendo Corporation, who made their system entirely child-oriented. The later boom of adult-centric systems heralded by the original Sony PlayStation showed that Generation X and younger cohorts would continue to play into adulthood, but the stereotype often lingers today, especially among members of the Baby Boom generation and older.

This same cultural sea change of the 1980s had a dramatic effect on where and how people played games. The thriving, if sometimes suspicious-looking video arcades, were eroded by public concerns over safety and hygiene (Herz 1997) in an era of conservative political values. Arcades slowly transformed into youth-oriented daycare facilities at shopping malls, while game players were driven into private home spaces. In reaction, multiplayer home game consoles boomed throughout the 1990s, and the pump was primed for the rise of home-based computer networks to link players with each other. So, as home computer prices dropped and diffusion rose, the audience of players was ready to adopt a new, networked game culture. This movement coincided with a larger cultural shift toward the home; with civic institutions on the decline and convenience driving entertainment consumption for a more and more overworked and separate populace (Putnam 2000), home game systems and computers took off. In fact, in the crucial decades of the 1980s and 1990s, games functioned as a stepping stone to the more complex and powerful world of home computers, *preceding* computers at every step of adoption, and have continued to be in more homes since their arrival (see Figure 10.1).

Modern gaming (2004–)

During the first decade of the twenty-first century, the percentage of American adults with access to the Internet increased from 37 percent in 2000 to 71 percent in 2010. Fast, broadband connections rose as well, with slower dial-up connections beginning to decline from 2001 (Smith 2010). Meanwhile, by the end of the decade, video games had become commonplace in the American household, cutting across age and gender demographics. In 2011, estimates placed 53 percent of all American adults and 72 percent of American households playing some form of video games (Entertainment Software Association 2011; Lenhart et al. 2008b). And despite the long-held stereotype of the young male gamer, both independent and university research (Griffiths et al. 2003; Williams et al. 2008; Yee 2006) found this stereotype not to be true. In fact, according to the Entertainment Software Association (Entertainment Software Association 2011), women aged 18 or older represent more of the game playing population (37 percent) than boys aged 17 or younger (13 percent).

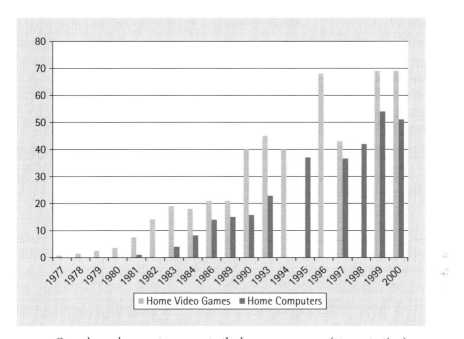

FIGURE 10.1: Consoles and computers come to the home, 1977–2000 (% penetration).

Data Source: Consoles, Nintendo of America, Amusement & Music Operators Assoc., *The Economist*, www.icwhen.com;
Computers, National Science Foundation, Roper surveys, Census Bureau, Statistical Abstracts of the United States

In addition to broadband surpassing dial-up for the first time, 2004 and 2005 saw three other important developments: the release of the most popular massively multi-player online game (MMO) of all time (also see *Virtual Worlds*, below), the first of a new generation of video game consoles, and the rise of social network sites.

World of Warcraft (*WoW*) was released during the holiday season of 2004 and became the best-selling computer game of 2005 (Entertainment Software Association 2006). It (or one of its subsequent expansions packs) was the best-selling computer game of 2005, 2006, 2007, and 2008 (Entertainment Software Association 2006, 2007, 2008, 2009), and would go on to be the best-selling MMO of all time—with more than 11.5 million monthly subscribers—and the third best-selling computer game of all time (Blizzard Entertainment 2008; Guiness World Records 2010). As of March 2011, Nielsen (2011) estimated that 7 percent of all game players play *WoW*, and 35 percent of all minutes spent playing non-casual PC games is spent on *WoW*, more than any other game. As a reference point, the game *League of Legends* ranks number two on the list, yet only occupies 5.5 percent of all minutes spent playing PC games.

The next year, in 2005, a new generation of consoles was launched, starting with Microsoft's Xbox 360, and subsequently followed by Sony's PlayStation 3, and Nintendo's Wii, both released in late 2006 (Shippy and Phipps 2009; Takahashi 2006). These new boxes featured several novel advances in features: the Xbox Live online gaming system created the largest online community and storefront for consoles; the PlayStation 3's powerful processor advanced graphics technology to impressive levels and doubled as a

Blu-ray disc player (at a time when standalone Blu-ray players were more expensive); and the Wii emphasized casual games and a popular motion-sensor controller (since copied by the other two companies in late 2010). As a result of this competition and innovation, the game industry saw a 60 percent increase in annual computer and video game sales between 2005 and 2008 (from 6.9 billion dollars to 11.7 billion dollars), after having held steady for most of the earlier part of the decade (Entertainment Software Association, 2011).

This was not the first generation of game consoles to have integrated Internet access, but was the first mainstream adoption: the previous generation's Sega Dreamcast (released in 1998) and Microsoft Xbox (released in 2001) had a built-in modem and Ethernet port, respectively, and Nintendo's GameCube (released in 2001) and Sony's PlayStation 2 (released in 2000) had optional accessories for online connectivity (Hagiwara and Oliver 1999; Takahashi 2002). Such a connection not only allowed for the playing of network games, but for the download and/or streaming of digital media. More importantly, the connection enables these increasingly powerful digital boxes to fulfill other roles within the household and to compete with other hardware categories. For instance, all three of these latest generation consoles allow for the streaming of movies using Netflix's proprietary Watch Instantly service. In addition, these consoles have some form of integrated web browser. In many ways, game systems are approaching the mythical convergence of set-top boxes prophesied in the 1990s (Negroponte 1996), and can be viewed as a Trojan Horse in the vicious corporate competition to get such a box into homes.

Another important event was the mid-decade launch and diffusion of social network sites (SNS); boyd and Ellison (2007) define SNS as "web-based services that allow individuals to (1) construct a public or semi-public profile within a bounded system, (2) articulate a list of other users with whom they share a connection, and (3) view and traverse their list of connections and those made by others within the system." While initially SNS had little relevance to gaming, as they matured and added more features the social connections afforded by the sites allowed for the development of casual games users could play with their friends in a persistent environment (Kirkpatrick 2010; Taylor 2010). A driving force of SNS games was Facebook, which initially was restricted to university students at elite universities, but by 2005 was open to all university and high school students worldwide. In late 2006 it became open to everyone (Kirkpatrick 2010). Since its founding, Facebook has seen exponential growth in its membership, with 845 million by the end of 2011 (Facebook 2012). In 2007, the site introduced the Facebook Platform, which allowed third-parties to develop applications that could take advantage of the social connections between friends. Despite the fact that Facebook thought games would not be viral enough to be widely adopted among its users, some of the early games, such as Texas HoldEm' Poker and Scrabulous (a Scrabble-like game), became quite popular very quickly (see A Casual Explosion, below).

With the rise of inexpensive (often free) casual games and a worldwide economic downturn, the trajectory of the gaming industry may again change. While it is hard to forecast games sales during a recession, some market research firms anticipate a decrease in retail sales of games in the coming years, both due to the state of the economy and the novelty of the latest generation of gaming consoles having worn off (especially the casual games of the Wii). After the steady increase in game sales, revenue decreased by 10 percent in 2009, and this trend is expected to continue (Entertainment Software Association 2010, 2011; Taylor 2010). However, usage of cheaper, less profitable (per user) social network games is expected to increase in the coming years (Taylor 2010), so while receipts may go down, overall play may actually increase.

The state of the industry may be in a transition period, but the widespread adoption of the Internet and social network sites has changed gaming. Networked gaming gives people more choices as to what games they can play and with whom they can play them. New games are often expected to be networked as a common feature, and much of the industry is interested in moving toward online gaming for both control and profiteering. Games that require connectivity to a centralized server system are more difficult to pirate, and piracy has been a particular challenge to the industry, especially from China. And, in addition to the social connectivity and networking of SNS sites, online gaming also offers the possibility of streaming services, meaning that the graphics processing formerly done by PCs or consoles might increasingly be moved to cloud-based server farms. Two start-ups, Gaikai and Onlive, began experimenting with technology and business models and revealed their advances in 2010. The future of gaming is thus likely to include a mix of social connectivity and continuing advances in technology as players seek each other as much as they seek games.

MAJOR ISSUES IN GAMES AND ONLINE GAMING

Virtual worlds

Virtual worlds originated from literary ideas, most notably the concept of cyberspace originating in the novels *Neuromancer* (Gibson 1984) and *Snow Crash* (Levin 2003; Stephenson 1992), then further popularized by movies ranging from *Tron* (Lisberger 1982) to *The Matrix* (Wachowski and Wachowski 1999). These fictions helped usher in the notion of a virtual space in which a representation of the user appeared on the screen in some way, either as a text-based character or a fully modeled 3D figure, or "avatar." The earliest incarnations were text-only games, usually called MUDs (multi-user dungeons), starting in 1978, in which networked players interacted in a fictional world. An important innovation was that the world was always on, or "persistent." Unlike most games with a start and an end, these ones kept going whether the players were there or not, giving them a more realistic feel. The first graphical version, *Meridan 59*, appeared in 1996 (Colker 2001), long before the Internet had become mainstream. These games began to be known as "massively" multiplayer online role playing games, or MMORPGs (often shortened to MMOs). "Massively" referred to the sudden appearance of very large player communities playing together. Other games capped out at 16 or 32 players, yet the

MMOs could have hundreds or even thousands on at the same time. This was a case where the change of scope changed the nature of the experience. Rather than small, occasional teams populating a space, virtual worlds fostered communities and small societies.

Meridian 59, and most games to follow, borrowed from the culture of *Dungeons & Dragons* and the fantasy novels of J. R. R. Tolkien (Pearce 2001). Even today, nearly 80 percent of all virtual world spaces are fantasy-oriented (White 2008). Early games such as *Ultima Online* and *EverQuest* eventually reached a niche profitability (Mulligan and Petrovsky 2003), but it was not until the highly successful *World of Warcraft* launched in 2004 that virtual worlds began to hit the mainstream. *WoW*, as it is still known by its 11.5 plus million players, is the most profitable and popular of the Western virtual worlds. Chinese and Korean markets are likely to be larger, but verifiable information in the sector is hard to come by. Eastern games also tend to operate by users buying time cards, where Western titles tend to use monthly subscriptions. This makes defining a "user" or "regular user" more art than science.

Who plays MMOs and why? Recent research suggests that the player base is typically 80 percent male, with a mean age of about 35. Most players are middle class, educated, and often technically savvy. They play for challenge, and to appreciate the virtual environment, but most often to interact with others (Griffiths et al. 2003; Kline and Arlidge 2002; Williams et al. 2008), and accordingly many titles have vibrant social communities, both on and offline. Estimates suggest that roughly a third of players knew each other before playing, with perhaps 5 to 10 percent of the new friendships migrating to the "real," face-to-face world (Williams et al. 2006; Yee 2006).

Coming as they did before the Facebook moment, these spaces were thus harbingers of the move to online social networks more generally. They have also been an attractive site for research, and perhaps more academic focus has been focused on them than is warranted by their sheer numbers. Scholars have studied them for their interpersonal interactions (Bailenson et al. 2005; Yee and Bailenson 2007; Yee et al. 2007), learning (Steinkuehler 2005), teamwork (Huang et al. 2009), cheating (Consalvo 2007; Keegan et al. 2010), community dynamics (Pearce 2009; Taylor 2006), identity and role playing (Nardi 2010; Williams et al. 2011), social networks (Huang et al. 2009), economics (Castronova 2001; Castronova et al. 2009), and many other topics.

Researchers have also flocked to study these spaces because they represent what Castronova has called "virtual petri dishes" (Castronova 2005, 2006). Social scientists have typically been able to get far more self-reported data than actual behavioral data, but these spaces suddenly presented a contained, observable environment populated by real people. This makes them potential proxies for studying offline behaviors in a safer, unobtrusive, and less expensive way, although there are certainly risks with doing such work badly (Williams 2010). Virtual worlds remain a vibrant genre within video games, but recently they have been surpassed in terms of raw numbers by a far more mainstream phenomenon, also online.

A casual explosion

Casual games are defined by their opposition to "hardcore" games. Where a hardcore game takes commitment and focus, and features cutting-edge graphics and complex game mechanics, casual games require no real dedication, feature simple graphics and are often easy to learn and play in a short time (Juul 2010). Yet despite the moniker, so-called "casual" gaming is the largest, most tectonic force in the history of the medium. It is also a case study in how supply, demand, cultural shifts, and new technologies can create an industry almost overnight. First, consider the numbers behind casual gaming. Whereas the target population of "mainstream" console gaming is males 18–35, casual games target everyone and attract a 60 percent female audience (Taylor 2010). Typical console games cost $15–25 million to develop, last about 3 months, and reach from 500,000 to four million players. Typical social and casual games cost $250–500 thousand to develop, last about 9 months and reach 10–50 million or more players (Taylor 2010). A console game is played for hours, a casual game minutes. In the US there are about 350 million dedicated game-playing devices, not including cell phones. These are home consoles and portable game players—in other words, the traditional, dedicated game-playing audience. From 2009–10, there were about 510 million accounts on social and casual games, up from virtually zero two years before. In other words, casual gaming in only two years appeared and rapidly surpassed the 35-year-old mainstream game industry.

Where did this movement come from? It's important to note that there have always been a lot of casual game players, but that they have been systematically prevented from playing by social and commercial forces. When early games burst onto the scene in the late 1970s and early 1980s as a cultural fad, the first players were not the stereotypical young men, but in fact were largely adults. The rise of Reaganite and Thatcherite social policies in the early 1980s coincided with a strong infantalization of games and electronic media in general. One theory is that social guilt over reduced time and resources spent on children manifested itself in animosity toward video games, VCRs, and cable television (Williams 2006a). These "electronic babysitters" caught most of the brunt of the guilt parents felt from spending less time with their children. More women working longer hours meant opportunities, but also significant fretting over child care. It was much easier to blame the devices which often took over the childcare role, than to look at the social forces and the bigger picture (Faludi 1991). So, it is perhaps not surprising that the same adults who happily plonked their quarters into *Ms. Pac Man* or *Asteroids* in 1981 would only two years later feel ashamed to admit it (Williams 2003). The middle-class dentist happily featured in a *Star Wars* game ad in 1980 was by 1982 replaced by quotes from an adult in an arcade in *Time's* cover story: "I'd really rather you didn't use my name. This is my secret place" (Skow 1982). By 1983, adults were effectively banned from arcades by social forces, and the simultaneous collapse of Atari and the home game industry made it appear that grown-ups were never again to be interested. Similar effects could be found among women, who were generally socialized away from technology already. The rise of Nintendo and its squarely child-centric marketing only reinforced these trends.

Yet another large force limiting adults has been the industry itself. Game development has been the province of hard-core game players who largely make games for themselves. The gradual corporatization of the games industry has moved developers towards thinking about audiences other than themselves, although this remains a challenge even today. Still, the exceptions tend to prove the rule: the biggest hits of the 1990s and 2000s tended to be "surprises" in that they sold a boatload of games to adults and especially to women. Games such as *The Sims*, *Myst*, and even the much-mocked *Deer Hunter* showed that the appetite for games was far broader than the supply had suggested, or developers realized.

However, the removal of those forces by corporate professionalization, demographic changes, and the rise of networks has demonstrated that what was lying dormant was in fact a tidal wave of interest. By the mid-2000s, those same children of the Nintendo era had become parents themselves and their desire for play had matured as well. The difference was that their time and their social networks were radically different. As Putnam (2000) wrote in his impactful *Bowling Alone*, adults have been largely sequestered from each other through media consumption and, we would add, arguably through the rise of atomized suburbs and a car-oriented culture. The combined effect is that there has been an immense demand for not just gaming for adults, but for social interactions in general (Williams 2006b, 2006c). To add to that, the original game players of the 1970s and 1980s have been able to "come out of the closet" so to speak, when geek is chic and gaming is acceptable. And, as Juul (2010) correctly notes, one need not be a hardcore gamer or devote hours on end to enjoy casual games. The brilliance of many casual titles is that they are accessible to anyone with a few minutes and a passing interest in either connecting with friends or even just killing some time. Rather than gamers trying to fit *their lives into* the requirements of complex games, casual games easily fit *into our lives* (Juul 2010).

Casual games are often (if not always) integrated into pre-existing social networks. Consider the case of a game player in three different eras. In 1990, the player had to find someone to come over, and that person had to commit to some significant time to learn and master the game. That was an effectively small roster of playmates, made tougher by the social constraint of not many people even admitting that they "play games." In 2000, with networks rising, that same player could probably do a lot better simply due to the fact that their potential playmates need not physically visit—although certainly that creates some of its own social capital costs and benefits (Shen and Williams 2011). Nevertheless, the player probably had a slightly larger roster. In 2010, the same player logs into Facebook and finds a system where nearly everyone they've ever met becomes a potential playmate, and the costs in time and effort have been dropped to near zero. This attracts the legions of the curious, the busy, and those who find games to be an excuse or a reason to stay connected to "real people," rather than the more anonymous spaces of virtual worlds.

This meteoric rise demonstrates that a massive pool of demand has been sitting untapped for decades. MMOs, the darlings of researchers, the press, and hard-core social players, collectively reached perhaps 45 million players worldwide by 2008, across roughly 100 titles. This was a massive expansion of online, networked play, and shocked many analysts. Contrast that with the 2009 case of game maker Zynga, who recorded 188 million players for *just one game*, *Farmville* (Taylor 2010) in just one year. Where most MMOs cost many millions of dollars to make and are considered successes with a few hundred thousand subscribers, Zynga introduced the cheap title *Treasure Island* in April of 2010 and had 24 million players after only three weeks (Taylor 2010).

These are changes of several orders of magnitude occurring to the game-playing base, and they are radically changing what it means to be "a gamer." Although the stereotype of the adolescent boy was broken by 2000 anyway, popular culture has been slow to realize it. This new cultural shift towards casual games and online social networking will continue to change that image. When combined with the demographic trends of new cohorts playing at 97 percent and above (Lenhart et al. 2008a; Lenhart et al. 2008b), gaming is unlikely to decline. Instead, it would appear more plausible that as older cohorts die off and take their lower playing rates with them, the overall rates of game play will only increase. Gaming is not simply here to stay, but is becoming more and more integrated with our daily lives, lived in the blurry space between online and off. What remains to be seen is how competitive forces will shape the casual game industry as the initial waves of novelty and first-mover advantages of the current market leaders dissolve.

Children's spaces

A 2010 report from the Kaiser Family Foundation (Ridehout et al. 2010) found that children aged 8–18 in the United States spent an average of an hour and a half each day playing interactive games, up twenty minutes from just five years earlier (Roberts et al. 2005). As with all child-oriented media, parents and policy-makers continue to be curious and suspicious about the effects video games may be having on children. The evidence is hotly disputed from the pages of academic journals to the halls of the US Supreme Court. Despite the fact that some scholars (Anderson et al. 2010) say the evidence for a causal link between game violence and aggression is greater than any other medium, other scholars have called the link into question or have questioned its degree of impact (Ferguson and Kilburn 2010; Sherry 2007). It may therefore be more useful to look at the use and importance of online play in everyday life. Indeed, Henry Jenkins and colleagues (2006) identify play and simulation as two of the essential skills necessary for youth to be literate and culturally competent in a new media landscape.

Ito and colleagues (2010), in bringing together a diverse range of ethnographic studies they conducted, identified at least five "genres of practice" among youths playing games. For some, games are just a means to kill time to fill in the gaps during their day. Others use games for socialization with friends and family. A third genre of youth game play is recreational game play, where competition is the primary motive. Related to this is organizing and mobilizing game practices, where social arrangements are necessary for competitive success (like guilds in MMOs). A fifth genre of game play is augmented game play, where gamers engage with secondary sources about the game, such as fan sites or modification hacks. Many of these genres are practiced in games intended for audiences of all ages, but there is no shortage of Internet games targeted for youth play.

One youth-oriented space that has been studied in depth is *Whyville*, an online virtual world/serious game (Kafai 2010). With over 4.2 million members aged 8 to 16 years old (68 percent female), it is one of the few youth-oriented virtual worlds designed for educational purposes. An average of 14,000 players log in each day, for an average for 40 minutes per login. Once online, players can customize their avatar and communicate with other users, much like any other virtual world (Kafai et al. 2010b). However unlike a typical virtual world, they can also participate in dozens of different educational activities. Players earn a virtual salary, and the most prominent way to build one's salary is through the successful completion of science games. These can range from single player games like Hot Air Balloon races (which require an understanding of the relationship between temperature and gas density and directional forces), to multiplayer collaborative games like Solstice Safari (where players work together to collect data about sunrise and sunset at different parts of the world), and multiplayer competitive games like Smart Cars races (where players must create light paths to navigate photosensitive tires, requiring an understanding of light, energy, and mechanical motion). In addition, *Whyville* has community science games, such as a virtual epidemiological outbreaks or virtual ecological disasters, that impact all users, who can then choose to engage in a new educational opportunity (Kafai et al. 2010a; Neulight et al. 2007).

Some sites/games, such as *Club Penguin* and *Neopets*, have been quite profitable, to the point that the former was purchased by Disney and the latter Viacom (Barnes 2007; Ito et al. 2010). *Club Penguin* is a typical virtual world, but instead of taking on human-like avatars, children create and move around the world as cartoon penguins that reside in personal igloos. Because the target audience is aged 6–14, *Club Penguin* places a heavy emphasis on child safety, by including automated filters in user chats and having moderators monitoring behavior. While basic game membership is free, players must pay a monthly fee in order to have full customization of their avatar. *Neopets*, a website that allows children to purchase and take care of virtual pets, is reminiscent of the Japanese toy Tamagotchi and the Pokémon franchise, as players can also train their virtual pets to fight one another. Players use virtual currency known as Neopoints (which can be won through game play) and Neocash (which can be purchased using real money). Games like *Neopets* have come under criticism for encouraging capitalism in youth by emphasizing the importance of earning and spending Neopoints (Grimes and Shade 2005; Seiter 2005), but Ito and colleagues (2010) argue that these spaces are often flexibly designed, allowing youth to explore different genres of play that best meet their interests and needs.

Serious games

Serious games are games with a primary purpose other than entertainment, such as education, training, or behavioral change (Ritterfeld et al. 2009). A movement towards designing and studying such games was spearheaded by Ben Sawyer and the Foresight and Governance Project at the Woodrow Wilson International Center for Scholars (Sawyer 2002). Drawing on the title of a 1970 book by Clark Abt (1987), Sawyer's Serious Game Initiative (and its subsequent spin-offs such as Games for Health and Games for Change) brought together scholars, practitioners, and designers with the goal "to help usher in a new series of policy education, exploration, and management tools utilizing state of the art computer game designs, technologies, and development skills" (<www.seriousgames.org>). Simultaneously, many academics had been thinking about the use of games as educational tools minus the specific label "serious games" (Gee 2003; Prensky 2006).

Multiple attempts have been made to come up with taxonomies for serious games. Sawyer and Smith (2008) classify them at the highest level based on the purpose (games for health, advergames, games for training, games for education, games for science and research, production, and games as work) and industry (government and NGO, defense, healthcare, marketing and communications, education, corporate, and industry). Each purpose further has its own unique sub-taxonomy. Ratan and Ritterfeld (2009) classify serious games on four dimensions: primary educational content (academic education, social change, occupation, health, military, and marketing); primary learning principle (practicing skills, knowledge gain through exploration, cognitive problem solving, or social problem solving); target age group (preschool and below; elementary school; middle and high school; and college, adult, and senior); and platform (computer and non-computer). Both Sawyer and Smith (2008) and Ratan and Ritterfeld (2009) also counted the number of titles that would fall into each of the proposed categories and found that serious games are predominantly geared towards academic education (it is hard to compare the taxonomies after that, as Ratan and Ritterfeld's second most populated category was games for social change, and many of these games Sawyer and Smith classified as advergaming).

While Ratan and Ritterfeld (2009) found that 90 percent of all serious games were PC games, they did not single out Internet versus non-Internet based games. It makes sense that they would not make this distinction, as educational games existed on the computer long before the Internet (Ito 2008). While online gaming can be leveraged for serious gaming purposes (Derryberry 2007; Gibson et al. 2007), the goals of many serious games do not inherently require online connectivity. In addition, some serious games will rely on the Internet for functionality, whereas other serious games will rely on the Internet for distribution only (Sawyer and Smith 2008).

One of the most popular first-person online shooter games is in fact a serious game: *America's Army* (Shilling et al. 2002). Developed as a recruitment tool for the US Army, the game was released Independence Day Weekend 2002 and had 400,000 downloads in its first day of availability. The game's website averaged 1.2 million hits per second in its first month (Lenoir 2002). Despite its entertainment value, its mainstream popularity, and its high ratings by leading game review magazines, it was thinly veiled to the audience as a serious game. The Army, facing a long decline in its recruiting goals, believed that exposing people to a simulation of basic training and the development of a military career in an emotionally entertaining fashion would spark the interest of game players. And in the process of getting people to download the game, the Army would also link players to other recruitment tools and websites (Li 2003). Part of its success was that it was a serious game that was also seriously fun (Shen et al. 2009).

Another serious game that harnessed the power of the Internet was *Darfur is Dying*, the winning entry in a competition sponsored by mtvU, the Reebok Human Rights Foundation, and the International Crisis group. Designed by graduate students at the University of Southern California, the online game (hosted on mtvU's website) depicts the hardships of living in the Darfur region in the Sudan, where the government supports the oppression and genocide of black Africans by the Janjaweed militia. Players assume the role of a Darfuri man, woman, or child, and try to find water and bring it back while avoiding militia jeeps. Players who fail are told of their character's likely fate, which usually involves beating and (in the case of females) rape. It also has a second part, where players learn to manage the scarce resources in a refugee camp. Integrated into the game are tools that allow people to email their friends and invite them to try the game for themselves and encourage them to write letters to their government officials to support pending legislations that would help resolve the humanitarian crisis in Darfur (Jones 2008; Raessens 2009; Thompson 2006).

Some (Bogost 2007; Brown 2007) have critiqued the effectiveness and rhetoric of games like *Darfur is Dying*, but one study found that Internet-based games for social change do have political impact. Neys and Jansz (2010) first interviewed developers of six political Internet games: *Airport Security* (a game about airport security policy), *Darfur is Dying*, *McDonald's Video Game* (a game that looks at McDonald's health and business practices), *Peacemaker Game* (a game about the Israeli-Palestinian conflict), *September 12th* (a game about Bush's War on Terror), and *Super Columbine Massacre RPG* (a game about the Columbine High School shooting). They found, in asking the developers their motivations, that these games serve three functions: informing players about an issue, persuasion (creating awareness and stimulating discussion), and engagement (inciting players to take action). After interviewing the developers, Neys and Jansz invited game players to try out one of these games. Before playing the game, participants were asked to write everything they knew about the topic. After playing, they were asked how playing the game affected their knowledge and opinion about the topic and whether they intended to learn more about the issue and/or tell their friends about the issue. The results suggested that these games did in fact lead to change (or at least self-reported, short-term change) in knowledge, opinions, and possible future actions. While the methodology could make few claims about external validity, this is one of the few empirical studies to look at the effectiveness of online serious games across multiple titles.

Serious games challenge the perceptions that video games are solely frivolous, leisurely activities or that they are bad for youth. As previously mentioned, Jenkins and colleagues (2006) see play and simulation as essential skills in the learning practices of youth. And serious games, such as *Darfur is Dying*, have the potential for social impact.

CONCLUSION AND RESEARCH DIRECTIONS

Video games have grown from a niche fad into a fully mature and commercialized medium, with all of the speedbumps and cultural conflicts that implies. From their earliest days as simple games played by only a handful of enthusiasts to their current position commanding billions of dollars and hundreds of millions of eyeballs, games have traced a history reflecting our own in modern industrialized societies—as we have become atomized into disparate communities and then reconnected in new forms via the Internet, so have games. Where games were once argued to be a medium that was as abominable as rock 'n' roll or comic books, they are nevertheless as inevitable as the seasons. This does not mean that they are embraced by all, or even understood by most. Video games—and all of the unknowns researchers have yet to discover about them—are now a cultural force simultaneously condemned for their corrosive effect on our values at the same time as they are embraced as a positive force for change, learning, and "real" experience.

This same sense of evolution, change, and novelty could just as easily be used to describe games research as well. The early days of research were marked by studies about "What do games do to us?" in communication research and a separate tradition around games and simulation with roots in military applications and table-top games. Today, the research community surrounding games comes from communication, psychology, cultural and critical studies, sociology, and now even business, economics, and computer science. It's not so much interdisciplinary as a collection of one-time refugees from these disparate fields now commonly linked by their interest, affection, or mistrust of the medium. Methodologies range from content analyses and experiments, to participant observation and textual analysis, to econometrics, and feature both quantitative and qualitative work. Whereas in 2000 there were few who would risk being labeled as "game researchers" for fear of being denied tenure or collegial respect, the field is now well out of the closet. It features more than a dozen conferences a year, healthy divisions within other major groups, a handful of active specialty journals, and a vibrant online community with listservs and growing archives for scholarship. The games bibliography site Digiplay Initiative (http://digiplay.info/digibiblio) now features over 3,000 citations across these various disciplines. Thus, as society comes to accept games, so also has the academy. It is conceivable that in the not-too-distant future, games studies will be a common department on college campuses, just as cinema transformed from a "low" art to one accepted as worthy of scholarly attention (Gabler 1999). This will be one more piece of evidence that the medium has entered the mainstream.

REFERENCES

Abt, C. (1987). *Serious Games*, Lanham, MD: University Press of America.

Anderson, C. A., Shibuya, A., Ihori, N., Swing, E. L., Bushman, B. J., Sakamto, A., Rothstein, H. R. and Saleem, M. (2010). "Violent Video Game Effects on Agression, Empathy, and Prosocial Behavior in Eastern and Western Countries: A Meta-Analytic Review," *Psychological Bulletin*, 136(2): 151–73.

Bailenson, J., Beall, A., Blascovich, J., Loomis, J., and Turk, M. (2005). "Transformed Social Interaction, Augmented Gaze, and Social Influence in Immersive Virtual Environments," *Human Communication Research*, 31(4): 511–37.

Barnes, B. (2007). "Web Playgrounds of the Very Young," *New York Times*, December 31. Available at <http://us.blizzard.com/en-us/company/press/pressreleases.html?id=2847816>. Accessed July 12, 2011.

Blizzard Entertainment (2008). "World of Warcraft Subscriber Base Reaches 11.5 Million Worldwide," Blizzard Entertainment Press Releases, November 21. Available at <http://us.blizzard.com/en-us/company/press/pressreleases.html?id=2847816>. Accessed July 12, 2011.

Bogost, I. (2007). *Persuasive Games: The Expressive Power of Videogames*, Cambridge, MA: MIT Press.

Borrow, Z. (2003). "The Godfather," *Wired*, 11(1): 103–4.

boyd, d. m. and Ellison, N. B. (2007). "Social Network Sites: Definition, History, and Scholarship," *Journal of Computer-Mediated Communication*, 13(1). Available at <http://jcmc.indiana.edu/vol13/issue1/boyd.ellison.html>. Accessed July 12, 2011.

Brown, J. G. (2007). "Teaching About Genocide in a New Millenium," *Social Education*, 71(1): 21–3.

Castronova, E. (2001). "Virtual Worlds: A First-Hand Account of Market and Society on the Cyberian Frontier", Center for Economic Studies and Institute for Economic Research. Available at <http://papers.ssrn.com/sol3/papers.cfm?abstract_id=294828>. Accessed July 12, 2011.

——(2005). *Synthetic Worlds: The Business and Culture of Online Games*, Chicago, IL: University of Chicago Press.

——(2006). "On the Research Value of Large Games: Natural Experiments in Norrath and Camelot," *Games and Culture*, 1(2): 163–86.

——Williams, D., Huang, Y., Shen, C., Keegan, B., Ratan, R., Xiong, L., Huang, Y., and Keegan, B. (2009). "As Real as Real? Macroeconomic Behavior in a Large-Scale Virtual World," *New Media & Society*, 11(5): 685–707.

Colker, D. (2001). "The Legend Lives On," *Los Angeles Times*, May 17: pp. T1, 6.

Consalvo, M. (2007). *Cheating: Gaining Advantage in Video Games*, Cambridge, MA: MIT Press.

Cowan, R. (1999). "The Consumption Junction: A Proposal for Research Strategies in the Sociology of Technology," in W. E. Bijker, P. Hughes, and T. Pinch (eds). *The Social Construction of Technological Systems*, Cambridge, MA: MIT Press, pp. 261–80.

Derryberry, A. (2007). "Serious Games: Online Games for Learning." Available at <http://www.adobe.com/resources/elearning/pdfs/serious_games_wp.pdf>. Accessed July 12, 2011.

Douglas, S. (1987). *Inventing American Broadcasting, 1899–1922*, Baltimore, MD: Johns Hopkins University Press.

Entertainment Software Association. (2006). "Essential Facts About the Computer and Video Game Industry." Available at <http://www.theesa.com/facts/pdfs/ESA_EF_2006.pdf>. Accessed July 12, 2011.

——(2007). "Essential Facts About the Computer and Video Game Industry." Available at <http://www.theesa.com/facts/pdfs/ESA_EF_2007.pdf>. Accessed July 12, 2011.

——(2008). "Essential Facts About the Computer and Video Game Industry." Available at <http://www.theesa.com/facts/pdfs/ESA_EF_2008.pdf>. Accessed July 12, 2011.

——(2009). "Essential Facts About the Computer and Video Game Industry." Available at <http://www.theesa.com/facts/pdfs/ESA_EF_2009.pdf>. Accessed July 12, 2011.

——(2010). "Essential Facts About the Computer and Video Game Industry." Available at <http://www.theesa.com/facts/pdfs/ESA_Essential_Facts_2010.PDF>. Accessed July 12, 2011.

——(2011). "Essential Facts About the Computer and Video Game Industry." Available at <http://www.theesa.com/facts/pdfs/ESA_EF_2011.pdf>. Accessed July 12, 2011.

Facebook (2012). "Statistics." Available at <http://newsroom.fb.com/content/default.aspx?NewsAreaId=20>. Accessed June 20, 2012.

Faludi, S. (1991). *Backlash: The Undeclared War Against American Women*, New York, NY: Crown Publishers.

Ferguson, C. J. and Kilburn, J. (2010). "Much Ado About Nothing: The Misestimation and Overinterpretation of Violent Video Game Effects in Eastern and Western Nations: Comment on Anderson et al.," *Psychological Bulletin*, 162(2): 174–8.

Gabler, N. (1999). *Life the Movie: How Entertainment Conquered Teality*, New York, NY: Alfred A. Knopf.

Gee, J. P. (2003). *What Video Games Have to Teach Us About Learning and Literacy*, New York, NY: Palgrave Macmillan.

Gibson, D., Aldrich, C., and Prensky, M. (eds.) (2007). *Games and Simulations in Online Learning: Research and Development Frameworks*, Hershey, PA: Information Science Publishing.

Gibson, W. (1984). *Neuromancer*, New York, NY: Ace Books.

Griffiths, M., Davies, M., and Chappell, D. (2003). "Breaking the Stereotype: The Case of Online Gaming," *CyberPsychology & Behavior*, 6(1): 81–91.

Grimes, S. M., and Shade, L. R. (2005). "Neopian Economics of Play: Children's Cyberpets and Online Communities as Immersive Advertising in Neopets.com," *International Journal of Media & Cultural Politics*, 1(2): 181–98.

Guiness World Records. (2010). *Guinness World Records Gamer's Edition*. Indianapolis, IN: BradyGames.

Hagiwara, S. and Oliver, I. (1999). "Sega Dreamcast: Creating a Unified Entertainment World," *IEEE Micro*, 19(6): 29–35.

Herman, L. (1997). *Phoenix: The Fall and Rise of Videogames*, Union, NJ: Rolenta Press.

Herz, J. C. (1997). *Joystick Nation*, Boston, MA: Little, Brown and Company.

Huang, Y., Shen, C., Williams, D., and Contractor, N. (2009). "Virtually There: The Role of Proximity and Homophily in Virtual World Networks," Paper presented at the IEEE-SocialComm-09, Vancouver, Canada.

Huang, Y., Zhu, M., Wang, J., Pathak, N., Shen, C., Keegan, B., et al. (2009). "The Formation of Task-Oriented Groups: Exploring Combat Activities in Online Games." Paper presented at the IEEE, SocialComm-09, Vancouver, Canada.

Ito, M. (2008). "Education vs. Entertainment: A Cultural History of Children's Software," in K. Salen (ed.), *The Ecology of Games: Connecting Youth, Games, and Learning*, Cambridge, MA: MIT Press, 89–116.

——Baumer, S., Bittani, M., boyd, d., Cody, R., Herr-Stephenson, B., et al. (2010). *Hanging Out, Messing Around, and Geeking Out: Kids Living and Learning With New Media*, Cambridge, MA: MIT Press.

Jenkins, H., Purushotma, R., Clinton, K., Weigel, M., and Robinson, A. J. (2006). "Confronting the Challenges of Participatory Culture: Media Education in the 21st Century." Available at <http://newmedialiteracies.org/files/working/NMLWhitePaper.pdf>. Accessed September 10, 2012.

Jones, R. (2008). "Saving Worlds with Videogame Activism," in R. E. Ferdig (ed.). *Handbook of Research on Effective Electronic Gaming in Education* (vol. 2), Hershey, PA: Information Science Reference, pp. 970–86.

Juul, J. (2010). *A Casual Revolution: Reinventing Video Games and Their Players*, Cambridge, MA: MIT Press.

Kafai, Y. B. (2010). "World of Whyville: An Introduction to Tween Virtual Life," *Games and Culture*, 5(1): 3–22.

——Fields, D. A., and Cook, M. S. (2010a). "Your Second Selves: Player-Designed Avatars," *Games and Culture*, 5(1): 23–42.

Kafai, Y. B., Quintero, M., and Feldon, D. (2010b). "Investigating the 'Why' in Whypox: Casual and Systematic Explorations of a Virtual Epidemic," *Games and Culture*, 5(1): 116–35.

Keegan, B., Ahmad, M., Srivastava, J., Williams, D., and Contractor, N. (2010). "Dark Gold: Statistical Properties of Clandestine Networks in Massively Multiplayer Online Games." Paper presented at the IEEE SocialCom-10, Minneapolis, MN.

Kent, S. (2000). *The First Quarter: A 25-year History of Video Games*, Bothell, WA: BWD Press.

Kirkpatrick, D. (2010). *The Facebook Effect: The Inside Story of the Company That is Connecting the World*, New York: Simon & Schuster.

Kline, S. and Arlidge, A. (2002). *Online Gaming as Emergent Social Media: A Survey*, Burnaby, BC: Simon Fraser University Media Analysis Laboratory.

Kline, S., Dyer-Witheford, N., and DePeuter, G. (2003). *Digital Play: The Interaction of Technology, Culture, and Marketing*, Montreal: McGill-Queen's University Press.

Lenhart, A., Jones, S., and Macgill, A. (2008a). "Over half of American Adults Play Video Games," Pew Internet & American Life Project, December 7. Available at <http://www.pewinternet.org/Reports/2008/Adults-and-Video-Games/1-Data-Memo/01-Overview.aspx>. Accessed June 20, 2012.

Lenhart, A., Kahne, J., Middaugh, E., Macgill, A., Evans, C., and Vitak, J. (2008b). *Teens, Video Games, and Civics*, Washington, DC: Pew Internet & American Life Project.

Lenoir, T. (2002). "Fashioning the Military-Entertainment Complex," *Correspondence: An International Review of Culture and Society*, 10: 14–16.

Levin, R. (2003). "Neal Stephenson Rewrites History," *Wired*, 12(9): 130–1.

Levy, S. (1994). *Hackers: Heroes of the Computer Revolution*, New York, NY: Penguin Books.

Li, Z. (2003). "The Potential of America's Army the Video Game as Civilian-Military Public Sphere." Unpublished Master's Thesis, Massachusetts Institute of Technology, Cambridge, MA.

Lisberger, S. (dir. and script). (1982). *Tron*, Walt Disney Productions.

Montfort, N. (2001). "Building 20," in V. Burnham (ed.). *Supercade: A Visual History of the Videogame Age 1971–1984*, Cambridge, Massachusetts: MIT Press, p. 34.

Mulligan, J. and Petrovsky, B. (2003). *Developing Online Games: An Insider's Guide*, Boston, MA: New Riders.

Nardi, B. (2010). *My Life as a Night Elf Priest: An Anthropological Account of World of Warcraft*, Ann Arbor, MI: University of Michigan Press.

Negroponte, N. (1996). *Being Digital*, New York, NY: Vintage.

Neulight, N., Kafai, Y. B., Kao, L., Foley, B., and Galas, C. (2007). "Children's Participation in a Virtual Epidemic in the Science Classroom: Making Connections to Natural Infectious Diseases," *Journal of Science Education and Technology*, 16(1): 47–58.

Neys, J. and Jansz, J. (2010). "Political Internet Games: Engaging an Audience," *European Journal of Communication*, 25(3): 227–41.

Nielsen Company. (2011). "Nielsen | Top 10 Video Games | Video Game Sales." Available at <http://www.nielsen.com/us/en/insights/top10s/video_games.html>. Accessed July 15, 2011.

Pearce, C. (2009). *Communities of Play: Emergent Cultures in Multiplayer Games and Virtual Worlds*, Cambridge, MA: MIT Press.

——(2001). "The Convergence of Creativity and Commerce: The Future of Interactive Game Arts." Paper presented at the Playing by the Rules Conference, Chicago, IL.

Prensky, M. (2006). *Digital Game-Based Learning*, New York, NY: McGraw-Hill.

Putnam, R. D. (2000). *Bowling Alone: The Collapse and Tevival of American Community*, New York, NY: Simon & Schuster.

Raessens, J. (2009). "The Gaming *Dispositif*: An Analysis of Serious Games from a Humanities Perspective," in U. Ritterfeld, M. Cody, and P. Vorderer (eds). *Serious Games: Mechanisms and Effects*, New York, NY: Routledge, pp. 486–512.

Ratan, R. and Ritterfeld, U. (2009). "Classifying Serious Games," in U. Ritterfeld, M. Cody, and P. Vorderer (eds). *Serious Games: Mechanisms and Effects*, New York, NY: Routledge, pp. 10–24.

Ridehout, V. J., Foehr, U. G., and Roberts, D. F. (2010). *Generation M^2: Media in the Lives of 8- to 18-Year-Olds*, Kaiser Family Foundation.

Ritterfeld, U., Cody, M., and Vorderer, P. (eds) (2009). *Serious Games: Mechanisms and Effects*, New York, NY: Routledge.

Roberts, D. F., Foehr, U. G., and Ridehout, V. J. (2005). *Generation M: Media in the Lives of 8–18 Year-Olds*, Kaiser Family Foundation.

Sawyer, B. (2002). "Serious Games: Improving Public Policy Through Game-Based Learning and Simulation." Available at <http://www.seriousgames.org/images/seriousarticle.pdf>. Accessed July 12, 2011.

——and Smith, P. (2008). "Serious Games Taxonomy." Available at <http://www.dmill.com/presentations/serious-games-taxonomy-2008.pdf>. Accessed July 12, 2011.

Schumpeter, J. A. (1943). *Capitalism, Socialism and Democracy*, New York, NY: Harper & Bros.

Seiter, E. (2005). *The Internet Playground: Children's Access, Entertainment, and Miseducation*, New York, NY: Peter Lang.

Sheff, D. (1999). *Game Over, Press Start to Continue: The Maturing of Mario*, Wilton, CT: GamePress.

Shen, C., Wang, H., and Ritterfeld, U. (2009). "Serious Games and Seriously Fun Games: Can They be One and the Same," in U. Ritterfeld, M. Cody and P. Vorderer (eds). *Serious Games: Mechanisms and Effects*, New York, NY: Routledge, pp. 48–61.

Shen, C. and Williams, D. (2011). "Unpacking Time Online: Connecting Internet and Massively Multiplayer Online Game Use With Psychosocial Well-Being," *Communication Research*, 38(1): 123–49.

Sherry, J. (2007). "Violent Video Games and Aggression: Why Can't We Find Links?," in R. W. Preiss, B. M. Gayle, N. Burrell, M. Allen and J. Bryant (eds) *Mass Media Effects Research: Advances Through Meta-Analysis*, Mahwah, NJ: Erlbaum, pp. 231–48.

Shilling, R., Zyda, M., and Wardynski, E. C. (2002). "Introducing Emotion into Military Simulation and Videogame Design: America's Army: Operations and VIRTE." Paper presented at the GameOn Conference, London.

Shippy, D. and Phipps, M. (2009). *The Race for a New Game Machine: Creating the Chips Inside the XBox 360 and the Playstation 3*, New York: Citadel Press.

Skow, J. (January 18, 1982). "Games that Play People: Those Beeping Video Invaders are Dazzling, Fun, and Even Addictive," *Time*, 50–8.

Smith, A. (2010). "Home Broadband 2010," Pew Internet & American Life Project, August 10. Available at <http://pewinternet.org/Reports/2010/Home-Broadband-2010.aspx>. Accessed June 20, 2012.

Steinkuehler, C. (2005). "Cognition and Learning in Massively Multiplayer Online Games: A Critical Approach." Unpublished Doctoral Dissertation, University of Wisconsin-Madison, Madison, WI.

Stephenson, N. (1992). *Snow Crash*, New York: Roc.

Takahashi, D. (2002). *Opening the Xbox: Inside Microsoft's Plan to Unleash an Entertainment Revolution*, Roseville, CA: Prima Lifestyles.

——(2006). *The Xbox 360 Uncloaked: The Real Story Behind Microsoft's Next-Generation Video Game Console*, Arlington, VA: Spiderworks.

Taylor, J. (2010). *2009–2010 Home Interactive Entertainment Market Update*, Portland, Oregon: Arcadia Investment Corp.

Taylor, T. L. (2006). *Play Between Worlds: Exploring Online Game Culture*, Cambridge, MA: MIT Press.

Thompson, C. (2006). "Saving the World, One Video Game at a Time," *New York Times*, July 23. Available at <http://www.nytimes.com/2006/07/23/arts/23thom.html>. Accessed July 12, 2011.

Vogel, H. L. (2001). *Entertainment Industry Economics: A Guide for Financial Analysis*, Cambridge: Cambridge University Press.

Wachowski, L. and Wachowski, A. (dirs. and script) (1999). *The Matrix*. Warner (Producer).

White, P. (2008). *MMOGData: Charts*, Gloucester. Available at <http://mmogdata.voig.com/Charts>. Accessed July 20, 2012.

Williams, D. (2002). "Structure and Competition in the U.S. Home Video Game Industry." *The International Journal on Media Management*, 4(1): 41–54.

——(2003). "The Video Game Lightning Rod." *Information, Communication & Society*, 6(4): 523–50.

——(2006a). "A Brief Social History of Game Play," in P. Vorderer and J. Bryant (eds). *Playing Video Games: Motives, Responses, and Consequences*, Mahwah, NJ: Erlbaum, 229–47.

——(2006b). "Groups and Goblins: The Social and Civic Impact of an Online Game," *Journal of Broadcasting and Electronic Media*, 50(4): 651–70.

——(2006c). "Why Game Studies Now? Gamers Don't Bowl Alone," *Games and Culture*, 1(1): 13–16.

——(2010). "The Mapping Principle, and a Research Framework for Virtual Worlds." *Communication Theory*, 20(4): 451–70.

——Ducheneaut, N., Xiong, L., Zhang, Y., Yee, N., and Nickell, E. (2006). "From Tree House to Barracks: The Social Life of Guilds in World of Warcraft," *Games and Culture*, 1(4): 338–61.

Williams, D., Kennedy, T., and Moore, R. (2011). "Behind the Avatar: The Patterns, Practices and Functions of Role Playing in MMOs," *Games and Culture*, 6(2): 171–200.

Williams, D., Yee, N., and Caplan, S. (2008). "Who Plays, How Much, and Why? A Behavioral Player Census of a Virtual World," *Journal of Computer Mediated Communication*, 13(4): 993–1018.

Yee, N. (2006). "The Demographics, Motivations and Derived Experiences of Users of Massively-Multiuser Online Graphical Environments," *PRESENCE: Teleoperators and Virtual Environments*, 15(3): 309–29.

——and Bailenson, J. (2007). "The Proteus Effect: Self Transformations in Virtual Reality," *Human Communication Research*, 33(2): 271–90.

——, Baileson, J., Urbanek, M., Chang, F., and Merget, D. (2007). "The Unbearable Likeness of Being Digital: The Persistence of Nonverbal Social Norms in Online Virtual Environments," *CyberPsychology & Behavior*, 10(1): 115–21.

CHAPTER 11

CROSS-NATIONAL COMPARATIVE PERSPECTIVES FROM THE WORLD INTERNET PROJECT

GUSTAVO CARDOSO, GUO LIANG,
AND TIAGO LAPA

INTRODUCTION: GLOBALLY NETWORKED RESEARCH ON THE INTERNET

THE World Internet Project (WIP) was initiated by a group of researchers who sought to understand the economic, political, and social impact of a global network.[1] Their project generated collaboration among dozens of countries around the world, each pursuing a common strategy for gathering common data. During the last decade, WIP has yielded data sets and analyses that address within nation, but also the cross-national, comparative aspects of the Internet's use and impact. Over time, it has advanced efforts to share and merge national data sets and to share insights with academics, governments, journalists, citizens, and business and industry around the world.

The project originated in 1999 at the Center for Communication Policy, University of California, Los Angeles, but in 2004 moved with the principal investigator to the University of Southern California's Annenberg School Center for the Digital Future. It was founded in collaboration with the School of Communication Studies at Nanyang Technological University in Singapore and the Osservatorio Internet Italia at Bocconi

[1] Up-to-date details about the World Internet Project can be found at <http://www.worldinternetproject .net> or <http://www.digitalcenter.org/>. Accessed May 11, 2011.

University in Milan, Italy. From this core set of countries, the project sought to incorporate nations from all regions of the world. The project sought partners among the most developed countries, before these nations grew too accustomed to the Internet; but it was considered equally important to work with developing countries, as they began to move online. The founders assumed that the influence of the Internet would rival television, and become one of the most important instruments of cultural influence of the twenty-first century. With that belief in mind, the WIP was designed to become the vehicle for tracking what happens as households and nations adopt and use the Internet.

The project was the first globally collaborative, longitudinal exploration of how life is being transformed by the Internet, with year-to-year comparisons of how people use this technology. While methodological and international collaboration proved to be time-consuming and complex to manage, the rationale was simple: track households as they go online and continue to follow them as their usage increases and becomes more comprehensive. By 2011 the project had attracted more than thirty partners. And by this time, it was arguable that, in some nations, the Internet had become comparable to television in its impact on work, school, and play, underscoring the value of the transnational longitudinal study of the Internet.

APPROACHES TO STUDYING THE WORLDWIDE DIFFUSION OF THE INTERNET

"Internet Studies" is an emerging field that takes a multidisciplinary perspective on the study of the Internet, but with a clearly articulated methodology. It does not pursue a homogeneous theoretical and methodological approach, since the scope of the Internet is potentially vast and is broadly defined. Instead, WIP research follows a pragmatic approach, one in which the collaborating partners seek to enable a global analysis of trends that can be commonly analyzed, while at the same time encouraging each partner to develop unique approaches to their own analyses, following their particular theoretical backgrounds.

The meaning of the Internet itself is purposely kept broad, as a network of networks, which includes related media and information and communication technologies (ICT), to reflect its ever-changing characteristics along with its unforeseen and unintended consequences. Since the Internet has brought changes in virtually all areas of social life—politics, culture, economy, education, interpersonal, and family relationships—it has brought researchers from different disciplines, in the social and behavioral sciences and elsewhere, into the wide field of Internet studies. This fosters innovation within the project, but also differences in theoretical perspectives and methods that are not always easily reconciled with each other.

Despite a focus on collecting data at the individual level, the diversity of the WIP permits partners to move across multiple levels of analysis, including theories of information and the network society, that have impacts in social theorizing as a whole, and focus on macro-level changes; studies of community or of regional changes associated with the meso-level of analysis; and studies of mediated interpersonal communication that are at a micro-level. Yet, as argued by Mouzelis (1995), this confinement to macro–micro analysis is over-simplistic, since personal interaction, for instance between heads of state, can and often does have consequences at the macro level that stretch both in time and space. The mediated interactions between agents, the mediated communication within a community of hackers, the blogging of key political figures or the posting of a video on YouTube by a single user, can all unlock a chain of events that have macro-level implications. In addition, the field of Internet Studies is as concerned with the analysis of *structures* (the shape of the networks, the constraints of access, and of the flow of information) as of the *agency* of those who act (Castells 2000).

There will continue to be controversies over the scope of Internet Studies and related fields such as New Media Studies. Therefore it is useful to keep a broad definition of Internet Studies that incorporates many aspects of these areas of research and teaching. Internet Studies is constantly on the move, at a rapid pace, looking for new objects of analysis and fresh perspectives, and new methodologies for the study of old objects. It acknowledges the complex interactions between the Internet and society and bridges technological, personal, and psycho-social changes without giving undue weight to one type of change over another.

Wellman (2004) has argued that there are three ages in Internet Studies. The first age was characterized by a great optimism about the changes that ICTs could bring, and about its significance in terms of technological progress and to human life as a whole. As Wellman put it: "The Internet was seen as a bright light, shining above everyday concerns. It was a technological marvel, thought to be bringing a new Enlightenment to transform the world" (2004: 124). Nevertheless, utopian visions also brought dystopian ones mirroring Umberto Eco's binomial distinction between Apocalyptic and Integrated views. Forfeiting social science knowledge led to gross misinterpretations of the significance of the Internet such as calling every interaction online a "community," catching on to Marshall McLuhan's notion that mass media was stitching the world together into a global village. Likewise, the focus on the *brave new world* of the Internet, neglects the intertwining between the offline social world and its community dynamics with online communication and relationships.

By the late 1990s, which was characterized by Wellman as the beginning of the second age, a series of actors, government policy-makers, commercial agents, and academics recognized the need of systematic documentation and investigation of users and how they made use of the new technologies. Since then, the worldwide rapid diffusion of Internet access and the repeated introduction of ever newer ICTs, often referred to by the buzzword "new media"—"shorthand for a volatile cultural and technology industry that includes multimedia, entertainment, and e-commerce" (Lievrouw and Livingstone 2002)—began to attract more attention from a number of social science and humanities disciplines, including the field of communication, resulting in a fertile ground for conceptual input. Some of these investigations, like the Pew Internet and American Life

Project and the WIP, framed the research in terms of traditional social science approaches, with a focus less on the technology than on users.

The focus remained, mainly, at the aggregate level and on global comparative research. But the Internet and networks themselves were not only viewed as mere objects of study: they have been used as a platform to boost cross-national and *networked* research, which facilitates the scientific exchange of procedures and results and the shared development of new hypotheses regarding the role of the Internet in changing human lives. Different research teams all over the world conduct long-term longitudinal studies of the impact of ICTs, using well-accepted social scientific survey methods and techniques. This is a great challenge but also a great opportunity that sets apart the social and technological conditions of the study of the Internet from the study of the traditional media, namely television (Cardoso et al. 2009: 3–4). The ongoing worldwide gathering of empirical results is paving the way to current theoretical scrutiny and conceptual refinements. Recent disciplinary developments correspond to what Wellman (2004: 127) saw as the dawning of the third age of Internet Studies, that is when "the real analysis begins with more focused, theoretically-driven projects" (2004: 127).

The study of the relationship between Internet and society provides a window on contemporary societies. This entails the study of social problems such as economic, political, and technological exclusion, and the social and personal implications of the dissemination of the Internet. Therefore, the worldwide research community is called upon to identify social problems or changes that result from the social shaping and social consequences of the Internet. But it is also a challenge to translate the impact of the Internet on society, and the influence of society on the Internet, into meaningful social theory. Just how the Internet is part of society remains subject to theoretical debate. Many of these discussions are not about technology but about how societies are changing, what are the key drivers of change, which changes are better or worse, how the Internet mediates the social changes and social relations, and what are its impacts on the state of democracy, culture, and social exclusion.

In research, studies often contextualize online social phenomena by looking at offline antecedents (demographics, user characteristics, power/access issues) of online activities, attitudes, and uses. These online practices can have, in turn, intended or unintended offline consequences at the individual, group, or societal level, whose consequences may be negative or positive, diffuse, or specific. There isn't a linear way to analyze the Internet and its social consequences. Nor is there a paradigmatic unity to look at this dynamic social cycle: offline antecedents → Internet activities → offline consequences.

This framework is closely connected with theoretical traditions in the empirical social sciences. These traditions lead research to view the offline world and its social, political, and economic structures from a positive viewpoint. This is more characteristic in the West, where it is more likely for researchers to regard the Internet as a tool to enhance positive aspects of liberal democratic societies. For instance, early utopian hopes of the development of the Internet argued that the offline positive antecedents of the Western world, such as individual liberty, pluralism, diversity, and the formation of communities, could be translated and even enhanced by online functioning of the Internet

(Kapor 1993). Therefore, the offline consequences of Internet activities would be beneficial to changing the lives of individuals (Rheingold 1993), which would complement their social connectivity through the Internet (Katz et al. 2001).

Conversely, authors who look to Western capitalism from a critical stance, notably Marxist scholars, such as Schiller (1996), were likely to see ICTs as technologies that reflect the social structure and can be used to enhance social inequalities. At the individual level, there were also reactions to the utopian views, since the Internet could be regarded as an escape mechanism to states of loneliness and depression, and to the lesser communication and individualization present in modern societies (Kraut et al. 1998). This perspective reintroduces the theme of alienation allegedly promoted by media technologies that could enhance and even endorse the loss of contact with the social environment (Nie and Erbring 2000) and have negative impacts on social capital and communities (Putnam 2000).

This debate called for a more neutral and dispassionate analysis of the Internet and its offline consequences, but it was also useful to highlight the complexities of the social study of ICTs. As DiMaggio et al. (2001) pointed out, research should look to the social structure of a given society and take into account the issues of power, inequality, and access. Furthermore, the offline consequences are also multifaceted and multilayered, given the wide range of influences in social life and structures. It is difficulty to isolate a clear main effect of the Internet as its impacts can have multiple manifestations and go both ways. As McKenna and Bargh put it: "Like the telephone and television before it, the Internet by itself is not a main effect cause of anything" (2000: 57).

Furthermore, the appropriation and domestication (Silverstone 2005) of the Internet in everyday life doesn't spread around the world in the same ways and has differentiated impacts in each dimension. Moreover, questions about the Internet are not restricted to the *media or technological landscape*: they encompass all dimensions. Indeed, we can conceptualize the Internet as a global social fact in a double sense: not only in Marcel Mauss' original notion, that is a social fact that encompasses all dimensions of the social, but also because it is a manifestation and a tool of globalization with far-reaching consequences. That doesn't mean that there aren't localized and specific consequences in particular societies. And to say that the social study of the Internet has encompassing effects in social structures doesn't mean that there aren't disjunctures from the flows of information between economic, cultural, and political structures.

But the necessity to put the Internet into context is not unproblematic, especially in its operationalization. On the one hand, the inception of a particular technology is, by itself, a social activity. As Livingstone puts it "before and indeed after any new medium is introduced there is a lengthy process of development and design, of the identification of a market and the construction of a 'need', all of these being fundamentally social activities rather than purely technical ones" (2002: 18). On the other hand, there is also the overzealous danger of completely neutralizing technology, undermining the attention given to its specific characteristics, semiotics, histories, and potentials. As MacKenzie and Wajcman (1999) explained, technological determinism is a partial truth since the specific features of Internet as a technology also matter. In general, Internet Studies has been contextualizing this new technology within the historical, economic, and culturally specific conditions of its development, dissemination, and social appropriation.

THE DIFFUSION OF THE INTERNET AND ITS USES AND IMPACTS WORLDWIDE

The research based on WIP data has shown that the diffusion of the Internet has rapidly increased during the last decade, but also that there remain major disparities across the world. Knowledge on the increased usage of the Internet has made us more aware of our commonalities than of our differences. Understanding worldwide differences will probably allow us to find out more about our own societies and our identity in the network society. There are many examples of the differences captured by the WIP surveys. For example, looking to WIP data from 2010, you can see that in Nordic European countries more than 80 percent of the population are using the Internet, which far exceeds other areas of the World, like Southern Europe, China, or Latin America. In Sweden, Internet access is high because of widespread access to broadband connections (97 percent of Internet users), with people spending a lot more time online (15.5 hours per week on average if both time spent at home and work are included). Usually, a high percentage of broadband connections go in hand with more time spent online; however, in the US, where there is a lower broadband penetration (around 80 percent of Internet users), people spend even more time online (19 hours per week on average).

There are also differences across studies concerning the consequences of the advancement of new media for the traditional media—newspapers and television. Nonetheless, recent changes are not only about new and traditional media competing for individuals' time and attention, or competing for advertising revenue. According to Cardoso and Araújo (2009), the Internet as a medium has an important role in our digital ecologies and has moved recently from being a space of keepers of knowledge into a space mainly built around the communication activities that configure the archetype of the communicator. The authors examine common traits found between words written about the Internet before 1997, and actions performed by users of the Internet in 2007. They argue that although we could frame the first studies in the fundamental opposition of uses between information spaces and social spaces or communities, after a decade of Internet usage communication has emerged as the major driving force in our daily uses of the Internet. Furthermore, the typological opposition between entertainment, information, and communication can be used to differentiate countries and groups of individuals within the same country. The researchers argue that if Asia is more "entertainment" driven in its uses of the Internet, the Anglo-Saxon speaking World is divided between Australia and US, where "entertainment" has a greater weight than in the UK, where in turn users focus more on "communication" and "information."

There has been an interest among WIP researchers in linking social demographics with usage patterns of the Internet. This is particularly important for the study of the digital divide within countries in terms of such factors as age, education, income, ethnicity, and geographic location. But research is not only carried out within the same society. Global comparative research takes into account country differences such as national wealth or the type of welfare state. There is also a different stance on social reality that comes with the democratization of access: the digital differentiation approach. Those with greater socio-economic, cognitive, and cultural resources, and skills, have tended to use the Internet more frequently as an information tool and as a social medium, and be less focused on entertainment.

The focus on access and frequency of use also leads to the issue of normalization versus stratification. When comparing the UK and Sweden, Reisdorf (2010) found that in some countries with a higher percentage of users diffusion is slowing, reaching a plateau where the digital divide persists as the outcome of exclusion because of social and economic constraints but also as the product of "choice" (Dutton et al. 2007).

The digital differentiation approach also looks at differences in Internet usage across "generations." Prensky argues that parents and educators are, at best, digital immigrants, "who speak an outdated language (that of the pre-digital age)," and "are struggling to teach a population [the digital natives] that speaks an entirely new language" (2001: 2). Indeed, Prensky reproduces Tapscott's (1998) argument in favor of drawing a clear line between generations, based on differentiated media socializations. However, Buckingham (2006) is cautious about this claim since the meanings and uses of technology vary according to various factors other than age. Also, he argues that to set the boundaries of a generation is a far more complex task than to simply define it through its relationship with a particular technology or medium (2006: 11). Moreover, techno-social changes affect children and adults alike. But studies that focus on Internet use and its effects among older adults seem to be fewer than those that focus on children—see the studies of University of Gothenburg (2009) and PewInternet (Madden 2010). According to Zimic (2009), who studied Swedish society, the notion of Net Generation might be misleading, since there are nuances under the stereotypical images. Major variances in Internet use across individuals of different ages are not denied but it's important to look beyond the "generational" differences. Differences within the same generation, such as with respect to experience online (Blank and Dutton 2012), are significant and there are big disparities within the so-called "Net Generation" regarding use of communication, entertainment, and information. Major differences are also present in a global scale that will be highlighted in the following sections.

Europe, the Americas, and Oceania

WIP research in Australia, by Ewing and Thomas, focused on the "'creative uses' of the net, ranging from relatively straightforward user-generated content such as sharing photographs to the distribution of more complex amateur-produced material" (Ewing and

Thomas 2009: 268). The Australian data indicates that the Internet's role as an entertainment source is much stronger among younger people, who are less likely to be watching as much television as others as a result. Ewing and Thomas suggest that the creative Internet bears some distinctive social features: an expanding user base, and notably more women, with usage slanted towards younger users who are more likely to be uploading and developing online content. They claim, however, that the understating of the creative Internet and its uses requires a broader context such as the relationship between the development of the "creative Internet" and broadband access. Australians with broadband access at home are almost twice as likely to consider the Internet as "important to their current way of life" and more likely to rate the Internet as a "very important source of entertainment." Such an analysis might highlight the differences between users in countries with generalized broadband use and countries with low levels of broadband access.

Goodwin et al. (2009) draw on the findings from the first WIP survey in New Zealand to argue that in a rapidly transforming global environment, monitoring the impact of technological change can inform interventions aimed at alleviating social inequalities. However, their analysis argues that the notion of a "digital divide" takes different meanings in countries where social and economic development is high, such as New Zealand, compared with countries with lower rankings, such as Colombia. First, whom the digital divide affects depends on the income, education, and other demographic profiles of countries such as the ethnic social composition: in New Zealand, those of Asian ethnicity have higher Internet access (94 percent) than Pakeha (77 percent), Pasifika (72 percent), and Maori (62 percent). Second, there is a digital divide among Internet users between those with broadband access and others, and between first generation users, tied to the pc in the household, and "next generation users" with multiple devices, some of which are portable (Dutton and Blank 2011). This suggests that there are different layers of digital divide.

Digital exclusion is a closely related concept that can take on different meanings within and across countries, since it encompasses various dimensions: access, motivations, knowledge, skills, and continuity in everyday practices. Helsper and Galácz (2009) point to evidence that countries with high socioeconomic inequality within Europe show strong links between social and digital exclusion: the UK showed strong links between low education, income, and digital exclusion. However, the UK has a higher broadband access than countries with lower socioeconomic inequality, such as the Czech Republic and Hungary. In these countries, there are more diverse links between digital and social exclusion. For instance, in Hungary ethnicity had a strong effect on digital engagement, which was considerably lower among the Roma population. Like others, they defend the fact that other variables, beyond income and education, such as gender, marital status, and children in the household, ethnicity, and even "soft" variables—skills, values and attitudes—promise to enrich the analyses that search for the complex links between social exclusion and digital engagement.

Other analyses that highlight the differences within countries between older and younger users show us that different contexts of use and experimentation make a difference. For example, Spain offers a more liberal approach to experimentation, reflected in Internet use, while Canada tends to bring to the online world many of the same constraints present in the offline audiovisual industry.

With respect to Canada, Caron and Caronia (2009), who look at the so-called new screens and young people's appropriation of entertainment content, state that although new information and communication technologies have become extremely dynamic, their content has been fairly controlled and regulated. They address how young people in Canada appropriate and evaluate content in traditional as well as new media environments, leading them to oppose the notion that young people are passive, easy to manipulate, unaware of their values, and lacking in critical thinking skills. Instead, their data lead them to be supportive of the notion of young people as active users, able to interpret, judge, and choose, and, consequently, capable of using knowledge and competencies.

In Spain, Tabernero et al. (2009) also investigated the relationship between media practices and the "connected lives" of young people. They found that widespread Internet use and the explosion of global mobile communication have opened the door to direct participation and to the emergence of user-driven participatory and collaborative culture(s). In this context, the young, as their lives unfold in an increasingly media- and technology-rich environment, are regarded as playing a fundamental role in socio-cultural transformations linked to media and communication practices. Among these, online social networking stands out as a powerful change-factor, both as a multimodal form of cultural consumption and a specific renewing set of media practices, supporting identity formation, status negotiation, and peer-to-peer sociality.

A third example is provided by Mexico. According to Gutiérrez and Islas (2009), Mexico has witnessed the rise of a new media ecology, with particular characteristics. They argue that the Internet is used more for informational purposes, while television is used more as an entertainment medium. Nevertheless, after television, Mexican Internet users regard the Internet as the second most important medium for entertainment. As in most other nations, Internet usage in Mexico was highly correlated with the socioeconomic level of individuals and strongly structured by age: around two-thirds of Internet users are 25 years old or less and almost 80 percent of users are under the age of 40.

What these three examples illustrate is that it is not just the age of users that defines Internet use in a given country, but also the institutional context and media culture. Such a combination tends to introduce more differences between countries than similarities.

Another example of cross-national diversity in WIP research can be found in the analysis of the relationship between Internet usage and the consumption of traditional media. The general assumption is that there is an inverse correlation between traditional newspaper reading and Internet use, since there are a lot of newspapers available online for free. Likewise, television viewing is expected to decline because people will have less time available to watch TV. But a more thorough analysis reveals that this is a spurious relationship, explained by other factors. For example, holding age constant, the correlation between Internet and other media use disappears. That is, for example, older people watch more TV and have lower levels of Internet use. There are changing media practices and habits among the younger generations, but changes are slow and not as profound as generally assumed.

To better understand what is happening over the years there is a need for longitudinal data that only research networks such as WIP might offer. On the whole, in Nordic countries and Japan the newspaper reach has remained high and TV viewing has not changed during the last ten years (Findahl 2009). However, the development of traditional media is not the same in all countries (Findahl 2009). In some countries, like the US, newspaper subscriptions have declined sharply, while in other nations sales have been rising.

The decline of newspaper reading began in the US in the 1960s, when television was introduced. Lunn and Suman (2009) argue that existing literature shows that the technology diffusion process is inherently complex, usually involving heterogeneous populations, and is correspondingly under-conceptualized through the use of single summary percent utilization figures. These authors identified the existence of several Internet usage dimensions: distinct adoption, non-adoption, discontinuance, and intermittent usage patterns. They claim that membership in different Internet adoption groups might be related to a systematic decline in the importance of newspapers as a source of information in the US. However, there remains a danger of enrolling in an analysis based on media centrism. There are many factors other than the Internet and the competition between media that have an impact on the decline or rise of a new or traditional medium, such as the economic climate. Also, the trust of users and perceived quality in the content of a specific medium exemplifies some of the many factors that could contribute to the success of new and traditional media. In addition, the mediascape doesn't change overnight.

The general conclusion of WIP findings to date is that the Internet has been more of a complement to the traditional media than a competitor, and that displacement effects are hard to find and aren't general or universal across countries. There are, of course, individual cases that point in another direction, such as in the US, but they are still rare and we cannot view them as the general case. Such an analysis is something that only global studies of the Internet like WIP can reveal.

Asia and the Middle East

Among two billion Internet users in the world, 44 percent are in Asia and 3.3 percent are in the Middle East. However, the Asian Internet penetration rate is only 23.8 percent, much less than North America (78.3 percent) and Europe (58.3 percent), and the world average (30.2 percent).[2] Nevertheless, Asia and the Middle East offer us other perspectives on the use of transnational and global studies of the Internet for the understanding of social, economic, political, and cultural change. For example, Allagui and Walters (2009) focus on the United Arab Emirates and the patterns of Internet usage in a

[2] See <http://www.Internetworldstats.com/stats.htm>. Accessed May 11, 2011.

multi-group society, from "locals" to "expats." They show us how people might have different patterns of Internet usage within their own country and as expats.

Another example comes from Japan, where Mikami (2009) argues that government policies and severe market competition have been boosting the spread of new media such as the Internet, mobile phones, and digital TV services since the mid-1990s. Based on WIP surveys of Japanese users, the Internet is not highly regarded as a source of information or entertainment, compared to traditional media such as television and newspapers. The country has an increasing Internet penetration rate, but those with mobile Internet far surpass those with only PC Internet—although usage of social media is higher in PC households. As a country with a very distinctive media ecology, particularly given its high reliance on mobile phones, Japan shows that the media ecology can influence the choices of users and vice versa.

Focusing on Singapore, Choi's (2009) analysis, on the link between the Internet and social life, looks at family relations and conflict resolution around Internet use. He states that differences in opinion exist with regards to whether or not the Internet is beneficial or harmful to family and social relationships and activities. Choi reviews two conflicting perspectives on this issue and his findings are twofold. His quantitative research did not support the pessimistic view that the Internet has negative effects on family relationships. But his detailed, qualitative research showed that the interaction around Internet use, parental awareness, and parenting style did increase the level of conflict, and the method of conflict resolution shapes the outcome of the parent-child conflict.

These previous two studies show that, when faced with cross-national comparative analyses, WIP does not simply obtain data on different countries, but also helps to raise new questions, such as in trying to identify the role of endogenous situations, such as national cultures and policy options in the adoption and use of the Internet.

Culturally, most Asian Internet users are in Eastern Asia, a region deeply influenced by Confucianism. Developed 2,500 years ago and based on agricultural society, Confucianism is mainly about social order and traditional inter-personal relations, such as a son obeying his father, and is also characterized by its collective and family-oriented values, in which individual rights are seriously neglected. This contrasts sharply with the culture of the Internet, which is an open system and a potentially revolutionary tool. Given this contrast, Eastern Asia, especially China, is a site for investigating the potential cultural implications of the Internet.

The process of modernization in China has been loosening traditional Chinese family ties. Young people leave their hometowns and villages, flocking into large cities. In addition to cell phone voice calls and SMS, Internet instant messaging is equally popular in China. Unlike Western netizens, who use the Internet communication both for work and personal purposes, Chinese netizens like to communicate with their family and friends more than their work ties. Whereas most Western Internet users use email, most Chinese Internet users prefer QQ, a Chinese version of ICQ (an instant chatting tool meaning I Seek You) provided by a Chinese company, Tencent, Inc. For example, in July 2011, 79.4 percent of Internet users in China were using instant messaging tools, according to the official China Internet Network Information Center (CNNIC).[3] By March 2010, Tencet announced that the number of registered QQ users reached 1 billion, with 100 million users simultaneously online.[4]

Analysis made under data collected in the WIP survey report of 2008 shows that a large percentage of users, in almost all of the WIP countries and regions, check their email daily. Only in urban China did fewer than 40 percent of users report checking their email daily. Compare this with Canada, New Zealand, and the United States where 80 percent or more of users use their email daily or several times a day.[5] In contrast, only a small number of Internet users in most of the WIP countries and regions routinely use instant messaging (WIP 2008: 327).

Traditionally, Chinese authority is not in a position to be challenged. Yet, with the open system of the Internet, more and more people are trying to openly express their opinion online, even though the discussion is limited and sometimes censored. One recent phenomenon in China is the rapid growth of public blogs, which conflicts with traditional Chinese culture that suggests individuals should not show off and young people should respect the elderly. There were 294.5 million blog users in China at the end of 2010.[6] Seventeen percent of Chinese Internet users write their own blogs, while 49 percent of Internet users read blogs, according to CNNIC.[7]

Mr. Han Han, a young Chinese professional racing car driver and a best-selling author, was elected by *New Statesman* as one of the "50 people that matter in 2010" for his most widely read and influential blog.[8] Next to those popular bloggers commenting on stock business, he ranked the seventh most popular blogger on sina.com.cn, the number one portal website in China. In addition to writing about his personal life, Mr. Han Han blogs on social events, and sometimes criticizes the government. His blog has already had 679 thousand active fans and reached 510 million hits by November 2011.[9]

Micro-blogging is also an important tool, not only for communicating with others but also for expressing personal opinions on public affairs. The number of registered micro-bloggers on sina.com reached 100 million at the end of March 2011. Another Chinese portal website, the most popular instant message (QQ) service provider, Tencent.com, also reported 100 million micro-bloggers. The top micro-blogger on sina.com, Yao Chen, had 7.4 million active fans by 2011.[10] The large user base has made the micro-blog a very strong communication tool for politics and public affairs. People share information and their opinion on international and domestic issues. Even some local governments and police departments communicate with citizens by micro-blogs.

---

[3] The 27th Internet survey report. See China Internet Network Information Centre at <http://www.cnnic.net/> p. 31. Accessed May 18, 2012.

[4] See <http://tech.qq.com/a/20100310/000298.htm>

[5] WIP (2008). The World Internet Project Report 2009, p. 322. Accessed May 11, 2011

[6] The 27th Internet survey report (see <http://www.cnnic.net/>) p. 32. Accessed May 18, 2012.

[7] Ibid p. 36.

[8] Available at *New Statesman*: <http://www.newstatesman.com/2010/09/han-china-matter-taken-200>. Accessed May 18, 2012.

[9] See <http://blog.sina.com.cn/twocold>. Accessed May 18, 2012.

[10] See <http://weibo.com/>. Accessed May 18, 2012.

According to the WIP survey report in 2008, relatively low percentages of users in most WIP countries/regions said the Internet "will give users more of a say in government actions." But while 25 percent or fewer respondents in five countries/regions said they agreed with this statement, respondents in urban China (46 percent) and Columbia (45 percent) reported far higher levels of agreement (WIP 2008: 186). This suggests that Chinese people perceive the Internet to be bringing some basic structural change to China's politics and society.[11]

METHODOLOGICAL OPPORTUNITIES AND PITFALLS FOR CROSS-NATIONAL INTERNET RESEARCH

The different WIP research teams conduct long-term longitudinal studies on the impact of computers, the Internet, and related technologies on families and society, using a combination of well-accepted survey research methods in the social sciences. Perhaps the greatest strength of WIP doesn't come from a unified theoretical approach but from a methodological strategy that mobilizes networked and cross-national comparative research. The search for global trends as well as for special cases in a diverse social reality across the globe has driven the WIP project teams.

As important as tracking Internet use is surveying non-users: to regularly track their social and cultural behavior, to see if and how attitudes and actions change as households obtain computers and Internet access. The WIP project has investigated why non-users do not participate and what their sense of the connected world is. In so doing, the project hopes to learn what compels many of them to become users later, and how their established patterns of media use, child-rearing, economic and political behavior, and other activities, then change. When, for example, and if, household penetration of the Internet reaches 90 percent, WIP hopes to be able to determine who the 10 percent non-users are, why they remain non-users, and how they do off-line what most of the world is doing online. More generally, the objective has been to coordinate a truly international effort to understand how both developed and developing countries are affected by the use of information technology.

However, it is difficult to coordinate and apply a survey worldwide, ensuring high-quality data collection, given the many methodological challenges in harmonizing multicultural, transnational research. National teams don't have the same material and human resources, the samples might not be obtained in the same way in each country, and each research team faces problems that are particular to their national context. In addition, the process of translating a survey isn't as straightforward as researchers would

---

[11] This theme of WIP research is supported by related research on global values and attitudes about the Internet (Dutta et al. 2011).

like since the same words and expressions might have particular meanings in a given cultural context.

One fundamental problem is to know if we are studying the same phenomena in different contexts; that is, quantitative surveys depend for their reliability on the principle of functional equivalence (Verba 1967). So the researcher has to question if the many differences between countries are scientifically meaningful and not methodological artifacts. Therefore, when facing odd results, we first question the reliability, validity, and comparability of the research procedures and do not jump straight away to substantive interpretations about "cultural" differences (Kohn 1987). Methodological artifacts might derive from different sample designs or reflect deficiencies on the linguistic, measurement, and conceptual equivalence in questions and in coding answers. This is particularly acute in world Internet research since, for instance, we are dealing with new terminology and Internet language that is not socially recognized in the same way across generations and across the globe and since most of that terminology was coined in the Anglo-Saxon world.

Allagui and Al-Shakaa (2009) needed to struggle to find funding in the UAE, to involve Arab academic institutions in the project, and address the cultural challenges in conducting the WIP survey. Nonetheless, the researchers point out the benefits of being the sole WIP partner conducting research within an Arab country: the possibility of enabling researchers within the Arab world to use data anchored in these societies, and the chance to motivate further research on the effects of ICT in Arab societies.

Comparability doesn't come from using the same theoretical approaches regardless of the social, political, and economical context. In fact, research in non-Western countries might add fresh perspectives that challenge the dominating scientific knowledge coming from the Western world.

Looking at the data on digital inclusion in Britain and Chile, Godoy-Etcheverry and Helsper (2010) challenge the concept of the "digital divide," arguing that it needs to go beyond the bipolar access/non access (digital) and want/do not want (decisional) divides. They state that the "digital divide" is a complex, evolving concept that should move to the notion of disengagement. One of their main conclusions is that to compare two different countries using the same variables about digital inclusion is not a straightforward task, since there are different varieties of inclusion and interpretations of engagement with ICTs. Therefore, the authors ask if the UK is really "ahead" of Chile simply because the UK has a larger proportion of people online, if they are really measuring the same social phenomena in both countries, or are they simply different?

With a cross-national approach it is useful to employ an analytical strategy close to a Durkheimian way of thinking, shedding light on crucial interpretive problems such as the limits of what has been learned about the world Internet. This way of conducting research might illuminate questions such as: what is the impact of cultural, political, and economic contexts on Internet "realities" from the US to the Middle East? What can we know and what kind of generalizations can we make? What are the special cases around the globe? What are the limits of our knowledge about the Internet and what questions would we like to answer? Such an approach might reveal not only intriguing differences between countries and cultures, but also aspects of one's own country and culture that would be obscured if one used only domestic data about the Internet.

It is also likely that cross-national studies are even more relevant today with moves towards transnational governance (Hantrais and Mangen 1996). From here we can use many dimensions of analysis. One dimension might concern the intra-societal variation of Internet usage patterns and representations about the Internet and its demographics. This dimension resembles one of the strategies of Kohn's typology (1987): to treat nations as objects of study, that is, to study nations for their own sake. Another dimension of analysis concerns the exploration of the world's cultural, political, economic, and institutional diversity. This focuses attention on the expectation of heterogeneous answers across societies. The two dimensions of analysis should be articulated since it is difficult to differentiate between both strategies of research, as Kohn acknowledges. In this way a researcher can hope to achieve the validity of interpretations derived from the analysis of single nations and find social regularities.

An example comes from the cross-national analysis of the Amichai-Hamburger and Hayat (2011) study, based on WIP data, on whether Internet use leads to a decline in social interactions and community involvement worldwide. Their results show, in line with other studies, that Internet use does not have a negative impact on the social lives of users and, in some aspects, it may even have positive effects.

Kohn (1987) argued that the substantive similarities between countries are less difficult to interpret and, in light of methodological dissimilarity, such similarities might even argue for the robustness of the findings. However, problems are more acute when interpreting inter-country differences in relationships. Jowell (1998) argues that even the greatest methodological precautions in the design and application of surveys doesn't prevent differences between nations from emerging as a consequence of matters of taxonomy and technique.

Issues surrounding the validity of measurement in surveys are relevant even beyond the research design. During the data analysis, the researcher should be aware that different languages are not merely means of defining and communicating ideas and concepts, but also reflect different thought processes, institutional frameworks, and underlying values (Harding, 1996). This is of particular importance in the study of items that measure attitudes and representations, but also Internet practices. In fact, one can pose the question: what is Internet usage? Does it mean having access to a computer or paying attention to the computer screen? But what about other uses that don't require the user's attention, such as leaving the chat open while absent or using a peer-to-peer file-sharing program? Regardless of the intention of the survey designers, one respondent can interpret a question about Internet usage as something different from another respondent. This is also an example of how theoretical problems can have a profound impact on methodological choices and design.

In this sense, Findahl (2010) compares the measurements between questionnaires, diaries, and traffic measurements, and finds consistent and significant differences between each measuring procedure. He also points out the benefits and shortcomings of each procedure. Questionnaires are always prone to human memory and time estimate errors.

Time and activity diaries, if filled in by the day, can give more accurate answers, but are restricted in scope. Measurements of the actual Internet traffic with a traffic management device give all traffic data, but the data is unsorted and has to be adapted, categorized, and summarized. He found that the data gathered in diaries and by traffic measurement is inconsistent and varies according to the period of the day. For example, the traffic measurement during the night period was much higher than the Internet activity recorded in diaries. Furthermore, the amount of time on the Internet at home indicated by users through questionnaire was much lower than the registered traffic measurement, even excluding peer-to-peer or background data exchange. Nevertheless, depending on the scope and aims of the research, it might be pertinent to make the methodological choice of excluding background data in measurements.

Concerning attitudes towards the Internet, these are often measured through Likert-type scales, which are prone to bias from several causes. The respondents might avoid the response categories at both ends of the scale (central tendency bias); concur with the presented statements (acquiescence bias); or avoid answers they perceive as politically or socially incorrect (social desirability bias)—for instance, pornography, file sharing of digital media, or other morally ambiguous practices. In relation to internal validity, attitudinal questions about the Internet are also more sensitive than factual questions (such as questions related to Internet access and concrete practices) to changes in wording, context, emphasis, and so on. One specific recommendation is to enhance the reliability of measurements with multi-item attitude scales related to the same construct or with further supporting evidence.

Another specific problem for survey researchers concerns non-response bias. If non-responses are random they can be less harmful, but if they are structured (non-response is higher in certain social groups) they lead to a biased representation of the target populations that might compromise a meaningful comparison between countries. Therefore, cross-national surveys routinely provide methodological reports that allow the researcher to access participating nation's procedures, methods, and success rates—highlighting rather than suppressing variations. With this information it is possible to make decisions such as to omit certain countries from comparisons or to qualify findings on grounds such as poor response rates, a non-conforming fieldwork period, or use of a different mode of interviewing or sampling method (Jowell 1998).

THE PARTICULAR CONTEXTS AND SINGULARITIES REGARDING INTERNET USE

Another limitation of cross-national analysis is that it often entails a level of abstraction from social contexts. According to Kohn, one might overlook cultural, political, and economic differences to explain the studied relationships between Internet practices, attitudes, and other variables. Yet, apparent similarities might mask profound differences, such as if the same outcomes emerged from very different social processes. Thus, when there isn't sound evidence or knowledge, Kohn (1987) recommends prudent explanations that limit the scope of interpretations. Furthermore, what can appear as differences may really be regularities when one changes the scope in terms of some larger, more encompassing interpretation. And the divergences observed within each country are at times more significant than those found between countries. In this case, to take a country as a unit of analysis might give us an unsatisfactory picture of a country's social reality, as the nation is not often the most important level of analysis.

That is the case of Cyprus, a country divided between the Turkish north and the Greek-speaking south, where there are evident methodological difficulties in conducting research, and challenges in analysis. Therefore, the analysis of Cyprus by Demertzis et al. (2009) does not refer to the Turkish part of the country occupied since 1974. Likewise, Liang and Bo (2009) present results regarding the use of ICT for interpersonal communication in urban China. To gather a representative sample of Chinese society as a whole would be impractical, given the vast rural regions with far lower levels of diffusion. But the reality of urban China gives us only a partial picture of the impact of the Internet in China as a whole.

In sum, it is essential to maintain a critical perspective in comparative approaches, being aware of the possibility that differences verified between countries in a certain region or continent can lose much of their analytical relevance if we compare the Western world with other areas in the world. One practical and powerful way to overcome these difficulties is to take advantage of networked research through the exchange of insights and knowledge about the academics' own societies, a key feature of the WIP.

CONCLUSION: BEYOND WORLD INTERNET PROJECTS?

In a world still very much dominated by national research on the Internet, in which our research paradigms seem to be national-driven and where only publishing seems to be fundamentally transnational, what is the role for projects such as the World Internet Project? There are two types of answers to this question. The first is that it is important to recognize the limitations of comparative studies, and explore new ways in which to deal with them. Despite the weaknesses and shortcomings noted in this chapter, WIP participants learn much from the comparative aspects of the work. The other is that we have done what we should have been doing with social analysis in the network society. That is, we have been promoting network research, and networks are not 100 percent stable because their nature is not one of immobility. So what we should do is to question an ever-changing reality. If that is the case, what should WIP be asking in the coming years in order to keep its scientific relevance?

Indeed, there is growing importance in analyzing the characteristics of "next generation users" (Dutton and Blank 2011; Blank and Dutton 2012) that access the Internet often on the move over multiple devices, and distinguishing between heavy users who are always connected to the Internet and frequent and mobile users. It is also relevant to distinguish between other modes of Internet use, namely to distinguish between active users and active producers, and between informational uses and social activities on social networks. Social reality itself, the changing social *technoscape*, poses a challenge and sometimes undermines the relevance and adequacy of survey questions about the Internet. Therefore, common questions should accommodate that changing reality: such as the advent of portable devices and tablets, which can become transformational in terms of Internet uses and impacts; and specific questions about social networks and popular applications and how people make choices in online environments. Another promising line of research concerns the development of questions and analyses about non-users and ex-users, and about emergent tendencies such as the diffuseness of "being online" in a era of widespread broadband connections.

To articulate a survey across many countries is a huge challenge since there are methodological differences and differentiated modes of scientific production and interests across national research teams. It isn't easy to reach a consensus concerning the relevance, accuracy, or validity of questions across countries. Thus, WIP partners have been discussing the development of optional modules besides the common core questions, which each research team can apply in their respective country, according to their own interests. Also, it would be very useful to develop a common bank of questions regarding the various themes concerning the use of the Internet that would be readily accessible, facilitating the design and construction of surveys beyond the WIP partners.

In terms of research about the Internet we certainly live at a unique moment. As David Pearce Snyder once pointed out, "this is the real McCoy—50–60 years from now whole history film clips will be devoted to this time, discussing how countries of the world either successfully or unsuccessfully exploited this moment." Global collaboration within the World Internet Project is needed as well as complementary studies with global reach.

References

Allagui, I. and Al-Shakaa, R. (2009). "The Emirates Internet Project: The Internet in UAE Year 1." Paper presented at World Internet Project conference, Macao, PRC, July 8–10.

—— and Walters, T. (2009). "From 'Locals' to 'Expats': Patterns of Internet Usage in UAE, a Multi-Group Society", in G. Cardoso, Angus Cheong, and Jeffrey Cole (eds). *World Wide Internet, Changing Societies, Cultures and Economies*, Macao, PRC: University of Macao Press, pp. 583–600.

Amichai-Hamburger, Y. and Hayat, Z. (2011). "The Impact of the Internet on the Social Lives of Users: A Representative Sample from 13 Countries," *Computers in Human Behavior*, 27(1): 585–9.

Blank, G. and Dutton, W. H. (2012). "The Emergence of Next Generation Internet Users," in J. Hartley, J. Burgess, and A. Bruns (eds). *Blackwell Companion to New Media Dynamics*, London: Wiley-Blackwell, ch. 7.

Buckingham, D. (2006). "Is There a Digital Generation?," in D. Buckingham and R. Willett (eds). *Digital Generations: Children, Young People, and New Media*, London: Routledge, pp. 1–17.

Cardoso, G. and Araújo, V. (2009). *Out of Information and into Communication: Networked Communication and Internet Usage*, LINI Working Papers No. 5. Available at <http://www.lini-research.org/np4/?newsId=11&fileName=GCARDOSO_VARAUJO_LINI_WP5.pdf>. Accessed June 5, 2011.

Cardoso, G., Cheong, A., and Cole, J. (eds) (2009). *World Wide Internet: Changing Societies, Cultures and Economies*, Macao, PRC: University of Macao Press.

Caron, A. and Caronia, L. (2009). "New Screens and Young People's Appropriation of Entertainment Content," in G. Cardoso, A. Cheong, and J. Cole (eds). *World Wide Internet: Changing Societies, Cultures and Economies*, Macao, PRC: University of Macao Press, pp. 296–330.

Castells, M. (2000). *The Rise of the Network Society*, Oxford: Blackwell.

Choi, A. (2009). "Internet Use, Family Relations and Conflict resolution," in G. Cardoso, A. Cheong, and J. Cole (eds). *World Wide Internet: Changing Societies, Cultures and Economies*, Macao, PRC: University of Macao Press, pp. 463–503.

Demertzis, N. et al. (2009). "The Internet in Cyprus 2009 Final Report," Department of Communication and Internet Studies, Cyprus University of Technology. Available at <http://www.worldInternetproject.net/_files/_Published/_oldis/CyprusWIPsemiFINAL.pdf>. Accessed June 16, 2011.

DiMaggio P., Hargittai E., Neuman W. R., and Robinson J. P. (2001). "Social Implications of the Internet," *Annual Review of Sociology*, 27: 307–36.

Dutta, S., Dutton, W. H., and Law, G. (2011). *The New Internet World: A Global Perspective on Freedom of Expression, Privacy, Trust and Security Online: The Gobal Information Technology Report 2010–2011*, New York: World Economic Forum, April. Available at <http://ssrn.com/abstract=1810005>. Accessed June 16, 2011.

Dutton, W. H. and Blank, G. (2011). "Next Generation Users: The Internet in Britain," The Oxford Internet Survey 2011 Report, Oxford Internet Institute, University of Oxford. Available at <http://www.worldinternetproject.net/_files/_Published/23/820_oxis2011_report.pdf>. Accessed June 16, 2011.

Dutton, W. H., Shepherd, A., and di Gennaro, C. (2007). "Digital Divides and Choices Reconfiguring Access: National and Cross-National Patterns of Internet Diffusion and Use," in B. Anderson, M. Brynin, J. Gershuny, and Y. Raban (eds). *Information and Communications Technologies in Society*, London: Routledge, pp. 31–45.

Ewing, S. and Thomas, J. (2009). "Creative Dynamics of the Broadband Internet: Australian Production and Consumption of Cultural Content," in G. Cardoso, A. Cheong, and J. Cole (eds). *World Wide Internet. Changing Societies, Cultures and Economies*, Macao, PRC: University of Macao Press, pp. 268–95.

Findahl, O. (2009). "The Internet as a Complement to Traditional Media. An International Comparison of Countries with High Newspaper Reach," in G. Cardoso, A. Cheong, and J. Cole (eds) *World Wide Internet: Changing Societies, Cultures and Economies*. Macao, PRC: University of Macao Press, pp. 51–74.

—— (2010). "How to Measure the Use of the Internet? A Comparison between Questionnaires, Dairies and Traffic Measurements," Paper presented at World Internet Project conference, Lisbon, Portugal, July, 6–8. Available at <http://www.lini-research.org/np4/?newsId=25&fileName=Sweden___Findahl___How_to_Measure.pdf>. Accessed June 5, 2011.

Godoy-Etcheverry, S. and Helsper, E. (2010). "Challenging and Deepening the Concept of Digital Exclusion: A Comparison between the UK And Chile," Paper presented at World Internet Project conference, Lisbon, Portugal, July, 6–8.

Goodwin, I. et al. (2009). "Internet Use in New Zealand: Implications for Social Change," in G. Cardoso, A. Cheong, and J. Cole (eds). *World Wide Internet: Changing Societies, Cultures and Economies,*" Macao, PRC: University of Macao Press, pp. 624–54.

Gutiérrez, F. and Islas, O. (2009). "Understanding the New Digital Ecology in Mexico: The organization and Arrangement of Complex Media Environments," in G. Cardoso, A. Cheong, and J. Cole (eds). *World Wide Internet: Changing Societies, Cultures and Economies,* Macao, PRC: University of Macao Press, pp. 75–92.

Hantrais, L. and Mangen, S. (eds) (1996). *Crossnational Research Methods in the Social Sciences,* London and New York: Pinter.

Harding, A. (1996). "Cross-National Research and the 'New Community Power'," in L. Hantrais and S. Mangen (eds). *Crossnational Research Methods in the Social Sciences,* London and New York: Pinter, pp. 184–194.

Helsper, E. and Galácz, A. (2009). "Understanding the Links between Social and Digital Exclusion in Europe," in G. Cardoso, A. Cheong, and J. Cole (eds). *World Wide Internet: Changing Societies, Cultures and Economies,* Macao, PRC: University of Macao Press, pp. 146–78.

Jowell, R. (1998). "How Comparative is Comparative Research?," Working Paper 66, Centre For Research Into Elections And Social Trends. Available at <http://www.europeansocialsurvey.org/index.php?option=com_docman&task=doc_view&gid=1&Itemid=80>.

Kapor, M. (1993). "Where is the Digital Highway Really Heading?," *Wired,* 94 July–August: 53–9. Available at <http://www.wired.com/wired/archive/1.03/kapor.on.nii_pr.html>. Accessed May 20, 2011.

Katz, J., Rice, R., and Aspden, P. (2001). "The Internet, 1995–2000: Access, Civic Involvement, and Social Interaction," *American Behavioral Scientist,* 45(3): 405–19.

Kohn, M. (1987). "Crossnational Research as an Analytic Strategy," American Sociological Association, 1987 Presidential Address, *American Sociological Review,* 52(6): 713–31.

Kraut, R., Lundmark, V., Patterson, M., Kiesler, S., Mukopadhyay, T., and Scherlis, W. (1998). "Internet Paradox: A Social Technology that Reduces Social Involvement and Psychological Well-Being?," *American Psychologist,* 53(9): 1017–31.

Liang, G. and Bo, G. (2009). "ICT's for Interpersonal Communications in China," in G. Cardoso, A. Cheong, and J. Cole (eds). *World Wide Internet: Changing Societies, Cultures and Economies,* Macao, PRC: University of Macao Press, pp. 504–25.

Lievrouw, L. and Livingstone, S. (2002). "The Social Shaping and Consequences of ICTs," in S. Livingstone and L. Lievrouw (eds). *Handbook of New Media: Social Shaping and Consequences of ICTs,* London: Sage, pp. 1–14.

Livingstone, S. (2002). "Part One: The Changing Social Landscape. Introduction," in S. Livingstone and L. Lievrouw (eds). *Handbook of New Media: Social Shaping and Consequences of ICTs,* London: Sage, pp. 17–21.

Lunn, R. and Suman, M. (2009). "A Longitudinal Examination of Internet Diffusion, Adopter Categories, and Ramifications of Internet Usage on the Importance of Newspapers," in G. Cardoso, A. Cheong, and J. Cole (eds). *World Wide Internet: Changing Societies, Cultures and Economies,* Macao, PRC: University of Macao Press, pp. 110–27.

McKenna, K. and Bargh, J. (2000). "Plan 9 From Cyberspace: The Implications of the Internet for Personality and Social Psychology," *Personality and Social Psychology Review,* 4(1): 57–75.

MacKenzie, D. and Wajcman, J. (eds) (1999). *The Social Shaping of Technology,* Buckingham: Open University Press.

Madden, M. (2010). "Older Adults and Social Media." Available online at <http://pewinternet.org/Reports/2010/Older-Adults-and-Social-Media.aspx>. Accessed June 18, 2011.

Mikami, S. (2009). "The Internet under a Changing Media Environment: Japan," in G. Cardoso, A. Cheong, and J. Cole (2009). *World Wide Internet. Changing Societies, Cultures and Economies*, Macao, PRC: University of Macao Press, pp. 93–109.

Mouzelis, N. (1995). *Sociological Theory: What Went Wrong?*, London: Routledge.

Nie, N. H. and Erbring, L. (2000). "Internet and Society: A Preliminary Report." Stanford Institue for the Quantitative Study of Society, Stanford, CA.

Prensky, M. (2001). "Digital Natives, Digital Immigrants," *On the Horizon* 9(5): 1–6.

Putnam, R. D. (2000). *Bowling Alone*, New York: Simon & Schuster.

Reisdorf, B. (2010). "Non-Adoption of the Internet: A Comparison of Britain and Sweden." Paper presented at World Internet Project conference, Lisbon, Portugal, July, 6–8.

Rheingold, H. (1993). *The Virtual Community: Homesteading on the Electronic Frontier*, Reading, MA: Addison Wesley.

Schiller, H. (1996). *Information Inequality: The Deepening Social Crisis in America*, Lonon: Routledge.

Silverstone, R. (2005). "Introduction," in R. Silverstone (ed.). *Media, Technology and Everyday Life in Europe: From Information to Communication*, Aldershot: Ashgate, pp. 1–18.

Tabernero, C., Sánchez-Navarro, J., Aranda, D., and Tubella, I. (2009). "Media Practices, Connected Lives," in G. Cardoso, A. Cheong, and J. Cole (eds). *World Wide Internet: Changing Societies, Cultures and Economies*. Macao, PRC: University of Macao Press, pp. 331–57.

Tapscott, D. (1998). *Growing Up Digital: The Rise of the Net Generation*, New York: McGraw-Hill.

University of Gothenburg (2009). "More Older People Active Online Now Than In Past," *ScienceDaily*, June 19. Available at <http://www.sciencedaily.com/releases/2009/06/0906 10074159.htm>. Accessed June 20, 2012. Survey, University of Gothenburg.

Verba, S. (1967). "Some Dilemmas in Comparative Research," *World Politics*, 20(1): 111–27.

Wellman, B. (2004). "The Three Ages of Internet Studies: Ten, Five and Zero Years Ago," *New Media & Society*, 6(1): 123–9.

WIP (2008). *The World Internet Project Report 2009*, WIP. Available at <http://www.world-Internetproject.net/?pg=reports&inHamtadId=463>. Accessed May 11, 2011.

Zimic, Sheila (2009). "Not so 'Techno-Savvy': Challenging the Stereotypical Images of the 'Net Generation.' *Digital Culture & Education*, 1(2): 129–44.

PART III

CREATING AND WORKING IN A GLOBAL NETWORK ECONOMY

....

CHAPTER 12

NEW BUSINESSES AND NEW BUSINESS MODELS

....

MICHAEL A. CUSUMANO AND ANDREAS GOELDI

INTRODUCTION

RESEARCH on the Internet has focused on technological change and increasingly on its societal implications. But the Internet and, in particular, the World Wide Web graphical user interface, have also had an enormous impact on existing businesses, as well as creating a variety of new business opportunities and ways to make money. Nevertheless, Internet Studies have not paid sufficient attention to the implications for business and business models. While there is a widespread recognition that the Internet has disrupted traditional institutions and ways of making money, we need more systematic research on the range and efficacy of different strategies and business models, and on how the Internet has encouraged the use of "platform" strategies and led to "Winner-Take-All-or-Most" market dynamics.

In this chapter, we review the general impact of the Internet on firm-level strategy (how to compete in particular markets) and business models (how to generate revenues and profits). This topic also touches on how the Internet has stimulated entrepreneurship and innovation. We conclude with a list of issues for future research.

IMPACT OF THE INTERNET ON STRATEGY AND BUSINESS MODELS

The Internet did not initially have much impact on business. In 1989, Tim Berners-Lee designed a browser and set of communications protocols primarily to improve communications and data sharing among academic experts (Berners-Lee 1999; Reid 1999).

Even the next major innovation did not directly have a commercial strategy behind it, but the implications would transform business and entrepreneurship in a variety of ways.

In 1993, Marc Andreessen and other college students working at the National Center for Supercomputer Applications (NCSA), based at the University of Illinois, developed the graphical Mosaic browser. This ran on Windows PCs and Macintosh computers as well as UNIX workstations. Like Berners-Lee, they did not have a strategy to make money from the Internet and still were targeting sophisticated computer users (Cusumano and Yoffie 1998). But after Andreessen co-founded Netscape in 1994, his company introduced the Navigator browser, a refined version of Mosaic. Browsers were relatively useless without servers containing web content and applications. But the new graphic features made access to the Internet possible for millions of average people. Then, in 1995, Microsoft bundled its Internet Explorer browser—which licensed the Mosaic technology—"free" with Windows 95. At the same time, Netscape and other companies began selling servers and application frameworks for building websites. The Internet, through the new World Wide Web, quickly became a new computing and communications platform for e-commerce, and then mass consumption of digital content and services by millions of people around the world. The emergence of the mass-market browser quickly led to new opportunities for software product firms and consulting services, and then for what would become a variety of "e-commerce" or "e-business" firms (Afuah and Tucci 2001).

Opportunities for new software products and services

In retrospect, we can say that the new web technology first created a business opportunity for companies selling new types of software products—browsers as well as a variety of server software, middleware programs to link websites with traditional databases and mainframe computers, new applications, and content management tools. For example, Netscape, Microsoft, and IBM, joined soon by newcomers such as BEA Systems, developed dozens of servers and programming tools to help individual users and companies create websites and distribute content, email, and applications such as for publishing and managing groups over the Internet. Sun Microsystems developed Java as a programming language especially well suited for building applications based on servers and accessed through Internet browsers. Various companies and open-source groups produced scripting languages that evolved beyond the original programming language of the Web, HTML (Hypertext Markup Language), to include JavaScript (developed at Netscape) and XML (Extensible Markup Language), developed between 1996 and 1998. These made it easier to build and link web pages and databases distributed via the Internet. Companies introduced new versions of operating systems, servers, and applications that accommodated new technical standards, driven by companies such as Cisco and Microsoft, and standards bodies such as the World Wide Web Consortium (WC3) and the Internet Engineering Task force (IETF), to make sure different networking systems and modes of communication were able to interoperate.

The World Wide Web especially created demand for new types of applications. By the end of the 1990s, trying to do business over the Internet—dubbed "e-business" or "e-commerce"—had become the equivalent of a modern-day gold rush. A new generation of "dot-com" entrepreneurs demanded software that enabled their new firms to do everything that was being done in the "old economy" on the Internet. This time, they hoped to take advantage of global scale economies and seemingly miniscule costs. Both the computer hardware and telecommunications industries benefited because most of the dot-com firms made large purchases of computer software, hardware, and telecommunications technology to create their websites and transaction capabilities, even if millions of paying customers never materialized.

During 2001–2, most dot-coms faded or failed due to the absence of sufficient customers and staggering infrastructure costs. But developing new products and services to enable firms to do business over the Internet became standard practice for "old economy" firms as well as newer firms. The need for integration and interoperability across different types of computers brought software producers for large machines closer to the PC software world, and prompted them to set up PC and e-business divisions that worked across the technologies. In the Internet era, it also became very common for software and IT consulting firms, ranging from IBM to start-ups like Razorfish and Sapient, to offer a new set of e-business services that combined consulting with systems design and software development.

Major types of Internet business strategies

The impact of the Internet on business largely has occurred through three types of strategies (Cusumano 2004: 114–9). The first strategy listed here is the simplest and tended to occur first chronologically in many industries, though the different strategies have also overlapped in time.

The most basic strategy is simply when companies decide to *use the Internet to enhance their existing business models and operations*, whether they are back-office functions, supply-chain management, or direct sales operations. For example, most enterprise software companies created browser-based versions of their applications. Usually, the new web software included improvements that made it easier for customers to use the programs or make changes themselves such as by customizing menus. This first strategy generated enormous work for software programmers and some new revenues as customers upgraded to Web-based versions of their products. In mid-2011, even Microsoft, a champion of traditional packaged software, finally introduced a new Web-based or "cloud" version of Office, accessed from central servers through an Internet browser (Jarzemsky 2011).

A second strategy is when companies decide to *use the Internet to create new products or services in traditional businesses*. Amazon and eBay are good examples here. Bookselling is an old business dating back to the Middle Ages, but Amazon uses unique software to create a virtual bookstore, with millions of titles. It also connects buyers with publishers, although it has built its own warehouses too. More interestingly, Amazon databases and software agents track what customers buy and might like to buy, and make suggestions. Likewise, auctions are an *ancient* business, dating back at least to Roman and Greek times. But eBay has developed software to enable them to take place electronically among hundreds and thousands of people located around the globe. In both cases there was no new business model, but the power of the Internet made it possible for entrepreneurs to offer new versions of traditional products and services.

The third strategy is when companies decide to *use the Internet to create totally new businesses*. This has been rarer. At a relatively simple level, Yahoo!, Google, Amazon, and other Internet "portals" fall into this category. They became virtual windows into a variety of information, products, and services available over the Internet, and generated revenues through advertising and transaction fees, and some pay-for-service fees. We could not really have global portal businesses without online networks such as the Internet. But this third strategy has also generated more unique examples of new businesses, again utilizing the computing and communications capabilities as well as the global network features of the Internet.

We should note, though, that making money from these new business models has been difficult. Take Napster for example, founded by Shawn Fanning, which illustrates the type of business enabled by the unique technology and scale of the Internet—peer-to-peer trading of, in this case, music. Fanning took advantage of MP3, an audio compression format that allowed users to send encoded music files over the Internet. At its peak in 2001, some 80 million people had downloaded the company's software. A very large percentage of these individuals were exchanging personal music files "for free." The recording industry started suing promoters of MP3 in 1999 and then targeted Napster in mid-2000. One problem for Napster was how to respect intellectual property rights and pay the artists or companies that owned the rights to the music. Another problem was how to make money from a technology and service that the company initially gave away for free. The original company never did find a solution. After lengthy court battles, Napster declared bankruptcy in May 2002 (Vance 2002; Denison 2002; Richtel 2002). In 2008, it reemerged as a pay-online music subscription service owned by US electronics retailer Best Buy.

Other types of pay services for music, using similar peer-to-peer technology, as well as various open-source software programs, became popular after Napster first appeared. Most notably, Apple introduced iTunes in 2001 to complement the iPod digital media player and later its iPhone and iPad devices. iTunes is not a peer-to-peer technology, but is a central repository for digital content. Apple shares revenues with the content creators. By 2010, iTunes had become the largest distributor of digital music and an industry-wide "platform" in its own right, working with smart phones and media players provided by Microsoft and other companies as well as Apple (Cusumano 2010). Apple also introduced a cloud-based version of iTunes in 2011, which enables users to access their music and video collections from multiple devices as long as they are connected to the Internet (Iwatani and Smith 2011).

Affiliate marketing over the Web is another Internet-only kind of business. Be Free, for example, a start-up founded in 1996, created technology to track "click-through" sales of a vendor's products to customers who came into the website from other sites, including Internet portals. The owners of the affiliated websites that transfer traffic get a percentage of the sales. The vendors that get the click-through sales pay for this broker service from their revenues. Be Free lost tens of millions of dollars in the first few years of operations and in 2002 merged with ValueClick (founded 1998), another provider of "cost-per-click" web advertising solutions.

Yet another new type of business only possible with the Internet, at least on its current scale, is social networking, led by companies or Internet sites such as Facebook, MySpace, LinkedIn, and Twitter. These firms primarily make money through selling advertisements. They have hundreds of millions of users and enormous amounts of personal and professional information that is highly attractive to advertisers as well as search engines. The social networking sites were also new kinds of platforms operating on top of the Internet, with thousands of independent software engineers creating applications that offered a wide variety of products and services. The largest social networking site in 2011 was Facebook, founded in 2004 by Mark Zuckerberg and his college roommates at Harvard University. By mid-2012, this site had more than 900 million individual users and several thousand applications from outside parties, as well as revenues in the billions of dollars.

As we look back, we see that entrepreneurs around the world believed the Internet would create magical scale economies as millions of users flocked to their websites. They did not anticipate the *millions of websites* that companies and individuals would create and *the great cost of getting customers to come to* any *one particular site*. During the later 2000s, Internet-related businesses experienced a major consolidation, similar to what the PC software industry has been experiencing since the mid-1990s (Cusumano 2008). Nonetheless, many of the firms that survived, as well as new ones such as in social networking, became powerful new businesses that affected both Internet commerce and the way individuals communicate and behave.

Fundamental drivers for the new strategies and business models

Several fundamental drivers have made new business strategies and business models on the Internet possible. These generally relate to the low marginal costs of digital goods and services, the ease of communicating and coordinating globally, and the broad potential differentiation in products and services, as well as pricing, that the Internet facilitates.

Marginal costs of distribution

Digital content is pure information, not bound to a particular physical form of distribution. Even a complex form of digital information, such as an entire movie, can be expensive to produce but distributed at very low cost over the Internet. Digital services exhibit similar economic characteristics. Developing the software and building the infrastructure for a major Internet search engine such as at Google and Microsoft, or for cloud computing services, is very expensive. But an additional search query or additional application user costs hardly anything.

High initial investments and low marginal costs, combined with a global network, are strong drivers for Internet business models and competitive strategies. In the world of physical goods, marginal costs tend to be high and may not benefit from economies of scale above a certain production volume, which puts a natural limit on the growth of any single manufacturer. But in the digital world, content and service providers have the ability and the incentive to spread their reach as widely as possible and often as quickly as possible. Every additional customer increases revenues by much more than it costs to serve that customer, and each additional product or service sold therefore decreases average costs.

Cost and speed of coordination

The cost and time required to coordinate market participants is an important factor in many economic transactions. In some cases, the sum of these transaction costs can be so high that the purchase of a product or service becomes economically unfeasible for the buyer. But the Internet provides access to information for small as well as large firms. This information and other technologies such as online payment systems can speed up coordination as well as potentially reduce costs by helping companies quickly find low-cost suppliers and monitor purchasing and delivery activities, often in real-time.

Versioning and price discrimination

Traditional microeconomic analysis suggests that vendors can maximize profits if they charge each buyer a different price for the same product, such as for airline tickets. Every buyer has a different willingness to pay, so charging the maximum possible from each individual would be ideal for the seller. Perfect price discrimination is probably impossible in the real world, especially given the logistical overhead of charging many different prices for the same goods and services. But computers and the nearly instant global communication made possible through the Internet—for both buyers and sellers, retail and wholesale—has enabled a much greater flexibility for price discrimination in a variety of markets.

First, digital goods can easily be sold in different versions that justify different prices. For instance, digitized music can be sold in several different quality levels, determined by the bit rate of the song file. Audiophiles are likely to pay a higher price for pristine quality, while most consumers will be satisfied with a "good enough" version of the same piece of music. Similar differentiation is possible for software products, online services, and almost all forms of digital content.

Second, websites are flexible enough to offer different prices to different users. An e-commerce shopping platform can show a specifically calculated price to each individual shopper, determined by factors like previous buying behavior, loyalty, or demographics. Large e-commerce vendors like Amazon occasionally experiment with varied prices for different users. However, we should note that the transparency of the Internet limits how much user-based price discrimination can be achieved. In some cases, users have protested against pricing experiments that they perceived as being unfair (Talluri and Van Rizin 2005: 15).

Probably the best example for very granular price discrimination on the Internet is Google's auction-based pricing of search advertising. In its AdWords system, Google charges a different price for each ad, depending on the popularity of the search keyword to which an ad message is attached. Competing advertisers bid on each keyword, so Google can take advantage of the different willingness to pay of each advertiser.

Intensifying competition around industry "platforms"

The Internet has also had a major impact on how companies compete, particularly in that the Web quickly became a new "platform" or foundation for computing and communications as well as conducting business. Accordingly, almost all entrepreneurs and managers who rely on the Internet have had to deal with the unique dynamics of platform markets in order to attract customers and generate sales and profits, either as platform leaders or leader-wannabes, or as "complementors" to some other firm's platform. Hence, any discussion of the Internet's impact on strategy as well as business models needs to consider the special role of industry-wide platforms and the impact of the Internet on this type of competition.

Many people use the term "platform" with reference to a base of common components around which a company might build a series of related products. This kind of in-house "product platform" became a popular topic in the 1990s for researchers exploring the costs and benefits of modular product architectures and component reuse (Meyer and Lehnerd 1997; Sanderson and Uzumeri 1996; Meyer and Utterback 1993; Ulrich 1995; Baldwin and Clark 1999). In the mid- and late 1990s, however, various researchers and industry observers began discussing technologies such as Windows and the personal computer, as well as the Internet (and the browser), as new "industry-wide platforms" for information technology. These new platforms competed with or replaced an older industry platform, the IBM System 360 family of mainframes.

But an industry platform such as Windows or the Internet has at least two essential differences from a company-centered product platform (Gawer and Cusumano 2002, 2008; Gawer 2009; Cusumano 2010). One is that, while it provides a common foundation or core technology that a firm can reuse in different product variations, an industry platform provides this capability as part of a technology "system." Moreover, the complementary products and services are likely to come from different companies (or maybe different departments of the same firm), which we can call "complementors." Second, the industry platform has relatively little value to users without these complementary products or services, ranging from software applications to digital content and broadband access, provided by outside companies, users, or the platform creator.

For example, the Windows-Intel personal computer or a smartphone are just boxes with relatively little value without software development tools and applications or wireless telephony and Internet services. The company that makes the platform is unlikely to have the resources or capabilities to provide all the useful applications and services that make the PC or the smartphone so compelling for users. Therefore, to allow their technology to become an industry-wide platform, companies generally must have a strategy to open their technology to complementors and create economic incentives (such as free or low licensing fees, or financial subsidies) for these other firms to join the same "ecosystem" and adopt the platform technology as their own.

A second distinguishing feature of an industry platform is the creation of "network effects," and here is where the Internet has had perhaps its biggest impact on platform-based competition. Network effects are positive feedback loops that can grow at exponentially increasing rates as adoption of the platform and the complements rise. The network effects can be very powerful, especially when they are "direct," such as when users of software applications or digital content are tied to a particular platform due to a technical compatibility or interface standard. This has existed, for example, between the Windows-Intel PC and Windows-based applications. The network effects can also be "indirect" and represent different "sides" of the market, not just the buying and selling of complementary applications. Sometimes these indirect effects are very powerful as well—such as when advertisers, content providers, or service providers adopt a particular platform (such as Google search, or the Apple iPhone versus Google Android smartphones, or Facebook versus MySpace in social networking) because they see so many more users and complementary applications appearing for a particular platform.

Most important with a network effect is that, the more external adopters in the ecosystem that create or use complementary innovations, the more valuable the platform (and the complements) become. This dynamic, driven by direct or indirect network effects, or both, encourages more users to adopt the platform, more complementors to enter the ecosystem, and more users to adopt the platform and the complements, almost ad infinitum.

There has been a growing amount of both theoretical and empirical research on industry platforms. Early work by economists focused on theory and mathematical models, with few detailed case studies. But the key concepts have remained central to our understanding of the Internet as a new platform: how platform industries or products are affected by standards and technical compatibility, the phenomenon of network or positive feedback effects, and the role of switching costs and bundling (David 1985; Farrell and Saloner 1986; Arthur 1989; Katz and Shapiro 1992; Shapiro and Varian 1998; Bakos and Brynjolfsson 1999). Switching costs and bundling have become strategically important because companies often can attract users to their platforms by offering many different features for one low price, and can keep users by making it technically difficult to move to another platform. This is why, for example, cable and telephone companies have competed to offer bundled voice, data, and video services to the home along with basic television, Internet, or phone service.

Multi-sided markets and "winner-take-all" dynamics

Another important insight for strategy and business models is that platform markets tend to have more than one "side" to them (Bresnahan and Greenstein 1999; Schmalensee et al. 2006; Rochet and Tirole 2003, 2006). We saw this clearly in the personal computer industry, before the Internet. Microsoft and Apple competed not merely to attract end users to their products. They also had to attract software and hardware firms to build applications products and peripheral devices, such as printers. With the increasing diffusion of the Internet, we saw Google, Yahoo!, Facebook, and many other companies compete not simply for end users and application developers, but also for a third side of the market—advertisers. Companies that sell video have an even more complicated market challenge. They have to attract not only end users, application developers, and advertisers, but also producers of content as well as aggregators of other people's content. Even in simple two-sided markets, strategy and pricing can get complicated quickly (Afuah and Tucci 2001; Yoffie and Kwak 2006; Adner 2006).

Related to the complexity of platform markets is other research on what makes for a "winner-take-all" (or most) scenario (Parker and Van Alstyne 2005; Eisenmann 2006; Eisenmann et al. 2006; Cusumano 2010). The conclusion seems to be that (1) as long as there is room for companies to differentiate their platform offerings, and (2) consumers can easily buy or use more than one platform, then it is unlikely for one dominant platform to emerge—unless (3) the direct or indirect network effects are overwhelmingly strong. For example, Internet search is dominated by Google in most countries around the world (in 2011, it had around 65 percent of the search traffic in the United States and more in some European countries). But Internet search did not have as strong network effects as existed with PC operating systems, where Microsoft achieved more than a 90 percent share, and there was still room for differentiation. It was also easy to use multiple search engines.

The broad range of Internet
business models

Entrepreneurs launching new companies in the Internet era, as well as managers in existing businesses, have found a variety of ways to make money from the technology and buying habits of Internet users. Again, most of these approaches probably would not be possible or not be as successful without the Internet's potentially powerful network effects, extremely low marginal costs, high speed of global communication and low costs of coordination, and ease of product versioning and price discrimination. What follows here is a sampling of the major business models we have observed.

Online performance marketing

The optimization of advertising is an inexact science, or as department store mogul John Wannamaker famously said: "Half the money I spend on advertising is wasted; the trouble is I don't know which half" (Ogilvy 1988). The Internet has changed this to some extent. User behavior on the Web can be tracked very precisely, and marketers can therefore measure the effectiveness of their marketing campaigns much more effectively than ever before. It is easy to track how many people clicked on a particular ad banner, and it is also possible with some precision to find out how much revenue resulted from these clicks. Some less direct effects of good advertising—in particular, putting a "brand message" in people's heads—can obviously not be measured as directly. But online advertising is almost certainly the most accountable marketing medium in the history of commercial promotion.

The first forms of online advertising followed the paradigm of the newspaper ad by putting advertising messages in a dedicated space on a web page. This so-called "banner advertising" or "display advertising" remained a crucial part of the online ad market even in 2012. In the late 1990s, the increasingly popular web search engines started to combine advertising with specific keywords that a user was searching for, showing only ads directly related to the researched topic. After a while, search engines started to charge their advertising customers only when a user actually clicked on an ad. Online performance marketing was born, and with it began Google's rise to the top of the Internet industry.

Online performance marketing tends to work best for established markets where a significant volume of demand exists and prospective buyers search actively for information. Entirely new products and low-involvement product categories (such as household cleaners or soap) typically need to rely on other forms of advertising. But thanks to its measurability and purely performance-driven costs, online performance marketing rapidly gained popularity with marketers. The most important forms are pay-per-click and pay-per-action advertising, as well as affiliate marketing.

Pay-per-click advertising

Google and other search engines make most of their money from pay-per-click advertising in combination with an auction mechanism for ad space. Advertisers bid a certain amount of money that they are willing to pay for every time a user clicks on their ad and therefore gets exposed to additional information provided by the advertiser. Since search ads are only shown when a user actively searches for a defined keyword, the targeting of the marketing message is very precise. The sequence in which ads are displayed on a search results page is determined by the height of the bid from each competing advertiser. However, Google is known to change this sequence by showing more popular ads (the ones that get a lot of clicks) first in order to optimize its own revenues (Davis 2006). In 2011, pay-per-click search advertising generated about 40 percent of all online advertising sales. The majority of this amount was captured by search engine market leader Google, with Microsoft a distant second.

The approximate click prices per keywords are public information and illustrate what amounts different industries are willing to spend on customer acquisition. For instance, data retrieved from Google's AdWords system in September 2010 indicated that a click on an ad for the keyword "mortgage refinancing" cost around $32 while a click on "digital camera" could be bought for $2 and "detergent" for less than a dollar.

Pay-per-action advertising

A user who clicks on an ad expresses general interest in the advertised product, but that does not necessarily mean that a sale results from this action. Often, advertisers pay significant amounts of money for clicks that never lead to more business and not even to the identification of a potentially interested customer.

This dilemma led to the development of an even more performance-oriented form of marketing, pay-per-action advertising (sometimes called pay-per-conversion). In this variation, advertisers only pay if a user performs a previously defined action. This could be as simple as signing up for an email newsletter, or as transaction-oriented as actually buying a product online.

Affiliate marketing

Affiliate marketing is a form of promotion that tries to capture highly focused traffic from the broader Internet, even from people who are not consciously searching for information on search engines. Affiliates typically operate niche-oriented content websites, such as blogs or communities that deal with fairly specific topics. They put advertising on these sites that could appeal to their target group. In most cases, affiliates are compensated on a pay-per-action basis, that is, they receive payment only if users buy something from an advertiser. But the commissions that affiliates receive for a completed transaction can be relatively high, and a whole niche industry makes money from this type of marketing. Affiliate networks, the middlemen between advertisers and affiliates, organize offers, track successful conversions, and handle payments for a cut of the commissions.

Free ad-supported services

In the 1990s, online advertising was primarily used by media companies to monetize their free content Websites and portals. In 2012, online advertising was increasingly used to finance online services and even online software. For example, Facebook is free to users and makes money predominately from advertising. Another example is web-based email from vendors such as Yahoo, Microsoft, and Google. In some markets, free ad-based services compete with paid services that charge their users a fee, such as in online dating services.

Many data points suggest that online advertising is a "winner-takes-most" market. Although a lot of niche services make adequate money from advertising, it seems difficult to finance a large-scale online service purely through ads, unless the vendor is one of the top two or three companies in its field.

Subscriptions for digital goods and services

Subscriptions—the repeated delivery of a service or product against the payment of a recurring fee—are nothing new. Newspapers, utilities, and telecommunication companies have used subscription models for a long time. But the Internet, with its low marginal distribution costs, opens the opportunity to use subscription models for new markets. In particular, the software industry and the music industry experienced fundamental change through the growing popularity of subscription-based pricing.

Software as a service and cloud computing

Traditionally, software installed on a user's computer is sold with a so-called perpetual license. The user pays an initial license fee upfront and gets the right to use the software in perpetuity under certain conditions. Enterprise software vendors often charge an additional annual maintenance fee of 15–25 percent of the original license price, which entitles the buyer to receive software updates and a defined level of customer service. Examples for this traditional way of selling software include packaged PC software such as Microsoft Office, infrastructure software such as an Oracle database, or enterprise-wide applications such as SAP ERP.

An alternative method of licensing software on a subscription basis without upfront payments has existed for a long time in certain niche markets. But only the economics of the Internet have made this approach of "renting" software practical for a broader mass market.

Subscription-based software products are often called "Software as a Service" (SaaS), or referred to as "cloud computing." Both terms imply that the vendors do not sell a product for an upfront fee, but rather provide the software product packaged and sold as a service. Users access the software over the Internet, typically through a standard web browser. All functionality and data resides on server infrastructure owned and run by the SaaS or cloud vendor.

There are some obvious advantages of SaaS and cloud computing for users. Since the software runs on the vendor's infrastructure, there is no need to invest in server computers and pay the personnel that is necessary to keep this infrastructure running. The absence of an upfront licensing fee means that companies with limited capital budgets can get access to sophisticated software on a more affordable pay-as-you-go basis. The main downside is limited control over the availability of the software and user-specific data. While most SaaS or cloud vendors guarantee a certain uptime of their own systems, outages in the public Internet can affect a user's availability to access the system. Furthermore, not every type of application is technically suited to be accessed remotely through a browser. However, the advantages seem to outweigh the concerns for many users. By 2010, SaaS or cloud-based versions of software products had become by far the most rapidly growing sector of the software industry (Gartner Group 2010), led by companies such as Salesforce.com, founded in 1999. Salesforce.com and other companies, including Google, Amazon, and Microsoft, were also competing to establish their infrastructure services, product, and service offerings, and software engineering tools, as new "platforms" for cloud computing (Cusumano 2010).

Streaming digital media

When Apple released the iPod in 2001, the normal method of buying music was to go to a record store and purchase a CD. Since then, the music market has changed fundamentally. In addition to Apple's iTunes, other vendors such as Amazon.com and even Wal-Mart have entered the market for online music (NPD Group 2010). At the same time, record store chains like Tower Records went out of business, and many music publishing companies struggled financially.

The Internet-based music market focused mainly on single downloadable tracks. In 2011, users paid somewhere between 60 cents and a few dollars per title and then received the right to download the track in digital form. In some cases, digital music is copy-protected to prevent users from spreading purchased music on the Internet. However, a new group of music vendors such as Pandora, Spotify, and Rhapsody changed the market again with a different approach to pricing: Instead of buying individual titles, users paid a monthly subscription fee for access to a large library of music that they could listen to on their personal computers or even mobile devices. In contrast to the iTunes model, users do not own the music in a permanently stored form on their hard disks, but can only access the music library over a "streaming" service as long as they pay the subscription fee.

Similar models existed for other types of media, particularly movies and TV shows. Mail-order DVD rental company Netflix expanded to offer online movie streaming as a standard part of its normal subscription. Hulu, a consortium of several TV networks, offers a subscription plan that enables customers to access a large library of TV show episodes through online video streaming.

"Freemium"

Thanks to the extremely low distribution costs for digital goods and the flexibility of online marketing, the Internet offers a very wide range of price discrimination possibilities. Maybe the most radical form is to give away certain forms of a product while charging different price levels for other editions of it. This strategy has come to be known as "Freemium"—a combination of "free" and "premium" (Anderson 2009: 26). The freemium model is used mainly for software, content, and platform services.

Giving away a product for free is only possible because the marginal costs of reproducing a digital product or providing a software-based online service are so low. Freemium business models rely on a certain percentage of users seeing enough value in an enhanced version of the product or service to pay for it, while many other users (often the majority) receive the product for free and are therefore subsidized by the paying users.

Freemium software products

A significant number of vendors of Software as a Service use freemium pricing to achieve greater scale and decrease marketing costs. The idea is that by giving away a basic version of the software, freemium vendors can attract an unusually large number of users through word-of-mouth marketing. Some of these users will convert to the paid version of the software because their requirements are more advanced. Many software companies also hope for positive network effects that might be achieved through the larger number of users gained through a freemium strategy.

Data on how many users of freemium software products actually end up converting to paid subscriptions is scarce. But anecdotal evidence suggests that most vendors see a conversion rate in the low single digit percentages (Anderson 2009; Darlin 2009). As a consequence, freemium strategies can only work if a service can be provided at minimal cost to non-paying users. Most freemium vendors therefore restrict the features and storage capacity provided by their free offerings at a level that makes the product just barely useful. For any serious usage, customers have to upgrade to the paid version. Most vendors offer several editions of their paid product at different price levels in order to further exploit different levels of user requirements and the resulting willingness to pay.

There are several variations of this pure freemium model. Some software vendors do not offer a perpetually free edition of their product, but provide a time-limited free trial to customers who want to evaluate the product. Others charge a nominal, very small amount for the simplest edition of their software. For instance, Salesforce.com offers a basic contact manager product for $5 per month, while its full product costs $65 per month.

Another strategy is to give away one component of a product for free and charge for a complementary component. A famous historical example is Netscape, which gave away its browser software for free while charging for the server component (Cusumano and Yoffie 1998). Another well-known case is Adobe, which gives away its PDF reader software but charges for its PDF generator products and other editing tools.

Digital media content

Many media companies offer their online content for free and try to make money from advertising. But some have successfully adopted a freemium business model for their online divisions. For instance, in 2011, the *Financial Times* granted an "allowance" of ten free articles per month to each user, but people who want to read more needed to buy a subscription. *The Wall Street Journal* offered article excerpts and in some cases entire articles for free, but made its full content available only to paying subscribers. Also, until it switched to a paying model in 2012 after viewing a certain number of articles, the *New York Times* provided most of its content for free online, but charged for its archive, as well as for more advanced ways of reading the paper, such as its PC-based New York Times Reader software.

Similarly, media companies outside the newspaper business experimented with free-mium models. Many record labels provided music videos for free on online platforms such as YouTube (owned by Google) or MTV.com, but still charged for downloadable versions of the same songs. Some publishing companies offered free e-books, but sold printed editions of the same books.

Market platforms and directories

Finally, several other types of online services are increasingly using freemium models. For instance, the social networking site LinkedIn.com provides its basic functionality for free, but makes advanced features such as direct messaging and advanced search only available to paying subscribers. Online classified advertising platform Craigslist does not charge for most of its ad types, but requires payment for job ads and real estate ads in some markets. And real-estate platform Zillow.com provides free real-estate list-ings, but also sells premium placements to real estate agents and brokers who want their ads to stand out.

Distribution platforms and the "long tail"

Unlike "brick-and-mortar" retail businesses, distribution platforms like Amazon, Apple's iTunes, or the web businesses of traditional stores, can access inventory and sell digital goods such as digitized music, movies, or e-books with almost no physical restric-tions. The availability of these huge selections led to a buyer behavior that is not readily observable in brick-and-mortar commerce: while some popular products, such as the latest "Harry Potter" book, might sell very well in both physical and digital form, the total range of products sold seems to be much larger in the digital domain (and, to a lesser extent, in online sales of physical products). Helped by the recommendation sys-tems that most e-commerce sites offer, customers can discover and compare obscure products (such as long out-of-print books or electrical components) that they would not otherwise be able to find.

The Internet has encouraged another phenomenon related to finding obscure prod-ucts. When all titles that an online bookshop offers are sorted by their sales in descend-ing order, there is typically a small "head" with a few hit titles that achieve very big sales. After that, sales drop off very rapidly. But the whole list or "tail" of titles that occasionally sell a copy is extremely long. Hence the name "long tail" that was assigned to this phe-nomenon (Brynjolfsson et al. 2003). The actual size of these "long tail" markets is diffi-cult to determine. But some research suggests that e-commerce companies like Amazon make up to 25 percent of their sales from relatively obscure niche products (Anderson 2006: 23).

Online auctions

Auctions are a very old method of price discovery and have been used since about 500 BC (Schneider 2009: 275). A main drawback of this type of coordination mechanism is that participants typically have to be physically present at the time when the auction takes place. The Internet has lifted this restriction. Online auctions allow participants from all over the world to submit their bids, and modern auction methods spread out the auction process over hours or days. As a result, online auctions have become a popular form of electronic commerce.

The most successful online auction platform is eBay. Founded in 1995, eBay remained one of the largest Internet companies, with revenues of $11.6 billion in 2011. The company started out as a sort of online flea market focused on collectibles. Over time, eBay's product range expanded dramatically to the point where nearly any kind of consumer product could be found on the site. eBay also allows sellers to set a fixed price for their products for customers who do not want to go through the bidding process.

In addition, eBay has achieved industry-platform status by building an ecosystem of third-party companies who use eBay as a sales channel. As early as 2007, according to some estimates, over 700,000 sellers in the United States were using eBay as their primary or secondary source of income (Wellman et al. 2007). Independent software companies also provide tools that enable users to sell on eBay more efficiently.

Virtual goods

As noted earlier, many business models from the traditional world of physical goods and services translate well into the online space, and most Internet business models initially were just a variation of these established ways of making money. But a truly new idea is to sell so-called "virtual goods." These are sold like physical products, for real money, but only exist digitally and provide value to the buyer only in the context of a certain online environment, for instance an Internet-based game. In 2012, the virtual goods industry was a multi-billion-dollar industry experiencing significant growth, mainly driven by gaming.

Frequently, users first have to use real money to buy some amount of virtual currency before they can buy virtual goods. This provides additional profits to vendors through interest on the pre-paid amounts of real money. Furthermore, there are psychological advantages of decoupling the pricing of virtual goods from real-world currency units. Buying something with "Linden Dollars" or "Farm Coins" (two forms of virtual currency used by successful vendors of virtual goods) is apparently easier to digest than buying something with real dollars, euros, or yen. Some examples of virtual goods are:

- Players in the popular multiplayer online game "World of Warcraft" can buy weapons and equipment to make their game character stronger.
- The virtual world "Second Life" offers all kinds of virtual products that users' virtual characters can use, including real estate.

The appeal of virtual goods to the companies selling them is obvious: Users are paying real money for something that has literally zero marginal cost to make. Once a game platform or virtual world is up and running, its owner can sell unlimited amounts of virtual goods. But even virtual goods answer to the laws of supply and demand. It is therefore not surprising that operators of virtual worlds have to be careful with their pricing and supply of virtual money. And not unexpectedly, some of these companies have come under significant scrutiny by financial authorities because producing virtual currency is not unlike traditional banking. For example, the Chinese government in 2009 banned the use of virtual currency for trading in real goods (Ministry of Commerce 2009).

Group buying

Organizing online group buying is a business model that has been tried in several waves throughout the existence of the Internet. The group-buying website acts as a middleman and negotiates discounts with vendors of the product that are then partially passed on to the buyers. Buyers profit from lower prices for a product that they want, while vendors get a guaranteed block of demand for which they are willing to give a discount. Group buying sites typically make money from charging a commission for their coordination services.

The most successful group buying sites offer a pre-selected, limited range of products or services to their members. For instance, Groupon.com, founded in 2008, sends a daily offer to its members—membership is free—specifying the conditions for which members can buy the offer. Typically, the seller offers an attractive discounted price if a certain minimum number of members decide to buy the product or service and prepay the offered price. Buyers then receive a voucher that they can exchange for the product or service. Sites of this type exist for a wide variety of products and services, covering markets such as electronics, designer clothes, travel, and restaurants.

Crowdsourcing

The coordination of work has traditionally been an important field for information technology (Olson et al. 2001). Internet-based crowdsourcing (a combination of "crowd" and "outsourcing") takes the coordination of distributed work resources to a new level by orchestrating work provided by geographically distributed, independent individuals in order to achieve a common goal. In its typical form, crowdsourcing starts with a well-defined problem posed by a client who is willing to pay a certain amount for a work result (Howe 2009). Crowdsourced tasks can range from very repetitive work to highly sophisticated research problems. A crowdsourcing service then broadcasts the work request on the Internet to an unknown group of potentially interested workers. Workers decide independently if they want to contribute to the work product for the conditions specified by the client. Crowdsourcing companies make money from either charging a percentage of the awarded payment or a fixed fee per project.

In some cases, crowdsourcing workers are simply paid by output, for example, per number of units completed in a repetitive job. E-commerce company Amazon offers a service called "Mechanical Turk" that specializes in this type of job. Typical examples are repetitive image recognition (e.g. "Do you see a human in this picture?"), data verification, or simple content production. In other cases, crowdsourcing takes the form of competitions where only the winner who provides the best solution is paid. This method is typically used for tasks that involve a creative or research component. For instance, businesses in need of a new corporate logo can use the platform 99designs.com to solicit logo designs from independent designers. Depending on the amount of money promised, clients can expect to choose from several dozen proposals, only one of which they are required to pay for.

Cloud computing infrastructure services

Outsourcing IT operations is a relatively old business that dates back to the era of mainframe computers in the 1950s and 1960s. The rise of the Internet, however, led to the formation of an entirely new industry of application hosting providers in the late 1990s. These companies own and operate data centers with thousands of computers that run websites and other online applications for customers. But yet another generation of infrastructure providers started to disrupt this hosting industry structure from around 2006, enabled by new virtualization technology that allows the operation of multiple "virtual" computers on the same physical machine. These so-called "cloud computing" providers offer a much more flexible model for the temporary purchase of computing power. One of the pioneers was e-commerce giant Amazon that started renting out surplus capacity in its data centers in 2006 (Thanos 2010).

A cloud-computing provider rents computing and storage capacity at very small increments, both in terms of the technical capacity and the time commitment needed. For instance, Amazon customers can rent a server computer for a minimum of just an hour. If a customer is willing to commit to a longer rental time span, prices get more attractive. But for many users of cloud computing, the high flexibility is the most interesting feature of these services. For instance, research teams use cloud computing services to temporarily increase computing capacity if they need to crunch numbers on a large data set. Vendors of online services use cloud capacity to service temporary spikes in demand. And thanks to cloud computing, many web start-ups now can sell their products and services to a broad audience without large capital expenditures for server machines and data centers.

Even though many larger and smaller companies have entered the cloud computing industry, the market is dominated by a few very big players—like Amazon, Google, Microsoft, and Rackspace. Cloud computing clearly benefits from scale economies, which reduce acquisition costs for the necessary infrastructure.

Many cloud computing providers are trying to differentiate themselves by offering "value-added services" on top of the pure computing infrastructure. For instance, both Amazon and Google provide simplified database storage engines that customers can use to develop their own applications more quickly and cheaply. The disadvantage for customers is that they lock themselves into a particular technical environment if they use these attractively priced services.

Conclusions

The Internet has revolutionized the way people live their daily lives, shop for goods and services, and communicate for personal and professional reasons. The cost and methods of doing business on the Internet also differ from the brick-and-mortar world. Consequently, it is no surprise that this technological innovation has both enhanced and disrupted traditional ways of doing business, as well as created many opportunities for entrepreneurs and established firms to create new businesses or expand existing markets. But there are several areas that researchers interested in the impact of the Internet on firm-level strategies and business models need to continue studying. This is not a comprehensive list but merely a sample of the problems that continue to vex managers and entrepreneurs who rely in whole or in part on the Internet.

First, is how to improve trust and authenticity, as well as general security, on the Internet. E-commerce has not led to a perfect "level playing field" or the radical "disintermediation" many predicted in the early days of the Web (Hagel and Armstrong 1997). The most important reason seems to be that the Internet does not provide a foolproof mechanism to evaluate the authenticity and trustworthiness of product-related information. For instance, many product reviews in blogs and online forums are planted by the manufacturer or a dealer. There are also many cases of fraudulent websites intended to gain access to credit card information, and other scams by criminal online merchants or "hackers" who gain access to confidential financial and personal information. The result is that many consumers continue to be cautious about online information and transactions, thereby limiting the spread of Internet commerce.

It is therefore not surprising that branded market platforms such as Amazon and Apple iTunes, or travel service providers such as Expedia, have an advantage in gaining consumers' trust. These platforms provide a controlled environment for online shopping and make sure that reviews are genuine and, for the most part, that customer data is secure. Driven by network effects, some of these platforms have become the dominant online retail channels in their industries. Trying to imitate this success, many start-up companies strive to become the dominant market platform for a specific sector, often using new marketing approaches such as group buying. To some extent, disintermediation has turned into re-intermediation. The efficiency gains compared to offline commerce are still considerable, but we need to know more about how to enable the Internet to realize its full potential as a transparent and secure market platform.

Second, is how to better manage digital property rights and price digital goods. This problem most obviously relates to books, magazines, and newspapers, as well as audio and video content such as music, movies, and television shows. It also relates to other digitized goods such as art work. How to value digital goods when the marginal cost of replication is zero may always remain a critical problem but it has inhibited the spread of businesses such as Netflix or Hulu.com that try to aggregate or distribute other firms' digital content via the Internet. Much of Apple's success with iTunes is due to the fact that it managed to get most music vendors to agree on a single price per song and thereby solved the highly complex problem of how to price music. Other firms such as the new Napster or Netflix have adopted subscription-based pricing for video and audio content, providing access for a fixed monthly fee. But we still do not know much about what is the best business model and pricing strategy for different types of digital content. In addition, we have seen software product companies, led by Salesforce.com, experimenting with subscription pricing as well for Software as a Service and other cloud computing businesses. Here as well, there is little data on which business model is likely to be more profitable, or encourage more revenue growth, or result in more satisfied customers.

Third, is the viability of "free" and ad-based business models for large numbers of firms over long periods of time. These strategies include variations such as giving away part or low-functional versions of a product for free and then trying to sell premium versions or sell professional and add-on services. Ads also provide information as well as disruptions, such as when friends are using a social network or playing an Internet game. Moreover, the reality of platform dynamics driven by network effects tends to result in a small number of players generating most of the web traffic, which is essential to be able to charge advertisers. We need much more research on when and where (which kinds of markets) free and ad-based business models work best, and how to make them, or variations such as freemium, work better for a larger number of firms.

Fourth, is how to integrate mobile devices more effectively into Internet commerce. Nearly every major market has an actual or potential mobile component, but most firms have not fully utilized the potential of mobile technology, especially when powered by fast and cheap Internet-based connections. The rise of smartphones and tablet computers running software from Apple, Google, RIM (Blackberry), Nokia, Microsoft, and ARM has created opportunities for thousands of companies to create small applications and sell them in the "App Stores" of these different companies. But we know relatively little about how important it is for one platform to have hundreds of thousands of applications available in its ecosystem versus a few "hit" applications, or how companies can effectively market their products and services and make a profit when there are thousands of competitors. Platform companies also tend to expand their features, bringing them into direct competition with their partners and complementors.

Fifth, is which entrepreneurial strategies are most successful in building businesses in the new markets enabled by the Internet (and similar disruptive technologies). Some of the most successful Internet businesses, such as Amazon, were built on an aggressive, high-growth "land grab" strategy that involved high initial losses in the race to dominate an untapped market. Others, such as Google and Facebook, started as small niche players and only found their successful business models after several years, recombining elements invented by others. And yet others, such as Apple, with its success in music and smartphones, entered a new market from an adjacent field, leveraging existing competencies and a long history of trial and error. But there are plenty of examples of competitors that failed with similar strategies. The mechanisms behind the success or failure of such strategies, and the positive or negative role of the Internet on business models, are still poorly understood.

In conclusion, from the consumer's viewpoint, the Internet has brought an almost unlimited ability to search the globe for the best products and services at the lowest prices. This seems to represent a dramatic increase in market efficiency. Established firms that were able to adapt survived and some have even thrived. Entrepreneurs also capitalized on the capabilities of the Internet to revolutionize old businesses and create new ones. But the flip side of the Internet is that customers can instantly compare and buy products and services from around the world. Inflexible or inefficient firms should disappear in a competitive market economy, and the Internet has facilitated this aspect of business as well as others.

REFERENCES

Adner, R. (2006). "Match Your Innovation Strategy to Your Innovation Ecosystem," *Harvard Business Review*, 84(4): 98–107.

Afuah, A. and Tucci, C. (2001). *Internet Business Models and Strategies: Text and Cases*, New York: McGraw Hill.

Anderson, C. (2006). *The Long Tail*, New York: Hyperion.

——(2009). *Free: The Future of a Radical Price*, New York: Hyperion.

Arthur, W. B. (1989). "Competing Technologies, Increasing Returns, and Lock-in by Historical Events," *Economic Journal*, 99 (March): 116–31.

Bakos, Y., and Brynjolfsson, E. (1999). "Bundling Information Goods: Pricing, Profits and Efficiency," *Management Science*, 45(12): 1613–30.

Baldwin, C. Y. and Clark, K. B. (1999). *Design Rules: The Power of Modularity*, Cambridge, MA: MIT Press.

Berners-Lee, T. (1999). *Weaving the Web: The Past, Present, and Future of the World Wide Web by Its Inventor*, London: Orion Publishing.

Bresnahan, T. and Greenstein, S. (1999). "Technological Competition and the Structure of the Computer Industry," *Journal of Industrial Economics* 47(1): 1–40.

Brynjolfsson, E., Smith, M. D., and Yu, H. (2003). "Consumer Surplus in the Digital Economy: Estimating the Value of Increased Product Variety at Online Booksellers," *Management Science*, 49(11): 1580–96.

Cusumano, M. A. (2004). *The Business of Software*, New York: Free Press.

——(2008). "The Changing Software Business: Moving from Products to Services," *IEEE Computer*, 41(1): 20–7.

——(2010). *Staying Power: Six Enduring Principles for Managing Strategy and Innovation in an Uncertain World*, Oxford: Oxford University Press.

Cusumano, M. A. and Yoffie, D. B. (1998). *Competing on Internet Time: Lessons from Netscape and Its Battle with Microsoft*, New York: The Free Press.

Darlin, D. (2009). "Using 'Free' to Turn a Profit," *New York Times*, August 29. Available at <http://www.nytimes.com/2009/08/30/business/30ping.html>. Accessed June 20, 2012.

David, P. (1985). "Clio and the Economics of QWERTY," *American Economic Review*, 75(2): 332–7.

Davis, H. (2006). *Google Advertising Tools*, Sebastopol: O'Reilly Media.

Denison, D. C. (2002). "Napster Files for Chap. 11, Hopes to Speed Relaunch," *Boston Globe*, June 4: D1.

Eisenmann, T. (2006). "Internet Companies Growth Strategies: Determinants of Investment Intensity and Long-Term Performance," *Strategic Management Journal*, 27(12): 1183–204.

—— Parker, G., and Van Alstyne, M. W. (2006). "Strategies for Two-Sided Markets," *Harvard Business Review*, 84(10): 92–101.

Farrell, J. and Saloner, G. (1986). "Installed Base and Compatibility: Innovation, Product Preannouncements and Predation," *American Economic Review*, 76(5): 940–55.

Gartner Group (2010). "Gartner Says Worldwide SaaS Revenue Within the Enterprise Application Software Market to Surpass $8.5 Billion in 2010," Gartner Report, July 22. Available at <http://www.gartner.com/it/page.jsp?id=1406613>. Accessed June 20, 2012.

Gawer, A. (ed.) (2009). *Platforms, Markets and Innovation*, Cheltenham/Northampton, MA: Edward Elgar.

—— and Cusumano, M. A. (2008). "How Companies Become Platform Leaders," *MIT Sloan Management Review*, 49(2): 29–30.

—— and Cusumano, M. A. (2002). *Platform Leadership: How Intel, Microsoft, and Cisco Drive Industry Innovation*, Boston: Harvard Business School Press.

Hagel, J. and Armstrong, A. G. (1997). *Net Gain: Expanding Markets Through Virtual Communities*, Cambridge, MA: Harvard Business Press.

Howe, J. (2009). *Crowdsourcing: Why the Power of the Crowd Is Driving the Future of Business*, New York: Three Rivers Press.

Iwatani, Y. and Smith, E. (2011). "Apple Readies iCloud Service," *Wall Street Journal*, June 1. Available at <http://online.wsj.com/article/SB1000142405270230365740457635721265774202024.html>. Accessed June 20, 2012.

Jarzemsky, M. (2011). "Ballmer Unveils Online Version of Office Software," *Wall Street Journal*, June 29. Available at <http://online.wsj.com/article/SB10001424052702304447804576413660894419054.html>. Accessed June 20, 2012.

Katz, M. and Shapiro, C. (1992). "Product Introduction with Network Externalities," *Journal of Industrial Economics*, 40(1): 55–83.

Meyer, M. H. and Lehnerd, A. P. (1997). *The Power of Product Platforms*, New York: Free Press.

—— and Utterback, J. M. (1993). "The Product Family and the Dynamics of Core Capability," *MIT Sloan Management Review*, 34(3): 29–47.

Ministry of Commerce (2009). "China Bars Use of Virtual Money for Trading in Real Goods," Press Release, People's Republic of China, June 29. Available at <http://english.mofcom.gov.cn/aarticle/newsrelease/commonnews/200906/20090606364208.html>. Accessed June 20, 2012.

NPD Group (2010). "Amazon Ties Walmart as Second-Ranked U.S. Music Retailer, Behind Industry-Leader iTunes," NPD Group Press Release, May 26. Available at <http://www.npd.com/press/releases/press_100526.html>. Accessed June 20, 2012.

Ogilvy, D. (1988). *Confessions of an Advertising Man*, London: Atheneum.

Olson, G. M., Malone, T. W., and Smith, J. B. (2001). *Coordination Theory and Collaboration Technology*, Mahwah, NJ: Lawrence Erlbaum Associates.

Parker, G. and Van Alstyne, M. W. (2005). "Two-Sided Network Effects: A Theory of Information Product Design," *Management Science*, 51(10): 1494–504.

Reid, R. H. (1999). *Architects of the Web: 1,000 Days that Built the Future of Business*, New York: Wiley.

Richtel, M. (2002). "Turmoil at Napster Moves the Service Closer to Bankruptcy," *New York Times*, May 14. Available at <http://www.nytimes.com/2002/05/15/technology/15MUSI.html>. Accessed October 5, 2010.

Rochet, J. C. and Tirole, J. (2003). "Platform Competition in Two-sided Markets," *Journal of the European Economic Association*, 1(4): 990–1029.

——and Tirole, J. (2006). "Two-sided Markets: A Progress Report," *RAND Journal of Economics*, 37(3): 645–67.

Sanderson, S. W. and Uzumeri, M. (1996). *Managing Product Families*. New York: Irwin.

Schmalensee, R., Evans, D., and Hagiu, A. (2006). *Invisible Engines: How Software Platforms Drive Innovation and Transform Industries*, Cambridge, MA: MIT Press.

Schneider, G. P. (2009). *Electronic Commerce*, Boston: Cengage Learning.

Shapiro, C. and Varian, H. (1998). *Information Rules: A Strategic Guide to the Network Economy*, Boston: Harvard Business School Press.

Talluri, K. and Van Rizin, G. (2005). *The Theory and Practice of Revenue Management*, New York: Springer.

Thanos, G. et al. (2010). "Grid Business Models," in K. Stanoevska-Slabeva, T. Wozniak, and S. Ristol (eds). *Grid and Cloud Computing: A Business Perspective on Technology and Applications*, Heidelberg: Springer, pp. 62–82.

Ulrich, K. (1995). "The Role of Product Architecture in the Manufacturing Firm," *Research Policy*, 24(3): 419–40.

Vance, A. (2002). "Judge Blocks Napster Sale," *Computerworld*, September 3. Available at <http://www.computerworld.com>. Accessed October 5, 2010.

Wellman, M. P., Greenwald, A., and Stone, P. (2007). *Autonomous Bidding Agents*, Cambridge, MA: MIT Press.

Yoffie, D. B. and Kwak, M. (2006). "With Friends Like These: The Art of Managing Complementors," *Harvard Business Review*, 84(9): 89–98.

CHAPTER 13

....

TRUST IN COMMERCIAL AND PERSONAL TRANSACTIONS IN THE DIGITAL AGE

....

REGINA CONNOLLY

INTRODUCTION

....

UNDERSTANDING the predictors and dynamics of consumer trust is an issue of enduring interest for both researchers and practitioners. The former seek to understand the antecedents of trust while the latter seek to build on this research to develop effective marketing strategies that will reduce perceived risk and engender trust beliefs in consumers. That interest derives from the understanding that trust is integral to transactions and its absence creates a chain reaction that manifests in lost sales, damage to reputation, and market share gains to competitors. In a commercial world that is becoming increasingly commoditized, consumer trust is the defining factor that characterizes winners, and, in its absence, losers. This has never been truer than in the online exchange context, a context that is characterized by perceived risk, lack of control, and increased consumer vulnerability.

Perceived risk is frequently cited as one of the key factors inhibiting online transactions (Chen and Barnes 2007). However, added to this, a new factor, the global economic crisis, has entered the equation, resulting in a consumer population that has far less disposable income than previously, a fact that has been manifested in sharply reduced online sales (ComScore 2009). These economic concerns have affected not only how much consumers are spending and from whom, but whether they will in fact purchase at all. A 2010 (Javelin) study reports that credit card usage fell dramatically from 2007 to 2008, with only 64 percent of consumers indicating they used a credit card in the month preceding the September 2008 survey, as compared to 87 percent of consumers in 2007—a 23 percentage point decline. This has implications for web vendors who are now competing for a reduced pool of available consumers. However, recent research reports (Mulpuru and Hult 2010) note that even amid a global financial crisis, US online retail sales are showing a 10 percent compound annual growth rate and are forecast to reach US$248.7 billion by 2014. They predict that growth in online retail sales will continue to outpace growth in offline retail sales, as low prices, convenience, and selection drive more shoppers to the Web. For web vendors seeking to gain and retain loyal market share, the imperative for them to ensure that consumers trust their brands and their transaction environments has never been greater.

Gaining that trust is not a simple task. The most recent European and World Values Survey shows that 70 percent of the survey respondents do not believe that people can be trusted (Hong and Bohnet 2007) while other studies have shown that between 60–75 percent of customers terminate their online transactions when asked to provide personal and financial credit card information as they do not trust the website (Rajamma et al. 2009). On a practical level, shopping cart abandonment, where individuals select a purchase, but fail to complete the purchase, represents approximately US$175 in lost sales to the online retailer, translating into a loss of more than US$6.5 billion per year for the total online retailing industry (McGlaughlin 2001). Clearly, a strong financial incentive exists for understanding how to successfully engender trust in online consumers. It is unsurprising therefore that eBay, which is consistently rated as the most trusted online company (Ponemon Institute and TRUSTe 2009), is equally one of the most financially successful online companies in the world. That perception of trustworthiness is not accidental, but derives from an acute awareness that trust drives the volume and value of every business transaction and is therefore the currency of success in an online environment. The fact that so few online companies are rated as trustworthy is indicative of the fact that there is limited understanding regarding the factors that engender trust beliefs in an online environment. This chapter seeks to address that problem and provide clarity in relation to the nature of the trust construct.

Research on trust in online environments is diverse and includes research on trust in global virtual teams (Mitchell and Zigurs 2009); trust in virtual organizations (Young 2008); trust in virtual communities (Johnson and Kaye 2009); trust in e-Government (Mutulu 2010); trust in IT artefacts (Wang and Benbasat 2008); as well as trust in e-commerce (Dutton et al. 2009; Connolly and Bannister 2007). This chapter focuses on the latter, but has implications for trust in a wider range of environments.

Despite its importance, the literature on trust in an online environment is comparatively sparse in contrast to the large body of work that exists on trust in the traditional, offline context. However, while it is true that the vast proportion of trust studies pertain to the offline environment, the findings of some of these studies transcend the distinction of traditional versus Internet commerce (Kracher et al. 2005) and, consequently, the extant literature should be viewed as a source of deep and valuable insights.

In order to progress and mature, online trust research requires a strong theoretical foundation. The objective of this chapter is to provide a holistic overview of the nature of the trust construct in order to contribute to the advancement of our understanding of trust in an online environment. The chapter is structured as follows: first, the differing conceptualizations of the trust construct and the problems that this presents are discussed. This is followed by a detailed review of research on the antecedents and contextual determinants that facilitate the production and maintenance of trust beliefs. While these two sections of the chapter draw from the established offline trust literature, the findings are germane to the online context as traditional and online environments share many commonalities in relation to the factors that can influence consumer trust responses and are therefore worthy of consideration by online trust researchers. The issues surrounding the conceptualization of online trust and some of the problems relating to trust research in an online transaction context are outlined. This is followed by a discussion of the role of experience, gender, and culture in relation to the generation of online trust beliefs. Finally, a number of fruitful research frontiers that need to be addressed by e-commerce trust researchers are proposed.

TRUST

The importance of trust and its contribution to interpersonal, inter-organizational, and transactional relationships is widely acknowledged. It is considered to be both an interpersonal and a collective phenomenon that facilitates human interactions and is consequently considered essential for psychological health (Young 2008). It serves as a means of reducing perceived risk in situations of uncertainty and complexity (Grabner-Kraüter and Kaluscha 2003; Mayer et al. 1995), such as an electronic commerce context. Sociologists (Gambetta 1988), psychologists (Deutsch 1973), organizational behavior scientists (Kramer 1999), as well as economists (Bradach and Eccles 1989), anthropologists (Ekeh 1974), and political scientists (Barber 1983) have contributed to the wide body of work that exists on this topic.

Defining trust

The most fundamental problem encountered when analyzing the trust literature is the lack of an agreed definition of the construct. The conceptual diversity is a consequence of the varying disciplines of the researchers and the foci of their research, as differing academic emphases, research objectives and insights have resulted in multiple conceptualizations of the construct. In an attempt to reduce the conceptual confusion, Brenkert (1998) points to three views of trust in the literature, which he identifies as attitudinal, predictability, and voluntarist views of trust. The attitudinal perspective stresses dispositional or attitudinal characteristics. It considers trusting behavior to be a function of attitude and inclination, based on a specific set of beliefs, rather than a cognitive state of mind. The predictability view of trust stresses the importance of expectations about the behavioral predictability of the other party, for example Dasgupta (1988: 51) emphasizes "expectations about the actions of other people." The voluntarist view of trust is that individuals voluntarily take the action of placing themselves in a position of vulnerability, believing that the other party has intentions of goodwill and not of harm. Although attempts to categorize trust in terms of perspective are useful in imposing structure on the research field and on the terms of analysis, they are limited in that they do not pay adequate attention to the influence of context on the individual's behavior. For example, the role of context is particularly significant when that context is electronically mediated and communication is via a website. A more comprehensive approach is provided by Sitkin and Roth (1993) who subdivide trust research into the four distinct categories of trust as an individual attribute, trust as a behavior, trust as a situational feature, and trust as an institutional arrangement. That approach reflects a more realistic understanding of the complex nature of the trust construct.

In spite of the diverse definitions and categorizations, some points of commonality are evident. For example, the view of trust as positive expectation, and trust as confidence, frequently emerge in the literature. Both views are predicated on the predictability of behavior and goodwill/positive intention of the trustee. Thus, researchers such as McAllister (1995) stress the use of positive trusting expectations as a determinant of subsequent behavior, while Good (1988) considers trust to be grounded in specific expectations relating to the other party's behavior based on claims of that party, and Deutsch (1973) stresses optimistic expectancy about another's behavioral motives. Moving beyond the concept of trust as a set of optimistic expectations, Golembiewski and McConkie (1975) instead perceive trust in terms of confidence. They posit that trust indicates confidence in some event, process, or person, based upon personal perceptions and experiences. Furthermore, they consider trust to be a dynamic rather than static phenomenon, which is strongly connected to overall optimism regarding the behavior of the other party (1975: 134). This indicates that trust evolves over time and can be influenced by positive experience. However, Brenkert (1998) makes the important distinction between the confidence that enables trusting behavior, and trustworthiness. He contends that trust is an attitude or disposition to put oneself into a situation of vulnerability that is dependent on the goodwill and good behavior of the other party, while trustworthiness is an evaluative appraisal of another party in terms of whether they are worthy of trust. This distinction is valuable as it separates out the twin issues central to any examination of trust when defined in terms of confidence, that is, the dispositional issues unique to the trustor and the perception that the target (e.g. the web vendor) is trustworthy. While some of these arguments seem quite theoretical in nature, their value lies in that they focus attention on the issues that are essential in any examination of trust issues, that is, that trustors are made to feel confident that their expectations will be satisfied because measures are in place to protect them against opportunistic behavior, and that the goodwill of the trusted party is effectively communicated to the trustor.

The antecedents of trust

Researchers who consider trust to be a dependent variable suggest that a perception of trustworthiness results from the perception of a number of characteristics (e.g. Lee and

Turban 2001). Many attempts have been made to identify these characteristics and while there may not be complete agreement, common themes such as the characteristics of ability, benevolence, and integrity consistently surface—albeit under differing titles and emphases.

Ability is perceived to relate to technical competence within a specific domain and has been defined (Mayer et al. 1995: 718) as "that group of skills, competencies, and characteristics that enable a party to have influence within some specific domain." In a computer-mediated marketplace environment, that ability is likely to be evaluated in terms of the technical characteristics of the website such as website design, ease of use, the presence of security features, the reliability of the website, the speed of the transaction, and the delivery of the correct product within the agreed time frame (i.e. transaction fulfillment).

Benevolence implies a perception of positive intent and good motives, which Mayer et al. (1995: 718) define as "the extent to which a trustee is believed to want to do good to the trustor, aside from an egocentric profit motive." In a computer-mediated marketplace context, the presence of privacy policies on websites (i.e. a guarantee that the vendor will not pass on information regarding customers to third parties) can reassure the consumer regarding the web vendor's benevolence and trustworthiness (Bandyopadhyay 2009).

Integrity is a derivative of the trustor's perception that the trustee behaves in a manner that indicates consistent and positive values. Factors which may influence the perception of trustee integrity include the consistency of the party's past actions, credible communications about the trustee from other parties, belief that the trustee has a strong sense of justice, and the extent to which the party's actions are congruent with his or her words (McFall 1987). In an online exchange context, the consumer's evaluation of a web vendor's integrity is influenced by communications from other parties (i.e. the experiences of the consumer's peers). In the absence of such communications, the vendor's integrity is likely to be evaluated in terms of whether the vendor provides product guarantees, no-quibble refunds and exchanges, does not overcharge, allows the customer to access their account history online, and most importantly of all, that in the event of a problem they stand by their guarantees.

Propensity to trust

In the literature, the effect of the propensity to trust characteristic on the individual's trust response is a matter of dispute. Personality-based psychologists (e.g. Hofstede 1980) contend that each person has a unique propensity to trust that is influenced by personality type, culture, and developmental experiences. They suggest that the individual's dispositional propensity to trust determines the amount and level of trust that a person has for another party in the absence of available or experiential information on which to base a judgment. On the other hand, organizational psychologists consider that situational factors exert a greater influence on the trust response than does the individual's tendency to trust (Kramer 1999). This raises the question as to whether examinations of trust in an online context should include a measure of dispositional trust as a control variable. While there is sufficient evidence to suggest that individuals differ greatly in their tendency to trust others (Lee and Turban 2001), a recent (Connolly and Bannister 2007) examination of the antecedents of trust in e-commerce found no evidence to support the influence of this characteristic on the individual's trust response. However, more research is required to determine whether the influence of this factor is culture dependent.

Trust and perceived risk

Trust is critical for the success of all social interactions that involve uncertainty and dependency. As Mayer et al. (1995; 711) note, "the need for trust only arises in a risky situation." For researchers such as Nooteboom et al. (1997: 316) that risk has two dimensions, which they define as *size of loss* and *probability of loss*. They contend that risk of opportunism can be restrained by measures such as direct supervision or by means of a legal contract. While these dimensions are relevant, equally important dimensions of risk such as the nature of the loss and the consequences of the loss should also be considered and are likely to be just as important to consumers as size and probability of loss. For example, online transactions involve a leap of faith, with the consumer being required to provide both personal and financial information, and trusting that it will not be misused. While much attention has been paid to consumers' online security concerns, it has been shown that the consequences of online privacy concerns include a lack of willingness to provide personal information online, rejection of e-commerce, or even unwillingness to use the Internet (Bandyopadhyay 2009).

While trust may increase the likelihood of risk-taking, not all risk-taking behavior results from trust or a willingness to be vulnerable to another party in a relationship. For example, in some online transaction situations a consumer might not trust a vendor at all but still purchase from that vendor. The cost of a breach of trust is insignificant to them. Another person with the same propensity to trust may act differently depending on their economic circumstances. In this case, the factor shaping the person's behavior is not the size of the risk or their propensity to trust but the relative economic impact of the loss to the person. The economic impact of that loss as perceived by that person "frames" their decision as to whether or not they should engage in risk-taking behavior. Based on these assumptions, the framing effect (rather than trust beliefs) may explain some risk-taking behavior.

Institutional trust production mechanisms

Institutional arrangements, social structures, processes, and norms have been described as "guardians of trust" (Shapiro 1987: 635) as they can have the effect of encouraging trusting behavior. Institution-based trust is considered to take two distinct forms—situational normality beliefs (Lewis and Weigert 1985) and structural assurance beliefs (Shapiro 1987). Situational normality beliefs stem from the appearance that things are "customary" (Baier 1986: 245) and everything seems in proper order (Lewis and Weigert 1985). These contextual cues make a transactional environment appear normal and thus engender trusting beliefs. Structural assurance beliefs (Shapiro 1987: 204) signify structural protections or governance mechanisms, such as policies, regulations, assurances, and contractual measures. Collectively, they facilitate the formation of trusting beliefs and risk-taking behavior. At a societal level, the presence of these guarantees, safety nets, and other supporting structures is evident through legal measures that protect the individual's rights and property and thus confer trust (Zucker 1986). However, some researchers (Sitkin and Roth 1993) suggest that institutional controls could potentially limit trust, as legal contracts and governance mechanisms reduce flexibility and create layers of formality. In fact, Zucker (1986) considers that institutional mechanisms reduce the opportunity for creating interpersonal trust, as when an exchange is formally structured to an extreme there is no need for individuals to trust. This raises the question as to whether institutional trust is simply a control mechanism or whether it does in fact support the formation of trust beliefs (Shapiro 1987).

Trust development is dependent on time (Doney et al. 1998); as common values, interdependent bonds, and shared norms cannot be established immediately, but require time to develop. Therefore, realistically, in many situations, such as in an online environment, the presence of governance mechanisms may be necessary to facilitate the formation of trust beliefs, particularly when the trustworthiness of one party is uncertain. However, as highly structured controls remove the need for trust formation, and thus may inhibit development of a trust relationship, for example progression from transaction to relationship, they have the potential to destroy what they set out to create. In fact, to a prospective trustor, the presence of highly structured controls may even have negative connotations, suggesting a complete absence of trust. In the context of online shopping, this means that while deterrence-based protection mechanisms are valued mechanisms in engendering initial trust beliefs, vendors must seek other measures to progress the relationship from simply being a strictly governed transaction to a relationship with the customer. What is important is to ensure that the trust relationship does not become permanently based on an awareness of sanctions and that attempts are made to progress it to a deeper and more stable trust form.

TRUST AND EXCHANGE

Trust has economic importance as it is a key facilitator of exchange; by increasing cooperation between transaction partners it reduces the need to implement controls and consequently lowers transaction costs (Wicks et al. 1999). This benefit is achieved by creating a sense of confidence in the other partners, diminishing the need for legal contracts, and increasing cooperative behavior. Thus, economists such as Hirsch (1978: 78) state that trust is "necessary for the success of economic transactions" and is viewed as the relationship facilitator between trading partners.

However, distinct differences exist between the offline and online transaction process in relation to the generation of trust beliefs. With the latter, technology mediates the transaction between the trustor and trustee (i.e. the object of trust), thus increasing its complexity for the trustor. Moreover, while factors such as perceived risk, complexity, and cost may restrict an exchange in an offline context, that exchange is typically simultaneous and involves face-to-face communication. However, in an e-commerce context, both a spatial and temporal separation exists between the vendor and consumer. The consumer is required to share sensitive personal and financial information with a vendor who may be based in a geographically remote location, and the consumer has limited (if any) control over the use of that information. Consequently, the perceived risk of the vendor behaving in an opportunistic manner and the resulting loss to the consumer is considerably greater in an e-commerce context.

TRUST IN INTERNET COMMERCE

Just as is the case in the offline environment, research on trust in an online context is beset by conceptual problems. Grabner-Krauter and Kaluscha (2003) observe that research in this area is limited by differing conceptualizations of the construct and a blurring of the distinction between trust and its antecedents. This results in difficulties when making comparisons (Shankar et al. 2002). Compounding the problem is the fact that many of the scales used in trust studies in an online context are neither theoretically grounded nor authenticated. The fact that the researchers' conceptualizations of trust differ is problematic as unless trust means the same thing to all who engage in e-commerce trust research, the results of these studies cannot be compared with any level of reliability. As Grabner-Krauter and Kaluscha (2003) note, some researchers ignore the relationship between trust and risk, others confuse trust with its antecedents and consequents, while other studies (e.g. Kim and Prabhakar 2002) contain definitional inconsistencies.

In an attempt to reduce the confusion, Corritore et al. (2003) propose two ways of defining online trust relationships. One approach is that taken by computer-mediated communication researchers (e.g. Olson and Olson 2000), which defines trust in an online context in terms of how one-to-one relationships are mediated by technology. The second approach is to define the technology (e.g. the vendor's website) as an object of trust (Shankar et al. 2002). Trust is the act of a trustor, which is to say that a person places trust in another person, organization, or object. In an online context, that object is computer technology and therefore computers and websites become the object of trust. This is confirmed by research which shows that people apply social rules and expectations to computers (Nass and Moon 2000), that they treat technology like a real person with a social presence (Reeves and Nass 1996), that they view the technology as a social actor (Nass et al. 1994), and interact with it in a similar way to offline trust relationships. This is in line with the early experimental work of Short et al. (1976) on social presence theory, which demonstrated that face-to-face communication is not superior to mediated communication and that a medium's social effects are principally caused by the degree of social presence that it affords to its users. More recent research has also confirmed that computer-mediated agents can influence trust relationships (Lee et al. 2007). However, Corritore et al. (2003) rightly point out that technology does not have intentionality (i.e. the ability to freely choose to refrain from opportunistic behavior and freely choose to behave in a trustworthy way). They suggest that at best the technology is a social actor in so far as it has a social presence to which individuals respond, and those characteristics of social presence are considered to be critical for the development of trust (Gefen and Straub 2003). Corritore et al. define online trust as "an attitude of confident expectation in an online situation of risk that one's vulnerabilities will not be exploited" (2003: 740). This definition encompasses all the key dimensions of the construct, such as confident expectations, perceived risk, and the potential for opportunistic behavior.

As previously discussed, the individual's need to trust relates directly to the risk involved in a given situation (Mayer et al. 1995). A greater degree of trust is required in an online transaction environment than in a physical shop due to the temporal difference between the exchange of money and receipt of the purchase, conflicting marketing messages, the requirement to provide sensitive information, and the uncertainty about what the retailer will do with the consumer's personal information (Grabner-Krauter and Kaluscha 2003). In fact, it has been shown that awareness of their lack of control over personal data can lead to consumers withholding information from companies and resisting the adoption of online purchasing (Goldsmith and Bridges 2000). To counter this, it has been suggested (Hoffman et al. 1999) that providing the consumer with a more interactive online experience by allowing them to have control over their personal information may facilitate the formation of trust beliefs, and this has been empirically confirmed by Bart et al. (2005) who found that consumer empowerment, that is, allowing consumers to manage information on the web vendor's website, exerts a positive influence on online consumer beliefs, which may in turn influence their decision to purchase online.

Hirshleifer and Riley's (1979) theory of information can be used to better understand the uncertainty that applies to the online purchase environment. This theory outlines two categories of uncertainty: *system-dependent uncertainty* and *transaction-specific uncertainty*. Both types of uncertainty exist in the online purchase environment. For example, the online consumer is dependent on the technological medium for the process to take place effectively and securely. However, the online consumer does not have any control over the medium or the transmission of the data (*system-dependent uncertainty*). *Transaction-specific uncertainty* relates to the fact that the product received may not be satisfactory. This may be due to the fact that the Internet cannot always represent products accurately, particularly in terms of colors and textures. In addition, the consumer often does not have any guarantee that the vendor will not sell their transaction and personal information to a third party. Even when guarantees are provided that customer data will not be passed on to third parties, the consumer does not have any guarantee that the vendor has measures in place to protect consumer data from employee theft. Hence, there is a high level of uncertainty related to the online purchase environment. Research has shown that customers frequently have legitimate anxiety about transaction confidentiality and anonymity (Ratnasingham 1998), but are willing to share more personal information about themselves when they have a trusted relationship (Giardano and Ponemon 2005). As each consumer is unique, the extent of perceived risk will be influenced by issues specific to the individual. For example, the extent to which online consumers are concerned about privacy and security issues is influenced by their education (Burke 2002), Internet experience, and interaction readiness (Miyazaki and Fernandez 2001).

Transaction-specific uncertainty can be reduced by creating a perception of vendor trustworthiness. However, perceptions in the online context differ from that of the traditional marketplace. The normal channels of direct and indirect visual cues, which are so important to the purchase process in the traditional marketplace, are not available to the prospective buyer in a web-based economic exchange. In the initial stages, when an online consumer has not had previous experience of the web vendor, what has been termed "cues of trustworthiness", such as security and privacy disclosures, have been shown to assist in the building of initial trust beliefs (Van Noort et al. 2008). Similarly, there is evidence that website quality and website brand affect consumers' trust and perceived risk, and in turn, consumer purchase intention (Chang and Chen 2008). However research by Schlosser et al. (2005) assert that even though privacy/security statements can influence certain trusting beliefs (i.e. benevolence and integrity beliefs), these measures do not necessarily increase searchers' willingness to buy online, thereby converting searchers into buyers. Instead, they found that website design plays a more important role in online purchase intentions as it serves as a signal that a firm's ability can be trusted, and it is this which they found to be the most significant driver of searchers' online purchase intentions. This finding is confirmed by the work of Bart et al. (2005) which showed that user-friendly navigation and presentation are particularly important influences on trust formation and consequently on behavioral outcome. The Schlosser et al. (2005) study is of particular significance for trust researchers as their findings highlight the importance of considering trusting beliefs separately to trusting intentions, as the former does not necessarily result in an increase in the latter. Their findings also highlight the need to separate signals from interpretation as not all consumers will interpret signals such as privacy statements in the same way and therefore their responses may vary considerably.

Online experience

The online consumer's trust beliefs are influenced by experience. Clearly a negative experience will diminish trust and a positive experience or series of experiences will positively influence the perception of vendor trustworthiness. Drawing on findings from the Oxford Internet Survey, Dutton and Shepherd (2006) found that experience was the primary factor shaping trust in the Internet, not prior dispositions shaped by a person's age or gender—and that bad online experiences may have a deterrent effect on using the Internet. Similarly, Connolly and Bannister (2007) have provided evidence that experience strongly moderates online consumers' perceptions of web vendors' competence, security, and integrity. Their findings showed that, not only is experience a strong predictor of online consumer trust beliefs, it is more influential than perceived vendor competence and evidence of vendor security controls. This finding is not surprising. The online purchase environment is fraught with risk, and even a single bad online transaction experience will almost invariably influence subsequent beliefs regarding that environment.

Exposure to the Internet also shapes trust beliefs, and Dutton and Shepherd (2006) found that even past Internet users, whom they term "internet-dropouts," have more confidence in the Internet than do non-users who have no experience with the technology. They also found that most predispositions to cybertrust that are associated with social and demographic characteristics tend to be mitigated over time, and can be accounted for by the lessons learned from experience online. Their analysis indicates that levels of cybertrust are related to an individual's patterns of use or non-use of the Internet over time, which supports the view that the Internet is an experience technology and is more accurately examined through a process-centric approach.

As an individual may have limited experience of online shopping, factors such as the web vendor's reputation and endorsements from independent third parties can influence the formation of consumer trust beliefs (Yoon 2002). In line with this, Smith et al. (2005) have shown that online peer recommendations have the potential to influence consumer purchase decisions and Urban et al. (2000) contend that advocacy features can increase transparency and consequently facilitate the formation of trust beliefs. Recently, Utz et al. (2009) have shown that judgments of trustworthiness in an online auction context are influenced by feedback comments: a finding that is particularly germane in light of research (Pavlou and Dimoka 2006) which indicates that the majority of eBay users read at least one page of text feedback comments about a seller.

Gender and online trust

While gender issues are not the focus of this chapter, there is some evidence to suggest that gender can affect IT perception and usage (Sanchez-Franco 2006) and that it also influences both trust and risk perceptions. We know that gender differences influence not only *how* we perceive risk, but also *what risks we perceive* (Nicholson 1997) and there is evidence that these differences apply to online trust as well. For example, the work of Rodgers and Harris (2003) shows that males report higher levels of trust in online shopping and had more positive attitudes about online shopping than is the case for females. Similarly, Van Slyke et al. (2004) have shown that male perceptions of website characteristics and the trustworthiness of online shopping is more positive than is the case for females and that men are more likely to use the internet for transactions. In addition, studies (Rodgers and Harris 2003) have found that the predictors of women's satisfaction with online shopping experience differ from those of men, and that females are more sensitive to affective cues. While women may have less positive attitudes towards online shopping, spend less time online and are less likely to purchase online (Garbarino and Strahilevitz 2004), recent research by Awad and Rogowsky (2008) provides the interesting insight that the effect of trust beliefs on intention to shop online is greater for women than for men. This has clear implications for web vendors. More recently, Riedl et al. (2010) used functional magnetic resonance imaging (fMRI) to examine whether online trust is associated with activity changes in certain brain areas in men and women. They found that most of the brain areas that encode online trustworthiness differ between women and men, with women activating more brain areas than did men. This finding, apart from confirming gender differences in relation to online trust beliefs, also brings the hitherto neglected dimension of biology into our understanding of online trust.

Culture and online trust

It has been suggested that national culture influences trust antecedents (Whitener et al. 1998). If this is the case, then the predictors of online trust may vary from one culture to the next and web vendors may find their trust-building measures ineffective. For example, Zhou et al. (2009) found that consumers in China lack trust in online banking and consequently resist its adoption, while Tariq and Eddaoudi (2009) found that trust concerns significantly influence Moroccan consumers' willingness to shop online. Similarly, the examination by Comegys et al. (2009) of the effect of consumer trust and risk on online purchase decision making in Finland and the United States found that United States' respondents with higher levels of trust towards online shopping tended to buy more, while Finish people with little trust towards web vendors reduced their online shopping over time.

Lewis and Weigert (1985: 456) define trust as a "reciprocal orientation and interpretative assumption that is shared," which implies that, to be effective, symbols used to signal trustworthiness (e.g. seals of approval, privacy policies, security symbols) must have shared meaning and equivalent recognition for all parties to the interaction. In the online purchase context, the parties to the interaction (i.e. online consumers and web vendors) are likely to have diverse backgrounds, norms, and cultural understandings. Therefore, unless website symbols have the same meaning and value for all consumers regardless of cultural differences, they are unlikely to be effective in generating trust beliefs. Were web vendors to have a more culturally sensitive understanding of the variables that predict a trust response, it is likely that they would be more effective at building trust relationships with consumers. However, Gefen and Heart (2006) note that, despite repeated theorizations of trust and national culture as intricately related constructs, online trust researchers have for the main part ignored the potential effects of national culture. They point out that the majority of online trust research has been conducted in the United States, a country that exhibits high levels of individualism and uncertainty avoidance (Hofstede 1980), and argue that conclusions based on studies conducted in one country cannot and should not be automatically applied to other cultures. There is clearly a need to expand online trust research in relation to culture, and Pavlou and Chai (2002) also question whether trust antecedent findings obtained in one country can be generalized to other cultural contexts. Support for this view has been provided by a study (Connolly and Bannister 2007) which applied an e-commerce trust model that had been developed and validated in Hong Kong to an Irish context, but found the model contained significant weaknesses when applied in a different national culture. Researchers are therefore advised to exercise caution and not assume that results obtained from trust studies conducted in one country are necessarily generalizable to other cultures.

In the main, studies of trust in online transaction environments have focused on identifying the antecedents of trust beliefs within a particular culture. Each study provides unique insights, and indicates cultural variations in online trust antecedents. For example, the work of Bart et al. (2005) has shown privacy and order fulfilment as the most influential determinants of trust for US online consumers using websites where both information risk and involvement are high, such as travel websites. The findings of Tang et al. (2008) confirm the importance of privacy signals as predictors of trust beliefs for US online consumers. However, studies of samples of online consumers outside of the US show variations in trust antecedents. For example, Connolly and Bannister's (2007) study of trust antecedents found that Irish consumers' trust in Internet shopping is the result of specific factors, the first of which relates to the vendor's perceived integrity (clearly defined terms, conditions, and guarantees), and the second of which relates to the vendor's perceived competence (as conveyed through an easy to use, reliable and secure web interface). The former encompasses social antecedents of trust, while the latter encompasses the technical antecedents of trust. In Taiwan, perceived usefulness, perceived security, perceived privacy, perceived good reputation, and willingness to customize have been shown (Chen and Barnes 2007) to be important antecedents to online initial trust, while studies of Malyasian online consumers (Alam and Mohd 2010) have found that perceptions of website security and privacy significantly influence online consumers' trust responses. The existence of such varying antecedents confirms the view of Gefen (2002) that trustworthiness and trust should not be regarded as a single construct with a single effect.

Remarkably few cross-comparisons of variations in online trust response across differing cultures (as opposed to differing countries) exist. The few cross-comparisons that are available have served to emphasize the fact that the antecedents of trust differ across cultures (Gefen and Heart 2006). For example, Kim (2008) found that transference-based antecedents of trust were more significant in Korea than in the US and that privacy concerns exerted a stronger influence on trust beliefs in the United States. Similarly, Cyr's (2008) comparison of samples across Canada, Germany, and China showed that the relative importance of a number of website design trust antecedents differed across cultures. Culture can vary even within a country, and Falicov (2001) has argued that Hispanics and Anglos (US consumers with Caucasian ethnicity) are cultures with different perceptions of trust, and consequently each group attributes differing levels of importance to aspects of the E-commerce experience. This contention has been supported by the recent work of Changchit et al. *(2009)* who compared Hispanic and Anglo cultures in the US in terms of their different trust perceptions, and found that Anglos place a stronger emphasis on aspects of trust such as perceived Internet security than is the case for Hispanics. Collectively, the insights obtained from studies such as these confirm that the antecedents of trust vary significantly across culture. They also indicate that collectivism and uncertainty avoidance are key elements of culture that influence trust antecedents (Gefen and Heart 2006), and indicate the need for further detailed cross-comparison research of variations in online trust across differing cultures.

WITHER TO FROM HERE? THE FUTURE
OF ONLINE TRUST RESEARCH

Since the dotcom bubble in the late 1990s, much research has been conducted on various aspects of trust in an online environment. The Internet is no longer a new unknown territory and many of the traditional trust barriers have been overcome. The focus of online trust issues has evolved and we now discuss the role of recommendation agents and avatars in trust building in the same way that the antecedents of trust received attention a number of years ago. That said, in comparison to the rich body of research that exists on trust in an offline environment, the literature on online trust is very much at an early stage of development. While much has been done, much remains yet to be done. Online trust researchers such as Urban et al. (2009) contend that there is a need for more precise research on the trust formation process and that this could be achieved through an examination of a longitudinal database of site visits and trust levels. They also argue that as overall trust cannot be measured via a single scale, there is a need for an attitude bank of questions that can be used to measure trust across multiple environments. This is pertinent and long overdue, as an attitude bank including the major trust components would provide stronger, more reliable trust measures, thereby facilitating more systematic examinations of online trust regardless of the researcher's base discipline. They also suggest the need for more research on: the importance of peer ratings on trust formation; whether manufacturer and dealer sites are trusted as much as third party sites; how online trust is affected in the presence of multiple outlets and channels; and how online presence interacts with personal selling efforts to build trust, privacy, and personalization.

Much of the extant online trust research is context and/or culture specific. Moreover, it is impossible to consider it time-independent—it is simply a snapshot in time. Research findings from studies a decade ago are not necessarily germane today, as technology, technical literacy, attitudes, and behaviors have also changed over this period. There is therefore a need for longitudinal surveys that would enable stronger conclusions to be drawn regarding causal relations and associations identified in trust research.

Having moved beyond the first stage of trust research over the past decade, we now need research that offers reliable contextual insights into "why" as well as "how" Internet users differ in their patterns of online trust. Dutton and Shepherd (2005) note that surveys are generally weak in providing detailed contextual knowledge and in unravelling the full complexity of individual beliefs, motivations, and actions. They therefore suggest that online trust survey analyses should be complemented by more qualitative research.

While the above are valid research possibilities and would provide insight into the gaps in our current knowledge in relation to online trust, they do not push the boundaries of our understanding. It has been contended that unravelling and gaining a better understanding of the many interrelated uncertainties related to trust tensions requires social research with a broad perception of the co-evolutionary nature of human, organization, and technological systems (Dutton and Shepherd 2005: 447). Urban et al. (2009) are in agreement and propose that the frontiers of online trust research lie in cross-disciplinary research that includes behavioral science and economics perspectives. They point to research on morphing, which is an attempt to communicate more effectively by imitative the online customer's cognitive style or cultural characteristics and research using fMRI to identify the areas of the brain that are activated by trust. Recently, Riedl et al. (2010) have done just this, enriching our understanding by using fMRI to examine whether neurobiological factors were associated with variance in trustworthiness decisions in online settings.

As previously mentioned, there has been very limited research examining gender-related differences in relation to trusting attitudes and trust behavior in an online context. As Dittmar et al. (2004: 423) note: "Given that men and women have been shown to differ in their attitudes toward both the Internet and shopping (in conventional environments), it seems surprising that there is little research that explicitly addresses gender differences in on-line buying." As a result of the work of Riedl et al. (2009) we know that women and men recruit different brain areas when facing uncertainty, processing information, and deciding which offer to trust. However, the reason why women and men are different on this neural level remains a matter of conjecture. Future research is necessary to determine whether socialization and experience determine these brain activation differences. The work of Riedl et al. points to the need for research to determine whether and in what ways text, presentation format, and color shape cognitive trust responses according to gender. The use of fMRI in future online trust research opens a new avenue of exploration for online trust researchers and is likely to provide valuable insights and progress our understanding of the dynamics surrounding online trust beliefs.

CONCLUSION

The number of people active online is increasing both in the United States and in Europe. For example, UK consumers are currently the most active Internet users in Europe and spend more time online than their US counterparts (ComScore 2009). This has clear implications for web vendors who seek to increase market share by converting website visitors into loyal customers. Gaining and maintaining consumer trust will be central to that conversion. Understanding how to generate consumer trust in a risk-fraught online environment is an imperative that will differentiate winners from losers.

Online trust research requires a strong theoretical foundation. This chapter contributes to the progression and maturing of the online trust field by providing a detailed overview of the nature of the trust construct, the differing conceptualizations of the construct, and their implications for online trust researchers, as well as the factors and dynamics that influence online trust formation. It is hoped that this chapter has provided online trust researchers with an understanding of some of the key issues that require consideration when researching trust in an online transaction context.

The field of online trust research is vibrant and presents many unique research possibilities. There is a need for multifaceted research that will expand existing theories of trust in online environments by examining the role of culture and gender, differing forms of trust, cognitive trust building agents, and the role of avatars and other recommendation agents on trust building. As trust responses comprise human beings, context, and the factors that influence their perceptions and their behavior, there is a particular need for cross-disciplinary research that incorporates both behavioral science and economics perspectives. Continuing advancements in the field will progress our knowledge and confer commercial benefits by increasing the effectiveness of marketing strategies.

REFERENCES

Alam, S. S. and Mohd, Y. N. (2010). "The Antecedents of Online Brand Trust: Malaysian Evidence," *Journal of Business Economics and Management*, 11(2): 210–26.

Awad, N. F. and Rogowsky, A. (2008). "Establishing Trust in Electronic Commerce Through Online World of Mouth: An Examination Across Genders," *Journal of Management Information Systems*, 24(4): 101–21

Baier, A. (1986). "Trust and Antitrust," *Ethics*, 96(2): 231–60.

Bandyopadhyay, S. (2009). "Antecedents and Consequences of Consumers' Online Privacy Concerns," *Journal of Business & Economics Research*, 7(3): 41–8.

Barber, B. (1983). *The Logic and Limits of Trust*, New Brunswick, NJ: Rutgers University Press.

Bart, Y., Shankar, V., Sultan, F., and Urban, G. L. (2005). "Are the Drivers and Role of Online Trust the Same for All Web Sites and Consumers? A Large-Scale Exploratory Empirical Study," *Journal of Marketing*, 69(4): 133–52.

Bradach, J. L. and Eccles, R. G. (1989). "Price, Authority, and Trust: From Ideal Types to Plural Forms," *Annual Review of Sociology*, 15: 97–118.

Brenkert, G. G. (1998). "Trust, Morality and International Business," in C. Lane, and R. Bachmann (eds). *Trust Within and Between Organisations*, Oxford: Oxford University Press.

Burke, R. R. (2002). "Technology and the Customer Interface: What Consumers Want in the Physical and Virtual Store," *Journal of the Academy of Marketing Science*, 30 (Fall): 411–32.

Chang, H. H and Chen, W. C. (2008). "The Impact of Online Store Environment Cues on Purchase Intention," *Online Information Review*, 32(6): 818–41.

Changchit, C., Garofolo, T., and Gonzalez, J. (2009). "E-commerce Trust: A Cultural Study on Hispanic vs. Anglo Perceptions," Paper presented at the ISOneWorld 8th Annual Conference, Las Vegas, NV, April 15–17.

Chen, Y. and Barnes, S. (2007). "Initial Trust and Online Buyer Behaviour," *Industrial Management and Data Systems*. 107(1): 21–36.

Comegys, C. H, Hannula, M, and Vaisanen, J. (2009). "Effects of Consumer Trust and Risk on Online Purchase Decision-making: A Comparison of Finnish and United States Students," *International Journal of Management*, 26(2): 295–308.

ComScore (2009). "U.S. Retail E-Commerce Declines 3 Percent in Q4 2008 versus Year Ago but Sales for Full Year Grew By 6 Percent." Available at <http://www.comscore.com/Press_Events/Press_Releases/2009/2/Q4_2008_Retail_E-Commerce>. Accessed September 10, 2010.

Connolly, R. and Bannister, F. (2007). "Consumer Trust in Internet Shopping in Ireland: Towards the Development of an Improved Model of the Antecedents of Trust," *Journal of Information Technology*, 22(2): 102–18.

Corritore, C. L., Kracher, B., and Wiedenbeck, S. (2003). "On-line Trust: Concepts, Evolving Themes, A Model," *International Journal of Human-Computer Studies*, 58(6): 737–58.

Cyr, D. (2008). "Modelling Website Design across Cultures: Relationships to Trust, Satisfaction and E-loyalty," *Journal of Management Information Systems*, 24(4): 47–72.

Dasgupta, P. (1988). "Trust as a Commodity," in D. G. Gambetta, (ed.). *Trust: Making and Breaking Cooperative Relations*, New York: Basil Blackwell.

Deutsch, M. (1973). *The Resolution of Conflict: Constructive and Destructive Processes*, New Haven, CT: Yale University Press.

Dittmar, H., Long, K., and Meek, R (2004). "Buying on the Internet: Gender differences in On-line and Conventional Buying Motivation," *Sex Roles*, 50(5–6): 423–44.

Doney, P. M., Cannon, J. P., and Mullen, M. R. (1998). "Understanding the Influence of National Culture on the Development of Trust," *Academy of Management Review*, 23(3): 601–20.

Dutton, W. H., Helsper, E. and Gerber, M. (2009). "The Internet in Britain 2009," Oxford Internet Institute, University of Oxford. Available at <http://www.oii.ox.ac.uk/research/oxis/OxIS2009_Report.pdf>. Accessed June 20, 2012.

—— and Shepherd, A. (2005). "Confidence and Risk on the Internet," in R. Mansell and B. S. Collins (eds). *Trust and Crime in Information Societies*, Cheltenham: Edward Elgar, pp. 207–244.

—— and Shepherd, A. (2006). "Trust in the Internet as an Experience Technology," *Information, Communication & Society*, 9(4): 433–51.

Ekeh, P. P. (1974). *Social Exchange Theory: The Two Traditions*, London: Heinemann Educational.

Falicov, C. (2001). "The Cultural Meanings of Money: The Case of Latinos and Anglo-Americans," *American Behavioral Scientist*, 45(2): 1–10.

Gambetta, D. G. (ed.) (1988). *Trust: Making and Breaking Cooperative Relations*, New York: Basil Blackwell.

Garbarino, E. and Strahilevitz, M. (2004). "Gender Differences in the Perceived Risk of Buying Online and the Effects of Receiving a Site Recommendation," *Journal of Business Research*, 57(7): 768–75.

Gefen, D. (2002). "Customer Loyalty in E-Commerce," *Journal of the Association of Information Systems*, 3(1): 27–52.

—— and Heart, T. (2006). "On the Need to Include National Culture as a Central Issue in E-Commerce Trust Beliefs," *Journal of Global Information Management*, 14(4): 1–30.

—— and Straub, D. (2003). "Managing User Trust in B2C e-Services," *e-Service Journal*, 2(2): 7–24.

Giardano, C. and Ponemon, L. (2005). *2005 Permission Management Study Canadian and U.S. Results*. Traverse City, MI: Ponemon Institute.

Goldsmith, R. E. and Bridges, E. (2000). "E-Tailing vs Retailing: Using Attitudes to Predict Online Buying Behavior," *Quarterly Journal of Electronic Commerce*, 1(3): 245–53.

Golembiewski, R. T. and McConkie, M. (1975). "The Centrality of Interpersonal Trust in Group Processes," in C. L. Cooper (ed.). *Theories of Group Processes*, New York: Wiley, pp. 131–85.

Good, D. (1988). "Individuals, Interpersonal Relations and Trust," in D. Gambetta (ed.). *Trust: Making and Breaking Cooperative Relations*, New York: Basil Blackwell, pp. 31–48.

Grabner-Krauter, S. and Kaluscha, E. A. (2003). "Empirical Research in On-line Trust: A Review and Critical Assessment," *International Journal of Human-Computer Studies*, 58(6): 783–812.

Hirsch, F. (1978). *Social Limits to Growth*, Cambridge MA: Harvard University Press.

Hirshleifer, J. and Riley, J. G. (1979). "The Analytics of Uncertainty and Information: An Expository Survey," *Journal of Economic Literature*, 17(4): 1375–421.

Hoffman, D. L., Novak, T. P., and Peralta, M. (1999). "Building Consumer Trust On-line," *Communications of the ACM*, 42(4): 80–5.

Hofstede, G. (1980). *Culture's Consequences: International Differences in Work-Related Values*, Beverly Hilly, CA: Sage.

Hong, K. and Bohnet, I. (2007). "Status and Distrust: The Relevance of Inequality and Betrayal Aversion," *Journal of Economic Psychology*, 28: 197–213.

Javelin Strategy and Research Report (2010). "Payment Card Issuer Strategies 2010: The Rise of the Cautious Consumer." Available at <https://www.javelinstrategy.com/uploads/1026.P_PaymentCardIssuerStrategies2010SampleReport.pdf>. Accessed April 27, 2012.

Johnson, T. J. and Kaye, B. K. (2009). "In blog we Trust? Deciphering Credibility of Components of the. Internet among Politically Interested Internet Users," *Computers in Human Behavior*, 25(1): 175–82.

Kim, D. J. (2008). "Self-Perception-Based Versus Transference-Based Trust Determinants in Computer-Mediated Transactions: A Cross-Cultural Comparison Study," *Journal of Management Information Systems*, 24(4): 13–45.

Kim, K. and Prabhakar, B. (2000). "Initial Trust, Perceived Risk, and the Adoption of Internet Banking," in *Proceedings of the Twenty-First International Conference on Information Systems*, Cairo, Egypt, December, pp. 537–43.

—— and Prabhakar, B. (2002). "Initial trust, perceived risk and trusting behavior in Internet banking." Proceedings of the 21st International Conferences on Information Systems, Brisbane, Australia, December.

Kracher, B., Corritore, C. L., and Wiedenbeck, S (2005). "A Foundation for Understanding Online Trust in Electronic Commerce," *Information, Communication, & Ethics in Society*, 3(3): 131–41.

Kramer, R. M. (1999). "Trust and Distrust in Organisations: Emerging Perspectives, Enduring Questions," *Annual Review of Psychology*, 50: 569–98.

Lee, M. and Turban, E. (2001). "A Trust Model for Consumer Internet Shopping," *International Journal of Electronic Commerce*, 6(1): 75–91.

Lewis, J. and Weigert, A. (1985). "Trust as a Social Reality," *Social Forces*, 63(4): 967–95.

McAllister, D. (1995). "Affect—and Cognition-based Trust as Foundations for Interpersonal Cooperation in Organizations," *Academy of Management Journal*, 38(1): 24–59.

McFall, L. (1987). "Integrity," *Ethics*, 98(1): 5–20.

McGlaughlin, M. (2001). "E-Tailers Seeking Fulfilment," High Beam Research, July 1. Available at <http://www.highbeam.com/doc/1G1-77825295.html>. Accessed September 6, 2011.

Mayer, R. C., Davis, J. D., and Schoorman, F. D. (1995). "An Integrative Model of Organisational Trust," *Academy of Management Review*, 20(3): 709–34.

Mitchell, A. and Zigurs, I. (2009). "Trust in Virtual Teams: Solved or Still a Mystery?," *Data Base for Advances in Information Systems*, 40(3): 61–83.

Miyazaki, A. D. and Fernandez, A. (2001). "Consumer Perceptions of Privacy and Security Risks for Online Shopping," *The Journal of Consumer Affairs*, 35(1): 27–44.

Mulpuru, S. and Hult, P., with Freeman Evans, P., Sehgal, V., and McGowan, B. (2010). "US Online Retail Forecast 2009 to 2014: Online Retail Hangs Tough For 11 percent Growth In A Challenging Economy." Available at: <http://www.forrester.com/rb/Research/us_online_retail_forecast,_2009_to_2014/q/id/56551/t/2>. Accessed September 10, 2010.

Mutulu, S. M. (2010). "A Model of Building Trust in E-Government," in E. E. Adomi, *Frameworks for ICT Policy, Government, Social and Legal Issues*, Hershey, PA: IGI Global Publishing, pp. 15–33.

Nass, C. and Moon, Y. (2000). "Machines and Mindlessness: Social Responses to Computers," *Journal of Social Issues*, 56(1): 81–103.

Nass, C., Steuer, J. S., and Tauber, E. (1994). "Computers are Social Actors," in *Proceeding of the Computer-Human Interaction (CHI) 1994 Conference*, pp. 72–8.

Nicholson, L. (ed.) (1997). *The Second Wave: A Reader in Feminist Theory*, New York: Routledge.

Nooteboom, B., Berger, H., and Noorderhaven, N. G. (1997). "Effects of Trust and Governance on Relational Risk," *Academy of Management Journal*, 40(2): 308–34.

Olson, J. S. and Olson, G. M. (2000). "I2i Trust in E-commerce," *Communications of the ACM*, 43(12): 41–4.

Pavlou, D. and Chai, L. (2002). "What Drives Electronic Commerce Across Cultures? A Cross-Cultural Empirical Investigation of the Theory of Planned Behaviour," *Journal of Electronic Commerce Research*, 3(4): 240–53.

Pavlou, P. A. and Dimoka, A. (2006). "The Nature and Role of Feedback Text Comments in Online Marketplaces: Implications for Trust Building, Price Premiums, and Seller Differentiation," *Information Systems Research*, 17(4): 391–412.

Ponemon Institute and TRUSTe (2009). "Ponemon Institute and TRUSTe Announce Results of Annual Most Trusted Companies for Privacy Survey." Available at <http://www.truste.com/about_TRUSTe/press-room/news_truste_ponemon_name_trusted_companies_08.html>. Accessed September 6, 2011.

Rajamma, R. K., Paswan, A. K., and Hossain, M. (2009). "Why do Shoppers Abandon Shopping Cart? Perceived Waiting Time, Risk, and Transaction Inconvenience," *Journal of Product & Brand Management*, 18(3): 188–97.

Ratnasingham, P. (1998). "Trust in Web-based Electronic Commerce Security," *Information Management and Computer Security*, 6(4): 162–8.

Reeves, B. and Naas, C. (1996). *The Media Equation: How People Treat Computers, Television, and the New Media like Real People and Places*, Stanford, CA: Cambridge University Press.

Riedl, R., Hubert, M., and Kenning, P. (2010). "Are there Neural Gender Differences in Online Trust? An fMRI Study on the Perceived Trustworthiness of eBay Offers," *MIS Quarterly*, 34(2): 397–428.

Rodgers, S., and Harris, M. A. (2003). "Gender and e-Commerce: An Exploratory Study," *Journal of Advertising Research* 43(3): 322–9.

Sanchez-Franco, M. J. (2006). "Exploring the Influence of Gender on the Web Usage Via Partial Least Squares," *Behaviour & Information Technology*, 25(1): 19–36.

Schlosser, A. E., Barnett White, T., and Lloyd, S. M. (2005). "Converting Web Site Visitors into Buyers: How Web Site Investment Increases Consumer Trusting Beliefs and Online Purchase Intentions," *Journal of Marketing*, 70(2): 133–48.

Shankar, V., Urban, G. L., and Sultan, F. (2002). "Online Trust: A Stakeholder Perspective, Concepts, Implications and Future Directions," *Journal of Strategic Information Systems*, 11(3–4): 325–44.

Shapiro, S. P. (1987). "The Social Control of Interpersonal Trust," *American Journal of Sociology*, 93(3): 623–58.

Short, J., Williams, E., and Christie, B., (1976). *The Social Psychology of Telecommunications*, London: Wiley.

Sitkin, S. B. and Roth, N. L. (1993). "Explaining the Limited Effectiveness of Legalistic 'Remedies' for Trust/Distrust," *Organizational Science*, 4(3): 367–92.

Smith, D., Menon, S., and Sivakumar, K. (2005). "Online Peer and Editorial Recommendations, Trust, and Choice in Virtual Markets," *Journal of Interactive Marketing*, 19(3): 15–37.

Tang, Z., Hu, Y., and Smith, M. D. (2008). "Gaining Trust Through Online Privacy Protection: Self-Regulation, Mandatory Standards, or Caveat Emptor," *Journal of Management Information Systems*, 24(4): 153–73.

Tariq, A. N. and Eddaoudi, B. (2009). "Assessing the Effect of Trust and Security Factors on Consumers' Willingness for Online Shopping Among the Urban Moroccans," *International Journal of Business and Management Science*, 2(1): 17–32.

Urban, G. L., Amyx, C., and Lorenzon, A. (2009). "Online Trust: State of the Art, New Frontiers, and Research Potential," *Journal of Interactive Marketing*, 23(2): 179–90.

——, Sultan, F., and Qualls, W. (2000). "Placing trust at the center of your Internet Strategy," *Sloan Management Review*, 42(1): 39–48.

Utz, S., Matzat, U., and Snijders, C. (2009). "Online Reputation Systems: The Effects of Feedback Comments and Reactions on Building and Rebuilding Trust in Online Auctions," *International Journal of Electronic Commerce*, 13(3): 95–118.

Van Noort, G., Kerkhof, P., and Fennis, B. M. (2008). "The persuasiveness of online safety cues," *Journal of Interactive Marketing*, 22(4): 58–72.

Van Slyke, C., Bélanger, F., and Comunale, C. (2004). "Factors Influencing the Adoption of Web-Based Shopping: The Impact of Trust," *The Data Base for Advances in Information Systems*, 35(2): 32–49.

——, Comunale, C., and Belanger, F. (2002). "Gender Differences in Perceptions of Web-based Shopping," *Communications of the ACM*, 45(7): 82–86.

Wang, W. and Benbasat, I. (2008). "Analysis of Trust Formation in Online Recommendation Agents," *Journal of Management Information Systems*, 24(4): 249–73.

Whitener, E. M., Brodt, S. E., Korsgaard, M. A., and Werner, J. M. (1998). "Managers as Initiators of Trust: An Exchange Relationship Framework for Understanding Managerial Trustworthy Behaviour," *Academy of Management Review*, 23(3): 513–30.

Wicks, A. C., Berman, S. L., and Jones, T. M (1999). "The Structure of Optimal Trust: Moral and Strategic Implications," *Academy of Management Review*, 24(1): 99–116.

Yoon, Sung-Joon (2002). "The Antecedents and Consequences of Trust in Online Purchase Decisions," *Journal of Interactive Marketing*, 16(2): 47–63.

Young, J. (2008). "Trust in Virtual Organisations: A Synthesis of the Literature," *International Journal of Networking and Virtual Organizations*, 5(3–4): 244–58.

Zhou, M., Dresner, M., and Windle, R. (2009). "Revisiting Feedback Systems: Trust Building in Digital Markets," *Information & Management*, 46(5): 279–84.

Zucker, L.G. (1986). "Production of Trust: Institutional Sources of Economic Structure, 1840–1920," in B. M. Straw and L. L. Cummings (eds). *Research in Organizational Behavior*, pp. 53–111.

CHAPTER 14

GOVERNMENT AND THE INTERNET: EVOLVING TECHNOLOGIES, ENDURING RESEARCH THEMES

PAUL HENMAN

INTRODUCTION AND OVERVIEW

GOVERNMENTS are on the Web—they use the Web and are increasingly defined by the Web. Throughout the world and through all levels of government, from the local to supranational, governments increasingly have a wider and deeper web presence. Since the dotcom era, government use of the Internet has evolved to become an essential space where government information is presented, transactions with government occur, and political and policy debates take place. Consequently, the way in which governments provide services and interact with citizens and businesses has changed remarkably. Technology alone does not fully explain these transformations, which are entangled with discourses on politics, public administration reform, and policy change, to which the Internet both shapes and is shaped by. Governments' web presence and activity is underpinned by the development of an even larger back office electronic infrastructure, including content management systems and administrative databases. The sheer significance of governmental usage of the Internet and other electronic technologies is also reflected in the cost to government, with over 1 percent of GDP being spent on electronic technologies by government (Margetts and Partington 2010: 48).

This chapter provides an overview of research on governmental use of Internet and related digital information and communication technologies (ICTs), a domain known as "e-Government." It begins by surveying key concepts of e-Government. It then charts the prehistory and evolution of Internet government, giving particular attention to the idea of evelopmental stages of online government and associated rankings. Following that, a range of key topics that have invigorated much research on government's use of the Internet and other ICTs are surveyed, and then some of the changes associated with the deployment of e-Government in public administration, service delivery, and public policy are examined. This is followed by a consideration of research on governments' emerging use of Web 2.0 tools and processes. The overview finishes with a consideration of e-Government as an academic discipline, in its own right, and as an arena of Internet Studies.

The chapter raises two clear themes around the dynamic nature of the technologies and issues surrounding e-Government. One is the constant state of change of the technology of government. The other is the enduring nature of the questions and issues in this area, despite technological change. It is in the juxtaposition of these apparently countervailing themes that the field of e-Government is developing as a strong field of Internet Studies.

Concepts

At first blush, the scope of governments' use of the Internet is clear. Yet the technological and conceptual boundaries of the Internet are not clear, as is well reflected in the various definitions of e-Government used within the literature.

The public emergence of the Internet generated a keen academic interest in government usage of electronic ICTs in the late 1990s, despite governments having used digital technologies for several decades previously. Various terms are used to articulate the use of the Internet by government, including, "electronic government," "e-Government," "digital government" and "virtual government." These terms emerged shortly after equivalent terms were applied to commerce, with "electronic government" first being mentioned in 1993 and "e-Government" somewhere between 1997 and 1999 (Heeks and Bailur 2007: n. 1; Henman 2010: 34). Contemporary parlance is usually "e-Government."

There is, however, no consistency in the meaning of these terms (Hu et al. 2010). Reflecting the Internet-inspired origin of this body of work, several authors define e-Government solely in terms of the Internet. Thus, the United Nations defines e-Government as "utilizing the Internet and the world-wide-web for delivering government information and services to citizens" (UN 2002: 1). Yet, governments' usage of the Internet and web tools is often inseparable with other, often older, electronic ICTs, such as administrative databases, and entangled with other contemporary technologies, such as mobile telephones, telephone call centers, smart chip cards and even Radio Frequency Identification technologies. In recognition of this complex web of electronic ICTs, a second group of e-Government definitions encompass a wider range of (digital) technologies. For example, Scholl and Klischewski define e-Government as "the seamless integration of computer-supported government services" (2007), and Silcock explains that "eGovernment is the use of technology to enhance access to and delivery of government services to benefit citizens, business partners and employees" (2001: 88).

Rather than the advent of the Internet defining a disjuncture in the use of electronic technologies by government, their uptake involves an ongoing evolution of technological government with continuities and discontinuities, similarities and dissimilarities. Being aware of the historical co-evolution of information technologies and government enables a historically-informed, critical account of emerging and future electronic government. Accordingly, this overview considers research on government's use of electronic ICTs both before and after the popular emergence of the Internet, though emphasizing the latter.

In addition to diversity in what technologies "e-Government" encompasses, there is also a mixture of descriptive and prescriptive definitions (Scholl 2003b: 1). While some definitions define e-Government in terms of the technologies deployed, many define it in terms of what the technologies are to achieve, namely a particular vision of government. There is an aspirational element in the use of electronic technologies, as is evident in Silcock's definition above.

This variety of e-Government definitions no doubt reflects the different publishers and audiences of e-Government literature, including governments, academics, and the IT industry, as well as the disciplinary variety of academic e-Government research (Heeks and Bailur 2007). Attempts thus far to provide a definitive e-Government definition or framework (e.g. Grant and Chau 2005; Hu et al. 2010) remain unsuccessful, suggesting that changing and varied definitions are a feature of the field.

History and evolution of e-Government

Pre-Internet e-Government from the mid-twentieth century involved the progressive installation of computer processing of government operations (Agar 2003; Cortada 2007; Smith 1985). Well-defined and quantitative-focused procedures involving large government or government critical activities were first to be computerized using mainframes, such as government accounting, taxation, and social security. Domains involving much discretion and human judgment were computerized later. Mainframe computer systems also evolved from overnight processing to online, real-time processing, and then the use of local area networks (LANs) and desk-top computers. These early compartmentalized mainframe systems, called "legacy" systems, made later policy reforms difficult. Accordingly, a key focus of 1980s' and 1990s' government computerization projects was the reordering of such systems to support government policy and service delivery reform, and to rationalize and centralize the details of client data.

Such pre-Internet developments are important in appreciating the development of online, transactional government, as online transactions typically relay data collected through secure online websites to back office mainframe database processing. Thus, the capacities of back office systems largely constitute the capacities of online government. Moreover, the research themes and insights gained from research into earlier government computerization have ongoing relevance to government Internet use.

Stages of e-Government: getting government online

A particular focus of e-Government research has been the evolution of e-Government, its diffusion and use, as well as the drivers and barriers to its development. A key aspect of this literature is the identification of different "stages" of e-Government, reflecting greater sophistication of the use of Internet technologies and capacities (Kaaya 2007). The e-Government stages approach has been used for assessing, comparing and ranking the level of e-Government development in different nations, international regions, and intra-national jurisdictions.

While there is no agreed model of the stages of e-Government, many models are influenced by the four-stage model articulated by the Gartner Group in 2000. Under that model, the first stage is an organization having a web presence used for publishing information like a billboard (i.e. one-way communication). Stage two involves website interaction between the government agency and user (i.e. two-way communication). Gartner's stage three is the capacity of government websites to undertake transactions, such as paying bills, or applying for licenses. Gartner's fourth stage is "transformation," by which the use of government websites involves a transformation in how government business is undertaken. By reconfiguring or extending governmental activities, this fourth stage contrasts with the three previous stages that involve enabling the conduct of previously existing government activities and ways of operating online. An early innovation was online portals to provide a more user-centric government (von Lucke 2007). Other e-Government stage models add new stages or redefine Gartner's. For example, many models append a final stage involving electronic, interactive "participation" or "democracy" (Scott 2001; Siau and Long 2005; West 2004).

The stages of e-Government approach has been very influential and has stimulated a vast academic and practitioner literature that uses the stages to measure and compare e-Government progression and to identify mechanisms that help or hinder such progress. Regular international comparisons have been undertaken by the United Nations since 2001 (e.g. UN 2010), Darrell M. West since 2000 (www.insidepolitics.org), and CapGemini for the European Union since 2001 (EC 2009). West also publishes e-Government assessments for each state of the United States. *The Economist* publishes national e-readiness rankings which reflect not so much e-Government development, but the national environment conducive to e-Government and e-business. Critical accounts of these benchmarking exercises and the validity of their results have been published (Ostermann and Staudinger 2007b).

Overall, the findings of these reports demonstrate a progressive increase in e-Government sophistication (with some exceptions). The UN found that the number of countries without a government website declined from 11 percent (of 190 countries) in 2001 to 2 percent (of 192 countries) in 2010 (UN 2002, 2010). Table 14.1 presents the ten countries with the most sophisticated e-Government development as assessed by the UN in 2010 and by West in 2008, which are largely wealthy countries. It has been observed that a country's wealth by GDP and/or ICT infrastructure is a leading contributor to

Table 14.1 Top 10 countries by e-Government development

Rank	UN E-government Development Index, 2010	West's E-government Country Rankings, 2008
1	Republic of Korea	South Korea
2	United States	Taiwan
3	Canada	United States
4	United Kingdom	Singapore
5	Netherlands	Canada
6	Norway	Australia
7	Denmark	Germany
8	Australia	Ireland
9	Spain	Dominica
10	France	Brazil

Source: UN (2010); West (2008)

e-Government sophistication (CS Transform 2010; West 2005). As the Internet is often associated with a culture of liberalism and political freedom, West (2005) considered whether national e-Government sophistication is related to the level of democratization within a country. He found that this is not so, and that authoritarian governments can progress e-Government through command-control centralization.

The UN's research reflects other benchmarking exercises in finding a historical trend of increased e-Government development with ongoing stark country and regional differences, with North America and Europe with high scores and Oceania and Africa the lowest scores (see Figure 14.1).

Measuring e-Government development typically involves an analysis of a selection of government websites. For example, the UN reports calculate a national e-Government Development or e-Government Readiness Index based on a combination of telecommunication infrastructure, human capital (i.e. education, literacy) and web maturity sub-indices, which are based on a country's national website and several national ministries' websites for their level of e-Government stage development and usability. The UN also reports a national e-Participation Index that assesses a national government's use of online technologies to interact, engage, and consult with its citizens.

E-Government research also involves more qualitative research to understand the complexities of comparisons within and between countries and regions: Europe (Gatautis 2007; Nixon et al. 2010), Asia and the Pacific (Dai 2007; Westcott 2010; Yong 2005) and Africa (Mutula 2008; Schuppan 2009). Within countries, state/provincial and local e-Government has been given particular attention in the USA (Drüke 2005; Scavo 2007; West 2005). E-Government research in developing countries emphasizes the very different economic, technological, and socio-cultural settings in which government operates, including stark differences in adult literacy, poor electricity and telecommunications infrastructures, and more kinship and clan-based engagement with government services.

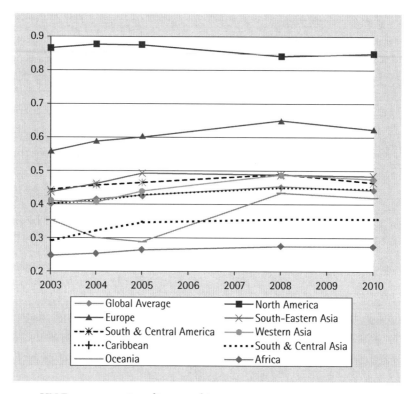

FIGURE 14.1: UN E-government readiness rankings, 2001–10

Source: Author's calculations from UN (2002–10).

E-Government aims and objectives

Just as e-Government has co-evolved with technological innovations, so too have the aims and objectives of e-Government. In the pre-Internet period from the mid-twentieth century to the early 1990s, the primary objective of government's use of digital ICTs was to increase the efficiency of government operations, thereby enabling cost reductions and/or enhanced customer service (Adler and Henman 2005). Computerization of bureaucratic processes was also commonly viewed as a way in which to enhance the responsiveness and flexibility of government bureaucracies to enable more frequent and more radical policy change. Automation was also aimed at improving the accuracy and consistency of administrative decision-making. Enhancing compliance of citizens as tax payers, welfare recipients, and so on, and reducing the scope of fraud and corruption have also been long-standing and ongoing objectives of e-Government. It would be wrong, however, to assume that computerization has been used by governments uniformly. Ingelstam and Palmlund (1991), for instance, found that while some countries used computerization to control employees through automating bureaucratic decision-making, other countries tended to computerize information flows to better support human bureaucrats.

E-Government in the 1990s and the early years of the twenty-first century has emphasized the importance of government getting onto the Internet and making use of digital networks for the electronic transfer of data. Once again efficiency objectives were important, but so too were the use of electronic ICTs to break down traditional government silos in order to provide "whole of government," customer-centric or personalized service delivery. The Internet was viewed as critical in enhancing service by making government available 24/7, and not limited to the opening hours of government buildings (Gil-Garcia and Helbig 2007). To enhance service, this period saw the rapid growth of telephone service centers (Ambriola et al. 2007) and one-stop-shops (Hagen and Kubicek 2000), and an emphasis on shared or collaborative service delivery.

Following the advent and proliferation of social media or Web 2.0 technologies in the first decade of the twenty-first century, the implications for such technologies for government were explored. The long-dominance of efficiency was notably replaced by an emphasis on government transparency and openness through the free disclosure of government data (Henman 2013; Zinnbauer 2007). A secondary objective of "Government 2.0" is the co-production of government services and practices (Leadbeater and Cottam 2010; Morison 2010). In some places, electronic processes are also linked to reducing public sector corruption (Ostermann and Staudinger 2007a).

E-Government objectives are not defined by the technology, though the technological capabilities shape what is possible. Wider discourses concerning public administration reform, political agendas, and citizen and business demands, as well as the interests of IT companies, all form part of the discourse to direct the government use of electronic ICTs. Much e-Government rhetoric of the 1990s and early years of the twenty-first century reflected reform objectives of New Public Management (Dunleavy et al. 2006; Henman 2010: ch 7). Citizens' experiences of electronic service delivery in businesses is also said to shape expectations that governments do the same. This idea of business (and citizen) led e-Government contrasts with the period from the 1950s to the 1980s when governments led businesses in the use of electronic ICTs (Cortada 2007).

E-GOVERNMENT RESEARCH FOCI

Research on government use of electronic ICTs has focused on a wide range of domains and issues that have resulted from the process of developing and deploying e-Government, both before and since the popular use of the Internet. Given that the technology under examination is a constantly evolving and proliferating substance, it is difficult to summarize the issues comprehensively. Having said that, many older issues and debates remain cogent today—albeit partly reconfigured by newer technologies and socio-political contexts—and are continually being revisited. Having a wide technological and historical perspective of specific research foci enables a critical perspective on recent and emerging directions and claims.

Organizational structure and the nature of power

One very early and enduring research topic has been the relationship between ICTs and changing organizational structure, the nature of organizational (and societal) power, and the experience of employees. While most early work focused on private sector organizations, studies within the public sector demonstrated similar observations.

Pre-Internet e-Government was first defined by central mainframes (from 1960s to 1980s), and still remain central to contemporary e-Government. Initially, computerization was largely focused on automating organizational processes to generate efficiencies and financial benefits. Flowing from this process were concerns about changing organizational structure and the centralization of organizational control and power—either towards central management or to the technical staff designing the information systems, with a consequent shift in the locus of decision making. Bovens and Zouridis (2002), for example, argue that by automating ever larger domains of public administration, human "street-level bureaucracies," in which frontline public servants make administrative decisions within the legislative framework and with the support of ICT, have evolved to "screen-level bureaucracies," in which ICT leads the activity of government officials whose administrative discretion is reduced as it becomes codified, and then to "system-level bureaucracies", in which frontline government officials become superseded by an integrated and all-encompassing, automated IT system. Evidence tends to broadly support this account, though not universally (Caputo 1988; Kraemer and Danziger 1990; Kraemer and King 1986; Laudon 1974). Related research foci included the changing nature of the work environment and the automation of jobs, with consequent deskilling or dismissal of staff, and industrial resistance to technological innovation. Research demonstrates that automation has indeed reduced administrative discretion and deskilled government administrators (Braverman 1974; Garson 1989; Karger 1986). However, massive job losses did not occur in the public sector, but the nature of jobs changed as automation enabled new forms of work. Researchers also discovered the significance of employee resistance to technological change. While this body of research is now quite old, it is far from dated. As automation through computers continues to expand into new and wider places, the concerns and insights remain enduring themes and questions that continue to be posed and re-posed.

From the 1980s, the development of online systems, Local Area Networks (LANs), data exchange networks operating across the boundaries of government agencies, and the Internet, generated a similar research foci on organizational structure, control, and power, albeit a belief in the distribution of power away from the center and diffused throughout society (Castells 1996; van Dijk 2006). While the Internet and other networked ICTs have helped to generate new and flatter organizational forms with dispersed power, it is also important to recognize that this is not the full story. States, hierarchical bureaucracies, and multinational companies retain their power, constitutional or otherwise (Dean 2007). Moreover, the expectation that free-flowing data through cross-institutional data networks would break down the traditional segmented nature of government into distinct, separate departments and agencies is very much a work in progress (Becker et al. 2009).

Privacy, surveillance, and data protection

Privacy, surveillance, and data protection is a second very early and enduring research theme on ICTs in government (see also Bennett and Parsons Chapter 23). The image of a central database on a massive mainframe computer generated ethical and policy questions about the growth of a "big brother," surveillance state (Davies 1992; Lyon 1994; Westin and Baker 1972). The development of networked computing and the Internet since the 1990s has only proliferated personal data collection and its circulation, and amplified the policy and ethical examination of these issues (Andrejevic 2009; Lyon 2007, 2009). Such research has had an impact. It has clarified the issues of concern and led governments worldwide to develop data protection and privacy policies, management procedures, and technical processes for both public and private sector organizations (Joshi et al. 2007; Raab 2009). Privacy, surveillance, and data protection remains a key research, political and policy concern.

Conceptual approaches to studying privacy and surveillance have advanced over the decades. The shadow of an authoritarian state, such as George Orwell's fictitious *1984*, has remained an enduring motif, reinforced by Michel Foucault's celebrated analysis of disciplinary Panoptic power (1977). These perspectives have been reinforced by the growth of data networks and Closed Circuit Television (Norris and Armstrong 1999). Individual privacy has been the central concept to counter apparent ubiquitous state power. Yet, the focus on privacy and "dataveillance" has been critiqued as too focused on individuals and not sufficiently sociological (Gilliom 2001). Data protection and access to services are two sides of the one coin (Davis 2005). In order to use and enhance electronic service delivery, the collection and circulation of personal data is essential, especially in creating citizen-centric services through inter-agency collaboration (Bellamy et al. 2005). In short, we participate in our own surveillance through readily sharing data. Other authors have demonstrated that we are not all equal in our data relationship with the state. E-Government is increasingly being used to differentially surveil the populace through data profiling and customer-relationship management (Elmer 2004; Henman and Marston 2008).

Efficiency

Despite universal claims of efficiency and effectiveness of computerization, and the long-standing e-Government objective of the same, e-Government projects have been plagued with cost over-runs and failures, both pre- and post-Internet (Margetts and Willcocks 1993; Organ 2003). Not only have IT projects often cost more than anticipated, but the realization of efficiency savings has been questioned.[1] Much has been written about the development of computer systems being poorly designed vis-à-vis formal and informal organizational processes. Jenner (2009) argues that much government IT business plans fraudulently overstate the benefits of IT projects, and benefits are rarely measured post-implementation. Bertot and Jaeger (2008) have warned that better services through electronic technologies do not necessarily cost less. Indeed, costs are more likely to increase when service delivery involves inter-agency collaboration. Instead of computerization simply speeding up previously non-automated organizational processes, computerization has led to the expansion of what governments do (Henman 1996). Organizational activities are not simply reproduced electronically, but the organization is reconstituted.

Enablers and barriers

A particularly strong theme of e-Government research is understanding the enablers and barriers to e-Government. This first involves consideration of building and developing government websites, the supply side of e-Government, and second of people and businesses using e-Government, the demand side of e-Government. There are many different approaches to categorizing enablers and barriers. To illustrate, a European Commission study characterized eight different barrier domains: legislative or constitutional barriers; leadership failures; financial inhibitors; digital divides and choice; poor coordination; workplace and organizational inflexibility; lack of trust; and poor technical design (EC 2007). Similar themes are found in West (2005: ch 4) where he identifies "legislative professionalism" (by which he means technically competent policy-makers) and fiscal capacity (or adequate resources) as important predictors of e-Government success.

Margetts and Dunleavy (2002) delineate several cultural barriers to successful e-Government development: organizational cultures, particularly negative attitudes towards technology; organizational values that constrain technological innovation, including formality, uniformity, and hierarchy; lack of organizational demand; and channel rivalry. These realities and aversion to public sector openness and public visibility are also viewed as cultural barriers to government use of Web 2.0 technologies (Gruen 2009).

Such e-Government research has led to countries using a range of mechanisms to advance e-Government (Dunleavy et al. 2006). These include targets for getting government agencies and services online; reforms of governance structures to support e-Government; the creation of e-Government champions or leadership positions, such as the now ubiquitous Chief Information Officer; and the location of such personnel towards the centre of government.

---

[1] With regard to computerization and efficiency more generally, renowned economist Robert Solow stated in 1987, "You can see the computer age everywhere but in the productivity statistics" (see Triplett 1999).

E-Government usage and the digital divide

Building government websites and offering electronic services is only one half of the equation. For e-Government to be successful, it needs to be used by citizens. A range of aspects enable or constrain end-user take-up of e-Government. Critically, citizens must have access to the Internet and the ability to use it. A key policy and research concern is unequal IT access and skills, or a "digital divide," as well as "e-inclusion" (see Hargittai, Chapter 7).

Capacity to use e-Government services and usage are two separate concerns. Internet users are not necessarily big users of online government. Figure 14.2 charts the increasing online availability of twenty basic public services in fifteen EU countries against the somewhat stable percentage of all individuals aged 16 to 74 who use the Internet for interaction with public authorities in those countries. Looking only at Internet users, the Oxford Internet Survey 2009 found that just over half of users (59 percent) had used online government services in the previous year (Dutton et al. 2009: 26; see also Gauld et al. 2010).

Various dimensions have been examined in understanding and responding to citizen non-usage of and concerns about e-Government, which largely reflect public concerns about the Internet and ICT in general. Trust in the government and the Internet is a key component of usage (Rowe 2007; Connolly Chapter 13). Trust is also very much connected to concerns about data protection, security, and privacy and surveillance, and disruption of security by viruses and hackers.

Another area of e-Government research concerns the usability and effectiveness of online government. Like wider web design research, much early research focused on the

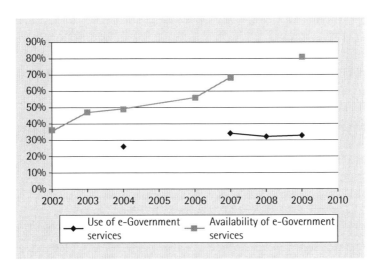

FIGURE. 14.2: Percentage of availability of government services online and percentage of users of online government services, EU(15), 2002–09

Source: Author's calculations from Eurostat tsiir130 and tsiir120

usability of government websites including layout, navigability and accessibility for people with disabilities, and low bandwidth speeds (Wu et al. 2009). Research attention quickly moved to the capacity of citizens and businesses to find the government information without a need to understand government organizational structure. Whole of government portals have been used to assist in this. It remains an unanswered question as to whether such portals offer better outcomes for users searching for online government information and services compared to generic websearch sites (Margetts and Partington 2010).

E-Government and changes
in government

E-Government research also examines the nature of change in government activities associated with the deployment of advanced electronic ICTs. Perri 6 (2004) delineates four different domains of e-Government—e-democracy, e-management (or public administration), e-service provision and e-governance (or policy-making)—which are used to structure the following section. As e-democracy is included in this collection under "Democracy and the Internet" by Helen Margetts (see Chapter 20), it is not further discussed.

Before proceeding, it is first important to observe conceptions of technology and change in the e-Government literature. There is no dominant conceptualization of the inter-relationship between technological change on the one hand, and social, political, organizational, and government change on the other hand. Early studies of computerization in government involving detailed and extended case studies yielded highly sophisticated, nuanced and multiple leveled understandings of this relationship. For example, Kraemer and King (1986: 464) observe that "computing fits within existing organizational life and exerts subtle influences" (see also Danziger et al. 1982).

Research since the mid-1990s tends to conceptualize the social-technological relationship implicitly. There is a wide range of views between technological deterministic accounts, in which technology drives change, to socially deterministic accounts, in which social actors are drivers. Heeks and Bailur's (2007) find that while most e-Government research recognizes both technology and social shaping factors, there is a sizeable minority with a crude technological deterministic perspective. They also find that a sizeable majority of e-Government research takes a "naive optimism" in approaching the impact of e-Government, with no surveyed research taking a solely pessimistic approach to the impact of e-Government. In addition, a substantial body of e-Government research contains a normative perspective on the use of ICTs in government. Instead of reporting research findings, such research advocates particular government innovations and e-Government visions (Henman 2010: ch 3; Scholl 2003a).

E-public administration

Digital technologies are used extensively in administering government activities and resources under the terms of government policy. E-public administration makes extensive use of database technologies and inter-organizational data networks, but also involves program management tools, financial and budgeting systems, email communication, performance and human resource management packages, and identity management systems. It includes digital technologies for compliance and fraud detection, such as data-matching, and e-procurement, and the use of the Internet for the announcing, submission of, and awarding of government tenders.

E-Government has variously affected public administration. Early effects of the Internet were found to include significant increases in client service, ways of contacting government, availability of government information, the capacity to receive and check customer data, the ability to update policy, and the speed of administrative decision-making, while decreases were observed in the level of contact between customer and government personnel (Adler and Henman 2005).

Digital technology contributes to public sector reform. Since the late 1980s, the New Public Management has been a dominant reform agenda globally. It involves the adoption of corporate management approaches to government. Research has examined the extent to which e-Government has enabled the fruition of these public sector reforms as well as the political, organizational, and technical factors that have impeded success (Bernardi 2009). Electronic information infrastructure has been important in establishing performance-measurement regimes, and electronic data networks have been critical in supporting purchaser-provider and outsourcing contractual arrangements. E-procurement is viewed as a critical technology to bring about a pan-European market for government consultancies and tenders (EC 2009).

Government IT services are subject to similar public sector reform agendas. In the 1990s and early twenty-first century, internal government IT services were often outsourced, often to oligopolies of very large international IT corporations. Dunleavy et al (2006) found that this undermined government IT and policy capacity, as well as increased overall costs. As a result, they argued that government IT practices are necessarily becoming more centralized, strategic, and internal, a setting they denote as "Digital Era Governance."

There is also a considerable body of research examining the contribution of digital and Internet technologies to the openness and accountability of government administration and government consultation processes (see also Margetts Chapter 20). While consultation and accountability have been long-standing themes in public sector innovation, the Internet and especially Web 2.0 technologies generated an increased focus on this topic. Much research focuses on the technological and informational mechanisms by which government data can be made more readily available and accessible (Chapman and Hunt 2006), while others assess the achievement of open and transparent government through digital technologies (Frick 2008; Meijer 2003).

Typically, it is automatically assumed that greater provision of data is good for government performance and trust in government. However, some studies demonstrate that high levels of transparency can be counterproductive (Grimmelikhuijsen 2010; Meijer 2007a). Other research topics concerning accountable and open government concern the use of open source software and the capacity of e-Government to reduce public sector fraud and corruption (Garcia-Murillo 2010; Pathak et al. 2009).

E-services

E-services encompass the full gamut of electronic delivery of government services. Melville (2007) notes that "e-service delivery...seldom involves the *physical delivery of services*," with a greater emphasis on information and advice, coordination and cash (Pirog and Johnson 2008). Some exceptions include telemedicine (Jennett et al. 2007), online counseling, and e-learning (see Davies and Eynon Chapter 16), though this is a rapidly evolving area.

E-Government has enabled developments in the public service delivery, and is now indispensable. One key development has been extending face-to-face and telephone access during normal business hours to 24/7 through the Internet. Online transactional services have been slower to develop for both technical and political reasons (Torres et al. 2005). A 2009 study demonstrated that online transactions involving generating government income were the most sophisticated, whereas online transactions for permits and licenses was the least developed area of e-services (EC 2009). Online registrations and citizens providing required data were moderately advanced.

A long-standing aim of e-Government is the creation of citizen-centric, holistic government that breaks down the traditional "silos of government," often through cross-agency collaboration and shared services and one stop shops (Dawes 1996; Dawes and Cook 2007). Research focuses on facilitators and inhibitors to joint working, such as data interoperability frameworks (dos Santos 2008), governance and management arrangements (Klievink and Janssen 2009), organizational dynamics, data protection and privacy protocols (Bellamy et al. 2005; Combe 2009). While the holistic delivery of services has often proved difficult, holistic information services have been more effective through whole of government or themed web portals (Daniel and Ward 2006; Leben et al. 2006).

E-Government is realizing the vision of citizen-centric services in another fashion. Instead of an agency delivering a uniform service, digital technologies are being used to personalize and target services to respond to the differential realities of citizens. Digital technologies assist in: identifying different service user groups or user profiles through data mining and analysis (Markellou 2007), which are then used to develop differentiated services; categorizing or profiling service users at the point of contact; and managing the more complex array of services. For example, employment services have become targeted to provide greater assistance to those at greater risk of long-term unemployment (McDonald et al. 2003). Research has examined the barriers to delivering targeted, personalized services using ICTs (Pieterson et al. 2007), the associated changed citizen–state relationship (Caswell et al. 2010), and corresponding policy and ethical tensions (Henman 2005).

The electronic delivery of services is fundamentally about citizens' relationship with government agencies (Lips 2010). As already noted, an enduring theme of e-Government research has been surveillance and control of citizens (see also Henman and Adler 2003). Conversely, there is also research about the extent to which digital technologies enhance greater citizen involvement in defining and reforming service delivery as well as in policy processes. Citizen interaction in processes of e-consultation (Stephens et al. 2006; Walsh 2007) and the co-production of services became a particularly strong research theme with the popularization of the Internet, and especially Web 2.0 technologies. Some e-Government research focuses on the "how to" of e-consultation, while other research finds open consultation ideals are often not met, or remain skeptical about their achievement (Medaglia 2007; Morison 2010). Successful use of Web 2.0 technologies in e-participation in service delivery is evident in the use of citizen feedback on local government services, whereby citizens report service problems through mobile GPS telephone images and online reports so that local government service teams can respond in real time (Miori and Russo 2009; Nasi 2009). Co-creation of services is also seen through government facilitation of consumer self-help groups (Allsop et al. 2004).

E-policy

The contribution of e-Government to policy processes or e-governance—namely, "the digital support for policy formulation and the scrutiny and oversight of the achievement of policy goals" (6 2004: 16)—has received far less research attention. As Margetts (2009) notes, the relationship between public policy and the Internet is not widely considered, though several strands of this relationship can be outlined.

One aspect is the development of policy responses to address problems arising from the Internet. These include policies to advance Internet access and use to bridge the digital divide, and policies to counter Internet-based crime and risks, including tax avoidance, cyber-bullying, online pedophilia, cyberchondria, and cyber terrorism (Haugen 2005). A second aspect is the use of the Internet and other digital technologies to administer public policies through databases, e-service delivery, and the like. A third area is the use of electronic technologies to support the policy process. This includes online public consultations (see also Margetts Chapter 20) to obtain the views of and feedback from stakeholders, the construction of computer policy modeling tools, wikis, and databanks of policy resources, and the operation of policy networks (McNutt 2007). In this regard, the Internet has been widely used in the process of rule-making in the US (Coglianese 2007; Shafie 2008). Fourth, the operation of e-Government can generate new forms of public policy, where it has been observed that e-Government has enabled the growth of greater targeting and personalization of public policy, an increase in the conditionality of public policy and greater policy complexity (Henman 2010). Indeed, digital technology has led to new ways of thinking about public policy and managing social problems. For example, Geographical Information Systems have stimulated and enhanced a spatial conceptualization of public policy (6 2004: 86–99), while Parton argues that the computerization of policy processes redefines policy intelligence from qualitatively rich social knowledge, to quantitative, "clean" data (Parton 2008).

Emerging e-Government: towards Gov 2.0?

With the advent and proliferation of Web 2.0 and social media technologies during the latter half of the first decade of the twenty-first century, governments began to consider and experiment with what these technologies might mean for their operations. Much early focus was on use of Web 2.0 for political activity and democratic participation (Carlson and Strandberg 2008; see also Margetts Chapter 20), rather than the conduct of government operations. Public sector data sets were progressively made freely available online for analysis, reuse, and mash-ups. Online ratings of citizen experiences of government schools and health services became possible. Blogs are being used by politicians and occasionally civil servants. Datamining of Web 2.0 data is used for policy and political purposes (Seifert 2007). This is a rapidly evolving work in progress, with government enquiries and reports being instituted to map new directions.

Serious academic scholarship is really yet to analyze Gov 2.0, with many publications enthusiastically articulating how government can be transformed by such technology (Eggers 2005; Lathrop and Ruma 2010; Noveck 2009). Such writings are infused with broader Web 2.0 values of openness and transparency, the idea of the "wisdom of crowds," and open-ended evolution ("perpetual beta"), with close associations with democratic movements. More measured research on Gov 2.0 has examined the ways in which governments can strategically incorporate Web 2.0 into their operations (Chang and Kannan 2008; Meijer and Thaens 2010; Osimo 2008), how data can be managed in an open data environment (Aichholzer and Strauß 2010; Warner and Chun 2009), and questioned the actuality of open consultation (Morison 2010).

In the early discussions about the future use of Web 2.0 technologies by government there is a view that such technologies will enable greater citizenship involvement in the formation of policy. This is seen to occur through electronic consultations with citizens on policy ideas and options, through feedback on services that critically gauge what is working and what is not, through greater openness and transparency of government performance as a driver for government innovation, and access to and analysis of public sector data through data mash-ups and the like to provide new and enhanced knowledge about policy problems and solutions (Henman 2013).

Alongside these Web 2.0 innovations are nascent developments in the government use of mobile computing (or "m-government"), such as Internet telephone applications, and in cloud computing, termed "Gcloud."

E-GOVERNMENT AS AN
ACADEMIC DISCIPLINE

Just as the birth of the Internet has given birth to a new multidisciplinary academic domain of Internet Studies, so too has e-Government co-evolved with a new multi-disciplinary e-Government discipline. To the long-standing journal of the European Association of Public Administration's study group on ICTs, initially established in 1991 and called *Informatization and the Public Sector* (now called *Information Polity*), many new journals were established in the first decade of the twenty-first century. Annual academic e-Government conferences are now held in Europe, North America, and internationally. There is also an academic Digital Government Society of North America.

Yet, the academic study of e-Government does not yet have a cohesive disciplinary identity. Quite disparate foci and perspectives exist, largely informed from the various disciplinary backgrounds of its academic participants. Key disciplines engaged in e-Government research are business/management, public administration, political science, computer science, and library and information studies (Heeks and Bailur 2007). Yet, at the same time, these disciplinary "homes" continue to treat e-Government as marginal concerns (Meijer 2007b). Apart from the stages of e-Government model, theoretic approaches to studying e-Government, when there is a conceptual approach, are drawn from other disciplines. This lack of conceptual and theoretical coherence is also reflected in the fact that there is no agreed conception of e-Government (Hu et al. 2010).

Heeks and Bailur (2007) observe that there is an overall paucity of critical analysis in e-Government research. Many e-Government publications are edited collections of poorly linked disparate papers, while most non-edited books are technical or practical "how-to's" of e-Government. The concerns about privacy and surveillance offer perhaps the most consistent critical perspective. There are also insightful, critical analyses using institutional theory (Fountain 2001), social studies of technology (Homburg 2008), information theory (Mayer-Schönberger and Lazer 2007), and post-Foucauldian governmentality (Henman 2010). There is certainly greater scope for research to examine the political economy of e-Government, including the ways e-Government discourses, agendas, and practices come to be defined by multinational IT companies, state power, broader business interests, and political movements (Dunleavy et al. 2006; Hood and Margetts 2007).

Methodologies for e-Government research are also quite varied. What is possible has evolved with the research tools enabled by the Internet. The case study is a long-standing and widespread method for studying e-Government. Often it may be a case study of the implementation and/or use of a new IT project in government, involving either "insider" ethnographic-style research, or "outsider" research using publicly available documents and data. Multiple case studies are used to allow comparisons and conclusions to be drawn. Surveys of e-Government personnel or citizens are also widely used. With the development of government websites, e-Government research rapidly conducted analyses of government websites using checklists. Webcrawling tools have also been used to investigate the nature of government websites and the networks in which they are positioned (Dunleavy et al. 2007; Petricek et al. 2006). Research methodologies will undoubtedly continue to evolve with technological innovations.

E-Government is a growing multidisciplinary field of study with a distinct history to the broader church of Internet Studies. However, there are clear connections, overlaps, and similarities. The advent and popularization of the Internet stimulated a wider interest in digital technologies in government and has created a new academic field of study. Just as with Internet Studies more broadly, new and emerging digital technologies will continue to initiate old questions in new circumstances of what these technologies mean for government and society. Yet there remain ongoing themes for critical investigation and debate. Being aware of these themes and earlier insights helps to keep our perspective and prevent us from getting carried away with all that is new.

References

6, P. (2004). *E-governance*, Basingstoke: Palgrave.

Adler, M. and Henman, P. (2005). *Computerisation and E-Government in Social Security*, Washington, DC: IBM Center for the Business of Government.

Agar, J. (2003). *The Government Machine*, Cambridge MA: MIT Press.

Aichholzer, G. and Strauß, S. (2010). "Electronic Identity Management in e-Government 2.0: Exploring a System Innovation Exemplified by Austria," *Information Polity*, 15(1–2): 139–52.

Allsop, J., Jones, K., and Baggott, R. (2004). "Health Consumer Groups in the UK: A New Social Movement?," *Sociology of Health and Illness*, 26(6): 737–56.

Ambriola, V., Bertagnini, S., and Pratesi, L. (2007). "Call Centre Evolution in the Digital Government," in A.-V. Anttiroiko and M. Mälkiä (eds). *Encyclopedia of Digital Government*, Hershey, PA: Idea Group Reference, pp. 158–62.

Andrejevic, M. (2009). *iSpy*, Lawrence: University Press of Kansas.

Becker, J., Niehaves, B., and Krause, A. (2009). "Shared Services Strategies and Their Determinants: A Multiple Case Study Analysis in the Public Sector." *AMCIS 2009 Proceedings*, Paper 14. Available at <http://aisel.aisnet.org/amcis2009/14/>. Accessed June 20, 2012.

Bellamy, C., 6, P., and Raab, C. D. (2005). "Joined-Up Government and Privacy in the United Kingdom: Managing Tensions between Data Protection and Social Policy: Part II," *Public Administration*, 83(2): 393–415.

Bernardi, R. (2009). "IT Enactment of New Public Management in Africa: The Case Study of Health Information Systems in Kenya," *Electronic Journal of e-Government*, 7(4): 311–26.

Bertot, J. C. and Jaeger, P. T. (2008). "The E-Government Paradox: Better Customer Service Doesn't Necessarily Cost Less," *Government Information Quarterly*, 25: 149–54.

Bovens, M. and Zouridis, S. (2002). "From Street-Level to System-Level Bureaucracies: How Information and Communication Technology is Transforming Administrative Discretion and Constitutional Control," *Public Administration Review*, 62(2): 174–84.

Braverman, H. (1974). *Labor and Monopoly Capital*, New York: Monthly Review Press.

Caputo, R. K. (1988). *Management and Information Systems in Human Services*, New York: Haworth Press.

Carlson, T. and Strandberg, K. (2008). "Riding the Web 2.0 Wave: Candidates on YouTube in the 2007 Finnish National Elections," *Journal of Information Technology and Politics*, 5(2): 159–74.

Castells, M. (1996). *The Rise of the Network Society*, Oxford: Blackwell.

Caswell, D., Marston, G., and Larsen, J. E. (2010). "Unemployed Citizen or 'At Risk' Client? Classification Systems and Employment Services in Denmark and Australia," *Critical Social Policy*, 30(3): 384–404.

Chang, A.-M. and Kannan, P. K. (2008). "Leveraging Web 2.0 in Government," IBM Center for The Business of Government. Available at <http://www.businessofgovernment.org/report/leveraging-web-20-government>. Accessed June 20, 2012.

Chapman, R. A. and Hunt, M. (2006). *Open Government in a Theoretical and Practical Context*, Aldershot/Burlington, VT: Ashgate.

Coglianese, C. (2007). "E-Rulemaking," in A.-V. Anttiroiko and M. Mälkiä (eds). *Encyclopedia of Digital Government*, Hershey, PA: Idea Group Reference, pp. 713–17.

Combe, C. (2009). "Observations on the UK Transformational Government Strategy Relative to Citizen Data Sharing and Privacy," *Transforming Government*, 3(4): 394–405.

Cortada, J. W. (2007). *The Digital Hand: How Computers Changed the Work of American Public Sector Industries*, vol. 3, New York: Oxford.

CS Transform. (2010). *e-Government Success*, London: CS Transform.

Dai, X. (2007). "e-ASEAN and Regional Integration in South East Asia," in A.-V. Anttiroiko and M. Mälkiä (eds). *Encyclopedia of Digital Government*. Hershey, PA: Idea Group Reference, pp. 416–21.

Daniel, E., and Ward, J. (2006). "Integrated Service Delivery: Exploratory Case Studies of Enterprise Portal Adoption in UK Local Government," *Business Process Management Journal*, 12(1): 113–23.

Danziger, J. N., Dutton, W. H., Kling, R., and Kraemer, K. L. (1982). *Computers and Politics*, New York: Columbia University Press.

Davies, S. (1992). *Big Brother*, Sydney: Simon and Schuster.

Davis, C. N. (2005). "Reconciling Privacy and Access Interests in E-Government," *International Journal of Public Administration*, 28(7–8): 567–80.

Dawes, S. S. (1996). "Interagency Information Sharing: Expected Benefits, Manageable Risks," *Journal of Policy Analysis and Management*, 15(2): 377–94.

—— and Cook, M. E. (2007). "Intergovernmental Digital Government through G2G Relationships and Applications," in A.-V. Anttiroiko and M. Mälkiä (eds) *Encyclopedia of Digital Government*, Hershey, PA: Idea Group Reference, pp. 1114–19.

Dean, M. (2007). *Governing Societies*, Maidenhead: Open University Press.

dos Santos, E. M. (2008). "Implementing Interoperability Standards for Electronic Government: An Exploratory Case Study of the E-PING Brazilian Framework," *International Journal of Electronic Government Research*, 4(3): 103–12.

Drüke, H. (2005). *Local Electronic Government*, London/New York: Routledge.

Dunleavy, P., Margetts, H., Bartholomeou, P., Bastow, S., Escher, T., Pearce, O. et al. (2007). *Government on the Internet*, London: National Audit Office Report by the Comptroller and Auditor General, HC 529 Session 2006–07.

Dunleavy, P., Margetts, H., Bastow, S., and Tinkler, J. (2006). *Digital Era Governance*, Oxford: Oxford University Press.

Dutton, W. H., Helsper, E. J., and Gerber, M. M. (2009). "The Internet in Britain 2009," Oxford Internet Institute, University of Oxford. Available at <http://www.oii.ox.ac.uk/research/oxis/OxIS2009_Report.pdf>. Accessed June 20, 2012.

EC (2007). *Breaking Barriers to eGovernment—A Legal and Institutional Analysis of Barriers to eGovernment*, Brussels: eGovernment Unit, EC. Available at <http://www.egovbarriers.org/?view=project_outputs>. Accessed June 20, 2012.

——(2009). *Smarter, Faster, Better eGovernment: 8th Benchmark Measurement*, Brussels: European Commission, Directorate for Information Society and Media.

Eggers, W. D. (2005). *Government 2.0*, Lanham, MD: Rowman and Littlefield.

Elmer, G. (2004). *Profiling Machines*, Cambridge, MA: MIT Press.

Foucault, M. (1977). *Discipline and Punish*, New York: Pantheon.

Fountain, J. E. (2001). *Building the Virtual State*, Washington, DC: Brookings Institution Press.

Frick, M. (2008). "Translucent States: Political Mediation of E-Transparency," *International Journal of Electronic Government Research*, 4(3): 81–102.

Garcia-Murillo, M. (2010). "The Effect of Internet Access on Government Corruption," *Electronic Government, an International Journal*, 7(1): 22–40.

Garson, B. (1989). *The Electronic Sweatshop*, Harmondsworth: Penguin.

Gatautis, R. (2007). "E-Government in Transition Economies," in A.-V. Anttiroiko and M. Mälkiä (eds). *Encyclopedia of Digital Government*, Hershey, PA: Idea Group Reference, pp. 554–9.

Gauld, R., Goldfinch, S., and Horsburgh, S. (2010). "Do They Want It? Do They Use It? The 'Demand-Side' of e-Government in Australia and New Zealand," *Government Information Quarterly*, 27: 177–86.

Gil-Garcia, J. R., and Helbig, N. (2007). "Exploring E-Government Benefits and Success Factors," in A.-V. Anttiroiko and M. Mälkiä (eds). *Encyclopedia of Digital Government*, Hershey, PA: Idea Group Reference, pp. 803–11.

Gilliom, J. (2001). *Overseers of the Poor*, Chicago: University of Chicago Press.

Grant, G. and Chau, D. (2005). "Developing a Generic Framework for E-Government," *Journal of Global Information Management*, 13(1): 1–30.

Grimmelikhuijsen, S. (2010). "Transparency of Public Decision-Making: Towards Trust in Local Government?" *Policy and Internet*, 2(1), Article 2. Available at <http://www.psocommons.org/policyandinternet/vol2/iss1/art2>. Accessed May 18, 2012.

Gruen, N. (2009). *Engage: Report of the Government 2.0 Taskforce*, Canberra: Department of Finance and Deregulation.

Hagen, M. and Kubicek, H. (eds). (2000). *One-Stop-Government in Europe*, Bremen: University of Bremen.

Haugen, S. (2005). "E-government, Cyber-Crime and Cyber-Terrorism: A Population at Risk," *Electronic Government*, 2(4): 403–12.

Heeks, R. and Bailur, S. (2007). "Analyzing e-Government Research: Perspectives, Philosophies, Theories, Methods, and Practice," *Government Information Quarterly*, 24(2): 243–65.

Henman, P. (1996). "Does Computerisation Save Governments Money?," *Information Infrastructure and Policy*, 5(4): 235–51.

—— (2005). "E-Government, Targeting and Data Profiling: Policy and Ethical Issues of Differential Treatment," *Journal of E-Government*, 2(1): 79–98.

—— (2010). *Governing Electronically*, Basingstoke: Palgrave.

—— (2013). "Governmentalities of Gov 2.0," *Information, Communication & Society*, 16(9): 1397–1418.

—— and Adler, M. (2003). "Information Technology and the Governance of Social Security," *Critical Social Policy*, 23(2): 139–64.

Henman, P. and Marston, G. (2008). "The Social Division of Welfare Surveillance," *Journal of Social Policy*, 37(2): 187–205.

Homburg, V. (2008). *Understanding E-Government*, Abingdon and New York: Routledge.

Hood, C. and Margetts, H. (2007). *The Tools of Government in the Digital Age*, Basingstoke: Palgrave.

Hu, G., Pan, W., and Wang, J. (2010). "The Distinctive Lexicon and Consensual Conception of e-Government: An Exploratory Perspective," *International Review of Administrative Sciences*, 76(3): 577–97.

Ingelstam, L. and Palmlund, I. (1991). "Computers and People in the Welfare State: Information Technology and Social Security in Sweden," *Informatization and the Public Sector*, 1(2): 5–20.

Jenner, S. (2009). *Realising Benefits from Government ICT Investment—a Fool's Errand?*, Reading: Academic Publishing.

Jennett, P. A., Smith, E. R., Watanabe, M., and Sharlene, S. (2007). "Adopting and Implementing Telehealth in Canada," in A.-V. Anttiroiko and M. Mälkiä (eds). *Encyclopedia of Digital Government*, Hershey, PA: Idea Group Reference, pp. 26–33.

Joshi, J. B. D., Joshi, S. R., and Chandran, S. M. (2007). "Identity Management and Citizen Privacy," in A.-V. Anttiroiko and M. Mälkiä (eds). *Encyclopedia of Digital Government*. Hershey, PA: Idea Group Reference, pp. 1019–25.

Kaaya, J. (2007). "Development Stages of Digital Government," in A.-V. Anttiroiko and M. Mälkiä (eds). *Encyclopedia of Digital Government*, Hershey, PA: Idea Group Reference, pp. 301–9.

Karger, H. J. (1986). "The De-Skilling of Social Workers: An Examination of the Industrial Model of Production on the Delivery of Social Services," *Journal of Sociology and Social Welfare*, 13(1): 115–29.

Klievink, B. and Janssen, M. (2009). "Realizing Joined-Up Government—Dynamic Capabilities and Stage Models for Transformation," *Government Information Quarterly*, 26(2): 275–84.

Kraemer, K. L. and Danziger, J. N. (1990). "The Impacts of Computer Technology on the Worklife of Information Workers," *Social Science Computer Review*, 8(4): 592–613.

Kraemer, K. L. and King, J. L. (1986). "Computing and Public Organizations," *Public Admnistration Review*, 46: 488–96.

Lathrop, D. and Ruma, L. (eds) (2010). *Open Government*, Sebastopol, CA: O'Reilly Media.

Laudon, K. C. (1974). *Computers and Bureaucratic Reform*, New York: John Wiley and Sons.

Leadbeater, C. and Cottam, H. (2010). "The User Generated State: Public Services 2.0." Available at <http://www.charlesleadbeater.net/archive/public-services-20.aspx>. Accessed November 4, 2010.

Leben, A., Kunstelj, M., Bohanec, M., and Vintar, M. (2006). "Evaluating Public Administration e-Portals," *Information Polity*, 11(3–4): 207–25.

Lips, M. (2010). "Rethinking Citizen–Government Relationships in the Age of Digital Identity: Insights from Research," *Information Polity*, 15(4): 273–89.

Lyon, D. (1994). *The Electronic Eye*, Minneapolis: University of Minnesota Press.

Lyon, D. (2007). *Surveillance Studies*, Cambridge: Polity Press.

—— (2009). "Surveillance, Power, and Everyday Life," in R. Mansell, C. Avgerou, D. Quah, and R. Silverstone (eds). *The Oxford Handbook of Information and Communication Technologies*, Oxford: Oxford University Press.

McDonald, C., Marston, G., and Buckley, A. (2003). "Risk Technology in Australia: The Role of the Job Seeker Classification Instrument in Employment Services," *Critical Social Policy*, 23(4): 498–526.

McNutt, K. (2007). "Virtual Policy Networks," in A.-V. Antiroiko and M. Mälkiä (eds). *Encyclopedia of Digital Government*, Hershy PA: IGI Global, pp. 1606–10.

Margetts, H. (2009). "The Internet and Public Policy," *Policy and Internet*, 1(1): 1–21.

—— and Dunleavy, P. (2002). *Cultural Barriers to E-Government*, London: National Audit Office.

—— and Partington, M. (2010). "Developments in E-government," in M. Adler (ed.). *Administrative Justice in Context*, Oxford/Portland, OR: Hart, pp. 47–71.

Margetts, H. and Willcocks, L. (1993). "Information Technology in Public Services: Disaster Faster?," *Public Money and Management*, 13(2): 49–56.

Markellou, P. (2007). "Web Mining for Public E-Services Personalization," in A.-V. Antiroiko and M. Mälkiä (eds). *Encyclopedia of Digital Government*, Hershy PA: IGI Global, pp. 1629–34.

Mayer-Schönberger, V. and Lazer, D. (2007). *Governance and Information Technology*, Cambridge, MA: MIT Press.

Medaglia, R. (2007). "Measuring the Diffusion of eParticipation: A Survey on Italian Local Government," *Information Polity*, 12(4): 265–80.

Meijer, A. J. (2003). "Transparent Government: Parliamentary and Legal Accountability in an Information Age," *Information Polity*, 8(1–2): 67–78.

—— (2007a). "Publishing Public Performance Results on the Internet: Do Stakeholders Use the Internet to Hold Dutch Public Service Organizations to Account?," *Government Information Quarterly*, 24(1): 165–85.

—— (2007b). "Why Don't They Listen to Us? Reasserting the Role of ICT in Public Administration," *Information Polity*, 12: 233–42.

—— and Thaens, M. (2010). "Alignment 2.0: Strategic Use of New Internet Technologies in Government," *Government Information Quarterly*, 27(2): 113–21.

Melville, R. (2007). "E-Social Policy and E-Social Service Delivery," in A.-V. Anttiroiko and M. Mälkiä (eds). *Encyclopedia of Digital Government*, Hershey, PA: Idea Group Reference, pp. 726–33.

Miori, V. and Russo, D. (2009). "QUIMBY: An Innovative Open-Source Solution for e-Democracy," in D. Remenyi (ed.), *9th European Conference on e-Government*, London, UK. Reading: Academic Publishing Limited, pp. 493–500.

Morison, J. (2010). "Gov 2.0: Towards a User Generated State?," *The Modern Law Review*, 73(4): 551–77.

Mutula, S. M. (2008). "Comparison of Sub-Saharan Africa's e-Government Status with Developed and Transitional Nations," *Information Management and Computer Security*, 16(3): 235–50.

Nasi, G. (2009). "E-Government and Local Service Delivery: The Case of Italian Local Governments," in C. G. Reddick (ed.). *Handbook of Research on Strategies for Local E-Government Adoption and Implementation*, Hershey, PA/London: Information Science Reference, pp. 735–51.

Nixon, P. G., Koutrakou, V. N., and Rawal, R. (2010). *Understanding E-Government in Europe*, London: Routledge.

Norris, C. and Armstrong, G. (1999). *The Maximum Surveillance Society*, Oxford: Berg.

Noveck, B. S. (2009). *Wiki Government*, Washington, DC: Brookings Institution Press.

Organ, J. (2003). "The Coordination of e-Government in Historical Context," *Public Policy and Administration*, 18(2): 31–6.

Osimo, D. (2008). *Web 2.0 in Government*, Luxembourg: Joint Research Centre, Institute for Prospective Technological Studies, EC.

Ostermann, H. and Staudinger, R. (2007a). "Corruption, Transparency, and E-Government," in A.-V. Anttiroiko and M. Mälkiä (eds). *Encyclopedia of Digital Government*, Hershey, PA: Idea Group Reference, pp. 251–9.

—— and Staudinger, R. (2007b). "Global Benchmarking of E-Governments," in A.-V. Anttiroiko and M. Mälkiä (eds). *Encyclopedia of Digital Government*, Hershey, PA: Idea Group Reference, pp. 869–80.

Parton, N. (2008). "Changes in the Form of Knowledge in Social Work: From the 'Social' to the 'Informational'?," *British Journal of Social Work*, 38(2): 253–69.

Pathak, R. D., Naz, R., Rahman, M. H., Smith, R. F. I., and Agarwal, K. N. (2009). "E-Governance to Cut Corruption in Public Service Delivery: A Case Study of Fiji," *International Journal of Public Administration*, 32(5): 415–37.

Petricek, V., Escher, T., Cox, I. J., and Margetts, H. (2006). "The Web Structure of e-Government—Developing a Methodology for Quantitative Evaluation," in *15th international conference on World Wide Web*, Edinburgh: ACM Press, pp. 669–78.

Pieterson, W., Ebbers, W., and van Dijk, J. (2007). "Personalization in the Public Sector: An Inventory of Organizational and User Obstacles towards Personalization of Electronic Services in the Public Sector," *Government Information Quarterly*, 24(1): 148–64.

Pirog, M. A. and Johnson, C. L. (2008). "Electronic Funds and Benefits Transfers, E-Government, and the Winter Commission," *Public Administration Review*, 68 (suppl. s1): S103–14. See <http://onlinelibrary.wiley.com/doi/10.1111/j.1540-6210.2008.00982.x/full>. Accessed May 2, 2012.

Raab, C. D. (2009). "Privacy Protection and ICT: Issues, Instruments and Concepts," in C. Avgerou, R. Mansell, D. Quah, and R. Silverstone (eds). *The Oxford Handbook of Information and Communication Technologies*, Oxford: Oxford University Press.

Rowe, N. (2007). "Trust in Digital Government," in A.-V. Antiroiko and M. Malkia (eds). *Encyclopedia of Digital Government*, Hershey, PA: Idea Group Reference, pp. 1572–6.

Scavo, C. (2007). "Development and Use of the World Wide Web by U.S. Local Governments," in A.-V. Anttiroiko and M. Mälkiä (eds). *Encyclopedia of Digital Government*, Hershey, PA: Idea Group Reference, pp. 296–300.

Scholl, H. J. (2003a). "E-government: A Special Case of ICT-enabled Business Process Change." Paper presented at the Proceedings of the 36th Annual Hawaii International Conference on System Sciences (HICSS'03). Available at <http://www.computer.org/portal/web/csdl/doi/10.1109/HICSS.2003.10015>. Accessed May 2, 2012.

—— (2003b). "Electronic Government: Make or Buy?" in R. Traunmüller (ed.) *Electronic Government: Second International Conference, EGOV 2003*, vol. 2739, Berlin/Heidelberg: Springer, pp. 220–7.

—— and Klischewski, R. (2007). "E-Government Integration and Interoperability: Framing the Research Agenda," *International Journal of Public Administration*, 30(8): 889–920.

Schuppan, T. (2009). "E-Government in Developing Countries: Experiences from Sub-Saharan Africa," *Government Information Quarterly*, 26(1): 118–27.

Scott, C. G. (2001). *E-Government in the Asia-Pacific region*, Manila: Asian Development Bank.

Seifert, J. W. (2007). "Data Mining and Homeland Security," in A.-V. Anttiroiko and M. Mälkiä (eds). *Encyclopedia of Digital Government*, Hershey, PA: Idea Group Reference, pp. 277–82.

Shafie, D. M. (2008). "Participation in E-Rulemaking: Interest Groups and the Standard-Setting Process for Hazardous Air Pollutants," *Journal of Information Technology and Politics*, 5(4): 399–410.

Siau, K. and Long, Y. (2005). "Synthesizing e-Government Stage Models—a Meta-Synthesis Based on Meta-Ethnography Approach," *Industrial Management + Data Systems*, 105(3–4): 443–58.

Silcock, R. (2001). "What is e-Government?," *Parliamentary Affairs*, 54(1): 88–101.

Smith, N. J. (1985). *Social Welfare and Computers*, Melbourne: Longman Cheshire.

Stephens, S., McCusker, P., O Donnell, D., Newman, D. R., and Fagan, G. H. (2006). "On the Road from Consultation Cynicism to Energising e-Consultation," *Electronic Journal of e-Government*, 4(2): 87–94.

Torres, L., Pina, V., and Royo, S. (2005). "E-Government and the Transformation of Public Administrations in EU Countries: Beyond NPM or Just a Second Wave of Reforms?," *Online Information Review*, 29(5): 531–53.

Triplett, J. E. (1999). "The Solow Productivity Paradox: What Do Computers Do to Productivity?," *Canadian Journal of Economics*, 32(2): 309–34.

UN (2002). *Benchmarking E-government: A Global Perspective*, Washington DC: UN.

—— (2010). *E-Government Survey 2010: Leveraging e-Government at a Time of Financial and Economic Crisis*, New York: UN.

van Dijk, J. A. G. M. (2006). *The Network Society*, 2nd edn., London: Sage.

von Lucke, J. (2007). "Portals for the Public Sector," in A.-V. Anttiroiko and M. Mälkiä (eds). *Encyclopedia of Digital Government*, Hershey, PA: Idea Group Reference, pp. 1328–33.

Walsh, L. (2007). "A Case Study of Public Servants Engaged in E-Consultation in Australia," *International Journal of Electronic Government Research*, 3(4): 20–37.

Warner, J. and Chun, S. A. (2009). "Privacy Protection in Government Mashups," *Information Polity*, 14(1–2): 75–90.

West, D. M. (2004). "E-Government and the Transformation of Service Delivery and Citizen Attitudes," *Public Administration Review*, 64(1): 15–27.

—— (2005). *Digital Government*, Princeton, NJ: Princeton University Press.

—— (2008). "Improving Technology Utilization in Electronic Government around the World," Brookings. Available at <http://www.brookings.edu/research/reports/2008/08/17-egovernment-west>. Accessed May 2, 2012.

Westcott, C. G. (2010). *E-Government in the Asia-Pacific Region*, Manila: Asian Development Bank.

Westin, A. F. and Baker, M. A. (1972). *Databanks in a Free Society*, New York: Quadrangle Books.

Wu, H., Ozok, A. A., Gurses, A. P., and Wei, J. (2009). "User Aspects of Electronic and Mobile Government: Results from a Review of Current Research," *Electronic Government*, 6(3): 233–51.

Yong, J. S. L. (ed.). (2005). *E-Government in Asia*, Singapore: Marshall Cavendish.

Zinnbauer, D. (2007). "Transparency and Information Disclosure in E-Government," in A.-V. Anttiroiko and M. Mälkiä (eds). *Encyclopedia of Digital Government*, Hershey, PA: Idea Group Reference, pp. 1566–71.

CHAPTER 15

DIGITAL TRANSFORMATIONS OF SCHOLARSHIP AND KNOWLEDGE

ERIC T. MEYER AND RALPH SCHROEDER

INTRODUCTION

SINCE the early days of computerization, the practice of research across disciplines and domains has been transformed by computational technologies and increasingly by the ubiquity of the Internet. For example, search engines such as Google have become a dominant source of information, not only among the general public but also for researchers (Bulger et al. 2011; Meyer et al. 2012). However, the possibilities of the Internet advancing research go far beyond basic information search. From massive physics collaboratories such as the European Organization for Nuclear Research (CERN) Large Hadron Collider, which relies on high-speed networks to distribute data around the world for analysis, to web-based resources such as Galaxy Zoo,[1] which is harnessing the power of citizen science to classify galaxies from the Sloan Digital Sky Survey (Lintott et al. 2008; Raddick et al. 2010), the Internet is increasingly embedded in developing science practices. Likewise, from genealogy enthusiasts researching family history (Crowe 2008; Yakel 2004), to individuals researching health information (Eysenbach et al. 2002; Hesse et al. 2005), the public can use a variety of digital technologies and access a vast range of resources via the Internet in the interests of research.

There are several topics that potentially fall under the rubric of "the digitization of research," including the Internet as a new social phenomenon in its own right, the use of the Internet as a source of information, and the Internet as a platform for social research (see Thelwall Chapter 4; Fielding et al. 2008). In this chapter, we concentrate

---

[1] See <http://www.galaxyzoo.org/>. Accessed December 8, 2011.

on a topic that has received far less scholarly study than it deserves, though it is a topic that will be absolutely central to scholarship in the twenty-first century: how the Internet is transforming academic research in the sciences, social sciences, and humanities. These transformations have attracted a number of labels, such as digital humanities, e-Social Science, cyberinfrastructure, and e-Science. However, in order to delimit our topic so as not to include all the changes that the Internet has brought to research (sending emails, for example), we define the digitization of research (or e-Research) as the use of digital tools and data for the distributed and collaborative production of knowledge (Meyer and Schroeder 2009). Thus we are primarily interested in various research frontiers where, we shall argue, a globally connected network of machines and people has had far-reaching consequences.

Despite some notable exceptions (e.g. Borgman 2007; Dutton and Jeffreys 2010b), this transformation has received little attention, partly due to the fragmentation of disciplinary perspectives which address this phenomenon. The digitization of scholarship has been analyzed from a variety of (inter)disciplinary perspectives. These include:

- the sociology of science and technology (STS), such as in studies of technological infrastructures (Jackson et al. 2007);
- media studies, such as how scholarly communication changes the publishing process (Boczkowski and Lievrouw 2008);
- political-institutional perspectives on the social shaping of technology (Dutton 2011);
- information and Web Science, such as in studies of sharing data (Borgman 2007);
- the fields of economics of innovation and research policy, where various issues surrounding intellectual property rights in multi-institutional collaborations have been discussed (David and Spence 2003);
- and in computer science and computer-supported collaborative work, where distributed work has received considerable attention (Olson et al. 2008).

Apart from the different topics covered, these disciplinary perspectives often have different aims: for example, contributing to the design of systems, addressing policy issues surrounding e-Research, or providing a critical approach to the claims about their transformative nature (see Fry and Schroeder 2010; Schroeder and Fry 2007).

This is only a partial list of topics covered from these (inter)disciplinary perspectives and their approaches. However, a key implication is that the diversity of perspectives, which is a characteristic of Internet Studies as a whole, is likely to persist. One way to nevertheless avoid a fragmented picture of digital transformations of research is to focus on a single substantive question, and then to illuminate this question from various disciplinary angles. In the case of the digital transformation of research, we argue that this question must be: how is scholarly knowledge changing as it moves into the online realm? Put differently, and in line with our definition, how do the distributed and collaborative uses of digital tools and data open up new avenues for research? As we shall see, the question of changes in knowledge is one that STS should be well-equipped to answer, but we shall argue that it does so only to a limited extent.

In this chapter, we will address this central question from a variety of perspectives, and come back in the concluding section to the issue of whether the diversity or pluralism of social science disciplinary perspectives can be overcome. One point to anticipate is that the digital transformation of scholarship would ideally be contextualized in a larger picture of how information and knowledge are being transformed by the Internet and related new media in society-at-large. These broader ideas about social change, often associated with terms like "the information society" or "knowledge society," are beyond the scope of this chapter, but we will come back to them in the concluding section.

The approach we take in this chapter is to provide a number of illustrations of some common shifts in how research is changing at the level of knowledge on the one hand and in scholarly practices on the other. Once we have done this, we will address the broader issue of different views on how scholarship is being transformed with e-Research, before concluding with some thoughts about how Internet Studies can grapple with these changes.

TRANSFORMING RESEARCH

There are literally thousands of examples of e-Research projects of varying size and impact. Some of these have arisen in response to various funding programs of research councils (see Dutton and Jeffreys 2010a), some are part of the attempts to build the e-Infrastructures or cyberinfrastructures supporting science and research (see also Barjak et al. 2013), and yet others represent "bottom-up" or "accidental e-Research" (see Meyer and Dutton 2009)—e-Research that has arisen independently when individuals or groups build their own tools for wider uptake or sharing and collaboration. In what follows, we will give examples that illustrate the range of e-Research, but we also use them to highlight in each case trends of how technology is used in research but also the changed research practices involved. This will allow us in the section thereafter to draw these together into larger patterns in how e-Research is contributing to the sciences and humanities.

Physics and large-scale data

We can begin with uses of the Grid and distributed computing in physics, which provides a good illustration of how the scaling up of organizational and technological complexity go together. The Large Hadron Collider (LHC) at CERN, and GridPP—a collaboration of particle physicists and computer scientists at nineteen UK universities, and Rutherford Appleton Laboratory—are good examples. The LHC is a large research instrument—a piece of technology, engineering, or a machine—that, put simply and crudely, smashes particles together. The experiment in this case consists of postulating a smaller particle than those that have been identified—this is the theoretical part. The practical part of the experiment is designed to undertake observation and measurement of these postulated particles. Computing plays a major role in this effort because the data generated by the experiment are large scale, requiring high throughput processing. The Grid is used to handle this volume of data using a multi-tiered structure, so that the parcels are delivered into what are called Tier 1 machines, which further parcel them out to Tier 2 machines, and so on. This grid computing effort has been partly enabled by research funding programs (in this case, the European Commission funded EGEE[2]/EGI[3]).

The organization of these complex and distributed computing operations in this case is highly bureaucratic in the sense of the hierarchical arrangement of this parceling out. However, it is also non-bureaucratic insofar as rather than having a top-down command structure, the assignment of tasks throughout the hierarchy takes place on the basis of memoranda of understanding that are relatively democratically arrived at—or what Shrum et al. (2007) describe as trust. The reason this way of doing research deserves the label e-Research—apart from this organization of sharing—is that the computing operations are scaled in order to highly parallelize the task of analyzing the data.

This effort also has its national constituent parts. GridPP,[4] for example, is the UK part of this effort. The UK has taken a sizeable share of the data from the current LHC experiment, and participates on all the tiers. To this end, the UK physics community has had to develop an organization to dedicate computing power to analyze these data in coordination with other physicists from around the world that are involved in exploiting the LHC data (see Zheng et al. 2011). The key feature of the LHC and GridPP to highlight is that physicists have for some time been a community that has had to coordinate research on a large scale and in teams with a high division of labor but also high degree of mutual dependence and task certainty (Whitley 2000). Physicists are well-placed to undertake complex tasks which parallelize computational data analysis across multiple levels and in a distributed manner. GridPP thus illustrates how physicists have had to adapt their organizational practices to fit around the highly distributed way in which their data need to be analyzed with—in this case "grid"—computing tools. In any event, this case shows that highly complex organizational and technological infrastructures are needed to cope with data on a scale that is unparalleled in other areas of research.

Public engagement via citizen science

A different example of computation on a large scale, though in this case with much less organizational and technological complexity—a much more "flat" and simple structure—are volunteer computing efforts, like Galaxy Zoo. As already mentioned, the Galaxy

---

[2] Enabling Grids for E-SciencE: <http://www.eu-egee.org/>. Accessed December 8, 2011.
[3] European Grid Infrastructure: <http://www.egi.eu/>. Accessed December 8, 2011.
[4] GridPP: <http://www.gridpp.ac.uk/>. Accessed December 8, 2011.

Zoo project makes use of citizen scientists to classify galaxies from the Sloan Digital Sky Survey (Lintott et al. 2008; Raddick et al. 2010) via a public website.[5] Unlike GridPP, which is using distributed computation to analyze data, Galaxy Zoo relies on distributed human cognition to classify data, a task for which human brains are still more suited than are computer algorithms. Citizen scientists are shown an image of a galaxy, and then are given a set of fairly simple choices, such as: is the galaxy smooth, or does it have features such as a disk? Is the galaxy clumpy or not? Does it appear to be a disk viewed edge on? None of these options are very difficult tasks for the human brain, but they are very difficult tasks to perform computationally. In addition, classifiers don't have to be highly skilled, since each image will be shown to multiple classifiers—if most of them agree in their classification, the likelihood that their classification is correct is quite high.

The scientists involved in the project (Lintott, personal communication) report that not only has this project surpassed their expectations, but it is making real contributions to science. Papers have been published with citizen scientists as co-authors,[6] and the project has resulted in new discoveries including famously *Hanny's Voorwerp*, a previously unknown astronomical object discovered by Galaxy Zoo participant and Dutch schoolteacher Hanny van Arkel.[7] What we see in this case is how a relatively simple technology—a website—can enable the distribution of tasks to a large number of volunteers, rather than distributing the task among computers as in the GridPP example. However, organizing the task in such a way that it attracts a lot of volunteers, and organizing the collection and analysis of the data are by no means minor tasks. Nevertheless, once the tool has been created for one application (astronomy), it has required less of an effort to develop a platform (Zooniverse) which has been used to distribute other tasks that require thousands of volunteers, and can be extended to others. In short, this kind of volunteer effort enables labor-intensive tasks to be distributed via the Web, but again, in an organizationally and technologically "flat" way, since this effort consists of thousands of volunteers logging into a website via their personal computers, and their efforts are aggregated within a single database.

The complexities of data sharing

A different way of harnessing digital resources, in this case from sensors, shows that it is nevertheless not straightforward to bring distributed data together: the Centre for Embedded Network Sensing (CENS) was set up to see how the availability of small and cheap sensing devices could be used to monitor environmental conditions. These sensors were deployed in the field in various settings and could provide streams of data back to scientists operating in the lab.[8] One of the findings of this project (Borgman et al. 2007)

---

[5] See n. 1 above.
[6] See <http://blogs.zooniverse.org/galaxyzoo/category/paper/>. Accessed December 8, 2011.
[7] See <http://www.hannysvoorwerp.com/>. Accessed December 8, 2011.
[8] CENS: <http://research.cens.ucla.edu/>. Accessed December 8, 2011.

is that the data generated by sensors was viewed differently by participants from different domains. For instance, the engineers on sensor projects were interested in performance data from the sensors (e.g. packet transmission information, battery state, and fault detection), scientists were interested in scientific data (e.g. water temperature, wind speed, and pH), and data managers and analysts were additionally interested in contextual data that could influence the scientific data (e.g. motor speed of the boat pulling the sensor, calibration data, and environmental conditions of the equipment connected to the sensors).

Unlike physics and volunteer computing for astronomy then, this kind of distributed computing effort demonstrates a different kind of complexity: Building data libraries that not only accommodate the needs of various kinds of researchers, but also allow for future use and reuse of the data, requires an understanding of the entire data lifecycle and an ability to integrate data from multiple sources (Borgman et al. 2007). In this case we can see that the main effort is not in the organization of the computational task (as in GridPP) or coordination of the task among many volunteers (as with Galaxy Zoo), but rather in implementing an extensive set of tools which require coordinating digital data over a heterogeneous set of instruments so that they provide a long-term data resource that is as consistent as possible. The major effort in this case lies in shaping organizations and their data practices.

Data practices have moved into the forefront of the challenges in e-Research, and the reason for this is not only the heterogeneity of data among different types of researchers. A different type of challenge lies simply in sharing data on a large scale among different groups, where this larger scale is a precondition for making scientific advances. A good illustration here is the Genetic Association Information Network (GAIN) project, which was an American effort starting in 2006 to do large-scale Genome-Wide Association Studies (GWAS) of six selected datasets related to a variety of medical conditions (Manolio et al. 2007). One of the innovative aspects of this program was that, unlike previous research where investigators would have exclusive use of their data for a period of time (often one year from the end of data collection), in GAIN, "results [were] made immediately available for research use by any interested and qualified investigator or organization" (Manolio et al. 2007: 1048), including organizations such as pharmaceutical companies. The attraction to researchers was the promise of large-scale high-quality genotyping of their research subjects, in exchange for contributions of DNA from blood and of diagnostic information.

The risk for researchers was that they could be beaten to publication on results from their own data, since other researchers could analyze their data at the same time. In other words, the contributing investigators had just a six-month exclusive publication window, after which anyone using the data could publish (Meyer 2009). This model of high-speed, high-stakes collaborative science suggests the potential to greatly speed up scientific discovery, but at a risk to individual scientific achievement. Nevertheless, the incentives whereby funding was made conditional on sharing data in a common pool in this case demonstrated that large-scale collaboration to produce datasets across research teams is possible. However, the result has been that the science of GWAS requires that even larger data-sharing efforts are needed in order to make progress in finding links between genes and the medical conditions in this study.

The GAIN project illustrates large-scale data sharing for a specific research goal. But e-Research also consists of much more ambitious efforts to develop data infrastructures which link different types of data at a population-wide level as a long-term infrastructure for research. Where this involves sensitive data, as with certain types of medical or social research, this poses the additional challenge of requiring the trust of populations that these data will not be misused in any way. A good example of such an effort is the Swedish e-Research program because it has embarked on precisely such an undertaking. One of the main preconditions which favors e-Research in Sweden is the availability of many high-quality datasets about the Swedish population that have been maintained for a long time, which have recently become the responsibility of the Swedish National Data Service (SND).[9] There are at least two further reasons why Sweden is uniquely well-equipped to embark on such an effort: one is that each person living in Sweden has a unique personal identifier (a person number) which is frequently and commonly used in everyday life and for record-keeping by the government and other bodies (for example, health records). This allows researchers to make links between different types of data that is typically difficult in other countries due to the heterogeneity of different types of datasets. Second, there exists a high level of trust between the Swedish population, researchers, and government. This is partly due to long-standing laws concerning (especially computer-supported) data protection, and partly due a number of widely publicized debates around the use of data in research.

These factors are currently being revisited by researchers in the development of e-Research capabilities at SND and more generally, with Swedish researchers well aware both of the unique circumstances in Sweden in terms of the quality and potential of its digital data, and of the need to maintain the trust that has been established and that will have to be maintained if this potential is to be fulfilled (Axelsson and Schroeder 2009). What we see illustrated in this example is that when sensitive data are involved, it is not just a question of organizing large-scale data collection and sharing (as with GAIN, where the data are anonymized). It is also a question of how data about whole populations requires a high level of trust between researchers, public authorities, and the public when these data derive value from linking different datasets and where this linking poses potential risks for research subjects. These conditions do not obtain in many countries, and it is an open question whether they will continue to do so in Sweden. For the moment, however, the relatively high level of trust in Sweden combined with the availability of many long-term datasets provides better preconditions for this type of e-Research than in most other countries. Put differently, the key in this case is not merely large-scale organizational efforts (as for GAIN), but also longer-term social enabling conditions.

[9] Swedish National Data Service: <http://www.snd.gu.se/en>. Accessed December 8, 2011.

The challenges of infrastructure across the academic-industry divide

Data-sharing and linking large-scale, heterogeneous, and sensitive datasets is not just a challenge in academic research. In recent decades, particularly in the life sciences, there has been increasing collaboration at the interface between academia and the private sector, and this raises further issues for research spanning different institutions. While such collaboration between industry and academia has not been extensively explored in the literature on e-Research, it is bound to become ever more significant. Here the SwissBioGrid project provides a good example inasmuch as it consisted of a collaboration between academic institutions and the private sector— in this case pharmaceutical companies (den Besten et al. 2009)—that was successful, albeit at a level of modest complexity.[10] The project involved a number of academic partners, including the Swiss Institute of Bioinformatics at the University of Basel and Swiss National Supercomputing Centre. The collaboration entailed two projects: proteomics data analysis and "virtual screening" to find new drugs for dengue fever. The core of the project was to develop tools for harnessing distributed computing power (in this case, partly using many idle PCs overnight) in pursuit of these aims in life sciences research, which succeeded in terms of demonstrating the technical capabilities required. It can be mentioned that in developing the software, SwissBioGrid drew on software developed for the CERN physics collaboration (discussed earlier) for some of the "middleware," i.e. the tools for distributed data management.

The project demonstrated that successful e-Research collaboration between the private sector and academic institutions is possible, and that distributed computing in the life sciences can provide useful research tools. On the other hand, despite its success, the project was limited insofar as there was, at the time, no larger infrastructure such as a national e-Infrastructure that it could become part of and be sustained by. Such Switzerland-wide efforts at resource sharing have since emerged in the shape of the Swiss National Grid Association (SwiNG). Yet, even if the project was prevented from being sustained within a larger infrastructure, it demonstrated the value of harnessing many PCs to perform a computationally intensive task, as with GridPP. Unlike GridPP, however, the main effort was not in coordinating the computing power of distributed organizations, but rather in coordinating several partner institutions to join, and in tailoring the software to the task of performing the analysis. And unlike the Swedish e-Research effort, which was begun by creating a national infrastructure for research, we can see the limitations of e-Research in the case of projects like SwissBioGrid that take place without embedding them in longer-term technical and organizational structures.

---

[10] Swiss BioGrid: <http://www.swissbiogrid.org/>. Accessed December 8, 2011.

Changing everyday practices and supporting users

E-Research requires not just new tools and organizational structures but also that researchers change their everyday practices. An example here is the Structure of Populations, Levels of Abundance, and Status of Humpbacks (SPLASH) project. This was "one of the largest international collaborative studies of any whale population ever conducted... [involving] over 50 research groups and more than 400 researchers in 10 countries" (Calambokidis 2010: 7). Using photo-identification techniques that use the fingerprint-like nature of humpback whale flukes (tails) to identify individual animals, scientists were able to start to answer population-level questions about the whales that individual scientists working alone could never hope to answer (Meyer 2009). Through this large collaboration, scientists were able to construct a much more complete picture of the current populations of Pacific humpbacks, and to understand more about their migrations and seasonal movements.

The project is a good illustration of how a large effort is required in changing research practices; in this case particularly in making the transition from non-digital to digital images. This is not so much a question of technological complexity, but rather of how many researchers can make the transition to handling and classifying digital images. Further, even though the amount of data is not large by the standards of research in astronomy or in physics, it nevertheless presented a daunting challenge in federating and analyzing these data, particularly given the large-scale and collaborative nature of the project (Calambokidis 2010; Calambokidis et al. 2008; Meyer 2009). And again, making this change across a number of organizations, as with the CENS example, requires a major level of coordination.

Changing practices requires not only making such a transition, but also expending the effort required in maintaining support to sustain these practices. This demands not just technological and organizational resources, but above all—in some cases—expertise dedicated to the task. A good illustration of this is the Virtual Observatory for the Study of Online Networks (VOSON), a web-based tool for studying online social networks based at the Australian National University.[11] This tool has been developed since 2005 to promote "webometric" approaches which measure, among other things, the visibility of websites in relation to the links (or hyperlinks) between them (Ackland 2009; Ackland et al. 2006). This tool allows social scientists to identify patterns of links between, say, environmental movements or political parties, in order to see how they are connected online—perhaps with implications for their offline networks and activities. VOSON has been developed as an open source tool and, using a Creative Commons license, researchers can not only use but also build upon and extend this tool. Thus VOSON has been used by a group of researchers worldwide who themselves belong to a wider community of researchers using "social network analysis," a community that includes researchers from beyond the social sciences and that often uses computationally intensive methods.

[11] VOSON: <http://voson.anu.edu.au/>. Accessed December 8, 2011.

VOSON continues to be developed and has been used in a number of publications, and it can be seen as part of a burgeoning engagement in e-Social Science. From the users' point of view, apart from requiring skills in the analysis of websites, to use the tool, it is only necessary to create an account and instructions are provided about how to use it. Nevertheless, the challenge with tools like VOSON is to maintain them (e.g. in making the tool compatible with other tools), and to provide support to users who often have queries. Unlike Galaxy Zoo, which requires minimal user support, web tools like VOSON require engagement with and ongoing support for a user community, a task that requires time as a key resource in addition to software expertise.

Engaging communities in the humanities

In yet other e-Research efforts, such specialist expertise may not be required, though the key may be to engage a community of contributors. We have already seen this in the example of Galaxy Zoo, which has been successful in enabling amateur contributions to astronomy. But volunteer efforts are not restricted to science. In the humanities, too, there have been a number of projects that have harnessed the power of "crowdsourcing." One such is the Pynchon Wiki, a wiki created with the purpose of annotating the works of the contemporary American novelist Thomas Pynchon (Schroeder and den Besten 2008).[12] One element of Pynchon's work is that his writing is full of allusions and obscure references, and this is the sort of work that invites a detective-like effort at producing annotated editions to help the reader understand these references.

But whereas Pynchon's previous novels had been annotated over a period of many years in book form, the members of the Pynchon Wiki effort were able to annotate the entirety of his new novel *Against the Day* in mere months after its release. The creation of this wiki involved hundreds of contributors. Apart from speeding up the process, the Pynchon Wiki has reconfigured how this effort takes place; namely, by contributors organizing themselves such that they find which parts of the novel have already been annotated, filling in the gaps that remain, and carrying out additional discussions if the entry for a particular term has already been "finalized." Thus it is not so much that literary studies become transformed as a discipline via this wiki, but that the wiki allows for both amateurs and non-academics to contribute, whereas previously this effort was carried out solely by academics.

Scholarly practices are further transformed insofar as the wiki allows some multimedia annotation (images and sound clips) to be added to text, but more importantly the task can be scaled to a large and open community of contributors since they can find out where annotation is needed, and locate and coordinate with others the parts that are in need of further work. Like Galaxy Zoo then, this tool allows a task to be highly distributed. And again like Galaxy Zoo, this web tool has subsequently been extended to a number of wikis for other Pynchon novels and wikis for the novelist David Foster

---

[12] Pynchon Wiki: <http://pynchonwiki.com/>. Accessed December 8, 2011.

Wallace and for the Beatles. Web-based research tools like these depend on enabling the scaling up of human effort much more than organizational and technological effort, and they can be applied to a variety of labor-intensive tasks.

Finally, e-Research is not just appropriate to knowledge-generating tasks on a large scale or for large communities of scholars or amateur contributors. The community of scholars that specializes in the study of Tibetan and Himalayan texts, for example, is quite small (500–700) and comes from several disciplines, including religious studies, anthropology, and philosophy. There have been a number of projects to digitize the texts and images used by these scholars that have previously been difficult to access due to the distributed nature of the collections, some of which are in remote locations (all material for this case is based on Madsen 2010). In terms of reorganizing the workings of this community, these projects have mainly been driven by a few individuals who have devoted themselves to this task, and the organizational challenge that remains here is to embed these projects within an organizational form that can sustain them (such as an institutional base and continued funding and staffing).

This small multidisciplinary specialism has not been dramatically transformed by the digitization of resources, although key staff digitizing texts have had to become experts in the software that is required. Moreover, although the main scholarly work in this area remains the interpretation of texts (and thus the main change in scholarly practices is in access), some scholars have also used the digital versions of text to undertake computational linguistic analyses such as frequency of terms, which had not been possible before. Hence this is one way in which the research front has changed. Another is that in a case of a relatively small community of specialist scholars, unlike the large numbers that have participated in Galaxy Zoo and the Pynchon Wiki, this project for accessing remote text requires the dedicated work of a few individuals with the requisite computing skills and, as with VOSON, a high level of effort to develop and maintain the tools.

STYLES OF SCIENCE IN E-RESEARCH

At this point, we can turn to some common characteristics of how e-Research has transformed knowledge and research practices. In doing this, we will develop some ideas in the sociology of science and technology. We will argue that what is distinctive in e-Research is how computing performs operations on digital materials: e-Research yokes the power of networked computing so that various operations can be scaled up, intensified, and organized in a complex way. We have illustrated this in relation to a number of projects and tools that, as we have seen, require quite different organizational and technological efforts. To analyze these modes of research at a more abstract level, we draw on Hacking's "styles of science" (2002)—Hacking, in turn, is following Crombie (1994)—though as we shall see, e-Research typically combines several styles, and there are additional styles that fall outside of and can be added to Hacking's.

What we can see is that e-Research harnesses networked computing and digital material in different ways. How does this advance scientific practice? Here it is necessary to make a distinction between science (representing and intervening, Hacking 1983) and how research technologies (refining and manipulating, Schroeder 2007) support science. Hacking has argued, based on a realist and pragmatist understanding of science and knowledge, that there are several "styles" of science—he says there are six—which underlie scientific enquiry. Several of these are exemplified by the kinds of e-Research that has been briefly described here: these include Hacking's (2009: 10) "experimental exploration and measurement of more complex observable relations"(LHC), "ordering of variety by comparison and taxonomy" (SPLASH), and "the statistical analysis of regularities of populations and the calculus of probabilities" (GAIN). Importantly, for Hacking, styles are "self-authenticating" (2009: 46–7): that is, they are validated by the style of reasoning that is used.

To this it needs to be added that in order to establish whether the e-Research efforts that have been mentioned here are contributing to the advancement of science, it would be necessary to determine if, within the community of researchers devoted to a particular object or set of objects (as Gläser 2006 has characterized it), e-Research has produced knowledge that has enabled a more powerful "interlocking of representing and intervening" (thus combining the method and its objects). In other words, to establish whether e-Research has advanced the research front within a scientific community. This criterion from Hacking's and Gläser's perspective within the sociology of science and technology could be used to gauge how knowledge and research practices are being enhanced.

This point can be elaborated by reference to the examples given in the previous section: in the experiments at the LHC, large amounts of data are being produced that need to be analyzed in a computationally intensive way, and in this case, this task is being distributed to many machines. Similarly, in the case of SwissBiogrid, the task—screening molecules—is organized so that it can be performed many times on many networked computers (parallelization). Or in the case of the CENS network, streams of data from different remote sources are fed into a single store in order to collect and detect patterns within and between these data sources. Similarly with SPLASH, though in this case the data are collected by digital cameras first and then brought together in a database in order to find patterns of whale migration. GAIN and VOSON both apply statistics (using the calculating capacity of computers): in the case of GAIN to find correlations between different datasets about illness, and for VOSON in identifying networks of hyperlinks. Still other cases entail databases and federated databases that can be analyzed to discover patterns and correlations (social science databases such as those of the Swedish National Data Service provide an example here).

The organization of computing tasks applies not only to organizing the data to enable the computer to sift through it and to calculate, but also to people: Galaxy Zoo and the Pynchon Wiki, for example, both mainly allow many people to do tasks that are accessible on a website—visually inspecting and classifying galaxies by their shape in one case, and contributing analyses of items to be annotated on pages of Pynchon's novels in the other. In these cases, it is more difficult to speak of Hacking's styles of *science* since these are e-Research efforts which do not (necessarily) involve the manipulation of digital data in the service of experiment (observation and measurement), taxonomy, statistical regularities—or Hacking's other three styles ("the simple postulation established in the mathematical sciences," "the hypothetical construction of analogical models," "the historical derivation of genetic development" (Hacking 2009: 10). We have not provided examples of these additional styles here for reasons of space, though examples in e-Research readily come to mind). Instead, these projects are examples of human interpretation of digital materials. So the Pynchon Wiki, for example, does not "intervene" in the physical world, but it provides a collection of materials for interpretation that are organized by technology for easy access. So this is e-Research but not e-*Science*, and the technology plays a supporting role. Such a role can be seen in all of the examples given here: distributed access, in the case of the Pynchon Wiki or Tibetan and Himalayan studies, to anyone with a PC and an internet connection. So it is not always the case that e-Research plays a role as in science, which tends to harness computers to manipulating data, but can consist of harnessing people to a common task in annotating or working on texts (as with the Pynchon Wiki or Himalayan texts). Nevertheless, even in this supporting role, the transformation of scholarship can lead to new directions in research (or the community of researchers orienting themselves to a new research object)—such as counting word frequencies in Pynchon's and in Himalayan texts.

Finally, we can therefore pinpoint the specific role played by research technologies in e-Research, since e-Research contributes to science in the sense of Hacking's styles in different ways (the data for the LHC experiment, to recall one of Hacking's styles, is produced by another technology, the collider; or the datasets in GAIN are gathered from patients, and so on) by providing more powerful research *technologies* (the ability to analyze the data in both these cases). The role of research technologies or instruments, in turn, points to the recognition that more powerful research instruments (technologies) are often responsible for driving science rather than the other way around (Schroeder 2008). In the case of the e-Research capabilities for the LHC and GAIN, the manipulation of large volumes of digital data (the research technology) plays a key role in this driving of science. Furthermore, we can recognize *how* technology does this—by developing a socio-technical core around which strong organizations can reproduce results. Hence research technologies gain their importance because they can be used in different domains, acting like passports that allow passage between them (Shinn and Joerges 2002). We have seen this illustrated particularly here in the cases (Galaxy Zoo and Pynchon Wiki) where research technologies have been extended to new domains.

In short, to get at the core of how e-Research contributes to knowledge, we can distinguish between the organizational role of e-Research technologies (providing people with access to organized materials) and its techno-scientific role (manipulating data more powerfully). These are the operations that take place in the "black box" of science, which is not so mysterious in relation to the contribution of the research technology here, but requires expertise in assessing the contribution that is made to advancing particular fields. In other words, how do digital data that have been analyzed—or data analyzed using digital tools—improve on existing data or findings? This latter question can only be answered, again, by reference to the research community and the research objects towards which scientists (or humanities scholars) are orienting themselves in each case (Gläser 2003). Moreover, whereas for some disciplines it is easier to ascertain whether such an advance has been made (those with a high degree of task certainty and mutual dependence; see Whitley 2000), in other disciplines this is more difficult to establish, or open to interpretation, or part of a contested terrain.

In any event, it is important to show, not just how research practices are changing, but also, from the point of view of the sociology of science and technology, if—and how—these changed practices are advancing knowledge. So far, however, the sociology of science and technology has failed to do this, partly because this disciplinary perspective currently rejects positions like Hacking's "realism" in favor of constructivist Actor-Network Theory, partly because it pays little attention to research technologies (which are at the centre of our argument), and finally because there is little by way of analysis of how the organization of science and scholarship is oriented towards a common research front, which in the case of e-Research is increasingly dominated and driven by research technologies.

Disciplinary differences in transformations of research

This way of understanding how knowledge is advancing in science and other types of research leads us to ask: What disciplinary differences are there in the take-up of digital technologies, and with what implications? Discussions of e-Research and disciplinarity must begin with "inter-" or "multidisciplinarity" since the introduction of digital technologies into research is typically regarded as an opportunity for greater collaboration between disciplines. It can be noted immediately, however, that there are two ways in which this collaboration is typically framed: either disciplines relax their boundaries and work successfully across them, or they are unable to do so and remain stuck in disciplinary silos. In fact, there is at least one further possibility, which is that e-Research becomes a new specialist discipline in its own right.

The traditional view of disciplines is as a hierarchy, with the "hard" natural sciences at the top (and perhaps physics, with its rigorous experimental methods, at the apex of these), the "softer" social sciences in the middle, and the humanities at the bottom with their greater pluralism and diversity but also weaker possibility for making progress. For our purposes, another perspective on disciplines is how they maintain their boundaries on the one hand and encroach on each other's institutional turf on the other (Becher and Trowler 2001; Fry and Schroeder 2010). In the case of digital technologies, the most immediate trend in this regard is how computer science (and its various subdisciplines) could be seen to be invading all other disciplines. At the same time, computer scientists deny this, claiming that they are merely supporting the other disciplines to do "better science" or "better research": they are merely the enablers. In view of what has already been said, this is at least sometimes a misleading view. Even if in some cases technology plays a supporting role (for example, in providing access to many contributors), in other cases, as we have seen, it is integral to research—as when the scale or scope of computation is itself driving or enabling how data are collected or how they are analyzed.

There are also a number of well-known differences between disciplines which relate to how e-Research is organized, such as whether researchers work in larger collaborative teams (as we have seen in the case of areas of physics) or in specialized laboratories (as in the life sciences; see Knorr Cetina 1999, for the contrast between physics and life sciences). However, our example of GAIN has shown that the life sciences can also scale up and share resources between laboratories, and the SwissBioGrid example illustrates that life sciences can go beyond specialist expertise to engage with computer scientists. A common view of humanities scholars, on the other hand, is that they work mainly as "lone wolves." But again, our examples of the Pynchon Wiki, and Tibetan and Himalayan studies, have shown that this view can be misleading. For digital research, we therefore ask: are there differences in the social organizations of research around different technologies?

In answering this question it is interesting to reflect how the very definition that we provided earlier rules out certain forms of digital research: for example, the researcher who makes a personal collection of digital materials (say, a Tibetan or Himalayan studies scholar digitizing images of rare manuscripts for analysis). If these remain purely the individual's own collection, without contributing to a shared resource that others can access, this would disqualify it from our definition. Note, too, that if this scholar should fully qualify for our definition of digital research, it should be necessary to use computing operations in the performance of research itself—and not simply build a shared collection of digital materials.

This has happened in at least some projects that use digital text material: as when the digital versions of the text allow text search, automated comparison of different text versions, word frequency counts, and the like. Traditional humanities are transformed in this case not just by technology but also disciplinarity: the interpretation of texts moves closer to the techniques of computational linguistics. One symptom of a discipline being transformed is when this type of scholarship becomes challenged as not being "real" humanities scholarship. Thus, for example, some scholars might argue that computational approaches to the text are not real research, or only represent superficial research— the real task should be to provide richer interpretations of the texts.

RESEARCH VISIBILITY AND ACCESS

The changes that have been discussed so far are on the "producer" side of research, which is the traditional focus of STS or of understanding changes in scholarly practices. What about the "consumer" side, or how knowledge is received? One change that is taking place here (see Meyer and Schroeder 2009) is how these two sides are becoming linked: academics are becoming increasingly aware of how their publications and other outputs are being received. This is because academic outputs are increasingly online and thus subject to measurement. Downloads can be counted, webometrics performed on the number of links to a particular web page, and scholars are aware of how they are accessed by means of search engines such as Google and Google Scholar. The automation of these ranking and measurement mechanisms produces a feedback loop whereby the "visibility" of scholarship feeds into academics' behavior (they ensure that they are highly "visible"), which ensures that they are more frequently accessed (see, for example, Willinsky 2005). Thus a new system is added to existing systems of research assessment or evaluation that adds online visibility to scientometric rankings of individuals and research institutions.

On the "consumer" side, there are also changing practices among researchers in how they access materials. Students, for example, search for information using search engines and increasingly rely on Wikipedia articles. Similarly scholars, although they also use specialized searches in journal and other databases, also use general search engines like Google to find material on specific topics and may be led towards articles on the open Web (Rieger 2009). Again, note the feedback loop: the more Wikipedia is relied upon, among other things, for students' and academics' research, the higher it will appear in search results. In this way, the boundary between academic research and the public is becoming somewhat blurred (Meyer and Schroeder 2009). This brings our argument full circle, for the proof that science and scholarship is being transformed cannot simply be in the creation of knowledge, but must also be evident in its impact and wider role in society. And while it would go too far to say that e-Research is contributing to a wider "knowledge" or "information" society, the various research fronts are certainly becoming more visible in the online realm, which is of course expanding, and not just among researchers, but in everyday life in society-at-large.

CONCLUSION

To say that the transformations of digitizing research are merely changes in scale or speed is misleading. When does quantitative change turn into qualitative change? Science—research—advances and gains more power. Perhaps beyond this advance it is only possible to gauge paradigm shifts or scientific revolutions, as Kuhn and Popper would have it, with the benefit of hindsight. Nevertheless, it is possible to chart how change takes place in a variety of ways—reorganizing disciplinary boundaries, changing day-to-day practices, shifting funding priorities, making more extensive and intensive use of computation, and more. These effects fan out across research fields, and gauging the cumulative gain in the power of research will tell us when a digital transformation has taken place. This is difficult to do across the board for all disciplines, though we have given a wide variety of examples. Instead, it is possible to examine advances in particular areas of research and by reference to the state-of-the-art in particular research communities.

This conclusion can be spelled out more fully: As we have seen, e-Research, like all research, consists of a constantly moving research front whereby scientists orient themselves towards the leading edge of the community to which they are contributing, and where they are competing to advance beyond the current state-of-the art within this community. The distinctiveness of e-Research in this regard is that the means by which researchers do so is that they create a physical networked structure that is aimed at this community's state-of-the-art, which therefore provides a persistent focus for all researchers working in this area. Whether this effort is successful or not cannot be known in advance, but the e-Research component has the advantage of enhanced visibility and of being able to build on this component—in addition to making use of more computationally intensive tools (one way to gauge whether e-Research constitutes an advance in this respect is to ask whether the opposite holds: that stand-alone computers may be more powerful, in which case it does not).

Putting these two characteristics (the core of a networked research instrument, and a community oriented to a common research front) together, e-Research involves the creation of a coherent network oriented towards the state-of-the-art of the community, a network which can be built upon and which provides computationally powerful manipulation of data within one of the styles of science, or of "representing and intervening." If this contribution advances beyond a current state-of-the art—typically in the case of disciplines with a high degree of mutual dependence and task certainty (Whitley 2000)—then e-Research will contribute to and become an established research instrument within the field. This chapter has shown how e-Research has made differences in respect to particular examples of how research is organized and carried out. The aggregation of these shifts can only be discerned as a fluid—but increasingly networked and digital—landscape of research aimed at advancing knowledge.

Yet it is also possible to make a broader point: in all of the projects described here across different areas, a physical core consisting of a network (the Internet and Web) and of manipulable data has been created that is maintained and used by a community or by groups of researchers. It is possible to distinguish this physical core from the organization of people that supports and makes use of it. In each case, this core produces new computationally intensive ways of doing research, whether by sorting materials, processing them, or performing numerical analysis such as statistics. It has been argued that these physical cores—of research instruments—typically enable scientists to mobilize around them (Fuchs 2001: 306, 330), in the case of e-Research consisting in the development and greater use of computational methods. Even if these are used only in specialized niches, it is likely that they will strengthen over time since—unlike the organization of people—they can be added to, extended, applied to other domains, and reconfigured. Again, we have documented this strengthening, and the resulting advances in niches in various fields. A more systematic analysis of how this strengthening around research instruments and these advances change the contours of research landscape is not possible here, both for reasons of space and because e-Research is still science- and knowledge-in-the-making. However, further research will be able to map these digital transformations of research—and how networked tools create new techno-scientific organizations (that always have a physical component) and promote the intensification of computational ways of producing knowledge—more fully.

One reason that Internet Studies has not been able to address the transformations that we have charted here is that, as we have shown, the sociology of science and technology, which should be central to the endeavor of explaining how knowledge is changing, does not have the conceptual tools to grapple simultaneously with how research communities are oriented to shared objects (in this case, digital objects that are computationally manipulated), how this affects various styles of science and knowledge, and how scholarly practices are therefore being transformed. Yet for the other disciplines that we mentioned at the outset—including media studies, political-institutional approaches, economics of innovation, and computer science fields—understanding how science and knowledge are being transformed and how they advance at the research front is not a core concern, even if they bring valuable perspectives to the topic of e-Research. The same applies to Internet Studies. Hence we have tried to put forward ideas that put the transformations of knowledge at the center, but also give an account of the technological cores around which communities focus and push research in new directions. This task is bound to remain elusive as it would entail understanding how various frontiers are advancing around computational techniques for manipulating digital objects, and how this focuses the research communities in various fields of scholarship—a larger topic than we can address here. Yet we have also identified a number of commonalities across these fields and how these foci of research communities can be generically understood from a social science perspective. This endeavor can hopefully bring different disciplines studying the Internet together around a shared object: transformations in knowledge. Whether such a shared object can overcome the fragmentation within the social sciences remains to be seen.

References

Ackland, R. (2009). "Social Network Services as Data Sources and Platforms for e-Researching Social Networks," *Social Science Computer Review*, 27(4): 481–92.

——O'Neil, M., Standish, R., and Buchhorn, M. (2006). "VOSON: A Web Services Approach for Facilitating Research into Online Networks." Paper presented at the 2nd International Conference on e-Social Science, University of Manchester, UK.

Axelsson, A.-S. and Schroeder, R. (2009). "Making it Open and Keeping it Safe: e-Enabled Data Sharing in Sweden," *Acta Sociologica*, 52(3): 213–26.

Barjak, F., Eccles, K., Meyer, E. T., Robinson, S., and Schroeder, R. (2013). "The Emerging Governance of e-Infrastructure," *Journal of Computer-Mediated Communication*, 18.

Becher, T. and Trowler, P. (2001). *Academic Tribes and Territories: Intellectual Inquiry and the Culture of Disciplines*, 2nd ed., Milton Keynes: Open University Press.

Boczkowski, P. J. and Lievrouw, L. A. (2008). "Bridging STS and Communication Studies: Scholarship on Media and Information Technologies," in E. J. Hackett, O. Amsterdamska, M. Lynch, and J. Wajcman (eds). *The Handbook of Science and Technology Studies*, Cambridge, MA: The MIT Press, pp. 949–77.

Borgman, C. L. (2007). *Scholarship in the Digital Age: Information, Infrastructure, and the Internet*, Cambridge, MA: MIT Press.

——Wallis, J. C., Mayernik, M. S., and Pepe, A. (2007). "Drowning in Data: Digital Library Architecture to Support Scientific Use of Embedded Sensor Networks." Paper presented at the 7th ACM IEEE-CS Joint Conference on Digital Libraries, Vancouver, BC, June 17–22.

Bulger, M., Meyer, E. T., de la Flor, G., Terras, M., Wyatt, S., Jirotka, M., Madsen, C. et al. (2011). "Reinventing Research? Information Practices in the Humanities," in *A Research Information Network Report*, London: Research Information Network.

Calambokidis, J. (2010). *Symposium on the Results of the SPLASH Humpback Whale Study: Final Report and Recommendations*, Olympia, WA: Cascadia Research.

——Falcone, E. A., Quinn, T. J., Burdin, A. M., Clapham, P., Ford, J. K. B., Maloney, N. et al. (2008). "SPLASH: Structure of Populations, Levels of Abundance and Status of Humpback Whales in the North Pacific," Final report for Contract AB133F-03-RP-00078, Seattle, WA: U.S. Department of Commerce.

Crombie, A. C. (1994). *Styles of Scientific Thinking in the European Tradition: The History of Argument and Explanation Especially in the Mathematical and Biomedical Sciences and Arts*, London: Duckworth.

Crowe, E. P. (2008). *Genealogy Online*, 8th edn., Columbus, OH: McGraw-Hill.

David, P. and Spence, M. (2003). "Towards Institutional Infrastructures for e-Science: The Scope of the Challenge," Oxford Internet Institute, Research Report No. 2. *Oxford Internet Institute Research Reports*. Available at <http://www.oii.ox.ac.uk/resources/publications/RR2.pdf>. Accessed October 29, 2007.

den Besten, M., Thomas, A., and Schroeder, R. (2009). "Life Science Research and Drug Discovery at the Turn of the 21st Century: The Experience of SwissBioGrid," *Journal of Biomedical Discovery and Collaboration*, 4(5). Available at <http://www.uic.edu/htbin/cgiwrap/bin/ojs/index.php/jbdc/issue/view/286>. Accessed May 18, 2012.

Dutton, W. H. (2011). "The Politics of Next Generation Research: Democratizing Research-Centred Computational Networks," *Journal of Information Technology*, 26: 109–19.

——and Jeffreys, P. (2010a). "World Wide Research: An Introduction," in W. H. Dutton and P. Jeffreys (eds). *World Wide Research: Reshaping the Sciences and Humanities*, Cambridge, MA: The MIT Press, pp. 1–17.

——and Jeffreys, P. (eds) (2010b). *World Wide Research: Reshaping the Sciences and Humanities*, Cambridge, MA: The MIT Press.

Eysenbach, G., Powell, J., Kuss, O., and Sa, E. R. (2002). "Empirical Studies Assessing the Quality of Health Information for Consumers on the World Wide Web: A Systematic Review," *Journal of the American Medical Association*, 287(20): 2691–700.

Fielding, N., Lee, R. M., and Blank, G. (eds) (2008). *The Sage Handbook of Online Research Methods*, London/Thousand Oaks: Sage.

Fry, J. and Schroeder, R. (2010). "Disciplinary Differences in e-Research," in W. H. Dutton and P. Jeffreys (eds). *World Wide Research: Reshaping the Sciences and Humanities*, Cambridge, MA: The MIT Press, pp. 257–75.

Fuchs, S. (2001). *Against Essentialism: A Theory of Culture and Society*, Cambridge, MA: Harvard University Press.

Gläser, J. (2003). "What Internet Use Does and Does Not Change in Scientific Communities," *Science Studies*, 16(1): 38–51.

——(2006). *Wissenschaftliche Produktionsgemeinschaften: Die Soziale Ordnung der Forschung*, Frankfurt: Campus Verlag.

Hacking, I. (1983). *Representing and Intervening*, Cambridge: Cambridge University Press.

——(2002). *Historical Ontology*, Cambridge, MA: Harvard University Press.

——(2009). *Scientific Reason*, Taipei: National Taiwan University Press.

Hesse, B. W., Nelson, D. E., Kreps, G. L., Croyle, R. T., Arora, N. K., Rimer, B. K., and Viswanath, K. (2005). "Trust and Sources of Health Information. The Impact of the Internet and its Implications for Health Care Providers: Findings from the First Health Information National Trends Survey," *Archives of Internal Medicine*, 165(22): 2618–24.

Jackson, S. J., Edwards, P. N., Bowker, G. C., and Knobel, C. P. (2007). "Understanding Infrastructure: History, Heuristics, and Cyberinfrastructure Policy," *First Monday*, 12(6). Available at <http://firstmonday.org/htbin/cgiwrap/bin/ojs/index.php/fm/article/view/1904/1786>. Accessed May 18, 2012.

Knorr Cetina, K. (1999). *Epistemic Cultures: How the Sciences Make Knowledge*, Cambridge, MA: Harvard University Press.

Lintott, C. J., Schawinski, K., Slosar, A., Land, K., Bamford, S., Thomas, D., Vandenberg, J. et al. (2008). "Galaxy Zoo: Morphologies Derived from Visual Inspection of Galaxies from the Sloan Digital Sky Survey," *Monthly Notices of the Royal Astronomical Society*, 389(3), 1179–89.

Madsen, C. (2010). "Communities, Innovation, and Critical Mass: Understanding the Impact of Digitization on Scholarship in the Humanities through Tibetan and Himalayan Studies" Doctoral thesis, University of Oxford, Oxford, UK.

Manolio, T. A., Rodriguez, L. L., Brooks, L., The Collaborative Association Study of Psoriasis, Ballinger, D., Daly, M., Collins, F. S. et al. (2007). "New Models of Collaboration in Genome-Wide Association Studies: The Genetic Association Information Network," *Nature Genetics*, 39(9): 1045–51.

Meyer, E. T. (2009). "Moving from Small Science to Big Science: Social and Organizational Impediments to Large Scale Data Sharing," in N. Jankowski (ed.). *E-Research: Transformation in Scholarly Practice*, New York: Routledge.

—— Bulger, M., Kyriakidou-Zacharoudiou, A., Power, L., Williams, P., Venters, W., Wyatt, S. et al. (2012). "Collaborative yet Independent: Information Practices in the Physical Sciences," in Bulger et al. (ed.), *A Research Information Network Report*, London: Research Information Network.

—— and Dutton, W. H. (2009). "Top-Down e-Infrastructure Meets Bottom-Up Research Innovation: The Social Shaping of e-Research," *Prometheus*, 27(3): 239–50.

—— and Schroeder, R. (2009). "The World Wide Web of Research and Access to Knowledge," *Journal of Knowledge Management Research and Practice*, 7(3): 218–33.

Olson, G. M., Zimmerman, A., and Bos, N. D. (eds) (2008). *Scientific Collaboration on the Internet*, Cambridge, MA: MIT Press.

Raddick, M. J., Bracey, G., Gay, P. L., Lintott, C. J., Murray, P., Schawinski, K., Vandenberg, J. et al. (2010). "Galaxy Zoo: Exploring the Motivations of Citizen Science Volunteers," *Astronomy Education Review*, 9(1). Available at <http://dx.doi.org/10.3847/AER2009036>. Accessed May 18, 2012.

Rieger, O. (2009). "Search Engine Use Behavior of Students and Faculty: User Perceptions and Implications for Future Research, *First Monday*, 14(12). Available at <http://firstmonday.org/htbin/cgiwrap/bin/ojs/index.php/fm/article/view/2716/2385>. Accessed May 18, 2012.

Schroeder, R. (2007). *Rethinking Science, Technology, and Social Change*, Stanford: Stanford University Press.

—— (2008). "e-Sciences as Research Technologies: Reconfiguring Disciplines, Globalizing Knowledge," *Social Science Information*, 47(2): 131–57.

—— and den Besten, M. (2008). "Literary Sleuths Online: e-Research collaboration on the Pynchon Wiki," *Information, Communication & Society*, 11(2): 167–87.

—— and Fry, J. (2007). "Social Science Approaches to e-Science: Framing an Agenda," *Journal of Computer-Mediated Communication*, 12(2): 563–582.

Shinn, T. and Joerges, B. (2002). "The Transverse Science and Technology Culture: Dynamics and Roles of Research-Technology," *Social Science Information*, 41(2): 207–51.

Shrum, W., Genuth, J., and Chompalov, I. (2007). *Structures of Scientific Collaboration*, Cambridge, MA: The MIT Press.

Whitley, R. (2000). *The Intellectual and Social Organization of the Sciences*, 2nd edn., Oxford: Oxford University Press.

Willinsky, J. (2005). *The Access Principle*, Cambridge, MA: MIT Press.

Yakel, E. (2004). "Seeking Information, Seeking Connections, Seeking Meaning: Genealogists and Family Historians," *Information Research*, 10(1). Available at <http://informationr.net/ir/10-1/paper205.html>. Accessed May 18, 2012.

Zheng, Y., Venters, W., and Cornford, T. (2011). "Agility, Paradox and Organizational Improvisation: The Development of a Particle Physics Grid," *Information Systems Journal*, 21(4): 303–333.

CHAPTER 16

STUDIES OF THE INTERNET IN LEARNING AND EDUCATION: BROADENING THE DISCIPLINARY LANDSCAPE OF RESEARCH

CHRIS DAVIES AND REBECCA EYNON

> New technologies and broadband Internet access offer formidable opportunities for increasing access to education. They make new learning opportunities possible. They add a new dimension to how we deliver literacy programs, train teachers, manage schools and share knowledge.[1]

THIS statement from the Director-General of UNESCO, delivered in June 2011, could have been made at any time since the end of the last century. While expectations of what the Internet might deliver for education have remained more or less the same throughout its life, its actual contribution to education has proved to be no more stable and predictable than any other aspect of its development since the World Wide Web came into being in the early 1990s. Indeed, much research in the field of educational technology in general, and with respect to the Internet in particular, has been driven by fairly speculative explorations of what technology might do for learning, reflecting a tendency within educational policy to see technology as the "fix" or "solution" for many educational challenges (Robins and

---

[1] From introductory remarks by the Director-General of UNESCO, Irina Bokova, to the Education Working Group of the Broadband Commission for Digital Development, June 6, 2011 at UNESCO Headquarters. See <http://www.unesco.org/new/en/unesco/themes/icts/single-view/news/education_at_the_broadband_commission/>. Accessed 13/6/11.

Webster 1989). It appears that the task of building a solid corpus of understandings about its educational potential is proving to be a slower process than expected.

Research in this field is not helped, either, by a lack of clear ownership of the research agenda concerning Internet-based learning and education. While such research might seem at first to belong in the domain of "educational technology," in reality this is a contested field, lacking any serious sense of coherence or location. This fluidity is demonstrated by the wide range of terms that are used to describe work that goes on in this somewhat ill-defined space (e.g. learning technology, instructional design, computer assisted learning, computer supported collaborative learning, technology enhanced learning, and e-learning), as well as the lack of agreement about ontology and epistemology, appropriate disciplinary choices, overall identity, and boundaries of the field (Czerniewicz 2008: 171).

One particularly interesting challenge for the identity of the field is the close relationship between academic work in this area and the practical implementation of technology into educational institutions. As Czerniewicz notes, "simultaneously and in overlapping ways, a new professional field is coming into being and a new knowledge field (or professional discipline) is emerging" (2008: 172). While in some ways this is an exciting and beneficial relationship we believe this can also have negative implications in terms of the research questions that tend to be asked, which may at times lack a critical perspective—concentrating instead on the practical issues involved around technology and learning.

Research in this emerging field tends to draw on a number of disciplines, including those already associated with the study of education throughout the twentieth century, such as psychology and sociology, and more recent areas of interest such as social psychology, sociometrics, computer science, Internet and media studies, and—quite recently—new literacy studies, a field which warmly embraced the Internet as a site for the study of multiple discourses. While such disciplines allow for research of a theoretically serious nature, there are nonetheless many areas of educational activity—those that find particularly strong resonance with the educational application of the Internet, such as professional development in commercial organizations, medical education, and language learning (e.g. Lam 2000)—which favor small-scale, localized case studies and small-scale studies incorporating experimental designs in the field. These kinds of methods are typically used to provide best practice examples and solutions to overcome the barriers to implementation, and to demonstrate the effectiveness of technology over other modes of learning. While these issues are important, such work tends to see technology as offering certain benefits which educators simply need to harness (Selwyn 2010; Oliver 2011).

In this chapter, we shall explore the ways in which the Internet is seen as potentially transforming the landscape of learning, and the ways in which research of various kinds is attempting to make sense of what is inevitably a disparate and unpredictable field of activity. In order to do so, we shall begin by distinguishing between different kinds of educational activity on the core dimension of formal and informal learning.

DISTINGUISHING BETWEEN FORMAL
AND INFORMAL LEARNING

By formal learning, we mean learning that is designated, designed, and managed by educators on behalf of learners, within institutions such as schools, colleges, and workplaces. By informal learning we mean what happens outside of the structures and boundaries of formal education, the topic or focus of which is determined by the person doing the learning, on their own or with others. This notion of informal learning also encompasses episodes of learning that are not initially, or perhaps ever, viewed by the learner as learning at all (sometimes referred to as pre-conscious learning or incidental learning; see Jarvis 2007: 22).

This distinction is less determined by where the work of learning is done than by how it has been generated. As Crook and Light argue, formal learning involves the application of certain cultural practices, such as focusing on texts, attending lectures and seminars, or working in laboratories (2002: 158), but the existence or otherwise of underlying curriculum motivation is key here. One might say that formal learning is bounded whereas informal is not. There are advantages and disadvantages to either state: the greatest difficulty faced by the self-motivated learner is in knowing where to start and when to stop, or whether they are on the right track at all. On the other hand, experienced teachers look for ways to make the required content of the curriculum feel like a choice learners have made for themselves in order to create a sense of ownership.

There is, of course, a close relationship between much formal and informal learning. While recognizing that "every aspect of life, at both the individual and the social level, offers opportunities for both learning and doing," the Delors Report for UNESCO (1996: 19) offers a traditional account of a learning trajectory over the life-course that moves smoothly from formal to informal, building on "a sound basic education" and encouraging "both the desire for, and pleasure in, learning, the ability to learn how to learn, and intellectual curiosity" (Delors 1996: 19). Within such a model, informal learning is seen as drawing on the same practices as formal, but in a context of increased individual choice once beyond the bounds of the formal.

Crook and Light, talking specifically of students in higher education institutions, see the relationship between formal and informal learning as rather more of a two-way process: "living in an educational context comprises the 'formal' and the 'informal.' This contrast is still broadly about life within the curriculum and life outside it, but the contrast seems more readily to admit a possibility of traffic between the activity settings" (2002: 158). It is likely that such two-way traffic, between the practices and cultures of formal and informal learning, will have increased substantially in the years since that study, as a direct consequence of the increased prominence of the Internet in students' lives.

While this distinction between formal and informal learning is not new (Coffield 2000), it is a crucial starting point for discussing the ways in which the Internet is reshaping the whole picture of learning because it is along that particular dimension that the ways in which it does so vary most vividly and significantly. This is something that has become increasingly apparent over recent years, and was not necessarily the case when serious efforts to engage the power and scope of the Internet for learning first began in earnest.

As far back as 1978, James Martin predicted with some accuracy that "[i]n the future a community with good schools may be expected to provide good computerized education via the community cables. Children will learn and do their homework with this facility, under direction of local schools" (1978: 233). He also saw considerable scope for the commercial expansion of education through new technologies, in terms very similar to those which briefly excited venture capitalists and educational software companies during the late 1990s: "the production of good computer-assisted instruction is a highly skilled, professional operation. One day a substantial industry will grow up to produce such programs. It may become an industry the size of Hollywood and just as professional" (1978: 234). Both he and Bill Gates (a number of years later) anticipated that new technologies, and especially the Internet, would make their greatest contribution to education through making well-produced traditional content and pedagogies available on a global scale, reflecting a widespread expectation that the key benefit would be the democratization of educational access:

> The highway will bring together the best work of countless teachers and authors for everyone to share. (Gates 1995: 185)

This, in fact, remained core to Microsoft's vision of what the role of the Internet might signify for learning throughout the first decade of the twenty-first century: instant access via a range of devices to beautifully produced content, alongside global connections to peers and excellent teachers (e.g. Zheng 2009). It does look though, as the second decade of this century gets underway, that the attractions of the Cloud, as a means of creating economically attractive technological and commercial solutions to data storage, sharing, and management, might rapidly shift the paradigm from enhanced learning resources to those that are less costly, far more widely available, and more easily accessed in different parts of the world:

> Make productivity easier by giving everyone endless ways to work and collaborate from anywhere at any time and on any device. In the cloud you make the rules.[2]

The Cloud actually consists of industrial-scale data centres located in various parts of the world that need to be marketed energetically within a range of markets, including education. Needless to say, this investment has lifted cloud computing to the current top of Gartner's hype curve (Gartner Group 2010), in the field of education as much as any.

The growth and constant morphing of the World Wide Web since its inception has led to a world of online practices—in largely unplanned and unmanaged ways—that provide a powerful context for accessing knowledge in very different ways from those

---

[2] Microsoft Cloud Power, <http://www.microsoft.com/en-ie/cloud/default.aspx>. Accessed June 20, 2012.

earlier somewhat top-down visions of making high status knowledge widely available.³ Such a shift in the dynamics of learning, from the long-established belief in formal education as the gold standard that defines and enables all further engagement with learning, towards modes of informal learning which are active, self-determined, potentially collaborative, not necessarily viewed as learning at all, and not necessarily developed out of the practices of formal learning, is more than democratizing existing notions of learning: it also has implications for the future of formal education itself.

This chapter looks next in more detail at how the Internet has been engaged to support and enable innovative practices in formal education at different levels. The subsequent section will then look at how the Internet has—via the World Wide Web—enabled the expansion in informal and incidental learning opportunities.

THE ROLE OF THE INTERNET
WITHIN FORMAL LEARNING

Post compulsory education

Greater strides towards incorporating the Internet into educational provision have been made in some parts of higher and continuing education than in other sectors. This is primarily because older students are normally able to make more flexible choices about modes of study than children can, and is also due to the diversity of the kinds of courses offered to a range of different students in post compulsory settings.

Reasons for using the Internet for learning and teaching in the post compulsory sector vary depending on the context, nature of the course, and the target audience. For example, the Internet is a particularly good way of supporting education that happens at a distance and which requires more flexibility (e.g. part-time courses, courses with a strong vocational element or for continuing professional development) and when used appropriately can offer a great deal of educational value compared to more traditional methods such as paper-based study packs or support via the telephone. For example, in developing economies such as in Brazil—with very large geographical distances between population centres, and many remote locations—the expansion of educational opportunity to include those who cannot hope to attend major educational centres in person is seen as key to its economic and cultural growth (*Portaria* 4.059 2004).

---

³ Foreseen, it appears, in 1995 in an article by J. Pickering (according to Gray 1999: 122), who advocated the potential of the Internet to enable new forms of learning, through the "post-modern curriculum of the Internet catalogue."

Online learning in the developed world

Many national systems see the emphasis on online education as a means of moving the work population and economy further along to a position where it can compete effectively in a global knowledge economy (Reich 1991; Jarvis 1999). While none of these assumptions should go unquestioned (Robins and Webster 2002; Selwyn 2007), this move can be seen in developed countries across the globe, including the United States. "Online enrolments have continued to grow at rates far in excess of the total higher education student population, with the most recent data demonstrating no signs of slowing" (Allen and Seaman 2010: 1). Between 2002 and 2008, enrollment in online courses has grown from 9.6 percent of total enrollment, to 25.3 percent, and the evidence suggests that the peak of such enrollment has not yet been reached. But despite this growth in demand, faculty acceptance of online courses, along with levels of training provided or taken up for teaching online, remains relatively low (Allen and Seaman 2010: 12).

Institutions with extensive familiarity in providing such courses tend to anticipate high drop-out rates (estimating higher than those without substantial experience), but it is likely that students enrolling in such courses tend to be coping with greater obstacles to study, such as holding down jobs, looking after families, or lack of resources. Furthermore, online learning at a distance presents a range of challenges to learners that can significantly affect their learning experiences and this needs to be considered (Hara and Kling 2002; Dabaj and Isman 2004), and will be discussed further below. Nonetheless, despite these challenges, the reality is that, for many individuals, this form of learning and teaching is the best option for them to gain access to further and higher education.

South Korea has focused particularly hard in this respect on making higher education widely available over the Internet. Hanyang Cyber University, which started operations in 2002 and now has 13,200 online students, focuses in particular on "fields and skills most in demand in the marketplace" and promises that its graduates will become leading figures of the twenty-first century knowledge society. All of South Korea's cyber universities appear to share the vision, expressed by the President of Daegu Cyber University, of seeking to achieve "the development and upgrading of the entire Korean society through the linkage role connecting the domestic to the outside globalizing world in the years to come" (Young Sae 2009).

The UK has also made efforts to develop online learning through its Online Learning Task Force, bringing together leading higher education institutions in the field of online learning such as the Open University, King's College London, and the University of Wolverhampton, with key commercial interests such as Microsoft, Apple, and Pearson. This focus is related to the economic downturn in 2009/10, with the recession leading "to many more people wanting flexible arrangements that allow them to combine work and study," according to the Task Force's chair (Attwood 2010). This has taken place in a context in which the UK's Open University has firmly established itself as the leading provider of online learning in the country, for reasons of educational quality as much as economic pragmatism, and continues to earn its positive reputation by having proved adaptable to changing conditions for learning, in terms both of economic problems and increased opportunity for online study:

> Many courses still have face-to-face tutorials, but more and more of the tuition is moving online....Intellectual exchange happens online, and tutors have to learn whole new ways to encourage interaction, moderate arguments and keep dialogue flowing, not to mention a whole new language of e-learning....Open University learning is a joy. (Horne 2010)

But while the Internet and other new technologies have long been viewed as providing ways of improving efficiency and effectiveness in a variety of aspects of educational provision, such as helping to improve personalization, access and flexibility, widening participation, promoting lifelong learning, and reducing costs (Buckingham 2007; Gell and Cochrane 1996), such optimistic expectations have not necessarily related as much to educational improvement as they do to economic benefit. For example, from an analysis of policy documents in the UK, Selwyn suggests that the promotion of new technologies in education was based more on the belief in efficiency drives than truly enhancing pedagogy (Selwyn 2008), along with the commercial drive from technology industries focusing on the education market.

Similarly, optimistic views of the power of technology meant little account was taken of the needs or experiences of learners in previous years of online learning provision. Such a view (for example in the case of initiatives that have tried to use new technologies to widen participation) have at times compounded and reinforced existing challenges and inequalities rather than reducing them (Conole and Oliver 2006). The UK's "eUniversity," (intended to promote the UK as a global leader in online education) is a classic example of policy-makers making unfounded assumptions about demands for online education. The initiative was pulled after £64m of Government money was committed and only 900 students enrolled in the first year (the target was 5,600) (Garrett 2004).

Approaches to online teaching have not necessarily developed in line with the expansion of infrastructure and take-up. The rhetoric of online higher education (and school education for that matter) has tried to move on from an approach that grew out of instructional design (Gagné 1977) to something claiming more of a social constructivist approach, but the logistics of wholly online delivery tend to undermine progress in these respects. It seems that hierarchically managed collaboration on the Internet does not necessarily lead to open dialogue, open knowledge sharing, or engaging co-construction of understanding.

Earlier attempts at using these tended to cause discomfort and anxiety among students unfamiliar with the conventions and practices of online communities. Hara and Kling describe the confusions and embarrassments for students of trying to engage in online discussions:

> Katie...was overwhelmed by her first experience of the fast pace of communication and felt frustrated at not being able to figure out why she could not operate her intended commands. (Hara and Kling 2002: 69)

In 1997, it seems the problems related to a combination of unreliable networks and unknown online social expectations, none of which would concern most students grounded in the more familiar social behaviors of Facebook ten years later: "I don't like...turning on the computer and finding that I have eleven messages on my e-mail....I mean to answer that many things, just talking in conversation would be so much easier, rather than replying and doing all the stuff you have to do." Around the same time, de Pourbaix's study of an online course in a Canadian university showed students learning how to cope with substantively different modes of expression and interaction:

> Initial essay type postings, possibly written to display skills, and directed, even if obliquely, at the course teacher under the guise of answering a topic-posting group's questions, evolved into meaningful interaction among community members....During the process of electronic discussion, expectations and standards—acceptable practices—evolved in terms of what was considered to be suitable content and format in postings. Role changes occurred, with corresponding changes in responsibility, both in group and individual identities. (de Pourbaix 2000: 135–6)

Online courses are built on notions of teaching that are easily replicable, and reflect approaches developed in distance learning courses prior to the widespread availability of the Internet. This has led to a relatively limited repertoire of pedagogical approaches, often reflecting the more negative aspects of the earlier days of the Open University model of teaching and learning, which was widely seen as being too dependent on "programmed learning, behavioural objectives, tight study deadlines and computer-marked assignments", leading to criticisms of "the commodification of knowledge" and a largely transmission-based approach to teaching (Woodley 2007: 59). Woodley optimistically suggests that "as we move into the a system of e-learning it seems that teaching methods could go in several directions," with heavily programmed learning at one extreme and students feeling free to construct their own learning at the other, especially through participating in networks with other learners.

More typically, online learning continues to be managed along more traditional pedagogic lines, in which collaboration between learners is designed into the learning experience by educators, for instance on the kind of basis illustrated by Salmon's five-part model (2002: 10), which places key importance on the teacher (or e-moderator in Salmon's terminology). Her model of learning offers structured progress through initial stages of participation, learning to engage socially online, and expansion of information exchange, towards the key goals of knowledge construction, individual development, and increasingly independent learning. Key to the success of such progression, according to Salmon, are appropriately designed activities at each stage, and the experienced support of e-moderators.

For the most part, online courses are managed via learning management systems, or virtual learning environments, which are more successful when it comes to administration of courses, recording participation, distributing resources, and providing resources such as discussion forums to large numbers of students, than they are at providing a context for progressive pedagogies, for establishing effective relations between teachers and learners, for maintaining engagement in study, and for assessing the outcomes of such learning in appropriate ways (Selwyn 2007). Such systems can fairly be said to "deliver" learning in abundance, but not necessarily to provide the quality assurance of what happens to it after it arrives.

Online learning in the developing world

Such concerns are as yet quite far down the line when it comes to the provision of online learning in many parts of the developing world, where digital inequality often prevents any form of access. This is an area of development that is gaining increased attention currently. For example, Gordon Brown, as a member of the board of Tim Berners-Lee's World Wide Web Foundation, has used his public profile since leaving his role as UK premier in 2010 to promote the economic and educational benefits of the Internet for Africa:

> I truly believe that the rapid expansion of internet access in Africa could transform how Africa trades, learns and holds political power accountable. (Brown 2010: 16)

Irina Bokova of UNESCO (whose speech to the Broadband Commission for Digital Development in June 2011 was quoted as the start of this chapter) suggested that Internet connectivity in countries such as Africa involves improvements in basic infrastructure as the condition for connectivity, partnerships between public and private sectors, better training of teachers, and content development and knowledge sharing through "digital libraries and open educational resources" (Bokova, cited in UNESCO 2011). But she also acknowledges the fundamental and essential fact that broadband access in much of the developing world is very poor, and disproportionately expensive:

> Despite encouraging trends, Africa continues to stand out for its relatively high prices. Fixed broadband Internet access in particular remains prohibitively high, and, across the region as a whole, still represents almost three times the monthly average per capita income. Only one out of ten people in Africa is using the Internet. (UNESCO 2011)

Stephane Boyera, from the World Wide Web Foundation, acknowledges that access to the Internet varies dramatically across Sub-Saharan Africa, especially between urban and rural areas. In rural areas, he suggests, the mobile phone appears to offer greater advantages for learning, although he knows of little actual evidence showing "where mobile has been a real platform for course delivery" (Boyera 2011). Most studies come to the same conclusion. In a technical evaluation report for the International Review of Research in Open and Distance Learning, Motlik questions the prospects of developing mobile learning as a solution for developing nations, making the point that if the "developed" nations of Asia are unable to properly implement e-learning projects, "what hope is there for the lesser developed nations of Asia and the world?" He considers that the best solution for many seems to lie in the expansion of mobile technologies in those very many parts of the world where Internet access is too costly to consider on any comprehensive scale.

While the diffusion of mobile phones lags behind many Asian countries, and notably China, Motlik claims that the educational use of mobile phones is "gaining momentum in Africa." He quotes a study by T. Brown in 2003 that suggested that mobile learning "has already started to play a very important role in e-learning in Africa," and that the growth of m-learning "has brought e-learning to the rural communities of Africa to learners that we never imagined as e-learning learners just a few years ago" (Motlik 2008: 11). The same possibilities are true for India which, although the world's third largest Internet population in 2010, nonetheless has one of the world's lowest Internet penetration levels, at 8.4 percent (Tan 2011). Again, though, there are very few substantial studies that demonstrate that mobile technologies, despite their massive superiority in terms of numbers and connectivity, are more viable in terms of providing and sustaining Internet-based learning.

A closely related issue has been the proliferation of initiatives to open up educational resources to increase access and participation in higher education in a range of country contexts. The Open Educational Resources (OER) movement is growing rapidly, with iTunes U, Academic Earth, the Open Courseware Consortium, MIT opencourseware and OpenLearn as just some of the plethora of examples of initiatives in this area. However, while such initiatives are to be applauded, important questions still remain as to the longevity of such projects (due to the large resources involved in opening up content), issues of interoperability and copyright, and, importantly, if and how OER is used both by individuals and institutions for supporting learning both in formal and informal contexts (OECD 2007). Indeed, in terms of the reuse of OER, take up and adaption is relatively low, both in developed and developing countries (Hatakka 2009).

Clearly, though, the expansion of connectivity in various ways, especially through mobile networks, constitutes a significant step towards equity on a global scale in terms of opportunities to gain new skills, qualifications, and some degree of participation in wider communities. Unfortunately, the weaknesses of distance online learning do not cease to be weaknesses just because the need for such provision is so much greater, and indeed the problems are possibly more acute in the developing world, and not necessarily amenable to following approaches used successfully in the developed world:

> The OU model has all too often been taken into quite a different context with little pragmatic adaptation to the local situation. (Kember 2007: 60)

Such necessary pragmaticism relates especially, according to Kember, to issues such as understanding the nature of the students following the online courses, in terms especially of their previous histories of study, and the ways in which these relate to core issues of how self-determined they need to be as learners, or how amenable to highly structured study. The matching of provision to local needs and conditions will prove to be as crucial, it is suggested, as the existence of networks to make such provision possible.

Face-to-face and blended learning

The notion of blended learning has become increasingly redundant as a specific term of art, in that it is difficult to envisage higher education that does not in some ways or other engage with a blend of new technologies within the primary context of face-to-face teaching and learning to some extent. The main form of such engagement, at the formal level, is via learning management or content management systems (known under a variety of acronyms in different parts of the world), which have become as much part of university resources and infrastructure now (in the developed world at least) as the library. Sometimes these systems are simply aspects of a university's intranet, making administrative, communicative, and academic resources conveniently available at all times. Increasingly, they are used to manage the submission and marking of student work, and as a vehicle for developing student e-portfolios (e.g. Mason et al. 2004; Conole and Warburton 2005).

As such, face-to-face teaching and learning is very usefully supported by a range of planning, content delivery, and communication tools that significantly enhance the experience of study, without in any profound way raising new possibilities in terms of epistemology, power relations, collaboration, or learner autonomy. In terms of pedagogy, it does not appear that the almost universal availability of online learning systems has changed very much about the nature of pedagogy or learning, so much as it has made those things easier and more efficient, and more capable of transmitting information and resources more rapidly than was possible before. In essence, the Internet is used to reinforce existing pedagogical practices rather than radically transform learning and teaching—similar to what Morrison and Svennevig (2001) term "functional amplifications."

Increasingly, also, they represent a means of organizing and making available learning materials. These systems have gradually been developed to allow students to have flexible access to course information and resources wherever they are, sometimes through mobile devices (e.g. Evans 2008). Attempts are often made to apply the kinds of tools for learning made available through distance learning versions of such systems—such as forums and chat-rooms—to the needs of face-to-face learning, but without marked success in many cases. Such attempts do in fact mark a key meeting point between formal and informal practices (another aspect, perhaps, of the two-way traffic that Crook and Light refer to), especially as students worldwide become immersed in their own informal networks through Facebook or alternatives.

There have been attempts from within the system to explore how technologies can contribute to a more radical rethinking of teaching and learning. Laurillard has long advocated a university pedagogy that is constructed upon iterative dialogue between teacher and student, which she argues is capable of transforming learning, even if it does leave existing power relations intact. Such dialogue should, she insists, address activities and media which are "discursive, adaptive, interactive and reflective," with the ultimate aim of linking "the world of experience and the world of academic representations of experience" (2002: 83–6). Her conversational framework, which applies rather more to face-to-face and blended learning than to distance, places the responsibility for making the learning happen firmly on university teachers.

While there is good evidence of improved learning experiences from the considerable number of projects exploring what technological solutions work best, and how best to implement these—for instance by the JISC (Joint Information Systems Committee) in the UK—there is little evidence of the contribution of network technologies amounting to significantly more than the provision of useful and valued tools to support and ease the processes of making learning happen. These are valuable innovations, but do not necessarily represent qualitative advances in the nature of learning and education.

Compulsory education

When the Internet first became widely available in schools, during the early 2000s, there was a great deal of talk of it enabling learners to take a more active role in their own learning. This was a vision that Seymour Papert had envisaged decades earlier, in which computers would replace what he, and many others, had characterized as the largely passive nature of classroom learning with "an empowering sense of one's own ability to learn anything one wants to know" (Papert 1982: 32). Such a vision lingered in the consciousness of educators who were advocating a rapid move to the creation of circumstances whereby young learners were expected to engage directly with the Internet once broadband became established in schools. In its "Vision for the Future of ICT in Schools," even the UK Government was expressing the hope that information and communications technology (ICT), through appropriate and effective application, could enable "pupils of all abilities to take greater control of their learning" (DfES/NGfL 2002: 8). Research at that time (Becta 2003) stated as one of the key benefits of ICT, alongside increased commitment and self-esteem, "increased independence and motivation for self-directed study," citing recent research that supported the prospect of broadband Internet helping pupils to "explore independently and to achieve their own goals" (ibid. 1).

In reality, progress towards embedding uses of the Internet into learning activities within the classroom is hampered by the need to show—to parents, school governing boards, and so on—that care is being taken to protect young people from undesirable content. This is not to say that there is no excellent Internet-enabled work ever done in classrooms, but more often the Internet serves as a fairly low level supplier of safe and largely pre-digested content, or a short reward for good work in the form of a more-or-less educational clip from YouTube. The baseline norm of Internet use in schools tends to revolve around the following:

- guided searching of teacher-preselected websites for specific projects or investigations
- some freestyle student searching of the Internet, without substantial guidance on how to formulate searches
- collection by students of short segments of information and images for inclusion in project work, essays, and PowerPoint presentations
- presentation of teacher and student presentations via the interactive whiteboard.

It appears that teachers now understand that students can use the Internet more freely at home than at school, and thus have learnt to set such activities for homework, obviously creating difficulties for students who have to stay behind and use school resources to do the same work. Resources within schools are variable at best (Warschauer et al. 2004), still tending to be found in large computer suites where access is dependent on internal power relations between different subject departments and teachers. Good work takes many forms: making podcasts for language learning, inter-school discussions for moral education, video and radio production, collaborative group blogs, and so on.

It has proved extremely difficult to deploy the web practices of Web 2.0 within the classroom in any kind of sustainable ways (Crook et al. 2008). Efforts by schools and individual teachers to deploy the Internet in order to enhance the lines of communications between school and home, especially with regard to homework assignments, are gradually gaining traction, although the majority of schools in the UK have encountered greater difficulties in getting these going than was originally intended. A UK study that compared innovation currently taking place in schools noted that the interactive whiteboard (IWB), which can readily be found being used in ways that fit squarely within the traditional teaching culture of classroom exposition and illustration, represented mainly low-level innovation, being seen generally as an "easy entry technology" in contrast with learning platforms (LPs), which more often were rapidly coming to be viewed as "problematic innovations," and tended to be "key to the spread of technology uptake across a school." On the other hand, learning platforms, when actually used, were proving to be associated with more dramatic improvements in practice, compared with interactive whiteboards (Underwood et al. 2010: 7).

The difficulties in embedding digital technologies into formal schooling are commonly experienced in many school systems. In Norway, Erstad et al. acknowledge that "schools seem to be struggling with implementing digital technologies into formal school activities" (2007: 183), reflecting discussions over many years by authors such as Cuban (2001) in the USA, Conlon and Simpson (2003) in Scotland, and Buckingham (2007) in the UK. Possible explanations include things like the lack of appropriate training and lack of "time to find out about appropriate resources" (Buckingham 2007: 58), but this seems to us to be a somewhat unconvincing and weak line of argument which pays insufficient attention to the central issue of whether or not classroom learning can *ever* constitute a suitable environment for the large scale use of network technologies at all. This is, in effect, a question of learning ecologies (Barron 2006), and in particular the very special kind of ecology created in classrooms. The teaching and learning that takes place in classrooms not surprisingly favors technologies which enable the teacher to manage and maintain the focus of attention and discourses within the classroom in ways that are not easy if individuals are privately engaged with their own trajectories of enquiry and interest, even if apparently working harmoniously as part of the larger group. In his paper "Has Classroom Teaching Served its Day," McIntyre explores the difficulties teachers face in dealing effectively with the complexity and information overload that are characteristic of a modern classroom, even without technology playing a part, but when that too comes into play he acknowledges that:

> Classroom teaching seems peculiarly ill-suited to most of the more exciting possibilities for using information technology to enhance the quality of learning in schools. (McIntyre 2002: 137)

He then moves on to what is still a more radical conclusion, noting "the strong boundary... between classroom learning and learning in other contexts" which he says has been accepted for long enough, suggesting that if they are to enhance their effectiveness and usefulness, "schools must... find ways of organizing learning activities so that these normally, not just exceptionally, relate to pupils' learning in other contexts" (McIntyre 2002: 137). To a limited but significant extent, the notion of the learning platform as it is conceived within school settings is beginning to enable just that kind of cross-context organization of learning, creating synergies between school learning practices and home learning practices (all within the ambit of formal learning).

But the real step forward, arguably, comes when the school's conception of learning becomes more responsive to the learning practices that are constructed quite independently entirely outside the contexts of formal learning. Most evident in this respect currently are the practices of information sharing, discussion, and collaborative problem solving that young people are managing for themselves through their Facebook networks, and some of these practices are also extending to incorporate uses of Twitter and other developing networks.

These are the kinds of possibility which emerge when we look more closely at informal practices online, which is the focus of the next section.

THE ROLE OF THE INTERNET WITHIN INFORMAL LEARNING

It is impossible to say when a degree of curiosity in or tentative exploration of new areas of knowledge or activity via the Internet can be described as informal learning (Sefton-Green 2004). At the very least, we would suggest that, to be recognized as learning, an activity must involve either a conscious and explicit effort to learn (regardless of outcome), or must result in a lasting change to the fund of what a person knows or can do (regardless of intent). People go online for all sorts of reasons, but the instant availability of information, knowledge, belief, assertionm and argument available on the Internet has resulted in an unprecedented explosion in the scope and availability of what might lead to informal learning—whether systematically pursued, vaguely hoped-for, or completely unintended—to the extent that learning might be seen as one of the primary activities taking place on the Internet, and one of the primary outcomes from using it.

The Internet allows for two quite distinct kinds of learning activity: solitary practices of exploration such as online information seeking (Rieh 2004), and networked modes of sharing (including: interacting and communicating via virtual communities or communities of practice, creating content (Rollett et al. 2007), playing games such as *World of Warcraft*, and engaging in other virtual environments like Second Life). The difficulties of deploying the Internet in classrooms point to a fundamental problem: using the Internet is not a spectator activity, but rather it is something that has to be individually driven. Groups work well together on the Internet when they are constituted of individuals dispersed across it, each managing their participation in front of their own screen. Given the fact that individualized exploration on the Internet is generally personalized, self-directed, and often haphazard, and given that the networks that most people belong to on the Internet are mainly non-hierarchical, there is considerable scope and stimulus on the Internet for people—of any age—to act differently from, and outside, the familiar bounds and practices of formal learning. This offers considerable scope for discovery, stimulus, and rapid progress, but not necessarily the sustained engagement with content and the gradual constructions of understanding by teacher and learners that are normally thought of as essential components of learning. Something quite different is taking place when people are learning in the non-formal contexts of the Internet.

Ito et al., in their influential report on the Digital Youth Project for the MacArthur Foundation, set the scene vividly for the new world of informal learning, which they describe as self-directed and peer-based, at least with respect to what young people do:

> Our focus is on describing learning outside of school, primarily in settings of peer-based interaction.... Our cases demonstrate that some of the drivers of self-motivated learning come not from institutionalized "authorities" setting standards and providing instruction, but from youth observing and communicating with people engaged in the same interests, and in the same struggles for status and recognition, as they are. (Ito et al. 2008: 11)

The report proposes three categories of youth engagement with the Internet, all of which have specific implications for learning: hanging out, messing around, and geeking out. Hanging out, the report explains, is the "desire to maintain social connections to friends," while messing around "represents the beginning of a more intense, media-centric form of engagement" in which young people begin to focus more on "looking around, searching for information online, and experimentation and play with gaming and digital media production"(Ito et al. 2008: 20). The report sees this stage as transitional between satisfying the desire for social connection and the more interest-driven participation that characterizes "geeking out," which involves "developing an identity and pride as an expert and seeking fellow experts in far-flung networks.... Rather than purely 'consuming' knowledge produced by authoritative sources, geeked out engagement involves accessing as well as producing knowledge to contribute to the knowledge network" (Ito et al. 2008: 29).

It is difficult to assess, though, quite how this plays out in reality: how large a proportion, in effect, of Internet users do actively participate in that process of sharing and building knowledge. A popular Internet trope proclaims the 90-9-1 principle, in which 1 percent of users are characterized as actually creating content, 9 percent as editing it, and the other 90 percent as merely consuming it (Nielsen 2006). Although this feels intuitively plausible in terms of the experience of many regular users, it conflicts sharply with the suggestion made by Jenkins et al. in their report for the MacArthur Foundation on participatory culture—drawing on a previous Pew Internet and American Life survey (Lenhardt and Madden 2005)—that "more than one-half of all teens have created media content, and roughly one-third of teens who use the Internet have shared content they produced" (Jenkins et al. 2006: 3). While one can dispute the definition of what it is to be creative online, there is evidence in current youth practices (and not confined to youth) of activity which certainly involves more than passive consumption of content. For instance, the expansion in 2009–11 of Facebook membership down through the age range, reaching into the pre-teen bracket, suggests widespread forms of engagement in online activities, networks, and culture that cannot be viewed as purely consumerist. All of these Facebook members need to learn to use the resources of the site to present and refine their individual identity, handle shared discourses, express opinions, participate in online communal activities, and evaluate resources of many kinds.

Over a similar period, an increasing number of adults have joined Facebook (Smith 2009; Eldon 2010). In the UK there was a significant jump between 2007 and 2009 in the number of adults engaging in social networking with 49 percent of employed Internet users using social networking sites in 2009 (compared to 89 percent of students and 12 percent of retired people) (Dutton et al. 2009). Similar increases can be seen in the US, where the percentage of 30–49 year old Internet users using social networking sites rose from 25 percent in 2008 to 61 percent in 2010 (Madden 2010)—so it would be a mistake to attribute these practices to young people alone. Nonetheless, it is still likely to be the case that senior Internet users (i.e. those aged 65 or older) are generally more comfortable with solitary knowledge-gathering activities, or tend to join more bounded special interest groups, and often lack the immediate peer support and encouragement to venture into the kind of open networks in which young people feel more at ease. This may change in time, as there is increasing attention towards finding ways of supporting older people in exploring the Internet with greater confidence.[4]

But we must be careful even with respect to younger people not to romanticize the extent of their membership of online peer networks, given the fact that in addition to economic barriers, as the Digital Youth Report points out, young people constantly encounter many obstacles—institutional, social, and cultural—to online participation:

[4] See e.g. <http://digitalunite.com/>. Accessed May 20, 2011.

> When kids lack access to the Internet at home, and public libraries and schools block sites that are central to their social communication, youth are doubly handicapped in their efforts to participate in common culture and sociability. (Ito et al. 2008: 36)

Similar problems have been identified in research in the UK context, that highlighted that those young people who did not have Internet access at home were more likely to use the Internet in more limited ways and to a lesser extent than other groups of young people (Livingstone and Helsper 2007; Eynon and Malmberg 2011). Long-established anxieties about the dangers of the Internet, and the supposed unreliability of sources of information such as Wikipedia, do not appear to be dissipating, so that many young people are taught by adults to be anxious about engaging in the opportunities for networking and seeking information online. Rather than assuming that young people's interactions with technology and new media are sufficient to generate engagement and new practices, in fact it now seems increasingly urgent that young people should be taught how to build productively on their spontaneous interests in the Internet. Indeed, as Jenkins warns, we cannot assume "that children and youth acquire…key skills and competencies on their own by interacting with popular culture" (Jenkins et al. 2006: 3), and neither is it sufficient to leave the initiative to those caught up in a largely anti-technicist agenda.

Blending the formal and the informal

The value of understanding people's uses of informal learning resides in the possibilities raised for exploring more hybridized approaches to Internet-related learning. To this extent, we should expect to see increasing focus not merely on the content of informal learning but also on the practices associated with them, in terms of how they can be made to connect with the concerns and goals of formal learning, and vice versa. In this respect, Jenkins' formulation of skills related to confident Internet use are highly relevant: experimentation, simulation, appropriation, multitasking, judgment, networking, and negotiation.

In effect, the impact of the Internet on learning should not be assessed simply in terms of its distinctive contributions to traditional formal and non-traditional informal practices, as separate entities. In terms of that simple opposition, the Internet's contribution to formal learning has been considerably less transformative than its contribution to informal learning. The contribution to formal learning has been wide-ranging and significant, in enabling greatly increased numbers of people to engage with learning in a wide variety of contexts; but the learning they experience there has so far tended to be fairly conservative and often traditional. On the other hand, the learning that takes place in informal settings, while often hard to identify and describe with any certainty, offers far greater choice and agency to the learner, and the possibility of breaking down disciplinary boundaries and encouraging learning practices.

Our argument, though, is that the value of this Internet-enabled informal learning—which very often tends, through its unbounded and undirected nature, to be unsustained and fragmentary—lies in the cross-over from informal online practices to formal educational practices, and in formal education's capacity to accommodate the core elements of informal online learning, such as high impact engagement, collaborative activity, and individual choice.

SUMMARY

This chapter began by claiming that research into the ways in which the Internet supports or transforms learning, in both formal and informal contexts, has tended towards the short-term and small-scale, and that there has been a failure to think sufficiently critically about the educational aspirations such research might be expected to address. There have been a wide range of disparate disciplinary engagements with the topic, but generally in the context of failing to engage with the rapidly changing nature of the Internet or understanding the much slower pace of development that the introduction of digital technologies into education has in fact necessitated.

While understanding how and why technologies facilitate effective learning is important, there is a growing call for a greater focus on understanding the actual realities of using new technologies for learning, at the same time examining the social, political, economic, and cultural contexts within which these activities take place. That is, the adoption of a more critical approach, where there is "a broader recognition of technology and education as a set of profoundly political processes and practices that are best described in terms of issues of power, control, conflict and resistance" (Selwyn 2010: 68). Appropriate methodologies here, could, for example, include longitudinal studies and in-depth ethnographies, and research designs that link the micro and macro levels of analysis in some way (Selwyn 2010).

Such a critical perspective shifts away from the technologically deterministic perspectives often seen in debates about learning and new technology towards the use of more social shaping theories of technology (MacKenzie and Wajcman 1985; Williams and Edge 1996; Selwyn 2010).[5] But even if research is moving on from the fundamentally determinist position of exploring how the technology will solve certain big educational problems, such as how to reach large numbers of students in the most economical ways possible, or how to utilize the Internet in order to connect the poor world with the kind of educational advantage that the rich world takes for granted, neither does the notion of the social shaping of technology look like providing the full answer either.

The Internet is not primarily an educational tool, but it self-evidently offers unique and unparalleled scope for the exploration of new forms of exploration and collaboration in the development and sharing of knowledge. In order to understand, and work productively with these opportunities, the interdisciplinarity that still does not come

---

[5] For a useful overview of some key trends and specific examples in the educational technology field, see Oliver 2011.

easily to the academy (but which comes somewhat more readily to the multiple discourses of the online world) must be fostered and opened up considerably further. This is not necessarily a choice that researchers are yet able to make, but it seems inevitable that study of the Internet and its users will continue to develop and intensify, forming new hybrids of sociology, psychology, communication and cultural studies, sociolinguistics, and multimodal analysis in order to understand how populations and individuals across the globe are making their own decisions about how to access and share knowledge, and what the implications of those informal practices might be for the more measured practices of formal education.

References

Allen, I. E. and Seaman, J. (2010). "Learning on Demand: Online Education in the United States, 2009," Babson Survey Research Group and Sloan Foundation. Available at <http://sloanconsortium .org/publications/survey/learning_on_demand_sr2010>. Accessed June 20, 2012.

Attwood, R. (2010). "Online Tuition Options Are Not Second-Rate, Says Task Force Chair," *Times Higher Education Supplement.* Available at <http://www.timeshighereducation.co .uk/story.asp?storycode=412768>. Accessed September 17, 2010.

Barron, N. (2006). "Interest and Self-Sustained Learning as Catalysts of Development: A Learning Ecology Perspective," *Human Development,* 49(4): 193–224.

Becta (2003). *What the Research Says About ICT and Motivation,* Coventry: Becta.

Brown, G. (2010). *Check Against Delivery.* Speech by the Right Hon Gordon Brown MP to African leaders, Kampala, July 24, 2010. Available at <http://www.gordonandsarahbrown .com/campaigns/the-campaigns/internet-access>. Accessed June 13 2011.

Buckingham, D. (2007). *Beyond Technology: Children's Learning in the Age of Digital Culture,* Cambridge: Polity Press.

Coffield, F. (2000). *The Necessity of Informal Learning,* Bristol: Policy Press.

Conlon, T. and Simpson, M. (2003). "Silicon Valley versus Silicon Glen: The Impact of Computers upon Teaching and Learning: A Comparative Study," *British Journal of Educational Technology,* 34(2): 137–50.

Conole, G. and Oliver, M. (2006). *Contemporary Perspectives in e-Learning Research: Themes, Methods and Impact on Practice,* London: Routledge.

Conole, G. and Warburton, B. (2005). "A Review of Computer-Assisted Assessment," *ALT-J,* 13(1): 17–31.

Crook, C. K. and Light, P. (2002). "Virtual Society and the Cultural Practice of Study," in S. Woolgar (ed.) *Virtual Society?—Technology, Cyberbole, Reality,* Oxford: Oxford University Press, pp. 153–75.

Crook, C., Fisher, T., Graber, R., Harrison, C., and Lewin, C. (2008). *Implementing Web 2.0 in Secondary Schools: Impacts, Barriers and Issues,* Becta Research Report, Coventry: Becta.

Cuban, L. (2001). *Oversold and Underused: Computers in the Classroom,* Cambridge, MA: Harvard University Press.

Czerniewicz, L. (2008). "Distinguishing the Field of Educational Technology," *The Electronic Journal of e-Learning,* 6(3): 171–8.

Dabaj, F. and Isman, A. (2004). "Communication Barriers in Distance Education: Textbased Internet-Enabled Courses," *International Journal of Instructional Technology and Distance*

Learning, 1(2). Available at <http://www.itdl.org/journal/Feb_04/article02.htm>. Accessed June 20, 2011.

de Pourbaix, R. (2000). "Emergent Literacy Practices in an Electronic Community," in D. Barton, M. Hamilton, and R. Ivanic (eds). *Situated Literacies*, London: Routledge.

Delors, J. (Chair) (1996). *Learning: The Treasure Within*, Paris: UNESCO.

DfES/NGfL (2002). *Transforming the Way We Learn*, London: DfES.

Dutton, W., Helsper, E. J., and Gerber, M. M. (2009). "The Internet in Britain 2009," Oxford: Oxford Internet Institute, University of Oxford. Available at <http://www.oii.ox.ac.uk/research/oxis/OxIS2009_Report.pdf>. Accessed June 15, 2011.

Dutton, W. H. and Loader, B. D. (2002). *Digital Academe: New Media in Higher Education and Learning*, London: Routledge.

Eldon, E. (2010). *Facebook's May 2010 US Traffic by Age and Sex: Younger Users Lead Growth*. Available at <http://www.insidefacebook.com/2010/06/03/facebook%E2%80%99s-may-2010-us-traffic-by-age-and-sex-younger-users-lead-growth/>. Accessed June 15 2011.

Erstad, O., Gilje, Ø., and de Lange, T. (2007). "Re-Mixing Multimodal Resources: Multiliteracies and Digital Production in Norwegian Media Education," *Learning, Media and Technology*, 32(2): 183–99.

Evans, C. (2008). "The Effectiveness of m-Learning in the Form of Podcast Revision Lecturers in Higher Education," *Computers and Education*, 50(2): 491–8.

Eynon, R. and Malmberg, L.-E. (2011). "A Typology of Young People's Internet Use: Implications for Education," *Computers and Education*, 56(3): 585–95.

Gagné, R.M. (1977). *The Conditions of Learning*, New York: Holt Rinehart and Winston.

Garrett, R. (2004). "The Real Story behind the Failure of the UK eUniversity, *Educause Quarterly*, 27(4): 4–6.

Gartner Group, The (2010). "Hype Cycles," Gartner Group Methodologies. Available at <http://www.gartner.com/technology/research/methodologies/hype-cycle.jsp>. Accessed June 16, 2011.

Gates, B. (1995). *The Road Ahead*, New York: Viking Penguin.

Gell, M. and Cochrane, P. (1996). "Learning and Education in an Information Society," in W. H. Dutton (ed). *Information and Communications Technologies: Visions and Realities*, Oxford: Oxford University Press, pp. 249–63.

Gray, D. E. (1999). "The Internet in Lifelong Learning: Liberation or Alienation?," *International Journal of Lifelong Education*, 18(2): 119–26.

Hara, N. and Kling, R. (2002). "Students' Distress with a Web-Based Distance Education Course," in W. H. Dutton and B. D. Loader (eds). *Digital Academe: New Media in Higher Education and Learning*, London: Routledge, pp. 62–84.

Hatakka, M. (2009). "Build It and They Will Come?—Inhibiting Factors for Reuse of Open Content in Developing Countries," *The Electronic Journal on Information Systems in Developing Countries*, 37(5). Available at <http://www.ejisdc.org/ojs2/index.php/ejisdc/issue/view/97>. Accessed June 20, 2011.

Horne, J. (2010). "Open University learning is a Joy," *The Guardian*, June 18. Available at <http://www.guardian.co.uk/commentisfree/2010/jun/18/open-university-learning-joy>. Accessed September 17, 2010.

Ito, M., Horst, H., Bittanti, M., Boyd, D., Herr-Stephenson, B., Lange, P., Pascoe, C. J., and Robinson, L. (2008). *Living and Learning with New Media: Summary of Findings from the Digital Youth Project*, Chicago: The John D. and Catherine T. MacArthur Foundation Reports on Digital Media and Learning.

Jarvis, P. (1999). "Global Trends in Lifelong Learning and the Response of the Universities," *Comparative Education*, 35(2): 249–57.

—— (2007). *Globalization, Lifelong Learning and the Learning Society: Sociological Perspectives*, London: Routledge.

Jenkins, H., Clinton, K., Purushotma, R., Robison, A. J., and Weigel, M. (2006). *Confronting the Challenges of Participatory Culture: Media Education for the 21st Century*, Chicago: The MacArthur Foundation.

Kember, D. (2007). *Reconsidering Open and Distance Learning in the Developing World. Meeting Students, Learning Needs*, London: Routledge.

Lam, W. S. E. (2000). "L2 Literacy and the Design of the Self: A Case Study of a Teenager Writing on the Internet," *Tesol Quarterly*, 34(3): 457–82.

Laurillard, D. (2002). *Rethinking University Teaching*, 2nd edn., London: Routledge Falmer.

Lenhardt, A. and Madden, M. (2005). "Teen Content Creators and Consumers", Pew Internet and American Life Project, November 2. Available at <http://www.pewInternet.org/PPF/r/166/report_display.asp>. Accessed September 17, 2008.

Livingstone, S. and Helsper, E. (2007). "Gradations in Digital Inclusion: Children, Young People and the Digital Divide," *New Media and Society*, 9(4): 671–96.

McIntyre, D. (2002). "Has Classroom Teaching Served its Day?," in B. Moon et al. (eds). *Teaching, Learning and the Curriculum in Secondary Schools*, London: Routledge-Falmer.

MacKenzie, D. and Wajcman, J. (eds) (1985). *The Social Shaping of Technology*, Milton Keynes: Open University Press.

Madden, M. (2010). "Older Adults and Social Media," Pew Internet and American Life Project, August 27. Available at <http://pewinternet.org/Reports/2010/Older-Adults-and-Social -Media.aspx>. Accessed September 17, 2011.

Martin, J. (1978). *The Wired Society*, New Jersey: Prentice Hall.

Mason, R., Pegler, C., and Weller, M. (2004). "E-portfolios: An Assessment Tool for Online Courses," *British Journal of Educational Technology*, 35(6): 717–27.

Morrison, D. E. and Svennevig, M. (2001). "The Process of Change: an Empirical Examination of the Uptake and Impact of Technology," in S. Lax (ed.). *Access Denied in the Information Age*, Palgrave: New York, pp. 125–39.

Motlik, S. (2008). "Mobile Learning in Developing Nations," *The International Review of Research in Open and Distance Learning*. Available at <http://www.irrodl.org/index.php/irrodl/article/view/564/1039>. Accessed June 15, 2011.

Nielsen, J. (2006). "Participation Inequality: Encouraging More Users to Contribute," *Jakob Nielsen's Alertbox*, October 9. Available at <http://www.useit.com/alertbox/participation_inequality.html>. Accessed June 15, 2011.

OECD (2007). *Giving Knowledge for Free: The Emergence of Open Educational Resources*, Paris: OECD.

Oliver, M. (2011). "Technological Determinism in Educational Technology Research: Some Alternative Ways of Thinking about the Relationship between Learning and Technology," *Journal of Computer Assisted Learning*, 27(5): 373–84.

Papert, S. (1982). "Tomorrow's Classrooms?," *Times Educational Supplement*, March 5: 31–2.

Portaria No. 4.059 (2004). Minister of Education amendment to the 81 of Law 9394 of December 20, 1996, and in art. 1 of Decree No. 2494 of February 10, 1998. December 10 (DOU of 13/12/2004, Section 1, p 34). Available at <http://portal.mec.gov.br/sesu/arquivos/pdf/nova/acs_portaria4059.pdf>. Accessed May 20, 2011.

Reich, R. (1991). *The Work of Nations: Preparing Ourselves for 21st-Century Capitalism*, New York: Vintage Books.

Rieh, S. (2004). "On the Web at Home: Information Seeking and Web Searching in the Home Environment," *Journal of the American Society for Information Science and Technology.* 55(8): 743–54.

Robins, K. and Webster, F. (1989). *The Technical Fix: Education, Computers, and Industry,* Basingstoke: Macmillan.

—— and Webster, F. (eds) (2002). *The Virtual University? Knowledge Markets and Management,* Oxford: Oxford University Press.

Rollett, H., Lux, M., Strohmaier, M., Dosinger, G., and Tochtermann, K. (2007). "The Web 2.0 Way of Learning with Technologies," *International Journal of Learning Technology,* 3(1): 87–107.

Salmon, G. (2002). *E-tivities: The Key to Active Online Learning,* London: Taylor and Francis.

Sefton-Green, J. (2004). *Literature Review in Informal Learning with Technology Outside School,* Bristol: NESTA Futurelab.

Selwyn, N. (2007). "The Use of Computer Technology in University Teaching and Learning: A Critical Perspective," *Journal of Computer Assisted Learning* 23(2): 83–94.

—— (2008). "Realising the Potential of New Technology? Assessing the Legacy of New Labour's ICT Agenda 1997–1007," *Oxford Review of Education.* 34(6): 701–72.

—— (2010). "Looking beyond Learning: Notes towards the Critical Study of Educational Technology," *Journal of Computer Assisted Learning,* 26(1): 65–73.

Smith, J. (2009). *Number of US Facebook Users Over 35 Nearly Doubles in Last 60 Days.* Available at <http://www.insidefacebook.com/2009/03/25/number-of-us-facebook-users-over-35-nearly-doubles-in-last-60-days/>. Accessed June 15, 2011.

Tan, F. (2011). "Internet Speed Declines in India in Favour of Coverage," *The next web,* May 12. Available at <http://thenextweb.com/in/2011/05/12/internet-speed-declines-in-india-in-favor-of-coverage/>. Accessed June 10, 2011.

Underwood, J., Banyard, P., Baguley, T., Dillon, G., Farrington-Flint, L., Hayes, M., Geyt, L. E., Murphy, J., and Selwood, I. (2010). *Understanding the Impact of Technology: Learner and School Level Factors. Final Report,* Coventry: Becta.

UNESCO (2011). "New Broadband Commission report seeks to bring high-speed connectivity to world's poorest communities," *UNESCOPRESS,* June 6. Available at <http://www.unesco.org/new/en/media-services/single-view/news/new_broadband_commission_report_seeks_to_bring_high_speed_connectivity_to_worlds_poorest_communities/>. Accessed June 13, 2011.

Warschauer, M., Knobel, M., and Stone, L. (2004). "Technology and Equity in Schooling: Deconstructing the Digital Divide," *Educational Policy,* 18(4): 562–88.

Williams, R. and Edge, D. (1996). "The Social Shaping of Technology," in W. H. Dutton (ed.). *Information and Communication Technologies: Visions and Realities,* Oxford: Oxford University Press, pp. 37–52.

Woodley, A. (2007). "The Open University of the United Kingdom: A British Eccentricity or a Model for the World?" in D. Kember (ed.). *Reconsidering Open and Distance Learning in the Developing World: Meeting Students' Learning Needs,* London: Routledge, pp. 29–61.

Young Sae, L. (2009). "Congratulatory Message from President of Daegu Cyber University," *Korea IT Times,* July 6. Available at <http://www.koreaittimes.com/story/4021/congratulatory-message-president-daegu-cyber-university>. Accessed September 24, 2010.

Zheng, L. (2009). "Microsoft's Future Vision Videos for Education," *I started something,* July 22. Available at <http://www.istartedsomething.com/20090722/microsofts-future-vision-for-education/>. Accessed June 15, 2011.

PART IV

COMMUNICATION, POWER, AND INFLUENCE IN A CONVERGING MEDIA WORLD

....

THEORETICAL PERSPECTIVES IN THE STUDY OF COMMUNICATION AND THE INTERNET

....

RONALD E. RICE AND RYAN P. FULLER

INTRODUCTION

SOCIAL science research and theory on computer-mediated communication (CMC), including the Arpanet and Bitnet, began in the early 1970s (Hiltz and Turoff 1978; Johansen et al. 1974; Rice 1980a, 1980b, 1992; among others). Social science articles specifically referring to the Internet first appeared in the early 1990s, and to the World Wide Web, in the early 2000s. Coverage of the Internet and the Web appeared earlier in technical, business, and popular publications (Rice 1984), but we consider only social science, communication-related academic journal articles here.

The first social science articles that used the word "Internet" in their titles and abstracts were about its history (Perry et al. 1988), NSFNET (Catlett 1989), library networks (Lynch 1989), and online security (Ryland 1989). The first appearances of "world wide web" in article titles considered use at work (Cheung et al. 2000), research information sharing (McCain 2000), and online representations of the Philippine diaspora (Tyner and Kuhlke 2000). Early articles with this term in the abstract analyzed citizen networks (Deibert 2000), privacy (Miller and Weckert 2000), and social isolation (Franzen 2000).

Growth in coverage of these topics in social science journals continued through about 2004, with slight increases since then, and a rise of articles with terms referring to more specific Internet and Web 2.0 media (Table 17.1). Similar searches for the terms "Internet" or "World Wide Web" during 2010 found them in 22,343 entries in the Web of Science for Social Sciences (which includes information science and computer science; 2,208

Table 17.1 Frequency of Internet, World Wide Web, and Web 2.0 terms in titles and abstracts of social science articles, 2000–2010

Year	Terms in Title	Terms in Abstract						
	Internet or World Wide Web	Internet or World Wide Web	(Internet or World Wide Web) and (communication)	Blog or weblog	Facebook or Myspace or Friendster	Twitter or microblog	Wiki	Instant Messaging
2000	318	560	105	0	0	0	0	0
2001	491	813	143	0	0	0	0	1
2002	551	942	145	0	0	0	0	5
2003	636	1428	222	1	0	0	1	7
2004	743	2438	300	5	1	0	0	20
2005	829	2703	358	26	1	0	1	22
2006	794	2650	344	31	6	0	6	25
2007	734	2955	341	56	16	0	5	59
2008	830	3174	413	78	57	0	12	46
2009	610	2593	303	53	68	8	25	40
2010	749	3091	383	111	131	45	34	38
Total	7285	23347	3057	361	280	53	84	263

were in the Communication subject area), and in 51,900 entries for Arts, Humanities, and Social Sciences (not separable) in Google Scholar (as of April 25, 2011).

This chapter describes the major theoretical/conceptual approaches to studying social aspects of the Internet during the period 2000–09, identifying the main theories, more general theoretical themes, and global theoretical themes, as well as meta-theoretical approaches, in 315 articles. The next section briefly summarizes the methodology. Then each global theme and its associated primary themes, as well as the theoretical frameworks, are described, and illustrated with representative articles.

METHOD

We searched the Social Science collection noted in Table 17.1, with ("Internet" or "World Wide Web") AND ("communication" and "theory"). We then searched all the International Communication Association (ICA) journals from the ICA website, from 2000 to 2009; all National Communication Association journals online; and *New Media & Society* and *Information, Communication & Society* (2000–09); and downloaded the full-text version where available. Finally, we added a few relevant reviews or meta-theoretical integrations from other journals within this period, resulting in an initial set of around 400 entries.

We used an inductive, consensual form of content analysis similar to the grounded theory method of inquiry (Charmaz 2006; Glaser 2004; Strauss and Corbin 1998), thus not using any pre-existing typology. Articles were initially coded for reference, abstract, primary theory, secondary theory(ies) and article type. Type 1 articles were "meta," that is at the theory level only, while Type 2 articles were "analyses," involving some kind of test or evaluation. All articles were coded for theories and themes, but the Type 1 articles were analyzed separately to see ways in which theories/concepts were treated. After multiple passes through the materials and codes, then we coded the final set of about 75 entries, following the same set of procedures, looking for additional primary theories, themes and possible global themes, recategorizing prior codes where appropriate, and then revising the themes and global themes. Our final sample consisted of 315 articles, from 46 journals.

GLOBAL AND PRIMARY THEMES (315 ARTICLES)

The following sections provide brief operationalizations for, and summarize each of, the twenty-seven themes within the six global themes, along with example primary theories (except the named theme theory itself), and brief examples from two articles each, illustrating as much as possible the range of primary theories, concepts, and contexts.

Global theme: media attributes (35)

Theme: Interactivity (12). Contexts of interactivity range from initial interpersonal interactions to the adaptation of new immigrants. Example primary theories in these articles include cultural variety, customization, discourse theory, interactivity model for initial interactions, and tailoring. One thread in these articles is the development, explication, or critique of interactivity typologies and dimensions (Downes and McMillan 2000). Another approach is to contextualize the implications of Internet interactivity, such as how teenage immigrants from the former Soviet Union to Israel, facing challenges of adaptation and loneliness, use the Internet to maintain a social support system of friends and family (Elias and Lemish 2009).

Theme: Media Attributes (23). Studies of media attributes range from multimodal communication to web design features (including design, genre, history, media ecology, or website features analysis; often linked to effects). Media attributes include characteristics and affordances such as media richness or website features, as well as more comparative media ecology approaches, and historical and genre approaches. Example primary theories include extended parallel processing model, information and communication technology (ICT) succession theory, media genres, real-virtual dichotomy, social construction of technology, social presence theory, and theory of channel complementarity.

One of the central debates in the literature concerns both the types of media attributes associated with the Internet, and how the Internet complements, substitutes for, or provides new channels and media genres. For example, a more historical approach finds Internet genres already existing in traditional media, adapted genres to incorporate linking and interactivity, and new genres developed to meet audience members' unique communication needs (Crowston and Williams 2000). The channel substitution approach is illustrated by Ledbetter (2008), who focuses on which channels tend to be used in association with others in best friend pairs, showing that postal mail use declined between 1987 and 2002, gradually replaced by email; telephone contact was a particularly important predictor of closeness, while face-to-face was a less stable indicator. These results were explained by two primary attributes—efficiency and convenience.

Global theme: media implications/use and understanding (75)

Theme: Credibility/Trust (5). Because an Internet source may be anonymous, temporary, or masked behind many levels, yet provide highly consequential information, issues of credibility and trust are a central concern of researchers, users, and policy-makers. These studies focus on message, source/sponsor, and medium credibility, as well as factors influencing perceptions of trust. Example primary theories in these articles include trust theory and cybertrust.

Media uses and perceptions of credibility and trust may vary depending on the genre and content of a website. For example, Flanagin and Metzger (2007) found that news websites were perceived as most credible, and personal websites were found to be least credible for message, site, and sponsor credibility, while e-commerce and special-interest websites were rated between these. The credibility assessments appeared to be due to web attributes, rather than to familiarity with sponsors. Perceived Internet credibility and trust also depend on traditional source characteristics such as gender; male bloggers (a website "characteristic") were perceived in one study to be more credible than female bloggers (Armstrong and McAdams 2009).

Theme: Diffusion of Innovations (12). Diffusion of innovation studies range from individual adoption of technology, to cross-cultural comparisons of ICT adoption, and to the role of the Internet in communicating innovations (Rice 2009). Example primary theories include actor-network theory, digital divide, mediamorphosis, network analysis, peer influence, radical/disruptive vs incremental innovations, social shaping of technology, and technology acceptance model.

This research applies a wide range of theories to help explain Internet adoption, diffusion, or rejection. For example, White and Scheb's (2000) study supports the concept of third-person perception, indicating that people believe general Internet use is higher than it is, fostering a sense of Internet anxiety. With world-wide adoption of the Internet, cross-cultural and macro-level analyses are increasing. Countries with higher levels of ICT adoption are associated with greater GDP, size of service sector, education, and governmental effectiveness (Billon et al. 2009). In developing countries adoption is positively associated with population age and urban population, and negatively associated with Internet costs.

Theme: Media Effects (19). Contexts of individual or psychological media effects (not explicitly represented by another theme) range from persuasive campaigns to organizational website design features, here emphasizing Internet-use outcomes. Example primary theories include agenda-setting, attribution theory, computers as social actors paradigm, flow, heuristic-systematic model, knowledge gap, social identification/deindividuation model, social information processing theory, and social presence.

Online group interaction can be studied or designed as an influence on attitudes about campaigns. David and colleagues (2006) report that interactants developed more pro-marijuana attitudes and subjective normative beliefs than those who viewed the ad only. Rather than outcomes, as in Diffusion of Innovation studies, adoption and usage are analyzed for their effect, such as on tolerance and diversity of opinions. For example, users are somewhat more tolerant, but there are differences across tolerance issues (racial, family, sexual, and political), according to Robinson and Martin's (2009) analysis of four General Social Surveys.

Theme: Media Use/Adaptation (12). Articles on media use continue a long tradition of identifying influences on particular media use (as an outcome variable), or comparing channel substitution/displacement/complementarity when additional media become available (as an explanatory variable). Articles specifically mentioning changes in sociality, or uses and gratifications theory, are included in those separate themes.

Example primary theories include actor-network theory, domestication theory, media substitution, social capital, social information processing theory, socio-technical perspective, and technological convergence.

An example of a more interpersonal approach to Internet use as an explanatory variable examines how parenting styles (authoritarian, authoritative, permissive, and uninvolved) and access to the Internet influenced mediation techniques (factual, evaluative, and restrictive) (Eastin et al. 2006). Focusing on usage as a dependent variable, Wilson and Tan (2005) apply ludenic newsreading theory and phenomenological analysis to assess how several Asian audiences engage with news websites as play, declarations of identity, consumption, navigation, and labor.

Theme: Possibly Harmful Internet Use (16). Possibly harmful Internet use consists of behaviors that violate norms, beliefs, or behaviors of a particular social group, including the specific "problematic Internet use" concept. This use and its implications have been an ongoing debate and concern. Contexts of possibly harmful Internet use range from individual addiction to inappropriate workplace behaviors. Example primary theories include addiction, interruption management, locus of control, moral panic, and third-person effect.

In the context of Internet pornography, Lee and Tamborini (2005) examine the influence of individualism-collectivism on the third-person effect. US-based participants perceived that the negative effects of pornography were greater on others than on themselves, and this perception was associated with greater support for Internet censorship, while collectivism diminished this third-person perception. Counter to the typical concerns about negative and harmful uses, Holmes (2009) questions the extent of young people's risks from Internet use (such as sharing personal information), instead emphasizing young people's competencies and the benefits of Internet use.

Theme: Uses and Gratifications (10). Certainly uses and gratifications theory has been increasingly applied to understand both motivations for, and gratifications from, using the Internet. Example primary theories associated with the Uses and Gratifications approach (U&G) include interactivity, social cognitive theory, socialization theory, and spiral of silence.

Many of these studies apply or extend traditional motivations or dimensions, such as Yang's (2000) study of Taiwanese academic gays' use of Internet for online news reading (and perceptions of its impartiality). The most influential motivations were social interaction and information, though they varied by the nature of Internet use. Other articles extend U&G theory by describing new motivations or analyzing Internet usage as a way to test more integrated models. For example, LaRose and Eastin (2004) integrated U&G with social cognitive theory to develop and test a strongly predictive model of "media attendance," moderated by Internet self-efficacy.

Global theme: participation (53)

Theme: Civic Engagement (19). Articles in this theme are concerned with democratization, interactions with government, voluntary organizations, non-governmental organizations, collective action, non-profits, social movements, religious groups, and participative online learning or collaboration. Example primary theories in these articles include civic engagement, collective action theory, democratic theory (deliberative democracy, liberal pluralism, radical participatory democracy), digital divide, participation, political engagement, public sphere, and theory of communicative action.

A central debate is whether the Internet may reinvigorate civic engagement through increased access to information and activities. Internet use directly affects political information, but indirectly affects civic engagement, due to the wider range of needs gratified through the Internet, increasing the contingent and contextual nature of Internet use (Xenos and Moy 2007). Politics is not the only form of civic engagement. Ho et al. (2008) examine factors influencing religious engagement online by Muslim web users in Singapore. Muslim web users tended to partake in online activities more for personal religious reasons than those related to institutional religion. Additionally, Internet self-efficacy, perceived social pressure, and religiosity were positively associated, and age negatively, with online religious activity.

Theme: Participatory Media/Users (4). The Internet has vastly increased the possibilities for formerly passive audiences to engage in creating content, "news," and fandom. Example primary theories associated with these studies include critical theory, cultural production, field theory, and participatory fandom.

One crucial issue is the extent to which Internet use can augment or even replace traditional news. For example, the coverage of the 2005 riots in France fostered much discourse about the nature and boundaries of news, journalists, and audience (Russell 2007). The nature and principles of participatory media are themselves up to debate. Indeed, Van Dijck and Nieborg (2009) critique the rhetorical strategies of Web 2.0 manifestos about collaborative culture and co-creation, showing problems with assigning equal creativity and motivations for use among users, capitalizing on relationships and social behavior of people clicking on sites, and the location of public collectivism within commodity culture.

Theme: Political Participation (8). Contexts of participation include democratization, voting, political engagement and awareness, and political action, such as online protests. Example primary theories include communicative action, political engagement, and social movement.

This research focuses on the Internet's role in increasing political participation. Some apply a broad, macro approach, such as Calenda and Meijer's (2009) analysis of relationships between Internet use, and offline and online political participation among young people in Spain, The Netherlands, and Italy, which provides evidence for both techno-deterministic versus social deterministic perspectives. Quite different approaches include micro-investigations of online political discussions, such as the influence of language style and source expertise (and other status cues) on perceptions of online discussants and their intentions to participate in political discussion (Tan et al. 2007).

Theme: Public Sphere (22). Concerns about the role of Internet in the public sphere–deliberative democracy, online political discussions, differential gains, journalism, voice, and selective exposure to political discourse–have become frequent topics of Internet Studies. Example primary theories include agonistic public space, civic engagement, deliberative democracy, differential gains, elaboration likelihood model, networked journalism, preferential attachment, and selective exposure.

One position is that Internet activities such as blogging foster a Habermasian public sphere. Opponents of this proposition, such as Cammaerts (2008), note that blogs do not provide a space where all participation is equal, and they politicize the private, due to four factors: colonization by the market; censorship by states, organizations, and industries (structural level); social control by citizens; and antidemocratic voices (individual level). As an empirical example of this critique, one state's e-democracy initiative to develop critical online public discourse used multiple channels, management approaches, and geographically bounded issues to overcome some barriers; however, it still has failed to compete with commercial sites, common-interest online communities, and liberal individualist political practices (Dahlberg 2001).

Global theme: social relations (89)

Theme: Community (25). Contexts of community range from virtual communities to cybercafés where users have Internet access, social movements, and online support. Example primary theories in these articles include collective identity, critical feminist perspective, exchange network theory, communicative action, hyperpersonal perspective, social networks, social support, and symbolic interactionism.

Two central issues in this research are the ways in which physically located communities differ or are similar to online communities, and how new media affect physical communities and shape online ones (Katz et al. 2004). Online spaces can provide virtual communities and even refuge to many groups, such as right-wing extremists bound by social rejection, stigmatization, and fatalism (De Koster and Houtman 2008).

Theme: Groups (12). Considerations of the group or team theme range from argument and decision-making to group identification in virtual teams. Example primary theories include adaptive structuration theory, attribution theory, channel use and online relationships in virtual teams, conflict resolution, and normative social influence.

Social identity and deindividuation (SIDE) theory appears in a number of the decade's Internet articles, and is especially salient in the group context. Consistent with SIDE theory, Lee (2004) found that when group identity was salient, uniform visual representation of participants triggered depersonalization and led to conformity, but when personal identity was salient, uniform virtual appearance reduced conformity. However, not all studies support this group identity influence. In a study of groups using Internet Relay Chat (Wang et al. 2009), confederates behaving likably were rated more attractive than those behaving dislikably irrespective of in- or out-group membership, and interpersonal dynamics provided stronger effects than intergroup dynamics.

Theme: Identity (19). Creating, testing, and communicating individual and group identity is especially salient because of users' ability to manage text, shift membership, mask or highlight their name or location, and interact with diverse others. Contexts of identity in these articles range from multimodal interpersonal communication to identity construction on weblogs, focusing on race, ethnicity, gender, sexual orientation, and community. Example primary theories include anonymity, avatars, critical race and culture theory, cultural identity, dialogical self theory, digital divide, discursive psychology, fandom, identity work, online trust, and symbolic interactionism.

Critical technocultural discourse analysis and racial formation theory enabled Brock (2009) to reveal four elements of construction of racial identity—cultural, Internet, ecological, and social—in blogs, websites, and their web-enabled audiences. Using a Foucauldian approach to examine the significance of texts in an electronic discussion group, and also what marginal groups do with the text and the Internet, Hung (2002) concluded that Hong Kong Chinese are not able to evade the power of dominant discourses, but are able to confirm their own specific identity.

Theme: Media Use and Sociality (9). The primary focus here is on whether, to what extent, and how, differences in Internet use are related to or affect changes in interaction, sociality, and connectedness (but without applying network analysis). Example primary theories include expectancy violations theory, hyperpersonal perspective, perpetual contact, relational quality, social control, social information processing theory, and social penetration theory.

At the interpersonal level, Birnie and Horvath (2002) apply computer-mediated social communication research, social network theory, social motives, and U&G to assess relationships between offline and Internet social communication, showing that online social communication is an extension of traditional social communication. Because sociality is shaped by, and an expression of, community, cultural, and national differences, such relationships between online and offline communication need to be compared cross-nationally. For example, while Internet use was positively associated with both offline civic engagement and interpersonal involvement, there were differences in strengths and socio-demographic influences across the four European countries/societies studied by Räsänen and Kouvo (2007).

Theme: Relational Management (4). The Internet has provided new venues for managing, as well as affecting, personal and family relations, including relational development, conflict and support, quality and outcomes, and self-disclosure.

Because the Internet (and associated devices) represents new household, family, and individual resources, new opportunities for identity management and external communication, and increased opportunities for covert or personal use and relationships, issues of relational management seem ripe for analysis. Applying family development and human ecology theory to investigate family conflicts associated with managing children's Internet use and possible negative consequences, Mesch (2006) found that such conflicts varied by the family development life-cycle. Relational maintenance strategy and equity theory provide frameworks to understand how college students maintain their face-to-face relationships through online communication (Johnson et al. 2008).

Theme: Social Capital (8). One argument about online communication is that it increases one's social capital, leading to both individual and collective benefits, by generating and maintaining access to more diverse resources and bridging and bonding relationships to others. Example primary theories include interpersonal trust, political participation, social resource motivation, and time displacement.

During and after Hurricane Katrina, Internet users within geographic locales were able to activate weak ties in their social networks, reduce uncertainty, and, especially for women, share expressive communication (Procopio and Procopio 2007). Some doubts about the advantages of the Internet for developing and applying social capital may be due to confounding informational uses of the Internet (and other media) versus social-recreational uses. The first tends to be positively related to social capital and the second negatively related, and for the youngest adult Americans, Internet use for information exchange had greater positive effects on social capital than did traditional print and broadcast news media (Shah et al. 2001).

Theme: Social Networks, Network Analysis (13). Individuals, institutions, and societies are embedded in social networks. The Internet, a network of networks, is one of the bases for the network society (Castells 2009), and thus presents a pervasive context for studying social networks, as a source of network data, and as a networking medium. Example primary theories include channel replacement, glocalized networks, network theory, collective identity and norms, and social support.

Developments include the application of network theory and methods for the study of hyperlink relationships among websites and blogs, and testing theories about online and offline social relationship patterns. For example, Caiani and Wagemann (2009) compare the hyperlink network structures of German and Italian extreme right organizations, complementing those analyses with detailed case studies of the organizations' offline characteristics, based on political opportunity structures and dominant societal discourses. And Haythornthwaite's (2005) synthesis of her research on online academic communities and distance education users combines measures of media use, network ties, and individual characteristics. Communicating pairs with stronger ties used more media to interact with each other, different tiers of media use supported social networks of different ties' strengths, and a new medium can develop latent tie connectivity that provides the means for activating weak ties.

Global theme: societal (47)

Theme: Boundary Crossing (7). Resonating with the concept of the Internet as both interconnected networks and foundation to the network society, several articles considered the role of the Internet in fostering or representing shifting and intersecting boundaries, in relation both to fundamental societal forces (economic, historical, political, and religious) as well as conceptual (time, space, and place). Example primary theories in these articles include liminality, metaphor, pragmatism, technological sublime, third place, and time.

Early Internet literature did not take into consideration the historical development of technology, the broader technological context, and the world of politics, economics, religion, and culture, which would reveal that new technology "overcomes many boundaries (of space and time, politics and economics), [but] other social borders may be created at the same time" (Carey 2005: 443). One of the broadest examples of boundary crossing is Gotved's (2006) visual matrix describing the embeddedness of cyber social reality in technology, time, and space.

Theme: Cultural Differences (3). Research in this theme emphasized cultural contexts of Internet use and effects. Example primary theories include apology, collectivism, and individualism.

The content and design of websites reflect, and are interpreted based on, cultural differences. Attitudes of American and Chinese Internet users toward web design reflect cultural backgrounds (Gevorgyan and Manucharova 2009). Thus cultural customization would be effective when users have strong ethnic identities. South Korea and the United States websites contain collectivist and individualist content and features (Kim et al. 2009). For example, South Korean websites were more likely to display polychromic time-management tendencies and preferences for high-context communication.

Theme: Digital Divide (16). Differences in access to, use, evaluation of, and benefits from the Internet—based on demographic and related variables—has been a fundamental research, social, and policy issue (Katz and Rice 2002). Contexts of digital divide research range from differential use of the Internet to differential adoption of specific types of websites. Example primary theories include disability divide, internet self-efficacy, network society, and theory of optimal slack.

Influences on such divides are not only individual and infrastructural, but also geographic and social. For example, usage patterns of individuals who live in more ethnically isolated regions more closely resemble usage patterns of their ethnic group (Agarwal et al. 2009). However, in spite of the deep and enduring digital divides within and across societies and nations, the Internet may also serve as a source of empowerment for individuals at the margins of society, including low-income families, sexual minorities, and African-American women (Mehra et al. 2004).

Theme: Political Economy/Policy (13). These articles take a more macro look at social and global implications of ICTs, the social shaping of technology, critical analyses of new media industries, public goods, and policy issues. Example primary theories include critical internet theory, digital divide, framing theory, knowledge society, public goods theory, and social shaping of technology.

The history of and influences on the Internet are often underestimated or narrowly defined. Simpson (2004) attempts to overcome this by explaining its evolution from a government research network to an electronic marketplace, applying neo-Gramscian concepts of consensus, hegemony, concessions, and international marketplace. A much more specific context for understanding these forces is early (and ongoing) tensions between blog news and traditional print and television news. McCoy (2001) applies the theory of news repair to explain the tensions, arguing that media "confluence" is a better term than "convergence."

Theme: Privacy (8). Privacy research here consists of concerns about protection of users' personal online data and identity. Contexts of online privacy range from social networks to trust. Example primary theories include communication privacy management, institutional trust, social exchange theory, and sociology of risk.

Consistent with communication privacy management theory, Metzger's (2007) analysis of privacy in an e-commerce relationship describes how online consumers form rules to decide when to reveal personal information. Extending this concern to a cultural relativism perspective, Cho and colleagues (2009) show that the ways in which individuals perceive and respond to online privacy issues are related to micro- and macro-level variables (i.e. age, gender, education, Internet experience, nationality, and cultural values).

Global theme: theory framework (referring to a specific theory) (16)

Theme: Critiques (7). One role of theoretical articles is to critique prior work to clarify differences and similarities among underlying concepts, and identify weaknesses or challenge assumptions, in order to revise and extend theories, and recommend future research agendas. This category included critiques, conceptual distinctions, recommendations, and research agendas. Example primary theories in these articles include disciplinarity, domestication theory, social capital, social identification/deindividuation model, social information processing, and technology clusters. Recommendations for extending the scope of research include more high-quality descriptive research to identify boundary conditions, highlight overlooked phenomena, attend to the global and international, move away from text-based to multimedia conceptualizations of CMC, and foster an ongoing mutual exchange of ideas. A second set emphasizes methodological approaches, such as to understand mixed-, multi-, and switched- modes, and use multiple lenses to guide research (such as use context, technology clusters, insights from prior technologies, multimedia aspects of new media, and boundary conditions to different theories about CMC). A third set centers on use and effects: consider the ongoing adaptation of technologies, pay more attention to public discourse about these new media, and distinguish short-term from long-term effects (Baym 2005; Parks 2009; Sawhney 2007; Scott 2009; Soukup 2000; Walther 2009).

Theme: Integrated or New Theoretical Models (2). Given the range of overlapping applicable theories, and new contexts and relationships associated with the Internet, more research should expand, revise, or integrate prior theories, and/or generate new theoretical perspectives. Example primary theories include infrastructure versus media attributes and theory of digital communication. Scolari (2009) developed a wideranging and integrative theoretical framework for studying digital media, emphasizing both continuities and discontinuities with prior theories, such as mass communication, cultural studies, political economy, social construction of technology, cybercultures, CMC, semiotics, hypertext, and others.

Theme: Reviews (7). These articles provided reviews, categorizations, and theoretical typologies for coding, to make the wide range of relevant research and theories more accessible, interpretable, and usable. Example primary theories include access and equity, development model of communication research, globalization, media attributes, network theory, privacy, social networks, and technological determinism. For example, Kim and Weaver (2002) group their extensive coding of research focus, developmental phases of research agenda, research method, and theoretical application within four stages of communication research development: 1) issues of the Internet itself, 2) uses and users, 3) effects, and 4) improvements of the Internet. Lievrouw et al. (2001) review ICT research on technology as artifacts/devices, and communication activities/practices, bringing to bear the social arrangements and organizations forming around those artifacts and practices.

Change in global theme focus

Given the recent rise of Web 2.0 technologies and related studies, possible changes in online social practices facilitated by these new media, the increase in Internet Studies overall, and the ongoing development of theoretical approaches, the focus of the global themes may have shifted from 2000 to 2009. We compared the articles published in the first half of the period (2000–04) to those in the second half period of the sample (2005–09). The total number of articles nearly doubled (from 115 to 200). As a percent of each of those totals, focus on participation themes doubled (from 10.4 percent to 20.5 percent), there was some decline in concern with social relations (32.2 percent to 26.0 percent) and media attributes themes (14.8 percent to 9.0 percent), but the other three themes (media implications/use and understanding, societal, and general theory framework) remained about the same. However, the overall chi-square (two periods, six themes) was not significant $(8.0, p=.15)$.

META-THEORY FRAMEWORKS (49)

Stepping back from the specific theories and themes, what were the major ways in which the "meta" articles treated these? A second coding included the above Theory Frameworks, which either did not deal with specific theories, or ranged widely over theories and concepts, as well as theory-specific articles that also used a Theory Framework. The same three primary themes and their operationalizations apply: Critiques, Integrated and New Theoretical Models, and Reviews.

Theme: critiques (20)

Richards (2000) critiques conceptualizations of hypermedia in developing an integrated model of electronic literacy, while Boyd (2003) uses a rhetorical lens to distinguish components of online trust. While many articles analyze influences and consequences of various forms of the digital divide, Gunkel (2003) critiques the terminology of the concept itself, questioning the presumed dichotomy and assumed technological determinism. Zhao and Elesh (2008), applying Goffman's and Giddens's theories of human interaction, tease out the contrasting dimensions and implications of co-presence versus co-location. Baym (2005) and Waskul (2005) argue for an increased focus on the intersection and borders of the Internet with other social, cultural, and social-psychological venues, including power. Mansell (2004) highlights the need to couch Internet theory and research in a political economy perspective of analyzing structural and processual power. Ruggiero (2000) makes a forceful argument for the appropriateness of a U&G approach to studying each new medium, and the need to integrate concepts such as interactivity, demassification, hypertextuality, and asynchroneity. Other primary theories in these articles include democratization, disciplinarity, domestication theory, electronic literacy, global civil society, liminality, possibly harmful Internet use, pragmatism, public sphere, social capital, social identification/deindividuation model, social information processing, technological sublime, technology clusters, trust theory, and ubiquitous connectivity.

Theme: integrated and new theoretical models (14)

Ramirez et al. (2002) focused on social information seeking in computer-mediated communication, integrating and extending the social identity model of deindividuation effects theory, social information processing theory, and hyperpersonal theory, including factors influencing the selection of particular strategies. Elmer (2003) critiqued recent attempts to outline a panoptic theory of surveillance, and developed one that questions the links among consumer, sales, distribution, and production data. Bimber et al. (2005) reconceptualize collective-action theory, arguing that collective action is a set of communication processes involving the crossing of boundaries between public and private life, both facilitated and challenged by the new media environment. Other primary theories/concepts considered in this category included critical Internet theory, diagrammatic theory of surveillance, discursive space, hyperpersonal perspective, interactional—new literacies, possibly harmful Internet use, social information processing theory, social networks, time, transformative democracy, and voice.

Theme: reviews (15)

Rice and Hagen (2010) synthesize research on social connectivity and social control of teenagers' and college students' use of the Internet and mobile phones. Laguerre (2004) proposes ways in which the Internet has changed our notions of time, employing concepts such as virtual time, the cyberweek, temporal boundaries, time fragmentation, and the behavioral decoupling of time zones, while Youngs (2001) reviews how gender and time are associated with ICTs. Other areas included in these reviews are access and equity, democratization, diffusion of innovations, digital divide, effects on language and communication, globalization, group dynamics, media attributes, mediamorphosis, metaphor, network theory, perpetual contact, privacy, public sphere, social context, social control, social structures and norms, social support, and technological determinism.

RELATIONS AMONG THE PRIMARY AND GLOBAL THEMES

Because of the interrelatedness of many theories, the applicability of multiple theories to any particular Internet issue, and the inherent interpretative nature of the coding process, articles in many of these formally mutually exclusive categories could overlap with other categories and their theories/constructs. So we identified the overall relationships among the 27 themes, based on the extent to which themes shared global themes, primary theories, and secondary theories (though only one entry for any particular secondary theory within a theme)—a total of 1,484 separate entries, representing 573 unique terms with multiple entries, from the 315 articles. The 573x27 term-by-theme matrix was converted to a 27x27 theme-by-theme correlation matrix, which was entered into UCINET multidimensional scaling (MDS) and optimization clustering analyses (Borgatti et al. 2002).

As Figure 17.1 shows, the MDS locates each theme in a two-dimensional space, which, because it is not a perfect representation (stress = .23), shows only one particular rotation, and takes into account cross-theme terms, but does not completely separate all themes exclusively into their global themes. The best clustering solution did produce the six global theme clusters (R^2 = .94, fit = .03) as expected, as each theme has its global theme term entry for all its articles. The five-cluster solution (R^2 = .84, fit = .08) included Interactivity and Media Attributes within the Integrated Theory and New Model cluster.

The theory frameworks of Reviews and Critiques are central to the entire theme network, and primarily associated with global themes of Social Relations and Participation, again emphasizing the core focus on interaction and involvement, two of the three main topics of Katz and Rice's (2002) multi-year study of the Internet. Integrated and New Models do relate to the Social Relations themes of Community, Social Capital, and Social Networks, but also to Boundary-Crossing and Political Economy (Societal), Participatory Media, Civic Engagement and Public Sphere (Participation), and Diffusion of Innovations and Media Use/Adaptation (Media Implications/Use and Understanding). As the second-level clustering showed, Interactivity and Media Attributes are related to Reviews

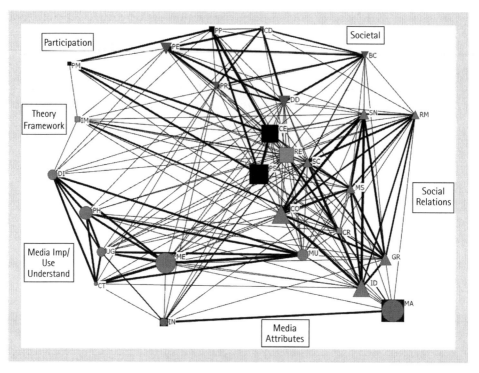

FIGURE. 17.1: MDS and cluster analysis of inter-relations among the 27 themes.
Note: Themes with same shapes are in same cluster, and size of Themes is proportional to the number of articles coded for that theme. Links are proportional to strength of correlations between Themes; thus, thin links are low correlations across global themes.
Note: BC: Boundary Crossing; CD: Cultural Differences; CE: Civic Engagement; CO: Community; CR: Critiques; CT: Credibility/Trust; DD: Digital Divide; DI: Diffusion Innovations; GR: Groups; ID: Identity; IM: Integrated and New Models; IN: Interactivity; MA: Media Attributes; ME: Media Effects; MS: Media Use/Sociality; MU: Media Use/Adaptation; PE: Political Economy/Policy; PH: Possibly Harmful Internet Use; PM: Participatory Media Users; PP: Political Participation; PR: Privacy; PS: Public Sphere; RE: Reviews; RM: Relational Management; SC: Social Capital; SN: Social Networks; UG: Uses and Gratifications

and Critiques, but also somewhat strongly to U&G, and then weakly (but usually jointly) to a variety of themes, such as Media Effects, Groups, and Relational Management. Themes in the Societal and Participation global themes are somewhat interrelated, primarily through Political Economy/Policy, Political Participation, and Cultural Differences. The Societal topic of Digital Divide, and the Media Implications/Use and Understanding topic of Media Use/Adaptation, are sort of ambassadors, or liaisons, to the Participation and Social Relations global themes.

The decade's communication articles on the Internet can be summarily described as consisting of two dimensions (with the most distinct example primary theories): *interpersonal* (right side: equity theory, family development theory and human ecology theory, relational dialectics) *versus media effects* (left side: actor-network theory, cultural production, participatory fandom, peer influence, technology acceptance model, vernacular web), and *societal* (top: apology, collectivism and individualism, communicative action, democratization, political participation and engagement, social movement) *versus media attributes* (bottom: media richness, schema theory, social construction of technology, structural isomorphism, tailoring). More parsimoniously, the bottom left diagonal of the space emphasizes *media* (use and attributes) while the top right diagonal emphasizes *people* (individual and societal relationships).

LIMITATIONS

Clearly, even the range of communication-related journals used here will not include examples of some kinds of communication-related theories and approaches about the Internet that are emphasized in other Communication journals (e.g. see the list by Levine 2010; Tomasello et al. 2010; the ISI Journal Citation Reports; or the Web of Social Science). Other journals, such as *Cyberpsychology, Behavior, and Social Networking*, are prominent sources of Internet articles, but were not included here because of their inaccessibility via library databases, and infrequent appearance in the general online search.

To provide some way to bound the extensive range of possible materials, this study does not consider books or book chapters. This, of course, also overlooks much central communication theory-related work, and both more specialist and more cultural and sociological topics; for book reviews on new media, see issues of *Information, Communication & Society* and *New Media & Society*, and the Resource Center for Cyberculture Studies (http://rccs.usfca.edu).

Nonetheless, we find some of the same major themes as other studies. As Lievrouw et al. (2001) concluded from their review, even a decade ago "network formations" was one of the three primary dimensions of communication and technology research. Also, Kim and Weaver (2002) noted that U&G, democratic theory, diffusion/adoption, and interactivity were among the most common theoretical perspectives in Communication journals from 1996 through 2000, similar to some of the most frequent theory themes in our analyses (they used the same search terms of "internet" and "World Wide Web" in the Communication Abstracts database). Peng et al. (2012) used text-mining tools to analyze 27,000 articles in Social Sciences Citation Index (SSCI) and arts and humanities citation index (A&HCI) journals from 2000 to 2009, finding four primary (global) themes, each with subthemes: e-healthcare (generic applications, specific behaviors), e-business (acceptance studies, management, marketing), social issues (social interactions, law/policy, communication), and human–technology interactions (psychological processing, information retrieval/knowledge, and learning). They also find emphases in the literature on the relationships between use and behaviors/attitudes/effects, social interaction, and network approaches.

Communication journals were in the top five most frequent subject categories for e-healthcare specific behaviors, ebusiness acceptance studies, and all three of the social science subthemes. Within the social science articles, example "hot topics" included some of the main themes identified in our study: online/virtual community, social capital, social community, social identity, political participation, digital divide, privacy, and communication use/behaviors.

Of course, the nature of the search terms ("Internet," "World Wide Web") and filtering via reading the abstracts and articles both focus and constrain the particular sample of articles. For example, Boler (2007) critically analyzed studies of text-based CMC (esp. MUDs and MOOs) to assess the hypes and hopes of mediated disembodiment. She did not use terms such as "Internet" or "World Wide Web" to search for candidate articles to review (personal communication), and her article itself did not meet the search criteria for this study. Her study generated several primary themes of our study, such as Identity or Accessibility, but also different ones, such as Space or Transcendence.

Conclusion

In the first decade of the twenty-first century, areas in communication-related social science articles distinct and frequent enough to represent their own theme included interactivity, media attributes, credibility, diffusion of innovations, media effects, media use, possibly harmful Internet use, uses and gratifications, civic engagement, participatory media/users, political participation, public sphere, channel use and sociality, community, groups, identity, relational management, social capital, social networks, cultural differences, digital divide, political economy/policy, and privacy. Some theoretical areas seem to be receiving more attention in this past decade, such as possibly harmful Internet use, civic engagement, public sphere, community, identity, social capital, political economy/policy, and privacy.

In sorting out approaches to applying theory to Internet phenomena, we can see areas that have received considerable attention, as well as those that warrant additional attention. Our review suggests that media attributes, public sphere, and community were the most popular theory themes. However, we do not suggest that these theory themes are oversaturated, because there is considerable theoretical breadth within each theme. Rather, we advocate that scholars balance breadth and depth, as they address topics in these themes. Based on the theory themes with the fewest instances, our review suggests opportunities for further theoretical development in the areas of credibility/trust, participatory media/users, relational management, and cultural differences. The phenomena in these themes complicate traditional notions of information, audience activity, relational strategies, and intercultural relations, and further development in these areas can revise scope conditions of theories, or bring about new theoretical approaches altogether. The general theme of participation received substantially increased coverage over the years, implying both an increased concern with and understanding of the active, more public role of Internet communication, and the increased presence of Web 2.0 interaction and activities.

The global theme typology/clusters, and the visual associations among themes based on shared terms, provide scholars with a useful tool to identify explicit and latent relationships among communication-oriented theories and concepts in the study of the Internet. For any particular study, these relationships can be used to broaden the context (such as in the literature review, or in model development), help focus the boundaries or provide the basis for conceptual differentiation, identify possibilities for further integration and boundary-crossing, locate areas of unexplored conceptual linkages, and provide guidance for area studies, meta-analyses, and literature reviews.

Perhaps the simplest, but most encouraging, conclusion is that while the early phase of CMC and Internet research was often criticized as being a-theoretical, an exceptionally wide range of primary and secondary theories, within more inclusive global themes, are being applied to understand social and communicative aspects of the Internet. More centrally, a large set of articles included theory frameworks, whether critiques, theoretical models, or reviews. As noted in the introduction, there has been much communication-related theory and many concepts about the Internet to read, review, critique, distinguish, integrate, and propose in the past decade. There will be more to come in the next.

NOTES

Articles with the listed words in title or in abstract of peer-reviewed journals in English, retrieved April 18, 2010 (and, for the 2010 entries, April 25, 2011) from relevant databases in CSA online Social Sciences collection (Communication Abstracts/CA, International Bibliography of the Social Sciences, PAIS (public affairs, international relations), PAIS International, PSYCArticles, PSYCInfo, Sociological Abstracts, Worldwide Political Science Abstracts). There are some duplicates within or across a search result (for example, an abstract may include both "facebook" and "instant messaging"), and even some quite specific terms such as "twitter" may have other references (such as the marmoset's or blackbird's twitter calls), though those were removed. Figures for 2010 are underestimates, as different journals take different numbers of months to be indexed and retrievable. Additionally, values in each cell may change in later searches, due to journals, volumes, or issues being added or deleted from the database. For example, CA was no longer included in the CAS collection by April 2011, so figures will be lower. We did run separate searches of the terms using the separate CA database in 2010 (for example, finding 119 entries for the title search). However, some journals are likely to be included in both CA and CAS, and we do not know when CA was dropped from CSA. So the numbers are not comparable.

The methods for our research, especially important in providing transparency in qualitative coding, can only be briefly summarized in this chapter. An extended account which includes lists of source journals, coded articles, primary theories, and secondary theories, is available online: <http://www.comm.ucsb.edu/faculty/rrice/RiceFuller Oxford HandbookInternetTheory2012Appendix.pdf.>.

Acknowlegments

An earlier version of this chapter was presented at the conference, *The Internet Turning 40: Never-Ending Novelty of New Media Research?*, The Chinese University of Hong Kong, June 2010. We thank Madison Crowley for her thoughtful help in initial coding. We thank InformaWorld for providing us a free full-text e-journal subscription to *Information, Communication & Society*. We thank Katy Pearce for the grounded theory advice, Megan Bolen for comments on a draft, and William Dutton for his encouragement and suggestions.

References

Agarwal, R., Animesh, A., and Prasad, K. (2009). "Social Interactions and the 'Digital Divide': Explaining Variation in Internet Use," *Information Systems Research*, 20(2): 277–94.

Armstrong, C. and McAdams, M. (2009). "Blogs of Information: How Gender Cues and Individual Motivations Influence Perceptions of Credibility," *Journal of Computer-Mediated Communication*, 14(3): 435–56.

Baym, N. (2005). "Introduction: Internet Research as It Isn't, Is, Could Be, and Should Be," *The Information Society*, 21: 229–32.

Billon, M., Marco, R., and Lera-Lopez, F. (2009). "Disparities in ICT Adoption: A Multi dimensional Approach to Study the Cross-Country Digital Divide," *Telecommunications Policy*, 33(10–11): 596–610.

Bimber, B., Flanagin, A. J., and Stohl, C. (2005). "Reconceptualizing Collective Action in the Contemporary Media Environment," *Communication Theory*, 15(4): 365–88.

Birnie, S. and Horvath, P. (2002). "Psychological Predictors of Internet Social Communication," *Journal of Computer-Mediated Communication*, 7(4). Available at <http://onlinelibrary.wiley.com/doi/10.1111/j.1083-6101.2002.tb00154.x/full>. Accessed October 12, 2011.

Boler, M. (2007). "Hypes, Hopes and Actualities: New Digital Cartesianism and Bodies in Cyberspace," *New Media & Society*, 9(1): 139–68.

Borgatti, S. P., Everett, M. G., and Freeman, L. C. (2002). *Ucinet for Windows: Software for Social Network Analysis*, Harvard, MA: Analytic Technologies.

Boyd, J. (2003). "The Rhetorical Construction of Trust Online," *Communication Theory*, 13(4): 392–410.

Brock, A. (2009). "Life on the Wire: Deconstructing Race on the Internet," *Information, Communication & Society*, 12(3): 344–63.

Caiani, M. and Wagemann, C. (2009). "Online Networks of the Italian and German Extreme Right," *Information, Communication & Society*, 12(1): 66–109.

Calenda, D. and Meijer, A. (2009). "Young People, the Internet and Political Participation," *Information, Communication & Society*, 12(6): 879–98.

Cammaerts, B. (2008). "Critiques on the Participatory Potentials of Web 2.0," *Communication, Culture & Critique*, 1(4): 359–77.

Carey, J. W. (2005). "Historical Pragmatism and the Internet," *New Media & Society*, 7(4): 443–55.

Castells, M. (2009). *The Rise of the Network Society: The Informage Age: Economy, Society, and Culture*, vol. 1, 2nd edn., Hoboken, NJ: Wiley-Blackwell.

Catlett, C. E. (1989). "The NFSNET: Beginnings of a National Research Internet," *Academic Computing*, 3(5): 19–21, 59–64.

Charmaz, K. (2006). *Constructing Grounded Theory: A Practical Guide through Qualitative Analysis*, London: Sage.

Cheung, W., Change, M. K., and Lai, V. S. (2000). "Prediction of Internet and World Wide Web Usage at Work: A Test of an Extended Triandis Model," *Decision Support Systems*, 30(1): 83–100.

Cho, H., Rivera-Sanchez, M., and Lim, S. S. (2009). "A Multinational Study on Online Privacy: Global Concerns and Local Responses," *New Media & Society*, 11(3): 395–416.

Crowston, K. and Williams, M. (2000). "Reproduced and Emergent Genres of Communication on the World Wide Web," *The Information Society*, 16(3): 201–15.

Dahlberg, L. (2001). "The Internet and Democratic Discourse: Exploring the Prospects of Online Deliberative Forums Extending the Public Sphere," *Information, Communication & Society*, 4(4): 615–33.

David, C., Cappella, J. N., and Fishbein, M. (2006). "The Social Diffusion of Influence among Adolescents: Group Interaction in a Chat Room Environment about Antidrug Advertisements," *Communication Theory*, 16(1): 118–40.

De Koster, W. and Houtman, D. (2008). "Stormfront is Like a Second Home to Me: On Virtual Community Formation by Right-Wing Extremists," *Information, Communication & Society*, 11(8): 1155–76.

Deibert, R. J. (2000). "International Plug'n' Play Citizen Activism, the Internet, and Global Public Policy," *International Studies Perspectives*, 1(3): 255–72.

Downes, E. J. and McMillan, S. J. (2000). "Defining Interactivity: A Qualitative Identification of Key Dimensions," *New Media & Society*, 2(2): 157–79.

Eastin, M. S., Greenberg, B. S., and Hofschire, L. (2006). "Parenting the Internet," *Journal of Communication*, 56(3): 486–504.

Elias, N. and Lemish, D. (2009). "Spinning the Web of Identity: The Roles of the Internet in the Lives of Immigrant Adolescents," *New Media & Society*, 11(4): 533–51.

Elmer, G. (2003). "A Diagram of Panoptic Surveillance," *New Media & Society*, 5(2): 231–47.

Flanagin, A. J. and Metzger, M. J. (2007). "The Role of Site Features, User Attributes, and Information Verification Behaviors on the Perceived Credibility of Web-Based Information," *New Media & Society*, 9(2): 319–42.

Franzen, A. (2000). "Does the Internet Make us Lonely," *European Sociological Review*, 16(4): 427–38.

Gevorgyan, G. and Manucharova, N. (2009). "Does Culturally Adapted Online Communication Work? A Study of American and Chinese Internet Users' Attitudes and Preferences toward Culturally Customized Web Design Elements," *Journal of Computer-Mediated Communication*, 14(2): 393–413.

Glaser, B. G. (2004). "Remodeling Grounded Theory," *Qualitative Social Research*, 5, art. 4.

Gotved, S. (2006). "Time and Space in Cyber Social Reality," *New Media & Society*, 8(3): 467–86.

Gunkel, D. J. (2003). "Second Thoughts: Toward a Critique of the Digital Divide," *New Media & Society*, 5(4): 499–522.

Haythornthwaite, C. (2005). "Social Networks and Internet Connectivity Effects," *Information, Communication and Society*, 8(2): 125–47.

Hiltz, S. R. and Turoff, M. (1978). *The Network Nation*, Menlo Park, CA: Addison-Wesley.

Ho, S. S., Waipeng, L., and Hameed, S. S. (2008). "Muslim Surfers on the Internet: Using the Theory of Planned Behaviour to Examine the Factors Influencing Engagement in Online Religious Activities," *New Media & Society*, 10(1): 93–113.

Holmes, J. (2009). "Myths and Missed Opportunities: Young People's Not So Risky Use of Online Communication," *Information, Communication & Society*, 12(8): 1174–96.

Hung, A. Y. H. (2002). "Identity Politics, Resistance and New Media Technologies: A Foucauldian Approach to the Study of the Hknet," *New Media & Society*, 4(2): 185–204.

Johansen, R., Miller, R. H., and Vallee, J. (1974). "Group Communication through Electronic Media: Fundamental Choices and Social Effects," *Educational Technology*, 14(8): 7–20.

Johnson, A. J., Haigh, M. M., Becker, J. A. H., Craig, E. A., and Wigley, S. (2008). "College Students' Use of Relational Management Strategies in Email in Long-Distance and Geographically Close Relationships," *Journal of Computer-Mediated Communication*, 13: 381–404.

Katz, J. E. and Rice, R. E. (2002). *Social Consequences of Internet Use: Access, Involvement and Interaction*, Cambridge, MA: The MIT Press.

——, Rice, R. E., Acord, S., Dasgupta, K., and David, K. (2004). "Personal Mediated Communication and the Concept of Community in Theory and Practice," in P. Kalbfleisch (ed.). *Communication Yearbook 28*, London: Routledge, pp. 315–70.

Kim, H., Coyle, J. R., and Gould, S. J. (2009). "Collectivist and Individualist Influences on Website Design in South Korea and the U.S.: A Cross-Cultural Content Analysis," *Journal of Computer-Mediated Communication*, 14(3): 581–601.

Kim, S. T. and Weaver, D. (2002). "Communication Research about the Internet: A Thematic Meta-Analysis," *New Media & Society*, 4(4): 518–38.

Laguerre, M. (2004). "Virtual Time: The Processuality of the Cyberweek," *Information, Communication & Society*, 7(2): 223–47.

LaRose, R. and Eastin, M. (2004). "A Social Cognitive Theory of Internet Uses and Gratifications: Toward a New Model of Media Attendance," *Journal of Broadcasting & Electronic Media*, 48(3): 358–77.

Ledbetter, A. M. (2008). "Media Use and Relational Closeness in Long-Term Friendships: Interpreting Patterns of Multimodality," *New Media & Society*, 10(4): 547–64.

Lee, B. and Tamborini, R. (2005). "Third-Person Effect and Internet Pornography: The Influence of Collectivism and Internet Self-Efficacy," *Journal of Communication*, 55(2): 292–310.

Lee, E.-J. (2004). "Effects of Visual Representation on Social Influence in Computer-Mediated Communication: Experimental Tests of the Social Identity Model of Deindividuation Effects," *Human Communication Research*, 30(2): 234–59.

Levine, T. R. (2010). "Rankings and Trends in Citation Patterns of Communication Journals," *Communication Education*, 59(1): 41–51.

Lievrouw, L. A., Bucy, E. P., Finn, T. A., Frindte, W., Gershon, R. A., Haythornthwaite, C., Kohler, T., Metz, J. M., and Sunder, S. Shyam (2001)."Bridging the Subdisciplines: An

Overview of Communication Technology and Research," *Communication Yearbook*, 24: Thousand Oaks, CA: Sage, pp. 271–95.

Lynch, C. A. (1989). "Linking Library Automation Systems in the Internet: Functional Requirements, Planning, and Policy Issues," *Library Hi Tech*, 7(4): 7–18.

Mansell, R. (2004). "Political Economy, Power and New Media," *New Media & Society*, 6(1): 96–105.

McCain, K. W. (2000). "Sharing Digitized Research-Related Information on the World Wide Web," *Journal of the American Society for Information Science*, 51(14): 1321–7.

McCoy, M. E. (2001). "Dark Alliance: News Repair and Institutional Authority in the Age of the Internet," *Journal of Communication*, 51(1): 164–93.

Mehra, B., Merkel, C., and Bishop, A. P. (2004). "The Internet for Empowerment of Minority and Marginalized Users," *New Media & Society*, 6(6): 781–802.

Mesch, G. S. (2006). "Family Characteristics and Intergenerational Conflicts over the Internet," *Information, Communication & Society*, 9(4): 473–95.

Metzger, M. J. (2007). "Communication Privacy Management in Electronic Commerce," *Journal of Computer-Mediated Communication*, 12(2). Available at <http://jcmc.indiana.edu/vol12/issue2/metzger.html>. Accessed June 20, 2012.

Miller, S. and Weckert, J. (2000). "Privacy, the Workplace and the Internet," *Journal of Business Ethics*, 28(3): 255–65.

Parks, M. (2009). "What will we Study when the Internet Disappears?," *Journal of Computer-Mediated Communication*, 14: 724–9.

Peng, T-Q., Zhu, J. J. H., Zhang, L., and Zhong, Z. (2012). "Mapping the Theme Structure of Internet Research: Text Mining of Social Science Journal Articles 2000–2009," *New Media & Society*.(forthcoming).

Perry, D. G. et al. (1988). "The ARPANET and DARPA Internet," *Library Hi Tech*, 6(2): 51–62.

Procopio, C. and Procopio, S. (2007). "Do You Know What It Means To Miss New Orleans? Internet Communication, Geographic Community, and Social Capital in Crisis," *Journal of Applied Communication Research*, 35(1): 67–87.

Ramirez, A., Walther, J. B., Burgoon, J. K., and Sunnafrank, M. (2002). "Information-Seeking Strategies, Uncertainty, and Computer-Mediated Communication: Toward a Conceptual Model," *Human Communication Research*, 28(2): 213–28.

Räsänen, P. and Kouvo, A. (2007). "Linked or Divided by the Web?: Internet Use and Sociability in Four European Countries," *Information, Communication & Society*, 10(2): 219–41.

Rice, R. E. (1980a). "The Impacts of Computer-Mediated Organizational and Interpersonal Communication," in M. Williams (ed.) *Annual Review of Information Science and Technology*, 15, White Plains, NY: Knowledge Industry Publications, pp. 221–49.

——(1980b). "Computer Conferencing," in B. Dervin and M. Voigt (eds). *Progress in Communication Sciences*, 2, New York: Ablex, pp. 215–40

——(1984). "New Media Technology: Growth and Integration," in R. E. Rice (ed.). *The New Media: Communication, Research and Technology*, Beverly Hills, CA: Sage, pp. 33–54.

——(1992). "Contexts of Research on Organizational Computer-Mediated Communication," in M. Lea (ed.). *Contexts of Computer Mediated Communication*, Hemel Hempstead: Harvester Wheatsheaf, pp. 113–44.

——(2009). "Diffusion of Innovations: Theoretical Extensions," in R. Nabi and M. B. Oliver (eds). *Handbook of Media Effects*, Thousand Oaks, CA: Sage, pp. 489–503

—— and Hagen, I. (2010). "Young Adults' Perpetual Contact, Social Connection, and Social Control through the Internet and Mobile Phones," in C. Salmon (ed.). *Communication Yearbook*, 34, London: Routledge, pp. 2–39.

Richards, C. (2000). "Hypermedia, Internet Communication, and the Challenge of Redefining Literacy in the Electronic Age," *Language Learning & Technology*, 4(2): 59–77.

Robinson, J. P. and Martin, S. P. (2009). "Social Attitude Differences between Internet Users and Non-Users: Evidence from the General Social Survey," *Information, Communication & Society*, 12(4): 508–24.

Ruggiero, T. E. (2000). "Uses and Gratifications Theory in the 21st Century," *Mass Communication & Society*, 3(1): 3–37.

Russell, A. (2007). "Digital Communication Networks and the Journalistic Field: The 2005 French Riots," *Critical Studies in Media Communication*, 24(4): 285–302.

Ryland, J. (1989). "Security: A Sleeper Issue Comes into its Own," *CAUSE/EFFECT*, 12(4): 8–13.

Sawhney, H. (2007). "Strategies for Increasing the Conceptual Yield of New Technologies Research," *Communication Monographs*, 74(3): 395–401.

Scolari, C. A. (2009). "Mapping Conversations about New Media: The Theoretical Field of Digital Communication," *New Media & Society*, 11(6): 943–64.

Scott, C. R. (2009). "A Whole-Hearted Effort to Get it Half Right: Predicting the Future of Communication Technology Scholarship," *Journal of Computer-Mediated Communication*, 14(3): 753–7.

Shah, D. V., McLeod, J. M., and Yoon, S.-H. (2001). "Communication, Context, and Community: An Exploration of Print, Broadcast, and Internet Influences," *Communication Research*, 28(4): 464–506.

Simpson, S. (2004). "Explaining the Commercialization of the Internet: A neo-Gramscian Contribution," *Information, Communication & Society*, 7(1): 50–68.

Soukup, C. (2000). "Building a Theory of Multi-Media CMC: An Analysis, Critique and Integration of Computer-Mediated Communication Theory and Research," *New Media & Society*, 2(4): 407–25.

Strauss, A. and Corbin, J. (1998). *Basics of Qualitative Research: Grounded Theory Procedures and Techniques*, 2nd edn., Thousand Oaks, CA: Sage.

Tan, K. W. P., Swee, D., Lim, C., Detenber, B. H., and Alsagoff, L. (2007). "The Impact of Language Variety and Expertise on Perceptions of Online Political Discussions," *Journal of Computer Mediated Communication*, 13(1): 76–99.

Tomasello, T. K., Lee, Y., and Baer, A. P. (2010). "'New Media' Research Publication Trends and Outlets in Communication, 1990–2006," *New Media & Society*, 12(4): 531–48.

Tyner, J. A. and Kuhlke, O. (2000). "Pan-National Identities: Representations of the Philippine Diaspora on the World Wide Web," *Asia Pacific Viewpoint*, 41(3): 231–52.

Van Dijck, J. and Nieborg, D. (2009). "Wikinomics and its Discontents: A Critical Analysis of Web 2.0 Business Manifestos," *New Media & Society*, 11(5): 855–74.

Walther, J. B. (2009). "Theories, Boundaries, and All of the Above," *Journal of Computer-Mediated Communication*, 14(3): 748–52.

Wang, Z., Walther, J. B., and Hancock, J. T. (2009). "Social Identification and Interpersonal Communication in Computer-Mediated Communication: What You Do Versus Who You Are in Virtual Groups," *Human Communication Research*, 35(1): 59–85.

Waskul, D. D. (2005). "Ekstasis and the Internet: Liminality and Computer-Mediated Communication," *New Media & Society*, 7(1): 47–63.

White, C. and Scheb, J. M. (2000). "Impact of Media Messages about the Internet: Internet Anxiety as a Factor in the Adoption Process in the USA," *New Media & Society*, 2(2): 181–94.

Wilson, T. and Tan, H. P. (2005). "Less Tangible Ways of Reading: A Ludic Surfing of Online Western News Sites," *Information, Communication & Society*, 8(3): 394–416.

Xenos, M., and Moy, P. (2007). "Direct and Differential Effects of the Internet on Political and Civic Engagement," *Journal of Communication*, 57(4): 704–18.

Yang, C.-C. (2000). "The Use of the Internet among Academic Gay Communities in Taiwan: An Exploratory Study," *Information, Communication & Society*, 3(2): 153–72.

Youngs, G. (2001). "The Political Economy of Time in the Internet Era: Feminist Perspectives and Challenges, *Information, Communication & Society*, 4(1): 14–33.

Zhao, S. and Elesh, D. (2008). "Copresence as 'Being With': Social Contact in Online Public Domains," *Information, Communication & Society*, 11(4): 565–83.

CHAPTER 18

....

TRADITION AND TRANSFORMATION IN ONLINE NEWS PRODUCTION AND CONSUMPTION

....

EUGENIA MITCHELSTEIN AND PABLO J. BOCZKOWSKI

NEWS media play a central role in the cultural, political, and economic lives of modern societies (Castells 1997; Luhmann 1996; Thompson 1995). Since the mid-1990s, online news has been incorporated into the media consumption routines of large segments of the population. For instance, nearly half (46 percent) of Americans got news from the Internet at least three days a week in 2010, compared to 2 percent in 1995 (Pew Research Center 2010). As online journalists and audiences have expanded and entered the mainstream, research about Internet news consumption and production has also increased and consolidated. Although there have been many studies analyzing narrowly defined aspects of online journalism and news consumption, there have been few thorough assessments (Boczkowski 2002; Kopper et al. 2000) of the findings revealed by these studies. This examination of research on Internet journalists and audiences intends, first, to fill this gap, providing an updated and comprehensive review of the scholarship on these topics, and second, to use this assessment as a basis to propose new directions of conceptual, methodological, and theoretical inquiry for the future.

The examination of the literature indicates that online news producers and consumers straddle between tradition and innovation in their daily practices. Although most journalists continue to prioritize their gate-keeping functions and work to control news content, some are more open to community-oriented functions and to acting as gate-openers. Audiences meanwhile: have increased their use of online news while maintaining traditional media as their main sources of information; exhibit both fragmentation and homogenization in their content choices; and, for the most part, have not taken up the opportunities offered to create their own news. The next two sections, which examine online news production and consumption respectively, delve into these matters. Tradition rather than innovation has also often characterized the dominant modes of inquiry on online news. This, in turn, might have hampered novel accounts of changes in online news production and consumption. Thus, the final section of this chapter is devoted to reflecting on the limitations in the research about Internet journalists and audiences, exploring how they are linked to fundamental organizers in the communication literature, and proposing ways to overcome these limitations in future research.

ONLINE NEWS PRODUCTION

This section is organized into five parts. The first examines research about contextual matters, such as the history and market environment of online news. The second part addresses analyses of the causes, dynamics, and consequences of innovation. The third part looks into research about changes in journalistic practice. The fourth focuses on occupational matters. The final part deals with the role of the user as a content producer.

The context of online news production

Scholarship on the historical development of online journalism has often focused on how competitive and institutional influences have shaped the evolution of Internet news. Research indicates that traditional media companies' main motivation to take up online news was their concern about new players in the digital arena (Dennis 2006; Gilbert 2005; Herbert and Thurman 2007; Salwen 2005). Nguyen characterizes mainstream media's initial participation in online journalism as fueled by "fear of the new being a disruptor of the near-monopoly (they) had been enjoying" (2008: 92). Boczkowski (2004a) proposes that these competitive dynamics have been related to a particular culture of innovation marked by reactive, defensive, and pragmatic traits. He argues that newspapers developed online operations as a reaction to prior moves by new competitors; they did so in a way that defended their existing territory rather than conquered new ones, and centered on making a profit in the short term rather than idealistically pursuing opportunities that could only pan out in the longer term.

Scholarship has also examined profitability, another key element of the online news market environment (Ahlers 2006; Chyi 2005; Greer 2004; Pavlik 2001). Research indicates that few online newspapers were making a profit by the early 2000s (Boczkowski 2004a; Singer 2003), and some scholars suggest that this was a consequence of the lack of an adequate business model (Cawley 2008; Chyi and Sylvie 2001; Stober 2004). Thurman and Myllylahti analyze the case of a Finnish financial newspaper, and find that canceling the print edition "did not result in an increase in online traffic" 2009: 704), and also led to a decrease of at least 75 percent in income due to the loss of print advertising and subscription revenue.

Research indicates that although online news organizations have straddled between resorting to traditional sources of income, such as advertising and subscription, and relying on new revenue-generating strategies made possible by the Internet, such as e-commerce, advertising has remained the primary source of revenue for most news sites (Bustamante 2004; Chan-Olmsted and Ha 2003; Herbert and Thurman 2007). In a survey of media executives conducted in 2009, 39 percent said the predominant business model was advertising-funded and 21 percent said it consisted of multiple revenue streams (Project for Excellence in Journalism 2010). However, studies have found that the advertising model does not guarantee substantive profits (Chyi 2005; Garrison 2005; Singer 2003). One reason for this conclusion is the relatively low level of expenditure on online advertisements. Filloux (2008) found that, in 2007, the *Washington Post* lost 77 million dollars in print ad revenue, while online advertising increased only by 6 million. The importance of advertising revenue is underscored by several studies that show that users are not prepared to pay for content (Chyi and Yang 2009; Gentzkow 2007; Herbert and Thurman 2007).

Historical conditions and market forces discussed above have influenced the development of online journalism. This development is also related to the process of innovation, shaped in turn by a host of social factors.

The processes of innovation in online journalism

Most scholars who study the role of technological change in the adoption of innovation in online journalism propose that innovations are shaped by initial conditions and contextual characteristics (Boczkowski 2004c; Conboy and Steel 2008; Haas 2005; Stober 2004). In an analysis of how journalism has changed, Deuze (2007: 153) proposes that "technology is not an independent factor influencing journalistic work...but must be seen in terms of implementation, and how it extends and amplifies previous ways of doing things."

Studies on the dynamics of innovation underscore the influence of organizational and institutional factors on how the process unfolds in different settings (Boczkowski and Ferris 2005; Gilbert 2005; Klinenberg 2005; Thurman 2008). For instance, DeWaal and Schoenbach find that non-newspaper sites "have been much faster to adopt the possibilities of online publishing" than newspaper sites, and suggest that "the disadvantage of having no ready-to-publish material resulted in a headstart...in terms of a progressive web design" 2010: 481). Scholars also examine the consequences of innovation for the media industry and society at large (Bolano et al. 2004; Bustamante 2004; Deuze 2006; Domingo 2008). Some studies indicate that established journalistic operations have tended not to realize the potential of new technologies (Deuze 2003; Garrison 2005; Quinn 2005; Steensen 2009). The tension between the established ways of producing news, and the changes in journalistic practices that the online medium affords, play out in distinct ways in different cultural and political settings (Dimitrova et al. 2005; Semetko and Krasnoboka 2003; Weber and Jia 2007). For instance, Kim and Hamilton look into the sociopolitical context of the emergence of the South Korean user-authored news site *OhmyNews* and argue that the site can only be fully understood "as a particular response to, and enabled by, very specific conditions" 2006: 547).

These dynamics of innovation have in turn been tied to transformations in the practices of gathering, producing, and publishing news.

The practices of online news production

Scholarship has mostly focused on four types of changes in journalistic practices: modifications in editorial workflow, alterations in news-gathering practices, acceleration of temporal patterns of production, and the convergence of print, broadcast, and online operations.

Researchers propose that online news has increased the pressure on journalists to perform multiple tasks and combine different media formats (Cawley 2008; Deuze 2004; Lawson-Borders 2006; Ursell 2001). Hermans and Vergeer indicate that "there is a greater demand for journalists able to work in a multimedia environment, requiring journalists to become multiskilled" (2009: 142). These workflow changes are tied to what Boczkowski calls the "de-reification of media options," as "the Web's multimedia potential moves media selection processes one step earlier by requiring journalists to choose what medium or media to use for a particular story" 2004a: 123).

Scholars have also argued that the existing technological capabilities and how journalists appropriate them contribute to shaping information-gathering practices (Millen and Dray 2000; O'Sullivan and Heinonen 2008; Pavlik 2000; Salwen 2005). Already in 1999, 92 percent of journalists in the United States gathered news online (Garrison 2001). However, use of the Internet for information seeking has not been homogenous across national contexts. Nicholas et al. (2000) found that nearly one-third of journalists in the United Kingdom surveyed in 2000 had no access to the Internet. Studies also indicate that journalists tend to distrust the Internet as a source (Cassidy 2007; Chan et al. 2006; Hermans and Vergeer 2009; Shin and Cameron 2003). This may be explained by the fact that reporters are susceptible to misinformation, as "the same digital systems that improve journalists' ability to do research in the office can also have perverse effects" (Klinenberg 2005: 56).

Research on Internet news production has also addressed the increased speed of communications in journalistic work. Many scholars propose that online journalism has contributed to the collapse of the twice-a-day news cycle (Boczkowski and de Santos 2007; García 2008; Karlsson and Strombäck 2009; Williams and Deli Carpini 2000). An examination of the period of data collection of various studies suggests that acceleration has deepened over time. Boczkowski (2004a) conducted research on the *New York Times on the Web* in 1998 and reported that editors published stories towards the end of the day, following the publishing cycle of the print *Times*. More recently, Rosenstiel (2005) has argued that acceleration has become a key feature of the contemporary news industry in the USA. However, increased speed is not an inevitable consequence of the shift to the online medium. In an ethnographic study of an Argentine online newsroom, Boczkowski (2010) finds that different units of the site followed varying temporal patterns: while in the "hard news" unit journalists produced six or seven new stories every day, at the "soft news" unit, journalists authored two or three new stories every week. He concludes that "acceleration in journalistic practice is not in the essence of online news but can vary greatly as a result of organizational and material factors, even within a single newsroom" 2010: 56).

Scholars have examined the organizational integration among print, broadcast, and online operations, usually under the rubric of "convergence" (Dennis 2006; Deuze 2007; Dupagne and Garrison 2006; Quinn 2005). Lawson-Borders (2006: 4) characterizes convergence as "the realm of possibilities when cooperation occurs between print and broadcast media for the delivery of multimedia content." Research indicates that the trend towards convergence has not been uniform across organizations and countries as a result of different patterns in the merging of the old and new logics of production (Boczkowski and Ferris 2005; Deuze 2004; Klinenberg 2005; Meier 2007). Thornton and Keith report the existence of a decline in the print-broadcast convergence model, and suggest that "newspapers and television stations were moving toward what might be called 'Webvergence'—a focus on each news organization producing multimedia content independently to feed its own Web site" 2009: 265).

These changes in news production practices are related to shifts in the professional identity of journalists.

Professional and occupational matters

Research about professional and occupational dynamics has focused on three key topics: the identity of journalism as a profession; the self reflection of journalists about changes to their professional identities; and the challenges posed by user-authored content to the jurisdictional space that news workers occupy.

Some researchers propose that the unresolved debate about who is a journalist has been exacerbated by the fact that journalism's occupational boundaries are more open to negotiation (Allan 2006; Deuze 2003; Dutton 2009; Robinson 2007). Other scholars propose that disputes over the professional identity of journalism could eventually lead to its demise as was known during the better part of the twentieth century (Boczkowski 2004b; Deuze 2007). Sousa examines the development of online journalism in Portugal and argues that "the economic and political conditions that brought journalism into existence will soon cease to prevail, and journalism, at least in its traditional form, with them" (2006: 379).

Scholarship about the self-perceptions of journalists has yielded varying results. Deuze and Paulussen surveyed online news workers in the Netherlands and Belgium and found that they believe that their profession is developing as a new type of journalism premised on ideas of immediacy, hypertext, and multimedia (2002). However, Quandt et al. (2006) found that American and German journalists continue to prioritize traditional information-oriented functions. This discrepancy might be an expression of the evolution of journalists' self-perceptions. For instance, in a survey of editors of the online operations of major American newspapers about online coverage of the 2000 elections, Singer reports a "normalization" process in which "information-oriented functions, particularly related to getting news out quickly, remain key components of their self-perceptions" (2003: 50). In a later study about online news sites during 2004 elections, Singer indicates that journalists appeared to re-imagine their role towards a partnership with consumers, conceptualizing the production of information "as a shared rather than an exclusive endeavor" 2006: 276). However, in a study of the 2008 election coverage, she finds a reassertion of traditional journalistic roles despite the increase in options for user input (Singer 2009).

Gatekeeping has been considered the principal marker of occupational jurisdiction in journalism since White's (1949) pioneering study. Some scholars have proposed that this jurisdictional claim might be challenged by the growing presence of users as content producers (Gillmor 2004; Lowrey 2006; McCoy 2001; Robinson 2007; Singer 2006). Gurevitch and colleagues suggest that, as citizens gain access to technologies through which they can create content, "the gate-keeping monopoly once enjoyed by editors and broadcasters is waning" 2009: 167). However, some authors contend that it might be too early to anticipate the end of gatekeeping (Allan 2006; Boczkowski and Mitchelstein 2010; Hujanen and Pietikainen 2004; Schiffer 2006). For instance, in their comparative study of audience participation opportunities in European and American newspapers, Domingo and his colleagues report that "journalists are retaining the traditional gatekeeping role in adopting user content in their websites" 2008: 340).

Scholars disagree on how best to characterize the broader societal consequences of these challenges to the occupational jurisdiction of journalists. On the one hand, some authors argue that these challenges could be beneficial for society (Deuze and Dimoudi 2002; Pavlik 2000; Russell 2001). Schudson examines news coverage of the 2008 presidential election in the United States and concludes that the new media "are sponsors of a new intensity, ubiquity, and anarchism in our mediated public world" (2009: 86). On the other hand, other studies raise concerns about the broader societal significance of these challenges (Salwen 2005; Singer 2001; Williams and Deli Carpini 2000). In their analysis of online newspapers, Nerone and Barnhurst (2001: 471) argue that the loss of journalists' gatekeeping function could replace "the benign dictatorship of the editor" with "the tyranny of the mouse."

The user as a content producer

The notion of news production as a collective effort between journalists and members of the public has captured the imagination of authors who study online journalism.

Analysts propose that the Internet allows a change in the relative position of reporters and audiences, from a one-way model of communication to a dialogical kind of journalism (Benkler 2006; Boczkowski 2004a; Dutton 2009; McCoy 2001; Tremayne 2007).

Research has examined how journalist- and user-generated content become combined on different sites. Some scholars suggest that news organizations are not enthusiastic about allowing audience members to become co-authors of content (Boczkowski 2004a; Schultz 2000; Thurman 2008; Ye and Li 2006). For instance, Williams and colleagues indicate that BBC reporters perceived audience material mainly as a source of information, and conclude that "truly collaborative relations between (journalists and audiences) remain rare exceptions" (2010: 11). In another dimension of the integration of production by professional reports and audience members, research shows that bloggers and citizen journalists rely heavily on journalists for information (Compton and Benedetti 2010; Haas 2005; Lowrey and Latta 2008; Reese et al. 2007). However, Anderson's account of a how the story of the arrest of four Philadelphia homeowners went from activist media to an alternative weekly to the local newspapers, and then to the local blogosphere, indicates that there is "neither informational anarchy nor the complete reemergence of an older, mass media dominated hierarchy, but a new model somewhere in between" (2010: 305).

Other studies have reported that members of the audience have shown limited interest in contributing content to online news sites (Chung and Nah 2009; Goode 2009; Hujanen and Pietikainen 2004; Thurman 2008). For instance, Boczkowski reports that the majority of news consumers in Argentina do "not read any blogs, forums, and comments appended to news stories," and that "the level of activity involved in contributing content to any of these user-authored options... is even lower than merely reading the content" (2010: 163). Furthermore, research indicates that most blogs do not cover public affairs topics (Lowrey and Latta 2008; Ornebring 2008; Trammell et al. 2006). Gans indicates that citizen journalists "cover the informally organized parts of society, the 'private' worlds of family, friends, compatible neighbors, work colleagues" 2007: 163). Some authors have proposed that the differences between users and reporters are due to organizational factors (Carlson 2007; Reich 2008; Rutigliano 2007). For instance, Lowrey analyzes the differences between journalist- and user-generated content and concludes that "the organization of production is the most fundamental distinction between journalism and blogging" 2006: 480). However, Dutton proposes that the characterization of citizen journalists as "spewing misinformation or trivial non-information... dismiss some of the same weaknesses of the traditional mass media, such as the 'if it bleeds it leads' focus on negative news stories" 2009: 13–14).

ONLINE NEWS CONSUMPTION

The tension between tradition and innovation is one of the defining characteristics of online news production. Research indicates that members of the audience also straddle between stability and change in their news consumption habits. Studies show that despite the proliferation of media outlets and technologies, most users are still influenced by past consumption habits. This assessment is presented in the next three sections. The first centers on research about whether online news complements or displaces traditional media use. The second addresses audience fragmentation and homogenization. The third looks at the links between online news and political knowledge and participation.

Does online news consumption complement or displace traditional media consumption?

Scholarship about the relationship between news consumption in online and traditional media is organized in two camps. The first stream of research indicates that the use of online news media complements the consumption of information in traditional media (Chyi and Lasorsa 2002; Kayany and Yelsma 2000; Livingstone and Markham 2008; Nguyen and Western 2007). For instance, Newell and colleagues analyze media use in the United States from 2003 until 2006 and find that consumers "can be characterized as adopting new media quickly, and dis-adopting incumbent media slowly, if at all" (2008: 137). Drawing on uses and gratification theory (Katz et al. 1974), a different perspective contends that users' goals and interests shape consumption more strongly than medium attributes (Flanagin and Metzger 2001). Thus, people focus on specific types of content, such as sports, politics, and entertainment in the multiple platforms used to access the respective stories (Dutta-Bergman 2004; Lin et al. 2005; Livingstone 2004).

An alternative research stream draws on the principle of relative constancy (McCombs 1972) to argue that use of traditional media has decreased, signaling a displacement effect (Gentzkow 2007; Gunter et al. 2003; Kaye and Johnson 2003). The Project for Excellence in Journalism (2010) reports that, in the US, newspaper circulation fell 10.6 percent between 2008 and 2009, compared to an increase of 14 percent in unique visitors to online news sites in the same period. There seems to be a complex relationship between complementarity and displacement that is, in part, dependent on temporal and socioeconomic factors. Some authors contend that audience behavior could change over time, as the appropriation of online technologies is normalized (Althaus and Tewksbury 2000; Metzger et al. 2003). Moreover, studies indicate that displacement effects are greater among better educated and younger users (Ahlers 2006; Althaus et al. 2009; Coleman and McCombs 2007; Lee 2006). De Waal and Schoenbach found that young users in the Netherlands are more likely to use online news than print newspapers, and suggest that "web newspapers serve similar needs to printed papers, but more easily or more attractively" (2010: 490).

Fragmentation and homogenization among online media audiences

Drawing on selective exposure theory (Zillmann and Bryant 1985), some scholars have argued that the diversification in online news supply may lead to polarization as people obtain their information increasingly from like-minded sources (Baum and Groeling 2008; Margolis and Resnick 2000; Stroud 2008; Sunstein 2001; Tewksbury and Rittenberg 2009). The possibility of polarized news audiences "has raised fears of political balkanization and break-down of the national political consensus" (Graber 2006: 376). However, Garrett tracks online news consumption patterns and reports that "there is little evidence that (citizens) will use the Internet to create echo chambers, devoid of other viewpoints" (2009: 278). Other analysts have proposed that a lack of interest in public affairs news is particularly problematic in relation to the fragmentation of the news supply (Davis 1999; Mutz 2006; Prior 2005). Prior examines the links between content preferences and the media environment and concludes that the proliferation of choices "causes increasing segmentation between news and entertainment fans" 2007: 274). On a related note, Tewksbury argues that "fragmentation may reduce the likelihood of sustained, widespread attention to political issues, thereby weakening the potential of consensus emerging around specific problems and policies" 2005: 346). A related stream of research suggests that online news audiences' content selection strategies are facilitated by the medium's characteristics, such as visible rankings and personalization features (Dimmick et al. 2004; Knobloch-Westerwick and Alter 2007; Knobloch-Westerwick and Meng 2009; Knobloch-Westerwick et al. 2005). Some scholars have tied audience fragmentation to socioeconomic factors (Dutton et al. 2004; Graber 1996; Papacharissi 2002). For instance, Zillien and Hargittai analyze a survey of Internet users in Germany and find that the odds of using the Internet for political information increased among respondents of higher socioeconomic status (2009).

The opposite camp contends that the public is not becoming increasingly fragmented (Chadwick 2006; Neuman 2001). Some authors have focused on the construction of the news agenda (Boczkowski 2010; Boczkowski and de Santos 2007; Lee 2007). Lim finds that the agendas of four major American online newspapers converge, and concludes that "online newspapers are able to influence people's cognitive process of determining important agendas, as their print counterparts do" (2010: 309). Other researchers have looked at the reception side (Coleman and McCombs 2007; Meraz 2009). For instance, Hindman has argued that audience distribution on the Web shows the existence of "a small set of winners that receive the lion's share of the traffic, and a host of tiny websites that, collectively, receive most of the remaining visitors" (2009: 134).

The consequences of online news consumption for political knowledge and participation

This section focuses on the ties between access to Internet news and political knowledge, the credibility of online information, and the influence of online news consumption on civic engagement. To some scholars influenced by Downs's economic theory of democracy (1957), the vast availability of online news makes it easier for citizens to access political information (Bimber 1998; Johnson and Kaye 2003; Neuman 2001; Weber et al.

2003). But others have argued that this availability might increase access to public affairs content only for those already interested (Graber 1996; Margolis and Resnick 2000; Nisbet and Scheufele 2004; Tolbert and McNeal 2003). Researchers have also studied whether online news consumption is more or less conducive to the acquisition of political knowledge than news consumption in traditional media. Some authors have argued that increased choice of online news reduces exposure to public affairs stories and, thus, knowledge and recall of current events (Althaus and Tewksbury 2002; Boczkowski et al. 2010; Dalrymple and Scheufele 2007). Boczkowski and Peer examined journalists and consumers' news choices in four American online news sites and suggest that "the pervasiveness and strength of consumers' preferences for nonpublic affairs stories…belie notions about a well-informed" online public (2001: 23).

However, other scholars indicate that access to Internet news does not lead to a decrease in knowledge of public affairs in contrast with traditional media, and might even have different cognitive effects (Drew and Weaver 2006; Eveland et al. 2002; Kenski and Stroud 2006; Xenos and Moy 2007). Kim found that while traditional news generally did not appear to have any influence, Internet news media "play a significant role in enhancing domain-specific knowledge" (2009: 276). A different stream of research indicates that access to the Internet might increase the likelihood of incidental news knowledge, as consumers are often exposed to online news during their general web use, which in turn can lead to greater awareness about public affairs' subjects (Lupia and Philpot 2005; Salwen 2005; Tewksbury et al. 2001).

Research has also examined the impact of online news consumption on democratic participation. Some authors have proposed that there are no significant links between online news consumption and civic participation (Bimber 2001; Kenski and Stroud 2006; Margolis and Resnick 2000; Weaver and Drew 2001). Scheufele and Nisbet surveyed Internet consumers in the US and found that informational uses played "a very limited role…in promoting levels of efficacy, knowledge, and participation" (2002: 65). However, the opposite camp contends that there is a positive relationship (Boulianne 2009; de Vreese, 2007; Johnson and Kaye, 2003). Tolbert and McNeal analyze data from the National Election Study in the United States and indicate that "the Internet may increase voter turnout by giving individuals greater access to political information, and in turn stimulating increased turnout" (2003: 179).

Other researchers have noted that the ties between online news consumption and civic participation may be mediated by political discussion (Eveland and Dylko 2007; Hardy and Scheufele 2005; Nisbet and Scheufele 2004; Xenos and Moy 2007). Shah et al. studied media consumption and civic participation during the 2004 US election and found that "media effects were largely indirect, channeled through political discussion and messaging" (2007: 696). Other scholars have argued that online discussion of public affairs is a form of civic participation, and have proposed that online media have lowered the cost of debating opinions in public (DiMaggio et al. 2001; Etzioni 2003; Papacharissi 2004; Wright 2007). However, studies of online discussion suggest that the dominance of loud minorities, the lack of rationality and civility in the exchanges, and the exclusion of dissenting voices, hampers deliberation (Boczkowski 2010; Davis 1999;

Margolis and Resnick 2000; Schultz 2000). Ye and Li looked at users' forums in American online newspapers and found that, given that the number of participants was low, postings were trivial, and public affairs topics were not the readers' first preference, "the value of forum messages is fairly limited, if measured by the high standards of democratic deliberation" (2006: 255).

DISCUSSION

The previous sections have critically assessed recent scholarship on online news production and consumption, focusing on eight key research topics: the historical context and market environment of online news; the processes of innovation; changes in journalistic practices; modifications to journalism's identity as a profession; the role of user-generated content; whether online news consumption displaces or complements traditional media consumption; audience fragmentation and homogenization; and the links between online news consumption and political knowledge and participation. This assessment shows that, as journalists and audiences have re-enacted their roles in the networked environment, they have straddled between tradition and innovation. Thus, it problematizes accounts of sweeping change in the production and consumption of news content that have tended to dominate discussion of online news. Moreover, the examination of the research suggests that the main scholarly approaches have been characterized by stability rather than change, which might have hindered a thorough examination of innovation in online news production and consumption. More precisely, these approaches have generated valuable insights, but have also exhibited four important limitations: the assumption of a division between print, broadcast, and online media; a narrow focus on online news that hinders comparisons with historical media developments and with changes in other industries; the inclination to concentrate on either ordinary or extraordinary patterns of phenomena but not on both within a single study; and the dearth of ethnographic studies on online audiences. The remainder of this section takes advantage of this discussion to propose avenues for future work and to reflect on the ways in which news producers' and consumers' practices and interpretation are also straddling between tradition and transformation.

The assumption of a division between print, broadcast, and online media has limited understanding of transformations in both news production and consumption. First, it has hindered appraisal of the transformations in journalistic work. Most studies focus on online sites of print newspapers (Cawley 2008; Dimitrova et al. 2005; Domingo et al. 2008; Singer 2003, 2006, 2009) and television stations (Chan-Olmsted and Ha 2003; Siapera 2004), or on recently converged operations (Lawson-Borders 2006), which has contributed to overemphasizing the differences rather than the growing similarities between the three kinds of media (Boczkowski 2004a; Thornton and Keith 2009). Second, this assumption has contributed to conflicting findings on whether the relationship between traditional and online media is one of displacement or complementarity.

The greater part of research has assumed that news consumption is divided between print, broadcast, and online media (Althaus et al. 2009; Chyi and Yang 2009, Gentzkow 2007; Kaye and Johnson 2003), and therefore has overlooked the ways in which audiences may integrate consumption of different media, by, for instance, posting comments on social network sites while watching broadcast news, or turning to the Internet to watch a news item or a documentary they missed on television.

Historical and comparative matters have not figured prominently in the scholarship about online news, which creates a void in registering the evolution of journalists' and audiences' behaviors, and their similarities with consumption and production processes in other industries. For instance, phenomena such as temporal acceleration (Klinenberg 2005), multiskilling (Bromley 1997), and prosumption (Ritzer and Jurgenson 2010) do not belong exclusively to media work. Comparing these processes in online news and in other settings would help to ascertain what might be unique to the journalistic field and what might be shared across other domains. Moreover, the dearth of historical perspectives on the political consequences of online news consumption runs the risk of underscoring novelty while downplaying continuity, and fails to provide depth to the empirical findings and associated theoretical conclusions of many studies. For instance, findings on incidental news knowledge (Tewksbury 2003; Lupia and Philpot 2005) echo Baum's (2003) research on the positive effects of soft news programs on the political information levels of television audiences, while evidence that the relationship between online news consumption and political engagement is mediated by discussion (Eveland and Dylko 2007; Shah et al 2007) evokes Katz and Lazarsfeld's (1955) seminal work on social influence. Research that takes into account the historical context in which media content is produced and consumed would contribute to make sense of the continuities and discontinuities (Boczkowski and Lievrouw 2007) in journalists' and audiences' behaviors.

Another limitation is scholars' tendency to focus on either ordinary or extraordinary patterns of behavior but not on both at the same time, which affects the appraisal of the market environment of online news production and may contribute to conflicting evidence on whether there is fragmentation or homogenization of online news audiences. For instance, studies about the feasibility of a subscription-based print model for online news usually focus on one elite newspaper, such as the *Financial Times* (Herbert and Thurman 2007) or the *Washington Post* (Gentzkow 2007), whereas research on the broader audience indicates that 35 percent of Internet news consumers have a favorite news site, and among those only 19 percent are willing to pay to access it (Project for Excellence in Journalism 2010). Rather than assuming that one business model should suit all outlets, scholarship on the market environment should distinguish between ordinary activities, such as surfing the Web for news, and extraordinary behaviors such as looking for a particular story or news site, which may entail willingness to pay for access. The distinction between ordinary and extraordinary activities would also help research on fragmentation and homogenization. On the one hand, some studies on politically interested news readers suggest that they do seek opinion-reinforcing information, which may lead to audience fragmentation (Baum and Groeling 2008; Sunstein 2001). On the other, findings about the news agenda of the most accessed sites indicates that news content is becoming increasingly homogenous, rather than less so (Boczkowski 2010; Lim 2010). Studying ordinary and extraordinary patterns of news consumption would provide more comprehensive and nuanced evidence on the tension between fragmentation and homogenization.

The dearth of ethnographic research on online media audiences may be related to lack of conclusive findings on the changing status of journalism as a profession and on the experiences of users as content producers. First, although several studies have examined the crisis of the jurisdictional space news workers occupy as gatekeepers of information (Allan 2006; Deuze 2003; Dutton 2009; Sousa 2006), most research is based on surveys and interviews with journalists (Quandt et al. 2006; Robinson 2007). Thus, it reflects news producers' perception of a challenge rather than audiences' questioning of journalism's occupational jurisdiction. Boczkowski's (2010) ethnographic study of media consumers constitutes an exception to this trend and provides evidence that, contrary to the widespread celebration of participatory audiences, consumers are not interested in either taking advantage of the opportunities to produce content or challenging journalistic authority. An extension of this approach would add depth and breadth to the study of the crisis of journalism as a profession. Second, scholarship about users as content producers has been limited by its overwhelming reliance on data gathered through surveys of contributors and content analysis of their contributions. In the same way that pioneering ethnographic accounts of journalistic work in the 1970s and 1980s helped to generate novel understandings of content creation within newsrooms (Fishman 1980; Gans 1980; Tuchman 1978), qualitative research on the activities and self-perceptions of bloggers and citizen journalists are needed to better understand the processes and politics of distributed forms of online content creation. For instance, Anderson's (2010) ethnographic account of journalistic networks that integrate professionals and amateurs provides a unique understanding of the interaction between journalists and users as content producers.

These limitations stem from long-dated conceptual and methodological settings in the study of news production and consumption. Deuze notes that "the literature in the field of journalism studies is largely informed by the standards of research, education, routines, rituals and practices set by print journalism" (2008: 199). Two of the most important organizers in communication studies have been the division between production and consumption, and the separation between mass and interpersonal communication. This organization of the scholarship is grounded on the one-way, unidirectional information architecture that dominated news media during the twentieth century. The transformation of the information environment in the networked society provides researchers with the opportunity to challenge these distinctions, examining differences and similarities with production and consumption in other settings, analyzing whether and when audiences integrate or divide the time they spend with different media, and differentiating between ordinary and extraordinary patterns of behavior. In this sense, the study of online news affords the opportunity to rethink some of the conceptual foundations in the scholarship of media and communication. Taking up this challenge might endow this area of inquiry with a mission and an importance beyond the intricacies of its object of study.

ACKNOWLEDGMENTS

This chapter builds on and also updates two articles published by the authors in *Journalism: Theory Practice and Criticism* (2009), and *New Media and Society* (2010). We are grateful to Bill Dutton and anonymous reviewers for most helpful comments on an earlier version of this chapter.

REFERENCES

Ahlers, D. (2006). "News Consumption and the New Electronic Media," *Harvard International Journal of Press-Politics*, 11(1): 29–52.

Allan, S. (2006). *Online News*, Maidenhead: Open University Press.

Althaus, S., Cizmar, A., and Gimpel, J. (2009). "Media Supply, Audience Demand, and the Geography of News Consumption in the United States," *Political Communication*, 26(3): 249–77.

Althaus, S. and Tewksbury, D. (2000). "Patterns of Internet and Traditional News Media Use in a Networked Community," *Political Communication*, 17(1): 21–45.

—— and Tewksbury, D. (2002). "Agenda Setting and the "New" News—Patterns of Issue Importance among Readers of the Paper and Online Versions of the New York Times," *Communication Research*, 29(2): 180–207.

Anderson, C. W. (2010). "Journalistic Networks and the Diffusion of Local News: The Brief, Happy News Life of the 'Francisville Four,'" *Political Communication*, 27(3): 289–309.

Baum, M. (2003). *Soft News Goes to War: Public Opinion and American Foreign Policy in the New Media Age*, New Haven: Princeton University Press.

—— and Groeling, T. (2008). "New Media and the Polarization of American Political Discourse," *Political Communication*, 25(4): 345–65.

Benkler, Y. (2006). *The Wealth of Networks: How Social Production Transforms Markets and Freedom*, New Haven: Yale University Press.

Bimber, B. (1998). "The Internet and Political Transformation: Populism, Community, and Accelerated Pluralism," *Polity*, 31(1): 133–60.

—— (2001). "Information and Political Engagement in America: The Search for Effects of Information Technology at the Individual Level," *Political Research Quarterly*, 54(1): 53–67.

Boczkowski, P. J. (2002). "The Development and Use of Online Newspapers: What Research Tells Us and What We Might Want to Know," in L. A. Lievrouw and S. Livingstone (eds). *Handbook of New Media: Social Shaping and Consequences of ICTs*, London: Sage, pp. 270–286.

—— (2004a). *Digitizing the News: Innovation in Online Newspapers*, Cambridge: MIT Press.

—— (2004b). "The Mutual Shaping of Technology and Society in Videotex Newspapers: Beyond the Diffusion and Social Shaping Perspectives," *Information Society*, 20(4): 255–67.

—— (2004c). "The Processes of Adopting Multimedia and Interactivity in Three Online Newsrooms," *Journal of Communication*, 54(2): 197–213.

—— (2010). *News at Work: Imitation in an Age of Information Abundance*. Chicago: University of Chicago Press.

Boczkowski, P. J., de Santos, M. (2007). "When More Media Equals Less News: Patterns of Content Homogenization in Argentina's Leading Print and Online Newspapers," *Political Communication*, 24(2): 167–80.

—— and Ferris, J. A. (2005). "Multiple Media, Convergent Processes, and Divergent Products: Organizational Innovation in Digital Media Production at a European Firm," *Annals of the American Academy of Political and Social Science*, 597(1): 32–47.

—— Boczkowski, P. J. and Lievrouw, L. A. (2007). "Bridging STS and Communication Studies: Scholarship on Media and Information Technologies," in E. Hackett, O. Amsterdamska, M. Lynch, and J. Wajcman (eds). *The Handbook of Science and Technology Studies*, Cambridge, MA: MIT Press, pp. 949–77.

—— and Mitchelstein, E. (2010). "Is There a Gap Between the News Choices of Journalists and Consumers? A Relational and Dynamic Approach," *International Journal of Press/Politics*, 15(4): 420–40.

—— and Peer, L. (2011). "The Choice Gap: The Divergent Online News Preferences of Journalists and Consumers," *Journal of Communication*, 61(5): 857–76.

——, Mitchelstein, E., and Walter, M. (2010). "Convergence across Divergence: Understanding the Gap in Online News Choices of Journalists and Consumers in Western Europe and Latin America," *Communication Research*, 38(3): 376–396.

Bolano, C., Mastrini, G., and Sierra, F. (2004). "Global Changes in the Economic System and in Communications: A Latin American Perspective for the Political Economy of Communications," *Javnost-The Public*, 11(3): 47–58.

Boulianne, S. (2009). "Does Internet Use Affect Engagement? A Meta-Analysis of Research," *Political Communication*, 26(2): 193–211.

Bromley, M. (1997). "The End of Journalism? Changes in Workplace Practices in the Press and Broadcasting in the 1990s," in M. Bromley and T. O'Malley (eds). *A Journalism Reader*, London: Routledge, pp. 330–50.

Bustamante, E. (2004). "Cultural Industries in the Digital Age: Some Provisional Conclusions," *Media Culture & Society*, 26(6): 803–20.

Carlson, M. (2007). "Blogs and Journalistic Authority," *Journalism Studies*, 8(2): 264–79.

Cassidy, W. (2007). "Online News Credibility: An Examination of the Perceptions of Newspaper Journalists," *Journal of Computer-Mediated Communication*, 12(2): 478–98.

Castells, M. (1997). *The Power of Identity*, Malden, MA: Blackwell.

Cawley, A. (2008). "News Production in an Irish Online Newsroom: Practice, Process and Culture," in C. A. Paterson and D. Domingo (eds). *Making Online News: The Ethnography of New Media Production*, New York: Peter Lang, pp. 45–60.

Chadwick, A. (2006). *Internet Politics: States, Citizens, and New Communication Technologies*, New York: Oxford University Press.

Chan, J., Lee, F., and Pan, Z. (2006). "Online News Meets Established Journalism: How China's Journalists Evaluate the Credibility of News Websites," *New Media & Society*, 8(6): 925–47.

Chan-Olmsted, S. M. and Ha, L. S. (2003). "Internet Business Models for Broadcasters: How Television Stations Perceive and Integrate the Internet," *Journal of Broadcasting & Electronic Media*, 47(4): 597–617.

Chung, D. and Nah, S. (2009). "The Effects of Interactive News Presentation on Perceived User Satisfaction of Online Community Newspapers," *Journal of Computer-Mediated Communication*, 14(4): 855–74.

Chyi, H. I. (2005). "Willingness to Pay for Online News: An Empirical Study on the Viability of the Subscription Model," *Journal of Media Economics*, 18(2): 131–42.

—— and Lasorsa, D. L. (2002). "An Explorative Study on the Market Relation between Online and Print Mewspapers," *Journal of Media Economics*, 15(2): 91–106.

Chyi, H. I. and Sylvie, G. (2001). "The Medium is Global, the Content is Not: The Role of Geography in Online Newspaper Markets," *Journal of Media Economics*, 14(4): 231–48.

—— and Yang, M. J. (2009). "Is Online News an Inferior Good? Examining the Economic Nature of Online News among Users," *Journalism and Mass Communication Quarterly*, 86(3): 594–612.

Coleman, R. and McCombs, M. (2007). "The Young and Agenda-Less? Exploring Age-Related Differences in Agenda Setting on the Youngest Generation, Baby Boomers and the Civic Generation," *Journalism & Mass Communication Quarterly*, 84(3): 495–508.

Compton, J. and Benedetti, P. (2010). "Labour, New Media and the Institutional Restructuring of Journalism," *Journalism Studies*, 11(4): 487–99.

Conboy, M. and Steel, J. (2008). "The Future of Newspapers," *Journalism Studies*, 9(5): 650–61.

Dalrymple, K. and Scheufele, D. (2007). "Finally Informing the Electorate? How the Internet Got People Thinking about Presidential Politics in 2004," *International Journal of Press-Politics*, 12(3): 96–111.

Davis, R. (1999). *The Web of Politics: The Internet's Impact on the American Political System*, New York: Oxford University Press.

de Vreese, C. H. (2007). "Digital Renaissance: Young Consumer and Citizen?," *Annals of the American Academy of Political and Social Science*, 611(1): 207–16.

De Waal, E. and Schoenbach, K. (2010). "News Sites' Position in the Mediascape: Uses, Evaluations and Media Displacement Effects over Time," *New Media & Society*, 12(3): 477–97.

Dennis, E. (2006). "Television's Convergence Conundrum: Finding the Right Digital Strategy," *Television Quarterly*, 37: 22–6.

Deuze, M. (2003). "The Web and its Journalisms: Considering the Consequences of Different Types of Newsmedia Online," *New Media & Society*, 5(2): 203–30.

—— (2004). "What is Multimedia Journalism?," *Journalism Studies*, 5(2): 139–52.

—— (2006). "Participation, Remediation, Bricolage: Considering Principal Components of a Digital Culture," *Information Society*, 22(2): 63–75.

—— (2007). *Media Work*, Cambridge: Polity.

—— (2008). "Toward a Sociology of Online News?" in C. A. Paterson and D. Domingo (eds). *Making Online News: The Ethnography of New Media Production*, New York: Peter Lang, pp. 199–209.

—— and Dimoudi, C. (2002). "Online Journalists in the Netherlands: Towards a Profile of a New Profession," *Journalism*, 3(1): 85–100.

—— and Paulussen, S. (2002). "Research Note: Online Journalism in the Low Countries," *European Journal of Communication*, 17(2): 237–45.

DiMaggio, P., Hargittai, E., Neuman, W. R., and Robinson, J. P. (2001). "Social Implications of the Internet," *Annual Review of Sociology*, 27(1): 307–36.

Dimitrova, D., Kaid, L., Williams, A., and Trammell, K. (2005). "War on the Web—The Immediate News Framing of Gulf War II," *Harvard International Journal of Press-Politics*, 10(1): 22–44.

Dimmick, J., Chen, Y., and Li, Z. (2004). "Competition between the Internet and Traditional News Media: The Gratification-Opportunities Niche Dimension," *Journal of Media Economics*, 17(1): 19–33.

Domingo, D. (2008). "Interactivity in the Daily Routines of Online Newsrooms: Dealing with an Uncomfortable Myth," *Journal of Computer-Mediated Communication*, 13(3): 680–704.

—— Quandt, T., Heinonen, A., Paulussen, S., Singer, J. B., and Vujnovic, M. (2008). "Participatory Journalism Practices in the Media and Beyond: An International Comparative Study of Initiatives in Online Newspapers," *Journalism Practice*, 2(3): 326–42.

Downs, A. (1957). *An Economic Theory of Democracy*, New York: Harper and Row.

Drew, D. and Weaver, D. (2006). "Voter Learning in the 2004 Presidential Election: Did the Media Matter?," *Journalism & Mass Communication Quarterly*, 83(1): 25–42.

Dupagne, M. and Garrison, B. (2006). "The Meaning and Influence of Convergence," *Journalism Studies*, 7(2): 237–55.

Dutta-Bergman, M. (2004). "Complementarity in Consumption of News Types across Traditional and New Media," *Journal of Broadcasting & Electronic Media*, 48(1): 41–60.

Dutton, W. (2007). "The Fifth Estate Emerging through the Network of Networks', *Prometheus*, 27(1): pp. 1–15.

—— Gillett, S., McKnight, L., and Peltu, M. (2004). "Bridging Broadband Internet Divides: Reconfiguring Access to Enhance Communicative Power," *Journal of Information Technology*, 19(1): 28–38.

Etzioni, A. (2003). "Are Virtual and Democratic Communities Feasible?," in H. Jenkins and D. Thorburn (eds). *Democracy and New Media*, Cambridge, MA: MIT Press, pp. 85–100.

Eveland, W. P. and Dylko, I. (2007). "Reading Political Blogs During the 2004 Election Campaign: Correlates and Political Consequences," in M. Tremayne (ed.). *Blogging, Citizenship and the Future of the Media*, New York: Routledge, pp 105–26.

Eveland, W. P., Seo, M., and Marton, K. (2002). "Learning from the News in Campaign 2000: An Experimental Comparison of TV News, Newspapers, and Online News," *Media Psychology*, 4(4): 353–78.

Filloux, F. (2008). "The Economics of Moving from Print to Online: Lose One Hundred, Get Back Eight," *Monday Note*, September 29. Available at <http://www.mondaynote.com/2008/09/29/the-economics-of-moving-from-print-to-online-lose-one-hundred-get-back-eight/>. Accessed September 24, 2010.

Fishman, M. (1980). *Manufacturing the News*, Austin: University of Texas Press.

Flanagin, A. J. and Metzger, M. J. (2001). "Internet Use in the Contemporary Media Environment," *Human Communication Research*, 27(1): 153–81.

Gans, H. J. (1980). "Deciding What's News: A Study of CBS Evening News, NBC Nightly News, Newsweek, and Time," Evanston, IL: Northwestern University Press.

—— (2007). "Everyday News, Newsworkers, and Professional Journalism," *Political Communication*, 24(2): 161–6.

García, E. P. (2008). "Print and Online Newsrooms in Argentinean Media: Autonomy and Professional Identity," in C. A. Paterson and D. Domingo (eds). *Making Online News: The Ethnography of New Media Production*, New York: Peter Lang, pp. 61–75.

Garrett, R. K. (2009). "Echo Chambers Online?: Politically Motivated Selective Exposure Among Internet News Users," *Journal of Computer-Mediated Communication*, 14(2): 265–85.

Garrison, B. (2001). "Diffusion of Online Information Technologies in Newspaper Newsrooms," *Journalism*, 2(2): 221–39.

—— (2005). "Online Newspapers," in M. B. Salwen, B. Garrison, and P. D. Driscoll (eds). *Online News and the Public*, Mahwah, NJ: Lawrence Erlbaum, pp. 3–46.

Gentzkow, M. (2007). "Valuing New Goods in a Model with Complementarity: Online Newspapers," *American Economic Review*, 97(3): 713–44.

Gilbert, C. G. (2005). "Unbundling the Structure of Inertia: Resource Versus Routine Rigidity," *Academy of Management Journal*, 48(5): 741–63.

Gillmor, D. (2004). *We the Media: Grassroots Journalism By the People, For the People*, Sebastopol, CA: O'Reilly.

Goode, L. (2009). "Social News, Citizen Journalism and Democracy," *New Media & Society*, 11(8): 1287–305.

Graber, D. A. (1996). "The 'New' Media and Politics: What Does the Future Hold?," *Political Science & Politics*, 29(1): 33–6.

—— (2006). *Mass Media and American Politics*, Washington, DC: CQ Press.

Greer, J. D. (2004). "Advertising on Traditional Media Sites: Can the Traditional Business Model be Translated to the Web?," *Social Science Journal*, 41(1): 107–13.

Gunter, B., Russell, G., Withey, R., and Nicholas, D. (2003). "The British Life and Internet Project: Inaugural Survey Findings," *Aslib Proceedings*, 55(4): 203–16.

Gurevitch, M., Coleman, S., and Blumler, J. (2009). "Political Communication—Old and New Media Relationships," *ANNALS of the American Academy of Political and Social Science*, 625(1): 164–81.

Haas, T. (2005). "From 'Public Journalism' to the 'Public's Journalism'? Rhetoric and Reality in the Discourse on Weblogs," *Journalism Studies*, 6(3): 387–96.

Hardy, B. and Scheufele, D. A. (2005). "Examining Differential Gains from Internet Use: Comparing the Moderating Role of Talk and Online Interactions," *Journal of Communication*, 55(1): 71–84.

Herbert, J. and Thurman, N. (2007). "Paid Content Strategies for News Websites," *Journalism Practice*, 1(2): 208–26.

Hermans, L. and Vergeer, M. (2009). "Internet in the Daily Life of Journalists: Explaining the use of the Internet by Work-Related Characteristics and Professional Opinions," *Journal of Computer-Mediated Communication*, 15(1): 138–57.

Hindman, M. (2009). *The Myth of Digital Democracy*, Princeton, NJ: Princeton University Press.

Hujanen, J. and Pietikainen, S. (2004). "Interactive Uses of Journalism: Crossing Between Technological Potential and Young People's News-Using Practices," *New Media & Society*, 6(3): 383–401.

Johnson, T. J. and Kaye, B. K. (2003). "A Boost or Bust for Democracy?: How the Web Influenced Political Attitudes and Behaviors in the 1996 and 2000 Presidential Elections," *International Journal of Press-Politics*, 8(3): 9–34.

Karlsson, M. and Strombäck, J. (2009). "Freezing the Flow of Online News," *Journalism Studies*, 11(1): 1–18.

Katz, E., Blumler, J., and Gurevitch, M. (1974). "Utilization of Mass Communication by the Individual," in J. G. Blumler and E. Katz (eds). *The Uses of Mass Communications: Current Perspectives on Gratifications Research*, Beverly Hills: Sage, pp. 35–49.

Katz, E. and Lazarsfeld, P. F. (1955). *Personal Influence: The Part Played by People in the Flow of Mass Communications*, New York: The Free Press.

Kayany, J. M. and Yelsma, P. (2000). "Displacement Effects of Online Media in the Socio-Technical Contexts of Households," *Journal of Broadcasting & Electronic Media*, 44(2): 215–29.

Kaye, B. K. and Johnson, T. J. (2003). "From Here to Obscurity?: Media Substitution Theory and Traditional Media in an On-Line World," *Journal of the American Society for Information Science and Technology*, 54(3): 260–73.

Kenski, K. and Stroud, N. (2006). "Connections between Internet Use and Political Efficacy, Knowledge, and Participation," *Journal of Broadcasting & Electronic Media*, 50(2): 173–92.

Kim, E. and Hamilton, J. (2006). "Capitulation to Capital? OhmyNews as Alternative Media," *Media Culture & Society*, 28(4): 541–60.

Kim, Y. (2009). "Issue Publics in the New Information Environment: Selectivity, Domain Specificity, and Extremity," *Communication Research*, 36(2): 254–84.

Klinenberg, E. (2005). "Convergence: News Production in a Digital Age," *Annals of the American Academy of Political and Social Science*, 597: 48–64.

Knobloch-Westerwick, S. and Alter, S. (2007). "The Gender News Use Divide: Americans' Sex-Typed Selective Exposure to Online News Topics," *Journal of Communication*, 57(4): 739–58.

—— and Meng, J. (2009). "Looking the Other Way.," *Communication Research*, 36(3): 426–48.

——, Sharma, N., Hansen, D. L., and Alter, S. (2005). "Impact of Popularity Indications on Readers' Selective Exposure to Online News," *Journal of Broadcasting & Electronic Media*, 49(3): 296–313.

Kopper, G., Kolthoff, A., and Czepek, A. (2000). "Research Review: Online Journalism—A Report on Current and Continuing Research and Major Questions in the International Discussion," *Journalism Studies*, 1(3): 499–512.

Lawson-Borders, G. (2006). *Media Organizations and Convergence: Case Studies of Media Convergence Pioneers*, Mahwah, NJ: Lawrence Erlbaum.

Lee, J. K. (2007). "The Effect of the Internet on Homogeneity of the Media Agenda: A Test of the Fragmentation Thesis," *Journalism & Mass Communication Quarterly*, 84(4): 745–60.

Lee, K. M. (2006). "Effects of Internet Use on College Students' Political Efficacy," *Cyberpsychology & Behavior*, 9(4): 415–22.

Lim, J. (2010). "Convergence of Attention and Prominence Dimensions of Salience among Major Online Newspapers," *Journal of Computer-Mediated Communication*, 15(2): 293–313.

Lin, C., Salwen, M. B., and Abdulla, R. A. (2005). "Uses and Gratifications of Online and Offline News: New Wine in an Old Bottle?," in M. B. Salwen, B. Garrison, and P. D. Driscoll (eds). *Online News and the Public*, Mahwah, NJ: Lawrence Erlbaum, pp. 221–36.

Livingstone, S. (2004). "The Challenge of Changing Audiences—Or, What is the Audience Researcher to Do in the Age of the Internet?," *European Journal of Communication*, 19(1): 75–86.

—— and Markham, T. (2008). "The Contribution of Media Consumption to Civic Participation," *British Journal of Sociology*, 59(2): 351–71.

Lowrey, W. (2006). "Mapping the Journalism-Blogging Relationship," *Journalism* 7(4): 477–500.

—— and Latta, J. (2008). "The Routines of Blogging," in C. A. Paterson and D. Domingo (eds). *Making Online News: the Ethnography of Online News Production*, New York: Peter Lang, pp. 185–97.

Luhmann, N. (1996). *The Reality of the Mass Media*, Stanford, CA: Stanford University Press.

Lupia, A. and Philpot, T. (2005). "Views from Inside the Net: How Websites Affect Young Adults' Political Interest," *Journal of Politics*, 67(4): 1122–42.

McCombs, M. (1972). "Mass Media in the Marketplace," *Journalism Monographs*, 24: 1–104.

McCoy, M. (2001). "Dark Alliance: News Repair and Institutional Authority in the Age of the Internet," *Journal of Communication*, 51(1): 164–93.

Margolis, M. and Resnick, D. (2000). *Politics as Usual: The Cyberspace "Revolution,"* Thousand Oaks, CA: Sage.

Meier, K. (2007). "Innovations in Central European Newsrooms," *Journalism Practice*, 1(1): 4–19.

Meraz, S. (2009). "Is There an Elite Hold? Traditional Media to Social Media Agenda Setting Influence in Blog Networks," *Journal of Computer-Mediated Communication*, 14(3): 682–707.

Metzger, M., Flanagin, A., and Zwarun, L. (2003). "College Student Web Use, Perceptions of Information Credibility, and Verification Behavior," *Computers & Education*, 41(3): 271–90.

Millen, D. and Dray, S. (2000). "Information Sharing in an Online Community of Journalists," *Aslib Proceedings*, 52(5): 166–73.

Mitchelstein, E. and Boczkowski, P. J. (2009). "Between Tradition and Change: A Review of Recent Research on Online News Production," *Journalism: Theory, Practice & Criticism*, 10(5): 562–86.

—— and Boczkowski, P. J. (2010). "Online News Consumption Research: An Assessment of Past Work and an Agenda for the Future," *New Media & Society*, 12(7): 1085–102.

Mutz, D. (2006). "How the Mass Media Divide Us," in D. W. Brady and P. S. Nivola (eds). *Red and Blue Nation?*, Wahington, DC: Brookings Institution Press.

Nerone, J. and Barnhurst, K. (2001). "Beyond Modernism—Digital Design, Americanization and the Future of Newspaper Form," *New Media & Society*, 3(4): 467–82.

Neuman, W. R. (2001). "The Impact of the New Media," in W. L. Bennett and R. M. Entman (eds). *Mediated Politics: Communication in the Future of Democracy*, Cambridge: Cambridge University Press, pp. 299–320.

Newell, J., Pilotta, J., and Thomas, J. (2008). "Mass Media Displacement and Saturation," *International Journal on Media Management*, 10(4): 131–8.

Nguyen, A. (2008). "Facing ' the Fabulous Monster '," *Journalism Studies*, 9(1): 91–104.

—— and Western, M. (2007). "Socio-Structural Correlates of Online News and Information Adoption/Use: Implications for the Digital Divide," *Journal of Sociology*, 43(2): 167–85.

Nicholas, D., Williams, P., Cole, P., and Martin, H. (2000). "The Impact of the Internet on Information Seeking in the Media," *Aslib Proceedings: New Information Perspectives*, 52: 98–114.

Nisbet, M. and Scheufele, D. (2004). "Political Talk as a Catalyst for Online Citizenship," *Journalism and Mass Communication Quarterly*, 81(4): 877–96.

Ornebring, H. (2008). "The Consumer as a Producer of What? User-Generated Tabloid Content in *The Sun* (UK) and Aftonbladet (Sweden)," *Journalism Studies*, 9(5): 771–85.

O'Sullivan, J. and Heinonen, A. (2008). "Old Values, New Media: Journalism Role Perceptions in a Changing World," *Journalism Practice*, 2(3): 357–71.

Papacharissi, Z. (2002). "The Virtual Sphere: the Internet as a Public Sphere," *New Media & Society*, 4(1): 9–27.

—— (2004). "Democracy Online: Civility, Politeness, and the Democratic Potential of Online Political Discussion Groups," *New Media & Society*, 6(2): 259–83.

Pavlik, J. (2000). "The Impact of Technology on Journalism," *Journalism Studies*, 1(2): 229–37.

—— (2001). *Journalism and New Media*, New York: Columbia University Press.

Pew Research Center (2010). *Pew Research Center Biennial News Consumption Survey*, Washington, DC: Pew Research Center for the People and the Press.

Prior, M. (2005). "News vs. Entertainment: How Increasing Media Choice Widens Gaps in Political Knowledge and Turnout," *American Journal of Political Science*, 49(3): 577–92.

Prior, M. (2007). *Post-Broadcast Democracy: How Media Choice Increases Inequality in Political Involvement and Polarizes Elections*, New York: Cambridge University Press.

Project for Excellence in Journalism (2010). "State of the News Media." Available at <http://www.stateofthemedia.org/2010/>. Accessed September 20, 2010.

Quandt, T., Loffelholz, M., Weaver, D., Hanitzsch, T., and Altmeppen, K. (2006). "American and German Online Journalists at the Beginning of the 21st Century," *Journalism Studies*, 7: 171–86.

Quinn, S. (2005). "Convergence's Fundamental Question," *Journalism Studies*, 6(1): 29–38.

Reese, S., Rutigliano, L., Hyun, K., and Jeong, J. (2007). "Mapping the Blogosphere: Professional and Citizen-Based Media in the Global News Arena," *Journalism*, 8(3): 235–61.

Reich, Z. (2008). "How Citizens Create News Stories," *Journalism Studies*, 9(5): 39–758.

Ritzer, G. and Jurgenson, N. (2010). "Production, Consumption, Prosumption: The Nature of Capitalism in the Age of the Digital 'Prosumer'," *Journal of Consumer Culture*, 10(1): 13–36.

Robinson, S. (2007). "Someone's Gotta be in Control Here," *Journalism Practice*, 1(3): 305–21.

Rosenstiel, T. (2005). "Political Polling and the New Media Culture: A Case of More Being Less," *Public Opinion Quarterly*, 69(5): 698–715.

Russell, A. (2001). "Chiapas and the New News: Internet and Newspaper Coverage of a Broken Cease-Fire," *Journalism*, 2(2): 197–20.

Rutigliano, L. (2007). "Emergent Communications Network as Civic Journalism," in M. Tremayne (ed.). *Blogging, Citizenship and the Future of Media*, New York: Routledge, pp. 225–37.

Salwen, M. B. (2005). "Online News Trends," in M. B. Salwen, B. Garrison, and P. D. Driscoll (eds). *Online News and the Public*, Mahwah, NJ: Lawrence Erlbaum, pp. 47–77.

Scheufele, D. A. and Nisbet, M. C. (2002). "Being a Citizen Online—New Opportunities and Dead Ends," *Harvard International Journal of Press-Politics*, 7(3): 55–75.

Schiffer, A. J. (2006). "Blogswarms and Press Norms: News Coverage of the Downing Street Memo Controversy," *Journalism & Mass Communication Quarterly*, 83(3): 494–510.

Schudson, M. (2009). "The New Media in the 2008 US Presidential Campaign: The New York Times Watches its Back," *Javnost-the Public*, 16(1): 73–86.

Schultz, T. (2000). "Mass Media and the Concept of Interactivity: An Exploratory Study of Online Forums and Reader Email," *Media Culture & Society*, 22(2): 205–21.

Semetko, H. and Krasnoboka, N. (2003). "The Political Role of the Internet in Societies in Transition—Russia and Ukraine Compared," *Party Politics*, 9(1): 77–104.

Shah, D. V., Cho, J., Nah, S., Gotlieb, M., Hwang, H., Lee, N. et al. (2007). "Campaign Ads, Online Messaging, and Participation: Extending the Communication Mediation Model," *Journal of Communication*, 57(4): 676–703.

Shin, J.-H. and Cameron, G. T. (2003). "The Interplay of Professional and Cultural Factors in the Online Source-Reporter Relationship," *Journalism Studies*, 4(2): 253–72.

Siapera, E. (2004). "From Couch Potatoes to Cybernauts? The Expanding Notion of the Audience on TV Channels Websites," *New Media & Society*, 6(2): 155–72.

Singer, J. B. (2001). "The Metro Wide Web: Changes in Newspapers' Gatekeeping Role Online," *Journalism and Mass Communication Quarterly*, 78(1): 65–80.

—— (2003). "Campaign Contributions: Online Newspaper Coverage of Election 2000," *Journalism & Mass Communication Quarterly*, 80(1): 39–56.

—— (2006). "Stepping Back from the Gate: Online Newspaper Editors and the Co-Production of Content in Campaign 2004," *Journalism & Mass Communication Quarterly*, 83(2): 265–80.

—— (2009). "Role Call: 2008 Campaign and Election Coverage on the Web Sites of Leading U.S. Newspapers," *Journalism & Mass Communication Quarterly*, 86(4): 827–43.

Sousa, H. (2006). "Information Technologies, Social Change and the Future: The Case of Online Journalism in Portugal," *European Journal of Communication*, 21(3): 373–87.

Steensen, S. (2009). "What's Stopping Them? Toward a Grounded Theory of Innovation in Online Journalism," *Journalism Studies* 10(6): 821–836.

Stober, R. (2004). "What Media Evolution Is: A Theoretical Approach to the History of New Media," *European Journal of Communication*, 19(4): 483–505.

Stroud, N. (2008). "Media Use and Political Predispositions: Revisiting the Concept of Selective Exposure," *Political Behavior*, 30(3): 341–66.

Sunstein, C. (2001). *Republic.com*, Princeton, NJ: Princeton University Press.

Tewksbury, D. (2003). "What do Americans Really Want to Know? Tracking the Behavior of News Readers on the Internet," *Journal of Communication*, 53(4): 694–710.

—— (2005). "The Seeds of Audience Fragmentation: Specialization in the Use of Online News Sites," *Journal of Broadcasting & Electronic Media*, 49(3): 332–48.

—— and Rittenberg, J. (2009). "Online News Creation and Consumption Implications for Modern Democracies," in A. Chadwick (ed.) *Handbook of Internet Politics*, London: Routledge, pp. 186–200.

——, Weaver, A., and Maddex, B. (2001). "Accidentally Informed: Incidental News Exposure on the World Wide Web," *Journalism & Mass Communication Quarterly*, 78(3): 533–54.

Thompson, J. B. (1995). "The Media and Modernity: A Social Theory of the Media," Cambridge: Polity Press.

Thornton, L. and Keith, S. (2009). "From Convergence to Webvergence: Tracking the Evolution of Broadcast-Print Partnerships through the Lens of Change Theory," *Journalism & Mass Communication Quarterly*, 86(2): 257–76.

Thurman, N. (2008). "Forums for Citizen Journalists? Adoption of User Generated Content Initiatives by Online News Media," *New Media & Society*, 10(1): 139–57.

—— and Myllylahti, M. (2009). "Taking the Paper out of News," *Journalism Studies*, 10(5): 691–708.

Tolbert, C. and McNeal, R. (2003). "Unraveling the Effects of the Internet on Political Participation?," *Political Research Quarterly*, 56(2): 175–85.

Trammell, K., Tarkowski, A., and Sapp, A. (2006). "Rzeczpospolita Blogów: Examining Polish Bloggers through Content Analysis," *Journal of Computer-Mediated Communication*, 11(3): 702–22.

Tremayne, M. (2007). *Blogging, Citizenship, and the Future of Media*, New York: Routledge.

Tuchman, G. (1978). *Making News*, New York: Free Press.

Ursell, G. (2001). "Dumbing Down or Shaping Up? New Technologies, New Media, New Journalism," *Journalism*, 2(2): 175–96.

Weaver, D. and Drew, D. (2001). "Voter Learning and Interest in the 2000 Presidential Election: Did the Media Matter?," *Journalism & Mass Communication Quarterly*, 78(4): 787–98.

Weber, I. and Jia, L. (2007). "Internet and Self-Regulation in China: The Cultural Logic of Controlled Cornmodification," *Media Culture & Society*, 29(5): 772–89.

Weber, L. M., Loumakis, A., and Bergman, J. (2003). "Who Participates and Why? An Analysis of Citizens on the Internet and the Mass Public," *Social Science Computer Review*, 21(1): 26–42.

White, D. M. (1949). "The 'Gatekeeper': A Case Study in the Selection of News," *Journalism Quarterly*, 27: 383–90.

Williams, A., Wardle, C., and Wahl-Jorgensen, K. (2010). "'Have They Got News For Us?' Audience Revolution or Business as Usual at the BBC?," *Journalism Practice*, 5(1): 1–15.

Williams, B. A. and Deli Carpini, M. X. (2000). "Unchained Reaction: The Collapse of Media Gatekeeping and the Clinton-Lewinsky Scandal," 1(1): 61–85.

Wright, S. (2007). "A Virtual European Public Sphere? The Futurum Discussion Forum," *Journal of European Public Policy*, 14(8): 1167–85.

Xenos, M. and Moy, P. (2007). "Direct and Differential Effects of the Internet on Political and Civic Engagement," *Journal of Communication*, 57(4): 704–18.

Ye, X. and Li, X. (2006). "Internet Newspapers' Public Forum and User Involvement," in X. Li (ed.). *Internet Newspapers: The Making of a Mainstream Medium*, Mahwah, NJ: Lawrence Erlbaum, pp. 243–59.

Zillien, N. and Hargittai, E. (2009). "Digital Distinction: Status-Specific Types of Internet Usage," *Social Science Quarterly*, 90(2): 274–91.

Zillmann, D., and Bryant, J. (1985). "Selective-Exposure Phenomena," in D. Zillmann and J. Bryant (eds). *Selective Exposure to Communication*, Hillasdle, NJ: Lawrence Erlbaum, pp. 1–10.

....

CHAPTER 19

THE INTERNET IN CAMPAIGNS AND ELECTIONS

....

DARREN G. LILLEKER AND THIERRY VEDEL

INTRODUCTION

....

THERE has been much written about political e-campaigning—the use of information and communication technology (ICT), especially the Internet, in coordinated action to mobilize and/or influence individuals. Early research into the role of the Internet in political campaigning was marked by peaks of idealism and troughs of disillusionment (for instance Hill and Hughes 1998; Bimber 2003). The idealistic argument is articulated by Joe Trippi (2004), the mastermind behind Howard Dean's revolutionary but unsuccessful bid for the 2004 US Democratic Party presidential nomination, who spoke of a revolution in electoral politics permitting the candidate to appeal directly to potential supporters, so negating strong media effects, and enabling any citizen to be better informed, find like-minded individuals and, within networked collectives, influence the course of a campaign or even the outcome of the election. Dean's innovation was to finance his campaign through public donations, but the ultimate failure of the campaign also perhaps showed the limits for the Internet's revolutionary potential. This debate between cyber-optimists and cyber-pessimists is played out over and again, but as the story develops the embeddedness of the Internet within campaigning strategy becomes ever deeper.

Studies in the 1990s focused on the potential of the Internet and its possible political effects, debates centering on the extent to which there was revolutionary potential or whether new media would simply reflect the traditional hierarchies of power, share of voice, and influence. However, research has not simply focused on evidence to support a specific set of hypotheses, but developed along three related strands: how the Internet can be used to inform, to mobilize, and to lead to interaction. While highlighting that there has been a significant impact on the forms and repertories of political communication, empirical studies reach mixed conclusions about its deeper impact on the political system.

Globally, however, there is a very mixed picture regarding the use of the Internet as a whole, as well as variations in online political communication styles. Variations are linked to national contexts, more especially the infrastructure, the institutional arrangements, the legal provisions, and the political culture that exist in each country. For instance, uses differ in countries with a proportional election system (which tend to promote a nationwide, party-led debate) and those with a majority system (which are usually more conducive to more localized and individualized electoral campaigns), hence different political uses of the Internet emerge.

The mixed picture that is electoral e-campaigning makes this a fascinating as well as complex area of academic study. This chapter will map the key developments in both practice and research to understand the role the Internet can and does play in the context of political campaigning, what we can learn from this about both political campaigning and the Internet, and where the research agenda needs to look to further develop our theoretical and empirical understanding.

THE POTENTIAL OF THE INTERNET
FOR CAMPAIGNING AND ELECTIONS

Research on the potential enhancements brought to political campaigning and elections center around three key areas (Vedel 2003). First, citizens can become better informed about and engaged with the processes of democracy through the capacity of the Internet to provide vast resources of data at any time to any wired location. Second, candidates and parties are able to build relationships with their supporters—and to more cheaply, effectively, and efficiently mobilize them to participate within a campaign. Third, but also most fundamentally for democracy, the Internet offers the potential to facilitate a broad public debate around a plethora of issues and so have direct input into a campaign agenda.

Information

The development of ICTs for political communication basically rests on the traditional argument that in a democracy citizens need full information and an enlightened understanding of situations to contribute to democratic deliberation and make good decisions (Dahl 1998). ICTs make enormous quantities of information available to the public. The reduction of publishing and dissemination costs allows access to fuller information, thus fulfilling a key element of democracy, which states decision-making should be transparent and accountable to the citizen. Equally, the decentralized structure and global nature of the Internet help provide greater pluralism of viewpoints. The Internet provides new channels for information and expression, which are to some extent in competition with the traditional mediation processes. Personal or collective blogs, video-sharing sites, and Wiki-type cooperative applications are making citizens more independent from the major daily newspapers and TV news broadcasts.

This change in quantity may result in a change in quality. Instead of getting limited and general information on political decisions, citizens can be provided with detailed data, preparatory reports, and expert advice, and can examine issues in greater depth. In the same way, instead of getting abstracts of politicians' statements or political platforms, citizens can get the full text and, therefore, have a better knowledge of what politicians really propose. Second, citizens can be active instead of passive recipients of news from a limited number of sources. Citizens can actively search out the information they want, compare sources, and look for alternative views. However, quantity may also result in problems finding information, due both to scale and the gatekeeping function of search engines, as well as in determining the veracity of information citizens find.

Mobilization and coordination

The Internet facilitates contact between individuals who share common interests and helps co-ordinate joint actions. The Internet has the potential to challenge traditional political organizations (parties, trade unions, and economic lobbies) in facilitating the formation of new political and social forces hitherto hindered by the lack of a struc-tured apparatus or low resources. Use of ICTs also encourages the consolidation of col-lective identities at a local community level or on a global scale, with the Internet providing the spaces for crystallizing and shaping social relations around a shared project (Melucci 1996).

The ability of ICTs to enable people who share common interests to get in touch despite distance or social barriers can lead to a whole new dimension for politics. People can escape geography (and marginalization) through global forums based on special-ized narrow interests. For example, it is difficult for people who belong to a minority to really count in a small city but, through the Internet, those people can acquire a sense of their identity and of their social or political weight at the global level. Once like-minded individuals have created a group, they can more easily exchange ideas in order to define their political platform and decide the kinds of action they want to engage in.

ICTs also make communication easy. Email updates can be sent regularly to members, and discussion forums can be established to discuss options. As these political groupings build their organization and reach they are then able to influence decision-makers or public opinion—for instance, by organizing email campaigns directed at government officials or politicians. Such tools, the potential of which have been demonstrated in stud-ies of pressure groups (Rodgers 2003), have equal application within election campaigns. Through ICTs, individuals can participate more actively, frequently, and quickly in the decision-making process of political parties and organizations. Individuals can publicly or privately communicate their opinions on parties' platforms, and express disagreements with parties' strategies or just comment on the campaign.

These developments, facilitated by technology yet adapted by those who are politically engaged online, lead us to focus on understanding the rise of a campaign communication ecosystem online: one that is connected, interdependent, open access, and chaotic. However, this is not necessarily evidence of a democratization of politics. Several surveys by the Pew Research Center have shown that Internet users interested in politics online have a considerably higher standard of education and social status than other Internet users, and even more so than the population as a whole. The Internet serves to "preach to the converted," as Pippa Norris put it (Norris 2003), increasing the capabilities of those who are most integrated into the political system. However, this can be a significant development for democracy.

Debate and discussion

The online communication ecosystem is founded on interconnected conversations taking place across platforms, forums, and public spaces around a given topic. It is argued that, as citizens become better informed and mobilized to seek further information, and to form collectives and engage with political decisions, this can also nurture more proactive civic behavior. Those empowered would be defined as the "connected people," what others have called a "fifth estate" of online activists (Dutton 2009). The Internet provides many spaces (discussion forums, blogs, and social networking or filesharing platforms) that facilitate the exchange of information, commentary, and ideas between individuals from different backgrounds who would probably never otherwise engage in joint discussions. This enables the Web to enlarge and/or revitalize the public sphere, so much so that some see it as a novel agora. In other words, the Internet would give rise to virtual communities, a notion popularized by Howard Rheingold (1993). This perspective runs through analyses of social relations within the networked society (Van Dijk 2006; Castells 2007) and many popular texts that claim to redefine the relations between politics, business, and society (Benkler 2006; Shirky 2009).

How to survey the political Web?
Methodological challenges

There has been a range of distinct and discreet methodological approaches to the study of political campaigning using the Internet. Schneider and Foot (2004) identified three ways of analyzing political parties and candidates' websites and categorized the studies as using content analysis, discourse analysis, and Web sphere analysis. All offer a range of advantages and disadvantages. A few studies have also surveyed party strategists and consultants, though issues of access, and the likelihood that this group will offer only post-hoc rationalizations limits their utility (Lilleker 2003). Hence most studies focus on analysis of what is physically created online in order to discover the role of the Internet in campaigns (Xenos and Foot 2005).

The most frequently employed method is content analysis, a quantitative technique that consists of developing a series of categories that can later be tested for their presence or absence, and counted within a specific website. The method is one that is highly object-ive and transparent and it can easily cope with a large sample. The problem with content analysis is that it can only categorize features and make assumptions about the experi-ences that are enabled, but not necessarily realized; it remains more difficult to assess what experiences are actually provided. This is particularly relevant when we consider the complexities surrounding interaction within environments built with Web 2.0 tech-nologies that can facilitate, but never achieve, extensive content co-creation by both the host and visitors.

However, content analysis provides the basis of much academic understanding of Internet use in politics. The coding schema developed by Gibson and Ward (2000) has helped create a rich picture of the role that the Internet has played within election cam-paigns globally (Ward and Gibson 2003; Tkach-Kawasaki 2003; Coleman and Ward 2005; Foot and Schneider 2006; Conway and Donard 2004; Schweitzer 2005; Stanyer 2006; Strandberg 2006; Kluver et al. 2007; Ward et al. 2008) and in political communi-cation generally (Jackson 2003; Gibson et al. 2003a; Ward and Lusoli 2005). Variations on the methodology have also been developed and adapted for web analysis. Videostyle (Kaid and Johnston 2001) in particular has been used for the analysis of presentational elements of candidates and parties (Trammel et al. 2006).

While content analysis focuses purely on counting, discourse analysis treats web-based communication as a rhetorical text (Davis and Brewer 1997). Text, taken to mean all features and layout (Fairclough 2003), is analyzed for its meaning using concepts bor-rowed from linguistics (Bergs 2006). With this approach the focus is on the message, in particularly the semiotics (Mayer 1998); however, this is often criticized as highly sub-jective. The advantages, however, are that within interactive environments we can assess the number of speakers and the nature of the conversations, for example the extent to which the host encourages dialogue (Rafaeli 1988). It has proven useful for measuring levels of interactivity on US Presidential Primary websites (Benoit and Benoit 2002) and government portals (Negroponte 1995; Boardman 2005), as well as in exploring the existence of an online public sphere (Chadwick and May 2003; Dahlberg 2001), includ-ing user-to-user interaction in social chat-rooms within virtual communities (Herring 2004), and plotting news stories between microblogs and the mainstream media (Chadwick 2011).

In contrast, web sphere analysis is an attempt to develop a grounded theory based on the network structure of websites (Schneider and Foot 2002; Kluver et al. 2007). In cam-paign studies, the method was used to compile over 50,000 different websites and inter-view 50 web producers in order to examine the political actions on, and traffic between, websites in the 2000 US election. The studies found that the presence of websites was transforming the way campaigns were conducted and that learning was cross-national, though the latter finding was also supported by using content analysis (Lilleker and Jackson 2011). Kluver et al. (2007) also predicted the impacts of user-generated content, ones we are only beginning to recognize. The definition of the web sphere as "not simply as a collection of Websites, but as a hyperlinked set of dynamically defined digital resources spanning multiple websites deemed relevant or related to a central theme or object" (Schneider and Foot 2004: 4) is significant for understanding the Internet within the context of election campaigning and placing the user at the center of research into online campaigning.

There has been a significant amount of research employing content analysis; less has taken a critical discourse analysis approach, and web sphere analysis is underused. Equally, only content analysis has been used to study election campaigning, and specifically the content of websites, hence this offers a more comprehensive method of exploring interactivity and its role within election campaigning and voter engagement.

However, there are broader questions relating to what specific media are important within the context of an election campaign. Is the collection of data from a website becoming pointless as browsers, and so campaigners, move into established social networks such as Facebook? In other words is communication taking place in various places and so is locating the heart of the online campaign becoming more difficult? Furthermore, in terms of how the browser might view the campaign, to what extent should user-generated political communication be recognized as part of the eco-system of a campaign and require as great attention, if not perhaps more, than official channels? The most important, but most difficult, question concerns the impact that the Internet is having on the attitudes and behavior of the voter: a significant amount or none at all? Capturing the impact of any campaign, or isolating the impact of any specific tool or aspect of a campaign, is at best a highly complex moving target. Influence is multi-directional, unique to the individual and governed as much by the individual's psychology as the design of the stimuli. Experiments remain underused and often produce mixed results. Yet, to fully understand the significance of new technologies and the ways in which they are employed within an election campaign, one needs to remember that at the heart of most election campaigns is the voter. Currently it is hard to find the voter as the central character within this strand of research.

THE EVOLUTION OF CAMPAIGNING

Modeling changes from pre-modern to post-modern campaigns

Colin Seymour-Ure (1977) suggested that political organizations adapt their communication to suit the dominant media of the day. This process of adaptation can lead to a simple re-orientation of communication or to significant changes to the organization itself. While societal pressures also have a key role in the shaping of politics, such as the consumerization of society leading to a marketization of politics (Lees-Marshment 2011), focusing on the relationship between political organizations and media is useful when considering how technological advances in communication lead to adaptations in the form and style of political communication.

In terms of the adaptations of political communication across the last half century, Norris' (2003) typology is in this context a useful heuristic. While the terminology is much contested, in particular the characterization of eras as pre-modern, modern, and postmodern (Negrine 2008), her schematic reinforces a shared conceptualization of change within a historical timeframe which elides with studies that introduce campaigning ages (Blumler 1990), campaign styles (Gibson and Römmele 2001), orientations (Lees-Marshment 2001), or organizational styles (Katz and Mair 2002).

The first or pre-modern age—prominent until the 1950s—was a time of easy access to a largely deferent media, when voters held fairly stable partisan attachments, and so parties could largely stand on a consistent product-oriented platform. Campaigns were local affairs, run by decentralized volunteer groups. This was the era of mass membership and so a labor-intensive campaign was both tenable and appropriate.

Television ushered in the modern era or second age. This led to campaigns developing a more national character, and the beginning of a centralization of strategy and a professionalization of communication. Campaigning became more sales-oriented, focused upon converting and persuading voters while also getting the loyalists out on election day. Rather than focusing on the partisan press, radio, posters, and interpersonal communication, television was supported by targeted direct mail.

The 1990s saw a further ramping-up of the professionalization, ushering in the postmodern campaign era. Political organizations adopted a market-orientation to their communication, as well as to some extent the design of key political messages and policy priorities (Lees-Marshment 2001). Post-modern campaigns also became more targeted and narrow-casted via direct channels of communication; these channels incorporated the mass media as well as email, online forums, and intranets (Norris 2003). In addition, organizations adopted a more bifurcated strategy for their campaigning: while the central campaign command set out the core messages, communication was also the responsibility of local organizations, with in particular the latter using local email lists, intranets, and forums to mobilize supporters (Gibson and Römmele 2001; Katz and Mair 2002; Norris 2003). Over time, local organizations would also become partially responsible for using social networking and microblogging tools to reinforce and make locally relevant the national campaign strategy.

This suggests a shift in organizational behavior, one perhaps driven both by new communication technologies as well as broad social changes. The extent to which the third or post-modern age is becoming the age of the Internet, as previous eras were interpersonal or television ages, is a moot point. Campaigns have clearly been adapted to a digital media landscape characterized by "abundance, ubiquity, reach, and celerity" (Blumler and Kavanagh 1999: 213). However, it is argued that even in 2011, it is the 24/7 mass media that remain dominant for campaigns, even within the US, yet new ways emerge of characterizing campaigning that are designed specifically for the integration of the online environment.

The Hypermedia campaign and new political repertoires

The political campaigning response to the social uses of technologies is the adaption of the tools of the postmodern campaign to incorporate digital communication technologies. Howard (2006) defines this as the hypermedia campaign, where communication is relayed across a wide range of outlets simultaneously, thereby meeting the demands of the postmodern media, the 24/7 news, and the global online audience (Davis 2010). Any single item of content will be tailored for multiple forms of consumption and disseminated in ways that can be collected by journalists, supporters, or web browsers alike at multiple communication junctions. While there will be an informational component within communication, a range of interactive actions are facilitated. Items are created to allow ease of sharing to facilitate messages going viral across the Internet (Boynton 2009) and can be commented on and adapted within the campaigns' ecosystem.

The hypermedia campaign must allow for and expect the "decomposition and recomposition of messages" (Howard 2006: 2). These communicative processes permit co-ownership of communication across a wider agora and for reach of messages to be multiplied across networks. While this appears to be beneficial for democracy, there are also threats associated with the use of technologies within the hypermedia campaign. Howard argues that the extensive use of data-mining and targeting will lead to a communicative divide. As noted in other critiques of political marketing and campaigning (Lilleker 2005; Savigny 2008), only a privileged few voters may be positioned at the heart of the campaign, having messages constructed for their consumption and being invited to offer their input.

This reductionist strategy of targeting those voters whose participation may swing the result leads to what Howard refers to as a "thin democracy," with engagement being managed through the process of targeted communication using email. This contrasts with perspectives that suggest that the broadening out of the ability to produce content can lead to a fatter, if no less unequal, form of democratic participation. The ability to wield political power and exert influence will depend on the size and reach of communication within social and communicative networks (Davis 2010: 98). Measurement of a network effect has been discussed widely, its value linked to the number of people within a network (Van Dijk 2006: 78), with the equation of the number of members squared referenced as one method of evaluation (Anderson 2007: 21); thus, the more connected members of the emergent polyarchy are, and the more they are able to disseminate and/or amplify a message, the wider their reach through the network.

However, real value is also related to the social capital of the network effect. The amplification of messages via a network does not simply increase reach but also adds credibility as individuals act as information hubs to their networks of contacts and friends.

These constitute a new information elite (Van Dijk 2006: 185), which can include established elites such as politicians and journalists as well as individual weblog authors (bloggers) or users deemed credible due to their propensity to share items among their friends and followers.

Thus for the meeting of campaign objectives, the hypermedia campaign strategist must harness the online and offline information elite simultaneously and create a synergistic communicative process between nodes within the network. Online actions by political actors (a post on Twitter for example) feed into communication by online and offline communicators (journalists and bloggers), and these draw hits to other online features such as a campaign website which generates further sharing or generates interaction, which in turn can create broader offline and online attention, or resources in the shape of volunteers or donations. The hypermedia campaign is thus the response to the twenty-first century campaign communication environment: it recognizes that to be successful one must both create and join the communication ecosystem.

Landmark campaigns from Dean to Royal to Obama

The evolution in adaptation to the hypermedia campaign can be traced through studying the campaigns of Howard Dean, Segolene Royal, and Barack Obama. The historiography of 2004–08, and the influence of these campaigns since, is instructive for understanding how a hypermedia campaign looks when executed. In most ways Howard Dean's unsuccessful bid for the Democratic nomination in 2004 was a typical insurgent campaign. The aim was to get a substantial amount of media coverage, so resulting in name recognition, and building support. Support would equate to donations, the lifeblood of any US electoral bid. However, unusually, Dean opted out of the federal government's match-funding scheme to avoid the campaign spending-cap. The reason for this was the confidence he had in focusing on small donations from a large support base (Lipsitz and Panagopoulos 2011). The key technological innovation adopted by Dean involved going to a site already used then by some five million Americans: Meetup.com. Meetup.com is a social networking platform that facilitates offline group meetings in various localities around the world. Meetup allows members to find and join groups unified by a common interest, such as politics, books, games, movies, etc. Dean harnessed the network effect of Meetup.com to organize supporter meetings and, importantly, fundraisers. Small donations of US$10–$100 flooded into his campaign coffers amounting to, at one point, US$4 million per day (Price 2004). Dean's campaign highlighted that a campaign could use the benefits of the new Web 2.0 technologies to its advantage and that potentially this could have an impact on the results (Towner and Dulio 2012).

The lessons from the Dean campaign, however, brought a new focus to incorporating the Internet into political campaigns, and in particular considering the benefits of the latest platforms. The 2007 French Presidential Campaign saw significant innovation in the use of ICTs. The eventual winner, Nicolas Sarkozy, focused on technological sophistication by building his own online video site (NSTV) and for a while created the second life *Isle de*

France environment where his presidential style could be tested out. However, it was the runner-up in the second round of voting that would best harness the social media environment and adapt to the norms of a hypermedia campaign. During the race to win the left vote in round one, Segolene Royal first allowed her supporters to contribute to a co-produced online manifesto. The *Cahiers d'espérance* (Notebooks of Hope), became a symbol of a more open style of campaigning and signifying a more collectivist presidential rule. This involved reaching out to those already politically active online and harnessing them to her campaign. The Segosphere was a tightly hyperlinked group of weblog authors who promoted her presidential bid and contributed to a wider political public sphere that centered on Royal's political platform. The Segosphere, which was created to target younger voters, linked together around 14,000 weblogs. This reflected the bottom-up communication style of Royal (Koc-Michalska and Vedel 2009), in which her website encouraged visitors to contribute to discussion groups and add to her platform.

It has been claimed that without Segolene Royal the Obama campaign would have been far less innovative; Obama's campaign was the first to utilize all aspects of the online communication environment, joining the existing political public sphere and creating his own ecosystem. Obama created presences across seventeen different social network profiles. Obama used YouTube as an online television service, making his videos available 24/7 but also facilitating browsers to express their support, by clicking the thumbs-up button to show liking, and through sharing via social networks. Twitter was utilized as a news feed, informing supporters where Obama was holding events as well as giving insights into his campaign. Alongside these "pull media," the Obama campaign proactively harvested mobile phone numbers, particularly by offering mobile subscribers the opportunity to be the first to learn whom Obama would have as his running mate. Thus, like Dean and Royal, Obama entered all the spaces where his potential voters might happen across political information and provided a space where they could engage with his campaign.

The key innovation was myBarackObama.com, or MyBO. This was a personal social network and public sphere where members could express support, comment on policy, ask questions, and be part of the Obama supporters' community. MyBO was not simply a space for friendship and chat, however; MyBO was a mobilization tool. Joining MyBO was about joining a community of activists, with activism orchestrated by the core campaign team but developed by community members (Harfoush 2009). Email was the key mobilization tool, both in directing traffic to the site and encouraging matching donations with other community members, facilitating holding fundraisers, providing training for canvassing, and getting out the vote. If we measure success in donations alone we should note that US\$711.7m was raised online (Hendricks and Denton 2010). The Obama campaign was the closest to a Web 2.0 campaign (Vaccari 2010; Lilleker and Jackson 2011: 78). The reason was that it was genuinely co-produced. The news weblog elicited huge numbers of comments, averaging eighty per item across 11,452 entries. In fact, it was almost impossible to find an Obama presence online that was not accompanied by public comment, though there was significant moderation. Obama's openness, matched by his success, placed the Internet on the map as a campaign tool and led many to ask how to "do an Obama" and replicate his "Internet magic" (Plehwe 2009: 173).

The Obama innovations were adopted, in adapted forms, in Germany, the UK, and elsewhere (Lilleker and Jackson 2011: 164).

Impacts on political participation and electoral outcomes

Any argument that the Internet can shape patterns of political participation, either activism or the formation of voter choices, must be moderated by the "preaching to the converted" thesis (Norris 2003). Hindman (2009) performs the widest survey of online behavior and finds that the most read weblog authors replicate offline sources of influence; they are largely white, male, highly educated, and politically active. These elite figures are also most likely to be able to have input into the broader political public sphere, shaping both the online and offline news agenda. Therefore the democratizing potential of the Internet, where anyone can have their voice, is significantly limited and reinforces the perspective that "it may be easy to speak in cyberspace, but it remains difficult to be heard" (Hindman 2009: 142).

Such findings are reinforced in a variety of studies that demonstrate the power of offline political elites in shaping both the content and sentiment of contributions within the online political communication ecosystem. Furthermore, the picture of who is heard online and who hears those voices offline is largely similar (Smith et al. 2009: 1). However, the report finds that the gaps in terms of age, income, and education level, where the politically active tend to be older, better off, and better educated, is narrowed within social networking sites. This is particularly the case with age, most online participation being the preserve of those over 35 but on social networks the age band is 18–24. However, those on lower incomes also make small donations to campaigns and the lower educated are as equally likely to participate by commenting, sharing, and liking as their better educated peers (Smith et al. 2009).

Yet, overall, there is still a stark inequality on most measures of civic engagement and participation online, which mirror more traditional means of being politically active. Therefore it seems that the greatest impact that the Internet has on campaigns is that it enables the campaigner to mobilize supporters and orchestrate fundraising more efficiently, so bringing the campaign and its supporters into a community; but it only reaches beyond a privileged and highly engaged minority at the margins on social networks.

Nevertheless, engagement with election campaigns is being reshaped by the Internet. Reviewing Internet use during the 2010 mid-term US elections, Smith (2011) found 58 percent seeking political information online, and for 32 percent it was the only information source. More importantly, 53 percent performed at least one action classified as civic engagement. The Internet is not, however, simply a media for reception. A majority of online users report that they feel it easier to connect with others who share their views politically, suggesting that people seek out communities of like-minded individuals. A majority also report that the Internet facilitates exposure to a wider range of political views than they can get in the traditional news media, so broadening knowledge and facilitating a more active public sphere.

These factors were argued to be of critical importance for the 2008 Obama campaign. As a result of his adoption of a hypermedia campaign strategy, the young in particular were mobilized more effectively than had had previously been the case. Barr (2009) notes the use of text messaging, Facebook, MySpace, email, and interactive platforms facilitated the establishment of a range of youth-led pro-Obama organizations that meant the campaign reached out further and got more young people registered to vote, developed peer-to-peer networks of youths, and offered a range of media that was attractive to the young.

However, these positives can also be balanced by a range of negatives. There has long been observable evidence of the growth of cyberghettoes (Sunstein 2007; Hindman 2009), where like-minded individuals group around quite narrow political ideas. Often these attempt to lock browsers into a network of web presences with a single ideological perspective. Equally, extremist movements can find a home on the Internet and are just as able to reach out to potential supporters as more mainstream and moderate movements.

When focusing on "impact," it is important to view a campaign holistically. The interplay of communication creates a rich campaign ecosystem with each aspect feeding the others. Broadcast media still play a huge role, as do a range of activities that occur below the radar and are often at a person-to-person level. Comments and conversations, liking and following, reflect a range of political and social trends that are occurring alongside the official campaign. The ability to share information gleaned from a telephone or doorstep conversation with a canvasser with a national or global audience adds texture to a campaign. Political activity online thus provides an immediate and visible element to a campaign.

The more active a campaign is, the more engaged a following they gain; this is also the case when measuring the impact of candidates' or parliamentarians' communication in terms of gaining fans, followers, or getting content shared within networks (Jackson and Lilleker 2011; Koc-Michalska and Lilleker 2012). The more posts made to Facebook or Twitter, the more weblog posts authored, the more likely they are to reach a wide audience and encourage participation. In this respect, if there is an impact from engaging through a hypermedia campaign, it is that the attention received can also be used as a predictor of votes. Tumasjan et al. (2011), based on a survey of sentiment within Twitter, notes that such tools "can be a valid indicator of the political landscape off-line" (Tumasjan et al. 2011: 414). Therefore winning in the battle to have the most proactive hypermedia strategy may also result in increasing awareness, engagement, and support; however, such a conclusion needs further rigorous testing.

FOUR LESSONS ON THE
INTERNET AND POLITICS

The research on models of campaigning and their impact offer four specific lessons regarding the limitations of academic predictions and the potential of the Internet as a campaign tool.

Ideology versus resources as predictors of usage

Explanations for the usage of the Internet as a campaign tool, and particularly the integration of interactive Web 2.0 era features and platforms into a hypermedia style campaign, usually focus on three elements: resources, incentives, and orientation (Margolis and Resnick 2000; Gibson et al. 2000; Norris 2003; Gibson et al. 2003a, 2003b; Solanet and Cardenal 2008). The incentives' dimension relates to the extent to which the Internet has the potential to reach significant numbers of actual and potential supporters, a factor seldom questioned across most democracies. The debate continues, however, as to whether physical resources such as finances or staff, or the orientation or ideology of the party or candidate, offer the most explanatory power for having an innovative online presence. Thus we find in literature two competing hypotheses: that candidates or organizations that have the greatest resources at their disposal, or those that are more center-left, are most proactive online.

The evidence to support either hypothesis is reliant on how the research was conducted. Sudulich, in a comparative study of Italy, Spain, the Republic of Ireland, and Great Britain found ideology was one factor, and that the left performed best in terms of interactivity (Sudulich 2009). Alternatively, Copsey (2003) argued that marginalized voices, and in particular those on the extreme right, find the Internet most appropriate for community building. When looking at the evidence from recent campaigns we can argue that both Royal and Obama, both center-left presidential candidates, utilized the Internet for more inclusive and interactive purposes than their center-right opponents. In Germany and the UK, however, we find the parties with the largest and most innovative presences as those with the largest parliamentary representation, and representing both centrist viewpoints. The outlier within the UK parliamentary contest was the far-right British National Party. Their website was the only one to match that of Obama in terms of its interactivity (Lilleker and Jackson 2011). This offers a highly mixed picture in terms of the impact of ideology.

Resources offer little indication of separating the main candidates in the 2007 French contest. Obama's fundraising gained him three times the spending power of his rival, McCain. Equally, parties with the greatest chance of winning also attract the greatest resources. This suggests that the level of resources is the key factor—and when considering the technical sophistication and person-hours to create, monitor, and maintain a sophisticated web presence, this makes sense. The outlier, once again is the British National Party. They relied on credit, leading to their highly sophisticated website being closed down on the morning of the 2010 election due to a failure to settle their account. Without resources, a sophisticated and innovative web presence is far more difficult.

A limited revitalization and enlargement of the public sphere

A longstanding argument has been that the Internet and related technologies can augment avenues for personal expression and promote citizen activity (Papacharissi 2002:

9–10; see also Negroponte 1995 and Rheingold 1993). The Internet, it is argued, has the capacity to provide substance to the idealized notion of the Habermasian public sphere based on open access to information and spaces for debate, discussion, and mobilization (Dahlgren 2005). Research tends to demonstrate, however, that this potential is largely unrealized (Papacharissi 2002). As we highlighted earlier, beyond the use of social media platforms, there is no evidence of a major broadening of political engagement as a result of campaigns adopting an online element (Norris 2003).

The uneasy diffusion of the Internet within political organizations

Independent of the incentives, there is much caution in adopting a hypermedia campaign. Stromer-Galley (2000) suggests two main reasons that have received some support by recent studies (Lilleker and Jackson 2011). The first is one of resources. Campaign strategists often struggle over questions relating to which media is most effective and efficient for meeting the objectives of the campaign. Offering basic web presences full of content repackaged from offline brochures can be seen as reasonably cost-neutral. More sophisticated presences require investment, and while the use of social networking platforms may be free, the creation of bespoke content is costly. Equally expensive is the monitoring of comments, removing attacks, and responding to those asking questions.

More fundamental issues relate to the nature of participation. The chaotic ecosystem that can form around a campaign is impossible to control. The centralist tendency to orchestrate a coherent, persuasive campaign can be undermined if the campaign becomes co-created. Each response to a post, text, or video contributes to further visitors' experiences, but also can undermine the persuasive impact of a message if it offers a negative perception. Similarly, erroneous material such as spam can be posted across open-access platforms and cause a distraction from the original content. More worrying for campaigns can be a loss of ambiguity over messages. Campaigns usually employ broad themes that capture the hopes and desires of the mass electorate. Potential supporters, however, often seek specific information relating to policy initiatives that may impact their own lives. Not only is answering such queries highly costly in terms of time, it can lead to electoral organizations making very specific promises, in public places, that it might not be able to keep if elected (Stromer-Galley 2000).

Drawing on a more party-centered perspective than that of Stromer-Galley, Lilleker et al. (2010) argue that the demands of citizen participation and internal party democracy must also be balanced. The external online audience can be involved but through weak interaction, such as by gauging opinion through simple polls. Forums that engage with an internal audience, open to members only, and concealed within Intranets, are viewed as more effective for good policy-making. Thus parties limit their adoption of such tools, and building a public sphere, as they do not want to invite an unmanageable mass to participate at the expense of those who they need to involve and should be at the heart of decision-making.

The media-mix: combining media and the Internet

The final lesson relates to the complex interplay within online and offline environments. Chadwick (2011) describes a hybridized media environment, which involves a range of actors, mass media, online media, independent or citizen journalists, weblog authors, and the broader users of social networks and microblogs. This ecosystem allows information to flow with fluidity, being adapted, refreshed, and elaborated alongside the usual news cycle. This process leads Chadwick to describe political information cycles as "complex assemblages in which the personnel, practices, genres, technologies, and temporalities of supposedly 'new' online media are hybridized with those of supposedly 'old' broadcast and press media. How this hybridization process occurs shapes power relations among actors and ultimately affects the flow of news" (2011: 7). The hypermedia campaign embraces this hybridized media environment and attempts to move within the political information cycle, recognizing the interplay between platforms and interdependence of a range of actors, the elite and emergent non-elite, in shaping the news agenda as well as the fortunes of a campaign.

AGENDA FOR FUTURE RESEARCH

There is much to learn, in particular as the role of the Internet as a campaign tool is constantly evolving, being adapted to campaign logics, while also causing campaign logics to adapt. There are three general ways in which the research agenda needs to develop to provide a foundation, both for future knowledge generation and the improvement of practice in this field.

First, there needs to be a shift from purely supply-side studies to ones which incorporate analysis of citizens' web usage and examine to what extent there is a demand for a more engaging, interactive, and sophisticated online campaign among candidates or parties seeking election. Such research should not only develop the experimental work that has taught us so much about the use of news, advertising, and posters for online environments, but also explore the political behavior of digital natives. What new forms of participation are being adopted, and to what extent they are perceived as civic engagement, are important questions that are currently underexplored; research needs to understand the psychology of online political participation.

Second, there is a need to better understand the interaction between off-line and online politics, and whether online activism changes the nature of political participation. Does the Internet usher in new forms of political engagement which are more flexible, contractual, and moral issue-oriented, in contrast to traditional activism, that is conceived as a permanent, ideological, even sacrificial, commitment (Ion et al. 2005). Some critics, such as Morozov (2011), have been prompt to mock the emergence of a slacktivism, described as the illusion of having a meaningful impact on the world without demanding anything more than joining a Facebook group. Also, we need to understand how the rise of online campaigns affects the transformation of parties. However, it would be useless to define online and offline political activities as being good or bad. It is more important to study their respective benefits and shortcomings, how they might interact, and how this transforms the functioning of political forces.

Finally there is the need for more comparative research on the extent to which not only organizational factors, resources, incentives, and orientation, shape Internet use but also the extent to which the political and social cultures, structures, and traditions impact upon campaign strategy.

In conclusion, political campaign communication has been transformed, but only to an extent. Campaigns have moved from an interpersonal, amateurish stage of campaigning, through the eras of the dominance of television to a hypermedia era. In the modern age the gulf between centralized and local is narrowing. Interpersonal communication, even face-to-face communication, can occur despite distances of millions of miles. There are new ways to be social, ones that involve being simultaneously isolated and connected. Politics has to be part of this environment, but candidates and parties cannot only be social in order to be elected. Being social involves resources and risks, which needs careful consideration; it also requires new skills that are slowly moving into the electoral arena. However, what is referred to as new media does not work in isolation from old media and the hybridization and merging of platforms creates a new communication ecosystem where influence is diffuse and consistency is hard to attain. There are many challenges facing political campaigners as they adapt to the online environment; there are also many benefits that are enabled. Perhaps we are at the cusp of a new age of campaigning and political engagement, or perhaps we are just witnessing a minor shift in politics as usual. E-campaigning is fertile ground for study, but an ever moving target; such is the challenge for this burgeoning field of study.

REFERENCES

Anderson, P. (2007). "What is Web 2.0? Ideas, Technologies and Implications for Education," JISC Technology and Standards Watch Report, February. Available at <http://www.jisc.ac.uk/media/documents/techwatch/tsw0701b.pdf>. Accessed June 20, 2012.

Barr, K. (2009). "A Perfect Storm: The 2008 Youth Vote," in D. Johnson (ed.). *Campaigning for President 2008: Strategy and Tactics, New Voices and New Techniques*, London: Routledge, pp. 105–25.

Benkler, Y. (2006). *The Wealth of Networks: How Social Production Transforms Markets and Freedom*, New Haven: Yale University Press.

Benoit, W. and Benoit, P. (2002). "The Virtual Campaign: Presidential Primary Websites in Campaign 2000," American Communication Journal, 3(3). Available at <http://ac-journal.org/journal/vol3/Iss3/rogue4/benoit.html>. Accessed May 10, 2008.

Bergs, A. (2006). "Analyzing Online Communication from a Social Network Point of View: Questions, Problems, Perspectives," Language@Internet, 3. Available at <http://www.languageatinternet.org/articles/2006/371>. Accessed on June 12, 2007.

Bimber, B. (2003). *Information and American Democracy: Technology in the Evolution of Political Power*, Cambridge: Cambridge University Press.

Blumler, J. (1990). "Elections, the Media and the Modern Publicity Process," in M. Ferguson (ed.). *Public Communication: The New Imperatives*, London: Sage, pp. 101–13.

—— and Kavanagh, D. (1999). "The Third Age of Communication: Influences and Features," *Political Communication*, 16(3): 209–30.

Boardman, M. (2005). *The Language of Websites*, London: Routledge.

Boynton, B. (2009). "Going Viral—The Dynamics of Attention," in Conference Proceedings of the YouTube and the 2008 Election Cycle in the United States Conference, the University of Massachusetts, Amherst, MA, April 16–17: pp. 11–38. Available at <http://scholarworks.umass.edu/cgi/viewcontent.cgi?filename=1&article=1000&context=jitpc2009&type=additional>. Accessed June 20, 2012.

Castells, M. (2007). "Communication, Power and Counter-Power in the Network Society," *International Journal of Communication*, 1(1): 238–66.

Chadwick, A. (2011). "The Political Information Cycle in a Hybrid News System: The British Prime Minister and the 'Bullygate' Affair," *International Journal of Press/Politics*, 16(1): 3–29.

—— and May, C. (2003). "Interaction Between States and Citizens in the Age of the Internet: 'e-Government' in the United States, Britain and the European Union," *Governance: International Journal of Policy, Administration and Institutions*, 16(2): 271–300.

Coleman, S. and Ward, S. (eds) (2005). *Spinning the Web: Online Campaigning During the 2005 General Election*, London: Hansard Society.

Conway, M. and Donard, D. G. (2004). "An Evaluation of New Zealand Political Party Websites," *Information Research*, 9(4). Available at <http://informationr.net/ir/9-4/paper196.html>. Accessed September 2, 2007.

Copsey, N. (2003). "Extremism on the Net: The Extreme Right and the Value of the Internet," in R. Gibson, P. Nixon, and S. Ward (eds). *Political Parties and the Internet: Net Gain?* London: Routledge, pp. 218–33.

Dahl, R. (1998). *On Democracy*, London: Yale University Press.

Dahlberg, L. (2001). "The Internet and Democratic Discourse: Exploring the Prospects of Online Deliberation Forums," *Information Communication and Society*, 4(4): 615–33.

Dahlgren, P. (2005). "The Internet, Public Spheres, and Political Communication: Dispersion and Deliberation," *Political Communication*, 22(2): 147–62.

Davis, A. (2010). *Political Communication and Social Theory*, London: Routledge.

Davis, B. H. and Brewer, J. P. (1997). *Electronic Discourse: Linguistic Individuals in Virtual Space*, Albany, NY: State University of New York Press.

Dutton, W. H. (2009). "The Fifth Estate Emerging through the Network of Networks," *Prometheus*, 27(1): 1–15.

Fairclough, N. (2003). *Analysing Discourse: Textual Analysis for Social Research*, London: Routledge.

Foot, K. A. and Schneider, S. M. (2006). *Web Campaigning*, Cambridge, MA: MIT Press.

Gibson, R. and Römmele, A. (2001). "Changing Campaign Communications: A Party-Centred Theory of Professional Campaigning," *Harvard International Journal of Press/Politics*, 6(4): 31–43.

—— and Ward, S. (2000). "British Party Activity in Cyberspace," in R. Gibson and S. Ward, (eds) *Reinvigorating Government? British Politics and the Internet*, Aldershot: Ashgate, pp. 155–207.

Gibson, R., Margolis, M., Resnick, D., and Ward, S. (2003a). "Election Campaigning on the WWW in the US and the UK: A Comparative Analysis," *Party Politics*, 9(1): 47–76.

——, Newell, J. L., and Ward, S. J. (2000). "New Parties, New Media: Italian Party Politics and the Internet," *South European Society and Politics* 5(1): 123–36.

——, Römmele, A., and Ward, S. (2003b). "German Parties and Internet Campaigning in the 2002 Federal Election," *German Politics*, 12(1): 79–104.

Harfoush, R. (2009). *Yes We Did: An Inside Look at How Social Media Built the Obama Brand*, Berkeley, CA: New Riders.

Hendricks, J. A. and Denton, R. E. (2010). *Communicator-in-Chief: How Barack Obama Used New Media Technology to Win the White House*, New York: Lexington.

Herring, S. C. (2004). "Computer-Mediated Discourse Analysis: An Approach to Researching Online Behaviour," in S. A. Barab, R. Kling, and J. H. Gray (eds). *Designing for Virtual Communities in the Service of Learning*, New York: Cambridge University Press, pp. 338–76.

Hill, K. and Hughes, J. (1998). *Cyber Politics: Citizen Activism in the Age of the Internet*, Oxford: Rowman and Littlefield.

Hindman, M. (2009). *The Myth of Digital Democracy*, New York: Lexington Books.

Howard, P. N. (2006). *New Media Campaigns and the Managed Citizen*, New York: Cambridge University Press.

Ion, J., Spyros, F., and Pascal, V. (2005). *Militer aujourd'hui*, Paris: Editions Autrement.

Jackson, N. (2003). "MPs and Web Technologies: An Untapped Opportunity?," *Journal of Public Affairs*, 3(2): 124–37.

—— and Lilleker, D. G. (2011). "Microblogging, Constituency Service and Impression Management: UK MPs and the Use of Twitter," *Journal of Legislative Studies* 17(2): 86–105.

Kaid, L. L. and Johnston, A. (2001). *Videostyle in Presidential Campaigns: Style and Content of Televised Political Advertising*, Westport, CT: Praeger/Greenwood.

Katz, R. and Mair, P. (2002). "The Ascendancy of the Party in Public Office: Party Organizational Change in Twentieth Century Democracies," in R. Gunther, J. R. Montero, and J. J. Linz (eds). *Political Parties*, Oxford: Oxford University Press, pp. 113–35.

Kluver, R., Jankowski, N. W. Foot, K. A. Schneider, S. M. (2007). *The Internet and National Election: A Comparative Study of Web Campaigning*, London: Routledge.

Koc-Michalska, K. and Lilleker, D. (2012) "Online Political Communication Strategies: MEPs e-Representation and Self-Representation," Journal of Information Technology and Politics, forthcoming.

—— and Vedel, T. (2009) "The Internet and French Political Communication in the Aftermath of the French Presidential Elections 2007." Paper presented at ECPR conference, Potsdam, 10–12 September.

Lees-Marshment, J. (2001). *Political Marketing and British Political Parties: The Party's Just Begun*, Manchester: Manchester University Press.

—— (2011). *The Political Marketing Game*, London: Routledge.

Lilleker, D. (2003). "Interviewing the Political Elite: Navigating a Potential Minefield," *Politics*, 23(3): 207–14.

—— (2005). Political Marketing: The Cause of an Emerging Democratic Deficit in Britain?," *Journal of Nonprofit & Public Sector Marketing*, 14(1–2): 5–26.

—— and Jackson, N. (2011). *Political Campaigning, Elections and the Internet: Comparing the US, UK, Germany and France*, London: Routledge.

—— Pack, M., and Jackson, N. (2010). "Political Parties and Web 2.0: The Liberal Democrat Perspective," *Politics*, 30(2): 105–12.

Lipsitz, K. and Panagopoulos, C. (2011). "Filled Coffers: Campaign Contributions and Contributors in the 2008 Election," *Journal of Political Marketing*, 10(1): 43–57.

Margolis, M. and Resnick, D. (2000). *Politics as Usual: The Cyberspace Revolution*, Walnut Creek, CA: AltaMira.

Mayer, P. (1998). "Computer-Mediated Interactivity: A Socio-Semiotic Perspective," *Convergence*, 4(3): 40–58.

Melucci, A. (1996). *Challenging Codes: Collective Action in the Information Age*, Cambridge: Cambridge University Press.

Morozov, E. (2011). *The Net Delusion: The Dark Side of Internet Freedom*, New York: Public Affairs.

Negrine, R. (2008). *The Transformation of Political Communication*, Basingstoke: Palgrave Macmillan.

Negroponte, N. (1995). *Being Digital*, New York: Free Press.

Norris, P. (2003). "Preaching to the Converted? Pluralism, Participation and Party Websites," *Party Politics*, 9(1): 21–45.

Papacharissi, Z. (2002). "The Virtual Sphere: The Internet as a Public Sphere," *New Media & Society*, 4(1): 9–27.

Plehwe, K. (2009). *Von der Botschaft zur Bewegung: Die 10 Erfolgsstrategien des Barack Obama*, Hamburg: Hanseatic Lighthouse.

Price, T. (2004). Cyberpolitics, *CQ Researcher*, 14(32): 757–80.

Rafaeli, S. (1988). "Interactivity: From New Media to Communication," in R. P. Hawkins, J. M. Wiemann, and S. Pingree, (eds). *Sage Annual Review of Communication Research: Advancing Communication Science*, 16, Beverly Hills, CA: Sage, pp. 110–34.

Rheingold, H. (1993). *The Virtual Community: Homesteading on the Electronic Frontier*, New York: Harper.

Rodgers, J. (2003). *Spatializing International Politics: Analyzing Activism on the Internet*, London: Routledge.

Savigny, H. (2008). *The Problem of Political Marketing*, London: Continuum.

Schneider, S. M. and Foot, K. A. (2002). "Online Structure for Political Action: Exploring Presidential Web Sites from the 2000 American Election," *Javnost (The Public)*, 9(2): 43–60.

—— and Foot, K. A. (2004). "The Web as an Object of Study," *New Media & Society*, 6(1): 94–102.

—— and Foot, K. A. (2006). "Web Campaigning by U.S. Presidential Primary Candidates in 2000 and 2004," in A. P. Williams and J. C. Tedesco (eds). *The Internet Election: Perspectives on the Web in Campaign 2004*, Lanham, MD: Rowman and Littlefield, pp. 21–36.

Schweitzer, E. J. (2005). "Election Campaigning Online: German Party Websites in the 2002 National Elections," *European Journal of Communication*, 20(3): 327–51.

Seymour-Ure, C. (1977). "Parliament and Mass Communications in the Twentieth Century," in C. A. Walkland (ed.). *The House of Commons in the Twentieth Century*, Oxford: Clarendon Press, pp. 527–92.

Shirky, C. (2009). *Here Comes Everybody*, New York: Allen Lane.

Smith, A. (2011). "Why Americans Use Social Media." Pew Internet & American Life Project, November 15. Available at <http://www.pewinternet.org/Reports/2011/Why-Americans-Use-Social-Media.aspx>. Accessed May 18, 2012.

—— Schlozman, K. L., Verba, S., and Brady, H. (2009). "The Internet and Civic Engagement." Available at <http://www.pewinternet.org/Reports/2009/15--The-Internet-and-Civic-Engagement.aspx>. Accessed May 18, 2012.

Solanet, P. A. and Cardenal, A. S. (2008). "Partidos y Politica en Internet: Un analysis de los websites de los partidos políticos Catalenes," *Revista de los Estudios de Derecho y Ciencia Politica de la UOC, IDP*, 6: 46–64.

Stanyer, J. (2006). "Online Campaign Communication and the Phenomenon of Blogging: an Analysis of Web Logs during the 2005 British General Election Campaign," *Aslib Proceedings*, 58(5): 404–15.

Strandberg, K. (2006). *Parties, Candidates and Citizens On-Line Studies of Politics on the Internet*, Abo, Finland: Abo Academy University Press.

Stromer-Galley, J. (2000). "Online Interaction and Why Candidates Avoid It," *Journal of Communication*, 50(4): 111–32.

Sudulich, M. L. (2009). "Do Ethos, Ideology, Country and Electoral Strength Make a Difference in Cyberspace? Testing an Explanatory Model of Parties' Websites." Paper presented at the ECPR Joint Workshops, Lisbon, April.

Sunstein, C. (2007). *Republic.com*. Princeton, NJ: Princeton University Press.

Tkach-Kawasaki, L. (2003). "Politics@Japan: Party Competition on the Internet in Japan," *Party Politics*, 9(1): 105–23.

Towner, T. L., and Dulio, D. A. (2012). "The Web 2.0 Election: Does the Online Medium Matter?," in C. Panagopoulos (ed.). *Strategy, Money and Technology in the 2008 Presidential Election*, London: Routledge, pp. 165–88.

Trammel, K. D., Williams, A. P., Postelnicu, M., and Landreville, K. D. (2006). "Evolution of Online Campaigning: Increasing Interactivity in Candidate Websites and Blogs Through Text and Technical Features," *Mass Communication*, 9(1): 21–44.

Trippi, J. (2004). *The Revolution Will Not Be Televised: Democracy, the Internet and the Overthrow of Everything*, New York: Harper Collins.

Tumasjan, A., Sprenger, T. O., Sandner, P. G., and Welpe, I. M. (2011). "Election Forecasts with Twitter: How 140 Characters Reflect the Political Landscape," *Social Science Computer Review*, 29(4): 402–18.

Vaccari, C. (2010). "Technology Is a Commodity: The Internet in the 2008 United States Presidential Election," *Journal of Information Technology & Politics*, 7(4): 318–39.

Van Dijk, J. (2006). *The Network Society*, London: Sage.

Vedel, T. (2003). "Political Communication in the Age of the Internet," in P. J. Maarek and G. Wolfsfeld (eds). *Political Communication in a New Era*, London: Routledge, pp. 41–59.

Ward, S. and Gibson, R. (2003). "Online and On Message? Candidates Websites in the 2001 General Election," *British Journal of Politics and International Relations*, 5(2): 188–205.

—— and Lusoli, W. (2005). "From Weird to Wired: MPs, the Internet and Representative Politics in the UK," *The Journal of Legislative Studies*, 11(1): 57–81.

—— Owen, D., Davis, R., and Taras, D. (eds) (2008). *Making a Difference: A Comparative View of the Role of the Internet in Election Politics*, Lanham, MD: Lexington Books.

Xenos, M. and Foot, K. (2005). "Politics as Usual or Politics Unusual? Position Taking and Dialogue on Campaign Web Sites in the 2002 U.S. Elections," *Journal of Communication*, 55(1): 169–85.

CHAPTER 20

....

THE INTERNET AND DEMOCRACY

....

HELEN MARGETTS

OF all socio-technological innovations, it is perhaps the Internet that has been most extensively associated with democracy. From across the field of Internet Studies—and to a far more limited extent, from within Political Science—the Internet has been identified as a possible stimulant for many of the "isms" of normative political theory and as offering the potential to transform the traditional institutions and political organization of democratic systems. It has also been viewed as having the potential to facilitate greater participation of individual citizens in democratic life, particularly through the facilitation of freedom of expression and through lowering the costs of obtaining the political information necessary to participate in democratic institutions and of organizing and contributing to collective action.

First, this chapter reviews the extent to which the Internet has the potential to play a role in alternative models of democracy, specifically republicanism, pluralism, and cosmopolitanism, the models that have been most associated with widespread use of the Internet. Second, it reviews the attention that has been paid to the relationship between the Internet and democratic institutions such as elections, political parties, legislatures, and interest groups. Third, it looks at how the Internet has been related to individual political behavior and what effect this relationship might have on democratic citizenship. Finally, in summary, it considers how the Internet might—or might not—be considered to contribute to the democratic principles of "popular control" and "political equality," and how the Internet's contribution to democracy might be assessed.

Most of the commentators on the relationship between the Internet and democracy come from the field of Internet Studies, broadly defined to include the disciplines of Communications and Media Studies. Political Science, the academic discipline most concerned with theoretical and empirical analysis of "democracy," has paid far less attention to the Internet. Of the sixty-three articles in the Web of Science database with "Internet" and "Democracy" in the title, only fourteen are published in politics or law journals, with the rest distributed across a range of other disciplines. However, there are some political scientists who have turned their attention to the Internet-related issues discussed below, and their work will be reviewed here. Some operate from the mainstream of the discipline and have concentrated on such issues rather fleetingly, while others have made it the main focus of their work; however, this latter group has tended to be somewhat ghettoized within Political Science. So for example, while most of the burgeoning list of Oxford Handbooks on topics relating to democracy (e.g. Katz and Crotty 2006; Loughlin et al. 2011) make little reference to the Internet, Chadwick and Howard's 2009 *Handbook of Internet Politics* is written by people from the field of Communications, with a scattering of political scientists who work solely on Internet issues.

So although there is an abundance of writing and research on the Internet and democracy, most of it comes from outside the academic discipline most usually associated with democracy, which is Political Science. There is an older tradition of writing on the impact of computing and telecommunication on politics and democracy, introducing such concepts as electronic democracy and teledemocracy long before use of the Internet became widespread (see Laudon 1977; Danziger et al. 1982; and Chadwick 2003, 2006). This body of work was consistently either ignored or ghettoized by mainstream Political Science (see Margetts 1999 for a discussion), perhaps one of the reasons why newer work on Internet-related technologies have also failed to reach the mainstream of the discipline. But some of the theories and concepts developed in this tradition have fed directly into the field of Internet Studies, particularly the "reinforcement" thesis arguing that information technologies reinforce existing patterns of political behavior, discussed below.

To make some kind of assessment or evaluation of the relationship between the Internet and democracy, it is necessary to identify a working definition of democracy. Such a definition should suggest key principles against which any given democracy might be judged, by looking at what evidence Internet research provides as to how the characteristics of what it means for a state to be democratic might be changing with widespread use of the Internet. One such definition that has been developed both normatively (by the political theorist David Beetham) and empirically (by the Demoractic Audit of the UK and IDEA, the Institute for Democracy and Electoral Assistance) is that democracy rests on two key principles: popular control, and political equality of that control (Beetham 1994; Beetham and Weir 2002). The conclusion of this chapter summarizes the research outlined here and assesses how these principles might be reinforced or challenged now that so much of political life takes place on the Internet. It considers other ways in which democracies have been assessed (using democratic indicators) and how the study of the Internet and democracy might develop in the future.

THE INTERNET AND MODELS OF DEMOCRACY

The Internet has long been associated with various models of democracy, and credited with making certain aspects of them more viable. Of the range of normative models for democratic political systems, there are three which have been most discussed within

Internet Studies and by some political scientists focusing on Internet-related issues: republicanism, pluralism, and cosmopolitanism. These three seem like the "best bet" for theoretical revival with widespread use of the Internet.

First, republicanism—perhaps the earliest model for political systems to emphasize the "rule of the many," rather than kings or other autonomous rulers—emphasizes political opinion and "will-formation," preserving democracy in terms of the "institutionalization of a public use of reason jointly exercised by autonomous citizens" (Habermas 1996: 23). The Internet has been particularly associated with Habermas's idea of the "public sphere," a "network for communicating information and points of view," where citizens in a republic can express their opinions, and deliberate and formulate some kind of common view or "will." There is a large literature within Communication and Media Studies on this topic, with over 150 articles with both "public sphere" and "Internet" as topics on the Web of Science (see Papacharissi 2009 for a review). The main ideas are based around the notion that the Internet provides a kind of "public sphere" for public discussion and deliberation, in the same way that the coffee houses of Vienna provided the forum for Habermas's original conception of the public sphere (Boeder 2005). Critics, however, for example Sunstein (2007), argue that the Internet actually works against the maintaining of a public sphere, with the capacity of the Internet to fragment public discourse into "echo chambers" of the interests of individual citizens—the "Daily Me" (Sunstein 2007; Negroponte 1995).

Pluralism, a model of democracy stressing the "many" as opposed to the "few" and based on interest groups as the building block of society, has also been associated with the Internet. Given the clear potential of the Internet to facilitate the formation of groups— matching people with similar beliefs and preferences, lowering coordination and organization costs, and allowing new forms of mass mobilization (such as email campaigns, electronic petitions, and a whole range of "weak-tie" associations)—it is inevitable that it has come to be associated with a revival of pluralist thought. As early (in Internet time) as 1998, Bruce Bimber was writing of "accelerated pluralism" through the Internet (Bimber 1998), in which the Internet would contribute to "the on-going fragmentation of the present system of interest-based group politics and a shift toward a more fluid, issue-based group politics with less institutional coherence" (see also Norris 2003).

Finally, cosmopolitanism, a model of democracy that works on the basis that all human groups belong to a single community, with a political structure that operates across different nations, has also been associated with the Internet, in part due to its link to the concept of globalization and the decreasing influence of the "nation state" as the Internet and related technologies facilitate trans-national and international interactions. In its strongest form, cosmopolitanism would imply the development of international law and "world government." In democratic terms, such a shift would be based on international organizations such as a World Parliamentary Assembly (Archibugi 2009) and a "global citizens movement," new institutional forms that, if they were really to encompass any notion of democracy, would rely heavily on Internet-enabled processes. Habermas (2004) himself has turned to cosmopolitanism as a concept, which could inform how a global citizen functions in an online digital environment (Papacharissi 2009).

DEMOCRATIC INSTITUTIONS
AND THE INTERNET

Any model of democracy relies on a number of democratic institutions that characterize what it means to be a democracy. For example, the democratic theorist Robert Dahl (1953, 1956, 1971) specified that a democratic "polyarchy" would include the following: free and fair elections; elected officials; the right to run for office; and alternative information and associational autonomy. Each of these institutions may be and has been associated with the Internet, usually with the idea that the Internet will facilitate greater involvement of more people in democratic processes.

First, with respect to *elections*, there is a range of literature looking at the relationship between elections, voting, and the Internet. Perhaps surprisingly, elections are probably the institutions that have changed least with the advent of widespread use of the Internet. In fact electoral administration in some countries remains remarkably resistant to Internet-enabled processes. In the UK, for example, polling stations are probably one of the only places that UK citizens still wield a pencil, to mark the cross on their ballot papers, and any information regarding the process or candidates tend to be "wild-west" style posters about electoral law and regulations rather than any electronic information aids. Although electronic voting machines are used in many countries— and even in the UK, electronic counting machines are used to work out the results of those elections not run under first-past-the-post—they do not tend to be linked to the Internet or use any of the communicative or interactive facilities that the Internet can provide, and indeed in some countries their use has been abandoned over concerns over privacy and openness associated with proprietary software (Oostveen and van den Besselaar 2006; Camp 2006). Although voting on the Internet has been piloted in various US states and is widely used in some smaller countries (such as Estonia, which became the first country to have legally binding general elections with Internet voting in 2005), it has not yet been associated with any positive democratic effects. In spite of early claims (Leadbeater and Mulgan 1997; Budge 1996; Morris 2001) that the Internet would lead to "direct democracy," with a plethora of referenda consulting the public on issues in between elections, there is little evidence that it has done so, although there has been a general rise in the use of referenda across liberal democracies over several decades (Reedy and Wells 2009).

Most elections are competed for through the auspices of *political parties*, and here there has been greater change and more analysis. Research dedicated to the relationship between parties and the Internet has concluded that Internet technologies have been used most for campaign coordination, fundraising, and voter targeting—for all of which activities it has proved itself an ideal mechanism, particularly in US primary elections—rather than as a mechanism for empowering members or enhancing internal communication channels (Gibson et al. 2003; Gibson and Ward 2009; Anstead and Chadwick 2009).

So, the Internet has challenged the dominance of parties as articulators of citizens' interests, rather than reinforcing their role. It has not brought about a return to the "golden age" of mass membership of political parties, mourned by many politicians and political scientists alike—indeed, the Internet changes people's expectations of organizations online and they certainly do not expect to pay for supporting a political party as was expected in the era of mass membership. However, a number of deep-rooted changes to party systems related to the Internet have been identified and analyzed. Some political parties (particularly the larger ones) have been rather slow to adapt to Internet culture, and it would be hard to associate the Internet with an increase in the internal cohesion of political parties; rather, it has been useful to informal factions within large parties, or looser associations of supporters concerned with particular elements of parties' agendas, or in reducing the entry costs and enhancing the visibility and sustainability of smaller parties. By 2012, it is clear the Internet lowers the entry costs for new and smaller parties, making for a more level playing field than previous media allowed; "while smaller parties do not have the capacity to offer voters and members the technology enriched experience that the larger parties can provide relative to other forms of media, it does appear to provide crucial assistance in disseminating an unedited message globally as well as allowing them a new 'space' for organizational co-ordination" (Gibson and Ward 2009: 10). Indeed, it might be argued that there is no reason why political parties should not exist almost wholly online, leading to a new "ideal type" of political party, labeled by this author as the "Cyber Party" (Margetts 2006), where the notion of membership is redefined to a looser type of supporter, as with US parties, not paying dues and self-selecting themselves to register support when they want to participate in some way (such as vote or donate money)—going back to the idea of Duverger (1964: 61) who points to a series of "concentric circles [of] ever-increasing party solidarity" providing a number of categories of party attachment.

Legislatures, the political institutions in liberal democracies most steeped in tradition and custom, were slow to adapt to the Internet age but legislative commentators have observed that the Internet has brought about a number of developments, particularly towards greater transparency and openness in what Stephen Coleman (2009) refers to as "the age of ubiquitous visibility." A growing literature focuses on the changing relationship between new media and legislatures; see, for example Coleman 2009; Dai and Norton 2007; Leston-Bandeira 2007; Gibson et al. 2005; Ward et al. 2006. This work shows how legislatures have adapted to a more transparent environment, but also, in many cases resisted and painfully negotiated the change. The UK parliament, for example, has "attempted to manage the terms of its own visibility" (Coleman 2009), but fights a "losing battle" as citizens adopt their own methods for scrutinizing and circumventing parliamentary processes.

With respect to the institutions of *executive government*, the Internet enhances the capability of citizens to convey and receive information to and from governments, so we might expect such institutions to become more "democratic." By 2009, in the UK and many other developed countries, a significant and growing proportion of citizens expect to go to the Internet first if they are to interact with government (Dutton et al. 2009; Dutton and Blank 2011). When asked, for example, where they would go first to find the name of their MP if they didn't know it, over half of UK respondents would go to the Internet first (Dutton et al. 2009). If governments want to encourage democratic input to policy-making, therefore, the Internet would be a key low-cost route, and many governments have embarked upon electronic consultations for new policy initiatives. But in general, these top-down initiatives, where government initiates the consultation, have been supplanted by a host of societal initiatives using the Internet to mobilize for or against policy change. The potential of such developments was illustrated when the UK Government introduced a petitions facility on the No. 10 Downing Street website in the early 2000s, which surprised policy makers in 2008 by attracting 1.8 million signatures on a petition against plans to introduce road-pricing. Since that time, there has been a marked rise in a range of policy-oriented online activism that have had an influence on policy in the UK, for example the pressure group 38 Degrees which claims to have been instrumental in reversing governmental plans to privatize UK forests.

Indeed, it is perhaps political organization in the form of *interest groups*, pressure groups, and looser forms of civic association that can illustrate the transformational possibilities of the Internet for democratic participation. The potential of the Internet to "promote the ability of people to associate freely with others who share their views and interests, regardless of where they are located … to share information with them, to make common cause with them, and to jointly advance their mutual political or other agendas" has long been recognized (Simon et al. 2002: 9). In general, certain types of interest groups have been innovative in capitalizing upon this potential, both in terms of how they communicate with supporters and how they apply pressure on governments. In addition, there is a range of theoretical and empirical work that shows how the Internet can reduce collective action problems associated with interest group activity (Lupia and Sin 2003; Bimber 2003; Bimber et al. 2006). In addition, by reducing the transaction costs of cooperative endeavors, the Internet seems to create new "communities" around new public goods, for example in the development of the freely available encyclopedia Wikipedia, with around 6 million registered contributors. Where such groups have a policy agenda, it is far easier than the original theorists of collective action (Olson 1965) ever imagined to overcome the collective action problems of large so-called latent groups, such as in the road-pricing lobby noted above, the anti-globalization movement, or the popular "Net Mums" site aimed at mothers of young children in the UK, which claimed to have played a significant role in the toppling of key figures in News International during the phone-hacking scandal in the UK in 2011.

What all these trends do is create larger, looser associations with political goals. The Internet blurs the boundaries between state and non-state, results in new organizational forms, and redefines what it means to be a pressure group, or indeed a political organization per se. Most political scientists would argue, for example, that a Facebook page where visitors may select a "like" option falls way short of the intensity required to participate politically. Indeed, the author Malcolm Gladwell in an extended *New Yorker* article in 2010 argued strongly and influentially that the kind of "weak ties" that social media allow would never result in "strong" forms of political activity, of the kind that formed the civil rights movement in the US, for example. However, even Gladwell himself might be questioning his own analysis after the events of the "Arab Spring" in 2011, where protestors and demonstrations in several Arab states were successful in, or came near to, overthrowing what seemed like firmly entrenched authoritarian regimes. In Egypt especially, Facebook was widely perceived to be influential, with the Facebook group "We are all Khaled Said" identified by some commentators as key in showing potential participants that a "critical mass" of demonstrators was being reached (Margetts 2011).

For some authors in Internet Studies, the importance of the Internet goes beyond its relationship with any particular institution and becomes the establishment of a "Fifth Estate" to join the traditional estates (the clergy, nobility, commons, and the media) with sufficiently distinctive and important features to warrant recognition as a separate institution, based in changing patterns of everyday Internet use around the world (Dutton 2009). According to Dutton, the Fifth Estate allows networked individuals to use the Internet to increase the accountability of the more traditional Estates, for instance by challenging government policies and Fourth Estate sources, thereby sustaining democratic vitality (Dutton 2009: 10).

THE INTERNET, POLITICAL BEHAVIOR, AND DEMOCRATIC CITIZENSHIP

So given the changes to political organization and democratic institutions outlined above, does research into the relationship between the Internet and democracy provide any evidence of changing political behavior relating to the Internet? Is there evidence that democracies have become more democratic due to Internet-enabled change, for example due to increasing voter turnout or political engagement? And have there been changes to the nature of democratic citizenship that would point to a changing model of democracy, closer to the ideals of republican, pluralist, or cosmopolitan political thought?

First, the process of acquiring *political information*, a critical resource for democratic citizenship, is clearly an activity that has been transformed by widespread use of the Internet. In the 2011 Oxford Internet Survey, over half of UK citizens said that they would "go to the Internet first" (rather than a telephone, directory or personal visit) to find the name of their MP if they did not know it, or to find information on schools or taxes. Over 70 percent of Internet users have used the Internet to look for health information, one of the fastest growing online activities (Dutton and Blank 2011). These data (which will be even higher in countries with higher Internet penetration) highlight a fundamental shift in information-seeking behavior, and cast new light on what we know about political knowledge. There is a long history in political science of measuring indicators of political knowledge, such as knowing basic facts about constitutional, institutional, and electoral arrangements and using them as key predictors of political behavior, and even in defining a "civic culture" (see e.g. Almond and Verba 1963; Dahl 1989; Dalton and Klingemann 2007). Such figures have been used to indicate a growing disengagement with politics in the UK (Hansard Society 2008). But the fact that people do not know the name of their political representative or details of electoral arrangements might no longer be a sign of a declining engagement with politics—for regular Internet users, it might be a rational response to a changing information environment. For non-Internet users, remembering such facts is more necessary, because the costs of finding them out, by means of more "physical" activities could be quite high. Thus trends in Internet use are bringing, not only enhanced capacity for gaining political knowledge, but also increasing inequalities through the differential costs of acquiring that knowledge.

Another shift in the interchange of information is in a kind of "democratization" of the dissemination of political information, which has the potential to de-institutionalize the "alternative sources of information" of which Dahl wrote, and conceptualized as the "Fifth Estate" by William Dutton (2009). Early discussion of the effect of the Internet on political communication focused on whether it makes it easier for "ordinary people" to participate in communication activities normally restricted to media organizations, with "news values" that favor state representative and institutional interests (Rheingold 2000; Bimber 2001). Certainly this seems to be the case, with growing use of blogs and micro-blogging sites (particularly Twitter), YouTube and, more locally, social networking sites. Information publicized on these social media is, at a certain level of attention, taken up by more traditional media, which emphasizes the effect. But another key difference in political communication is that various kinds of "news" are spread through a series of point-to-point connections in online networks, rather than broadcast from central media. Already classic examples are the video clip of an Iranian girl dying amid the 2009 demonstrations in Tehran (an image that some compared to the photograph published in 1972 of a young Vietnamese girl running naked and burning, arguing that this image could be equivalently influential), or the image of Khaled Said, a young man brutally murdered by police in Cairo, taken on mobile phones and spread virally across the world on the Internet, as noted above.

When we go beyond information exchange to more deliberative activities, some research has gone beyond the normative work on the public sphere noted above to tackle the question of whether deliberation is on the rise. Recent research suggests that Internet use does in fact promote exposure to political disagreement and deliberation among citizens of the kind that the original architects of the concepts of republicanism and the public sphere (Arendt 1968; Habermas 1989) have argued to be essential (Brundidge and Rice 2009). Empirical research has demonstrated that such deliberation seems to be leading to increased political learning and a sense of legitimacy for democratic outcomes (Price et al. 2002a, 2002b). However, in general the evidence from the literature on online deliberation is mixed (Reedy and Wells 2009), with some studies finding strong evidence of deliberation (Kim 2006) and others finding few benefits from online political discussion (Janssen and Kies 2005; Smith et al. 2013).

The key democratic act that most citizens undertake is *voting*. Indeed, voter turnout is often included as one of the most important democratic indicators by political scientists attempting to develop indices of democracy (e.g. Vanhanen 1990) and declining turnout in liberal democracies, particularly among young people, is a major concern of contemporary politics (Hansard Society 2008; Stoker 2010). So has the Internet impacted at all on people's incentives to vote? The most likely candidate for the Internet having a positive impact on turnout is through the provision of political information, hypothesized by political scientists since Anthony Downs (1957) to be positively associated with higher turnout. Through changing patterns in information-seeking behavior and the far greater range of political information available to average citizens, the Internet could help to increase turnout. Horiuchi et al. (2005) tested this hypothesis by considering the effect of policy information provided through party websites in the Japanese 2004 election, finding that voters were less likely to abstain when they received such information, although these effects were greater among voters who were planning to vote anyway, but were undecided about the party for which to vote. Tolbert and McNeal (2003) found access to the Internet and online election news to be positively associated with voting and other forms of political participation. Johnson and Kaye (2003) and more recently Drew and Weaver (2006) identified exposure and attention to online political information as being positively related to campaign knowledge and interest, themselves indications of propensity to vote. Although demonstrating causal effects in the relationship between Internet and turnout is hard, there is an increasing range of evidence to suggest that it is playing a part in at least halting turnout decline in liberal democracies.

Increasing *participation*, particularly in protest and demonstration, looks like another "democratic" trend arising from widespread use of the Internet, although there has been much debate over this trend. Early debates over the relationship between the Internet and political participation revolved around the "normalization" and "reinforcement" theses, with their origins in previous work on the political implications of computers and telecommunications predating Internet Studies (such as Danziger et al. 1982). Proponents of the former argued that the Internet would only intensify the participation of people who already participate, with individuals doing (or not doing) online what they used to do (or not do) offline (Margolis and Resnick 2000). Proponents of the "reinforcement" thesis argued that the Internet acted as a reinforcement for those who have traditionally participated in democratic life (Norris 2001; Bimber 2001), meaning that inequalities in democratic participation would become greater. Later research, however, has started to evidence the "new mobilization" thesis, arguing that the Internet may be facilitating the mobilization of new individuals and groups of individuals who have traditionally not participated (Tolbert and McNeal 2003; Gibson et al. 2005; Anduiza et al. 2010a, 2010b; Borge and Cardenal 2011). These studies provide evidence that groups previously regarded as participating at lower levels, such as young people, are participating more, and that increases in forms of unconventional participation (such as protest or product boycotts) are due in part to those who normally participate more conventionally embarking on unconventional forms of participation. The biennial Oxford Internet Survey, the most comprehensive analysis of changes in Internet use from 2003 to 2011 does not record a steadily rising propensity in the most commonly observed measures of political or civic participation, such as signing a petition or donating to charity, either offline or online. But it does show the rapid entry of new forms of participation that take place only online, such as contributing to a blog or micro-blogging site (such as Twitter) or expressing a political opinion on a social networking site, which were carried out by 9 percent of Internet users (Blank and Dutton 2012).

Other evidence includes a demonstration that Internet skills are joining the traditional resources of time, money, and civic skills (Borge and Cardenal 2011) in predicting whether people will participate politically (Anduiza et al. 2010a, 2010b; Gibson et al. 2005). Norris (2009), in an analysis of nineteem countries, used the European Social Survey to analyze the relationship between Internet use and political activism, finding that regular Internet users are significantly more politically active across all twenty-one indicators of activism captured in the survey; it was not possible to establish any causal effect, but use of the Internet continued to be significantly related to political activism, even when controlling for prior social or attitudinal characteristics of Internet users such as age, education, and civic duty. After these factors, use of the Internet proved the next strongest predictor of activism, more important than other indicators such as social and political trust or use of any news media. And recent research from Spain has demonstrated an association between general Internet use and political participation, with the authors arguing that by reducing participation costs, use of the Internet diminishes the role of political motivation in participation, leading frequent and skilled Internet users to participate in politics even without political motivation (Borge and Cardenal 2011).

So if they continue, would these trends of more interchange of political information and discussion, higher levels of voting, and greater levels of political participation amount to a new form of *democratic citizenship*? Various researchers have tackled this question, particularly in terms of how inequalities in Internet access and skills work against any kind of digital citizenship and the capacity to participate in society online (Mossberger 2009). Mossberger (2009: 173) defines digital citizens as those who use the Internet every day, with regular means of access (usually at home), some technical skill, and the educational competencies to find and use web-based information and communicate with others on the Internet (Mossberger et al. 2008). Her argument is based on the assumption that the explosion of political information and opportunities on the Web mean that "digital citizenship is an enabling factor for political citizenship, whether practiced online or offline." The research of Mossberger and others (Norris 2001; Mossberger et al. 2008; Warschauer 2003) reveals a number of inequalities relating to "digital divides" in both access and use, with wide variation in the ability to participate online, structured by age, education, income, race, and ethnicity (Mosserger 2009: 184).

The above discussion has centered on liberal democracies, but a discussion of the Internet and democracy would not be complete without some consideration of the impact of the Internet on non-democratic—that is, *authoritarian*—states. Indeed, there is a range of recent work in this area (including Goldstein and Wu 2008; Howard 2011; Drezner 2010; and Morozov 2011), discussing the role of the Internet in authoritarian states and the possibilities for it to play a role in democratization. Much of this discussion focuses on the question of whether the Internet strengthens authoritarian regimes, for example through Internet censorship, filtering or the non-availability of Internet access—or whether it weakens them, through the facilitating of mass demonstration and protest, and more general activism to subvert state control. For the former, Deibert et al. (2008) show how authoritarian regimes are using filtering and censorship strategies to control information flows both within and across borders, while Drezner (2010) argues that regimes based on repression and surveillance are actually being strengthened by the Internet. Morozov (2011) argues that the democratizing potential of the Internet is a myth, and that authoritarian regimes such as Iran and China are as stable as before, using the Internet to disseminate propaganda and pacify "citizens" with digital entertainment.

Set against this argument, are analyses by Best and Wade (2005), who argue that Internet use is more important in explaining variation in democratization than literacy rates, even when controlling for geographic region, economic level, and social development. Groshek (2009) also argued that there is a positive relationship between Internet diffusion and democratization, while Howard (2011) found from research in Muslim countries an explicit link through which technology diffusion can contribute to democratization. Also in this category must come the events of 2011, where mass demonstrations broke out in several repressive regimes. At the time of writing, it is too early to judge (although see Howard 2011) the outcome for democracy of the revolutions that have already taken place (such as Tunisia and Egypt), or of those that are still underway (as in Syria). In those countries where the revolutions were deemed to have been successful, there is already disillusionment with the moves towards creating democratic institutions that have been promised by temporary regimes. But the arguments of (for example) Morozov (2011) and Gladwell (2010) are clearly challenged by the wave of mobilizations across these states, in which online social networks sustaining huge numbers of "weak ties" played such a varying but important role, particularly in Egypt and Tunisia where penetration of Facebook and other social media sites was high.

CONCLUSION

To conclude, it is helpful to consider the work reviewed here under the headings provided by Beetham (2002)'s definition of democracy; popular control, and political equality. With respect to *popular control*, it seems to be the case that the Internet facilitates a "way in" for citizens in a democracy to acquire information about, engage with, and even influence the key institutions that make up a democratic polity. It greatly enhances the acquisition of the political information required to participate meaningfully in elections, "democratizes" the dissemination of information, and provides voters with more choice, by opening up possibilities for a greater range of political parties for which to vote. The Internet has forced legislatures to become more transparent, making more information freely available to citizens, and at least having the potential to offer more avenues for engagement more meaningfully with them. For executive government also, there are more possibilities for citizens to know what is going on and to contribute to policy-making. The Internet opens up new channels for collective action and political participation, with some evidence to suggest that use of the Internet for non-political purposes is actually generating new forms of political participation. These trends have reshaped the ecology of interest groups, creating new organizational forms and new patterns of looser association that are really making a difference in some states. Although this difference is most evident in the authoritarian regimes involved in the so-called "Arab Spring," it is also evident in the oldest of liberal democracies, where protest, demonstration, and mass mobilization seem to be on the rise. In the UK, for example, Prime Minister David Cameron's Big Society has come to life most clearly in the form of mass demonstrations against student tuition fees and, public sector cuts, or well-orchestrated online campaigns against the privatization of forests or NHS reform, where it has had real policy impact.

For *political equality*, the prospects are a little less bright. There is an abundance of research to suggest that the Internet may actually reinforce the disadvantages of lower income and low levels of education and these demographics may overtake age as the most important demographic for understanding Internet use. As the Internet becomes increasingly entwined with democratic life, it inevitably means that democratic citizenship relies upon digital citizenship.

Another way to assess the democratic potential of the Internet would be to look at work that develops "democratic indicators" for cross-national comparison of states, such as Vanhanen's "democratization index" (Vanhanen 1990, 1997, 2003), which led to a dataset of 187 countries over the period 1810 to 2000; the Economist Intelligence Unit's Democracy Index; or the more controversial Freedom House index of liberal democracy (www.freedomhouse.org). If, for example, we were to take Vanhanen's two principle indicators of "degree of electoral competition" (the share of vote by the largest party) and the degree of electoral participation (turnout), both of which have been positively associated with the Internet in the evidence amassed above, we might start to point to a generalized "Internet effect" on democratization. But given a wider body of evidence suggesting a relationship between economic development, modernization, and democratization (Przeworski 2000), and the clear relationship between Internet penetration and these other variables, it would be impossible to point to any causal effect. Such quantitative cross-national attempts to assess the relationship could only work in combination with detailed studies on specific Internet effects, of the kind outlined above.

With regard to the normative models of democracy outlined at the start of this chapter, there is perhaps most evidence for a revival of the pluralist dream, through a revival of large-scale interest groups and more widespread political participation, particularly if the Internet continues to blur the boundaries between state and non-state actors.

For republicanism, early fears of the fragmentation of the "public sphere" and gloomy predictions of individual citizens isolated in narrow echo chambers of their own choosing seem unfounded. But the idea of a deliberative and representative virtual "public sphere" seems over-optimistic, given the inequalities that persist. And while tentative moves towards cosmopolitanism exist, such as the existence of transnational diaspora and the flows of information and influence from one country to the other (in the Arab Spring for example), they do not really amount to a new global order. There is no meaningful "world governance" and indeed the only truly international organization with legitimate authority is the International Criminal Court (which remains unrecognized by the US) (Dunleavy and Dryzek 2009).

Most of the authors and researchers whose work has been reviewed here come from Internet Studies, rather than Political Science, the "home" discipline of democracy. The extensive research that has been carried out in specific sub-fields (such as electoral campaigning, political parties, legislatures, collective action, and political participation) needs feeding back to the mainstream of political science. Increasingly, this research involves developing and using new methods which make the most of the "big data" that the Internet, particularly social media, can provide: transactional data about what participatory acts people are undertaking (such as signing petitions), or directly expressed public opinions, unmediated by a survey. Dealing with data can pose challenges to social scientists; it is the kind of data more commonly found in "hard" scientific research and requires technologically sophisticated tools to capture, analyse, and present (Margetts 2009). But as democratic life moves online, political scientists in general may find an increasing need to incorporate such methods and tools into their own research.

REFERENCES

Almond, G. and Verba, S. (1963). *The Civic Culture*, Princeton, NJ: Princeton University Press.

Anduiza, E., Cantijoch, M., Gallego, A., and Salcedo, J. (2010). "*Internet y Participación Política en España*," Colección Opiniones y Actitudes, 63, Madrid: CIS.

Anduiza, E., Gallego, A., and Cantijoch, M. (2010). "Online Political Participation in Spain: The Impact of Traditional and Internet Resources," *Journal of Information, Technology and Politics*, 7(4): 356–68.

Anstead, N. and Chadwick, A. (2009). "Parties, Election Campaigning and the Internet," in A. Chadwick and P. N. Howard (eds). *Handbook of Internet Politics*, London: Routledge.

Archibugi, D. (2009). *The Global Commonwealth of Citizens: Toward a Cosmopolitan Democracy*, Princeton, NJ: Princeton University Press.

Arendt, H. (1968). *Between Past and Future: Eight Exercises in Political Thought*, New York: Viking.

Beetham, D. (ed.) (1994). *Defining and Measuring Democracy*, London: Sage.

Beetham, D. and Weir, S. (2002). *Democracy under Blair: A Democratic Audit of the United Kingdom*, London: Politicos.

Best, M. and Wade, K. (2005). *The Internet and Democracy: The Global Catalyst or Democratic Dud?*, Cambridge, MA: Berkman Center for Internet and Society.

Bimber, B. (1998). "The Internet and Political Transformation: Populism, Community and Accelerated Pluralism," *Polity*, 31(1): 133–60.

—— (2001). "Information and Political Engagement in America: The Search for Effects of Information Technology at the Individual Level," *Political Research Quarterly*, 54(1): 53–67.

—— (2003). *Information and American Democracy: Technology in the Evolution of Political Power*, Cambridge: Cambridge University Press.

—— Flanagin, A. and Stohl, C. (2006). "Reconceptualizing Collective Action in the Contemporary Media Environment," *Communication Theory*, 15(4): 365–88.

Blank, G. and Dutton, W. H. (2012 forthcoming). "The Emergence of Next Generation Internet Users," in J. Hartley, J. Burgess, and A. Bruns (eds). *Blackwell Companion to New Media Dynamics*, London: Wiley-Blackwell.

Boeder, P. (2005). "Habermas' Heritage: The Future of the Public Sphere in the Network Society," *First Monday*, 10(9). Available at <http://firstmonday.org/htbin/cgiwrap/bin/ojs/index.php/fm/article/view/1280/1200>. Accessed June 20, 2012.

Borge, R. and Cardenal, A. (2011). "Surfing the Net: A Pathway to Participation for the Politically Uninterested?," *Policy and Internet*, 3(1): 1–29.

Brundidge, J. and Rice, R. E. (2009). "Political Engagement Online: Do the Information-Rich get Richer and the Like-Minded more Similar?," in A. Chadwick and P. N. Howard (eds). *Handbook of Internet Politics*, London: Routledge.

Budge, I. (1996). *The New Challenge of Direct Democracy*, London: Polity.

Camp, J. (2006). "Varieties of Software and their Implications for Effective Democratic Government," in C. Hood and D. Heald (eds). *Transparency: the Key to Better Government*, Oxford: Oxford University Press.

Chadwick, A. (2003). "Bringing E-Democracy Back In," *Social Science Computer Review*, 21(4): 443–55.

—— (2006). *The Internet and Politics*, Oxford: Oxford University Press.

—— and Howard, P. N. (2009). *Handbook of Internet Politics*, London: Routledge.

Coleman, S. (2009). "Making Parliamentary Democracy Visible: Speaking to, with, and for the Public in the Age of Interactive Technology," in A. Chadwick and P. N. Howard (eds). *Handbook of Internet Politics*, London: Routledge.

Dahl, R. (with C. E. Lindblom) (1953). *Politics, Economics, and Welfare*, Chicago: University of Chicago Press.

—— (1956). *A Preface to Democratic Theory* (new edn. 2006), Chicago: University of Chicago Press.

—— (1971). *Polyarchy: Participation and Opposition*, New Haven: Yale University Press.

—— (1989). *Democracy and its Critics*. New Haven: Yale University Press.

Dai, X. and Norton, P. (eds) (2007). "The Internet and Parliamentary Democracy in Europe," *Journal of Legislative Studies*, 13(3): 342–53.

Dalton, R. and Klingemann, H. (eds) (2007). *The Oxford Handbook of Political Behaviour*, Oxford: Oxford University Press.

Danziger, J., Dutton, W., Kling, R., and Kraemer, K. (1982). *Computers and Politics: High Technology in American Local Governance*, New York: Columbia University Press.

Deibert, R., Palfrey, J., Rohozinski, R., and Zittrain, J. (2008). *Access Denied: The Practice and Policy of Global Internet Filtering*, Cambridge, MA: MIT Press.

Downs, A. (1957). *An Economic Theory of Democracy*, New York: Harpers and Row.

Drew, D. and Weaver, D. (2006). "Voter Learning in the 2004 Presidential Election: Did the Media Matter?," *Journalism and Mass Communication Quarterly*, 83(1): 25–42.

Drezner, D. (2010). "Weighing the Scales: The Internet's Effect on State–Society Relations," *Brown Journal of World Affairs*, 16(2), 31–44.

Dunleavy, P. and Dryzek, J. (2009). *Theories of the Democratic State*, Basingstoke: Palgrave Macmillan.

Dutton, W. H. (2009). "The Fifth Estate Emerging through the Network of Networks," *Prometheus*, 27(1): 1–15.

—— and Blank, G. (2011). "Next Generation Users: The Internet in Britain", Oxford Internet Institute, University of Oxford. Available at <http://www.oii.ox.ac.uk/publications/oxis2011_report.pdf>. Accessed June 20, 2012.

——, Helsper, E. J., and Gerber, M. M. (2009). "The Internet in Britain 2009," Oxford Internet Institute, University of Oxford. Available at <http://www.oii.ox.ac.uk/research/oxis/OxIS2009_Report.pdf>. Accessed June 20, 2012.

Duverger, M. (1964). *Political Parties: Their Organization and Activity in the Modern State*, London: Methuen.

Gibson, R. and Ward, S. (2009). "Parties in the Digital Age—A Review Article," *Representation*, 45(1): 87–100.

——, Nixon, P., and Ward, S. (eds) (2003). *Net Gain? Political Parties and the Internet*, London: Routledge.

——, Lusoli, W., and Ward, S. (2005). "Online Participation in the UK: Testing a 'Contextualised' Model of Internet Effects," *British Journal of Politics and International Relations*, 7(4): 561–83.

Gladwell, M. (2010). "Why the Revolution will not be Tweeted," *New Yorker*, October 4. Available at <http://www.newyorker.com/reporting/2010/10/04/101004fa_fact_gladwell>. Accessed June 20, 2012.

Goldstein, J. and Wu, T. (2008). *Who Controls the Internet? The Illusions of a Borderless World*, New York: Oxford University Press.

Groshek, J. (2009). "Freedom and 'New' Media: Examining the Relationship between Communication Technologies and Democracy Cross-Nationally from 1946 to 2003," PhD Dissertation, Indiana University, DAI-A 69/08, February.

Habermas, J. (1989). *The Structural Transformation of the Public Sphere*, T. Burger and F. Lawrence (trans.), Cambridge, MA: MIT Press.

—— (2004). *Der Gespaltene Westen*, Frankfurt am Main: Suhrkamp.

—— (1996). "Three Normative Models of Democracy," in S. Benhabib (ed.). *Democracy and Difference*. Princeton: Princeton University Press, pp. XXX–XXX.

Hansard Society (2008). *Audit of Political Engagement 5*. London: Hansard.

Horiuchi, Y., Imai, K., and Taniguchi, N. (2005). "Estimating the Causal Effects of Policy Information on Voter Turnout: An Internet-based Randomized Field Experiment in Japan," Working Paper. Available at <https://digitalcollections.anu.edu.au/handle/1885/43124>. Accessed June 20, 2012.

Howard, P. (2011). *The Digital Origins of Dictatorship and Democracy: Information Technology and Political Islam*, New York: Oxford University Press.

Janssen, D. and Kies, R. (2005). "Online Forums and Deliberative Democracy," *Acta Politica*, 40(3): 317–35.

Johnson, T. and Kaye, G. (2003). "A Boost or Bust for Democracy? How the Web Influenced Political Attitudes and Behaviours in the 1996 and 2000 Presidential Elections," *Harvard International Journal of Press-Politics*, 8(3): 9–34.

Katz, D. and Crotty, W. (eds) (2006). *Handbook of Party Politics*, London: Sage.

Kim, J. Y. (2006). "The Impact of Internet Use Patterns on Political Engagement: A Focus on Online Deliberation and Virtual Social Capital", *Information Polity*, 11(1): 35–49.

Laudon, K. (1977). *Communications Technology and Democratic Participation*, New York: Praeger.

Leadbeater, C. and Mulgan, G. (1997). "The End of Unemployment", in G. Mulgan (ed.). *Life After Politics*, London: Fontana.

Leston-Bandeira, C. (2007). "The Impact of the Internet on Parliaments: A Legislative Studies Framework," *Parliamentary Affairs*, 60(4): 655–74.

Loughlin, J., Hendriks, F., and Listrom, A. (eds) (2011). *The Oxford Handbook of Local and Regional Democracy in Europe*, Oxford: Oxford University Press.

Lupia, A. and Sin, G. (2003). "Which Public Goods are Endangered? How Evolving Communication Technologies Affect the Logic of Collective Action," *Public Choice*, 117(3–4): 315–31.

Margetts, H. (1999). *Information Technology in Government: Britain and America*, London: Routledge.

—— (2006). "Cyber Parties," in R. S. Katz and W. J. Crotty (eds). *Handbook of Party Politics*, London: Sage, pp. 528–35.

—— (2009). "The Internet and Public Policy," *Policy and Internet*, 1(1), Article 1.

—— (2011). "The Net Effect", Economic and Social Research Council Web Site: Features and Findings, March 1. Available at <http://www.esrc.ac.uk/impacts-and-findings/features-casestudies/features/14808/opinion-the-net-effect.aspx>. Accessed June 20, 2012.

Margolis, M. and Resnick. D. (2000). *Politics as Usual: The "Cyberspace Revolution,"* Thousand Oaks, CA: Sage Publications.

Morozov, E. (2011). *The Net Delusion: The Dark Side of Internet Freedom*, Washington, DC: Public Affairs.

Morris, D. (2001). "Direct Democracy and the Internet," *Loyola of Los Angeles Review*, 34(3): 1033–53. Available at <http://digitalcommons.lmu.edu/llr/vol34/iss3/5>. Accessed June 20, 2012.

Mossberger, K. (2009). "Toward Digital Citizenship: Addressing Inequality in the Information Age," in A. Chadwick and P. N. Howard (eds). *Handbook of Internet Politics*, London: Routledge.

—— Tolbert, C. J., and McNeal, R. S. (2008). *Digital Citizenship: The Internet, Society, and Participation*, Cambridge, Massachusetts: The MIT Press.

Negroponte, N. (1995). *Being Digital*, London: Hodder and Stoughton.

Norris, P. (2001). *Digital Divide: Civic Engagement, Information Poverty and the Internet Worldwide*, Cambridge: Cambridge University Press.

—— (2003). "Preaching to the Converted? Pluralism, Participation and Party Websites," *Party Politics*, 9(1): 21–45.

—— (2009). "The Impact of the Internet on Political Activism: Evidence from Europe," in C. Romm and K. Setzekorn (eds). *Social Networking Communities and E-Dating Services*, New York: I-Global.

Olson, M. (1965). *The Logic of Collective Action: Public Goods and the Theory of Groups*, Cambridge: Harvard University Press.

Oostveen, A. and van den Besselaar, P. (2006). "Non-Technical Risks of Remote Electronic Voting," in A.-V. Anttiroiko and M. Malkia (eds). *The Encyclopedia of Digital Government*, Hershey, PA: Idea Group Inc., pp. 502–7.

Papacharissi, Z. (2009). "The Virtual Sphere 2.0: the Internet, the Public Sphere and Beyond," in A. Chadwick and P. Howard (eds). *The Routledge Handbook of Internet Politics*, London: Routledge.

Price, V., Cappella, J. N., and Nir, L. (2002a). "Online Deliberation and its Influence: The Electronic Dialogue Project in Campaign 2000," *Information Technology and Society*, 1(1): 303–29.

——, Cappella, J. N., and Nir, L. (2002b). "Does more Disagreement Contribute to More Deliberative Opinion?," *Political Communication*, 19(1): 95–112.

Przeworski, A. (2000). *Democracy and Development: Political Institutions and the Well-Being of the World*, New York: Cambridge University Press.

Reedy, J. and Wells, C. (2009). "Information, the Internet, and Direct Democracy," in A. Chadwick and P. Howard (eds). *The Handbook of Internet Politics*, London: Routledge.

Rheingold, H. (2000). *The Virtual Community*, Cambridge, MA: MIT Press.

Simon, L., Corrales, J., and Wolfensberger, D. (2002). *Democracy and the Internet: Allies or Adversaries*, Washington: Woodrow Wilson Center Press.

Smith, G., John, P., and Sturgis, P. (2013 forthcoming). "Taking Political Engagement Online: An Experimental Analysis of Asynchronous Discussion Forums," *Political Studies*.

Stoker, G. (2010). "The Rise of Political Disenchantment," in C. Hay (ed.). *New Directions in Political Science*, London: Palgrave Macmillan.

Sunstein, C. (2007). *Republic.com 2.0*, Princeton, NJ: Princeton University Press.

Tolbert, C. J. and McNeal, R. S. (2003). "Unraveling the Effects of the Internet on Political Participation?," *Political Research Quarterly*, 56(2): 175–85.

Vanhanen, T. (1990). *The Process of Democratization: A Comparative Study of 147 States, 1980–88*, New York: Crane Russak.

—— (1997). *Prospects of Democracy: A Study of 172 Countries*, London: Routledge.

—— (2003). *Democratization: A Comparative Analysis of 170 Countries*, London: Routledge.

Ward, S., Lusoli, W., and Gibson, R. K. (2006). "Reconnecting Politics? Parliament, the Public and the Internet," *Parliamentary Affairs*, 59(1):1–19.

Warschauer, M. (2003). *Technology and Social Inclusion; Rethinking the Digital Divide*, Cambridge, MA: MIT Press.

PART V

GOVERNING AND
REGULATING THE
INTERNET

CHAPTER 21

....

ANALYZING FREEDOM OF EXPRESSION ONLINE: THEORETICAL, EMPIRICAL, AND NORMATIVE CONTRIBUTIONS

....

VICTORIA NASH

INTRODUCTION

....

THE continuing reinvention and worldwide diffusion of the Internet has made it an increasingly central medium of expression in the twenty-first century, challenging the role of traditional mass media, including radio, television, and newspapers. By 2011, more than two billion people worldwide—over one quarter of the world's population—were using the Internet.[1] As the geographic spread of this global network of networks has expanded, so it has become more embedded in every aspect of everyday life, bringing with it major societal implications, and reshaping global access to information, communication, services, and technologies (Dutton 1999). As these changes have been wrought, so traditionally separate disciplines have converged to study problems or enduring issues of common interest, albeit from very different perspectives. In this context, debates around the protection of fundamental communication rights, and in particular challenges to freedom of expression, have benefited significantly from the rich and varied insights of literature from different disciplines in Internet Studies.

[1] Current worldwide statistics on usage at <http://www.internetworldstats.com/stats.htm>. Accessed August 18, 2011.

For example, research in communications and sociology has revealed how global diffusion of the Internet, along with a continuing stream of innovations enabling easy production as well as consumption of content, are making the Internet increasingly pivotal to the communicative power of individuals, groups, and institutions (Dutton 2005; Castells 2009). At the same time, research in law, politics, and regulation has highlighted countervailing trends, outlining increasing efforts to restrict and control the use of the Internet for information, and communication on political, moral, security, and other grounds, including mitigating risks to children, to privacy or intellectual property rights. Nor are the contributions limited to social science: computer science has advanced our understanding of the efficacy (or otherwise) of many technical measures used to block or limit content online, while humanities research in media or cultural studies has shed light on questions of how online communication shapes and is shaped by factors such as social norms, technical affordances, and legal frameworks.

While it would be impossible to give a detailed account of the contributions made by each discipline in all these broad areas, this chapter will highlight the most important ways in which research from across Internet Studies combines thematically to offer a vivid picture of the challenges facing freedom of expression in the twenty-first century, as well as the need for broader theoretical frameworks.

FREEDOM OF EXPRESSION:
A FUNDAMENTAL RIGHT

Representatives of global institutions and national governments around the world have long embraced freedom of expression as a basic human right with the most symbolic endorsement being its instantiation in the United Nations Universal Declaration of Human Rights in 1948.[2] As well as being enshrined in international rights instruments, the right to freedom of expression is recognized in many other regional human rights' charters such as the African Charter on Human and People's Rights or the European Convention on Human Rights (ECHR), and in many national constitutions, including China, India, and Pakistan.

Insofar as rights are devices that demarcate the boundaries of legitimate state intervention in individuals' lives, the right to freedom of expression or "free speech" can be defined as the right to speak or write without state censorship. However, this does not mean that such a right has to be "absolute" or without exception. The ECHR, for example, guarantees everyone the freedom to hold opinions and to get and pass on information and ideas, but it also allows a number of qualifications, stating that these rights:

> may be subject to such formalities, conditions, restrictions or penalties as are
> prescribed by law and are necessary in a democratic society, in the interests of

[2] Article 19 states: "Everyone has the right to freedom of opinion and expression; this right includes freedom to hold opinions without interference and to seek, receive and impart information and ideas through any media and regardless of frontiers." See: <http://www.un.org/en/documents/udhr/>. Accessed August 18, 2011.

national security, territorial integrity or public safety, for the prevention of disorder or crime, for the protection of health or morals, for the protection of the reputation or rights of others, for preventing the disclosure of information received in confidence, or for maintaining the authority and impartiality of the judiciary.[3]

In reality, most rights are limited in law even if the degree of exception varies from one state to another. In the United States, freedom of expression is enshrined in the First Amendment to the US Constitution as part of the Bill of Rights, and is famously interpreted by the courts in more absolute terms than in many other nations. The Amendment states:

> Congress shall make no law respecting an establishment of religion, or prohibiting the free exercise thereof; or abridging the freedom of speech, or of the press; or the right of the people peaceably to assemble, and to petition the government for a redress of grievances.[4]

Even here, there are still exceptions: obscene materials, subject to a narrowly drawn definition[5], are not protected, nor are libelous words or expression, which indicates "imminent lawless action."[6] In practice, however, many federal laws seeking to limit access to certain forms of content, especially by minors, have been overturned in the United States on grounds that they are unconstitutional, often on the basis that they are either too indiscriminate in the range of content to be blocked, or that they are indiscriminate in failing to capture only the targeted group[7].

In many states, the right to free expression is augmented by rights to freedom of information, providing citizens with a legal right to request and access government-held information, and imposing duties on states to publish open records. The close connection between these rights is obvious, namely that the value of free expression is significantly weakened if it cannot be exercised in consideration of key political information relating to how citizens are governed and taxes spent. The importance of this connection was expressed by Viviane Reding (2007), Commissioner for Information Society and Media in the European Commission, in saying: "Freedom of expression is one of the most fundamental rights of our European democracies" ... but that "without freedom of information, freedom of expression often remains meaningless." These recent developments reinforce the commitment of international institutions, such as the United Nations Education, Scientific, and Cultural Organization (UNESCO), which "promotes freedom of expression and freedom of the press as a basic human right."[8]

---

[3] Article 10 see <http://conventions.coe.int/Treaty/en/Treaties/Html/005.htm>. Accessed April 30, 2012.

[4] First Amendment, see: <http://www.law.cornell.edu/constitution/constitution.billofrights.html>. Accessed April 30, 2012.

[5] The "Miller Test" determining whether the materials meets one of three possible criteria, drawn from *Miller v. California*, 413 U.S. 15 (1973).

[6] *Brandenburg v. Ohio*, 395 U.S. 444 (1969).

[7] See *ACLU v. Mukasey*, 534 F.3d 181 (3d Cir. 2008) and broader discussion of its case history at <http://www.mediacoalition.org/ACLU-v.-Mukasey>. Accessed July 31, 2012.

[8] See: <http://www.unesco.org/new/en/communication-and-information/freedom-of-expression/>. Accessed May 10, 2012.

Despite being recognized internationally as a fundamental human right (that is, a right which all human beings should enjoy regardless of whether or not their state has chosen to implement such rights), there is surprisingly little practical or theoretical consensus as to why we value free speech rights so highly. Most discussion of this issue has broadly fallen into three camps:

- Arguments for knowledge and social progress (e.g. Mill 1859). This instrumentalist argument suggests that without unfettered public debate and the right always to question accepted views or theories, knowledge, truth, and even society cannot progress. Although initially formulated as an attack on religious dogma, the argument still stands as a key principle of academic freedom and provides a fundamental critique of social conservatism.
- Arguments for democracy (e.g. Meiklejohn 1965). This argument, also an instrumental one, places heavy emphasis on political speech, arguing that the free flow of ideas and exchange of views is critical to democratic processes and institutions, underpinning the ability of citizens to vote in an informed way and to hold their governments and other public institutions to account.
- Arguments for personal autonomy (e.g. Rawls 1972). This argument broadens the debate to claim both that free speech has more than instrumental value, as an intrinsic aspect of individual autonomy, and further that such speech rights apply to all forms of speech, not solely political. Clearly, the perceived weight of this principle will vary cross-culturally depending on how individual autonomy is valued in relation to collective goals. For example, a focus on individual autonomy might support the role of the individual in choosing what to filter. In contrast, a focus on collective good could support a greater role for state filtering to protect shared values.

While these principles, drawn from political theory and jurisprudence, may seem obscure, it is worth being aware of the different theoretical perspectives when exploring the way in which research from different disciplines is contributing to our understanding of the interplay between freedom of expression and digital communication. Indeed, as will be seen, in some cases radically different assumptions appear to be made, not only about the supposed rationale for prioritizing speech rights, but the way in which trade-offs are to be balanced with other policy goals.

FREEDOM OF EXPRESSION
IN A NETWORK SOCIETY

In the digital era of networked communication, our conceptions of freedom of expression entail two general categories of rights but are closely associated with at least two more. In 2003, the United Nations' World Summit on the Information Society (WSIS) sought to find some agreement between governments, business, and civil society groups as to the values and goals of a global information society. While the Declaration of Principles that emerged has no legally binding status, it does serve to elucidate some of the aspirations of players in seeking more social equity and a re-focusing on human rights in the digital era (Mansell 2005). The Declaration is particularly helpful in unpacking what might be meant by freedom of speech in a network society, stating that:

> We reaffirm, as an essential foundation of the Information Society, and as outlined in Article 19 of the Declaration of Human Rights, that everyone has the right to freedom of opinion and expression; that this right includes freedom to hold opinions without interference and to seek, receive and impart information and ideas through any media and regardless of frontiers. Communication is a fundamental social process, a basic human need and the foundation of all social organization. It is central to the information society. Everyone, everywhere should have the opportunity to participate and no one should be excluded from the benefits the Information Society offers. (WSIS 2003: para. 4)

There seem to be at least four aspects to freedom of speech in this context. The first focuses on the rights of individuals and groups to use various media to express views and opinions. This is most often associated with freedom of the press and the freedom to associate with others, but is increasingly being extended to the freedom to use the Internet and Information and Communication Technologies (ICTs) to shape and define personal values and identity, as well as to engage in or even lead public debate, particularly as individual Internet users increasingly take on many roles formerly played by the press.

The second aspect concerns rights of access to the means of expression. Theorists of rights and liberty have previously argued that freedom is not meaningful unless it can actually be exercised (Taylor 1991). In the age of digital networking, this increasingly translates into the requirement of access to the Internet—Hilary Clinton's "freedom of connection" (Clinton 2010)—as it becomes a primary interface between individuals and the world (Dutton 1999). It is not clear how this requirement should be interpreted—as a right of universal Internet access, or merely a policy justification for supporting the global diffusion of the Internet.

As well as protecting freedom of expression, many states also provide legal guarantees for a right to freedom of information that is the third aspect of freedom of expression in the information society set out in the WSIS Declaration. Such rights ensure that citizens have the right to access information about how government operates, and in many cases they also impose duties on government to be transparent in operation, providing "open records" of publicly accessible data. In so far as freedom of expression is deemed to be one of the fundamental civil rights supporting democratic processes, freedom of information is required in order to ensure that citizens can vote in an informed way, and that they can hold their governments accountable through public scrutiny.

It has also been argued that there is a fourth right very closely linked to freedom of expression, albeit one not set out in the Declaration above, namely the right to communicate. This concept has been the subject of both theoretical and political controversy in a historic debate that reflects some of the most divisive elements of Internet governance (Mueller et al. 2007; Hamelink and Hoffman 2008). Embodying fundamental concerns for equality and voice in an era of inequitable media flows, the UNESCO-commissioned McBride report argued for a new right to communicate which would involve "the extension of specific rights such as the right to be informed, the right to inform, the right to privacy, the right to participate in public communication" (UNESCO 1980). Perhaps unsurprisingly, this report, although initially sympathetically received, became associated with challenges to Western dominance of media markets and was seen as a possible threat to free trade. It is notable that since that point, calls for the international recognition of a new right to communicate have been dropped in favor of less antagonistic demands for a strengthening of existing "communication rights" such as the three outlined above (Movius 2008).

The Internet's contribution to freedom of expression

As a global "network of networks" the Internet enables people to inform and educate themselves, express their views, and participate in civil society and democratic processes to an extent never before possible. The rich variety of communication tools and platforms it offers enables users to search for, read, share, generate, manipulate, and even co-produce information. In such ways, the Internet has complemented more traditional forms of one-to-many broadcast communication by providing opportunities for many-to-many and many-to-one forms of communication as well as new broadcast models, such as Twitter.

However, this potential for the Internet to enhance freedom of expression is not universally welcomed. For example, some worry that the Internet could undermine traditional media practices and institutions by eroding standards of broadcasting, or undermining the business models supporting national and local media. In other cases there are concerns about particular information or content that might be disseminated online, perhaps on the basis of national security, or on political or moral grounds. In such cases, it is unfortunately clear that the Internet offers just as many opportunities for digital surveillance or censorship as it does for free expression, a point too often forgotten by cyber-utopians (Morozov 2011).

While state-led filtering or censorship may be the most obvious and feared threat to freedom of expression online, the most numerous challenges stem from the daily decisions of multiple different actors pursuing a diverse range of policy goals, many seemingly unrelated to freedom of speech at all. In some cases, the pursuit of particular goals can enhance freedom of expression. For example, the push towards economic progress by developing countries has been a major impetus behind the worldwide diffusion of the Internet, as it has become a central infrastructure for local and global economic transactions and trade. In other cases, the pursuit of different goals can lead, directly or indirectly, to restrictions of freedom of expression, such as where intellectual property legislation limits the free exchange of scientific research. It is in the pursuit of these diverse objectives that governments, regulators, corporations, and even non-governmental organizations (NGOs) can (with or without intent) expand or limit citizens' enjoyment of freedom of expression. It will be argued in the rest of this chapter that the most helpful contribution of Internet Studies in furthering our understanding of freedom of expression in the digital age has been to expose and illuminate the many different forces that restrict or expand our opportunities to speak and communicate.

ACCESS AND INEQUALITY

One of the most positive developments shaping the role of the Internet in opening up new channels of expression has been the continuing pace of worldwide innovation and diffusion, which has been well mapped both academically, such as through the World Internet Project,[9] and for policy purposes, such as through the International Telecommunications Union (ITU).[10] By 2011, over 30 percent of the world's population had access to the Internet, growing from 6 percent in 2000.[11] This corresponds to over 2 billion users. Internet diffusion has reached almost every region of the world with the exception of Africa, which has remained comparatively low in levels of Internet access at just 11.5 percent penetration in 2011.[12] At the same time, mobile penetration rates are also improving. Figures for Africa still lag behind at just 45 subscriptions per 100 inhabitants in 2010, compared to 95 per 100 in the Americas,[13] but as mobile communication converges rapidly with Internet communication this will help diminish, but by no means erase, the divide across world regions.

Studies that map penetration statistics can hide fundamental inequalities in Internet access and use between groups and individuals that will clearly impact on whether or not enhanced opportunities for communication and expression are delivered to those that need them most. While large-scale surveys of Internet penetration have been invaluable in helping to elucidate the extent to which citizens in different states face very different communication infrastructures, Internet Studies has also seen the emergence of a rich vein of work fleshing out the concept of access. Thus lack of physical or material access is distinguished from the paucity of digital skills or information literacy, often drawing on research from educational studies (e.g. Warschauer 2003). Studies in communications and sociology identify other factors which potentially hamper Internet use, including lack of mental access, resulting from too little digital experience and confidence, or a lack of "usage access," where individuals face few opportunities for using the Internet in their daily lives, such as in the workplace (van Dijk and Hacker 2003).

---

[9] See <http://www.worldinternetproject.net/#news>. Accessed April 21, 2012.

[10] See <http://www.itu.int/itu-d/ict/>. Accessed April 21, 2012.

[11] Data given for March 31, 2011. Taken from: <http://www.internetworldstats.com/stats.htm>. Accessed April 21, 2012.

[12] Data given for March 31, 2011. Ibid.

[13] Data taken from ITU World Telecommunication/Ict Indicators Database: <http://www.itu.int/net/pressoffice/stats/2011/03/index.aspx>. Accessed April 21, 2012.

Others in sociology have warned of the dangers of focusing too much on the "digital divide" where the haves and have-nots are clearly separated on dichotomous measures of access, failing to appreciate the degrees of digital inequality that might exist between Internet users (DiMaggio and Hargittai 2001; Hargittai and Hsieh Chapter 7). Such studies are important as they highlight the extent to which, even in countries with very high levels of Internet penetration, not all individuals will reap the potential benefits of increasing diffusion, on the basis that they lack other key resources.

Legal and regulatory initiatives have underpinned increasing worldwide access to the Internet and the information, communication, and services that it enables. The Internet's worldwide diffusion has not been the inevitable outcome of the technology itself, but of a series of technological, economic, and social innovations shaped by policy and practice. For example, the Internet was developed early on as the ARPANet (Advanced Research Projects Agency Network), supported by funding from the US Department of Defense. However, it was developed within universities and research institutions primarily as a tool for scientists to share computing resources, not as a tool for national defense (Naughton 1999; Dutton 2008).

Previously, skills and infrastructures necessary to produce and disseminate content for many media, such as the press, radio, and television, were highly centralized. The potential of the Internet and advances in related technologies such as video, Web 2.0 applications, and mobile devices have enabled a more decentralized production of content. However, access to the Internet does not automatically translate into its use for the production of new content. Most users are primarily consumers of Internet services, rather than producers of original content. The potential of the Internet, like other ICTs, to "reconfigure access" (Dutton 2005), is not always realized. This is one reason why many nations are aggressively pursuing initiatives designed to enhance the proficiency and literacy of Internet users. This could not only enable more people to benefit from the vast array of information online, but also allow them to contribute original and local content to the World Wide Web. The McBride Commission might have recognized the long-term potential of new technologies to reconfigure global information flows, but this potential has never before been as technically feasible as it is today; ensuring the appropriate skill levels remains a major challenge.

In contrast to the mass media of film and television, the Internet has a greater potential to transform the geography of production and consumption, enabling a more decentralized production and more diverse flows of content around the world. However, it could also further centralize content production, given the concentration of media skills in major centres, such as Los Angeles and London. Research on the geography of content production and consumption is in its early stages, but it is a clear priority of research on the Internet.[14] Increasingly, as access becomes more widespread, debate will undoubtedly turn back to the themes that gripped mass media studies after the McBride Commission around worldwide information flows, equality of voice, and the correlative debate about communication rights.

---

[14] See <http://www.oii.ox.ac.uk/research/projects/?id=89>. Accessed July 31, 2012.

TECHNOLOGIES OF DISCONNECTION

If Internet Studies has contributed a great deal to our understanding of the concept, drivers, and demography of access to the Internet, it has also helped to illuminate how access is denied. The use of Internet filtering and other means of restricting full access to the Internet has led to a number of efforts to track and monitor its prevalence, including work done by NGOs such as Freedom House (2009), and academic research such as that undertaken by the OpenNet Initiative (Deibert et al. 2008).

Many different actors can restrict freedom of expression online. Individuals decide what to read and what to delete or filter by installing spam filters on their own devices, while parents, corporate IT departments, and public institutions like schools or libraries all have a role in deciding what content is available to users in different social contexts. In general, however, studies of censorship and filtering and freedom of expression are most often concerned with state-level censorship. Governments can directly or indirectly restrict freedom of expression by regulating access to the Internet or to particular Internet content. Many civil society advocates of freedom of expression are concerned that such state-supported restrictions are increasing and threatening freedom of expression online.

The most extensive empirical research project which examines government filtering and website blocking suggests that these practices have increased since 2002 (Deibert et al. 2008, 2010) and these trends are supported by other studies (Dutton et al. 2011; Freedom House 2009; and Reporters without Borders 2010).

How filtering works

In parallel with advances in technology underpinning greater access to the Internet and mobile communication technologies, there have been innovations in technological approaches to controlling the flow of information over these networks. This has been driven by the need to maintain and improve the quality and security of services, such as by screening out spam and viruses, but also by efforts to block unwanted content as judged by individuals, parents, NGOs, corporations, or governments. As information and communication flows online, it may use several Internet-related protocols and services and pass through various points in the Internet network as well as the end user's device. As a result, filtering methods can be applied at various "choke points" throughout the network ranging from state-directed filtering schemes where blocking is carried out at the level of the Internet backbone, to filtering by Internet Service Providers (ISPs) or search engines, down to filtering at households or institutional level. Most concern is focused on state-sponsored or enforced filtering, but even when mandated by the government it can be implemented at different levels and by various different parties. Concerns to maximize the civil liberties of Internet users suggest that filtering decisions should be made at the lowest possible level—as close as possible to the individual user.

Most forms of filtering require some inspection of either data content, such as the words, strings of words, or images in the message or on the website, or of the routing or header information derived from the identity of the source. There are also other approaches to filtering such as blocking by DNS (Domain Name System) record, or through hybrid and proxy-based approaches that efficiently combine other forms of filtering. The definition or identification of content to be blocked may stem from three different sources. Blacklists (or "deny" lists) are configured to pass traffic by default unless they contain certain content, names, or keywords on the list. Such lists may be updated by public reports of illegal content or responses from law enforcement as with the "Cleanfeed" system operated by British Telecom (BT) in the UK, which prevents access to child abuse sites identified by the Internet Watch Foundation (IWF). If blocking takes place within a certain network, such as within a company, the network administrator is often the person who manually defines the filtering parameters. In contrast, many defense filters or virus scanners bought or installed by users will normally use pre-defined criteria to filter content automatically.

Critiques of content filtering

Content regulation may be a very widespread practice, often undertaken with well-meaning intentions such as preventing the distribution of illegal child abuse images. However, even efforts to restrict access to illegal content are open to controversy, with freedom of expression campaigners calling for heightened prevention and prosecution measures as well as removal of illegal content at source, rather than what is seen as paternalistic filtering activity. But it is not just illegal content that is subject to blocking: in many states, content or speech deemed to be harmful is also blocked. Such actions are a source of even greater controversy and a variety of critiques of filtering can be found in Internet Studies literature, some of which draw on arguments other than freedom of expression. Examples would include:

- Concerns about the imprecision or inefficacy of filtering techniques. Many contemporary filtering tools are blunt instruments, often leading to some level of over- or under-blocking. Further, many technologically savvy users can find alternative methods to access blocked material as the content itself is not erased from the Internet, creating a cat and mouse game between actors seeking to gain or block access to particular content (Zittrain and Palfrey 2008).
- "Slippery slope" arguments claiming that even limited filtering of strictly illegal content opens the door to potentially more widespread censorship. It is notable that even within the category of "illegal content" there is more consensus around the filtering of some types (say, child abuse images) than there is about others (pirated or illegally copied content, for example). So one concern might be that the scope of state-sponsored filtering will expand, either within the category of "illegal content" or beyond. Should filtering move beyond the illegal to cover legal

but potentially "harmful", the concern would be that censorship becomes ever more politically and socially accepted. These fears are supported by examples of states introducing wide-ranging censorship defended on the basis of more acceptable justifications such as blocking child abuse images (Akdeniz and Altiparmak 2008).

- Claims that certain types of filtering (those applied at levels beyond an individual's control) remove the responsibility of autonomous decision-making. This rather more theoretical objection suggests that applying technical "fixes" for essentially social or moral problems can have a detrimental impact on individual moral character, by removing the opportunity for us to choose not to break the law (Brownsword 2008).

- Concerns about the damaging effect of any form of censorship on other Internet "goods" such as creativity and innovation. According to this argument, the problem of Internet filtering is that it risks damaging the very things we value about being online (Zittrain and Palfrey 2008).

ALTERNATIVES TO FILTERING[15]

In addition to filtering measures, government agencies have used a number of techniques to deny access or censor particular types of online content in ways that differ from filtering. These include:

- Denial of service attacks, which produce the same end result as other technical blocking techniques—blocking access to certain websites—although only temporarily. This is more often used by non-state actors seeking to disrupt services;

- Restricting access by installing high barriers (costs, personal requirements) to register a domain or even to get Internet access; such measures may also be targeted at certain "vulnerable" members, as with age verification measures imposed to limit access by minors.

- Taking-down or removal of illegal websites from servers is one of the most effective ways of regulating content. To do so, regulators need to have direct access to content hosts, or the legal jurisdiction over the content hosts, or an ability to force ISPs to take down particular sites. In several countries, where authorities have control of domain name servers, officials can deregister a domain that is hosting restricted content (Deibert et al. 2008).

One creative approach to addressing content concerns is to enter Internet conversations. This approach is most in tune with the spirit of free expression, but only if it is transparent. For example, the US State Department has initiated an effort to respond to what

---

[15] The following three subsections draw on material from the author's earlier UNESCO Report (Dutton et al. 2011).

they view as misinformation and inaccurate accounts of US policy and actions on Arab language blogs and websites by commenting on blogs, and explicitly identifying themselves as representatives of the US State Department (Khatib et al. 2012). In many respects, this is a modern form of public diplomacy, adapted to Web 2.0 technologies and in keeping with open access to more diverse sources of information.

However, some regimes have increasingly resorted to guiding or influencing online discussion without being transparent, such as through the clandestine use of paid pro-government commentators or the financing of entire websites and blogs. Freedom House (2009) pins this offence on the Chinese government for employing "50 Cent Party" commentators, Russia for using Kremlin-affiliated "content providers," and Tunisia for using similar approaches to "subvert online conversations." Governments may also seek to counter particular political movements or to guide online opinion by producing online publications or "propaganda" such as pro-government websites.

Control of online expression and content may also make use of offline measures. Content can be influenced by introducing rules, or laws, or by instilling social norms among content producers. This can be enforced by the threat of legal action, but also by social pressure (see for example, discussion of the limited filtering which occurs in Singapore, in Deibert et al. 2008: 366–7). Arrest or detention of content producers is perhaps the most traditional and repressive form of content control, and one that is now supported by an increasingly sophisticated range of surveillance and monitoring methods. In recent years, there has been a worrying increase in the arrests of journalists, bloggers, and Internet users in several of the more repressive regimes (Freedom House 2011). The next section explores the accumulated effect of all these techniques to highlight international variations in the protection of online freedom of expression.

INTERNATIONAL PATTERNS OF INTERNET FREEDOM

Research in Internet Studies has provided ample insights into international trends relating to enjoyment of freedom of expression online, just as they have into patterns of access and exclusion on a global scale. These findings present some surprises, with both authoritarian and democratic states imposing threats on freedom of expression online, as detailed below.

Internet filtering and censorship

As noted above, in the early years of the twenty-first century, an increasing number of governments have taken steps to block or regulate Internet access or content. In 2002, the OpenNet Initiative reported on just a few governments that were blocking online content, while by 2007 they estimated that at least forty countries used methods to do so (Deibert et al. 2008). Freedom House's 2011 report noted that since its 2009 study, the scores for Internet freedom had declined in nine of the fifteen countries covered in both years, while Internet freedom had also been undermined in more democratic states such as Brazil, India, and the UK (Freedom House 2011: 7). Thus, national regulation of the Internet appears to be increasing, with inevitable implications for freedom of expression.

It is often assumed that content control systems are only established in undemocratic countries or by authoritarian regimes wishing to control political speech or criticism. In fact, such measures are prevalent in most liberal democracies and are often undertaken with very good intentions. A meta-analysis of existing surveys illustrates that many nations are likely to exercise some level of control, but that only a minority exhibit pervasive levels of censorship (Dutton et al. 2011). Australia, Canada, China, Finland, France, Germany, Japan, Kyrgyzstan, Saudi Arabia, the UK, the US, and Uzbekistan are just a few countries who have implemented national filtering systems or have presented legislation to approve filtering practices.

In this context it is important to take into account not just the quantity of material that is restricted but also its significance, although this is an area much better suited to discrete and detailed country studies rather than comparative research at the macro level. In democratic societies, issues of copyright infringement, hate speech, defamation, privacy protection, and child protection are at times a basis for Internet filtering or other content control. It could be argued that filtering for such purposes does not represent as significant a threat to freedom of expression as the deliberate blocking of political speech or information and communication for certain social minority groups. Others, who see freedom of expression as an absolute right of fundamental importance, would disagree.

The states most consistently identified as operating extensive filtering practices are China, Cuba, Myanmar (Burma), Iran, Tunisia, Saudi Arabia, and Vietnam (Dutton et al. 2011; Freedom House 2011; Deibert et al. 2008). These nations fall primarily in three regions: East Asia, the Middle East and North Africa, and Central Asia. Nevertheless, there is great diversity in filtering practices within these regions. In the Asia-Pacific region, much has been written about the "Great Firewall of China," and there is widespread agreement that China has one of the most sophisticated and pervasive filtering systems for Internet censorship.[16] Vietnam follows many similar practices. Myanmar (Burma) famously shut down the Internet in the fall of 2007, during disturbances, and held an opposition candidate, Aung San Suu Kyi, under house arrest, although she has since been released and permitted to have a Facebook account. In South Korea, the Internet is generally free, except in the area of national security, where there are tight controls. Pakistan and Sri Lanka restrict politically sensitive sites.

[16] A website was available that enabled users to "[t]est any website and see real-time if it's censored in China." However, the site now notes that: "Because of the ever stricter measures of censorship Chnia imposes on the Internet, the team … at present can no longer vouch for the reliability of its test tool." See <http://www.greatfirewallofchina.org/>. Accessed April 21, 2012.

Although no significant restrictions were reported in the studies used for the meta-analysis, filtering in North America and Western Europe is mostly targeted at child sexual abuse images or hate speech and propaganda (Zittrain and Palfrey 2008). In Central and Eastern Europe there is high regional diversity, with some states being quite open and others taking steps to block access (Belarus and Kazakhstan compared to Turkmenistan). In the Middle East and North Africa, the blocking of websites is fairly extensive, especially in Syria and Iran. On the African continent, the lack of access to the Internet is the greatest obstacle to expression. In addition, while the Internet is only now beginning to play a major role due to financial and infrastructural constraints, Gambia and Ethiopia have already started to block sites and restrict access.

EXPANDING THE FRAMEWORK
OF DISCUSSION

The preceding sections outline how Internet Studies has elucidated the ways in which changing patterns of Internet access and restrictions on online activity are shaping freedom of expression online. While this body of research has played a vital role in informing policy and exposing the worst forms of repression, there is actually a much wider body of research that should be brought to bear on this topic. The primary theme of this chapter is that it is helpful to broaden the context in which "freedom of expression" is conceptualized. Not only does the pursuit of other values shape freedom of expression, but the pursuit of freedom of expression can also itself serve a variety of other values and interests, from democratizing communication to reinforcing vested interests. A useful framework for this purpose is based on the concept of an "ecology of games."

The idea of an "ecology of games" (EoG) was introduced in local community studies within Political Science during the 1950s (Long 1958) and was then adapted for communication technology and policy issues in the 1990s (Dutton 1992). The concept was used to focus on a key weakness of dominant elite and pluralist perspectives on community power, arguing that few actors sought to control communities per se. Instead, actors sought to achieve a wide array of more specific objectives, from making their neighborhood safer to enhancing the quality of schools, to getting a promotion. In other words, there exists an ecology of actors, each pursuing particular objectives, and each making choices in the pursuit of those objectives that shape the development of a community. From this perspective, community development is a largely unplanned process driven by the unanticipated interactions of multiple players or stakeholders within overlapping "games." The unfolding history of such separate but interdependent games is then driving the evolution of local communities.

The use of the concept of "games" is not meant to trivialize their importance. Games have a set of objectives, rules, and values, with a range of players and prizes. Likewise, actors in public policy and regulation also have objectives, and compete or cooperate with others to achieve their objectives under a set of rules. Success can also mean that they are rewarded—there are prizes. However, the games of policy and regulation are different from games played for entertainment in that their outcomes shape critical aspects of everyday life and work, even the protection of fundamental rights such as freedom of expression.

A new framework: the ecology of freedom of expression

The ecology of games perspective has been refined and applied to a variety of policy areas including transport (Lubell et al. 2010), science and technology (Brandon 1994), and education (Stone 1995). Dutton (1992) applied this framework to tele-communications policy and later to computerization and Internet governance (Dutton and Peltu 2007), where it can be seen as particularly appropriate, given the unusual character of the policy landscape. While much of the debate about the Internet's "regulability" has been caught between cyber-utopian claims of citizen empowerment and institutionalism's focus on the emergence of new transnational governance organizations (Mueller 2010), the ecology of games framework can engage with developments on both levels (Dutton et al. 2011). The players of games in Internet policy and regulation can be traditional political actors such as states and international bodies, as well as increasingly influential bodies such as corporations or NGOs, or even individual users. Similarly, in any one game, those different players may have objectives on radically differing scales, as in the copyright game, where states and international trade bodies pursue goals relating to maximizing trade receipts, but are pitted against individuals simply seeking to use and reuse creative content.

A report for UNESCO provided a new perspective on the study of freedom of expression, by viewing these freedoms as the outcome of an ecology of choices made, not only about freedom of expression, but also a variety of other objectives (Dutton et al. 2011). Table 21.1 below (adapted from that report) illustrates how the wide range of separate but interrelated goals being pursued by a variety of different actors (governments, NGOs, industry), employing an array of strategies, might influence the state of freedom of expression on the Internet.

In some cases, actors such as those from civil society are explicitly seeking to achieve greater freedom of expression, but others are focused on restricting freedoms, such as through the use of Internet filtering, the censorship of news and mass media, or efforts to silence journalists or bloggers. More indirectly, some actors are focused on quite different goals altogether, such as protecting children from harmful content, management of critical networks or infrastructure, or even promoting the vitality of an economy. The more the Internet has become central to communication, the more it has played a role in helping multiple actors to achieve their various goals, which explains the wide variety of policy areas listed below.

Table 21.1 Examples illustrating an ecology of freedom of expression on the Internet

Policy Areas	Policy Goals and Objectives	Actors
Digital Rights	Expanding access to the Internet	National and local governments, international bodies, NGOs, Local SMEs and international corporations
	Maximizing or restricting freedom of expression	NGOs, press and media, national governments
	Data protection	Courts, law enforcement, government agencies, national and regional governments.
	Protecting privacy	Corporations, NGOs, government agencies.
Protecting national interests	Intellectual Property Rights (IPR): copyright and patents	Creative industries, WIPO, national governments, NGOs, ISPs, users.
	Innovation and market growth	National, regional, and local government, venture capital industry, SMEs, large industry
	Competition and market development	National and regional governments, regulators, consumer groups
	National security	Governments and national security agencies, law enforcement, ISPs, Internet industry
User-Focused	Child Protection	Law enforcement, NGOs, national governments, international bodies, parents and educators
	Decency: Pornography	Adult content industry, national regulators, governments, NGOs, ISPs
	Libel: Defamation	Courts, lawyers and law enforcement, press and media
	Hate Speech	Governments, NGOs, international bodies
Internet-Focused	Internet Governance and Regulation	Governments, international bodies, corporations, NGOs, national regulators
	Domain Names and Numbers	ICANN, registries, individuals and firms
	Standard Setting: Identity	W3C, national and regional governments, IETF
	Net Neutrality	ISPs and mobile operators, national governments and regulators, NGOs

Three examples of games impacting on freedom of expression[17]

i) Privacy versus national security: Blackberry

Companies providing services that encrypt user communications or data have often been challenged by courts and governments to provide access to private information in the name of national security. Research in Motion (RIM), the Canadian makers of the

---

[17] This following section draws on material from the author's earlier report for UNESCO (Dutton et al. 2011).

Blackberry, received such requests from government representatives in the United Arab Emirates, Saudi Arabia, Indonesia, India, and Bahrain, who argued that RIM's encryption of Blackberry messages posed national security threats and that the routing of data to RIM's offshore servers put control over data beyond the scope of national regulators and law enforcement. In 2010 Saudi Arabia and the United Arab Emirates went so far as to threaten a shutdown of Blackberry services within their respective national borders if RIM could not find a technical solution that would enable security services to monitor Blackberry communications.

Making a decision on such an ethically complex issue is very difficult for any organization, and in this case was further complicated by several other factors, ranging from the economic to the practical. The Blackberry's routine encryption feature—designed to make messages more difficult for anyone (including RIM) to monitor—is a major selling point of the device, and market pressures pushed RIM towards technical monitoring, with stock shares falling as governments threatened shut-downs, and rising on news of technical solutions for monitoring. Like most handset manufacturers, RIM is also dependent on service providers in other nations to provide cellular access for their Blackberry devices, so where these service providers were more tightly controlled by government agencies they would have provided additional pressure for monitoring.

It is worth noting that such complex tensions between individual privacy, national security, and corporate economic success are not only found in more authoritarian states. During the UK riots of 2011, information about the location of proposed civil action was believed to be passed via free one-to-many encrypted Blackberry Messenger systems, leading to calls from media and politicians that RIM identify the ringleaders, alongside calls for access to social networking sites such as Facebook and Twitter to be restricted in such emergencies (Cameron 2011).

ii) Child protection

The Internet is an increasingly central component in the lives of children and young people in the developed world and cannot be seen as an "adults-only" environment. It is in this context that some of the most emotive debates around freedom of expression online arise, at the point where the laudable regulatory goal of protecting minors pushes up against the noble ideal of free speech for all (including children). Many, possibly even most states, have introduced some regulatory tools to protect children online, at least in terms of prohibiting illegal activity; the question remains as to how much regulation is enough, and how much is too much. In many jurisdictions, this debate hinges in large part on the distinction between activities that are illegal and those that are harmful.

In attempting to combat activity that is clearly illegal, many countries have expressed revulsion at the production, dissemination, and use of child sexual abuse images, and in most countries the removal of these images is deemed to be a justified limitation to freedom of expression. Despite this agreement however, regulatory responses vary, with many countries still without legislation that specifically addresses child sexual abuse images. Even within countries with strong domestic legislation that enforces notice and take-down of such material, the challenge of dealing with images hosted on foreign servers is significant. Blocking of such images through the use of blacklists and filters at ISP or search engine level is one very obvious response, but one which has its own limitations, as previously outlined. Should Internet content be controlled by law enforcement agencies or should it rather be a responsibility undertaken by ISPs and search engines? If so, should this occur with or without government support and mandates? Removal of child abuse images at source may still be subject to some controversy, but filtering is even more problematic, although it remains one of the few tools available to limit the continuing re-victimization of those abused.

Once discussion of child protection moves beyond preventing what is clearly illegal towards what is potentially harmful or inappropriate for some users, tensions between rights becomes greater. In countries as diverse as Denmark, South Korea, the United States, and Afghanistan, schools and libraries are required to use filtering software to protect children who use their systems. While the ability for consenting adults to opt out of using these filters varies between countries, such censorship falls primarily upon disadvantaged people who must use public facilities to access the Internet. The extent of state responsibilities in protecting children is very much a matter of debate. Some experts argue that regulation may not be the most efficient solution and that parents, teachers, and childcare workers should have primary responsibility for dealing with online child protection issues (Thierer 2007). Others, however, have pointed out that household inequalities are associated with experience of online harm, implying that such support networks may not reach all those most at risk (Livingstone and Haddon 2009).

No matter where governments decide to limit freedom of expression rights in the name of child protection, it is important that such regulation be transparent, focuses on specific potential risks, and is measured by its effectiveness. In doing so, governments can employ tools to protect the most vulnerable while lessening risks that their efforts be perceived as serious repression of speech (Hills et al. 2010).

iii) Protective regulation: net neutrality

Principles of net neutrality require that ISPs do not discriminate against users through access fees, favor one type of content or content provider over another, or charge content providers for sending information to consumers over their broadband cables (Hogendorn 2007). As digital media evolve with the creation of new applications and services, the escalating need for bandwidth has made the net neutrality debate more prominent. It is attractive to many as a possible solution to managing existing bandwidth more efficiently as demands begin to exceed supply, rather than simply expanding available bandwidth. However, it is also a strategy to enable providers to find additional revenue from video on demand services, which fuels debate over the commercialization of the Internet.

Net neutrality has often been viewed as a North American issue, though regulatory policy in Europe and elsewhere would indicate otherwise (Marsden 2010). The Internet is increasingly being threatened by privatization, and net neutrality has become linked with approaches to vertical integration between content and conduit (Wu and Yoo 2007).

This has raised concerns about potentially discriminatory actions and the possibility of a two- or multi-tiered Internet. Other commentators have noted that ISPs have already employed discriminatory practices such as throttling, but with a broad public interest aim of ensuring that exceptionally high bandwidth users do not slow down overall Internet traffic. This has distanced them from concepts of net neutrality, albeit in the interests of improving service.

Part of the debate is determining what constitutes "good" and "bad" discrimination (Wu and Yoo 2007) and what kind of policy or set of laws governments should adopt in order to ensure fair access. There is no clear agreement in the academic literature on this point. Some have argued that net neutrality regulation will incentivize ISPs to invest in broadband infrastructure at a more socially optimal level (Cheng et al. 2011), while others recommend that policy-makers promote new market entries by adopting policies that boost the size of "best-efforts" broadband connections (Atkinson and Weiser 2006) or simple market-based solutions backed up by light-touch regulation (Marsden 2010).

IMPLICATIONS OF APPLYING THE
ECOLOGY OF GAMES FRAMEWORK

The preceding examples serve to highlight how policy actors focused on goals or objectives other than promoting or limiting freedom of expression may ultimately have a significant impact on citizen enjoyment of this fundamental value. They also reveal the great range of actors involved in this process. In some cases (such as net neutrality) national governments may take a conscious decision not to act, leaving policy to be set by the actions or explicit self-regulation of industry players. In other cases (such as efforts to reduce the distribution of child abuse images), governments may choose to act, and may even align interests internationally to achieve certain goals.

It is often assumed that the absence of government intervention is necessarily a good thing, and when the openness of the Internet is at stake, less regulation is definitely preferable to more. However what is often ignored is the role being played in this context by other actors such as industry or NGOs. Self-regulation is often perceived as a more flexible, less obtrusive means of resolving policy problems (Tambini et al. 2008). However, as the preceding examples make clear, it may also be more difficult to protect fundamental rights if unaccountable non-state actors are ultimately responsible for shaping how individuals use the Internet.

In this light, Internet Studies has a particular responsibility to play in this ultimately normative debate. The investigation and measurement of the extent of freedom of expression is a vital foundation, but it is also important that more effort is devoted to empirical study of the myriad different policy "games" which impact on citizens' enjoyment of this core value. With these solid research foundations we will be better placed to understand and, if necessary, to change the status quo.

CONCLUSIONS

Research from across the many disciplines covered by Internet Studies highlights the tensions inherent in the Internet's contributions to freedom of expression. On the one hand, studies of access and patterns of global diffusion reveal how the Internet's steady expansion and the growing ease of producing as well as consuming content are opening up ever more opportunities for communication and expression. On the other hand, studies in the legal or political frame note that this augmentation of individuals' communicative power has spawned greater efforts to restrict and control the use of the Internet for information and communication on political, moral, cultural, security, and other grounds. It is also leading to ever more regulatory initiatives aimed at limiting risks to children, to privacy, to national security, and so on, which can indirectly, and even unintentionally, limit freedom of expression.

As a consequence, defenders of freedom of expression have raised growing concerns that legal and regulatory trends might be constraining freedom of expression at the very time that the Internet has become more widely recognized as a major medium for fostering global communication. It is clear that technological innovation will not necessarily enhance freedom of expression; indeed, research from across the many disciplines covered by Internet Studies suggests that such fundamental freedoms will be diminished unless we pay more attention to the full array of policy "games" that shape outcomes in this area, and the normative frameworks of discourse and theory which provide the values ultimately guiding those games.

Thus, what is needed is a broader theoretical framework that can encompass the range and variety of actors, objectives, and strategies involved in shaping freedom of expression online. The ecology of games framework is sufficiently flexible to do just this, and its application will help us to more systematically monitor the wide range of legal and regulatory developments that directly—and indirectly—shape the future of free expression on the Internet in local and global contexts.

ACKNOWLEDGEMENT

This chapter draws on and updates an earlier report completed for UNESCO: Dutton et al. (2011).

REFERENCES

Akdeniz, Y. and Altiparmak, K. (2008). "Internet: Restricted Access: A Critical Assessment of Internet Content Regulation and Censorship in Turkey." Available at: <http://privacy.cyber-rights.org.tr/?page_id=256>. Accessed July 31, 2012.

Atkinson, R. D. and Weiser, P. (2006). "A 'Third Way' on Network Neutrality," *The New Atlantis*, 13. Available at <http://www.thenewatlantis.com/publications/a-third-way-on-network-neutrality>. Accessed May 10, 2012.

Brandon, R. N. (1994). "Establishing Long-Term Science and Technology Goals: Providing Vision for an Ecology of Games," *Technology in Society*, 16 (4): 373–87.

Brownsword, R. (2008). "So What Does the World Need Now? Reflections on Regulating Technologies," in R. Brownsword and K. Yeung (eds), *Regulating Technologies*, London: Hart.

Cameron, D. (2011). PM Statement on Disorder in England, August 11. Available at <http://www.number10.gov.uk/news/pm-statement-on-disorder-in-england/>. Accessed May 10, 2012.

Castells, M. (2009). *Communication Power*, Oxford: Oxford University Press.

Cheng, H. K., Bandyopadhyay, S., and Guo, H. (2011). "The Debate on Net Neutrality: A Policy Perspective," *Information Systems Research*, 22 (1): 1–27.

Clinton, H. R. (2010). "Internet Freedom." The prepared text of U.S. of Secretary of State Hillary Rodham Clinton's speech, delivered at the Newseum in Washington, DC, 21 January. Available at <http://www.foreignpolicy.com/articles/2010/01/21/internet_freedom?page=full>. Accessed July 31, 2012.

Deibert, R., Palfrey, J., Rohozinski, R., and Zittrain, J. (eds) (2008). *Access Denied: The Practice and Policy of Global Internet Filtering*, Cambridge, MA: MIT Press.

——, Palfrey, J., Rohozinski, R., and ittrain, J. (eds) (2010). *Access Controlled: The Shaping of Power, Rights, and Rule in Cyberspace*, Cambridge, MA: MIT Press.

DiMaggio, P. and Hargittai, E. (2001). "From the 'Digital Divide' to 'Digital Inequality': Studying Internet Use As Penetration Increases." Princeton University Centre for Arts and Cultural Policy Studies Working Paper #15. Available at <http://www.princeton.edu/~artspol/workpap15.html>. Accessed May 10, 2012.

Dutton, W. H. (1992). "The Ecology of Games Shaping Communications Policy," *Communication Theory*, 2(4): 303–28.

—— (1999). *Society on the Line*. Oxford: Oxford University Press.

—— (2005). "The Internet and Social Transformation: Reconfiguring Access," in W. H. Dutton, B. Kahin, R. O'Callaghan, and A. W. Wyckoff (eds). *Transforming Enterprise*, Cambridge, MA: MIT Press, pp. 375–97.

—— (2008). "Social Movements Shaping the Internet: The Outcome of an Ecology of Games," in M. Elliott and K. L. Kraemer (eds). *Computerization Movements and Technology Diffusion: From Mainframes to Ubiquitous Computing*, Medford, NJ: Information Today, Inc.

——Dopatka, A., Hills, M., Law, G., and Nash, V. (2011). *Freedom of Connection, Freedom of Expression: The Changing Legal and Regulatory Ecology Shaping the Internet*, Paris: UNESCO.

Dutton, W. H. and Peltu, M. (2007). "The Emerging Internet Governance Mosaic: Connecting the Pieces," *Information Polity*, 12(1–2): 63–81.

Freedom House (2009). "Freedom on the Net 2009." Available at <http://www.freedomhouse.org/template.cfm?page=383&report=79>. Accessed May 10, 2012.

—— (2011). "Freedom on the Net 2011." Available at <http://www.freedomhouse.org/report/freedom-net/freedom-net-2011>. Accessed May 10, 2012.

Hamelink, C. and Hoffman, J. (2008). "The State of the Right to Communicate," *Global Media Journal*, 7(13). Available at <http://lass.purduecal.edu/cca/gmj/fa08/gmj-fa08-hamelink-hoffman.htm>. Accessed July 31, 2012.

Hargittai, E. and Hsieh, Y. P. (2012). "Digital Inequality," in W. Dutton (ed.). *The Oxford Handbook of Internet Studies*, Oxford: Oxford University Press.

Hills, M., Powell, A., and Nash, V. (2010). "Child Protection and Freedom of Expression Online." Oxford Internet Institute Discussion Paper no. 17. Available at <http://www.oii.ox.ac.uk/publications/FD17.pdf>. Accessed July 31, 2012.

Hogendorn, C. (2007). "Broadband Internet: Net Neutrality Versus Open Access," *International Economics and Economic Policy*, 4(2): 185–208.

Khatib, L., Dutton, W. H., and Thelwall, M. (2012 forthcoming). "Public Diplomacy 2.0: An Exploratory Case Study of the US Digital Outreach Team," *Middle East Journal*, 66(3)

Livingstone, S. and Haddon, L. (2009). *EU Kids Online: Final Report*, London: LSE. Available at <http://eprints.lse.ac.uk/24372/>. Accessed July 31, 2012.

Long, N. E. (1958). "The Local-Community as an Ecology of Games," *American Journal of Sociology*, 64: 251–61.

Lubell, M., Henry, A. D., and McCoy, M. (2010). "Collaborative Institutions in an Ecology of Games," *American Journal of Political Science*, 54(2): 287–300.

Mansell, R. (2005). "Introduction—Human Rights and Equity in Cyberspace," in M. Klang and A. Murray (eds). *Human Rights in the Digital Age*, London: Glasshouse Press.

Marsden, C. T. (2010). *Net Neutrality: Towards a Co-Regulatory Solution*, London: Bloomsbury Academic.

Meiklejohn, A. (1965). *Political Freedom: The Constitutional Powers of the People*, New York: Oxford University Press.

Mill, J. S. (1859). "On Liberty." Reproduced in J. S. Mill, *Utilitarianism* (1990) (M. Warnock ed.), London: Fontana.

Morozov, E. (2011). *The Net Delusion*, London: Penguin.

Movius, L. (2008). "Global Debates on the Right to Communicate," *Global Media Journal*, 7(13). Available at <http://lass.purduecal.edu/cca/gmj/fa08/graduate/gmj-fa08-grad-movius.htm>. Accessed July 31, 2012.

Mueller, M. (2010). *Networks & States: The Global Politics of Internet Governance*, Cambridge, MA: MIT Press.

——, Kuerbis, B., and Page, C. (2007). "Democratizing Global Communication? Global Civil Society and the Campaign for Communication Rights in the Information Society," *International Journal of Communication*, 1(1): 267–96.

Naughton, J. (1999). *A Brief History of the Future*, London: Weidenfeld & Nicholson.

Rawls, J. (1972). *A Theory of Justice*, New York: Oxford University Press.

Reding, V. (2007). "The Importance of Freedom of Expression for Democratic Societies in the Enlarged European Union." Speech given at a press conference on the conclusion of a Framework Agreement between the International Federation of Journalists and WAZ Mediengruppe, 9 July. Available at <http://europa.eu/rapid/pressReleasesAction.do?reference=SPEECH/07/478&format=HTML&aged=1&language=EN&guiLanguage=en>. Accessed May 10, 2012.

Reporters without Borders (2010). *Enemies of the Internet: Countries Under Surveillance*, Paris: Reporters without Borders. Available at <http://www.rsf.org/IMG/pdf/Internet_enemies.pdf>. Accessed May 10, 2012.

Stone, C. N. (1995). "School Reform and the Ecology-of-Games Metaphor," *Journal of Urban Affairs*, 17(3): 303–7.

Tambini, D., Leonardi, D., and Marsden, C. (2008). *Codifying Cyberspace: Communications Self-Regulation in the Age of Internet Convergence*, Abingdon: Routledge.

Taylor, C. (1991). "What's Wrong with Negative Liberty?," in D. Miller, *Liberty*, Oxford: Oxford University Press.

Thierer, A. D. (2007). "Rep. Bean's 'Safer Net Act': An Education-Based Approach to Online Child Safety," *SSRN eLibrary*. Available at <http://papers.ssrn.com/sol3/papers.cfm?abstract_id=975507>. Accessed July 31, 2012.

UNESCO (1980). *Many Voices, One World. Report of the International Commission for the Study of Communication Problems*, Paris: UNESCO.

Van Dijk, J. and Hacker, K. (2003). "The Digital Divide as a Complex and Dynamic Phenomenon," *Information Society*, 19(4): 315–26.

Warschauer, M. (2003). *Technology & Social Inclusion*, Cambridge, MA: MIT Press

WSIS (World Summit on the Information Society) (2003). "Declaration of Principles: Building the Information Society: A Global Challenge in the New Millennium," WSIS-03/GENEVA/DOC/0004. Available at <http://www.itu.int/wsis/docs/geneva/official/dop.html>. Accessed July 31, 2012.

Wu, T. and Yoo, C. S. (2007). "Keeping the Internet Neutral?: Tim Wu and Christopher Yoo Debate," *Federal Communications Law Journal*, 59(3): 575–592.

Zittrain, J. and Palfrey, J. (2008). "Internet Filtering: The Politics and Mechanisms of Control," in R. Deibert, J. Palfrey, R. Rohozinski, and J. Zittrain (eds). *Access Denied: The Practice and Policy of Global Internet Filtering*, Cambridge, MA: MIT Press.

CHAPTER 22

CULTURAL, LEGAL, TECHNICAL, AND ECONOMIC PERSPECTIVES ON COPYRIGHT ONLINE: THE CASE OF THE MUSIC INDUSTRY

MATTHEW DAVID

INTRODUCTION

ATTEMPTS to represent file-sharing as theft, piracy, and an aid to terrorism have largely failed, and have often backfired, as when the piracy label has come to be celebrated by many, rather than vilified. The absence of a coherent philosophical foundation for copyright and diversity in its historical and geographical construction is mirrored today in the weakness of substantive attempts to enforce a formal regime on global intellectual property rights. While technical scope for distributed exchange gives asymmetric advantage to sharers over defenders of copyright monopolies, encryption and surveillance technologies, in their symmetrical application by all sides in such disputes, tend to cancel themselves out. As a result, sharing has not been stopped by cultural, legal, or technical means. What then are its economic consequences? In relation to file-sharing, what Castells (2000) calls "timeless time," "the space of flows", and "real virtuality" manifest themselves as threats to straightforwardly capitalist network enterprises. In the music industry, for example, new business models based on free information exchange, such as by fostering better rewards for "live" performance, represent "perestroika from below." Alternative business models present themselves in some fields, but have yet to stabilize in others. Online sharing hit recorded music first and hardest. Alternatives here are also most developed. Challenges to business as usual in film, television, journalism, publishing, and computer gaming emerged later but parallel those in music.

THE RHETORIC OF THEFT: THE SHIFT FROM CIVIL TO CRIMINAL LIABILITY

"Cyber-crimes" are mainly online techniques for attaining traditional unlawful ends in the "real" world, but new digital ends create scope for new crimes (Wall 2007; Yar 2006). Unlicensed sharing of copyrighted material has long been unlawful. However, the Internet makes the civil offense of sharing more significant than the criminal offense of commercial piracy. Technical, economic, cultural, and legal distinctions blur in the various attempts to maintain and/or challenge business as usual. The most pervasive worldwide "anti-piracy" commercial features an opening image of a man breaking into a car followed by the text "You wouldn't steal a car!" What follows is a sequence of similar image and text couplets, which then lead to a final set of images concerning the free downloading of copyrighted materials and a set of text-based assertions equating file-sharing with the preceding series of criminal acts. These commercials are pervasive, but pervasive inversion and parody challenges any simple equation of pervasive and persuasive. William Patry (2009) views this campaign as a classic moral panic. He notes that such moral entrepreneurship primarily sought legislative action, not popular "panic," but such a focus upon the legislative nexus is of limited value if laws cannot be enforced any more than can the popular consciousness be moulded successfully.

Such commercials suggest ideas are like objects, and the act of copying is stealing. Copying does not remove the original. Copyright defenders claim what has been stolen is not the expression itself, but rather the utility that such an expression might afford its owner if they retained control over its use or distribution. Academically, Stan Liebowitz (2006) articulates the recording industry's claim (BPI 2008) that file-sharing causes falling CD sales and that lost income reduces creativity. If property rights and markets best distribute scarce resources, weakening such rights dampens creativity (Kerr 2002). This view is contested by those who believe creativity requires a free and common culture (Lessig 2004; Vaidhyanathan 2003). The case study discussed in this chapter suggests, first, that copyright, at least in relation to copies for personal use, can no longer be defended robustly, and second, that this failure will not reduce rewards to musicians. While Liebowitz is right to say file-sharing damages record companies, Lawrence Lessig is right to suggest that this is not necessarily harmful to artists and creativity.

Earning potential drops when monopoly control is suspended. Is this stealing? The monopoly has been stolen. The tenuous equation with stealing has been playfully inverted in a myriad of parody anti anti-piracy commercials circulating on the Internet. Implosive strategies carry the intended meaning of corporate messages to such an extreme that they collapse under the weight of their own hyperbole. "You wouldn't steal a baby." "You wouldn't shoot a policeman." "File-sharing is terrorism." Explosive strategies parody by analogy, wherein the rhetoric of invisible and virtual stealing is transferred to corporations, banks, political elites, and military actions of dominant states. "You wouldn't steal an election" (George W. Bush being sworn in as president); "You wouldn't lie to congress" (Colin Powell asserting the existence of Iraqi weapons of mass destruction); and "You wouldn't steal a pension fund" (Enron and Anderson executives in handcuffs). Ubiquity enables parody and its scope for inversion. The relationship between pervasiveness and persuasiveness is complex and sometimes contradictory.

COPYING ISN'T STEALING ANYWAY: CONDEMNATION BY DUBIOUS CONFLATION

Making a copy for personal use is not a criminal act of piracy, but a civil offense of copyright infringement. The question of piracy is dealt with below. Mark Poster (2006) has highlighted the rapid escalation of recorded incidents of so called "identity theft" online, such as the "stealing" of someone's personal identification details so as to take hold of that person's assets, such as money in bank accounts, to gain a passport, or to take out credit in someone's name. Lobby groups representing the recording and film industry (such as the Federation Against Copyright Theft and the Recording Industry Association of America) routinely equate "identity theft" with the "theft" of intellectual property. Commercial piracy seeks to pass its copies off as authorized originals. It engages in a form of identity theft (trying to pass as the copyright holder). Those sharing material online do not pretend to be who they are not. Online sharing is not identity theft. There have even been attempts (Film Education 2012) to equate online sharing with plagiarism. The claim that such circulation is plagiarism is misleading at best. Educational institutions encourage the free circulation of ideas in exchange for credit in the form of citation not payment. The attempt by commercial lobby groups to equate free circulation with theft and to equate educational and commercial contexts is problematic. If students were to search and catalogue their reading and reference their essays as assiduously as they do their freely acquired music collections, that would most likely be a good thing, academically.

"PIRACY FUNDS TERRORISM AND WILL DESTROY OUR SOCIETY AND YOUR FUTURE ENJOYMENT" (UK FEDERATION AGAINST COPYRIGHT THEFT CINEMA COMMERCIAL 2004)

Linked to the attempt to persuade people that copyright infringement through online sharing is a criminal offence, are attempts to link such activities with other crimes. The most prominent of these attempts was in relation to piracy, and the second was with terrorism. Other campaigns have attempted to make connections with people-smuggling and illegal immigration, drug trafficking, and drug dealing as well as prostitution and online paedophile grooming (David 2010). While the above quote from the Federation Against Copyright Theft (FACT) starts with reference to piracy, the promotional material linked to it equated such commercial copying with online sharing under the label of "piracy." Similarly, the president of the Motion Picture Association of America (MPAA), Jack Valenti (Bagchi 2003), testified before the United States House Judiciary Committee's Subcommittee on Courts, the Internet and Intellectual Property, and again (Valenti 2004) to the Senate Committee on Foreign Relations, that there was a strong link between international counterfeiting organizations and the funding of international terrorism. In both Valenti's statements and in those made by elected representatives on the committees to which he spoke, the equation of commercial piracy and online sharing was asserted and not questioned. Both FACT and MPAA president, Valenti, cited as evidence for the link between "piracy" and terrorism the firm convictions of police officers from various national and international forces that such a link existed, and their strong pronouncements about such links made at international conferences on the subject sponsored by organizations such as their own. Police force representatives around the world cited each others' conviction as to the reality of the link. Lobby groups then created the impression that the link (rather than just the belief in it) was widespread and well established.

However, when called to account by the UK Advertising Standards Authority over the claim that "piracy funds terrorism," FACT, after initial resistance to revealing its sources on the grounds that this might undermine ongoing security investigations, admitted that the only confirmed instance of such a link was that of a Northern Irish paramilitary group, who, after the 1998 Good Friday Peace Agreement had become involved in the commercial counterfeiting of DVDs. A threat to blow up the offices of the Northern Irish Anti-Counterfeiting and Racketeering Office had been made. Whether this group were still active political terrorists; whether such a link warranted (unqualified) the claims that were being made regarding the link between piracy and international terrorism, especially in the post- 9–11 context; and whether the equating of commercial counterfeiting with file-sharing (branded as "online piracy") was reasonable were questions that were not asked. Rather, a convenient representation was constructed and promoted in the United States (Patry 2009) and the United Kingdom (Birmingham and David 2011): panic messages resonate more readily with legislators than the public.

Again, parody and counter arguments over the claimed link between terrorism and "piracy" (however defined) flourish online. Claims by FACT and others that up to one third of the CDs and DVDs being sold, including those sold in shops, were pirate copies, and the claim that such pirate sales might be funding terrorism, led to the assertion that the only way to avoid funding terrorism was to download songs and film for free via the Internet. This avoids any risk of giving money to terrorists.

But is free circulation in fact piracy?

Piracy, in the legal sense, if not in its popular usage, is commercial infringement. Where bootlegging (Marshall 2005) is the production of copies for sale, such copies are distinguished from "piracy" in so far as bootlegged material does not seek to pass itself off as the "original." Most bootlegs are recordings of live performances or compilations of recording studio out-takes otherwise not commercially available. Bootleg copies of material also released by the copyright holder are less common and are distinguishable from legal copies by their idiosyncratic packaging. Bootlegs don't replicate legal packaging, or they would become "pirates." Bootlegs supplement rather than substitute.

To the extent that online digital file-sharing makes available everything that exists in a digital format, it acts to distribute both supplements and substitutes, and in the latter sense does the same thing as do pirates. However, in so far as file-sharing networks do not charge for making copies they do not fulfill the legal criteria for being designated pirates, which is that their actions be commercially based; and because they do not seek to pass themselves off as selling on behalf of the copyright holder, neither are they engaged in identity theft, which pirates do when they sell items with forged holograms, replica packaging, trademarks, and other legal, technical, and/or cultural identification markers.

However, while copies are not for sale, the legal definition of piracy in most countries that have introduced into domestic legislation the conditions of the Trade Related Intellectual Property and Services treaty (TRIPS) (see below) also include provisions for defining piracy to include not only unauthorized copying for commercial gain, but also unauthorized copying intended to produce large-scale and intentional commercial damage. While this may be seen as primarily designed to prohibit a competitor flooding the market with free copies of another competitor's copyrighted material, it could be used to target large-scale up-loaders, individuals who make available large volumes of material for others to copy.

This is legally problematic, first because it is hard to prove that any individual up-loader's action directly contributed to any serious economic harm suffered by a copyright holder whose work was being made available. While the advent of file-sharing coincided with very large-scale declines in the overall volume and price of recorded music, this correlation is not a proven causal relationship, especially not at the level of individual actions. Second, when courts started convicting up-loaders for such acts as "piracy," up-loaders simply migrated from peer-to-peer networks to peer-to-peer torrent services, which did not require downloading from any one identifiable individual.

Isabella Alexander (2007) compares lobby group rhetoric around the UK's 2006 Gowers' Review of Intellectual Property and that within the 1906 Copyright Act. In both cases "piracy" was associated with the supposed threat of illegal migrants from Eastern Europe, people trafficking, exploitation of children, sedition/terrorism, and economic ruin. In both cases those labeled "pirates" actively embraced the term. However, it should be noted that those targeted in 1906 were commercial hawkers of sheet music, not free-sharers. They were "pirates," legally speaking. The Gowers' review remained resistant to further extensions of copyright, even hinting at the need to extend legal protection to forms of personal sharing. These recommendations were however set aside in the subsequent, rhetorically forceful, substantively limited, and highly contested, UK Digital Economy Act 2010 (Dutton 2010).

HOLLYWOOD HATES PIRATES
UNLESS THEY'RE JOHNNY DEPP!

The most famous website actively, and in some senses successfully, targeted for "piracy" is The Pirate Bay, a bit torrent service. Torrent services eliminate the need for a one-to-one relationship between one up-loader and one down-loader. The down-loader instead downloads from a torrent of up-loaders, compiling a complete copy from many sources. This means there is no single legally liable source, and pursuing individual downloaders is the worst case scenario for copyright enforcers as it is like catching air with a butterfly net.

What is of interest here is the fact that *The Pirate Bay* (TPB) chose to embrace the term pirate despite disputing almost everything else being claimed by the recording and film industry lobbies about online sharing. Even in the act of being prosecuted, and in being sentenced to prison sentences, TPB's designers rejected the claim that they were commercially benefiting from unlawful copying even as they still celebrated the pirate label that their prosecutors wanted to legally pin on them. TPB's legal defense, of only exchanging users' requests to locate others with material they wanted to copy, rather than actually trafficking the infringing material itself (which is what the original Napster had done and was closed down for doing), was tantamount to the claim that they were not "pirates" in the legal sense. This was, in its own terms, correct. However, TPB had actively promoted their site as a vehicle for copyright infringement, and had actively advocated such violation, and this, combined with commercial gain from advertising revenues, allowed authorities to successfully prosecute them for actively promoting and directly profiting from commercial harm to mainstream record companies.

The success of the prosecution led to TPB moving its servers to other jurisdictions, and had the effect of further promoting the practice of copyright infringement as rebellious piracy rather than simply a way to save money. That those labeled by the authorities as "pirates" have been so happy to embrace the label, despite its dubious legal standing, is interesting. While TPB actively proclaimed their support for the violation of intellectual property rights, most file-sharers and the peer-to-peer/peers to peer services that support them actively avoid direct admission of such intentions, yet the label confers more positive than negative value in a culture where pirates are viewed more as playful heroes than as the selfish privateers (free-entrepreneurs) of the past and present high seas. The popularity of T-shirts carrying a skull and crossed electric guitar heads, or with TPBs signature galleon with mainsail bedecked with a scull morphed cassette and crossed bones, or even with the slogan "Internet Piracy is Killing the Recording Industry: And It's Fun!" highlight the cache of "rebel sell" (Heath and Potter 2004).

Just as Hollywood has romanticized the very pirate identity it also seeks to use as a pejorative label in its conflict with file-sharers; so the music industry, with its use of royalties rather than direct payment to artists sought to create a distance between the artist and the commercial production system which profits from the sale-ability of that artist's alleged authenticity. As Lee Marshall (2005) observes, the romantic mythology of the creative artist at one step removed from the instrumental machine that surrounded them enabled fan identification with the artist as "keeping it real," even as the relationship between artist and fan was being ruthlessly exploited.

The thing that separates the "artist" from the "jobbing musician for hire" is the system of royalties rather than wages. As royalties are paid at around 12 percent of net sales, and as the cost of production, promotion, and a host of other legal, management, and other expenses are recouped from royalties, most "artists" end up in debt to their record companies even when the remaining 88 percent of net sales produce profits for the labels they are signed to (David 2010). That many prominent recording artists actively advocate online file-sharing as record sales make so little contribution to artists' income, rather like Hollywood's moonlighting pirates, had the effect of further inverting the message recording and film industry lobby groups were seeking to achieve in their promotion of the pirate label. Once again pervasive does not equal persuasive.

So far we have noted the marked failure of a range of cultural strategies to reign in the free circulation of copyrighted materials on the Internet. In part the failure to enforce a particular interpretation of events, even as formal qualities of messages and labels have clearly spread widely, is in part down to the character of the medium itself. An editorial nexus through which powerful cultural players (such as the film and recording industries) can act to control the distribution and articulation of messages is absent. In such conditions lobbies have been unable to prevent their preferred readings of events being inverted. Stan Cohen's (1972) conception of "moral panic" has undergone numerous modifications over its forty-year history, not least in relation to broadcast and print media diversification (McRobbie and Thornton 1995). Yet, the observation that media diversification limits the power of moral entrepreneurs to control public perception of an issue, and hence the public's disposition towards "panic," a diversification that new media takes to a qualitatively new level, should be set against Cohen's original observation that public reactions are rarely as strong as media coverage invites. He was more interested in how moral panic media messages acted to warrant control agencies' reactions, a focus that Patry (2009) and others suggest continues to be legitimate. Legislative reactions have reflected panic messages irrespective of public belief or otherwise in the threat of "piracy." Yet, the attempt to bypass persuasion by legal prohibition may yield little success if the Internet presents no clearer legislative nexus by which to block sharers than it does an editorial one by which to control communication.

OWNING KNOWLEDGE: PHILOSOPHICAL AND HISTORICAL ORIGINS AND CURRENT INTERPRETATIONS

Copyright based intellectual property rights (IPRs) are those most threatened by the Internet's capacity for free distribution. Trademark forms of IPRs are also vulnerable, but are less significant. Global brands seek to evict "cyber-squatters" (Dyer-Witheford 2002) who register domain names that might be confused with corporate products. Corporations claim such web addresses should be theirs, to avoid confusing the public, even if others got there first. This rather inverts their typical assertions that ownership of creative expression should be enforced on a "first come first served" basis rather than on the basis of general social benefit. Trade secrets, such as the recipe for Kentucky Fried Chicken batter, are no doubt available online, but this seems to have ruffled few feathers.

Some pharmaceutical firms have claimed they are considering registering new drugs through copyrighting their chemical formulae, rather than patenting them (Dutfield 2008; Dutfield and Suthersanan 2005). Patent requires a demonstration of mechanism, utility, originality, and non-obviousness. Such public disclosure makes it easier for competitors in developing countries to "pirate" such innovations, and in the absence of strong enforcement this allows cheaper derivative drugs to enter the market, such as in the case of HIV inhibiting drugs which can be made at a fraction of the prices charged by patent-holding corporations (Light and Warburton 2005; May and Halbert 2005). Copyright is easier to register, has a longer duration (and is getting longer), and the level of evidence necessary to demonstrate infringement is lower—and getting lower (Lessig 2004; Vaidhyanathan 2003). The fact that most computer software is registered under copyright of creative expression rather than under patent of technical innovation does suggest at least the perceived advantage of one over the other. However, current troubles experienced by copyright holders in enforcing such rights, however easily acquired in principle, may make patent holders feel less envious.

In a knowledge economy, where the value of information inputs increase relative to physical inputs, barriers to market entry fall. This is most rapid in relation to copyright protected goods where the expression itself is what is being sold, while most patented products still tend to require a non-trivial level of physical manufacture. Networked computers enable every terminal to become a factory for the reproduction of creative expressions. Thereby marginal physical unit costs for such goods tend towards zero. Only contriving scarcity prevents the price of such goods also tending towards zero. Such scarcity can only be contrived through legal monopoly or technical inhibitions. It is for this reason that copyright issues around the Internet have become increasingly significant in recent years, with the former used to maintain a scarcity based exchange system inadvertently challenged by the latter.

The British Statute of Anne, in 1710, granted licenses to publishers in exchange for an obligation to uphold crown censorship, but was resisted by revolutionaries in the American War of Independence, leaving the emergent United States deeply hostile and suspicious of copyright. As the world's leading advocate of strong global copyright today, it is worth remembering that the United States did not fully recognize foreign copyright claims until the 1990s. Post-revolutionary France and the US tended towards an enlightenment belief in the value of knowledge as shared culture, whereas Britain tended to the view that creative expression was property—though the owner of that property shifted from publisher to author (at least in principle) in the 1830s (Marshall 2005). Just when the United States and Germany moved in the 1870s to allow companies to claim ownership over ideas generated by employees, the Dutch and the Swiss suspended IPRs in order to encourage the diffusion of innovation. At the same time *The Economist* magazine advocated the abolition of IPRs in the interests of growing international trade, while John Stuart Mill defended IPRs as natural rights, just as would be assumed for physical things.

Chris May and Susan Sell (2005) note the division between utilitarian and romantic justifications for property rights in ideas. Where the former emphasize the value of property rights in motivating the creative process, romanticism has come to be associated with the notion of a natural right of creative genius over ideas in parallel with John Locke's (1988) inalienable rights to life, liberty, and property. Yet this division fragments further on inspection. Utilitarian doctrine advocates the maximum advantage for the maximum number, balancing incentives to innovate with affordable access to subsequent benefits. Hence monopoly rights have limited duration, unlike rights in other forms of property. But there is no natural or necessary equilibrium as it is impossible to calculate objective measures of the different values of competing utilities.

Utilitarian principles are deployed to argue for everything from complete suspension of IPRs, if they are believed to stifle collaborative and developmental innovations (Shiva 1998), to their near perpetual extension if monopoly rents are believed to provide a strong foundation for future high cost research and development. Likewise, romantic writers, like William Wordsworth, initially rejected ownership of ideas, as creativity was said to flow through the artist from the wellspring of nature, community, or tradition. He only came to advocate copyright later in life on the premise that creativity was the product of individual genius (David 2006). Utilitarian and romantic principles can be applied one way or the other.

Historically, geographically, and intellectually divergent, and often contradictory, the foundations of today's IPRs framework, as it reaches towards some degree of global integration, should remind us of its contingent and fragile character. This is particularly important when confronted with questionable claims as to either its natural or its draconian character.

IS THERE A NEW GLOBAL INTELLECTUAL PROPERTY "REGIME"?

Given the fractured nature of the debate over IPRs in relation to foreign trade at the end of the nineteenth century, the emergence in 1883 and 1886 of the Paris and Berne treaties, dealing with technical (patentable) and creative (copyrightable) ideas respectively was highly significant (May 2007b), though the exclusion of the United States from the Berne treaty was perhaps more so. It refused to fully recognize copyright on creative works not physically manufactured in the United States up until the advent of the World Trade Organization and its TRIPS treaty. This shift indicates a changed attitude among US policy-makers after the Cold War to the view that the United States would benefit more from global regulation as a mature IPR gamekeeper than it would have done as a developing poacher.

Young nations, individuals, companies, and fields/genres tend to the view taken by the emerging US, that poaching from established players is their right and key to development. More established nations, individuals, companies, and fields/genres tend to the view taken by the United States, that property rights in ideas is their right and key to continued prosperity (David 2010: 56). This should not surprise anyone. What is interesting is the extent to which contending parties to disputes over such divergent rights are persuaded or compelled to conform to interests other than their own. During the Cold War the United States actively encouraged the development of the Asian Tiger economies through a relaxed attitude to their near universal disregard for Western IPRs. Since 1996, most developing countries have signed up to TRIPS, despite their vocal opposition to its one size fits all conception of IPRs (May 2004).

Chris May (2007b) suggests that the World Intellectual Property Organization (WIPO), an off-shoot of the Paris and Berne treaties, plays a significant role in the building of a global intellectual property rights regime. The World Trade Organization requires states to sign into domestic legislation their strong support for foreign IPRs on pain of powerful economic sanctions if they do not. In so doing the WTO has brought states together to legislate at a common baseline standard, at least on paper. WIPO, which is nominally affiliated to the United Nations, is however funded and staffed by the very states and companies with patents and copyright claims to be enforced. This is reflected in WIPO's strong claims regarding the common benefits of even stronger and more universal IPRs. It pursues a policy of ratcheting up from the WTO's baseline by a combination of lobbying, training, and coordinating between those it represents and the states it wishes to bring around to its point of view.

WIPO promotes the view that a strong IP regime is the best way for developing states to develop. This is on the premise that developed states and powerful corporations support such a regime and are said to represent the model for developing countries to emulate. WIPO claims its advocacy of a strong and universal IPR regime is compatible with its UN affiliate obligation to support the legitimate development goals of less well-off countries. Critics (May 2007b) point out that today's developed societies might support strong IP now, but that their development was in almost every case built upon the suspension of IPRs, especially those of developing rivals. The success of WTO and WIPO in shaping the current global IPR framework has led Brian Holmes (2003) to warn of an "immaterial imperialism." At one level such an order is coming into existence. However, at the level of free exchange on the Internet of supposedly copyright protected material by hundreds of millions of people worldwide, such imperialism remains relatively immaterial, at least in its consequences.

LEGAL GENEALOGY

Signed into law in 1998, the Digital Millennium Copyright Act (DMCA) fulfilled the United States' obligation under TRIPS to pass into domestic legislation the principles set out in the 1996 WIPO Copyright Treaty. The DMCA specifically targeted the Internet and technologies that enabled IP infringement online. Its most notable early target was the original Napster, which, having been established in 1999 was forced to cease trading in 2001 and declared bankruptcy in 2002. Under the conditions of the act, Napster was charged with contributory infringement for "trafficking" infringing files between sharers through its central server. Napster's defense, that it was not responsible for what users exchanged any more than a postal or telephone service, was rejected. The DMCA was drafted to make Internet technology providers liable for the uses to which their innovations were put. Napster's closure seemed to provide a decisive victory for copyright defenders. However, Napster's closure promoted services that allowed users to exchange materials and later to locate potential sharers without the need to direct information through the software provider's server. These were the first truly peer-to-peer forms of file-sharing. They lost Napster's legal Achilles heel: its direct mediation of peer-to-peer exchanges.

In 2003 and 2004 peer-to-peer file-sharing software providers Grokster and Morpheus successfully defended themselves on the basis that it was unlawful to prohibit a technology on the grounds that it had non-legal uses if it also had legal ones. They cited the principle of "dual use" which had been established in US law in the case of Sony versus the Motion Picture Association of America. In 1984 Sony successfully claimed that while their video recorders could be used to infringe copyright, the fact that they had legal applications meant that Sony was not responsible for what users chose to do with them, and that the state had no right to prohibit the sale of such record-ers. The principle of "dual use" stands in strong contrast to that of "staple [or predom-inant] use" proposed by Prasad and Agarwala (2008) whereby something is illegal if it is mainly used for illegal acts. These authors also propose the principle of "positive leg-islation" where the law defines what it is seeking to protect (in this case intellectual property) rather than the specifics of what it seeks to prohibit. While central to the strong wording of the DMCA and other post TRIPS legislation, the idea that law should prohibit anything not already defined as legal, or which has the potential to be used unlawfully, violates more fundamental legal principles, not least the idea that law regu-lates action rather than prescribing it.

In 2005 the US Supreme Court did find Morpheus and Grokster guilty of actively pro-moting unlawful use of their products, and for actively routing contacts between users through their servers. The principle of dual use was not rejected. Rather, the defendants were found guilty of actively promoting the unlawful use of their services. Grokster closed down; but Morpheus modified its promotional material, required users to tick a box indicating they understood that it was unlawful to exchange copyrighted material without permission, adding an indicator that Morpheus did not want to encourage such actions, and adopting underlying software that allowed users to find each other inde-pendently of the software provider. Again, legal prohibitions and restrictions had the effect of furthering the distributed character of peer-to-peer exchange rather than reducing it.

Failure to limit file-sharing through the targeting of software providers led content industry representatives to target individual uploaders, those making files available for others to download. In the United States tens of thousands of Internet users have been threatened with pre-court demands for large sums of money for alleged infringement. Internet service providers in the US have been largely compliant with copyright holders' demands for the real world identities of Internet users suspected of uploading.

While initially successful, this approach has been doubly limited. First, outside of the United States, Internet service providers have countered demands from copyright hold-ers to identify users with appeals to human rights legislation that protects both privacy and freedom of expression. Okechukwu Benjamin Vincents (2007) compares court interpretations of US (first amendment) and EU (Personal Data Directive) legislation in balancing privacy law and copyright enforcement. He concludes that US courts have been more prone to copyrights, whereas in the EU greater emphasis is placed on privacy rights through data protection.

Second, the development of torrent based downloading services no longer requires that a copy be made of any single uploaded file. Rather, downloaders compile a copy from a cloud of bits such that no one individual can be said to have provided a copy. It is not unlawful to provide a snippet online, just as it is not unlawful to photocopy less than 5 percent of a book in the library. By the time the UK Digital Economy Bill became law in 2010 its provisions regarding the requirement of Internet service providers to cooperate more fully with copyright holders in identifying up-loaders was already one step behind the technical reality. Robert Danay (2005) notes that invasion of privacy in the name of copyright protection, as allowed for in the 1988 UK copyright act, has been challenged successfully by reference to the privacy provisions of the 1998 Human Rights Act, which passed the European Convention on Human Rights into UK law. Provisions within the Digital Economy Bill to warrant invasions of privacy in the name of copyright protection have been similarly blunted. Initially the Act enabled 'bulk' requests (ten thousand identities per £350 application). However, within months, the High Court deemed such requests 'speculative lawyering', restricting applications to single individuals, choking off the practice (Wall 2014). ISPs also write to implicated users. Whilst 'cooperating' with rights holders, such letters may simply promote less visible infringement.

In Canada legislators have interpreted their requirement to accord with the 1996 WIPO Treaty in such a way that only exchanges that were contained fully within Canada's borders would be dealt with domestically (Leong and Saw 2007). This radically restricts the scope for realistic action as exchange networks flow across borders. The provisions of the European Union Human Rights Act severely limit the scope for hardline interpretations of copyright enforcement activities. Even in Sweden, where years of conflict over the interpretation of competing rights and protections ended with prison sentences for the founders of The Pirate Bay, the sentences have only had the effect of fostering a profusion of less publicity-seeking torrent services, and requiring TPB to relocate its servers to other countries.

Fair use exemptions that allow a US citizen to copy the contents of a CD onto an MP3 player for personal use while traveling are technically not allowed in the UK. Claims by leaders of the G8 in July 2008 (David 2010) that airport security would be rolling out scanners to check the contents of digital players for illegal downloads highlighted problems with any idea of a global IP regime at the level of digital music copying. Would UK airports delete contents from incoming US citizens' iPods that would have been legal when they got onto the plane, only to become illegal when they got off? As legal CDs are not encrypted anyway it would be impossible to tell whether material on a digital player was from a file-sharing site or burned from a CD.

Privacy issues would also have complicated matters. Would searching be indiscriminate and, if not, what selection criteria would be legitimate? The scheme never got past the sound bite stage. The attempt to look tough ended up making advocates of such digital surveillance look both silly and weak. Far from highlighting the potential of an integrated global IP regime, attempts to regulate the most globally integrated spaces (airports) came to highlight its opposite. The Internet continues to demonstrate the extent to which file-sharing networks are better integrated globally than are IPRs enforcement.

The above example illustrates how attempts to target MP3 players at airports because of their staple use as carriers of copyright infringing materials fell foul of assumptions about "fair use" and the realities of "dual use." There is an irony here, as it is assumed by many that US fair use law applies everywhere. "Law as myth" (Litman 1991) works in reverse. The very influence of global big business that Lessig (2004) rightly suggests is squeezing fair use by the letter of the law at home is accidentally promoting it in practice everywhere else.

TECHNICAL SHIFTS: DISTRIBUTION, ENCRYPTION, AND SURVEILLANCE

Does technology have consequences? Few today would suggest technology simply has effects on society, while the view that novel artifacts passively mirror the social conditions of their creation is almost as unpopular. Novel artifacts afford changes in the relative scope of different forms of action by different groups (Hutchby 2001). However, such groups may reconfigure themselves around newly afforded possibilities for alliance and opposition (Latour 2005). Existing social relationships and strategies of action will shape and continue to shape innovations and their uses even while being modified in the process (May 2002).

On the question of increasingly distributed networks, each new attempt to legislate file-sharing out of existence by targeting the network at its narrowest point had the effect of encouraging engineering solutions that bypassed the need for that particular bottleneck. If attempts to drive the cork back into the bottle at the narrowest point only encourage the dismantling of such bottlenecks, what was driving this counter pressure? In part this may be explained simply in terms of what Himanen (2001) calls "the hacker ethic," a geek aesthetic driven by the desire to simply push technology to its limits. Yet this does not explain the direction towards disclosure, when political hacktivism is as much concerned with preserving privacy as it is with releasing hidden information.

Castells' (1996) assertion that the digital infrastructure beneath the network capitalist mode of production has a technical mode of development that is relatively autonomous from the social relations of ownership and control that seek to harness them parallels Himanen's view. Yet, again, the suggestion of a relatively autonomous technical developmental process does not explain why technologies such as digital recording, compression, and circulation, initially developed for commercial purposes, should have then facilitated such a wholesale challenge to commercial imperatives, while commercial responses have, for all their resources, seemed relatively powerless.

The counterfactual example to file-sharing, that of social networking, which also began in 1999, to this day continues to operate using central servers through which users interact with each other. It is not by any technical necessity, a logic of network distribution, that file-sharing came to adopt increasingly distributed architectural forms. Commercially, a central server model is far more attractive as it makes it easier to stream advertising to users. This is the common source of income for social networking sites, as it was for the original Napster, and for The Pirate Bay tracker site. That file-sharing networks use increasingly distributed forms is simply because any hub becomes a legal target. The Internet facilitates such distribution, while limiting the capacity of authorities to restrict the flow of exchanges. This changed the balance of possible actions, but does not determine choices.

That the Internet changes the balance of possibilities between those seeking to maintain scarcity in informational goods and those seeking to share that information suggests that it does have an effect. Encryption and surveillance, taken individually when used by both sides in file-sharing disputes or when taken together when used in opposition to one another by conflicting parties, appear to have no effects as they cancel themselves out. The ability to encrypt a file, disc, or network is the ability to prevent surveillance, and the ability to surveil is the ability to get past what encryption might be set in place to prevent such surveillance. As such, surveillance and encryption are two sides of the same communications coin.

Technical strategies to protect digital rights have taken both forms: strong digital rights management refers to the ability to encrypt securely while weak digital rights management refers to the ability to deploy surveillance strategies to detect those engaged in forms of infringement (May 2007a). The other side of the coin is the attempt by those participating in online file-sharing networks to conceal the content of what they are sharing by means of encryption, and the attempt to use counter surveillance to identify and avoid services designed to identity and entrap file-sharers. Both sides in the dispute over filesharing have made bold claims as to their abilities to encrypt what they seek to distribute (whether commercially or by sharing networks) and to identify those they wish to either catch or avoid being caught by.

On the encryption side of the equation, claims on both sides have been exaggerated. For reasons of market competition, no encryption format was agreed for the release of CDs as this would have required a consensus over the choice of de-encryption to be fitted on all CD players. In the 1980s record companies did not agree any common format, either among themselves or with the manufacturers of players. At the time there was no large-scale threat to bring players together. As such the billions of CDs sold since 1982 were and remain unencrypted.

By the time DVDs were released encryption formats were agreed, but these were almost immediately broken and the necessary codes circulated widely (David and Kirkhope 2006). Attempts to prosecute the hacker responsible failed on the grounds that the code was itself a mathematical formula that was not itself open to copyright protection. The same hacker, Jon Johansen, was also responsible for the repeated hacking of the Fair Play encryption used to offer protection to copyright holders by Apple when it introduced its iTunes downloading service. From 2008 Apple abandoned its attempt to encrypt iTunes on the pretext that such efforts were useless, but also because Apple felt such a requirement inhibited iTunes market development when faced with competition from unencrypted CDs sales and file-sharing alternatives as sources of material to download onto MP3/4 players.

Such an inability to maintain encryption demonstrates the ability of open-source/hacker software communities to outstrip their commercial research rivals. However, claims by The Pirate Bay to be able to roll out a totally encrypted darknet through which sharers could exchange without fear of being caught is also technical exaggeration.

Sheer volume of traffic offers the greatest anonymity to even the best protected sharer, even if various additional technical measures can also significantly reduce the chance of being caught.

Even if a totally robust form of encryption were to be developed it would only offer as much protection to those seeking to restrict access for commercial purposes as it would to sharers who could then use the same technology to share with impunity, even if it would require some rather old-fashioned recording techniques to make initial copies from the copyright holder's encrypted version onto the sharer's version (though it may not have to be as crude as just holding a microphone next to a loudspeaker).

The double-edged character of surveillance is similar. Proxies acting for copyright holders trawl the Internet looking for IP addresses that appear to be exchanging large volumes of material, or pose as sharers looking to download material so as to identify users who are making material available. Sharers, in return, can draw upon a range of counter-surveillance software in order to steer themselves away from sites engaged in what appears to be trawling behavior, or which are identified as proxies for copyright enforcers. Banerjee et al. (2006) found file-sharers could reduce their chances of being identified many hundred fold by using counter-surveillance techniques. The use of torrent services makes the identification of participants within networks increasingly meaningless anyway.

The asymmetrical architecture of the Internet makes circulation easier than regulation. Encryption and surveillance tend to cancel themselves out. May (2007a) is right to suggest that threats and ignorance may deter non-natives of the network age, but such a demographic is shrinking and of limited commercial value. May parallels Lessig (2004) in suggesting that technical barriers to action will enforce, extend, and even replace legal and culturally agreed norms, substituting debate over balance with mechanical and non-negotiable blocks. While Lessig's concern for the replacement of legal freedoms by technical forces reflects a legitimate concern over the rise of a "culture of permission" relative to a "free culture," it is worth noting that technical systems have proved no less "permissive" than courts and legislatures in formally democratic societies (David and Kirkhope 2006; see also Mayer-Schönberger 2008).

NEW TIMELESS TIME—LIVE-STREAMING NOW!

For Manuel Castells (1996), the development of network infrastructure has forced and facilitated the development of network capitalism. His attention is focused upon the rise of the network enterprise and its part in what he calls "capitalist perestroika." "Timeless time" (the instantaneous quality of action at a distance enabled by digital communications); "the space of flows" (the increased mediation of place by mobility); and "real virtuality" (the growing significance of mediated/disembodied experience), Castells suggests characterize the network society, and it is the network capitalist enterprise he believes that has best adapted to this new reality (1996, 2009). This focus of attention upon corporate adaptation tends to overlook limits, challenges, and alternatives.

The most recent manifestation of online sharing is live-streaming. This extends the dynamic of distribution observed in the conflict between file-sharers and copyright defenders discussed above, but takes distribution into the realm of timeless time. File-sharers challenged centralized monopoly controls with de-centralized forms, which then, when threatened, shifted to increasingly distributed forms. Live-streaming stations allow users to stream whatever they have access to via a channel made available by the station. As such, this is particularly good for the streaming of live events, such as sporting events and concerts. Anything that is being broadcast in one location can be instantly re-routed and made available everywhere. Commercial television channels are often required not to air events live in the country where they are being staged as direct competition between ticket sales and television access will depress ticket prices. However, the same companies often sell live broadcast rights into foreign markets. Live-streaming simply enables anyone in that other location to re-broadcast the programme on the Internet. It is then free to watch anywhere in the world.

Attempts to close down live-streaming sites have run into the problem of timeless time. The English Premier League and Football Association (EPL and FA) have sought to prevent the live-streaming channel Justin.TV facilitating the streaming of live EPL games, as they see this as a threat not only to gate receipts but also to the future of very lucrative arrangements for commercial television rights. Setanta, one of the two broadcast rights holders for EPL matches, declared bankruptcy in 2009. This was in large part the result of its failure to gain enough subscribers to repay the cost of buying the broadcast rights in the first place. It had overestimated audience numbers and their willingness to pay. The existence of free alternatives broadcast at the time matches were actually being played is likely to have been significant in this (Birmingham and David 2011; David 2011).

Justin.TV has offered to fully cooperate with the FA and EPL. As soon as they are notified of any perceived infringement of copyright on any one of the thousands of channels made available through its hub, Justin.TV promise to investigate and act appropriately. Of course this takes time. Unlike early versions of Napster, Grokster, Morpheus, The Pirate Bay, and others, Justin.TV actively offers to comply with the law, but it is in the character of timeless time across the network that live events are streamed instantly, while legal and administrative attempts to identify and switch them off are less instantaneous, and only come into effect after the event has stopped and the stream terminated anyway.

Having fueled rampant player fee/salary inflation since 1992, growth in digital television rights revenues has created conditions where half of the EPL clubs are technically insolvent, even as gate and season ticket prices have spiraled with most subscription matches not broadcast live domestically. The bankruptcy of digital subscription sports channel Setanta in 2009, when an escalation in use of live-streaming channels significantly contributed to Setanta's failure to meet expected and sufficient subscriber growth, may best be described as digital television's Napster moment.

A WIDER SPACE OF FLOWS—VIRTUAL PROXY NETWORK/SERVERS

Digital networks increase the impact of mediations and mobility in the composition and conduct of life in any given place, undermining what boundaries particular places might have to maintain a degree of self-governance and autonomy. The paradigmatic illustration for Castells is the networked corporation and its ability to evade the regulative power of particular jurisdictions while able to exert pressure on less mobile actors to comply with its strategic interests. While certainly important, what has been highlighted above is that such network corporations are themselves outflanked by sharer networks with even greater scope to deterritorialize in the face of attempts to pin them down.

Many of the tools that enable such flows were developed for business by business, to enable greater mobility and distributed forms of production. Digital storage, processing, and compression standards were all developed to allow commercial production to be better integrated even while more easily distributed (David 2010). Protocols for Internet and web communication were developed by a combination of state, academic, and commercial bodies. Yet these same technologies have been inverted just as effectively against their original intentions to create a space of flows that is more like glasnost (free communication) and perestroika (economic reconstruction) from below than Castells' "capitalist perestroika." Global knowledge-based enterprises (in music, computing, film, television, agribusiness, and pharmaceuticals) retain highly bureaucratic and hierarchical characteristics, and depend upon the maintenance of monopoly controls over knowledge (anti-glasnost) and over its application (anti-perestroika). They are not the lithe and mercurial spirits of the ideal typical "network enterprise." For this we are better advised to look at their challengers from below.

Controversies over virtual proxy networks/servers (VPNSs) illustrate the inversion of Castells' conception of the space of flows in challenging network capitalism. Initially developed to allow business travelers to access from abroad services that were restricted to apply within national firewalls, VPNSs allow someone in one country to log onto a server in another and thereby pass themselves off as being in that second country, thereby being able to access material that would otherwise not be available to them. While initially developed for business, VPNSs have become crucial vehicles for those seeking to access and communicate information from within repressive regimes and for those seeking to access information and services restricted to within particular jurisdictions. As proxy services proliferate rapidly, because they have legal as well as infringing uses, and because most states support their use against regimes they disapprove of and only disapprove of their use against their regulative frameworks, attempts to limit VPNSs remains localized.

REAL VIRTUALITY: THE ECONOMICS
OF POST-SCARCITY, OPEN ACCESS,
AND GREATER REWARDS

The new economy of sharing online has led to artists receiving greater rewards than ever before by means of a curious twist in what Castells refers to as real virtuality, the increasing impact of virtual relationships in the formation of "real world" identities, interests, and activities. Contrary to what we might expect in conditions of timeless time and the new space of flows, the increasing free availability of informational goods online is having the effect of increasing the demand for live performance in the arena of performing arts at least. Here, the possibility of post-scarcity at the level of information itself seems to have led to increased competition for access to what remains particular and limited, that is, presence at "unique" performances. Money that would have been spent on recordings appears to be redirected to the same performer, only more directly, as the proportion of revenues that go to the performer is greater from live performance than it is for recording. As material valuation of live performance increases relative to recording, so aesthetic valuation of the creativity of the unique live performance relative to that associated with recording increases (David 2010: 141–2).

Alan Krueger (2004; and Krueger and Connolly 2006) neatly confirms the validity of the singer David Bowie's view that the future of music lies in performance not recording, and that free distribution is the best thing that ever happened to musicians. Krueger uses Pollstar data to identify total ticket sales and their prices to calculate overall live performance revenues for artists in the US in years before and just after the millennium. Taking inflation into account, overall revenues remained flat until a small spike in 1996, with rapid and sustained increases from 1999; 1996 saw relatively cheap CD burners while 1999 saw the advent of filesharing, and Krueger concludes that the decline of parallel competition between recordings and live performance has migrated spending from one to the other.

The universal availability of recordings has not hurt artists. Rather, their overall incomes have increased. Concert ticket prices have risen many fold since the advent of file-sharing. In addition, concert halls, new arenas, stadiums, and festival venues have grown in response to increased demand. Free circulation of recorded music offers no opportunity cost, and, as good advertising, promotes music-related spending. Revenues increase, costs fall, and the proportion going to artists rises. Record companies appear economic and promotional impediments. Their traditional five functions of production, manufacture, distribution, promotion, and rights management have all been undercut (David 2010: 130–41). Networks of free content and publicity also offer opportunities for new forms of non-copyright based capitalist exploitation. Free content and the streaming of adverts made Rupert Murdoch's purchase of MySpace very profitable. Paralleling live music's revival, cinema attendance has grown since the 1984 Sony ruling.

Digital multiplexes combine choice with something akin to the "being their together" of going out to a live concert.

Conclusions

In linking file-sharing and piracy, copyright defenders have added rebel cool to the practice. Philosophical, jurisdictional, and interpretational differences in relation to other rights have stifled legal attempts to stop it. Earlier legal victories only promoted more distributed, and thereby less legally targetable, systems of sharing. Surveillance and encryption cancel themselves out. Cultural, legal, and technical attempts to prevent Internet sharing have failed. The Internet makes every computer an infinite copying machine and one hard to disconnect from every other. Maintaining scarcity, and hence price, becomes problematic. Copyright and bypassing it are not new. The relative importance of intellectual relative to physical property in an informational economy and the ease by which such intellectual property rights can be bypassed are new. The mercurial affordances of the Internet enabled capitalist enterprises to deterritorialize and hence limit the regulative force of welfare taxing nation-states. The outmaneuvering of states, and competitors, by more flexible network enterprises, is what Castells calls "capitalist perestroika." Yet capitalist enterprises built on intellectual property monopolies cannot abandon central and hierarchical control. Channeling information and payment through the nexus of their business remain essential, whether by technical requirement (limiting distribution by encryption and surveillance), legal compulsion (through copyright enforcement), or cultural persuasion (by means of editorial control). Peer-to-peer networks limit the force of all three regulative strategies. Timeless time (live-streaming), the space of flows (file-sharing and VPNSs), and real virtuality (as with the rebirth of live performance, and the growth of cinema attendance) represent perestroika from below, challenging the assumption that creativity requires scarcity. The music industry has been hit first and hardest by online sharing, and shows the clearest signs of successful adaptation, even if the traditional record company may not survive. Later manifestations of digital capitalist perestroika, such as subscription based sports television, are beginning to witness online sharing challenges. Newspapers, academic, and non-academic publishing, as well as computer gaming, face similar challenges to "business as usual." The lesson from the music industry is to offer something that people will pay for even when they can get the informational content for free.

References

Alexander, I. (2007). "Criminalizing Copyright: A Story of Publishers, Pirates and Pieces of Eight," *Cambridge Law Journal*, 66(3): 625–6.

Bagchi, J. (2003). "File-Sharing and Piracy Linked to Terrorism?" *Kuro5hin: technology and culture, from the trenches*, March 15. Available at <http://www.kuro5hin.org/story/2003/3/14/234939/956>. Accessed August 6, 2008.

Banerjee, A., Faloutsos, M., and Bhuyan, L. N. (2006). "P2P: Is Big Brother Watching You? Technical Report." Available at <http://static.cs.ucr.edu/store/techreports/UCR-CS-2006-06201.pdf>. Accessed June 20, 2012.

Birmingham, J. and David, M. (2011). "Live-Streaming: Will Football Fans Continue to be More Law Abiding than Music Fans?," *Sport in Society*, 14(1): 69–80.

BPI (British Recorded Music Industry) (2008). *More than the Music*, London: BPI. Available at <http://www.bpi.co.uk/music-business/article/music-social-responsibility.aspx>. Accessed June 20, 2012.

Castells, M. (1996). *The Rise of the Network Society*, Oxford: Blackwell.

——(2000). "Materials for an Exploratory Theory of the Network Society," *British Journal of Sociology*, 51(1): 5–24.

——(2009). *Communication Power*, Oxford: Oxford University Press.

Cohen, S. (1972). *Folk Devils and Moral Panics*, London: MacGibbon and Kee.

Danay, R. (2005). "Copyright vs. Free Expression: The Case of Peer-to-Peer File-Sharing of Music in the United Kingdom," *Yale Journal of Law and Technology*, 8: 32–62.

David, M. (2006). "Romanticism, Creativity and Copyright: Visions and Nightmares," *European Journal of Social Theory*, 9(3): 425–33.

——(2010). *Peer to Peer and the Music Industry: The Criminalization of Sharing*, London: Sage.

——(2011). "Music Lessons: Football Finance and Live Streaming," *Journal of Policy Research*, 3(1): 95–8.

——and Kirkhope, J. (2006). "The Impossibility of Technical Security: Intellectual Property and the Paradox of Informational Capitalism," in M. Lacy and P. Witkin (eds). *Global Politics in an Information Age*, Manchester: Manchester University Press, pp. 80–95.

Dutfield, G. (2008). "Delivering Drugs to the Poor: Will the TRIPS Amendment Help?," *American Journal of Law and Medicine*, 34(2–3): 107–24.

——and Suthersanan, U. (2005). "DNA Music: Intellectual Property and the Law of Unintended Consequences," *Science Studies*, 18(1): 5–29.

Dutton, W. (2010). "Aiming at Copyright Infringers and Hitting the Digital Economy," *Prometheus*, 28(4): 385–8.

Dyer-Witheford, N. (2002). "E-Capital and the Many-Headed Hydra," in G. Elmer (ed.). *Critical Perspectives on the Internet*, Boulder, CO: Rowman and Littlefield, pp. 129–64.

Film Education (2012). "Switched On: Learning in ICT." Available at <http://www.filmeducation.org/switchedon/>. Accessed July 30, 2012.

Gowers, A. (2006). "Gowers' Review of Intellectual Property," The Stationery Office. Available at <http://www.official-documents.gov.uk/document/other/0118404830/0118404830.asp>. Accessed June 20, 2012.

Heath, J. and Potter, A. (2004). *The Rebel Sell*, Mankato MN: Capstone Press.

Himanen, P. (2001). *The Hacker Ethic and the Spirit of the Information Age*, London: Secker and Warburg.

Holmes, B. (2003). "The Emperor's Sword: Art under WIPO." World-Information.Org, December 2003. Available at <http://world-information.org/wio/readme/992007035/1078488424>. Accessed September 1, 2008.

Hutchby, I. (2001). *Conversation and Technology*, Cambridge: Polity.

Krueger, A. (2004). "The Economics of Real Superstars: The Market for Rock Concerts in the Material World," Industrial Relations Sections Working Paper no. 484, Princeton University. Available at <http://dataspace.princeton.edu/jspui/handle/88435/dsp016108vb25k>. Accessed October 1, 2008.

—— and Connolly, M. (2006). "Rockonomics: The Economics of Popular Music," in V. Ginsberg and D. Throsby (eds). *Handbook of the Economics of Art and Culture*, Amsterdam: North-Holland, pp. 667–720.

Kerr, O. (2002). "A Lukewarm Defence of the Digital Millennium Copyright Act," in A. Thierer and C. Crews (eds). *Copyfights*, Washington, DC: Cato, pp. 163–70.

Latour, B. (2005). *Reshaping the Social*, Oxford: Oxford University Press.

Leong, S. and Saw, C. (2007). "Copyright Infringement in a Borderless World—Does Territoriality Matter? Society of Composers, Authors and Music Publishers of Canada v Canadian Association of Internet Providers [2004] 2 SCR 427," *International Journal of Law and Information Technology*, 15(1): 38–53.

Lessig, L. (2004). *Free Culture*, New York: The Penguin Press.

Liebowitz, S. (2006). "File-Sharing: Creative Destruction or just Plain Destruction?," Center for the Analysis of Property Rights. Working Paper No. 04–03. Available at <http://papers.ssrn.com/sol3/papers.cfm?abstract_id=646943>. Accessed April 19, 2011.

Light, D. and Warburton, R. (2005). "Extraordinary Claims Require Extraordinary Evidence," *Journal of Health Economics*, 24(5): 1030–3.

Litman, J. (1991), "Copyright as Myth," *Pittsburg Law Review*, 53(1): 235–49.

Locke, J. (1988). *Two Treatises of Government*, Cambridge: Cambridge University Press.

McRobbie, Angela and Thornton, Sarah (1995). "Rethinking Moral Panic for Multi-Mediated Social Worlds," *British Journal of Sociology*, 46(4): 559–74.

Marshall, L. (2005). *Bootlegging*, London: Sage.

May, C. (2002). *The Information Society*, Cambridge: Polity.

—— (2004). "Cosmopolitan Legalism Meets 'Thin Community': Problems in the Global Governance of Intellectual Property," *Government and Opposition*, 39(3): 393–422.

—— (2007a). *Digital Rights Management*, Oxford: Chandos.

—— (2007b). *The World Intellectual Property Organisation*, London: Routledge.

—— and Halbert, D. (2005). "AIDS, Pharmaceutical Patents and the African State: Reorienting the Global Governance of Intellectual Property," in A. Petterson (ed.). *The African State and the AIDS Crisis*, Burlington: Ashgate, pp. 195–217.

May, C. and Sell, S. (2005). *Intellectual Property Rights*, Boulder, CO: Lynne Rienner Publishers.

Mayer-Schönberger, V. (2008). "Demystifying Lessig," *Winsconsin Law Review*, 2008(4): 713–46.

Patry, William (2009). *Moral Panics and the Copyright Wars*, Oxford: Oxford University Press.

Poster, M. (2006). *Information Please*, Durham NC: Duke University Press.

Prasad, A. and Agarwala, A. (2008). "Whodunit! Assessing Copyright Liability in Cyburbia: Positing Solutions to Curb the Menace of Copyrighted 'File-Sharing' Culture," *Journal of International Commercial Law and Technology*, 3(1): 1–12.

Shiva, V. (1998). *Biopiracy*, London: Green Books.

Vaidhyanathan, S. (2003). *Copyrights and Copywrongs*, New York: New York University Press.

Valenti, J. (2004). "Testimony of Jack Valenti President and CEO Motion Picture Association of America, Before the Committee on Foreign Relations, United States of America," June 9. Available at <http://foreign.senate.gov/testimony/2004/ValentiTestimony040609.pdf>. Accessed August 1, 2008.

Vincents, O. B. (2007). "When Rights Clash Online: The Tracking of P2p Copyright Infringements Vs. the EC Personal Data Directive," *International Journal of Law and Information Technology*, 15(3): 270–96.

Wall, D. (2007). *Cybercrime*, Cambridge: Polity.

—— (2014: forthcoming). "Copyright trolling and the policing of intellectual property in the shadow of law," in M. David and D. Halbert (eds.), *Sage Handbook of Intellectual Property*, London: Sage.

Yar, M. (2006). *Cybercrime and Society*, London: Sage.

CHAPTER 23

PRIVACY AND SURVEILLANCE: THE MULTIDISCIPLINARY LITERATURE ON THE CAPTURE, USE, AND DISCLOSURE OF PERSONAL INFORMATION IN CYBERSPACE

COLIN J. BENNETT AND CHRISTOPHER PARSONS

INTRODUCTION

THE governance of privacy now comprises a large and growing "issue network" of private and public sector actors at domestic and international levels, as well as a range of national and international policy instruments (Bennett and Raab 2006). The protection of personal data has also assumed a place as a critical trade-related question to be resolved within the interplay of broader forces and interests in the international information economy (Newman 2008). The ranges of issues associated with the capture, processing, and dissemination of personally identifiable information are recognized as established policy sectors in every advanced industrial state and in many emerging economies as well.

There is no question that the contemporary prominence of the issues is attributable in large measure to the explosive impact of digitally mediated communications systems which extend the risks to privacy and the potential for ubiquitous and routine surveillance (Deibert and Rohozinski 2010; Lyon 2007; Solove 2007). To what extent, in what ways and to whom, do individuals actually surrender their "personal" information when they surf, search, blog, email, and network has been extremely controversial for over 20 years. A series of privacy disputes about governmental plans and corporate proposals have shaped the profile of the privacy issue, the experience of privacy advocates and regulators, and the nature of the Internet itself. Issues such as encryption policy, identification of processor chips, identity management systems, behavioral advertising, retention of search data, and data breaches have raised highly technical questions to levels of political and corporate controversy and intense media attention (Bennett 2008: ch. 5).

Internet privacy is not just another policy "issue" to be resolved and balanced according to the prevailing preferences of dominant political actors. Instead, questions associated with this issue strike to the heart of the medium itself: Is the prevailing assumption of the Internet one of surveillance or one of privacy? Do we need an entirely different set of assumptions for analyzing and understanding the capture and processing of personal data on the Internet? Can the language of privacy and "data protection" policies sufficiently address the range of privacy issues encountered in our globalized, networked, and digitized environment? Do individuals even believe that they should be allowed to control the circulation of their personal information, or should they behave as if they "have zero privacy anyway, and get over it," as Scott McNeally, Chairman of Sun Microsystems, once asserted?

While of momentous importance to the future of the Internet, these questions are also of extraordinary technical complexity. The circumstances under which "others" might monitor our online behavior depend on a complicated set of conditions relating to personal behavior, technical defaults, fluctuating corporate motivations and policies, as well as international and domestic legal provisions. The Internet confuses many traditional processes of identification along with the very nature of personally identifiable information itself. "Others" may not need to know whether we are Colin Bennett or Christopher Parsons to "know" what we are doing online, and to manipulate, profile, match, and transfer that information to remotely accessible databases. This raises the possibility that the Internet could be a surveillance medium and yet beyond the regulatory capacity of privacy and data protection law.

Most social scientists would agree that meaningful analyses of social problems like privacy necessitate broad conceptions of technology that comprise not just the "apparatus," but also the whole variety of associated social and organizational practices. Technologies are not mere aids to human activity: they constitute powerful forces that reshape human activity and its meaning (Winner 1989). Analyses must transcend causes and effects and investigate how technologies become deeply insinuated into people's perceptions, thoughts, and behavior. This approach is essential given the Internet's characteristics of being ubiquitous, distributed and mobile, and as a technical apparatus that can be embedded in material objects through the "Internet of things." Individuals no longer need to "go online" to be affected by the digital processes coursing along the Internet. Thus, the details of technological form and architecture affect society while simultaneously embodying political qualities and consequences. One role for social scientists, therefore, is to try to understand the "valence" of the Internet—the structural configurations that lead towards certain values over others.

What does academic research tell us about these issues? We first consider the broad question of how the Internet has, and has not, influenced the interdisciplinary literature on surveillance studies. What does this literature tell us about how the Internet has changed the nature of personal surveillance? Next, we consider the relationship between key structures of the Internet and the literatures on privacy and surveillance. How have the hardware devices and software code guiding the pulsations of packets across the Internet been affected by the conflicting demands for privacy and surveillance? Third, what does the literature say about risk and the perception of risk? Has the Internet reshaped perceptions of individual and collective risk? Are the privacy risks and harms in the online world qualitatively and quantitatively different from those in the offline world? Finally, we turn to the literature on the role of international, legal, self-regulatory, and technological policy instruments in protecting personal information online. How have the policy solutions been adapted to these new conditions, and with what effect?

"The Internet" and surveillance studies

Although these complex issues tend to get framed in terms of the language and policies of "privacy," there are many scholars who insist that these questions must be conceived on a broader scale, and particularly in terms of the discourse and politics of "surveillance" (Lyon 2001; Haggerty and Ericson 2006). "Privacy" and all that it entails is argued to be too narrow, overly grounded on liberal assumptions about subjectivity and human rights, insufficiently sensitive to the collective and discriminatory aspects of surveillance, inordinately embroiled in spatial metaphors about "invasion" and "intrusion," and too focused on the harm to individuals (Bennett 2011). As a concept, and as a way to frame the various global challenges encountered within "surveillance societies," privacy can never capture the broader social and institutional harms resulting from the persistent observation of our actions, movements, preferences, and behaviors. Thus, privacy is not, and can never be, the "antidote to surveillance" (Stalder 2002). The advent of the Internet has occurred within a context of deepening concern about the level and nature of surveillance, which is rendering our lives, activities, movements, and behaviors increasingly transparent to a growing number of individuals and organizations. In the popular mind "surveillance" implies espionage or video monitoring. In scholarly circles, however, it is often regarded as a broader and multi-directional phenomenon that structures relations between individuals and organizations, and between individuals and individuals. According to Lyon, it comprises "any collection and processing of personal data, whether identifiable or not, for the purposes of influencing or managing those whose data have been garnered" (2001: 2).

For many scholars, surveillance has been essential to the nation-state's development, to global capitalism, and to de-centered forms of disciplinary power and "governmentalities" inherent to modern society. The phenomenon is central to the sociological debates about the nature of modernity and post-modernity, and generates significant disputes over concepts, theory and method (Wood 2009). These scholars have recognized for some time that contemporary surveillance cannot be accurately captured by metaphors offered by Orwell's "Big Brother" or Foucault's "panopticon" because the networked information environment enables diffuse and elusive patterns of surveillance that erode traditional institutional and functional distinctions and hierarchies (Haggerty and Ericson 2006). Today we are faced with porous and less discrete systems that compose a "surveillant assemblage." This assemblage operates by abstracting human bodies from their territorial settings, and separating them into a series of discrete flows. These flows are then reassembled in different locations as discrete and virtual "data doubles" (Haggerty and Ericson 2000: 605), leading to a progressive "disappearance of disappearance" (ibid. 619).

The literature often paints a picture of a vulnerable subject who engages in typical activities of modern societies—checking into a hotel, using a credit card, booking an airline ticket, or surfing the net—who unknowingly leaves traces of data behind. Surveillance is now about the "monitoring of everyday life" (Lyon 2001): who we are, what we are doing, and where we are doing it. Everybody surrenders personal information for a range of perceived benefits. Sometimes that surrender is voluntary or transparent; sometimes it is secretive or coercive. The point is that one does not have to be a "suspect" any more to be a subject of surveillance.

Surveillance is also global in nature and therefore analyzed as a central feature and condition of globalization (Zureik and Salter 2005). With the rise of transnational corporations that employ private and public international networks, as well as the advent of "cloud computing," surveillance becomes a process that might originate from anywhere. Hence the capacities of any one jurisdiction or organization to regulate the flows of personal data are inescapably linked with the actions of public and private organizations operating beyond their borders.

These trends are accompanied by more general pressures towards securitization, a process whereby more issues, problems, behaviors, and phenomena get defined in "security" terms and subjected to the "protectionist reflex" (Beck 1998). If an issue is successfully securitized it is possible to legitimize extraordinary means to solve the perceived problem(s), with the corollary that the issue becomes an inappropriate topic for critical debate or resistance (Buzan et al. 1998). In this context, the particular dynamics of the attacks of September 11, 2001 (9/11) have boosted the national and international legal mechanisms that legitimate practices such as the monitoring of online communications and the retention of communications traffic data (Lyon 2003; Monahan 2010).

The development and growth of the Internet are universally acknowledged as both a cause, and an effect, of these larger trends. The nature of the Internet is entirely consistent with the metaphor of the "surveillant assemblage." Personal information is routinely captured on the Internet. The flows are increasingly remote and global. And Internet communications and activities have progressively been defined as a matter of risk assessment and securitization. On the other hand, there is a striking paucity of analysis of the actual processes of information capture and processing on the Internet within the surveillance literature. Most scholars of surveillance studies tend not to be technically astute or sensitive to the complexities of technical standards and protocols, the distinctions between the various forms of "cookie" technology, the sources of spyware, the uses of deep packet inspection by providers, the distinction between synchronous and asynchronous encryption and secure socket layers (SSL), and so on. Generalizations about the Internet as a surveillance medium tend, therefore, to be quite metaphorical. This conclusion is supported by the indexes of some of the most prominent, and recent, surveillance studies collections, in which there are remarkably few explicit references to the Internet and to the phenomenon of cyber-surveillance (e.g. Zureik and Salter 2005; Haggerty and Ericson 2006; Monahan 2006; Lyon 2007).

This suggests that most authors regard the Internet as a pervasive and integrating communication medium that may connect with existing social activities. Internet surveillance tends to be framed in terms of traditional institutions and practices: monitoring email in the workplace; controlling Internet activity in schools; integrating online applications with electronic health records; targeted marketing and advertising; and capturing online communications for national and international law enforcement. These issues generate distinctive sets of privacy problems, not because of the Internet, but because of the unique sets of questions raised by different information sensitivities and institutional contexts (Nissenbaum 2009). But are there quite separate surveillance practices that occur on the Internet, and nowhere else? We must look to literature from other disciplines to find out.

PRIVACY, SURVEILLANCE, AND THE INFRASTRUCTURE OF THE INTERNET

In examining the literature on the relationship between privacy, surveillance, and Internet infrastructure, we consider two central research questions. How does the Internet's actual infrastructure integrate with advertising, government surveillance, and the various techniques of control? How has the visualized Web, the domain for search and online commerce, been drawn into the debates about surveillance and privacy?

Internet infrastructure

The companies that create the hardware and essential software required for the Internet to exist are an emerging sector for surveillance providers. Central to these modes of surveillance is the complicity of Internet Service Providers (ISPs) who work with corporate vendors to perform the analysis of data packets coursing through their networks. This equipment is used for government surveillance, advertising, and the analysis of content for network management purposes (Parsons 2011).

The prominence of infrastructure-based surveillance was most recently brought to light following the 2006 revelations about the warrantless wiretapping provisions within the Bush Administration's Terrorist Surveillance Program. The National Security Agency (NSA) reportedly established "listening rooms" in Internet Exchange Points around America, using data traffic analyzers to precisely target email, chat, calendaring, draft folders, and other elements of data traffic (Bamford 2008; Wolfson 2007). In the UK, Detica (a subsidiary of BAE Systems Ltd.) manufactures the "strange black boxes" that enable British intelligence services to siphon material off the Internet as it passes through ISP gateways (Aldrich 2010).

These Western surveillance appliances are primarily designed to monitor information flows, whereas differently configured appliances in other areas of the world conduct intensive filtering and direct censoring of content (Deibert et al. 2008, 2010). Obvious filtering and censorship are identified as part of the first generation of infrastructure-based surveillance that shape information accessibility. More elaborate filtering and censorship entails "managing networks through denial that is highly selective and event based, and that *shapes* access to the sources of information and means of communication in a manner that could plausibly be explained by errant technical failures or other random network effects" (Deibert and Rohozinski 2010: 21–2). Such capacities for surveillance, and uses of infrastructure-driven power, endanger democratic values as code overcomes or bypasses law (Lessig 2006), colonize the Internet with particular nationalistic territorial values (Saco 1999), and provide authoritarian nations with instruments to significantly undermine freedoms of speech and association (Wagner 2009).

Governments are not alone in using Internet infrastructures for surveillance. Advertisers also monitor and profile web surfers. Working alongside ISPs, advertising companies deploy hardware appliances in ISPs' networks to track browsing behavior, modify data in transit, and subsequently issue advertisements (Clayton 2008; Topolski 2008). Some network appliances monitor ISPs' networks for copyright infringement to develop "piracy indices" in a manner that avoids associating infringement with any particular customers (Parsons 2009). Unquestionably, these data packets are being subjected to surveillance, insofar as they are subject to "the focused, systematic and routine attention to personal details for purposes of influence, management, protection, or direction" (Lyon 2007: 14). It is less clear, however, that all surveillance of this type violates data protection laws if personally identifiable information is never processed (Clayton 2009).

In addition to working with and for government and partnering with advertisers, ISPs themselves have vested interests in surveying data traffic. They have deployed equipment identifying what programs are transmitting data to the Internet, to mediate the speed of data transmissions in their networks. Such equipment is part of an "integrated technology of control" that arguably undermines technical simplicity, political freedom, and economic openness (Bendrath 2009). In a similar vein, McKelvey (2010) argues that algorithms driving hardware-based surveillance appliances reveal a struggle over the ongoing constitution of the Internet itself, and that the logics of control might overcome the Internet's anarchic and participatory culture. This concerns Zittrain (2008) and Lessig (2006) on the basis that changes to the Internet's infrastructure can be leveraged to enforce traditional and code-based "law." Using these tools, data is increasingly labeled and filtered to facilitate its discovery, cross-referencing, and consumption.

Seeking to correct the power asymmetry between individuals, governments, and ISPs, Ian Kerr argues that the connection between ISPs and their customers establishes a fiduciary relationship. As a result, ISPs should be required to "act in the best interests of their users" and "safeguard a user's personal information and private communications in spite of a reluctance to do so" (2002: 12). Unfortunately, in only a few cases have ISPs protected the privacy of their users when approached by the government. We have yet to see Kerr's defense of customers become a common (or legally required) business practice.

Search, advertising, and online commerce

In addition to surveillance processes being embedded into the Internet's infrastructure, there is a competitive business environment encouraging "Big Data" companies to collect personal information to map patterns of online behavior (Franzak et al. 2001). Search companies are voracious in their appetite for data. For example, Google knows "how often each word is searched for, how many searches per session any one user issues on average, how much time there is between sessions and individual searches, how many advertisements are clicked on per session, and how often advertisements are expected to be clicked by a given user" (Soghoian 2003: 310; Jones et al. 2007). These massive aggregations of data are meant to "perfect" search, but also give rise to "the concentrated surveillance, capture, and aggregation of one's online intellectual and social activities by a single provider" (Zimmer 2008).

The capacity to hide (especially with a unique or prominently promoted name) is challenging in the era of the large data set. These challenges were highlighted by AOL's release in 2006 of anonymized search data to researchers, who could develop detailed user profiles that included states of pregnancy, mental and psychological conditions, marital relations, and medical information (Hillyard and Gauen 2007). Despite the subsequent withdrawal of the dataset, it rapidly spread across the Internet, and the privacy of AOL users was unrecoverable. The ability to re-identify data demonstrates the dangers in releasing granular information about search terms, even if formal identifiers such as IP addresses and usernames are deleted. Indeed, some have argued that true anonymization is a myth (Ohm 2009). Thus, quantitative collections of data are promoting qualitative changes in the questions we ask about our lives: Who knows what about me? Why do they know this information? How can I control the flow of my personal information to, and between, other parties?

Of course, it is valuable to step beyond the large datasets and consider search companies' actual privacy practices. In doing so, we see that the world's largest advertisers rarely limit the possibility of information disclosures to governments and other third parties, despite their publicly stated commitments to protect user data (Soghoian 2011). Echoing McKelvey's statements about control, though in a different context, Abelson and colleagues maintain that search is "a new form of control over information" (2008: 313). There is a politics, sociology, and ethics to search, needing careful inter-rogation if we are to understand the dynamics of information transmission in the digital information ecosystem.

Search companies are not alone in profiling Internet users. While cookies and web bugs have long been used to monitor people's movements (Bennett 2001) zombie-like Flash cookies are used by shadowy advertisers. Flash cookies "respawn" after they are deleted, making it impossible for individuals to control the flow of their browsing infor-mation to advertisers (Soltani et al. 2009). Web-based applications generally default to disclosing users' online behaviors and disempower users to the benefit of online infor-mation brokers (Elmer 2004). User profiles entrench information and power asym-metries between corporations and individuals (Gandy 1995) and, somewhat pessimistically, Gandy maintains that the "best we can hope for is transparency—that citizens and consumers are routinely and effectively informed about the nature and extent to which their options and opportunities are being shaped by the application of statistical techniques" (2006: 279).

Maintaining control over personal information is increasingly important as the web of things—the linking of physical objects in our daily environment to the Internet—comes closer to reality. Moreover, as the seams between the analogue and digital are bridged, and mobility and Internet monitoring are drawn together, critics are begin-ning to consider the ethics of building these bridges (Ratto 2007), and to investigate the systems of anonymity and identity associated with our bio-digital environments (Van de Ploeg 2003).

In summary, the literature on surveillance at the level of the Internet infrastructure tends to paint a quite pessimistic picture of the potential, if not the actual reality, of pervasive analysis and manipulation of online behavior. There are clearly strong govern-mental and corporate incentives to monitor Internet activity and it increasingly appears that the Internet has become a fundamentally "surveillance-ready" technology (Roberts and Palfrey 2010). What then are the risks and how have these been conceived and addressed in the literature?

Cyber-surveillance and the Assessment of Risk

Risks on the Internet come in many controversial forms. Consider a few examples. A young woman lets her dog defecate in a subway car and refuses to clean up the mess. A fellow pas-senger snaps a picture of the woman and dog and posts it to the Internet. The image goes viral, leading the woman to drop out of university from the resulting harassment. Did the young woman have a reasonable expectation of privacy on the subway? Did her fellow pas-senger engage in an invasive surveillance practice by capturing her action? One UK ISP has tested a service that "follows" people around the Internet to develop a composite of harmful and non-harmful websites in anticipation of a future harm prevention service. The ISP does not inform its customers, but avoids recording identifying information linking customers to web traffic. Is this an invasion of privacy? Does the (supposed) delinking of personal information from browsing habits absolve the ISP of liability? So, what are the sources and effects of harm on the Internet from the processing and disclosure of personal information? They are both individual and collective.

Individual harms

The Internet, as a series of interlinked hardware and software processes, is becoming deeply integrated into the structures of social life. Whereas privacy by obscurity once largely kept indiscretions confined to the locales they occurred in, this is less the case in a digital ecology that defaults to remembering (and, increasingly, sharing) everything (Palfrey and Gasser 2008: ch. 3; Solove 2004). Youth and adults alike are "at risk" for the rest of their lives from their digital excursions.

In their examinations of Facebook and other social network services, Chew and colleagues (2008) identify three ways harms can arise. First, the lack of control over activity streams can lead to information being "leaked" to stream viewers. Second, unwelcome linkage between spaces where different facets of one's identity are revealed can compress these identities into a single digital portfolio. Finally, the merging of social graphs—combining information held by multiple social network sites—can lead to the de-anonymization of pseudonoymous and anonymous profiles alike. Of course, the crossing of identity boundaries is not a new phenomenon (Friedman 2007), but the ability to massively, and easily, do so in the digital era is a significant innovation and represents a normative shift in social expectations of privacy. Further, online social environments, such as blogs, lack the traditional media's norms of restraint. Some contend that the "less-well-developed-norms" of social networking need to be reconstituted with a widely adopted code of ethics that significantly returns control of personal information to individuals (Solove 2007). Failure to reconstitute these borders can cause significant harms and provoke psychic trauma (Jameson 2008). The disclosure of locational information might reveal, for example, when homes are vacant and therefore vulnerable (Perez 2010).

Information asymmetries can drive certain misunderstandings about privacy online to the detriment of individuals. Incomplete notification complicates individual decision-making about privacy, and leads individuals to rely inappropriately on default settings when deciding to reveal facets of their lives online. As an indication of the complexity of online revelations, research by Acquisti and Grosslags has found that individuals tend to only have vague and limited notions of actions that can protect personal information online; their actions can have unpredictable effects; relational consequences of information revelations are likely unknown; desirable actions and information may be unavailable; and privacy invasions are often by-products of other transactions (Acquisti and Grossklags 2008).

Carey and Burkell provide a set of heuristics to trace the motivations for revealing personal information, recognizing that heuristics are helpful in risk analysis because they "allow the decision maker to bypass complex calculations regarding probability" (2009: 74). The affect heuristic recognizes that positive perceptions associated with information disclosure result in services themselves being trusted. The availability heuristic acknowledges that individuals' perceptions of risk increase with direct experience of negative outcomes and thus provide personal information when perceptions of risks are low. The representativeness heuristic sees individuals often shield their membership in vulnerable groups. While these heuristics may allow individuals to make privacy-related decisions, they prevent individuals from making effective and nuanced choices given the complexity of many privacy decisions. Ignorance and inaccurate risk-assessment are key, but unsurprising, sources of privacy-related harms, given the complexity and expansiveness of technological systems.

The development of such heuristics highlights an ongoing tension between sharing information and retaining control over it. The new political economy of Internet surveillance threatens the establishment and development of trust (Wall 2006). In a case study, Karyda and Kokolakis (2008) found that individuals believe that selectively interacting with others is the best way to protect themselves, but developing this kind of trust can be challenging. In terms of the "trust" that individuals place in technological systems, few users can conduct genuine reputation analyses or detect technical misbehavior which they can communicate in a meaningful way to other Internet users. Their "relationship" with the system is largely limited to "does the system appear to work for me?"

That individuals willingly provide information to third-parties online while claiming to highly value privacy is an oft-cited paradox, upon which scholarship has shed light (Dutton and Meadow 1987). According to Karyda and Kokolakis, people join communities to enjoy a sense of community, in anticipation of reciprocity, or for recognition. Where the community is seen as part of one's social life, individuals "may not wish to shelter themselves from it. This could explain the fact that membership in digital communities is exponentially growing and, at the same time, privacy is among the primary concerns Internet users have" (2008: 257). Similar attitudes are reflected in Marwick and colleagues' literature review of youth and privacy: youth spending time online desire private spaces for "socialization, exploration, and experimentation away from adult eyes" (2010: 65) and want granular privacy controls. The cognitive dissonance of this paradox is taken up by Kerr et al. (2009: 18–20) who contend that such dissonance addresses how "people seek to alleviate the discomfort they experience" from divulging personal information online by using one of three techniques: trivializing competing cognitions and convincing themselves that a privacy violation is insignificant or privacy itself overvalued; selectively seek information that assuages the concern, such as seeing that a data collector has a privacy policy and thus is securing people's privacy; and changing their entire attitude, opinion, or behavior concerning privacy online.

Thus, there may be significant psychic and social harms, or a concerted cognitive effort to "simply" ignore the problem. Of course, where individuals suffer objective injuries as a result of information being made available online—the inability to work, the persistent psychological fear of stalking, the dissemination of intimate facts that lead to harassment—it is considerably harder, if not impossible, to just ignore the problem. Solove (2008) and Nissenbaum (2009) have both established frameworks to identify harms, enabling legislators and judges to determine whether privacy violations have occurred or surveillance processes are unduly onerous. For others, the detection of harm is an important initial step that must be complemented by a broader ethic of surveillance and data protection (Marx 1999).

Collective harms

The routine surveillance by stealth, extended and deepened by the information left by the unwary browser, has broader democratic consequences. Paul Schwartz has warned of the "widespread, silent collection of personal information in cyberspace…that cloaks in dark uncertainty the transmutation of Internet activity into personal data that will follow one into other areas and discourage civic participation" (Schwartz 1999). Others have warned of the chilling effect of actual and perceived covert surveillance on freedom of speech and association (Strandburg 2008). In studying the effects of government surveillance of Muslim-Americans, Sidhu found that a limited section of his sample had made changes to their online activities (Sidhu 2007).

In addition to chilling effects, information asymmetries are seen as a widespread issue affecting most Internet users. In recognition of the challenges posed by the development of digital dossiers, Solove (2004) maintains that protecting privacy "is a question of social design" to correct "architectures of vulnerability" to reflect broader social values. Architectures of vulnerability "cause harm not only by creating emotional distress and anxiety but also by increasing our risks of being victimized by identity theft, fraud, stalking, or other crimes" (Solove 2008: 120–1). New architectures will only emerge with a new regulatory system that is "akin to the ones we have in place regulating our food, environment, and financial institutions" (Solove 2004). In a similar vein, Mayer-Schonberger (2008) argues that collected data should gradually be forgotten to alleviate some of the memory-related problems associated with the default "remember" of digital storage.

Simmons has examined how governments perform end-runs around constitutional safeguards by laundering data collection and processing to non-governmental actors (Simmons 2009: 1004). Palfrey and Gasser (2008) suggests that laws should let individuals force third-party data collectors to delete information held about the individual. And Kreimer (2004) recommends better administrative processes for government surveillance, including access controls, audit trails, data access officials, and sunset provisions. These authors are struggling to resolve issues emerging from massive data availability on the Internet, indicating their doubts about the effectiveness of privacy protection regimes developed over the past decades. It is to these regimes that our discussion turns in the following section.

MANAGING CYBER-SURVEILLANCE
THROUGH PRIVACY PROTECTION

While there have been creative attempts to address problems of online risk, the entire panoply of individual and collective harms is also framed as a policy problem that needs to be addressed through national and international privacy regimes, which comprise a range of policy instruments (Bennett and Raab 2006): transnational instruments, regulatory instruments, self-regulatory instruments, and technological instruments. What has the academic literature had to say about the application of these policy solutions to issues of cyber-surveillance?

Transnational instruments

Regulators recognized as early as in the 1970s that data knew few boundaries. Consequently, harmonized privacy and data protection regulations have been developed by the Council of Europe (1981), the Organization for Economic Cooperation and Development (OECD) (1981), the European Union (EU) (1995), and more recently the Organization for Asia-Pacific Economic Cooperation (APEC) (2005). Such regulations aim to influence national law and regulate conditions under which personal data might be exported from one jurisdiction to the next. By far the most important is the 1995 directive from the European Union, which dictates that personal data should not flow from European countries to states lacking an "adequate level of protection." With the rise of Internet communications, and especially "cloud computing," these questions have assumed a renewed urgency and complexity. And questions about the viability of these instruments, the meaning of export or transfer, and the larger trade implications, have been a matter of expert analysis within the legal literature (Reidenberg 2005; Schwartz 2009; Schaffer 2002).

A larger question is whether or not the involvement of international organizations has, or can, produce policy convergence (Bennett 1992, 1997; Maclay 2010). While principles and instruments of privacy protection have grown increasingly alike and been adopted by a greater number of countries, Reidenberg (2000: 1340) contends that convergence obscures profound differences rooted in "distinct visions of democratic governance" and cultural perspectives on the "role of the state in protecting the rights of citizens and the ability of the market to assure the fair treatment of citizens." Also questioning the ongoing nature of convergence, Farrell (2008: 382) argues that "if an epistemic community of privacy experts helped drive the international convergence on data protection principles at an earlier juncture, officials in justice, home affairs, and security ministries and agencies are now playing a similar—but much less privacy friendly—role in driving many pertinent areas of policy." Farrell's comments are reinforced by Newman's research, where policy networks associated with the EU's third pillar undermined

European data protection commissioners' attempts to limit the transfer of EU citizens' airline information to the America security establishment (Newman 2008: 132–40). Thus, prior achievements are not written in stone. The logic of the risk economy and of securitization threatens to undermine hard-won international policy harmonization.

A parallel with this technological complexity is observed in organizational complexity. It is common for several different organizations, located in different jurisdictions, to be involved in any one transaction over the Internet. The company from which one buys a product might be located in one country, the bill-payment system in another, the organization that services the website in other, the ad-placement agency in another, and so on (Reidenberg 2000). The international privacy problems of the 1980s and 1990s were described as "transborder data flows" implying identifiable moments when data was sent from organization A in country A, to organization B in country B. The rise of "cloud computing" confuses such "direct" data transmissions, leading many corporations to develop specific contractual devices or "binding corporate rules" to implement privacy obligations wherever the data reside.

Legal instruments and regulatory agencies

Privacy law embodies a rich and evolving body of constitutional, tort, and statutory provisions, all of which have come under scrutiny in relation to Internet communications. At a constitutional level, "unreasonable search and seizure" provisions in American and Canadian constitutions have been tested with respect to issues such as the interception of email and ability to access inappropriate websites in the workplace. An expanding body of legal analysis accompanies these, and other, cases (Ciocchetti 2001; Hornung 2005).

With respect to the existing body of data protection statutes, which are based on a common set of fair information principles (FIPS), major Internet-related issues arise with respect to questions of data retention, either for commercial purposes as is the case with the search data retained by Google (Kirk 2010), or for law enforcement purposes, as with legislation in many countries mandating ISPs to retain "traffic data" for possible use in criminal investigations. The volume of data flowing through Internet gateways often leads governments to turn to traffic, rather than content, analyses (Diffie and Landau 2007). These analyses enable government surveillance, require less stringent legal authorization, and evade constitutional limitations on searches and seizures. Such evasions have led some scholars to postulate that freedom of association, rather than freedom from illegitimate searches, might be more effective in preserving privacy (Standburg 2008; Crump 2003).

A fundamental question for data protection authorities is whether the IP Address, the foundation identifier for all Internet communications, constitutes "personally identifiable information" (PII). Virtually all data protection law applies only when an individual can, or potentially can, be identified. Data protection authorities have not reached an international consensus on this question, though scholarly commentary and analysis

(McIntyre 2011; Lah 2008; Schoen 2009) has tried to integrate existing and disparate case law to find a common ground that identifies when an IP address constitutes PII.

Over and above these vexing policy questions, others have critiqued the continued relevance of the principles upon which data protection legislation has been based. Daniel Weitzner and colleagues contend that the traditional approach has been falsely based on a principle of "containment." This "hide it or lose it approach," they argue, is increasingly inadequate "for a connected world where information is easily copied and aggregated and automated correlations and inferences across multiple databases uncover information even when it is not revealed explicitly" (2008: 84). They prefer a regime based on the principle of accountability, in which the dominant concern addresses how personal information is used, and for what purposes. These ideas have influenced recent thinking concerning how to regulate international flows of personal data (Center for Information Policy Leadership 2009).

Yet, even before the complexity of Internet communications rose to the agenda of the privacy regulators, there had been considerable uncertainty about the efficacy and relevance of data protection law. Gellman (1997: 212) concludes that "[I]t is difficult to say whether the law is really an effective device for protecting privacy. Different attempts have produced a mixed bag of results." Lyon worries that data protection laws and their associated agencies merely promote a "culture of care regarding personal information" (Lyon 2007: 173). He contends that legislation does not "significantly reduce or mitigate the amount of potentially damaging social sorting that occurs," nor does it effectively alleviate the questions of human dignity or collective solidarity that arise when individuals are regarded as best suited to looking out for themselves (Lyon 2007: 115–6).

Self-regulatory instruments

In recognition of the complexity of the issue, a range of self-regulatory and co-regulatory instruments has also appeared on national and international agendas. Over the last two decades, organizational and sectoral codes of practice, privacy impact assessments, privacy trustmark schemes, and certifiable privacy standards have entered the discourse of the privacy policy community and the repertoire of policy instruments (Bennett and Raab 2006: 153–167). International pressures—such as the Safe Harbor requirement negotiated between the US and the EU—also drive self-regulatory approaches. Some insist that privacy is in the interests of the responsible corporation (Cavoukian and Hamilton 2002). Others remain skeptical, insisting that appetites for data are driven by the logic of the capitalist enterprise (Gandy 1995) or of bureaucratic organizations more generally (Rule et al. 1980). Probably the incentives for adopting and implementing self-regulatory measures are contingent upon several international and national dimensions such as the level of public exposure, the extent to which an organization is exposed to international trade and e-commerce, the structure of the industry, the level of techno-logical innovation, and so on (Bennett and Raab 2006: 170–5).

Good test cases are the privacy trustmark programs designed to give websites good housekeeping seals of approval. These programs vary with respect to the level of oversight and procedures for complaint investigation. Some seals are backed by detailed standards and independent audits; others just require payment. Some seals include a free dispute resolution service for complaints; others have no complaint mechanisms, or charge consumers for lodging complaints. A recent evaluation has concluded that it is difficult to see how consumers can trust the value of the seals or the practices of the organizations displaying them (Galexia 2009).

Some argue that domestic regulatory bodies should be empowered to investigate compliance with self-regulated practices, issuing fines or criminal sanctions on the basis of false advertising where practices are not followed (see Leon et al. 2010). Fischer-Hübner et al. (2008) provide a scheme of user interface designs that visually reveal the implications of privacy policies and, in a similar vein, Kelley et al. (2010) have found that standardized "privacy labels" that borrow from nutrition labeling assist individuals in quickly, and accurately, comparing privacy characteristics. Perhaps a more granular control system, backed by formal (if limited) regulatory oversight, would be better suited to manage individuals' control over sharing their information with others. Control systems can raise awareness and promote a sense of agency, though both skill and experience can modify individuals' actual assertions of agency. Thus default privacy positions and their ease of modification are important issues for policy-makers, corporations and scholars to address (boyd and Hargittai 2010).

Technological instruments

While part of the "privacy problem" on the Internet is surely derived from technology, technology can also mitigate privacy and surveillance related concerns. Privacy Enhancing Technologies (PETs) are useful complements, or secondary tools, to existing regulatory and self-regulatory approaches (OECD 2002: 25). They were first recognized in the early 1990s with the advancement of public-key cryptography and creation of "blind signatures" for e-commerce (Chaum 1992; Diffie and Landau 2007). The aim was to "eliminate the use of personal data altogether or to give direct control over revelation of personal information to the person concerned" (Burkert 1997: 125).

PETs operate at various levels: systemically, they can operate at the level of network technical standards and protocols; collectively, they can operate as a result of government development of public-key infrastructures; and individually, they can operate as instruments of empowerment by requiring end-users to make explicit choices (Bennett and Raab 2006: 181). Successful PETs have all demonstrated four key characteristics: (1) ease of use; (2) ease of deployment and integration into people's daily tools; (3) the delivery of promised benefits; and (4) optimal operation in non-ideal environments (Goldberg 2008). The potential of PETs is now embraced by the slogan "Privacy by Design" and advocated by prominent privacy commissioners and professionals (Cavoukian 2008).

With the proliferation of these technologies, they have occasionally been championed as alternatives, rather than supplements, to existing privacy laws and protections, especially in the United States. Given the broad range of uses of PETs, their minimal adoption by consumers, and occasional criticism of them by privacy advocates (EPIC 2000), their more general role as mechanisms to promote privacy on the Internet remains in some doubt.

Conclusion: the Internet
and identity

The Internet is predicated, in many respects, on robust vulnerability. Its basic operations depend on a kind of radical trust that is dependent on control by computer protocol itself. Network design emphasizes packet delivery instead of infrastructural or data security, leaving networks, and their users, incredibly vulnerable to exploitation. As a result, the Internet's protocols have disrupted traditional conceptions of personal information control. Moreover, the extension of surveillance into the very ecosystem of the Internet demands that we raise normative questions about the composition of contemporary digital networks: what form the Internet should assume, and what the broader effects of this format are on the future of privacy.

Friedman argues that we face two "huge" privacy problems: the capacity to snoop and intrude in the name of overriding public policies, such as the protection of intellectual property, and the ability to squeeze exemptions out of existing legal systems for such intrusions (2007: 168). This is evidenced in the processes that governments and corporations have undertaken to legitimize the surveillance of citizens and customers online. These processes demonstrate the shift from personal forms of surveillance—which historically have focused on issues of criminal behavior—to mass surveillance oriented towards social control (Clarke 1988). Such mass surveillance is grounded in the protocological nature of the Internet. Its freedoms arise from control "based on openness, inclusion, universalism, and flexibility. It is control borne from high degrees of technical organization (protocol), not this or that limitation on individual freedom or decision making" (Galloway 2004: 142). In effect, the delivery of Internet traffic requires that data packets conform to key organizational principles and technical features, with the result that individual freedoms are threatened and decisions by users problematized. Thus, we are now witnessing an exploitation of technical organizations to influence and limit individuals' rights using Internet-based surveillance technologies.

The rise of Internet-enabled surveillance and information control is significant. Databases linked to the Internet, which facilitate this mass surveillance, promote the adjustment and readjustment *ad infinitum* of the norm of individuality (Poster 1990: 91). By exploiting individuals as communicating entities, and defining who they are based on reprocessed data profiles, the definition of what constitutes individuality is drawn into doubt. Certainly, questions around the ontological boundaries of the self are not new, but the Internet raises these questions in new ways. Service providers have often incorporated the radical trust upon which the Internet relies into their product offerings and left information readily available to other parties. This default mode of sharing information—of being forced to extensively disclose personal information—is arguably out of alignment with how users want their information treated (boyd 2007; Solove 2007: ch. 7) and destabilizes individuals' abilities to sequester their experiences. This "disappearance of disappearance" raises central moral dilemmas for human beings as domains previously excluded from social life are drawn to public attention (Giddens 1991: ch. 5).

In conclusion, the various literatures perhaps paint an inconclusive picture as to whether the valence of the Internet does, or will, point in any particular direction or the other. The story of privacy and surveillance over the last twenty years is episodic and reflective of quite frenzied attempts to come to grips with unprecedented technological transformations in the light of the most recent scandal or controversy. It is also very difficult to separate the academic analyses from the more prescriptive discussions of how we should make the Internet a safer place. The literature does not belong in any one academic tradition. Research is inherently multidisciplinary, emanating as much from the labs of major companies, the agencies of government, and the organizations of civil society, as from the traditional scholarship of academia.

It is important to avoid fetishizing the Internet by exaggerating the dangers and potentials of Internet-based technologies (Mosco 2004). Concerns of privacy are certainly attenuated by the availability of data and the ease of transmitting it, but many of the normative concerns we have raised are old problems in a new garb. Basic information privacy principles have become widely accepted, creating a common consensus about how responsible organizations should collect and process PII. More and more organizations in more and more countries have to be open about their policies and practices; only collect personal information for defined and relevant purposes; only use and disclose that information in ways that are consistent with those purposes; grant access and correction rights to individuals; and keep the data secure. And there is a common understanding that these principles should apply regardless of the institution and regardless of whether or not personal data is collected, processed, and distributed over the Internet.

While questions remain concerning the effectiveness of such principles and processes, it is clear that central points of agreement about the terms and implications of the debate do exist. Further, it is evident that the Internet is not an "uncivilized" or undisciplined space as some have asserted. It is a domain enmeshed in existing and emerging forms of governance. It is a domain that is being shaped by a multitude of stakeholders that remain active in trying to understand, engage with, and respond to the ongoing privacy issues raised by the integration of digital systems into the daily activities of individuals around the globe. And it is a domain that will continue to be shaped by conflicts over this crucial human right—the right to personal privacy.

REFERENCES

Abelson, H., Ledeen, K., and Lewis, H. (2008). *Blown to Bits: Your Life, Liberty, and Happiness After the Digital Explosion*, Toronto: Addison-Wesley.

Acquisti, A. and Grossklags, J. (2008). "What Can Behavioural Economics Teach Us About Privacy," in A. Acquisti and S. Gritzalis (eds). *Digital Privacy: Theory, Technologies, and Practices*, New York: Auerbach Publications, pp. 363–80.

Aldrich, R. K. (2010). *GCHQ: The Uncensored Story of Britain's Most Secret Intelligence Agency*, London: Harper Press.

APEC (Asia-Pacific Economic Cooperation) (2005). *APEC Privacy Framework*. Available at <http://www.apec.org/Groups/Committee-on-Trade-and-Investment/~/media/Files/Groups/ECSG/05_ecsg_privacyframewk.ashx>. Accessed April 26, 2012.

Bamford, J. (2008). *The Shadow Factory: The Ultra-Secret NSA from 9/11 to the Eavesdropping on America*, New York: Doubleday.

Beck, U. (1998). *World Risk Society*, Cambridge: Polity.

Bendrath, R. (2009). "DPI as an Integrated Technology of Control—Potential and Reality," Office of the Privacy Commissioner of Canada: Essays. Available at <http://dpi.priv.gc.ca/index.php/essays/dpi-as-an-integrated-technology-of-control-potential-and-reality/>. Accessed April 26, 2012.

Bennett, C. (1992). *Regulating Privacy: Data Protection and Public Policy in Europe and the United States*, Ithica: Cornell University Press.

—— (1997). "Convergence Revisited: Toward a Global Policy for the Protection of Personal Data," in P. Agre and M. Rotenberg (eds). *Technology and Privacy: The New Landscape*, Cambridge, MA: MIT Press, pp. 99–123.

—— (2001). "Cookies, Web Bugs, Webcams and Cue Cats: Patterns of Surveillance on the World Wide Web," *Ethics and Information Technology*, 3(3): 195–208.

—— (2008). *The Privacy Advocates: Resisting the Spread of Surveillance*, Cambridge, MA: MIT Press.

—— (2011). "In Defense of Privacy: The Concept and the Regime," *Surveillance and Society*, 8(4): 486–496.

—— and Raab, C. (2006). *The Governance of Privacy: Policy Instruments in Global Perspective*, Cambridge, Mass.: The MIT Press.

boyd, d. (2007). "Why Youth (Heart) Social Network Sites: The Role of Networked Publics in Teenage Social Life," in D. Buckingham (ed.). *MacArthur Foundation Series on Digital Learning—Youth, Identity, and Digital Media Volume*, Cambridge, MA: MIT Press, pp. 119–42.

—— and Hargittai, E. (2010). "Facebook Privacy Settings: Who Cares?" *First Monday* 15(8). Available at <http://firstmonday.org/htbin/cgiwrap/bin/ojs/index.php/fm/article/view/3086/2589>. Accessed June 20, 2012.

Burkert, H. (1997). "Privacy Enhancing Technologies: Typology, Critique, Vision," in P. Agre and M. Rotenberg (eds). *Technology and Privacy: The New Landscape*, Cambridge, MA: MIT Press, pp. 125–42.

Buzan, B., Wæver, O., and de Wilde, J. (1998). *Security: A New Framework for Analysis*, Boulder CO: Lynne Rienner Publishers.

Carey, R. and Burkell, J. (2009). "A Heuristics Approach to Understanding Privacy-Protecting Behaviors in Digital Social Environments," in I. Kerr, V. Steeves, and C. Lucock (eds). *Lessons From the Identity Trail: Anonymity, Privacy and Identity in a Networked Society*, Toronto: Oxford University Press, pp. 65–82.

Cavoukian, A. (2008). *Privacy and Radical Pragmatism*, Toronto: Information and Privacy Commissioner/Ontario.

Cavoukian, A. and Hamilton, T. (2002). *The Privacy Payoff: How Successful Businesses Build Consumer Trust*, Toronto: McGraw-Hill Ryserson.

Center for Information Policy Leadership (2009). "Data Protection Accountability: The Essential Elements." Available at <http://www.huntonfiles.com/files/webupload/CIPL_Galway_Accountability_Paper.pdf>. Accessed April 26, 2012.

Chaum, D. (1992). "Achieving Electronic Privacy," *Scientific America, Inc.*, August: 96–101.

Chew, M., Balfanz, D., and Laurie, B. (2008). "(Under)mining Privacy in Social Networks," *Proceedings of W2SP Web 20 Security and Privacy*: 1–5.

Ciocchetti, C. (2001). "Monitoring Employee E-Mail: Efficient Workplaces vs. Employee Privacy," *Duke Law and Technology Review* 0026. Available at <http://scholarship.law.duke.edu/cgi/viewcontent.cgi?article=1025&context=dltr>. Accessed June 20, 2012.

Clarke, R. (1988). "Information Technology and Dataveillance," *Communications of the ACM* 31(5): 498–512.

Clayton, R. (2008). "The Phorm 'Webwise' System," Light Blue Touchpaper: Security Research, Computer Laboratory, University of Cambridge, May 18. Available at <http://www.cl.cam.ac.uk/~rnc1/080518-phorm.pdf>. Accessed April 26, 2012.

—— (2009). "Objecting to Phorm," at *Office of the Privacy Commissioner of Canada: Collection of Essays*. URL: <http://dpi.priv.gc.ca/index.php/essays/objecting-to-phorm/>. Last accessed April 26, 2012.

Council of Europe (1981). *Convention for the Protection of Individuals with Regard to Automatic Processing of Personal Data (Convention 108)*, Strasbourg: Council of Europe.

Crump, C. (2003). "Data Retention: Privacy, Anonymity, and Accountability Online," *Stanford Law Review* 56(1): 191–229.

Deibert, R. and Rohozinski, R. (2010). "Control and Subversion in Russian Cyberspace," in R. Deibert, J. Palfrey, R. Rohozinsky, and J. Zittrain (eds). *Access Controlled: The Shaping of Power, Rights, and the Rule in Cyberspace*, Cambridge, MA: MIT Press, pp. 15–34.

——, Palfrey, J., Rohozinski, R., and Zittrain, J. (eds) (2008). *Access Denied: The Practice and Policy of Global Internet Filtering*, Cambridge, MA: MIT Press.

——, Palfrey, J., Rohozinski, R., and Zittrain, J. (eds) (2010). *Access Controlled: The Shaping of Power, Rights, and the Rule in Cyberspace*, Cambridge, MA: MIT Press.

Diffie, W. and Landau, S. (2007). *Privacy on the Line: The Politics of Wiretapping and Encryption, Updated and Expanded Edition*, Cambridge, MA: MIT Press.

Dutton, W. H. and Meadow, R. G. (1987). "A Tolerance for Surveillance: American Public Opinion Concerning Privacy and Civil Liberties," in K. B. Levitan (ed.). *Government Infostructures*, Westport, CT: Greenwood Press, pp. 147–70.

Elmer, G. (2004). *Profiling Machines: Mapping the Personal Information Economy*, Cambridge, MA: MIT Press.

EPIC (Electronic Privacy Information Center). (2000). "Pretty Poor Privacy: An Assessment of P3P and Internet Privacy." Available at <http://epic.org/reports/prettypoorprivacy.html>. Accessed April 27, 2012.

EU (European Union) (1995). Directive 95/46/EC of the European Parliament and of the Council on the Protection of Individuals with regard to the Processing of Personal Data and on the Free Movement of Such Data, Brussels: OJ No. L281. October 24. (The EU Data Protection Directive.)

Farrell, H. (2008). "Privacy in the Digital Age: States, Privacy Actors, and Hybrid Arrangements," in W. Drake and E. Wilson (eds). *Governing Global Electronic Networks: International Perspectives on Power and Policy*, Cambridge, MA: MIT Press, pp. 375–400.

Fischer-Hübner, S., Sören Pettersson, J., and M. Bergmann, M. (2008). "HCI Designs for Privacy-Enhancing Identity Management," in A. Acquisti and S. Gritzalis (eds). *Digital Privacy: Theory, Technologies, and Practices*, New York: Auerbach Publications, pp. 229–52.

Franzak, F., Pitta, D., and Fritsche, S. (2001). "Online Relationships and the Consumer's Right to Privacy," *Journal of Consumer Marketing*, 18(7): 631–42.

Friedman, L. M. (2007). *Guarding Life's Dark Secrets: Legal and Social Controls over Reputation, Propriety, and Privacy*, Stanford: Stanford University Press.

Galexia. (2009). "Trustmark Schemes Struggle to Protect Privacy (2008)." Available at <http://www.galexia.com/public/research/assets/trustmarks_struggle_20080926/trustmarks_struggle_public-Introduc.html>. Accessed April 27, 2012.

Galloway, A. R. (2004). *Protocol: How Control Exists After Decentralization*, Cambridge, MA: MIT Press.

Gandy Jr., O. H. (1995). "It's Discrimination Stupid!," in J. Brook and I. A. Boal (eds). *Resisting the Virtual Life: The Culture and Politics of Information*, San Francisco: City Lights, pp. 35–48.

—— (2006). "Data Mining, Surveillance, and Discrimination in the Post-9/11 Environment," in K. D. Haggerty and R. V. Ericson (eds). *The New Politics of Surveillance and Visibility*, Toronto: University of Toronto Press, pp. 79–110.

Gellman, R. (1997). "Conflict and Overlap in Privacy Regulation: National, International, and Private," in B. Kahin and C. Nesson (eds). *Borders in Cyberspace*, Cambridge, MA: MIT Press, pp. 255–82.

Giddens, A. (1991). *Modernity and Self-Identity: Self and Society in the Late Modern Age*, Stanford: Stanford University Press.

Goldberg, I. (2008). "Privacy-Enhancing Technologies for the Internet III: Ten Years Later," in A. Acquisti and S. Gritzalis (eds). *Digital Privacy: Theory, Technologies, and Practices*, New York: Auerbach Publications, pp. 3–28.

Haggerty, K. D. and Ericson, R. (2000). "The surveillant assemblage," *British Journal of Sociology*, 54(1): 605–22.

—— and Ericson, R. (2006). "The New Politics of Surveillance and Visibility," in K. D. Haggerty and R. V. Ericson (eds). *The New Politics of Surveillance and Visibility*, Toronto: University of Toronto Press, pp. 3–34.

Hillyard, D. and Gauen, M. (2007). "Issues Around the Protection or Revelation of Personal Information," *Knowledge, Technology and Policy*, 20(2): 121–4.

Hornung, M. S. (2005). "Think Before You Type: A Look at Email Privacy in the Workplace," *Fordham Journal of Corporate and Financial Law*, 11(1): 115–60.

Jameson, S. (2008). "Cyberharassment: Striking a Balance Between Free Speech and Privacy," *CommLaw Conspectus: Journal of Communications Law and Policy*, 17(1): 231–66.

Jones, R., Kumar, R., Pang, B., and Tomkins, A. (2007). "I Know What You Did Last Summer—Query Logs and User Privacy," *Proceedings of the Sixteenth ACM Conference on Information and Knowledge Management*: 909–14.

Karyda, M. and Kokolakis, S. (2008). "Privacy Perceptions among Members of Online Communities," in A. Acquisti and S. Gritzalis (eds). *Digital Privacy: Theory, Technologies, and Practices*, New York: Auerbach Publications, pp. 253–66.

Kelley, P. G., Cesca, J., Bresee, J., and Cranor, L. F. (2010). "Standardizing Privacy Notices: An Online Study of the Nutrician Label Approach," Carnegie Mellon University CyLab, January 12. Available at <http://www.cylab.cmu.edu/files/pdfs/tech_reports/CMUCyLab0 9014.pdf>. Accessed April 27, 2012.

Kerr, I. (2002). "Online Service Providers, Fidelity, and the Duty of Loyalty," in T. Mendina and B. Rockenback (eds). *Ethics and Electronic Information*, Jefferson, North NC: McFarland Press.

——, Barrigar, J., Burkell, J., and Black, K. (2009). "Soft Surveillance, Hard Consent: The Law and Psychology of Engineering Consent," in I. Kerr, V. Steeves, and C. Lucock (eds). *Lessons From the Identity Trail: Anonymity, Privacy and Identity in a Networked Society*. Toronto: Oxford University Press, pp. 5–22.

Kirk, J. (2010). "Europe warns Google, Microsoft, Others about Search Data Retention," *Computerworld*, May 27. Available at <http://www. computerworld. com/s/article/9177424/ Europe_warns_Google_Microsoft_others_about_search_data_retention>.

Kreimer, S. (2004). "Watching the Watchers: Surveillance, Transparency, and Political Freedom in the War on Terror," *University of Pennsylvania Journal of Constitutional Law* 7: 133–81. Available at <https://www.law.upenn.edu/cf/faculty/skreimer/workingpapers/7JofConstLaw133. pdf>. Accessed June 20, 2012.

Lah, F. (2008). "Are IP Addresses Personally Identifiable Information?," *I/S: A Journal of Law and Policy for the Information Society*, 4(3): 676–703.

Leon, P. G., Cranor, L. F., McDonald, A. M., McGuire, R. (2010). "Token Attempt: The Misrepresentation of Website Privacy Policies through the Misuse of P3P Compact Policy Tokens," Carnegie Melon University CyLab, September 10. Available at <http://www.cylab .cmu.edu/research/techreports/2010/tr_cylab10014.html>. Accessed April 27, 2012.

Lessig, L. (2006). *Code: Version 2.0*, New York: Basic Books.

Lyon, D. (2001). *The Surveillance Society*, Buckingham: Open University Press.

—— (2003). *Surveillance after September 11*, Cambridge: Polity Press.

—— (2007). *Surveillance Studies: An Overview*, Cambridge: Polity Press.

McIntyre, P. (2011). "Balancing Expectations of Online Privacy: Why Internet Protocol (IP) Addresses Should Be Protected As Personally Identifiable Information," *DePaul Law Review*, 60(3): 895–936.

McKelvey, F. (2010). "Ends and Ways: The Algorithmic Politics of Network Neutrality," *Global Media Journal—Canadian Edition*, 3(1): 51–73.

Maclay, C. M. (2010). "Protecting Privacy and Expression Online: Can the Global Network Initiative Embrace the Character of the Net?," in R. Deibert, J. Palfrey, R. Rohozinski, and J. Zittrain (eds). *Access Controlled: The Shaping of Power, Rights, and the Rule in Cyberspace*, Cambridge, MA: MIT Press, pp. 87–108.

Marwick, A. E., Murgia-Diaz, D., and Palfrey Jr., J. G. (2010). "Youth, Privacy and Reputation (Literature Review)," Berkman Center Research Publication No. 2010–5; Harvard Law Working Paper No. 10–29. Available at <http://papers.ssrn.com/sol3/papers.cfm?abstract_id=1588163>. Accessed April 27, 2012.

Marx, G. (1999). "Ethics for the New Surveillance," in C. J. Bennett and R. Grant (eds). *Visions of Privacy: Policy Choices for the Digital Age*, Toronto: University of Toronto Press, pp. 39–67.

Mayer-Schonberger, V. (2008). *Delete: The Virtue of Forgetting in the Digital Age*, Princeton, NJ: Princeton University Press.

Monahan, T. (ed.) (2006). *Surveillance and Security: Technological Politics and Power in Everyday Life*, New York: Routledge.

—— (2010). *Surveillance in the Time of InSecurity*, New Brunswick: Rutgers University Press.

Mosco, V. (2004). *The Digital Sublime: Myth, Power, and Cyberspace*, Cambridge, MA: MIT Press.

Newman, A. L. (2008). *Protectors of Privacy: Regulating Personal Data in the Global Economy*, London: Cornell University Press.

Nissenbaum, H. (2009). *Privacy in Context: Technology, Privacy, and the Integrity of Social Life*, Stanford, CA: Stanford University Press.

OECD (Organization for Economic Cooperation and Development) (1981). *Guidelines on the Protection of Personal Information and the Transborder Flows of Personal Data*, Paris: OECD.

—— (2002). "Directorate For Science, Technology and Industry," in *OECD Guidelines for the Security of Inforamtion Systems and Networks: Towards a Culture of Security*, Paris: OECD.

Ohm, P. (2009). "Broken Promises of Privacy: Responding to the Surprising Failure of Anonymization," *UCLA Law Review* 57(6): 1701–77.

Palfrey, J. and Gasser, U. (2008). *Born Digital: Understanding the First Generation of Digital Natives*, New York: Basic Books.

Parsons, C. (2009). "Aggregating Information About CView," *Technology, Thoughts, and Trinkets*, December 17. Available at <http://www.christopher-parsons.com/blog/privacy/aggregating-information-about-cview/>. Accessed April 27, 2012.

—— (2011). "Is Your ISP Snooping on You?," in M. Moll and L. Shade (eds).*The Internet Tree: The State of Telecom Policy in Canada 3.0*, Canadian Center for Policy Alternatives, pp. 83–91.

Perez, S. (2010). "Location-Based Social Networks: Delightful, Dangerous, or Somewhere in Between," *ReadWriteWeb*, March 30. Available at <http://www.readwriteweb.com/archives/location-based_social_networks_delightful_dangerous.php>. Accessed April 27, 2012.

Poster, M. (1990). *The Mode of Information: Poststructuralism and Social Context*, Chicago: University of Chicago Press.

Ratto, M. (2007). "Ethics of Seamless Infrastructures: Resources and Future Directions," *International Review of Information Ethics*, 8(8): 20–7.

Reidenberg, J. (2000). "Resolving Conflickting International Data Privacy Rules in Cyberspace," *Stanford Law Review*, 52(5): 1315–71.

Reidenberg, J. (2005). "Technology and Internet Jurisdiction," *University of Pennsylvania Law Review*, 153: 1951–1974.

Roberts, H., and Palfrey, J. (2010). "The EU Data Retention Directive in an Era of Internet Surveillance," in R. Deibert, J. Palfrey, R. Rohozinski, and J. Zittrain (eds). *Access Controlled: The Shaping of Power, Rights, and Rules in Cyberspace*, Cambridge, MA: MIT Press, pp. 35–54.

Rule, J., McAdam, D., Stearns, L., and Uglow, D. (1980). *The Politics of Privacy: Planning for Personal Data Systems as Powerful Technologies*, New York: Elsevier.

Saco, D. (1999). "Colonizing Cyberspace: National Security and the Internet," in J. Weldes, M. Laffey, H. Gusterson, and R. Duvall (eds). *Cultures of Insecurity: States, Communities, and the Production of Danger*, Minneapolis, MN: University of Minnesota Press, pp. 261–92.

Schaffer, G. (2002). "Reconciling Trade and Regulatory Goals: The Prospects and Limits of New Approaches to Transatlantic Governance through Mutual Recognition and Safe Harbor Agreements," *Colombia Journal of European Law*, 9: 29–77.

Schoen, S. (2009). "What Information is 'Personally Identifiable'," *Electronic Frontier Foundation, Deeplinks Blog*, September 11. Available at <http://www.eff.org/deeplinks/2009/09/what-information-personally-identifiable>. Accessed April 27, 2012.

Schwartz, P. (1999). "Beyond Lessig's *Code* for Internet Privacy: Cyberspace Filters, Privacy Controls and Fair Information Practices," *Wisconsin Law Review* 2000: 743–88.

—— (2009). "Managing Global Data Privacy: Cross-Border Information Flows in a Networked Environment," *The Privacy Projects*. Available at <http://theprivacyprojects.org/wp-content/uploads/2009/08/The-Privacy-Projects-Paul-Schwartz-Global-Data-Flows-20093.pdf>. Accessed April 27, 2012.

Sidhu, D. S. (2007). "The Chilling Effect of Government Surveillance Programs on the Use of the Internet by Muslim-Americans," *University of Maryland Law Journal of Race, Religion, Gender and Class* 7: 375–94.

Simmons, J. L. (2009). "Buying You: The Government's Use of Forth-Parties to Launder Data about 'The People'," *Columbia Business Law Review*, 2009(3): 950–1012.

Soghoian, C. (2003). "The Problem of Anonymous Vanity Searches," *I/S: A Journal of Law and Policy for the Information Society*, 3(2): 299–18.

—— (2011). "An End to Privacy Theater: Exposing and Discouraging Corporate Discloser of Data to the Government," *Minnesota Journal of Law, Science & Technology*, 12(1): 191–38.

Solove, D. J. (2004). *The Digital Person*, New York: New York University Press.

—— (2007). *The Future of Reputation*, New Haven, CT: Yale University Press.

—— (2008). *Understanding Privacy*, Cambridge, MA: Harvard University Press.

Soltani, A., Canty, S., Mayo, Q., Thomas, L., and Hoofnagle, C. J. (2009). "Flash Cookies and Privacy." Available at <http://ssrn.com/abstract=1446862>. Accessed April 27, 2012.

Stalder, F. (2002). "Privacy is not the Antidote to Surveillance," *Surveillance and Society*, 1(1): 120–4.

Strandburg, K. J. (2008). "Surveillance of Emergent Associations: Freedom of Associations in a Network Society," in A. Acquisti and S. Gritzalis (eds). *Digital Privacy: Theory, Technologies, and Practices*, New York: Auerbach Publications, pp. 435–58.

Topolski, R. (2008). "NebuAd and Partner ISPs: Wiretapping, Forgery and Browser Hijacking," Free Press and Public Knowledge. Available at <http://www.publicknowledge.org/pdf/nebuad-report-20080618.pdf>. Accessed April 27, 2012.

Van de Ploeg, I. (2003). "Biometrics and the Body as Information: Normative Issues of the Socio-technical coding of the Body," in D. Lyon (ed.). *Surveillance as Social Sorting*, London: Routledge, pp. 57–73.

Wagner, B. (2009). "Study: Deep Packet Inspection and Internet Censorship," *Global Voices Advocacy: Defending Free Speech Online*, June 25. Available at <http://advocacy.globalvoicesonline.org/2009/06/25/study-deep-packet-inspection-and-internet-censorship/>. Accessed April 27, 2012.

Wall, D. S. (2006). "Surveillance Internet Technologies and the Growth in Information Capitalism: Spams and Public Trust in the Information Society," in K. D. Haggerty and R. V. Ericson (eds). *The New Politics of Surveillance and Visibility*, Toronto: University of Toronto Press, pp. 340–62.

Weitzner, D. J. et al. (2008). "Information Accountability," *Communications of the ACM*, June, 51(6): 84.

Winner, L. (1989). *The Whale and the Reactor: A Search for Limits in the Age of High Technology*, Chicago: University of Chicago Press.

Wolfson, S. M. (2007). "The NSA, AT&T, and the Secrets of Room 641A," *I/S: A Journal of Law and Policy for the Information Society*, 3(3): 411–41.

Wood, D. M. (2009). "Situating Surveillance Studies," *Surveillance and Society*, 19(7): 52–61.

Zimmer, M. (2008). "The Externalities of Search 2.0: The Emerging Privacy Threats when the Drive for the Perfect Search Engine meets Web 2.0," *First Monday* 13(3). Available at <http://firstmonday.org/htbin/cgiwrap/bin/ojs/index.php/fm/article/view/2136/1944>. Accessed June 20, 2012.

Zittrain, J. (2008). *The Future of the Internet: And How to Stop It*, New Haven, CT: Yale University Press.

Zureik, E. and M. Salter (eds) (2005). *Global Surveillance and Policing: Borders, Security, Identity*, Cullompton: Willan Publishing.

....

CHAPTER 24

DIGITAL INFRASTRUCTURES, ECONOMIES, AND PUBLIC POLICIES:

Contending Rationales and Outcome Assessment Strategies

....

ROBIN MANSELL AND W. EDWARD STEINMUELLER

INTRODUCTION

....

INVESTMENTS in the physical infrastructures of society, including transport and communication, are signposts of particular episodes of historical development. This experience suggests that such investments may be a means of fostering economic development and social change. Canals, railways, electricity, telegraph, and telecommunication networks—universally and sometimes selectively—at various times, have been the central focus of national and regional developmental aspirations. A debate concerning the appropriate balance between public and private expenditure and initiative has accompanied almost all of these episodes. This debate draws upon many theories and empirical studies in the social sciences, although the discipline of economics often predominates because of its claims to be able to measure the benefits and costs that might accrue from such policies.

Infrastructures typically rely upon advances in specific industries to provide key technological inputs. For example, railroads soon require steel rails, electricity ever-larger generators, and telecommunication networks, ever more capable methods of switching and transmitting signals. Because of their scale and the inter-dependence of the technological features of infrastructures, their successful development often involves interventions in the course of technological development or the timing and nature of demand. Such interventions may include technical standards that favor particular technologies or procurement policies that increase demand above levels that would otherwise prevail in markets. In promoting an infrastructure, it is also often necessary to change the "rules of the game" governing social and economic activity. For example, many infrastructures rely upon a restructuring of property rights that grant the builders or operators of infrastructure facilities unique privileges or rights. Those companies that construct transport and communication corridors must be able to conscript the routes, and those companies that would employ the radio frequency spectrum must be granted exclusive rights. Some infrastructures additionally require legal regulation to support universality goals or non-discriminatory terms in the provision of access so as to prevent profit-maximizing monopolistic behavior.

The mix of industrial policies, institutional change (altering the rules of the game), and the nature and extent of regulation differ depending upon prevailing ideological fashions (sometimes more liberal or laissez faire and at other times more dirigiste or collective). While many industrial policy interventions are aimed at infrastructure development, two types of interventions have assumed an increasingly central position in recent years.[1] The first is the strengthening of the position of a particular industry in an effort to support "self-financed" infrastructure development. The second is the establishment of government-industry partnerships in order to socialize the risks, participate in the control, and share in the benefits of infrastructure development.

These two interventions are most often rationalized within the liberal or market-driven zeitgeist of the early twenty-first century by using the argument of market failure. For example, government investment may be justified based on the argument of un-appropriated and positive "spillover" effects—that producers are unable to extract adequate revenues from infrastructure users to fund the level of investment that would maximize social welfare. In these circumstances, the government may attempt to "sweeten" the incentives for private investment or serve as a partner in infrastructure development—assuring that investment resources are available and risks are shared. For a particular infrastructure project, a central question then becomes whether private sector investment will be adequate or needs to be stimulated through concessions or subsidies from public authorities (whether state, municipal, or regional). In certain cases, this justification may extend to public ownership and operation, although this option has been employed rarely in the industrialized countries in recent years.

The economic crisis which overtook the world in 2008 has given a strong boost to the information and communication technology (ICT) industrial policies and to specific government interventions supporting infrastructure investment that were already present at the beginning of the twenty-first century. Policies to foster the upgrading of networks to higher capacities and speeds have gained high visibility alongside the diffusion of the Internet and digital technologies and services. This contrasts with the experience early in the decade when a more specific financial collapse, the

---

[1] We focus only on those interventions and rationales that have been prominent in discussions of ICT policy, rather than attempting a comprehensive review of industrial policy. Broader reviews may be found in Bianchi and Labory 2006.

bursting of the dot.com bubble in 2000, caused enthusiasm for the digital economic initiatives to temporarily wane. In those years, uncertainties about whether future supply would meet demand (expressed in economic terms or in terms of citizen preferences for an improved Internet experience—always available, mobility, etc.) were seen as creating major financial risks for investors, both public and private. By contrast, with the larger economic crisis at the end of the decade, supply is seen as having the potential to create demand, and infrastructure development policies are key components in the economic stimulus packages devised by the governments of many countries. Broadband infrastructure development is often identified as a category deserving urgent policy action. This is the case in Europe and North America, the regions we focus on in this chapter. We examine claims about the social and economic benefits and disadvantages of privileging infrastructure investment in this way. In considering the scholarly literatures upon which these are based, we specifically examine the factors understood by social scientists to be influencing these developments, highlighting differences between economists' and other social scientists' viewpoints. These differences influence the ways in which the outcomes of these industrial policy initiatives might be assessed, which we also discuss in this chapter.

NETWORK INFRASTRUCTURE POLICIES

In contemporary industrialized countries, the infrastructures receiving greatest interest are advanced digital ICTs and the "digital economy" networks and applications they support.[2] Policies supporting the construction and operation of these infrastructures have been in place for several decades, although in the US, with a strong commitment to market-led initiatives, there is a reluctance to refer to policy initiatives as industrial policy. By contrast, the success of the newly industrializing Asian economies in both the ICT and network industries, and especially Japan and South Korea as the leader in broadband take-up, is often attributed to technology-led and government coordinated industrial policies (Cambini and Jiang 2009; Fransman 2006; Menon 2011). Regardless of whether accounts of policy interventions acknowledge or diminish the role of government intervention and policy, the assessment of progress in infrastructure development has focused on issues of access, cost, and coverage.

Policies to achieve the improved accessibility and affordability of telecommunication networks and services have a long history in the broader context of support for the production and consumption of ICTs. These policies find support in both academic analysis and the assertions made by policy makers (Bar and Riis 2000; Lehr and Pupillo 2009; NRC 2009). Beginning with efforts in the US to promote the "Information Superhighway" and the subsequent adaptation of this term in other regions of the world,

---

[2] Other infrastructures receiving increasing interest include "intelligent" electricity distribution systems and systems for recycling waste.

the term "global information infrastructure" emerged. This term proved difficult to understand and another technical term, "broadband," has become widely employed and will be used in this chapter.

The addition of broadband connectivity to the list of candidates for various forms of industrial policy promotion did not arise until most industrialized countries transitioned from narrow to broadband Internet services. Broadband refers to telecommunication networks operating at speeds exceeding those of the "narrowband" networks constructed for purposes of voice telephony but later used for data communication with the, increasingly obsolete, acoustic modem. Since broadband is defined in terms of a basic or floor network data exchange capacity, its actual capacities constantly change as technologies and services advance, such as with discussion of "super-fast broadband." Initially limited by the methods used to expand the data communication capacity of copper wire networks, broadband policy typically encompasses network infrastructure including the replacement of copper with optical fiber networks, digital services, and even digital literacy initiatives, as well as very high capacity computing networks used for scientific research purposes. Economic analysis underpins industrial policy initiatives in this area, emphasizing the relationships between investment in broadband, productivity, economic growth, and market competitiveness (OECD 2009b).

The OECD has emphasized broadband diffusion through competitive market-led solutions. In practice, however, the OECD member countries as well as other countries have promoted and continue to promote the supply of, and to a lesser extent, the demand for, broadband networks as central features of twenty-first century economic policy in the US and Europe (Preston 2001). In Europe and in the US there are differences in the arguments used to defend such policies and what will be expected, respectively, of private and public actors. However, a common feature of these policies is neglect of the non-technical and non-economic factors that influence the extent to which societies are becoming dependent on digital networks and information. Issues of democracy and governance, cultural diversity, and social interaction are some of those that influence the relationship between technology development and the features of societies emerging as a result of promotion of digital infrastructures.

Technology policies, in this area as in others, inevitably rely upon trends in the cultural, political and social spheres as well as in the economic sphere. Academic analysts based in the social sciences often are able to explain the relative importance of these contributing factors after they have, collectively, produced outcomes, but such explanations are rarely applicable for predicting the next set of developments. This means that when policy-makers turn to academics for answers to the policy dilemmas they face, they are often disappointed in the equivocal answers they receive, or they are perplexed by the barrage of claims and counterclaims from different academics choosing to weight possible influences in different ways. In this weighting process, values and aspirations for society play important roles, and thus academic analysis is not immune from political belief or hope.

One set of criteria for assessing the outcomes of broadband (or more generally infrastructure) policy initiatives is whether they yield social benefits such as improving the condition of the environment, workplace safety, or health. Another is whether they yield widespread economic growth benefits. If private investors are reluctant to develop new networks and services on the time-scale required, or with the desired social benefits, the question is whether, and to what extent, governments should become more involved in their development. Each of these areas is controversial and provides illustrations of how the weights that are placed on competing explanations and expectations fundamentally influence the conclusions that may be reached.

Promoting ICTs, the Internet,
and Broadband

The challenges of digital infrastructure and service development have been scrutinized by the OECD from the perspectives of technology, innovation, and regulatory policy since the initial moves to introduce competition into national and global telecommunication markets (OECD 1988). As the political impetus to privatize and liberalize these markets gained momentum in the 1980s, the main theme of policy in this area has been an emphasis on the benefits of competition as the key stimulus to investment and innovation in ICTs. However, this neo-liberal approach to market-led growth has been challenged by evidence of persistent gaps in access to and the use of networks, including the Internet. Whether rural and remote areas or excluded groups are the targets, OECD policy guidance has suggested the need for policy intervention (OECD 2009a).

In the case of Europe, by 1993 the European Commission had set a goal of acquiring a leading competitive position in the information society (European Commission 1993a). The rapid development of broadband networks and interactive information and audio-visual services were to support this goal while also ensuring that such developments would bring desirable social outcomes. In the decade of the 1990s, the deployment of the first generation of broadband networks was described as a "race" between Europe and other regions of the world (Bohlin and Granstrand 1994). Within Europe, emphasis was given to the need to improve coordination between the member states so as to construct harmonized trans-European networks. However, industrial and regulatory policy initiatives were slowed by competing political and economic interests among the major actors (Mansell 1997). Further concerns were raised about whether liberalized telecommunication markets would maintain the universal (telephone) service obligations of the former monopoly incumbent operators.[3] European Commission policy focused both on universal service and provisions to stimulate investment in advanced trans-European networks. The perceived need to upgrade networks to support broadband was clearly in

---

[3] These changes in policy in Europe were reflected in a series of directives issued by the European Commission on universal service.

evidence in the Commissions spending on research and development (R&D) in the ICT domain (1993b).

A decade later, the European Union Lisbon Strategy of 2000 aimed to make the European Union the most competitive economy in the world by increasing the level of R&D in individual member states as well as through other measures and to achieve full employment by 2010, objectives that, in retrospect, were entirely out of reach. This coincided with the eEurope Initiative of 2000 and various action plans for the Information Society. Initially, the Information Society was regarded as being synonymous with new ICTs, emphasizing a technology-led strategy. These initiatives called for supply and demand-side policy measures, aiming to foster a European information society for all. The Lisbon Strategy was re-launched in 2005, giving rise to the i2010 strategy for ICTs. The latter called for the creation of a single European information space, innovation and ICT R&D, and greater citizen inclusion. These developments were buttressed by a 2009 Directive augmenting earlier Directives on universal service and users' rights relating to electronic communication networks and services (European Commission 2005, 2009b)

In the wake of the recession in Europe, in 2008, the European Economic Recovery Plan asserted that "Equipping Europe with this modern infrastructure is as important as building the railways in the nineteenth century" (European Commission 2008: 16), and that public funds would be needed to provide broadband access to under-served and high cost areas where market actors would not choose to provide service. Technology investment was central to this plan as evidenced in the European Strategy for ICT R&D and Innovation in Europe (European Commission 2009a: 5) which stated that Europe is expected to lead in the development of the "Future Internet" and that to do so, Europe would need to "raise its game." A sense of urgency was fostered through recognition that the European Union's ICT business sector was spending less than half as much on R&D as its US counterpart.

In the response to the 2008 crisis and its lingering aftermath, it became clear that public sector intervention in support of broadband was to be welcomed. Specifically with regard to the broadband Internet, the European Digital Competitiveness Report for 2009 stated that broadband Internet "is essential to businesses, public services and to making the modern economy work" (European Commission 2009c: 8).

By 2010, the European Union had a new Digital Agenda in place, the overall aim of which was "to deliver sustainable economic and social benefits from a digital single market based on fast and ultra fast internet and interoperable applications" (European Commission 2010a: 3). The agenda is intended to take forward the Europe 2020 strategy (European Commission 2010b) which called for smart, sustainable and inclusive growth, achieving this through an economy based on knowledge and innovation, a greener and more competitive, high-employment economy. However, these aims required even more effective use of ICTs in Europe than elsewhere because the direct contribution of ICTs to economic growth has remained lower in Europe at 5 percent of GDP, as compared to 6.4 percent in the US and 6.8 percent in Japan (European Commission 2010c).

The Digital Agenda is one of several pillars in the 2020 strategy. The objectives were strikingly similar to those announced in 2008, although its authors observed that Europe is still a patchwork of online national markets and, importantly, that more would need to be done "to facilitate investment in the new very fast open and competitive internet networks that will be the arteries of a future economy," (European Commission 2010a: 6) and to ensure that broadband targets will be met.

In the United Kingdom, the notion that governments have a role to play in identifying and promoting emerging and generic technologies has a long history. This notion has been applied in the promotion of digital technologies and services for several decades, although not without controversy. From the 1980s digital information started to be regarded as an opportunity to devise new business models leading to enhanced economic growth (Guy and Arnold 1989; ITAP 1983). The policies of the 1980s are echoed by many of the digital inclusion initiatives in subsequent years. Following public consultation in 2009, the government published its *Digital Britain* Report with a ministerial foreword claiming that: "The move from analogue to digital technology is one of those revolutionary changes. It will define the competitiveness of our economy and change dramatically the way we lead our lives" (BIS-DCMS 2009: 1). The wide-scale implications of ICTs for the economy and society were acknowledged without hesitation. The goal of government policy was clarified as being to strengthen the competitive position of the United Kingdom by complementing and assisting the private sector to deliver a modern communication infrastructure, building on new digital technologies.

The focus on broadband as the agent of economic transformation and social change is very clear. It is claimed that the first generation of broadband connectivity yielded a boost to GDP of 0.5–1.0 percent annually and that there is a clear case for the universal availability of networks with speeds of 50mbp/s and above (BIS-DCMS 2009: 13). A number of methods of financing this were considered, including a surcharge of 50 pence per month on all fixed copper lines. The surcharge was estimated to enable expansion in coverage of Next Generation Access (NGA), that is, the next step in upgrading the capacity of networks accessible to citizens, to the large majority of the British population. The overall conclusion was: "we are moving into a world where not having broadband access creates social and economic disadvantage" (BIS-DCMS 2009: 52). The Digital Economy Act of 2010 (UK Government 2010) took forward many of the provisions outlined in the *Digital Britain* report. Questions were raised about whether demand would be sufficiently strong to support investment in super-fast broadband networks and about the political viability of proposed government subsidies aimed at ramping up private-sector investment (House of Commons 2010: 21).

In the US, a digital investment policy theme has been apparent in government policy for some time, and it has often emphasized broadband. The need to encourage infrastructure and service development was discussed in the 1990s in the context of the need for a National Information Infrastructure (NII) to improve national productivity and quality of life, and an agenda for action followed (US Government 1990, 1993). The emphasis was on building the "information superhighway" through strategic alliances between the major industry players, and on analyzing the ways in which investment in ICTs would enhance the performance of the service industries (CSTB 1994; Gore 1995). Government sponsored reports pointed to the potential of the *Emerging*

Digital Economy (Department of Commerce 1999) and the Federal Communications Commission (FCC) made numerous decisions about whether there was a need for government to accelerate the deployment of advanced networks, finding that the market should lead deployment of upgrades to telecommunication networks, although some steps might be taken to ensure improved access (FCC 1999). During the decade of the 1990s, some analysts argued that policy based on features other than intense market competition between private investors would be needed for the US to maintain its role as leader in the production and consumption of ICTs and to benefit from widespread Internet (broadband) use (Kahin and Wilson III 1997).

By 2009, in the wake of the financial crisis, Title VI of the American Recovery and Reinvestment Act of 2009 (US Government 2009) initiated the "Broadband Technology Opportunities Program." This was designed to provide public funding for initiatives to improve access to broadband service in unserved or under-served areas and to provide broadband education, access, equipment, and assistance for schools, libraries, healthcare providers, and vulnerable groups in society. Demand-side policy was emphasized to a greater extent than in earlier initiatives. Alongside many other government agencies, the FCC was expected to play a major role in facilitating the stimulus program for broadband.

Harvard University's Berkman Center for Internet and Society was commissioned by the FCC to evaluate the evidence on the relatively mediocre performance of the US in achieving leadership in broadband network provision compared to other leading countries. Its report, *Next Generation Connectivity* (Berkman Center 2010), confirmed that broadband performance had declined relative to other countries over the past decade and provided a summary of the announced costs associated with broadband policies in selected countries, demonstrating how widely levels of government support vary in both absolute and per capita terms (from a claimed European Union average of US$912 per capita, to 6,330 per capita in South Korea, 46,000 per capita in Australia, and 7,200 per capita in the US in 2009). It also emphasized the need for demand-side policies and profiled, among others, initiatives underway in South Korea, the country widely acknowledged as the leader in individual use of high bandwidth Internet access. The range of initiatives included skills training; funding for public Internet access sites; and other measures to validate and promote Internet use (Berkman Center 2010).

Although this report was met with criticism for its failure to identify trade-offs faced by broadband policy makers (Bauer 2009), the FCC set out its *Connecting America: The National Broadband Plan* (FCC 2010) in response to the government mandate provided by the Recovery and Reinvestment Act, arguing that digital exclusion would grow in the absence of government action. Under the Obama Administration, a much wider range of industrial policy initiatives has been envisaged than under previous administrations. The FCC Broadband Plan discussed government influence over the communication "ecosystem", including the traditional emphasis on market competition, but also contemplating renewed use of procurement policies and an extension of universal service provisions. It called for 100 million homes to have affordable access to download speeds of 50 mbp/s and upload speeds of 20 mbp/s by 2015 (FCC 2010).

In the case of South Korea, the success of initiatives such as the Korean Information Infrastructure initiative launched in 2005 aimed at constructing a high-speed backbone network, has been attributed to a combination of policies aimed at stimulating competition between telecommunication and cable platforms and demand-side stimulus policies (Fransman 2006; Picot and Wernick 2007). Several countries included measures to boost broadband access in their economic stimulus packages in the wake of the financial crisis of 2008 in addition to those discussed above (Canada, Germany, Portugal, and Finland) and others introduced plans specifically aimed at broadband development (Australia, France, Ireland, Japan, and Singapore, in addition to the renewed efforts of South Korea) (Qiang 2010). In most of these cases, the aim was to stimulate the private sector to invest more than it would otherwise have done in the absence of some government investment.

All of these bold initiatives claim evidence from research as the basis for action. To what extent can the policies discussed here be justified on the basis of academic evidence? How disinterested is this academic evidence base?

JUSTIFYING BROADBAND POLICY

It has been claimed that ICTs are "General Purpose Technologies" (GPTs). Economists argue that GPTs are technological innovations, such as electricity or digital technology, whose impacts on the economy and society are so extensive and disruptive that they have a profound economy-wide influence. The general theory of GPTs was developed in the 1990s (Bresnahan and Trajtenberg 1995), but the specific transformational potential of the ICT revolution was discussed earlier by Perez and others (Freeman 1988; Perez 1983). As these technologies diffuse widely, investment leads to disruptive effects on the structure of the ICT producing industries and to the need for adjustment of government policies and regulation. The models of diffusion guiding these views on the impact of digital ICTs are also drawn from sociological theories of the diffusion process, elaborating on the qualitative insights, but relying increasingly on quantitative modeling techniques to assess rates of diffusion and the impacts of ICTs (Antonelli 2003; Mansell et al. 2007; Rogers 1962). Digital technologies have been nominated as important contributors to industrial development strategy for regions and for stimulating innovation and competition more broadly (Braczyk et al. 1997; Justman and Teubal 1995).

As in the case of all investment strategies—whether sponsored by the public or private sector—there is always the risk that demand will not be responsive to supply. In the late 1980s, for example, when broadband initiatives to build the ISDN (Integrated Services Digital Networks) were promoted, there were major questions about whether the capacity of new data networks would exceed demand (David and Steinmueller 1990). These questions have remained relevant, although the same optimist and pessimist views are present. For the enthusiasts, research and development leading to innovative digital technologies and applications are essential elements in any framework of industrial policy (Geuna et al. 2003). For the pessimists, a technologically driven focus on the economy or society suggests that citizens' opportunities to shape their communication environment will be foreclosed by the decisions of those designing and promoting the new technologies (Silverstone and Mansell 1996).

From the perspective of economists—mostly optimists—a major challenge is to understand why some countries forge ahead economically and others fall behind (Abramovitz 1986). The evidence that a major share of long-term economic growth in recent decades is associated with knowledge accumulation and the apparent link between knowledge and the use of ICTs, leads to calls for technology policies in which new ICTs play an ever greater role (Abramovitz and David 1996; Metcalfe 1997). The nature of these dynamics has been extensively studied, with an emphasis particularly on the interactions between the "old" and the "new" economy and on interactions between older and newer network technologies and communication practices (Christensen and Maskell 2003; Steinmueller 1995). The importance of digital technologies in enabling the convergence of formally separate industry segments (e.g. broadcasting, telecommunication, software and computing) has led scholars to call for new approaches to policy for the ICT sector and, more broadly, for all ICT-using sectors of the economy including services (Miles 2010). On the basis of these arguments, the evidence in support of industrial policies and regulatory measures to promote ICTs and broadband networks seems strong; but is it?

Policies, evidence, and politics: Building a critical perspective

Two broad categories of public policy initiatives are used to stimulate broadband adoption: 1) policies assisting the build-up of broadband networks and 2) policies aimed at enhancing competition through telecommunication market openness and access to infrastructures. Policies aimed at financially assisting telecommunication providers, establishing public–private partnerships (i.e. through public sector demand aggregation), and building government-owned networks, are in the first category, together with policies to enable access to computers.

The rapid and sustained pace of ICTs is clearly believed by policy-makers to be opening up new frontiers for commercial and non-commercial activities. The potential of these innovations is large, but they call into question long-accepted assumptions about how best to organize markets for the production and consumption of new products. Policy choices are necessary, and regulatory environments are needed to foster appropriate incentives and rules. The economic issues include the organization of the markets for supplying these technologies, the growth and structure of demand, and the response of private actors to the rules and incentives established by government policy. Each of these issues has political features—both in terms of accountability and priority.

The ability to measure and assess whether promised potentials are being fulfilled is the basis for policy accountability. It is essential to be able to evaluate whether the claims made for these policies, and specifically for those with respect to the Internet and broadband, are the empty promises of zealous promoters or credible approximations of the transformations that lie ahead. Establishing accountability is the most important step in refining and innovating in the process of industrial policy and regulation. Unless we know how information societies are capable of failing to meet the aspirations of different stakeholders, there is little likelihood that policy initiatives will enhance their benefits, re-direct them from misguided paths, or mitigate their negative consequences, except by accident or through a tortuous re-appraisal conducted in hindsight.

Accountability brings the need for an evidence-base and it is here that all branches of the social sciences and the humanities can play a key role, although the political and contested nature of that role needs to be acknowledged. In the case of broadband, the parameters for accountability are reasonably clear. Policy-makers need evidence for deciding among the possibilities of: 1) monopoly-based network integration with political intervention to achieve economic and social goals; 2) free market competition leading to the possibility of more rapid innovation at the cost of network fragmentation with the possibility of social exclusion; and 3) oligopolistic dominance of markets leading to higher rates of investment at the risk of market fragmentation, a denial of the need for regulation (compared to monopoly-based network integration), and social exclusion. It is important to note that each of these options raises possibilities of social exclusion unless mitigating regulatory intervention is undertaken. Policy-makers also need to consider the "public interest" implications of the spread of the Internet and broadband networks for democratic processes and social and cultural development, as well as for economic efficiency and innovation.

The theoretical frameworks used by academics to assess the "performance" of economies undergoing technological change often do not lend themselves to normative (what should be done) conclusions. Alternatively, the frameworks themselves may contain prior judgments of normative positions that are either not transparent or, when they are explicit, are presented as if they contained no politically contentious issues. In the case of the *Next Generation Connectivity* report noted in the preceding section (Berkman Center 2010) there are instances where the authors conflated the results of academic studies with normative policy prescriptions that do not necessarily follow from the quantitative and qualitative evidence base. Evidence of the politically charged environment in which assessments of broadband policies are undertaken is also present in the response to a report of the Directorate of the European Commission responsible for Employment and Social Affairs on *Building the European Information Society for Us All* (European Commission 1997) which was based on the work of leading academics and warned against an overemphasis on technology and simplistic notions of social and economic adjustment. The policy recommendations called for attention to the way technological developments are shaped by social forces and values, and to the complexity and non-linearity of this relationship. The R&D technology-led Directorates of the Commission concerned directly with the competitiveness of the economy downplayed this recommendation in subsequent iterations of European ICT policy.

Policy-makers appear to be absorbing some of the more sophisticated economic reasoning concerning the pervasive effects of changes accompanying growing ICT use and incorporating this reasoning in their plans. For example, the FCC, the OECD and the European Commission refer to insights arising from the GPT characteristics of ICTs in their more recent plans and strategies. Absent, however, is evidence that they have understood that it is exactly the general purpose nature of these technologies that not only creates positive disruption, but also negative disruption, such as rapid shifts in employment opportunities, liquidation of established business models, and the possibility of a structural crisis of adjustment as the new technologies diffuse widely throughout the economy. There is continuing evidence of a striking inability on the part of policy-makers to hear and act as a matter of priority upon evidence of a critical component of these developments.

The problem of deciding what evidence is relevant for inclusion in policy assessment (or planning) is accompanied by the problem of establishing a causal relationship between policy interventions and outcomes. Policy announcements and prescriptions for intervention generally do not acknowledge the complexity of the relationships that are affected by public policy interventions. They posit a linear relationship between a given action or set of actions and a set of outcomes. This attribute is common in policy statements suggesting that investment in ICTs will produce productivity growth; that broadband Internet access will lead to citizen empowerment in democratic practice; or that public investment in high bandwidth infrastructure inevitably will lead to economic growth.

The difficulty in foreseeing policy outcomes is sometimes acknowledged as in the case of the 2010 FCC plan for broadband where it is noted that market dynamics are likely to change in unpredictable ways (FCC 2010: 151). This difficulty is similarly present in the European context when it is acknowledged that the test of whether there is a need for public investment is subject to future incentives arising from changes in the competitiveness of the marketplace (Cave and Hatta 2009). Public subsidies may be justified to meet industrial policy goals and as enablers of economic and social benefits across sectors, but all policies represent trade-offs between providing incentives for building networks and for promoting competition, once they are built (Bauer 2010). Whether policy measures seeking to promote investment in broadband have desired effects depends on the design of the policy instruments and the situation of specific organizations and individuals. Many economic studies are rooted in equilibrium models that make it difficult to capture these dynamic "interdependencies," the economists' shorthand for all the features of the political, cultural, and social environment that influence policy outcomes.

Given the complexity and uncertainty associated with policy interventions to stimulate broadband, policy-makers are inclined to rely upon economists for guidance. What such guidance is likely to be, however, is worth investigating.

Can economics define the future?

In policy planning and assessment, recourse is often made to studies of the impact of ICT investment on the economy as a whole, to discern how it influences changes in productivity (Jorgenson 2001; Jorgenson and Stiroh 2000). A productivity gap between the US and Europe is well documented (Van Ark et al. 2008) but the reasons for its persistence are not clear. Aggregate studies do not provide sufficiently fine-grained insight into the factors—apart from investment in technology—that explain the persistent differences. To do so means that evidence must be gathered that is far more fine-grained and that analysis must stray beyond the boundaries of macro-economic analysis. For instance, Van Reenen et al. provide a state-of-the-art examination of European firm level evidence on the economic impact of ICTs, finding that labor and product market regulation may be significant determinants of cross-country differences in the impact of ICT. As they observe, "Rather than being focused on correcting market failures in ICT investment, policies in this area need to focus on assisting the accumulation of a number of complementary factors, principally organizational capital and skills" (Van Reenen et al. 2010: 10). The principal issue is not technology or investment but issues of institutional structure and reform, organization and management, including culture, and education, that is, the preferences and behavior of human beings. Van Renan et al.'s observations for Europe are consistent with the results of studies conducted in the US that emphasize the importance of learning to use ICTs more effectively through skills development (see Hargatti and Hsieh Chapter 7).

Addressing these issues should be a central economic issue rather than an incidental or peripheral concern in assessing broadband industrial policies. There are, however, many examples of studies that use the ICT "treatment effect" to infer such impacts by seeking a causal link between investment in infrastructure and economic growth, invariably over-emphasizing technology supply over demand considerations (Koutroumpis 2009). The treatment effect has been employed to examine other economic variables than growth and productivity, such as the potential for job creation yielding results indicating either job destruction and displacement or incremental job creation, depending on the assumptions made for the purposes of the analysis (Katz and Suter 2009).

In summary, the most common approach of economists attempting to deal with the problems of the ICT and Internet "revolutions" is to assume that these massive technological changes represent an augmentation to productivity and, therefore, an impetus to economic growth. There appears to be little patience, at least as reflected by the balance of papers, with attempting to sort out the industry by industry effects of technological change, the changes in human capital associated with greater use of ICTs and the Internet, or the other intervening intermediate good supply and demand features that lead to uncertainty about the likely impact of policies aimed at stimulating broadband investment. While some of these detailed features may be of little aggregate consequence, it seems hazardous to proceed directly to the assumption that disruptions and dislocations disappear simply because of new production processes or organizational arrangements. Economists, however, are responding to the demands by policy-makers for a rationale and justification for promoting the uptake of infrastructure. It will not do to reply that this is a very complicated issue for which researchers have insufficient evidence or that "time will tell" (after all the intermediating changes which produce disequilibrium are resolved). It may be better to take the treatment effect model, with its assumption of a shift in equilibrium outcomes as a result of ICT investment, as a starting assumption and an approximation of likely changes, rather than waiting to map out the pattern of change as it emerges. This solution runs the risk of downplaying or excluding consideration of cultural, social, or political issues that are of substantial importance in shaping the outcomes of policy for the societies that emerge.

Demand considerations; more complexity

The emphasis in broadband policy-making is on technological innovation and supply in the marketplace, but technology diffusion requires effective demand. In the case of ICTs and the Internet, demand analysis remains a poor cousin to supply analysis in the justifi-cations for industrial policy initiatives. This is partially a consequence of the interaction between policy-makers' demands for answers and the willingness of economists to sup-ply them, with, but mostly without, appropriate qualifications about the complex ways in which ICTs and the Internet become embedded in the economy and society. Unfortunately, there is no untapped reservoir of research that might better illuminate the contingencies and traps that policy-makers face in attempting to respond to the chal-lenges of rapid changes in ICT and the Internet. There are many beginnings and pointers, but there is little of the substance that might enable a systematic approach to negotiating the turbulent processes that constitute the reality of these rapid changes. Many academic analysts have stressed the importance of developing improved understanding of demand for new technologies and criticized the general tendency to over-emphasize investment in physical infrastructure, while neglecting the implications of ICTs and the Internet for empowerment and participation, information access, and lifelong learning, for example (Mansell and Steinmueller 2000; Melody 2005; Siegen University 2010).

Many of the demand side developments are associated with the growing potential for the co-production of content using the tools of the Web. Others are facilitated by access to high capacity networks for downloading and uploading of content (legally or illegally). These activities enable Internet users—as citizens and as consumers—to experiment and learn—facilitating a more participatory culture (Jenkins 2006; Jenkins et al. 2009). In a "remix" culture, amateur creativity becomes a substantial resource for the economy and society, and research on e-participation and on e-living shows that a key feature of these changes is the way broadband technologies and applications offer attractive environ-ments for experimentation in formal and informal settings (Aichholzer and Westholm 2009; Anderson et al. 2006; Lessig 2008). Community-based strategies developed by local governments also influence the way broadband network access develops, and local governments may become involved in stimulating broadband access (Josgrilberg 2008; Powell and Shade 2006). Initiatives aimed at stimulating demand have been shown to be effective only when they are responsive to local priorities and social contexts.

Opportunities offered by the availability of the Internet are strongly influenced by the strategies of the large content-providing firms and the network operators which may influ-ence the demand for broadband as a result of pricing strategies, the bundling of services, and limitations on the bandwidth that is available to the Internet Service Provider subscriber. There also is a need for caution in interpreting studies aimed at demonstrating the potential demand for broadband in the light of findings indicating that users shape their take up in unexpected ways (Castells 2009; Silverstone 2005; van Dijk 2005). The assessment of demand for broadband needs to be examined critically in the light of research findings suggesting that the contexts of online use influence the users' experience, suggesting that online experience is associated with major changes in sociability and in some cases in psychological well-being. This suggests that policies aimed at stimulating demand for broadband need to be considered in the light of broader social goals for society and complemented by policy intervention in areas of digital literacy, as well as in areas relating to Internet users' offline experiences (Baym 2010; Turkle 2011).

Studies of demand for broadband and related ICT applications highlight important developments that hint at starting points for sustained research on the complexity of the interactions between supply and demand for the applications and services that increasingly fast broadband networks can make available for citizens and consumers. Existing works offer some tentative generalizations, many of which are at a level of abstraction that is difficult to translate easily into the specific implications that can be used to inform policy. They do suggest, however, that policy-making should be informed by research that yields new ideas about the nature of the "impacts," "effects," and "treatments" resulting from the process of technological change.

THE EVIDENCE-BASE AND THE ASSESSMENT OF OUTCOMES

The evidence base supporting broadband policies is unsurprisingly inconsistent because it starts from different theoretical premises, employs different methods, and has recourse to very different qualities of data—both qualitative and quantitative. It is also inconsistent because of the politics of research and the pressures to read normative conclusions from results, as well as the inevitability that normative values are built (implicitly or explicitly) into research designs and methodologies. The evidence base justifying policy initiatives has been controversial, but the evidence base for assessing broadband policy outcomes has been even more contested.

International agencies and countries around the world are developing metrics for measuring the take-up and use of broadband technologies. For the most part, these involve indices that track access, prices, and to some extent, types of use.[4] Over time, a relatively nuanced profile of broadband patterns of supply and use is emerging, but these

---

[4] The OECD publishes data on penetration, usage, coverage, prices, services, and speeds. The European Commission collects information about rural coverage, competition, price, quality, and take-up of advanced services and socio-economic context. The EuroBarometer Surveys examine types of use, issues of safety on the Internet, etc.

results cannot provide definitive answers to questions about the direct relationships between broadband policy initiatives and their outcomes, and they are generally focused on the diffusion of technologies rather than on the qualitative changes that promote or suppress demand for new applications and services. Some authors suggest greater attention to the unexpected outcomes associated with broadband policies, to changes in cultural and social life, and to the way the legal and regulatory environment influences the potential for experimenting with digital information (Melody 2005; Preston et al. 2007; Ramirez 2007). Experimentation is likely to be suppressed when regulation fails to curtail the market power of incumbent suppliers evident, for example, in digital content markets when suppliers seek to limit access through tactics to restrain copyright infringement, and in infrastructure markets where economies of scale in network supply may be encouraging a new stage of market concentration (Mueller 2010; Wu 2010). These developments are occurring in the context of the global reach of ICT markets, raising issues for trade in equipment and services and for the intensity of competition which, in turn, creates uncertain investment incentives for the roll-out of broadband networks (Cowhey and Aronson 2009). These are all considerations that influence the assessment of the outcomes of broadband policies.

Conclusion

Industrial policy aimed at stimulating investment in infrastructure, understood broadly to include both its physical components and the institutional and social arrangements for its provision and use, is a controversial, but not uncommon means through which governments seek to extend facilities and services to their populations. Broadband policy is often justified in this context both as a means of stimulating economic growth and as a means of enhancing the quality of life. These rationales are much in evidence in Europe and the US as digital infrastructures have come to be regarded as being increasingly pivotal in the societies of the twenty-first century. The question asked by policymakers is whether private sector investment will be adequate to meet future needs, in the absence of a stimulus provided by the state.

The need for a response has become urgent in the wake of the recession that began at the end of the first decade of the twenty-first century. Broadband investment has been incorporated into the core of stimulus packages, designed to speed economic recovery, as well as in the longer-term development plans of countries experiencing rapid economic growth or achieving the status of late-comer industrialization (such as Korea, Taiwan, and Brazil and, to a lesser extent China, India, and Russia). Academic analyses addressing policy-makers' needs for answers have been given greater visibility, particularly if they serve to help to rationalize these policies. Policy-makers also turn to scholarly research as a means of monitoring the outcomes of their policy initiatives in this area, more often to seek new ways to hasten the speed of development than to discover ways in which these developments can be shaped to increase or broaden social benefits.

We have examined arguments provided by academic research as a basis for policy prescription and assessed whether the evidence base is robust as a means of providing accountability for government initiatives. Academics are not always well positioned to assess whether industrial policies, which are invariably technology-led in the ICT field, are likely to yield social or economic benefit. Nevertheless, the promotion of ICTs, the Internet, and broadband connectivity is assumed by many policy-makers to be directly and causally related to economic growth through productivity gains and to other social outcomes, including improved quality of life, improved education, and more responsive government services. There are signs that in both Europe and in the US, research has contributed to the realization that ICTs (and broadband) are GPTs, and that they are capable of contributing to extensive and pervasive changes in the economy and society. However, in policy terms, this realization has implied a predominant focus on the effects of broadband supply and ICT diffusion, with the treatment of demand as an incidental feature of the supply and demand equation.

Policy initiatives in Europe and the US demonstrate greater understanding of the multiple variables involved in this relationship, but there is continued reliance principally on the insights of economists with respect to technology and investment employing treatment effects models, despite the fact that some economists and other social scientists have insisted on the necessity of examining issues such as institutional structure, organizational practice, education, and cultural distinctions. The richness of insights of researchers from other disciplines that insist on the importance of political, cultural, social, and economic trends in explaining developments in broadband markets is difficult to make palatable for policy-makers. A productive route towards improved accountability of broadband (and other) industrial policy initiatives requires research aimed at considering the contributions of these strategies from a variety of disciplinary perspectives.

The values and assumptions built into the research conducted independently by academics or under sponsorship by those with an interest in the outcome need to be acknowledged so as to achieve improved accountability through an explicit acknowledgement of the political nature of research, just as the political nature of policy-making itself is commonly understood. In this context, the insights of some of those working in the economics discipline and most of those working in other social science disciplines point to a vital need to better understand demand for higher capacity networks and their applications. The research agenda needs to be aimed at considering broadband investment options in the context of the social and economic aspirations of citizens so as to contribute more effectively to policy judgments about how far the public sector should proceed to meet those aspirations ahead of what the private sector is likely to achieve.

ACKNOWLEDGMENT

We are grateful to Bill Dutton for helpful comments on an earlier version of this chapter. We are responsible for any errors or omissions in the text.

References

Abramovitz, M. (1986). "Catching Up, Forging Ahead and Falling Behind," *Journal of Economic History*, 46(2): 385–406.

—— and David, P. A. (1996). "Technological Change and the Rise of Intangible Investments: The US Economy's Growth-Path in the Twentieth Century," in D. Foray and B.-Å. Lundvall (eds). *Employment and Growth in the Knowledge-based Economy*, Paris: OECD, pp. 35–60.

Aichholzer, G. and Westholm, H. (2009). "Evaluating eParticipation Projects: Practical Examples and Outline of an Evaluation Framework," *European Journal of ePractice*, 7(3): 1–18.

Anderson, B., Brynin, M., Raban, Y. and Gershuny, J. (eds) (2006). *Information and Communications Technologies in Society: E-Living in a Digital Europe*, London: Routledge.

Antonelli, C. (2003). "The Digital Divide: Understanding the Economics of New Information and Communication Technology in the Global Economy," *Information Economics and Policy*, 15(2): 173–99.

Bar, F. and Riis, A. M. (2000). "Tapping User-Driven Innovation: A New Rationale for Universal Service," *The Information Society*, 16(2): 99–108.

Bauer, J. M. (2009). "Comments of Johannes M Bauer on 'Next Generation Connectivity,' Broadband Study conducted by the Berkmann Center for Internet and Society," Washington In the Matter of International Comparison and Consumer Survey Requirements in the Broadband Data Improvement Act; A National Broadband Plan for Our Future; and Inquiry Concerning the Deployment of Advanced Telecommunications Capability to All Americans in a Reasonable and Timely Fashion, NBP Public Notice No. 13, Federal Communications Commission. Available at <http://ecfsdocs.fcc.gov/filings/2009/11/16/6015499155.html>. Accessed June 20, 2012.

—— (2010). "Regulation, Public Policy, and Investment in Communications," *Telecommunications Policy*, 34(1–2): 65–79.

Baym, N. K. (2010). *Personal Connection in the Digital Age: Digital Media and Society Series*, Cambridge: Polity Press.

Berkman Center (2010). *Next Generation Connectivity: A Review of Broadband Internet Transitions and Policy from around the World*, Boston MA: Berkman Center for the Internet and Society, Harvard University.

Bianchi, P. and Labory, S. (eds) (2006). *International Handbook on Industrial Policy*, Cheltenham: Edward Elgar Publishing.

BIS-DCMS (2009). *Digital Britain: Final Report*, London: Department for Business Innovation and Skills, Department for Culture Media and Sport, June.

Bohlin, E. and Granstrand, O. (eds) (1994). *The Race to European Eminence*, Amsterdam: Elsevier.

Braczyk, H.-J., Cooke, P., and Heidenreich, M. (eds) (1997). *Regional Innovation Systems*, London: University College London Press.

Bresnahan, T. and Trajtenberg, M. (1995). "General Purpose Technologies: 'Engines for Growth,'" *Journal of Econometrics*, 65(1): 83–108.

Cambini, C. and Jiang, Y. (2009). "Broadband Investment and Regulation: A Literature Review," *Telecommunications Policy*, 33(10–11): 559–74.

Castells, M. (2009). *Communication Power*, Oxford: Oxford University Press.

Cave, M. and Hatta, K. (2009). "Transforming Telecommunications Technologies—Policy and Regulation," *Oxford Review of Economic Policy*, 25(3): 488–505.

Christensen, J. F. and Maskell, P. (eds) (2003). *The Industrial Dynamics of the New Digital Economy*, Cheltenham: Edward Elgar.

Cowhey, P. F. and Aronson, J. D. (2009). *Transforming Global Information and Communication Markets*, Cambridge, MA: MIT Press.

CSTB (1994). *Information Technology in the Service Society: A Twenty-First Century Lever*, Washington, DC: National Academy Press for Computer Science and Telecommunications Board, Commission on Physical Sciences, Mathematics, and Applications, and National Research Council, Committee to Study the Impact of Information Technology on the Performance of Service Activities.

David, P. A. and Steinmueller, W. E. (1990). "The ISDN Bandwagon is Coming, But Who Will be There to Climb Aboard?: Quandaries in the Economics of Data Communication Networks," *Economics of Innovation and New Technology*, 1(1–2): 43–62.

Department of Commerce (1999). *The Emerging Digital Economy II*, Washington DC: Department of Commerce, June.

European Commission (1993a). "Growth, Competitiveness, Employment: The Challenges and Ways Forward into the 21st century." White Paper, Brussels: European Commission, COM(93)700 final.

——(1993b). *Trans-European Networks—Integrated Broadband Communications*, Brussels: Commission of the European Communities, DGXIII, RA933510/T.

——(1997). *Building the European Information Society for Us All: Final policy report of the high-level expert group, DGV for Employment and Social Affairs*, Luxembourg: European Commission.

——(2005). *i2010—A European Information Society for Growth and Employment, Communication from the Commission to the European Parliament, the Council, the European Economic and Social Committee and the Committee of the Regions*, Brussels: European Commission COM(2005)229, 1 June.

——(2008). *A European Economic Recovery Plan, Communication from the Commission to the European Council*, Brussels: European Commission COM(2008)800 final, 26 November.

——(2009a). *Communication from the Commission to the European Parliament, the Council, the European Economic and Social Committee and the Committee of the Regions: A Strategy for ICT R&D and Innovation in Europe: Raising the Game*, Brussels: European Commission SEC(2009)289; COM(2009)116 final.

——(2009b). Directive 2009/136/EC of the European Parliament and of the Council of 25 November 2009, amending Directive 2002/22/EC on universal service and users' rights relating to electronic communications networks and services, Directive 2002/58/EC concerning the processing of personal data and the protection of privacy in the electronic communications sector and Regulation (EC) No 2006/2004 on cooperation between national authorities responsible for the enforcement of consumer protection laws, Brussels: European Commission Official Journal, L337/11.

——(2009c). *Europe's Digital Competitiveness Report: Main Achievements of the i2010 Strategy 2005–2009*, Brussels: European Commission COM(2009)390.

——(2010a). *A Digital Agenda for Europe: Communication from the Commission to the European Parliament, the Council, the European Economic and Social Committee and the Committee of the Regions*, Brussels: European Commission COM(2010)245 final.

——(2010b). *Europe 2020: A European Strategy for Smart, Sustainable and Inclusive Growth*, Brussels: European Commission, Communication from the Commission, COM(2010)2020, March 3.

——(2010c). *Europe's Digital Competitiveness Report, Commission Staff Working Document*, Vol. 1, Brussels: European Commission SEC(2010)627.

FCC (1999). *In the Matter of Inquiry Concerning the Deployment of Advanced Telecommunications Capability to All Americans in a Reasonable and Timely Fashion, and Possible Steps to Accelerate*

Such Deployment Pursuant to Section 706 of the Telecommunications Act of 1996, CC Docket No. 98–146, Washington DC: Federal Communications Commission, February 2.

FCC (2010). *Connecting America: The National Broadband Plan*, Washington DC: Federal Communications Commission.

Fransman, M. (ed.) (2006). *Global Broadband Battles: Why the US and Europe Lag While Asia Leads*, Stanford, CA: Standford University Press.

Freeman, C. (1988). "Information Technology and the New Economic Paradigm," in H. Schutte (ed.). *Strategic Issues in Information Technology: International Implications for Decision Makers*, Berkshire: Pergamon Infotech, pp. 159–75.

Geuna, A., Steinmueller, W. E., and Salter, A. J. (eds) (2003). *Science and Innovation: Changing Rationales for the Public Funding of Research*, Cheltenham: Edward Elgar.

Gore, A. (1995). *Global Information Infrastructure—Agenda for Cooperation*, Washington, DC: Vice President of the United States and R. H. Brown, Secretary of Commerce and Chairman, Information Infrastructure Task Force.

Guy, K. and Arnold, E. (1989). *Government IT Policies in Competing Countries: A Review of Policies Affecting the IT Sectors of the USA, Japan and the EEC, France, West Germany and the UK*, London: Electronics EDC of the National Economic Development Office, June.

House of Commons (2010). *Broadband: Fourth Report of Session 2009–10: Report, together with formal minutes, oral and written evidence*, London: House of Commons Business Innovation and Skills Committee.

ITAP (1983). *Making a Business of Information*, London: Cabinet Office Information Technology Advisory Panel, HMSO.

Jenkins, H. (2006). *Convergence Culture: Where Old and New Media Collide*, New York: New York University Press.

——Purushotma, R., Weigel, M., Clinton, K., and Robison, A. J. (2009). *Confronting the Challenges of Participatory Culture: Media Education for the 21st Century*, Cambridge, MA: MIT Press for John D. and Catherine T. MacArthur Foundation Reports on Digital Media and Learning.

Jorgenson, D. W. (2001). "Information Technology and the US Economy," *American Economic Review*, 91(1): 1–31.

——and Stiroh, K. J. (2000). "Raising the Speed Limit: U.S. Economic Growth in the Information Age," *Brookings Papers on Economic Activity*, 31(1): 125–211.

Josgrilberg, F. B. (2008). *Muni-Wi: An Exploratory Comparative Study of European and Brazilian Municipal Wireless Networks*, Saõ Paulo: Report prepared for Fundacao de Amparo a Pesquisa de Sao Paulo, Graduate Communication Department, Methodist University of Saõ Paulo.

Justman, M. and Teubal, M. (1995). "Technological Infrastructure Policy (TIP): Creating Capabilities and Building Markets," *Research Policy*, 24(2): 259–81.

Kahin, B. and Wilson III, E. J. (eds) (1997). *National Information Infrastructure Initiatives: Vision and Policy Design*, Cambridge, MA: MIT Press.

Katz, R. L. and Suter, S. (2009). *Estimating the Economic Impact of the Broadband Stimulus Plan*, New York: Columbia Business School, Columbia Institute for Tele-Information.

Koutroumpis, P. (2009). "The Economic Impact of Broadband on Growth: A Simultaneous Approach," *Telecommunications Policy*, 33(9): 471–85.

Lehr, W. H. and Pupillo, L. M. (eds) (2009). *Internet Policy and Economics: Challenges and Perspectives*, 2nd edn., Dordrecht: Springer.

Lessig, L. (2008). *Remix: Making Art and Commerce Thrive in the Hybrid Economy*, London: Bloomsbury.

Mansell, R. (1997). "Technical Innovations, Policy and Strategy," in A. Dumort and J. Dryden (eds). *The Economics of the Information Society*, Luxembourg: European Commission, pp. 219–24.

—— Avgerou, C., Quah, D., and Silverstone, R. (eds) (2007). *The Oxford Handbook of Information and Communication Technologies*, Oxford: Oxford University Press.

Mansell, R. and Steinmueller, W. E. (2000). *Mobilizing the Information Society: Strategies for Growth and Opportunity*, Oxford: Oxford University Press.

Melody, W. H. (2005). "Regulation and Network Investment: A Framework for Analysis," in A. K. Mahan and W. H. Melody (eds). *Stimulating Investment in Network Development: Roles for Regulators*, Lyngby: Technical University of Denmark for IDRC, infoDev and LIRNE.net, pp. 19–37.

Menon, S. (2011). "Policy Agendas for South Korea's Broadband Convergence Network Infrastructure Project," *Info: The Journal of Policy, Regulation and Strategy for Telecommunications*, 13(2): 19–34.

Metcalfe, J. S. (1997). "Technology Systems and Technology Policy in an Evolutionary Framework," in D. Archibugi and J. Michie (eds). *Technology, Globalisation and Economic Performance*, Cambridge: Cambridge University Press, pp. 268–96.

Miles, I. (2010). "Service Innovation," in P. P. Maglio, C. A. Kieliszewski, and J. C. Spohrer (eds). *Handbook of Service Science*, New York: Springer, pp. 511–34.

Mueller, M. (2010). *Networks and States: The Global Politics of Internet Governance*. Cambridge, MA: MIT Press.

NRC (2009). *Assessing the Impacts of Changes in the Information Technology R&D Ecosystem: Retaining Leadership in an Increasingly Global Environment*, Washington, DC: National Academies Press for US National Research Council.

OECD (1988). *New Technologies in the 1990s: A Socio-Economic Strategy*, Paris: OECD.

—— (2009a). *Network Developments in Support of Innovation and User Needs*, Paris: OECD Working Party on Communication Infrastructures and User Needs, DSTI/ICCP/CISP(2009)2/final.

—— (2009b). *OECD Communications Outlook 2009*, Paris: OECD.

Perez, C. (1983). "Structural Change and Assimilation of New Technologies in the Economic and Social-Systems," *Futures*, 15(5): 357–75.

Picot, A. and Wernick, C. (2007). "The Role of Government in Broadband Access," *Telecommunications Policy*, 31(10/11): 660–74.

Powell, A. and Shade, L. R. (2006). "Going Wi-Fi in Canada: Municipal and Community Initiatives," *Government Information Quarterly*, 22(2–4): 381–403.

Preston, P. (2001). *Re-shaping Communications: Technology, Information and Social Change*, London: Sage Publications.

——, Cawley, A., and Metykova, M. (2007). "Broadband and Rural Areas in the EU: From Technology to Applications and Use," *Telecommunications Policy*, 31(6–7): 389–400.

Qiang, C. Z.-W. (2010). "Broadband Infrastructure Investment in Stimulus Packages: Relevance for Developing Countries," *Info: The Journal of Policy, Regulation and Strategy for Telecommunications*, 12(2): 41–56.

Ramirez, R. (2007). "Appreciating the Contribution of Broadband ICT with Rural and Remote Communities: Stepping Stones Toward an Alternative Paradigm," *The Information Society*, 23(2): 85–94.

Rogers, E. M. (1962). *The Diffusion of Innovations*, New York: Free Press.

Siegen University (2010). *Study on the Social Impact of ICT (CPP No. 55A—SMART No 2007/0068) Final Version*, Siegen: Fachbereich Wirtschaftsinformatik und Neue Medien.

Silverstone, R. (ed.) (2005). *Media, Technology and Everyday Life in Europe: From Information to Communication*, Aldershot: Ashgate.

Silverstone, R. and Mansell, R. (1996). "The Politics of Information and Communication Technologies," in R. Mansell and R. Silverstone (eds). *Communication by Design: The Politics of Information and Communication Technologies*, Oxford: Oxford University Press, pp. 213–27.

Steinmueller, W. E. (1995). "Technology Infrastructure in Information Technology Industries," in M. Teubal, D. Foray, M. Justman, and E. Zuscovitch (eds). *Technological Infrastructure Policy: An International perspective*, Dordrecht: Kluwer Academic Publishers, pp. 117–39.

Turkle, S. (2011). *Alone Together: Why We Expect More from Technology and Less from Each Other*, New York: Basic Books.

UK Government (2010). *Digital Economy Act 2010 (c.24)*, London.

US Government (1990). *S.2800, Communications Competitiveness and Infrastructure Modernization Act of 1990*, Washington DC: United States Senate Report No. 101–456, 101st Cong., 2nd Sess.

—— (1993). *National Information Infrastructure: Agenda for Action—Realizing the Information Future*, Washington, DC: Information Infrastructure Task Force.

—— (2009). *American Recovery and Reinvestment Act of 2009*, Washington, DC: 111th Congress of the United States of America, Senate and House of Representatives.

Van Ark, B., O'Mahoney, M., and Timmer, M. (2008). "The Productivity Gap Between Europe and the United States: Trends and Causes," *Journal of Economic Perspectives*, 22(1): 25–44.

van Dijk, J. A. G. M. (2005). *The Network Society: Social Aspects of New Media Second Edition*, London: Sage.

Van Reenen, J., Bloom, N., Draca, M., Kretschmer, T., and Sadun, R. (2010). *The Economic Impact of ICT SMART No. 2007/0020*, London: Enterprise LSE.

Wu, T. (2010). *The Master Switch: The Rise and Fall of Information Empires*, New York: Alfred A. Knopf.

CHAPTER 25

THE INTERNET AND DEVELOPMENT: A CRITICAL PERSPECTIVE

TIM UNWIN

THIS chapter explores research on the complex interrelationship between the Internet and "development," focusing especially on the effects of the Internet on the lives of some of the poorest people and most marginalized communities. Much of the literature on Information and Communication Technologies for Development (ICT4D) suggests that the Internet can indeed bring very significant benefits in the "fight against poverty" (see e.g. Weigel and Waldburger 2004; Rao and Raman 2009; Unwin 2009), but other research is marshaled in this synthesis to challenge this assumption. In essence, I argue that the expansion of the Internet serves very specific capitalist interests, and that unless conscious and explicit attention is paid to designing interventions that will indeed directly serve the needs of the world's poorest people, then the Internet will only replicate and reinforce existing structures of dominance and control. This argument supports the need for more research that challenges taken-for-granted assumptions about the Internet and development.

THE INTERNET AND DEVELOPMENT: ECONOMIC GROWTH, SOCIAL EQUALITY, AND POLITICAL FREEDOM

Differing trajectories

Access to the Internet varies hugely across the world. As Figure 25.1 highlights, the *difference* between the number of Internet users per 100 people in "developed" and "least

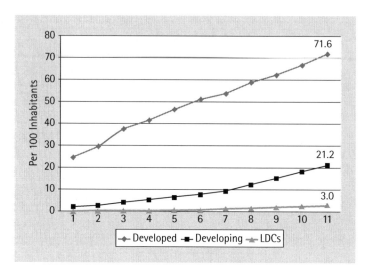

FIGURE 25.1: Internet users per 100 inhabitants, 2000–2010.

Source: International Telecommunication Union (2011: 28).

developed" countries has risen from around 25 to more than 68 between 2000 and 2010 (International Telecommunication Union 2011). Access has thus become considerably more differentiated over the last decade. If Internet access is meant to contribute to development then it does not seem to have done so very successfully. The poorest and most marginalized have yet to benefit appropriately.

This chapter seeks to explore why this is so. If the most marginalized are to benefit from the transformatory impact of the Internet, new research agendas are necessary specifically to identify the information and communication needs of the world's poorest people. This research must then be used effectively to influence the policies and practices that purport to use information and communications technology (ICTs) to contribute to development.

The Internet

From its beginnings in the 1960s and 1970s, the Internet was fundamentally a means through which interconnections were made between computer networks (Abbate 1999); fundamentally, it was a technology. However, over the last decade, use of the term has widened considerably (Dutton and Jeffreys 2010; Leiner et al. 2003). Increasingly, it has come to subsume not only hardware and software, but also the traffic that flows across them, and the ways that human society is changed through engagement with them. Whereas the World Wide Web was once seen as being distinct, referring to the body of resources accessed through the Internet by hyperlinks, increasingly the medium and the message have become merged into a single over-arching conception of "the Internet." Most users simply see the Internet as the totality of the digital technologies that permit them to access information and to communicate electronically.

This broad definition, though, is more problematic outside the developed world. In rich countries, where connectivity is more or less ubiquitous, it seems to matter little as to whether the technology is distinct from the information and communication to which it enables access. However, where connectivity is absent, where networks of digital technologies are not interconnected, and where people are insufficiently literate to be able to read and write, the distinction between the infrastructure, hardware, and software that enable digital devices to be interconnected on the one hand, and information and communication needs of poor people on the other, remains of considerable significance.

Geography still matters. There are many parts of central Africa or Asia, for example, where there is limited connectivity, and even in the richer parts of the world, poor people and marginalized communities either do not have, or cannot afford, access to the Internet. In the absence of such basic connectivity, none of the wider potential of the Internet that so many now take for granted can be realized. Rural areas are thus less connected than urban ones; women generally have less access than men. Thus, in her research on how low-literate people in Ethiopia and Malawi interact with ICTs, Geldof (2010) was able to capture some of the ways in which youths in these countries conceived of the Internet. Young men in Malawi, for example, gave the following responses:

- "Internet, you can use if for typing things" (referring to a picture of a computer);
- "Internet, you write the message and send via the Internet. I haven't seen the Internet. I heard about it on the radio" (referring to ways of communicating with people);
- "An Internet for receiving messages" (referring to a picture of a printer) (Geldof, pers. comm. August 11, 2010).

In contrast, none of the women in her survey mentioned the Internet at all.

... and "Development"

Figure 25.1 serves as a stark reminder of the significant differences that exist across the world between those who have, and those who are without. Whereas 77 percent of people in North America are Internet users, only 11 percent of those in Africa are, albeit that this latter figure grew by 2,357 percent between 2000 and 2010. How such figures are interpreted, depends on the lens of "development" through which they are considered.

Notions of "development" have long been contested (see for example Rostow 1960; Easterley 2006; Kothari 2006; Pieterse 2010), and indeed much recent academic discourse has explicitly focused on post-developmentalism as a critique of the entire development project (Escobar 1995; Rahnema and Bawtree 1997). The dominant hegemonic model of development practice at the beginning of the twenty-first century is one where "development" is primarily interpreted as being the elimination of poverty through economic growth. This notion underlay the formulation of the Millennium Development Goals (MDGs) adopted in 2000 (United Nations no date), and has driven much development practice ever since (United Nations 2010). Such emphasis on the economic dimensions of development has been particularly popularized by economists such as Jeffrey Sachs (2005), who has advocated the need for the richer countries of the world to give much greater amounts of aid to the poorer ones in order to kick-start their economic development. For this to be effective, though, most bilateral donors and international agencies agree on the need for systems of good governance to be in place aligned with the principles of liberal democracy and a free market (see e.g. DFID 2009).

This belief that development is fundamentally concerned with the elimination of poverty through economic growth is nevertheless premised on the highly problematic aspiration that poverty can indeed be eliminated (Unwin 2007). It is also driven primarily by the economic interests of global corporations and private capital. Most current definitions of poverty revolve around crude economic indicators such as the proportion of people whose income is less than US$1.25 a day, which is now used as the key measure for the first MDG. Proponents of this approach, such as the United Nations (2010) point to the "success" of the global community in reducing this figure.

If, though, poverty is seen in terms of relative inequalities (O'Boyle 1999; Madden 2000), it becomes much more difficult to argue that it can ever be eliminated—only reduced (Unwin 2007). According to a relative perspective, the highest economic poverty is to be found where there are the greatest differences in income levels or access to resources. Under such conditions, economic growth can actually be associated with an expansion of poverty, as the rich outpace the poor in their acquisition of wealth. Moreover, while absolute definitions of poverty tend to focus on individual success criteria, relative definitions pay much more attention to social equality and cooperation (O'Boyle 1999).

The distinction between absolute and relative poverty is central to an understanding of the role of technology, and the Internet in particular, in development. A view of development as being synonymous with the elimination of absolute poverty through economic growth legitimates a focus on the ways in which the Internet has helped achieve this, concentrating largely on individual success and economic growth. If, in contrast, development is seen as being concerned with a reduction in relative poverty, then attention needs to be placed on the ways in which the Internet has reduced inequalities and encouraged increasing social interaction and cooperation. Given the dominance of the economic growth agenda, it is scarcely surprising that most of the focus of research and practice at the interface between development and the Internet has so far been on the former (see e.g. UNCTAD 2007).

However, there remain many other definitions of "development", and each of these also has specific implications for any consideration of its intertwined relationship with the Internet. One of the most influential of these alternative approaches has been Sen's (1999; see also Sen 1976) conceptualization of development as being concerned with the freedoms that people have to realize their capabilities, rather than with growth in any particular economic indicator (see also United Nations 1996). Sen suggests that a society's level of development should be measured primarily by people's freedoms and capabilities to live the lives they value, rather than merely being a measure of economic standards of living (see also Levine 2004). This introduces an important new layer of ethical and political considerations into any discussion of the Internet and development, and is pursued further towards the end of this chapter.

The Internet and development

Any enquiry into the Internet and development has to be steered by the choice of definitions used. In particular, it is important not just to assume that one definition of "development" is correct, or even that development is itself somehow a "good thing"(Escobar 1995). This chapter therefore examines the implications of the relationships between the Internet and "development" in terms of development as economic growth, development as social equality, and development as political freedom. The paths chosen lead to very different outcomes, both intellectually and in terms of practical implications for poor and marginalized people. In the past, too much research undertaken on ICTs and development has been blinkered to the complexities of development theory and practice, and as a result the implementation of well-intentioned ICT for development projects has all too often failed (Sreekumar and Rivera-Sánchez 2008; Unwin 2009; Pieterse 2010).

THE INTERNET AND ICTS; TECHNOLOGY, DEVELOPMENT, AND EMPOWERMENT

The above discussion raises two other important issues at the research interface between the Internet and "development": the place of Internet Studies within the context of research on ICTs and development more generally; and the wider relationship between technology and development.

The Internet, ICTs, ICT4D, ICTD ...

The increasing prominence of digital technologies and their role in the processes of globalization has led to much research on the ways in which all kinds of ICTs influence, and are influenced by, wider development processes (see e.g. Castells 2000; Mansell and Wehn 1998; Weigel and Waldburger 2004; Samarajiva and Zainudeen 2007; Rao and Raman 2009; Unwin 2009). Television and radio, for example, remain critically important in providing some of the world's poorest people with both entertainment and information. The successful TV drama series, *Makutano Junction*, which began in 2005, and which attracted more than 7 million viewers in Kenya alone, provides a wealth of information for peri-urban dwellers on health, education, and rural development issues (http://www.mediae.org/makutano_junction). Over time, it veloped an interactive mobile SMS/Text interface, and in conjunction with its website this enabled viewers to obtain follow-up information about the key development issues that the program tackled each week. This is an example of how the benefits of more traditional media have been enhanced by the Internet, but it also highlights the difficulties in attributing development impacts to any one technology alone. The Internet is one of a number of complementary infrastructures, making specific Internet interventions more difficult to identify. Indeed, the rapid expansion of mobile broadband offers much potential for empowering the poor, although it cannot be attributed simply to the Internet.

One of the exciting things about research at this interface is that it has been approached from many different conceptual backgrounds, each of which has its own particular take on the field. Heeks (2010), for example, has drawn up league tables of specialist journals in the field of ICT4D, originating from a wide diversity of disciplines. There are nevertheless three fundamental problems with such disciplinary diversity. First, there is a tendency for those within a single discipline to focus inwards, and not to recognize the importance of research undertaken in different disciplines with interests in ICT4D. Far too often, publications in one field make no acknowledgment of closely similar research previously published in another field. Second, there is a somewhat unhealthy competition between journals and groups of academics from different disciplinary backgrounds, each seeking to be the "top" journal, and thereby imprinting their own particular disciplinary "take" on the wider ICT4D/ICTD field. Third, there is a dominance of English language publication. If scholars working at this interface are truly going to make an impact in the field of development, they need to find ways of incorporating a diversity of languages so that everyone can learn from the research of colleagues whose native language is not English, as through the fostering of multilingual websites that provide ready access to research from across the world.

While the Internet has enabled many of the changes discussed in research published in these journals, much of their content focuses not so much on the Internet itself, but rather on the services provided through the Internet as well as on other ICTs. In many instances, the notion of the Internet has also, somewhat problematically, taken on an overarching identity of its own. Many working in the field of development, and particularly advocates of the use of networked computers in delivering development outputs, have tended to use the word "Internet" to refer to the whole package of deliverables offered by ICTs more generally. All too often it is the Internet that is seen as being the key innovation that is necessary for development, rather than focusing on the information and communication requirements of poor people and marginalized communities (Unwin 2009).

This has had damaging effects. As Mercer (2006: 243) has commented: "A discourse which constructs the Internet as an inclusive development tool that can be deployed in strategies for modernizing Africa has become hegemonic among development donors and telecommunications organizations." In the instance of Tanzania, for example, she differentiates between the ways in which elites and others conceptualize and use the Internet, highlighting once again the important distinction between, on the one hand, the use of the Internet in contributing to development as economic growth, and on the other the Internet as being an enabler of social and cultural development. It can indeed do both. What is of most interest, though, is to explore the conditions that determine which pathway is followed, and the interests that underlie such choices.

It is commonly argued that the main reasons for failure of projects designed to use ICTs and the Internet to support development objectives is that they are top-down, supply-led, and externally implemented (Unwin 2009). Such arguments can also be applied to much of the research that has been undertaken in the multidisciplinary field of ICT4D. As Figure 25.2 seeks to summarize, although there is a spectrum of research at the interface between the Internet and development, there is a strong tendency for there to be a separation between research developed by those from a technological, physical science background and those from a social science or "development" background.

Much technological research, especially that undertaken in North American and European institutions, tends to be top-down, supply-led and elitist, as indicated to the left of Figure 25.2. Innovative ideas and technologies that "should" apply in developing countries are all too often developed in well-funded laboratories, far away from the reality of poverty on the ground in Africa or Asia. They are then trialled "on," rather than "with," people in developing areas, and to the real surprise of the well-intentioned academics who have been involved in their development, they all too often either fail immediately or are unsustainable in anything but the short term.

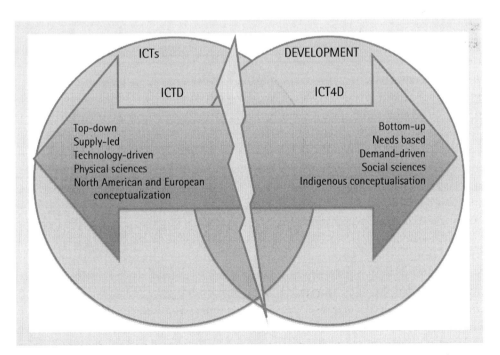

FIGURE 25.2: A spectrum of research and practice at the interface between development and ICTs

Much of the research that goes under the name ICTD (ICT *and* Development) tends to be to the left of the diagram, whereas those who lay claim to ICT4D (ICT *for* Development) have a tendency to be towards the right. This binary divide also to some extent parallels the distinction between development seen as economic growth, which is most usually linked with the technological model to the left of Figure 25.2, and development seen as being concerned with social equality which is more closely aligned to the right side.

In trying to bridge the gap both in research and in practice between these two domains, it is crucial to focus on two important issues. First, one of the most exciting aspects of the field is its very necessary multidisciplinary character. Innovative ideas and solutions often come from the clash of epistemologies and practices of people from very different disciplines and cultures. Second, it is important for all those involved in this critical area to retain a sense of humility. In an increasingly intellectually fragmented world, few individuals have the training or capacity in the diversity of skills and knowledge necessary to understand or implement effective Internet and development initiatives. A crucial task for those working at the interface between the Internet and development is thus to find ways of supporting the intellectual and practical experience of committed people so that they can indeed combine such expertise.

Technology and development

The Internet is one of the most pervasive technologies of the late twentieth and early twenty-first centuries. For Castells (2000: 31), for example, it is only in this new Information Age, enabled by the Internet, that there is a "cumulative feedback loop between innovation and the uses of innovation." Not all, though, agree, instead suggesting with Harvey (2000: 62) that "it is easy to make too much of this. The newness of it all impresses, but then the newness of the railroad and the telegraph, the radio and the telephone in their day impressed equally" (see also Wallerstein 2000). Such arguments serve as a reminder that, although the Internet is a relatively new phenomenon, much of the well-established academic debate over the role of technology and development applies equally to discussions about the Internet. At the heart of such debate is the question of whether technologies are generally developed and used by the rich and powerful, to enable them better to exert their control over the societies that they dominate, or whether they can instead be used to serve the common good, enabling the poor and the marginalized to have greater control over their lives (Habermas 1978).

With the Internet, one of the key questions that therefore needs to be explored is whether it has enabled powerful states and corporations to increase their global economic, cultural, and political dominance, or whether instead it has actually served to shift the balance of power towards poorer and more marginalized peoples, states, and communities (Sreekumar and Rivera-Sánchez 2008). Building on the framework of Figure 25.2, those working more to the right side of the spectrum have tended to believe in the latter, whereas those to the left frequently seem to serve the interests of the former. This chapter seeks to tread the delicate path of the lightening bolt between the two.

The evidence increasingly suggests that many early advocates of ICT4D were naïvely optimistic, and that the anarchic potential of the Web has been deliberately crushed by those with an interest in retaining their positions of economic and political power (Pieterse 2010). The Internet may not be as disruptive a technology as many would have us believe (Latzer 2009; Flew and Wilson 2010).

There is a long established tradition of argument that science and technology can indeed be a sustained force for economic growth and development (Baker 2004; Sachs 2005), However, as Conway and Waage (2001: xix) comment,

> At one extreme, some see science and technology providing the principle means for reducing poverty, eliminating disease and improving well-being. At another extreme, science is seen as part of an imposed, external regime, associated with industrial exploitation and suppression of indigenous knowledge.

They conclude positively, though, that science and technology, particularly through the power of the Internet, can have a beneficial impact on development (Conway and Waage 2010). Such arguments are based on the belief that science and technology are value free, and do not represent the interests of any particular group of people. The historical reality, however, is very different. As Habermas (1978) has argued so cogently, all types of science are underlain by particular interests, and the hegemonic model of positivist (empirical-analytic) science effectively serves the interests of those in power: "by making a dogma of the sciences' belief in themselves, positivism assumes the prohibitive function of protecting scientific enquiry from epistemological self-reflection. Positivism is philosophical only insofar as is necessary for the immunization of the sciences against philosophy" (Habermas 1978: 7).

While the Internet has undoubtedly served to enable new systems of social interaction, its primary impact has been in the economic sphere, enabling vastly swifter flows of information across the world, and in particular making a very significant qualitative difference in the speed through which financial transactions can take place. This has transformed economic activity, not only in terms of employment, but more significantly through the speed at which capital can circulate and accumulate. By enabling capital to become increasingly footloose, the Internet has vastly sped up the rate at which profit can be accumulated.

Critics of capitalism argue that the owners of the means of production have two primary objectives: to reduce their labor and raw materials costs, and to realize their profits through expanded markets. The Internet has been crucial to speeding up these processes, and thus to shaping the distinctive evolution of capitalism over the last twenty years. It is no coincidence that the rapid expansion of the Internet only took place in the early 1990s once the private sector had persuaded governments to let them rip it from the hands of the researchers who had created and nurtured it, thereby enabling commercial businesses to use it to generate profit. Likewise, it is no coincidence that the Internet itself developed in its early stages primarily through the work of the US government's Defense Advanced Research Projects Agency. The economic and political interests of US capital have underlain the origins and evolution of the

Internet since its very beginning, and until the twenty-first century there has been little reason to doubt that this would change.

Politics and implementation: the global agenda of WSIS, the IGF, and ICANN

The UN decision to host the World Summit on the Information Society (WSIS), was the catalyst that brought together much existing research on the interface between the Internet and development, and sought to turn this into practical action (Kelly 2004; Souter 2007a; Souter 2007b; Unwin 2009). WSIS was an unusual summit both because it was held in two phases, in Geneva in 2003 and then in Tunis in 2005, and also because it was the first major UN summit at which the private sector, and to a lesser extent civil society, were also actively involved. This latter point is particularly significant, since the summit's focus on the need for partnerships between states and the private sector to create an effective information society, meant that almost for the first time the private sector was at the very center of international discourses on development issues (Abida 2009). Many civil society activists asserted that both phases of WSIS thus marginalized their interests, and failed sufficiently to address issues of human rights and the democratization of the so-called information society (Mueller et al. 2007; Souter 2007b).

Led by the International Telecommunications Union (ITU), the first phase of WSIS focused primarily on the overall role of broadly defined ICTs in development, the relationship between human rights and ICTs, the financing of future ICT4D initiatives, and the governance of the Internet. Progress in Geneva on the first two of these was relatively good, since there was much previous work to build on, but the latter two proved to be more controversial and became the focus of attention for the second summit to be held in Tunis in 2005. The Geneva process was, though, much more productive than many had anticipated, and it led to a set of eleven principles and a plan of action for their delivery that have subsequently helped shape much of the international agenda on ICT4D activities.

With respect to funding, civil society organizations and the private sector argued, albeit for very different reasons, for the creation of a digital solidarity fund to provide very large sums of money to implement the agreed plan of action. For civil society, this would enable their aspirations of a truly democratic and open information society, where everyone had explicit rights to knowledge, to be fulfilled. For the private sector, the creation of such a fund would provide a bonanza to enable them rapidly to expand their markets across the poorer countries of the world. Arrayed against both of these sets of interests were the donor governments and agencies in the international community, who had little appetite for the creation of a new fund, particularly because it ran counter to their emphasis on general budget support mechanisms (Unwin 2004), and also because of the perceived problems with the implementation of other global funds such as the Education For All Fast Track Initiative and the Global Fund to Fight AIDS, Tuberculosis and Malaria (Unwin 2009). In order to address this, a Task Force on Financial Mechanisms was created (MacLean 2005), but little progress was made with the Digital Solidarity Fund.

Debates over the way in which the Internet should be governed, led to the creation of the Internet Governance Forum (http://www.intgovforum.org), following the Tunis phase of WSIS. Its activities shed considerable light on the intersection between the Internet and development with which this chapter is concerned (Souter 2007a). From the creation of the Internet, the US has dominated its control, and since 1998 this has been exercised through the Internet Corporation for Assigned Names and Numbers (ICANN), a not-for-profit public-benefit corporation "dedicated to keeping the Internet secure, stable and interoperable" (http://www.icann.org/en/about/; Kleinwächter 2004; Koppell 2005).

However, between the two WSIS Summits, opposition to the perceived US dominance of the global Internet grew considerably, and civil society organizations, notably the Association for Progressive Communications (APC), lobbied extensively that ICANN should be turned into a more global body (MacLean 2004). During the Summit, the US refused to give ground over its control of ICANN, but tensions were mollified through agreement to set up an Internet Governance Forum (IGF) (http://www .intgovforum.org) as a new forum for multi-stakeholder policy dialogue to resolve these issues.

A widely applauded feature of the way in which the IGF has operated has been its openness to a diversity of participants, including governments, the private sector, and civil society, and particularly the way in which these have been encouraged to participate through remote participation. As Gurumurthy (MacLean 2009: 388) has commented: "The IGF is a unique institution attempting to measure up to the realities of a transnational political community. As a UN forum, it allows people excluded from other spaces and arenas where Internet policies are being shaped to participate equally in the dialogues implicating their own lives." However, the IGF is primarily a multi-stakeholder forum, and without any formal decision-making authority it has as yet remained essentially an arena for discussion.

This brief review of some of the more important institutions to have emerged over the last decade is only partial, focusing especially on the Internet, and has not in any way covered the earlier work of the UN's ICT Task Force out of which many of the ideas that were developed in WSIS emerged, or indeed of other post-WSIS bodies such as the Global Alliance for ICTs and Development (GAID) (http://un-gaid.org/) and the WSIS Forums (http://www.wsis.org/forum). However, it has sought to emphasize three key aspects of the global institutional context that have helped shape the intersection between the Internet and Development over the last decade.

First, the private sector has gained unprecedented access to involvement in UN and other global institutions through its role in the field of ICTs. This is highly unusual, and reflects, not only the complexity of delivering ICT-based development interventions, but also the necessity of private sector involvement therein to implement the technological roll-out. This has meant that public–private partnerships have become a central feature of many ICT4D initiatives, although more recently the term multi-stakeholder partnerships has been introduced to emphasize the need to include civil society organizations in such initiatives for them to be effective (Unwin 2005, 2009).

Second, many of these institutions have primarily taken the form of arenas for discussion, with frustratingly little action having been taken directly by them. For all of its successes in bringing diverse partners together to consider issues such as Internet governance for development, the IGF has not yet, for example, directly led to any fundamental change in the ways in which the Internet is governed.

Third, this discussion has also highlighted once again how discussion of the Internet has tended to dominate the arena of ICTs and development. As Souter has cautioned,

> The Internet is merely one of a number of information and communication media around which the current debate about the role of ICTs revolves. Its potential for extending information and communication resources has led some to give it pre-eminence within the range of ICTs becoming available within development. In practice, however, Internet use has spread much less rapidly in low-income countries than other ICTs. (2007a: 32–33)

The remainder of this chapter explores in more detail how the Internet has indeed intersected with development practices. In so doing, it argues that it has been no coincidence that the Internet has dominated this discussion, because of the crucial role that the US government and companies have played, not only through ICANN, but also through the powerful commercial interests of US computer manufacturing, component, and software companies, combined with the interests of networking companies such as Cisco, whose 2009 Annual Report is simply entitled *The Connected World*. The Internet did not just happen. It was shaped and developed explicitly by the commercial interests largely of US capital.

THE INTERNET AND DEVELOPMENT AS GROWTH

There is extensive evidence to suggest that the Internet has contributed significantly to economic growth. A recent report for the Telenor Group (Boston Consulting Group, 2009), for example, has concluded "increased adoption of Internet can accelerate business productivity, thereby generating income, jobs and government revenues in emerging economies." (Telenor 2009, unpaginated) Likewise, UNCTAD (2007) has emphasized a wide range of ways in which ICTs can contribute to economic growth, including generating higher sales per employee, expanding exports (see also World Bank 2006), enhancing the adoption of new technologies, cost savings through Voice over Internet Protocol (VoIP), facilitating online payments, and enabling developing countries to participate more fully in the global information economy.

In general terms, the Internet contributes to economic growth through three main means: expanding access to information, rapidly increasing the pace of transactions, and providing a demand for the raw materials required in the production of the equipment that drives it. Theoretically, through the Internet, anyone with access to a computer can access information stored on all of the other computers in the world; financial transfers now take fractions of a second, whereas in the nineteenth century it could take weeks for money to be transferred across the world by sea. Those with access to the Internet, and with sufficient skills to take advantage of the opportunities that it offers, are thus indeed likely to gain economic benefits from so doing. Best et al. (2007), for example, have shown clearly how Internet access has helped to create new businesses and opportunities in villages in post-conflict zones, thereby contributing to economic growth (see also Best and Kenny 2009; Zhao, 2008). Access to information has been crucial to the success of businesses at a range of scale, and much evidence suggests that the Internet has indeed been of positive benefit (Qiang et al. 2006), particularly for marketing, gathering product information, and speeding up financial transactions.

However, for the smallest micro-entrepreneurs, there is increasing evidence that mobile phones, without any Internet connections or functionality, may be of more importance. Ilavarasan and Levy (2010) in a rigorous and detailed study of entrepreneurs in Mumbai, for example, show that few micro-entrepreneurs use Internet cafés for business purposes, whereas nearly all of them used their mobile phones. Likewise, Internet access has not yet been as beneficial for rural farmers in China as might be assumed (Zhao 2008). Furthermore, Kenny and Kenny (2010: 3) argue convincingly that the benefits of rolling out new high-speed fiber networks "have been grossly overstated." Qiang et al. (2003), Qiu (2010), and Enough Project (2010) all highlight further problems associated with the dumping of computer waste, and labor exploitation associated with the rapid expansion of the IT industry in areas of rapid economic growth such as Malaysia and China.

The relationship between the Internet and economic growth is therefore not quite as clear-cut as many advocates would suggest. It is commonplace to read about how Internet penetration in developing countries is increasing apace, as though this were some kind of "natural" process (see e.g. UNCTAD 2007). However, there is nothing "natural" about it at all: it is nothing to do with countries "catching up." Rather, it represents very careful and cold decision-making among the major corporations that drive the Internet industry. Indeed, once penetration levels of existing technologies become increasingly saturated in more developed countries, the only real way of expanding the market for such products is into poorer countries, while continuing to evolve newer more advanced products that can be sold at a higher price to those living in richer countries. Hence, global corporations have invested very considerable sums of money in encouraging governments and civil society organizations in poorer countries to adopt computers with Internet access for a wide range of activities, including education, health, governance, and rural development.

The Internet and development
as equality

While Figure 25.1 can be interpreted as a success story in terms of economic growth, at least for many of the world's developed and developing countries, it can also be seen as a failure in terms of equity. The last decade, rather than seeing a closing of some kind of digital divide, has actually seen a very rapid increase therein. The populations of developed countries have indeed been able to access what advantages the Internet may provide, whereas those in the world's least developed countries have become even more marginalized as far as the Internet is concerned.

This is even more striking in terms of the differences within poor countries. While major towns across Africa do now have reasonable connectivity, with the submarine cable having transformed the ease with which content can be downloaded and VoIP and video conferencing undertaken across the continent, the reality for those living in peripheral rural areas, far from the path of the fibre backbone that is now rapidly being laid across the continent, is that the Internet is as distant as ever. This is despite the effort of organizations such as First Mile Solutions (http://www.firstmilesolutions.com/), which seek to use WiFi and digital storage to make the Internet accessible to rural communities. Furthermore, there is now convincing evidence that in many countries, ICTs are reinforcing and exacerbating gender divides rather than enabling everyone to benefit from them (Gurumurthy 2004; Huyer and Hafkin 2007).

The Mobile Internet may offer increasing opportunities for people in the poorer countries of the world to access information and use other benefits of the Internet (Wray 2009), and the arrival of submarine cables off the east coast of Africa in 2009 has already done much to open up the continent to faster and more reliable connectivity. However, it is interesting to note that African users are not so much using the Mobile Internet for economic benefits, but are rather using it as a means of social networking, with Facebook being the most popular African destination on the mobile Web (Opera 2009). There is a growing body of evidence suggesting that poor people actually place most emphasis on social connectivity when using ICTs. The ITU (2011) thus comment that very poor families in South Africa can spend up to 20 percent of their income on mobile telephony, simply so that they can keep in touch with their family networks.

Another important dimension of equality and the social dimensions of the Internet, though, is the issue of Net Neutrality, which has become increasingly controversial in recent years. Indeed, it is but one example of the ways in which the Internet as a more mature economic phenomenon is likely to become increasingly fragmented. Net Neutrality has been a central principle of the Internet ever since its foundation, and has held that those providing Internet services should treat all sources of data equally. As Google (2006) commented in 2006: "Today the Internet is an information highway where anybody—no matter how large or small, how traditional or unconventional—has equal access. But the phone and cable monopolies, who control almost all Internet access, want the power to choose who gets access to high-speed lanes and whose content gets seen first and fastest. They want to build a two-tiered system and block the on-ramps for those who can't pay." However, by 2010, Google and Verizon appeared to have changed positions on this, essentially proposing a two-tier system that could offer a broadband network of premium services while also maintaining an otherwise open Internet (Google 2010; see also Waters and Gelles, 2010). This controversial proposal was made within the context of the contentious discussions led by the US Federal Communications Commission with broadband providers and other interested groups about the future of the Internet in the US. How these are resolved will have a major influence on the Internet across the world, and reflect once again the present dominance of the US in shaping the Internet, both in terms of its political and its economic power. In this respect, it will be interesting to see how the rapid expansion of Internet usage in China in recent years will affect this, with Baidu taking on Google, and QQ challenging Facebook.

Much has been written about the potential of the Internet to contribute to the lives of poor people (Rao and Raman 2009; Unwin 2009), but the reality is that, despite the efforts of many well-intended initiatives, much of its usage for development purposes remains as a means of sharing information among an elite of development experts. For example, the potential of Open Education Resources made available across the Internet (see e.g. UNESCO 2010; OER Africa 2010) is huge, but remains largely driven by "experts" from the richer countries of the world, and is largely unused, even by academics, in poor countries (similar arguments apply in the context of the critically important Free/Libre and Open Source Software movement). Likewise, the Food and Agriculture Organization's (FAO) exciting e-agriculture initiative (http://www.e-agriculture.org), designed as a community of practice to enhance sustainable agriculture, most certainly enables dialogue amongst agricultural experts across the world, but how this then feeds down into changed practices for landless laborers in poor countries remains much less clear.

One particularly exciting interactive dimension of the social dimensions of the Internet in development practice has been the use of crowd sourcing, particularly as expressed through the work of Ushahidi (http://www.ushahidi.com/; Hersman 2010). Ushahidi, meaning "testimony" in Kiswahili, was born in the aftermath of the violence associated with the 2007 elections in Kenya, and is an excellent example of the ways in which an organization that dislikes hierarchy and being told what cannot be done can use the Internet to help poor people have better life opportunities. The initial deployment of Ushahidi had 45,000 users in Kenya, and was a website that mapped incidents of violence and peace efforts based on reports submitted by mobile phones and the Web. It was subsequently rolled out more widely, receiving particular prominence in the aftermath of the Haiti earthquake in 2010, where it represented the most up-to-date map available to the humanitarian community, mapping some 3,584 incident reports (http://haiti.ushahidi.com/reports). Building on this success, the Ushahidi team have subsequently launched Huduma (http://huduma.info), which uses crowdsourcing to enable people to report on the effectiveness of the delivery of government sources in Kenya.

As Hersman (2010: np) concludes: "We've learned that technology does overcome inefficiencies, but that it still takes people to make it happen. We've learned that more people need to buck the status quo; that questioning everything makes us better. We've learned that Africans can build world-class software, and to expect nothing less." Critical to Ushahidi's success has been recognition that the Internet is unavailable in many parts of the world, and therefore that mobile phones had to be the primary means through which people could send details of crisis incidents and receive updates. That having been said, it is clear that the crowd still remains to those who have access to digital technologies and the knowledge how to use them.

The Internet and development as freedom

Sen's (1999) notion that development should be about the freedoms that people have to live the lives that they want, raises a third alternative way of considering the Internet and development. Indeed, one of the most intriguing aspects of the relationship between the Internet and development concerns the balance between anarchy and control, between top-down and bottom-up approaches to development. This was particularly highlighted during the so-called Green Revolution in Iran following the 2009 Presidential elections, when opponents of President Ahmadinejad launched an extensive campaign using social networking media such as Twitter over the Internet to express their opposition. While this attracted much publicity in the US and Europe, subsequent reflections suggest that this said as much about interests in the technology as it did about realities in Iran (Weaver 2010). The more recent dramatic changes in North Africa nevertheless raise at least a glimmer of hope that the Internet can indeed contribute to political and social transformation. At the time of writing in mid 2011, the long-term outcome of the so-called Facebook revolutions in Egypt and Tunisia remains unclear, but it is evident that many of those involved did indeed see the Internet as contributing significantly to their struggles. Wael Ghonim, the Google executive who became one of the figureheads of the Egyptian "revolution," thus claimed that "If there was no social networks it would have never been sparked... Without Facebook, without Twitter, without Google, without YouTube, this would never have happened." (http://www.dawn.com/2011/04/25/egypt-revolution-hero-to-leave-google-set-up-ngo.html)

Despite such claims, not all regimes have been as susceptible to change as were those in Tunisia and Egypt, and the fundamental cause of the protests had little to do with the existence of the Internet, but rather reflected underlying social issues, not least the rising food prices and urban youth unemployment. Only some 21 percent of the Egyptian population and 34 percent of Tunisians were Internet users in 2010, and the poorest citizens of both countries had little access to this form of political protest. Indeed, it is tempting to wonder just how much influence the companies cited by Ghonim, including his employer Google, had to play in promulgating these attempted political transformations. It is no coincidence that sites such as www.movements.org, which specifically incites activists to use new technologies to make social change have been sponsored by companies such as Google, Pepsi, and CBS News, as well as the USA's Department of State and the UK's Home Office.

It is not only activists, though, who have sought to use the Internet to overthrow states that they deem to be oppressive. Karlekar and Cook (2009: 1) thus note that: "As the Internet and other new media come to dominate the flow of news and information around the world, governments have responded with measures to control, regulate, and censor the content of bogs, websites, and text messages." They argue that it is not only in what they describe as "some of the world's most repressive regimes, like China and India," but also in "more democratic countries—such as the United Kingdom, Brazil, and Turkey" where Internet freedom is increasingly being undermined; as they conclude, "On the whole, threats to Internet freedom are growing and have become more diverse, both in the array of countries that impose restrictions and in the range of methods employed" (Karlekar and Cook 2009: 1).

While there have been a plethora of e-Government initiatives, designed in principle to make government more open, transparent, and responsive to the needs of the poor (Guida and Crow 2009), there is little evidence that conclusively confirms that this has indeed been the general outcome (Kakabadse and Kakabadse 2009; Unwin 2010). Indeed, both so-called democratic and oppressive regimes are increasingly expanding their control, through new forms of censorship, monitoring, and technical attacks, which have been greatly facilitated by the Internet (Karlekar and Cook 2009). This is typified by debates over the introduction of biometric identity cards and the use of digital technologies in censuses. India thus planned to introduce biometric digital processes for its fifteenth census in 2011. Every person over the age of 15 was to be photographed and would also have all of their fingerprints taken so as to create a national biometric database, information from which will be used to issue identity cards that will contain personal data and proof of identity such as fingerprints or iris scans (http://censusindia.gov.in/2011-Common/IntroductionToNpr.html). The government sees this as offering significant benefits, but it raises difficult ethical questions. While a government remains benign, it can reasonably be argued that it has the best interests of its people in mind. However, many of the world's governments are not of this kind, and it does not take much imagination to think what a government in possession of digital information about every individual in a country, accessible over the Internet, might choose to do with it, particularly if it was intent on inciting ethnic or social conflict.

While the founders of the Internet intended that it would be open, thereby encouraging people from many different backgrounds to benefit from enhanced access to information and communication, the balance has swung in recent years to one where powerful states are increasingly exerting their control. As Karlekar and Cook (2009) conclude, three future trends seem likely: more governments as in China and Iran, are likely to channel mobile Internet traffic through the same gateways as traditional Internet traffic, thereby enabling them to restrict or control it; increasingly sophisticated censorship and filtering methods are likely to be introduced by governments to monitor Internet activity; and many more legal controls are likely to be imposed alongside increased violations of user rights.

One final worrying aspect concerning the relationships between the Internet and freedom has been the rapid increase in what has been termed "Internet addiction" in many of the poorer countries of the world, especially in Asia. While research on this subject is in its early stages, Hechanova and Czincz (2008) estimate that as many as 12 percent of youths in China and Korea are addicted to the Internet (see also Chen et al. 2007). Likewise, a report by IDRC (2008) notes that problems associated with cyberslacking, cybergambling, and cyberpornography are common across other Asian countries, such as India, the Philippines, and Thailand. What is important about this evidence is that many people seem unable to control their use of the Internet, and that this causes psychological and social difficulties in their lives. If these claims are true, rather than being liberating, the Internet in such instances seems actually to be damaging human freedom. There is an evident need for considerably more research to explore these issues, so that evidence-based policies can be adopted that will minimize the risk facing such people. Closely linked to this is the increasing risk of cyber-attacks on governments and organizations across the world, including those in poor countries. In response, a growing number of international initiatives, such as IMPACT (the International Multilateral Partnership Against Cyber Threats, http://www.impact-alliance.org/), have been launched to try to address the challenge, and this is likely to feature much more prominently in the years to come.

CONCLUSION

Four important and inter-related conclusions can be drawn from this short overview of research on the Internet and development. First, it must be remembered that the Internet is but one of a number of new digital ICTs. While many have given it predominance, "Internet use has spread much less rapidly in low-income countries than other ICTs— notably broadcast radio . . . and television and, more recently, mobile telephony" (Souter 2007a: 33). As Souter (2007a: 33) goes on to emphasize, ultimately "the potential of the Internet can only be achieved if effective access is available," and this requires the availability of the ICT infrastructure and reliable electricity at an affordable price for the poor, and that it provides relevant information that is not available more cheaply through other means. If the world's poor are truly to benefit from the Internet, then far more attention needs to be paid explicitly to ways in which they can indeed use it to their real advantage, thereby enabling them to benefit at the expense of the world's rich. Only then will relative poverty be reduced.

Second, the success of the Internet in delivering development objectives depends very much on how such objectives are defined. Much research and practice has focused on the hegemonic notion that development is about economic growth, and there are convincing arguments that the Internet can indeed contribute to such an objective. However, even here, it is evident that the presence of the Internet alone will not in most instances contribute to the economic well-being of the poorest and most marginalized. From a relativist perspective, focusing particularly on social equality, the evidence is far more uncertain. Numerous studies (Huyer and Hafkin 2007), for example, show how women in patriarchal societies are increasingly marginalized by their exclusion from access to the Internet. Likewise, if development is seen as being concerned with freedoms, then the ambivalent character of the technology of the Internet is once more revealed.

A third important characteristic of the Internet in the context of development has been its dehumanizing and alienating effects. Just as factory production in the nineteenth century made humans appendages of machines (Lukács 1923), so too in the twenty-first century has the Internet made people ever more the appendages of computers. In so doing, users are becoming further alienated from the physical world of nature and creativity, and ever more constrained by those who design the virtual realities of which we are part. What is remarkable about this is that in the name of progress, such virtual worlds are accepted and applauded as being "good" and where the future lies (Carr 2008). Such arguments need to be strongly countered if we are to retain the very essence of what makes us human. By enabling people to work away from their offices, by dramatically reducing the constraints of time and space on production, consumption, and exchange, the Internet has enabled owners of capital to exploit their workforces far more efficiently and effectively than ever before, while at the same time making them think that they are enjoying it. Imagine a world where one was not expected to answer the hundred or so emails that arrive every day, and where one actually had time to think, be creative, and enjoy the physical experience of being human! Paradoxically, the poor and marginalized, those without access to the Internet, may ultimately actually be richer than the bankers, traders, and business executives who have become the new proletariat of the digital age, quite simply because the poor without access to the Internet are not bound by its dehumanizing, unspoken, and constraining rules.

This chapter has sought to highlight the ambivalent character of the Internet. Rather than being an independent force with a life of its own, or a silver bullet that can be used to fight poverty, it is but a technology that is used by those with access to it to pursue the ends that they seek. As other chapters of this book highlight, there are undoubted benefits that people gain from access to the Internet. That is why its potential role in development is so important. However, what I have sought to argue here is that if we are really to address development challenges we need to explore a research agenda that is rather different from that which is usually advocated.

First, we should work with those who do not already have access to the Internet to explore how their information and communication needs and wants can best be addressed. How, for example, can the Internet best benefit those with disabilities (see e.g. http://www.e-accessibilitytoolkit.org) or the poorest landless laborers living in rural areas? Second, we need to place much greater emphasis on ways through which connectivity, implying both bandwidth and electrical power, can be made available to people living in the most inaccessible areas. Unless there is truly universal access, then the Internet can only but exacerbate the differences between those who do not have access to it, and those who do. This is as much to do with developing new insights into effective regulatory environments as it is concerned with creating innovative technical solutions.

Finally, we need to place much more emphasis on the social, cultural, and political dimensions of the Internet in development practice than has heretofore been the case. For the poorest people, access to ICTs and their uses thereof are very often not driven primarily by economic reasons.

Development is about so much more than simply economic growth, and greater research on how the Internet can contribute to this wider agenda must be undertaken if we have a serious interest in changing existing balances of power across the world that have until now tended to be reinforced rather than transformed by the Internet.

Acknowledgements

I am especially grateful to Marije Geldof, Bill Dutton, and Mark Graham for their comments on an earlier version of this chapter. Mike Trucano, Laurent Elder, Ken Banks, Uduak Okon, Erik Hersman, and Ugo Vallauri have also provided important insights into the interface between the Internet and development that have shaped my thoughts on this subject, and I would here like to acknowledge their significant contribution to my evolving ideas.

References

Abbate, J. (1999). *Inventing the Internet*, Cambridge, MA: MIT Press.

Abida, M. (2009). "The World Summit on the Information Society: A Reflection," in T. Unwin (ed.). *ICT4D: Information and Communication Technologies for Development*, Cambridge: Cambridge University Press, pp. 142–3.

Baker, K. M. (2004). "Translation of Condorcet, Sketch for a Historical Picture of the Progress of the Human Mind: Tenth Epoch," *Daedalus*, 113(3): 65–82.

Best, M. and Kenny, C. (2009). "ICTs, Enterprise and Development," in T. Unwin (ed.). *ICT4D: Information and Communication Technologies for Development*, Cambridge: Cambridge University Press, pp. 177–205.

Best, M. L., Jones, K., Kondo, I., Thakur, D., Wornyo, E. and Yu, C. (2007). "Post-Conflict Communications: The Case of Liberia," *Communications of the ACM*, 50(10): 33–9.

Boston Consulting Group (2009). *Towards a Connected World: Socio-Economic Impact of Internet in Emerging Economies*, Boston, MA: Boston Consulting Group.

Carr, N. (2008). *The Big Switch: Rewiring the World, from Edison to Google*, New York: W.W. Norton.

Castells, M. (2000). *The Rise of the Network Society*, 2nd edn., Oxford: Blackwell.

Chen, P., Liu, S., and Luo, L. (2007). "A Study on the Psychological Health of Internet Addiction," *Chinese Journal of Clinical Psychology*, 15: 40–2.

Conway, D. and Waage, J. (with Delaney, S.) (2010). *Science and Innovation for Development*, London: UKDS.

DFID (2009). *Eliminating World Poverty: Building our Common Future*, Norwich: The Stationery Office.

Dutton, W. H. and Jeffreys, P.W. (eds) (2010). *World Wide Research: Reshaping the Sciences and Humanities*, Cambridge, MA: MIT Press.

Easterley, W. (2006). *The White Man's Burden: Why the West's Efforts to Aid the Rest Have Done so Much Ill and so Little Good*, New York: Penguin.

Enough Project (2010). Raise Hope for Congo: Our Initiatives. Available at <http://www.raisehopeforcongo.org/content/initiatives/our-initiatives>. Accessed May 24, 2012.

Escobar, A. (1995). *Encountering Development: The Making and Unmaking of the Third World*, Princeton, NJ: Princeton University Press.

Flew, T. and Wilson, J. (2010). "Journalism as Social Networking: The Australian Youdecide Project and the 2007 Federal Election," *Journalism*, 11(2): 131–47.

Geldof, M. (2010). "Literacy and ICT: Social Constructions in the Lives of Low-literate Youth in Ethiopia and Malawi." PhD Thesis, Royal Holloway, University of London.

Google (2006). "A Note to Google Users on Net Neutrality." Available at <http://www.google.com/help/netneutrality_letter.html>. Accessed May 24, 2012.

——(2010)."Facts About Our Network Neutrality Policy Proposal." Available at <http://googlepublicpolicy.blogspot.com/search/label/Net%20Neutrality>. Accessed May 24, 2012.

Guida, J. and Crow, M. (2009). "E-Government and E-Governance," in T. Unwin (ed.). *ICT4D: Information and Communication Technologies for Development*, Cambridge: Cambridge University Press, pp. 283–320.

Gurumurthy, A. (2004). *Gender and ICTS: Overview Report*, Brighton: IDS.

Habermas, J. (1978). *Knowledge and Human Interests*, 2nd edn., London: Heinemann.

Harvey, D. (2000). *Spaces of Hope*. Oxford: Blackwell.

Hechanova, R. M. and Czincz, J. (2008). "Internet Addiction in Asia: Myth or Reality." Unpublished paper, Ateneo de Manila University, Philippines.

Heeks, R. (2010). ICT4D Journal Ranking Table. Available at <http://ict4dblog.wordpress.com/2010/04/14/ict4d-journal-ranking-table/>.

Hersman, E. (2010). "Making Ushahidi." See <http://whiteafrican.com/2010/08/12/making-ushahidi/comment-page-1/#comment-252430>. Accessed May 24, 2012.

Huyer, S. and Hafkin, N. (2007). *Engendering the Knowledge Society: Measuring Women's Participation*, Montreal: Orbicom.

IDRC (2008). "Workshop on Internet Addiction Research in Asia." Unpublished report, Ottawa: IDRC.

Ilavarasan, P. V. and Levy, M. R. (2010). "ICTs and Urban Microentrepreneurs: Identifying and Maximizing Opportunities for Economic Development: Final Report," Ottawa: IDRC.

International Telecommunication Union (2011). *The Role of ICT in Advancing Growth in Least Developed Countries*, Geneva: International Telecommunication Union.

Kakabadse, N. and Kakabadse, A. (2009). "The Citizen and the State: A Progressively Subversive, State Determined and ICT Mediated Relationship," in A. Kakabadse, N. Kakabadse, and K.N. Kalu (eds). *Citizenship: A Reality Far From the Ideal*, Basingstoke: Palgrave Macmillan, pp. 145–70.

Karlekar, K. D. and Cook, S. G. (2009). "Access and Control: A Growing Diversity of Threats to Internet Freedom," in Freedom House, *Freedom on the Net: A Global Assessment of Internet and Digital Media*, Washington, DC: Freedom House, pp. 1–11.

Kelly, T. (2004). "World Summit on the Information Society (WSIS) and the Digital Divide," Presentation to the KADO/APWING Digital Opportunity Conference, Seoul, November 24. Available at <http://www.itu.int/osg/spu/presentations/2005/kelly-wsis-digital-divide-24-nov-04.pdf>. Accessed May 24, 2012.

Kenny, R. and Kenny, C. (2010). "Superfast: is it Really Worth a Subsidy?," Communications Chambers. Available at <http://charleskenny.blogs.com/files/overselling_fibre_1127.pdf>. Accessed May 24, 2012.

Kleinwächter, W. (2004). "Beyond ICANN vs ITU: How WSIS Tries to Enter the New Territory of Internet Governance," *International Communication Gazette*, 66(3–4): 233–51.

Koppell, J. G. S. (2005). "Pathologies of Accountability: ICANN and the Challenge of 'Multiple Accountabilities Disorder," *Public Administration Review*, 65(1): 94–108.

Kothari, U. (2006). *A Radical History of Development Studies: Individuals, Institutions and Ideologies*, London: Zed Press.

Latzer, M. (2009). "Information and Communication Technology Innovations: Radical or Disruptive?," *New Media and Society*, 11(4): 599–619.

Leiner, B. M., Cerf, V. G., Clark, D. D., Kahn, R. E., Kleinrock, L., Lynch, D. C., Postel, J., Roberts, L. G. and Wolff, S. (2003). *A Brief History of the Internet.* Available at <http://www internetsociety.org/internet/internet-51/history-internet/brief-history-internet/>. Accessed May 24, 2012.

Levine, D. (2004). "Poverty, Capabilities and Freedom." *Review of Political Economy*, 16(1): 101–15.

Lukács, G. (1923). *History and Class Consciousness*, London: Merlin Press, 1963.

MacLean, D. (ed.) (2004). *Internet Governance: A Grand Collaboration. An Edited Collection of Papers Contributed to the United Nations ICT Task Force Global Forum on Internet Governance, New York, March 25–26, 2004*, New York: UN ICT Task Force.

—— (2005). *A Brief History of WGIG.* Available at <http://www.wgig.org/docs/book/A_Brief_history_of_WGIG.html>. Accessed May 24, 2012.

MacLean, D. (ed.) (2009). *Internet for All.* Proceedings of the Third Internet Governance Forum, Hyderabad, India, 306 December 2008. New York: United Nations.

Madden, D. (2000). "Relative or Absolute Poverty Lines: a New Approach," *Review of Income and Wealth*, 46(2): 181–99.

Mansell, R. and Wehn, U. (1998). *Knowledge Societies: Information Technology for Sustainable Development*, Oxford: Oxford University Press.

Mercer, C (2006). "Telecentres and Transformations: Modernizing Tanzania through the Internet," *African Affairs*, 105/419: 243–64.

Mueller, M. L., Kuerbis, B. N., and Pagé, C. (2007). "Democratizing Global Communication? Global Civil Society and the Campaign for Communication Rights in the Information Society," *International Journal of Communication*, 1(1): 267–96

O'Boyle, E. J. (1999). "Toward an Improved Definition of Poverty," *Review of Social Economy*, 57(3): 281–301.

OER Africa (2010). "OER Africa: Building African Education Through Openness." Available at <http://www.oerafrica.org/>. Accessed May 24, 2012.

Opera (2009). "State of the Mobile Web." Available at <http://www.opera.com/smw/2009/11/#chart_pages>. Accessed May 24, 2012.

Pieterse, J. N. (2010). *Development Theory*, 2nd edn., London: Sage.

Qiang, C., Pitt, A., and Ayers, S. (2003). *The Contribution of Information Communication Technologies to Growth*, World Bank Working Paper 24, Washington DC: World Bank.

Qiang, C. Z.-W., Clarke, G. R., and Halewood, N. (2006). "The Role of ICT in Doing Business," in World Bank (ed.). *Information and Communications for Development: Global Trends and Policies*, Washington DC: World Bank.

Qiu, J. L. (2010). "Network Labour and Non-elite Knowledge Workers in China," *Work Organisation, Labor and Globalization*, 4(2): 80–95.

Rahnema, M. and Bawtree, V. (eds) (1997). *The Post-Development Reader*, London: Zed Books.

Rao, M. and Raman, N. (2009). *ICT4D: Learnings, Best Practices and Roadmaps from the PAN Asia ICT R&D Grants Programme*, Singapore: AMIC and Nanyang Technological University.

Rostow, W. (1960). *The Stages of Economic Growth: A Non-Communist Manifesto*, Cambridge: Cambridge University Press.

Sachs, J. (2005). *The End of Poverty: How we can Make it Happen in our Lifetime*, London: Penguin Books.

Samarajiva, R. and Zainudeen, A. (2007). *ICT Infrastructure in Emerging Asia: Policy and Regulatory Roadblocks*, New Delhi and Ottawa: Sage and IDRC.

Sen, A. K. (1976). "Poverty: An Ordinal Approach to Measurement," *Econometrica*, 44(2): 219–31.

—— (1999). *Development as Freedom*, Oxford: Oxford University Press.

Souter, D. (2007). "Internet Governance and Development: Another Digital Divide," *Information Polity*, 12(1–2): 29–38.

—— (with Jagun, A.) (2007). *Whose Summit? Whose Information Society? Developing Countries and Civil Society at the World Summit on the Information Society*, Melville, South Africa: Association for Progressive Communications.

Sreekumar, T. T. and Rivera-Sánchez, M. (2008). "ICTs and Development: Revisiting the Asian Experience," *Science Technology Society*, 13(2): 159–74.

Telenor (2009). "Internet Boosts Economic Growth and Social Welfare." Available at <http://www.telenor.com/en/news-and-media/press-releases/2009/Internet-boosts-economic-growth-social-welfare>. Accessed May 24, 2012.

UNCTAD (2007). *Information Economy Report 2007–2008: Science and Technology for Development—The New Paradigm of ICT*, New York: United Nations.

UNESCO (2010). "Welcome to the wiki of the UNESCO OER Community: Open Educational Resources." Available at <http://oerwiki.iiep.unesco.org/index.php?title=Main_Page>. Accessed May 24, 2012.

United Nations (1996). *Human Development Report 1996*, New York: United Nations/Oxford: Oxford University Press.

—— (2010). *Millennium Development Goals Report*, New York: United Nations.

—— (no date). "We Can End Poverty 2015 Millennium Development Goals." Available at <http://www.un.org/millenniumgoals/bkgd.shtml>. Accessed May 24, 2012.

Unwin, T. (2004). "Beyond Budgetary Support: Pro-Poor Development Agendas for Africa," *Third World Quarterly*, 25(8): 1501–23.

—— (2005). *Partnerships in Development Practice: Evidence from Multi-Stakeholder ICT4D Partnership Practice in Africa*, Paris: UNESCO for the World Summit on the Information Society.

—— (2007). "No End to Poverty," *Journal of Development Studies*, 43(5): 929–53.

—— (2009). *ICT4D: Information and Communication Technologies for Development*, Cambridge: Cambridge University Press.

—— (2010). "ICTs, Citizens and the State: Moral Philosophy and Development Practices," *Electronic Journal on Information Systems in Developing Countries*, 44(1): 1–16.

Wallerstein, I. (2000). "Globalization or the Age of Transition? A Long-Term View of the Trajectory of the World System," *International Sociology*, 15(2): 249–65.

Waters, R. and Gelles, D. (2010). "Google Deal Splits Industry Over Net Neutrality." *The Financial Times*, August 12, 2010. Available at <http://www.ft.com/cms/s/2/5eb2e902-a59f-11df-a5b7-00144feabdc0.html>. Accessed May 24, 2012.

Weaver, M. (2010). "Iran's 'Twitter Revolution' was Exaggerated." *The Guardian*, June 9. Available at<http://www.guardian.co.uk/world/2010/jun/09/iran-twitter-revolution-protests>. Accessed May 24, 2012.

Weigel, G. and Waldburger, D. (eds) (2004). *ICT4D—Connecting People for a Better World*, Berne and Kuala Lumpur: Swiss Agency for Development and Cooperation and Global Knowledge Partnership.

World Bank (2006). *Information and Communication for Development: Global Trends and Policies*, Washington, DC: The World Bank.

Wray, R. (2009). "Africa Sees Massive Growth in Mobile Web Usage," *The Guardian*, December 22. Available at <http://www.guardian.co.uk/technology/2009/dec/22/mobilephones-Internet>. Accessed May 24, 2012.

Zhao, J. (2008). "Integrating the Internet into Farming Activities: A Study of Farmer Users in Shandong Province, China," *Science Technology Society*, 13(2): 325–44.

CHAPTER 26

THE EMERGING FIELD OF INTERNET GOVERNANCE

LAURA DENARDIS

INTERNET governance scholars focus on what is at stake in the design, administration, and manipulation of the Internet's protocological and material architecture—a departure from Internet research focused on Internet content and usage. This technical architecture is not external to politics and culture but, rather, deeply embeds the values and policy decisions that ultimately structure individual freedom online and the pace of Internet innovation. An important set of questions exists at this level of complex technological design and governance, which is orthogonal to content and generally outside of public view.

"Governance" in the Internet context requires qualification because relevant actors are not only governments. Governance often refers to the efforts of nation states and traditional political structures to govern. Sovereign governments do perform certain Internet governance functions such as regulating computer fraud and abuse, performing antitrust oversight, enforcing intellectual property laws, and responding to Internet security threats. Sovereign governments also unfortunately use content filtering and blocking techniques for surveillance and censorship of citizens. Many other areas of Internet governance, such as Internet protocol design and coordination of critical Internet resources, have historically not been the exclusive purview of governments but of new transnational institutional forms and of private ordering. Without this qualification, the Internet governance nomenclature might incorrectly convey that this type of scholarship focuses primarily on government policy or advocates for greater government control of the Internet (Johnson et al. 2004).

The study of Internet governance is concerned with a number of overarching questions. How are we to understand the role of private industry in determining communicative contexts of political and cultural expression? How can conflicting values be balanced: for example, the desire for interoperability versus the need to limit some exchanges based on authentication and trust? How should critical Internet resources be allocated, and by whom, to maximize technical efficiency but also achieve social goals? How do repressive governments "govern" the Internet through filtering, blocking, and other restraints on freedom of expression? What is the appropriate relationship between sovereign nation-state governance and non-territorial modes of Internet governance? What are the connections between Internet protocol design, innovation, and individual civil liberties? To what extent are the problems of Internet governance creating new global governance institutions and what are the implications?

Internet governance research brings these important public interest issues to light and produces the theoretical and applied research that influences critical public interest debates. This chapter offers a taxonomy for understanding themes and controversies in Internet governance and presents a canon of interdisciplinary Internet governance scholarship. The following are the key governance areas this chapter describes: control of critical Internet resources; Internet protocol design; Internet governance-related intellectual property rights; Internet security and infrastructure management; and communication rights. Internet governance decisions in these areas have enormous public interest implications but, unlike Internet Studies areas that are content-related, these decisions have a concealed technical complexity that renders them largely out of public view. The chapter explores the nature of this governance by, largely, private ordering and posits that all key Internet governance debates contain an inherent tension between forces striving for interoperability and openness and forces striving for proprietary approaches and information enclosure.

An Internet governance framework

"Internet governance" is a contested term with various definitions (Hoffman 2005). As Milton Mueller suggests, Internet governance debates have often reduced into an exaggerated dichotomy between the extremes of cyberlibertarianism and cyberconservativism (Mueller 2010a). The former can resemble utopian technological determinism and the later is basically a state sovereignty model that extends traditional forms of state control to the Internet with the goal of adequately serving the public interest. The cyberlibertarian and cyberconservative perspectives are indistinguishable in one way. They both disregard the governance sinews already permeating the Internet's technical architecture. While the relative malleability of content and the distributed nature of the Internet can misleadingly convey the impression that no one controls the Internet, coordination—sometimes, centralized coordination—occurs in several technical and administrative areas necessary to keep the Internet operational. In fact, Internet governance functions historically predate the term Internet governance, never mind the debates over what constitutes Internet governance (Abbate 1999).

To dismiss possible misconceptions, *Internet governance is not merely about domain names*. Because of the late 1990s controversies that led to the formation of the Internet Corporation for Assigned Names and Numbers (ICANN), a number of Internet governance examinations address domain names and debates about the role of ICANN in managing critical Internet resources (e.g. Wu et al. 2007). Domain names are also the one part of Internet governance that can "be seen" by general Internet communities so they have received disproportionate press coverage and attention in civil society.

Internet governance is also not only about institutions. One approach to studying Internet governance involves institutional ethnographies examining the organizations involved in Internet governance functions—e.g. the Internet Engineering Task Force (IETF), ICANN, the Regional Internet Registries (RIRs), the International Telecommunication Union (ITU), etc. Relegating Internet governance examinations to these institutions has limitations. First, it can omit private sector governance and the role of private industry contracts in ordering the flow of information on the Internet. Second, it can omit the role of self-governance, the possibility of co-regulation, and even the role of the traditional nation state in aspects of Internet governance and regulation.

Internet governance is also not the United Nations Internet Governance Forum (IGF). Much discussion of Internet governance has focused on the IGF and the World Summit on the Information Society (WSIS) process that led to its formation[1] (e.g. Drake 2006; Malcolm 2008). Some of this scholarship focuses on issues of new institutional forms, issues of multistakeholderism, analyses and critiques of agenda-setting processes, assessments of the efficacy of relevant actors, or examinations of cross-cultural collaboration. Scholarship examining the IGF process has been excellent, but the IGF is less critical than the actual arenas of Internet governance. The IGF supports a dialog (i.e. a series of conferences) with no policy-making authority or traditional powers such as taxation, judicial recourse, or enforcement mechanisms. Even as a dialog alone, some critiques of the IGF process have noted that it has sometimes eschewed divisive topics such as intellectual property rights, government censorship, and privacy (Malcolm 2008; Dutton et al. 2007). The practice of Internet governance is what has continued to occur outside of this discourse in institutions, in emerging government Internet policies, and in private decision-making.

Internet governance generally refers to policy and technical coordination issues related to the exchange of information over the Internet. There are many options for creating taxonomies of Internet governance functions (see, e.g. Dutton and Peltu 2007). The following sections present five (sometimes overlapping) themes in Internet governance and highlight key global policy debates in each area, as outlined in Table 26.1.

---

[1] The World Summit on the Information Society (WSIS) was a two-phase process organized by the United Nations in Geneva, Switzerland in 2003 and Tunis, Tunisia in 2005. A dominant source of contention in the WSIS process was the issue of United States government oversight of ICANN and the prospect of further internationalizing this authority. One outcome of this impasse was the formation of the Internet Governance Forum (IGF), which would have no decision-making authority but which would continue the multi-stakeholder dialog.

Table 26.1 Key topics of Internet governance

Topics	Some Specific Issues
Critical Internet Resources	Distribution of Internet Addresses IPv4 Address Scarcity The Domain Name System Domain Name Trademark Dispute Resolution Autonomous System Numbers Institutions of Control (ICANN, IANA, RIRs)
Internet Protocol Design	Institutions of Control (IETF, ISO, ITU, W3C, etc.) Interoperability and the Economics of Standards Public Interest Implications of Protocol Design The Transition to IPv6 Open Standards Debates Debates over Role of Government
Intellectual Property Rights	Domain Name System as Copyright Enforcement Trade Secrecy in Information Intermediation Standards-Based Patents Digital Rights Management The Role of Network Operators in Enforcement Global Trademark Dispute Mediation
Security and Infrastructure Management	National Security/Critical Infrastructure Protection Securing Routing and Addressing Infrastructures Public/Private Security Approaches and CERTs Politics of DDoS Attacks Network Management Economics of Internet Exchange Points
Communication Rights	Universal Access Policies and Net Neutrality Privacy Policies of Information Intermediaries Government Filtering and Blocking Use of Deep Packet Inspection by ISPs Government "Kill Switch" Policies Circumvention and Technologies of Dissent

Control of Critical Internet Resources

"Critical Internet Resources" are a central theme in Internet governance research and in global debates over control of the Internet (see e.g. Weber 2009). Critical Internet Resources (CIRs) usually refer to Internet-unique logical resources rather than physical infrastructure or virtual resources not exclusive to the Internet. Physical infrastructure such as the power grid, fiber optic cables, routers, and Ethernet switches are certainly critical Internet infrastructure but not CIRs per se. There are several explanations for this distinction. As will be described, CIRs must meet a technical requirement of global uniqueness, requiring some central coordination. In contrast, there are no coordination requirements limiting the dissemination of privately owned and operated physical infrastructure. Another distinction is that the physical infrastructure components can be used for other, non-Internet applications, but the logical resources that will be discussed are unique to the Internet and essential for its operation, regardless of underlying physical architecture. Similarly, virtual resources that are not unique to the Internet, such as those associated with electromagnetic spectrum allocation and management, are usually addressed outside of policy discourses about Critical Internet Resources, although there is nothing inherently fixed about this distinction. The main Internet governance concern over CIRs involves logical, software-defined resources unique to Internet architecture rather than physical architecture or virtual resources not unique to the Internet.[2] This section briefly describes three types of Critical Internet Resources—Internet addresses, the Domain Names System (including the root zone file and domain names), and Autonomous System Numbers (ASNs)—and will explain some of the substantive policy issues in each of these areas.

One common characteristic of CIRs, as historically engineered, is their role as globally unique identifiers. Meeting this criterion of global uniqueness requires some central coordination, a condition at the heart of debates over who controls these resources and how they are distributed. Unlike other types of technologically derived resources (e.g. electromagnetic spectrum), CIRs have never been exchanged in free markets, nor directly regulated by sovereign governments. They have primarily been controlled by institutions and have therefore always invoked questions about institutional legitimacy.

Internet Protocol (IP) addresses are a fundamental resource required for exchanging information over the Internet. Each Internet device possesses a unique binary number identifying its virtual location, either assigned temporarily for a session or assigned permanently. Routers use these addresses to route packets over the Internet, somewhat analogous to the postal system's dependence on unique physical addresses. Under the prevailing Internet address standard, Internet Protocol version 4 (IPv4), each binary address is a fixed 32 bits in length. This provides a reserve of 2^{32}, or approximately 4.3 billion unique Internet addresses. In 1990, the Internet standards community identified the potential depletion of addresses as a crucial design concern and the IETF recommended a new protocol, Internet Protocol version 6 (IPv6), to expand the number of available addresses. IPv6 extends the length of each address from 32 to 128 bits, supplying 2^{128} or 340 undecillion addresses. Despite the longstanding availability of IPv6, the upgrade to IPv6 has barely begun on a global scale. The distributed and decentralized nature of the Internet's technical architecture precludes the possibility of a coordinated, rapid transition. One problem is that the new protocol is not directly backward compatible with the prevailing protocol, in that a computing device exclusively using IPv6 cannot natively exchange information with a device exclusively using IPv4. (See DeNardis 2009a for a complete explanation.)

---

[2] Other definitions of Critical Internet Resources, such as the definition from the United Nations Working Group on Internet Governance (WGIG), include issues directly related to telecommunications infrastructure, interconnection, and peering.

Historically, there have been significant Internet governance policy questions about IP addresses, primarily addressed within the Internet Assigned Numbers Authority (IANA, a function under ICANN) and the regional Internet registries (RIRs)[3] to which IANA allocates addresses for regional assignment. Who should control the assignment and allocation of Internet addresses and on what basis do they derive their legitimacy? Should resources be directed toward first mover advantage, market efficiency, distributive justice, or some other objective?

A pressing question about IP addresses involves how to extend the life of the IPv4 address space. The exhaustion of the IPv4 address reserve has significant implications, especially in parts of the developing world without large existing stores of IPv4 addresses. One historical debate has involved the question of what type of market intervention or government regulation might be necessary, if any at all, to free up IPv4 addresses that are allocated but not used or provide incentives for upgrading to IPv6 (DeNardis 2009a).

The Domain Name System establishes the domain name space in the same way that the Internet Protocol establishes the Internet address space. The DNS translates between alphanumeric domain names and their associated IP addresses necessary for routing packets of information over the Internet. The DNS, through this address resolution process, handles billions of queries per day. It is an enormous, hierarchical database management system (DBMS) distributed globally across countless servers. The Internet's root name servers contain a master file known as the root zone file itemizing the IP addresses and associated names of the official DNS servers for all top-level domains (TLDs): generic ones like .com, .edu, .gov, etc. and country codes, or ccTLDs such as .cn for China or .uk for the United Kingdom. The IANA function under ICANN is ultimately responsible for managing the assignment of domain names, although delegated through Internet registrars, and for controlling the root server system and the root zone file. Milton Mueller's *Ruling the Root* (2002) provides an excellent analysis of the evolution of ICANN and the Domain Name System and associated governance debates.

The most high-profile Internet governance controversies in this area have involved struggles over DNS control and corresponding issues related to legitimacy and jurisdiction (Mueller 2002; Paré 2003). The controversy over US ties to ICANN and control of the Domain Name System continues to be a heated topic in international policy debates about Internet governance (e.g. Mayer-Schönberger and Ziewitz 2009).

There have been other substantive policy issues related to domain names. For example, the DNS was originally restricted to ASCII characters, precluding the possibility

[3] The five Regional Internet Registries are the African Network Information Centre (AfriNIC), the Asia Pacific Network Information Centre (APNIC), the American Registry for Internet Numbers (ARIN), the Latin America and Caribbean Network Information Centre (LACNIC), and Europe's RIPE Network Coordination Centre (RIPE NCC). The RIRs are private, nonprofit institutions that employ a contract-oriented administrative model of governance. They serve large geographical areas, managing the address space allocated to them by IANA, under ICANN.

of domain names in scripts that are the basis of such languages as Arabic, Chinese, or Russian. The introduction of internationalized domain names (IDNs) in the opening decade of the twenty-first century enabled country code top-level domains in native language scripts. The relationship of domain names and freedom of expression is another recurrent topic, as well as DNS security and trademark dispute resolution for domain names. For example, what are the legal remedies for addressing trademark-infringing domain name registrations and what is the responsibility of domain name registries for infringement? National legal remedies have not always been helpful because of jurisdictional complexities such as where a trademark is registered, where a server is located, or where a trademark infringing entity resides. Traditional legal intervention in trademark disputes is also too lengthy a process relative to the quick pace of Internet developments. ICANN's Uniform Domain-Name Dispute-Resolution Policy (UDRP) has served as a mechanism for trademark protection in the sphere of domain names but, like many of ICANN's activities, has long been controversial (Geist 2001).

Autonomous System Numbers (ASNs) are another Critical Internet Resource. Roughly speaking, an autonomous system (AS) is a network operator. More accurately, an AS is made up of a unique collection of routing prefixes used within a network system connected to the Internet. This virtual resource is a central currency of the Internet's routing system. Each autonomous system must have a globally unique ASN for use in Border Gateway Protocol (BGP) routing. BGP is a core Internet protocol that maintains a directory of network prefixes that establish how packets are routed among network operators.

Similar to IP addresses, IANA assigns blocks of ASNs to regional Internet registries, which in turn allocate numbers to network operators. ASNs have evolved similarly to the IP address space in that the original 16-bit number, allowing for only 2^{16} unique numbers, has been expanded to 32-bit numbers to provide orders of magnitude more globally unique network identifiers.[4] Many policy concerns about IP addresses are relevant to ASNs: who is eligible for an ASN, how are resource constraints shaping the political economy of these numbers, and what are the global implications of the proliferation of private Autonomous System Numbers that are designed to conserve globally unique ASNs but that cannot be used to access the global Internet? Internet governance research has not addressed the issue of Autonomous System Numbers as expansively as other Critical Internet Resources, so there is a great need for research in this area. This theme of control over technologically derived resources is not unique to Internet governance. What may be unique about Critical Internet Resources, and in particular IP addresses, is that they are completely global rather than geographically bounded resources and they require central coordination because of the technical criterion of each resource serving as a globally unique identifier.

---

[4] See Request for Comment 4893, "BGP Support for Four-octet AS Number Space." Available at <http://tools.ietf.org/html/rfc4893>. Accessed June 14, 2011.

Internet protocol design

Another Internet governance function is the development of Internet protocols, the standards that enable interoperability among information technologies. The Internet "works" because it is universally based upon a common protocological language. Protocols are sometimes considered difficult to grasp because they are intangible and often invisible to Internet users. They are not software or material hardware. They are closer to text (Galloway 2004). Protocols are literally the blueprints that developers use to manufacture products that will be compatible with other products based on the same standards. Routine Internet use involves hundreds of standards ranging from Bluetooth, Wi-Fi standards, the MP3 format for encoding and compressing audio files, VoIP protocols, HTTP, and the TCP/IP protocols on which the Internet relies at the network and transport layer. The Internet Protocol (mentioned above) is part of the TCP/IP protocol suite. These are just a few of the protocols that represent information in common formats, encrypt or compress information, provide error detection and correction, and provide common addressing structures.

The IETF has developed the core networking protocols for the Internet, including TCP/IP, so much scholarship about protocols has focused on this entity (e.g. Froomkin 2003). But IETF standards are only part of a vast protocol ecosystem required to provide end-to-end interoperability for voice, video, data, and images over the Internet. The World Wide Web Consortium (W3C) sets application-layer standards for the Web. The International Telecommunication Union (ITU) sets standards in areas such as security and voice over the Internet. The Institute of Electrical and Electronics Engineers (IEEE) developed Ethernet and the Wi-Fi family of standards. Countless other entities develop specifications that collectively enable the transmission of information over the Internet: including the Motion Picture Experts Group (MPEG); the Joint Photographic Experts Group (JPEG); the International Organization for Standardization (ISO); and the Standardization Administration of China (SAC).

Internet protocols not only serve technical functions, but have significant political and economic implications (Morris and Davidson 2003; Garcia 2005). The economic effects of information technology standards have been studied since before the advent of the Web (David and Greenstein 1990). Web accessibility standards make decisions about the extent of access for the hearing impaired and those with other disabilities. Authentication and encryption standards intersect with individual privacy online and mediate between competing values of individual civil liberties and national security and law enforcement functions. Internet governance research examines how values are embedded in protocol design; on what basis private standards-setting institutions have the legitimacy to make policy choices; and what the responsibilities of governments to encourage conditions that promote certain types of standardization processes are.

A traditional debate in Internet governance policy involves what constitutes an open standard (Ghosh 2005; Krechmer 2005; DeNardis 2011). This is a controversial issue with much at stake for Internet innovation and for technology companies whose success is dependent upon a particular definition of open standards. As Phil Weiser describes,

"The most formidable regulatory regime that has governed the Internet to date is the institution of open standards that has allowed the Internet to grow exponentially as a network of networks" (Weiser 2001). Questions about standards openness exist in several areas. The first is the question of openness in standards development, meaning who is permitted to participate in standards design or permitted to access information about the development of a standard and associated deliberations, minutes, and records. A second set of questions addresses the degree of a standard's openness in its implementation, meaning whether the standard itself is published, whether the standard can be accessed for free, and to what extent the standard has underlying intellectual property restrictions for implementation in products. A third set of questions addresses the openness in a standard's use, meaning the resulting extent of product competition and user choice of technologies based on the standard. If one considers application-layer standards for voice, images, and video, the degree of openness of Internet-related standards is a complicated spectrum requiring a great deal of research.

Another global Internet governance debate involves the question of the appropriate role of governments in promoting certain types of standards. Governments (e.g. Japan, the European Union, and China) have attempted to promote the national adoption of the IPv6 protocol. Governments also increasingly try to encourage the adoption of open standards, often through electronic government interoperability frameworks (e-GIFs) specifying information technology standards for e-Governance infrastructures.

Internet governance-related intellectual property rights

Another Internet governance concern involves intellectual property rights (IPR) such as patents, copyright, trademarks, and trade secrecy. Whereas intellectual property rights enforcement online is designed into and implemented in technical architecture, such as the DNS, copyright filtering or digital rights management (DRM) technologies (Benoliel 2004; Gillespie 2007), or executed by network operators, such as "three strikes laws" and notice and takedown approaches, these technical protection measures are a direct concern of Internet governance. Many intellectual property issues address technical measures for control content, but others more directly address the Internet's actual technical architecture and specific areas of Internet resource coordination. For example, the issue of domain name trademark dispute resolution was mentioned above in the discussion of Critical Internet Resources. This section will provide a brief sample of a few of the other intellectual property rights issues that intersect with Internet governance functions. These will include: the use of the Domain Name System for copyright and trademark enforcement, standards-embedded patents, trade secrecy in information intermediation, and Internet three-strikes laws.

The Internet's Domain Name System has historically served a straightforward function of translating between alphanumeric domain names that humans use and the Internet addresses that digital devices use. It has also been identified as a resource for intellectual property rights' enforcement. One technique has involved the seizure of domain names associated with websites deemed to be infringing intellectual property rights. The intended targets of the seizures, usually carried out by Internet registries or registrars, are websites that illegally distribute digital content such as pirated movies or sell counterfeit goods such as luxury handbag knockoffs. In the United States, for example, domain name seizures have been carried out by US Immigration and Customs Enforcement (ICE), an investigative law enforcement agency of the Department of Homeland Security.[5] While too complex an issue to address briefly here, this technique, like many Internet governance areas, implicates conflicting public interest values such as freedom of expression versus law enforcement, complexities of national jurisdiction of cross-border infrastructures, as well as technical concerns about the stability and security of infrastructures of Internet governance.

Another ongoing Internet governance debate involves royalty-bearing patent claims embedded in Internet standards (DeNardis 2009b). The Internet has experienced rapid innovation and growth in part because of its underpinning of openly available technical protocols with minimal intellectual property restrictions. The evolution of the Internet's architecture and of Internet governance has created more complicated IPR conditions. A single device integrates countless functions—voice, video, text messaging, and imaging, and is able to connect to multiple networks like GSM cellular networks, Wi-Fi, or global positioning systems. These devices embed hundreds of standards, many of them royalty-bearing. This integration of royalty-bearing standards into the Internet landscape can have effects on innovation, on economic competition, and on costs to end-users (Kobayahi et al. 2009). Intellectual property scholar Mark Lemley has described the problem of patent owner holdup, particularly in the technical standardization context, as "the central public policy problem in intellectual property law today" (Lemley 2007: 149). An additional complexity is that standards-setting institutions, even those in the same industry, all have different policies about IPR (Lemley 2002). A related issue is the use of intellectual property laden standards as global trade barriers (Gibson 2007). The extent to which intellectual property rights are increasingly embedded in Internet-related standards, and the empirical implications of this phenomenon, is a critical topic for Internet governance scholarship.

The use of trade secrecy laws in Internet search and other information intermediation is another area of Internet governance concern, particularly within architectural components of the Internet that organize or manipulate information. Search engines provide a prime example of this because they use trade-secret protected techniques related to the algorithmic sorting and ranking of information. Search engine companies can invoke trade secrecy to protect themselves, particularly in litigation matters, from disclosing information about how these technologies and algorithms work (Grimmelmann 2007). To the extent that Internet governance refers to policy and coordination issues related to the exchange of information over the Internet, the direct mediating power of

---

[5] See US Immigration and Customs Enforcement Press Release, "'Operation In Our Sites' targets Internet movie pirates," June 30, 2010. Available at <http://www.ice.gov/news/releases/1006/100630losangeles.htm>. Accessed June 14, 2011.

search engines in ordering information on the Internet is an Internet governance concern. Like all technologies, search engines are not disembodied, neutral tools but reflect editorial control decisions of designers. Policy controversies about search engines revolve around such issues as the possibility of search engine bias (Goldman 2006), as well as state censorship implemented via search technologies. Some suggest that greater transparency of algorithmic ordering, possibly legislatively mandated transparency, or other legal remedies, might be necessary to assess possible degrees of search engine bias (Pasquale 2006). Here the issue of trade secrecy can conflict with public interest concerns related to transparency and fairness. However, loosening trade secrecy protections in this area might itself have unfortunate consequences such as making it easier to game search engine results, particularly by search engine spammers. Trade secrecy issues will increasingly arise in other areas of Internet governance, such as within the private agreements and techniques shared among carriers at Internet exchange points discussed later in this chapter.

Network operators, such as Internet service providers (ISPs), serve a number of Internet governance functions related to access policies, network management, and security. But they too—like registrars and registries—have been drawn into the front lines of intellectual property rights enforcement. So-called three-strikes laws, also called graduated response, is an approach some countries have taken to curb online copyright infringement, particularly illegal file-sharing. At the request of media content industries and required by law in some countries, network operators take action against users allegedly engaged in illegal file-sharing by either completely disconnecting users from the Internet or deploying a variety of punitive technical measures such as blocking access to certain sites, portals, and protocols, monitoring communications, or throttling back bandwidth. For example, France introduced a statutory measure that implemented a three-strikes approach. As is the case in other Internet governance functions related to intellectual property rights' enforcement, this approach raises questions such as the economic burden of these measures on network operators, the implications of these techniques to freedom of expression, and the civil liberties implications of network operator surveillance on individual privacy.

Internet security and infrastructure management

Securing critical Internet infrastructure is one of the most critical areas of Internet governance and one that involves a variety of solutions and problems related to authentication, critical infrastructure protection, encryption, worms, viruses, denial of service attacks, and data interception and modification. Internet governance scholars address a number of questions related to problems of cybercrime and cybersecurity. Is the Internet's underlying routing and addressing system adequately secure? How vulnerable is the DNS to a major service disruption? What is the relationship between national and international approaches to Internet security and how is this coordinated? What are the responsibilities of the private sector, individual users and technical communities, and where does government fit in this framework (Brown and Marsden 2007)? What is the political economy of certain hacking techniques such as the distributed denial of service attacks carried out by Anonymous and others?

Some describe Internet security as part of a "peer production of Internet governance" framework, meaning that individuals and the companies operating networks are primarily responsible for securing the Internet (Johnson et al. 2004). It is true that the private sector develops and implements the majority of Internet security measures. Businesses selling products online implement voluntary authentication mechanisms such as public key cryptography to secure online transactions. Service providers, business Internet users, and individual users implement their own access control mechanisms such as firewalls. But this view of the peer production of Internet security also extends to the multi-stakeholder institutions that design the protocols intended to secure information (e.g. encryption protocols), authenticate users (e.g. public key cryptography), and secure Internet infrastructure (e.g. IPsec, DNSsec).

This is also one area of Internet governance in which governments are quite involved. Most national governments enact policies for critical infrastructure protection and cybersecurity. For example, the US Department of Homeland Security operates a Computer Emergency Response Team (CERT) that works in conjunction with private industry to identify security problems and coordinate responses. Detecting and responding to Internet security problems is a complicated area of public-private interaction and also one requiring transnational coordination. There are hundreds of CERTs around the globe, many of which are hybrid public-private institutions. The coordination of information and responses to attacks among these public-private entities is a critical Internet governance concern. This is one area that benefits from conceptual frameworks of Internet governance that address co-production processes involving a complexity of actors (Levinson 2010).

Internet governance scholarship in this area also extends well beyond the end user Internet security problems that are most visible to the public such as viruses and worms. Many types of attacks target the Internet's underlying infrastructure. One example involves distributed denial of service attacks (DDoS) that hijack computers and deposit code that unknowingly makes these computers work together to disable a targeted computer by flooding it with requests. The targets of these attacks have included the Internet's root servers, high-profile commercial websites, WikiLeaks, and government servers. These are all significant Internet governance concerns, but especially attacks on the Domain Name System, which can potentially affect large parts of the Internet. Two Internet security concerns addressing underlying Internet infrastructure involve securing the DNS itself (Kuerbis and Mueller 2007) and securing the Internet's routing and addressing infrastructure (Mueller and Kuerbis 2010).

At the level of infrastructure management, there are a number of Internet governance areas. Scholarship has primarily focused on access and "last mile" issues of interconnection. For example, network neutrality papers focus primarily on last mile and home Internet use. Much less scholarly attention has been given to the Internet's backbone infrastructure. The Internet is a collection of networks owned and operated by private telecommunications companies (e.g. British Telecom, Korea Telecom, Verizon, AT&T, Comcast). These companies operate hundreds of thousands of miles of transmission facilities, including terrestrial fiber optics, microwave facilities, submarine fiber cable, and satellite links. These backbone facilities aggregate Internet traffic and transmit bits over backbones at rates upwards of 40 Gbps (e.g. OC-768 fiber optic transmission). For the Internet to successfully operate, these Internet backbones obviously must interconnect.

Commercial networks conjoin either at private Internet connection points between two companies or at multi-party Internet exchange points (IXPs). These IXPs are the physical junctures where different companies' backbone trunks interconnect, exchange Internet packets, and route them toward their appropriate destinations. One of the largest IXPs in the world, based on throughput of peak traffic, is the Deutscher Commercial Internet Exchange (DE-CIX) in Frankfurt, Germany. DE-CIX was founded in 1995 and is owned by the non-profit "eco Internet Industry Association."[6] DE-CIX connects hundreds of companies, including content delivery networks, web hosting services, and Internet service providers. For example, Google, Sprint, Level3, and Yahoo! all connect through DE-CIX, as well as to many other IXPs. Other interconnection points involve private arrangements between two telecommunications companies to connect their respective IP networks for the purpose of exchanging Internet traffic. Making this connection at private interconnection points requires physical interconnectivity and equipment but it also involves agreements about cost, responsibilities, and performance. There are generally two types of agreements—*peering* agreements, whereby no money is exchanged among companies agreeing to exchange traffic at interconnection points, and *transit* agreements in which one company agrees to pay a backbone provider for interconnection. Transit agreements often involve a smaller company paying a larger company in exchange for this interconnection. There is no standard approach for peering agreements, with some interconnections involving formal contracts and others just verbal agreements between companies' technical personnel. Interconnection agreements are unseen in that there are no directly relevant statutes, there is no regulatory oversight, and there is little transparency in private contracts and agreements.

These interconnection points have enormous implications. One area of inquiry involves the *critical infrastructure implications* of whether Internet backbone architectures have sufficient redundancy, capacity, and performance to meet requirements for the Internet's growth and reliability. Problems with peering and transit *agreements*, not just problems with physical architecture, can produce network outages. For instance, in 2008 there was an Internet outage stemming from an interconnection dispute between Cogent and Sprint (Weiser 2009), and in 2010, from a peering dispute between Comcast and Level 3.

Another area of inquiry involves *competition and antitrust* implications of peering and transit agreements. Unlike other telecommunications services, there have been almost no regulations of interconnection points. Market forces, coupled with some

---

[6] Background information about DE-CIX is available at <https://www.de-cix.net/>. Accessed June 14, 2011.

antitrust oversight, have historically been considered sufficient to discourage anti-competitive behavior in backbone interconnection agreements (Kende 2000). Others have cited concerns about lack of competition in Internet backbones, dominance by a small number or companies, and peering agreements among large providers that are detrimental to potential competitors (Kesan and Shah 2001). Developing countries have complained about transit costs to connect to dominant backbone providers.[7]

These interconnection points, because they concentrate the flow of traffic between network operators, are also obvious potential *points of government filtering and censorship*. Having greater transparency and insight into the arrangements at these sites of potential government intervention is an area in need of additional Internet governance research. Finally, the emerging area of *interconnection patents* is a critical area of Internet governance scholarship. For example, several companies successfully sued Vonage for infringing on patents for VoIP interconnection techniques (Werbach 2009).

Internet governance-related communication rights

Freedom of expression and association are increasingly exercised online but the same technologies that expand freedom of expression have created unprecedented privacy concerns and opportunities for governments to censor and filter information. Internet governance scholarship often invokes a "rights" framing to address substantive issues. On one side are the Internet governance issues that address the prospect for governments to promote the public interest through interventions such as universal access policies, broadband incentives, and network neutrality regulations (Yoo 2004; Wu 2005; Felten 2006; Wu and Yoo 2007). On the other side are mounting concerns about government censorship and surveillance, and ways in which suppression of freedom of expression is increasingly designed into or enabled by Internet infrastructure (Dutton et al. 2011). Technical measures such as infrastructure disabling, content filtering, digital rights management techniques, and blocking access to websites are techniques that repressive governments use to restrictively govern the flow of information on the Internet (Deibert et al. 2008). To the extent that government policies as well as architectural design and implementation decisions determine communication rights and civil liberties online, this area is an important part of Internet governance research.

Governance, in the traditional sense of the actions of sovereign nation states, has had immediate implications to freedom of expression online, particularly beginning in the early twenty-first century. These actions include filtering and blocking techniques enacted through the Great Firewall of China, online censorship regimes in countries such as Iran, Cuba, and Syria, and even more extreme approaches that completely sever Internet infrastructure for political reasons. For example, the Nepalese government cut

---

[7] See the Organization for Economic Co-operation and Development (OECD) paper "Internet Traffic Exchange and the Development of End-to-End International Telecommunication Competition" (2002) URL (last accessed in July 2010) <http://www.oecd.org/dataoecd/47/20/2074136.pdf.>

off international Internet connections during the martial law declared by the King in 2005.[8] The Burmese government severed Internet connectivity in 2007 in response to political protests and to stop citizens and journalists from sending images and other information making the world aware of the government's violent suppression of protests and other human rights violations.[9] The entire world watched as the Internet went dark in Egypt in 2011. Also in 2011, Internet infrastructures were intentionally disrupted in the United States, in San Francisco, California, when the Bay Area Rapid Transit (BART) agency shut down its in-station cell phone service in a preemptive effort to impede a planned protest. Internet governance scholars study both the technical aspects of these so-called "kill switch" approaches and questions about the conditions, if any, under which government termination of communication networks is permissible or advisable.

Private industry Internet governance over platforms and infrastructure also raises issues related to communication rights. Social media companies like Facebook make decisions that influence individual privacy online (e.g. the Beacon controversy). Recall how Yahoo! settled a lawsuit brought in the US by several Chinese dissidents who alleged they were persecuted for political speech after Yahoo! revealed their identities to the Chinese government. The United States government asked Twitter to delay scheduled service maintenance during the protests following the 2009 Iranian presidential election so that online dissent and citizen journalism could continue unabated. Google initially took criticism from international human rights organizations for complying with requests to delete politically sensitive YouTube videos or to filter content. These circumstances have raised public questions about corporate social responsibility as well as the ethical and legal consequences potentially faced by corporations involved in these controversies.

Private industry also intersects with communication rights at even less visible levels, such as the use of deep packet inspection by network operators. Bendrath and Mueller (2010) have described deep packet inspection (DPI) as a "potentially disruptive technology, one with the ability to dramatically change the architecture, governance and use of the Internet." DPI is a capability manufactured into firewall technologies that scrutinizes the entire contents of a packet, including the payload (i.e. information content) as well as the packet header. ISPs and other information intermediaries have traditionally used packet headers to route packets. It has not always been technically viable, or necessary, to inspect the content of packets because of the enormous processing speeds and computing resources this requires. ISPs use DPI to perform network management functions as well as copyright enforcement in cooperation with intellectual property rights holders. DPI can help identify viruses, worms, and other unwanted programs embedded

---

[8] See OpenNet Initiative's dispatch "Nepal: Internet Down, Media Censorship Imposed." Available at <http://opennet.net/blog/2005/02/nepal-internet-down-media-censorship-imposed>. Accessed March 21, 2011.

[9] See the account of Burma Internet shutdown in OpenNet Initiative Bulletin, "Pulling the Plug: A Technical Review of the Internet Shutdown in Burma," Report. Available at <http://opennet.net/sites/opennet.net/files/ONI_Bulletin_Burma_2007.pdf>. Accessed March 21, 2011.

within legitimate information and help prevent denial of service attacks. The most publicized instances of DPI have involved ad-serving practices of service providers to provide highly targeted marketing based on what a customer views or does on the Internet.[10] Some scholars have raised concerns about state use of deep packet inspection for Internet censorship (Wagner 2008).

The use of DPI is an area with historically almost no transparency. Regardless of whether DPI is used for ad serving, copyright enforcement, law enforcement, traffic prioritization for competitive gain, or routine network management functions, this type of information surveillance raises privacy implications for citizens using the Internet, as well as concerns about the chilling effects this surveillance would have on free expression, democratic participation, cultural production, and possibly innovation.

THE TENSION BETWEEN INTEROPERABILITY AND INFORMATION ENCLOSURE

This chapter has conveyed how Internet governance functions carry significant public interest implications and how these functions are diffusely distributed among new institutional forms, the private sector, and more traditional forms of governance. Network management via deep packet inspection raises privacy concerns; protocol design makes decisions about accessibility, interoperability, economic competition, and individual freedom; critical resource administration has implications for the future of the Internet's architecture as well as the pace of economic development; governments use technologies such as filtering and blocking for censorship and surveillance.

Despite the significant public interest implications, Internet governance is largely hidden from public view (not intentionally hidden but hidden nevertheless). User engagement with content, and the relative malleability of content, can convey the false impression that there is a great deal of public oversight of the Internet. Concerns about securing the Domain Name System and routing and addressing infrastructures are similarly invisible to the public. The general public is not aware about what occurs at IXPs, in search engine algorithms, or in the open standards debates. This "concealed complexity," to use Langdon Winner's phrase, all but precludes the ability of users to have oversight and input into these areas. Internet governance scholars and Internet scholars generally, have a responsibility to bring this largely hidden world to a wider audience and explain why citizens, and other scholars, should be critically engaged in these debates.

---

[10] For example, in 2008, Charter Communications announced that it would begin offering advertisers information to help target its customers with marketing information tailored to the contents of Internet searches. Under pressure from privacy advocates, lawmakers, and citizens, Charter decided to suspend its ad program.

Internet governance as a field is inherently interdisciplinary. Examining research questions related to control and governance of the Internet's underlying architecture requires a significant degree of technological knowledge. Many Internet governance scholars have backgrounds in computer science and engineering, either educationally or experientially. As evident in the literature review underlying this chapter, scholars most directly examining Internet governance are situated in interdisciplinary information schools and Internet centers,[11] communication schools, the field of science and technology studies (STS), and the legal academy. Traditional academic disciplines have somewhat circumvented Internet governance topics. For example, political scientists accustomed to studying the governance structures of nation states have not collectively embraced the study of more hybridized and diffuse Internet governance institutions (Mueller 2010b).

Internet governance research is also inherently global, addressing issues that obviously transcend national boundaries and nation-state governance structures. A global community of Internet governance scholars has coalesced around the Global Internet Governance Academic Network (GigaNet). This scholarly community was formally launched in the spring of 2006 in conjunction with the inauguration of the United Nations Internet Governance Forum. GigaNet has four principal objectives: "to: (1) *support* the establishment of a global network of scholars specializing in Internet governance issues; (2) *promote* the development of Internet governance as a recognized, interdisciplinary field of study, (3) *advance* theoretical and applied research on Internet governance, broadly defined; and (4) *facilitate* informed dialogue on policy issues and related matters between scholars and Internet governance stakeholders (governments, international organizations, the private sector, and civil society)."[12]

One important overarching theme in Internet governance research is the large role of private ordering in determining online public policy. Private industry has always played a crucial role in the design and administration of the Internet. Representatives from technology companies actively participate in standards-setting organizations; private companies operate and manage the wired and wireless telecommunications infrastructures underlying the Internet; private corporate Internet users are responsible for securing Internet transactions with customers. As even newer forms of private Internet governance emerge, it is critical for society (and scholars) to assess the potential consequences. The positive aspects of private industry Internet governance are the same as they have always been—the prospect of technical expediency and the promise of market-driven innovation.

All areas of Internet governance are sites of debates over competing values. These debates contain an inherent tension between forces striving for interoperability and openness and forces striving for proprietary approaches and information enclosure. To a greater or lesser degree, this inherent conflict enters nearly all of the contemporary

---

[11] For example, the Berkman Center for Internet and Society at Harvard University, the Oxford Internet Institute, and the Information Society Project at Yale Law School.

[12] From the founding statement of principles of the Global Internet Governance Academic Network (2006).

controversies in infrastructure policy, Critical Internet Resources, security, standards, and intellectual property rights. This tension is especially present in private industry Internet governance contexts. The tradition of Internet designers has been to publicize information about the decisions that led to design choices and administrative procedures. But trade secrecy in information intermediation is inherently closed. The escalation of interconnection patents at IXPs is another move toward more proprietary norms. The use of deep packet inspection has marked a shift away from traditional Internet values. Internet governance techniques can inherently be techniques to gain competition advantage. Standards-based patents, search engine trade secrecy, and competitively motivated prioritization of traffic can all have consequences for competition and innovation.

The implication of this tension between openness and enclosure always raises the prospect of a resurgence of proprietary communication norms and a diminishment of Internet governance transparency. One important role of Internet governance research is to assess the implications of this tension between forces of openness and forces of enclosure, examine the implications of the privatization of governance, and bring to public light the key issues at stake at the intersection of technical expediency and the public interest.

References

Abbate, J. (1999). *Inventing the Internet*, Cambridge, MA: MIT Press.

Bendrath, R. and Mueller, M. (2010). "The End of the Net as We Know it? Deep Packet Inspection and Internet Governance." Available at <http://ssrn.com/abstract=1653259>. Accessed August 23, 2012.

Benoliel, D. (2004). "Technological Standards, Inc. Rethinking Cyberspace Regulatory Epistemology," *California Law Review*, 92: 1069.

Brown, I. and Marsden, C. (2007). "Co-Regulating Internet Security: The London Action Plan." Paper presented at Global Internet Governance Academic Network Second Annual Symposium, Rio de Janeiro, Brazil.

David, P. and Greenstein, S. (1990). "The Economics of Compatibility Standards: An Introduction to Recent Research," *Economics of Innovation and New Technology*, 1(1): 3–41.

Deibert, R., Palfrey, J., Rohozinski, R., and Zittrain, J. (eds) (2008). *Access Denied: The Practice and Policy of Global Internet Filtering*, Cambridge, MA: MIT Press.

Drake, W. J. (ed.) (2006). "Reforming Internet Governance." Working Group on Internet Governance (WGIG). Final Report. Available at <http://www.wgig.org/docs/book/toc2 .html>. Accessed July 20, 2010.

DeNardis, L. (2009a). *Protocol Politics: the Globalization of Internet Governance*, Cambridge, MA: MIT Press.

——(2009b). "Open Standards and Global Politics," *International Journal of Communications Law and Policy*, 13 (Winter). Available at <http://www.ijclp.net/files/ijclp_web-doc_9-13-2009 .pdf>. Accessed June 23, 2010.

——(ed.) (2011). *Opening Standard—The Global Politics of Interoperability*, Cambridge, MA: MIT Press.

Dutton, W. H. and Peltu, M. (2007). "The Emerging Internet Governance Mosiac: Connecting the Pieces," *Information Polity*, 12(1–2): 63–81.

——, Dopatka, A., Hills, M., Law, G., and Nash, V. (2011). "Freedom of Connection—Freedom of Expression: The Changing Legal and Regulatory Ecology Shaping the Internet," Paris: UNESCO.

——, Palfrey, J., and Peltu, M. (2007). "Deciphering the Codes of Internet Governance: Understanding the Hard Issues at Stake," *Oxford Internet Institute Forum Discussion Paper* No. 8, Oxford: University of Oxford.

Felten, E. W. (2006). "Nuts and Bolts of Network Neutrality," Woodrow Wilson School of Public and International Affairs, Princeton University. Available at <http://itpolicy.princeton.edu/pub/neutrality.pdf>.

Froomkin, M. A. (2003). "Habermas@discourse.net: Toward a Critical Theory of Cyberspace," *Harvard Law Review*, 116(3): 749–873.

Galloway, A. (2004). *Protocol: How Control Exists after Decentralization*, Cambridge, MA: MIT Press.

Garcia, L. (2005). "Public and Private Interests in Standard Setting: Conflict or Convergence," in S. Bolin, *The Standards Edge: Future Generations*, Anne Arbor, MI: Bolin Group. Available at <http://dlindagarcia.com/wp-content/uploads/privatepublicinterests.pdf>. Accessed August 24, 2012.

Geist, M. A. (2001). "Fair.com?: An Examination of the Allegations of Systemic Unfairness in the ICANN UDRP." Available at <http://papers.ssrn.com/sol3/papers.cfm?abstract_id=280630>. Accessed August 24, 2012.

Ghosh, R. (2005). "An Economic Basis for Open Standards." Available at <http://flosspols.org/deliverables/FLOSSPOLS-D04-openstandards-v6.pdf>. Accessed June 12, 2012.

Gibson, C. S. (2007). "Technology Standards—New Technical Barriers to Trade?," in S. Bolin (ed.). *The Standards Edge: Golden Mean*. Available at <http://ssrn.com/abstract=960059>. Accessed July 20, 2010.

Gillespie, T. (2007). *Wired Shut: Copyright and the Shape of Digital Culture*, Cambridge, MA: MIT Press.

Goldman, E. (2006). "Search Engine Bias and the Demise of Search Engine Utopianism," *Yale Journal of Law and Technology*. Available at <http://papers.ssrn.com/sol3/papers.cfm?abstract_id=893892>.

Grimmelmann, J. (2007). "The Structure of Search Engine Law," *Iowa Law Review*, 93(1): 3–63.

Hoffman, J. (2005). "Internet Governance: A Regulatory Idea in Flux," English translation. URL (last consulted June 2010): <http://duplox.wzb.eu/people/jeanette/texte/Internet%20Governance%english%20version.pdf>.

Johnson, D. R., Crawford, S. P., and Palfrey, J. G. Jr. (2004). "The Accountable Internet: Peer Production of Internet Governance," *The Virginia Journal of Law and Technology*, 9(9): 2–33.

Kende, M. (2000). "The Digital Handshake: Connecting Internet Backbones," FCC Office of Plans and Policy Working Paper No. 32. Available at <http://www.fcc.gov/Bureaus/OPP/working_papers/oppwp32.pdf>. Accessed July 20, 2010.

Kesan, J. P. and Shah, R. C. (2001). "Fool Us Once Shame on You—Fool Us Twice Shame on Us: What We Can Learn From the Privatizations of the Internet Backbone Network and the Domain Name System," *Washington University Law Quarterly*, 89. Available at <http://papers.ssrn.com/sol3/papers.cfm?abstract_id=260834>. Accessed July 20, 2010.

Kobayashi, B. H. and Wright, J. D. (2009). "Intellectual Property and Standard Setting," George Mason Law & Economics Research Paper No. 09-40; ABA Handbook on the Antitrust Aspects of Standards Setting, 2010; George Mason Law & Economics Research Paper No. 09-40.

Krechmer, K. (2005). "Open Standards Requirements." Available at <http://www.csrstds.com/openstds.pdf>. Accessed August 24, 2010.

Kuerbis, B. and Mueller, M. (2007). "Securing the Root: A Proposal for Distributing Signing Authority," Internet Governance Project White Paper. Available at <http://www.internet-governance.org/pdf/SecuringTheRoot.pdf>. Accessed August 24, 2010.

Lemley, M. (2002). "Intellectual Property Rights and Standard-Setting Organizations," *California Law Review*, 90: 1889. Available at <http://papers.ssrn.com/sol3/papers.cfm?abstract_id=310122>. Accessed July 20, 2010.

—— (2007). "Ten Things to Do about Patent Holdup of Standards," *Boston College Law Review*, 48: 149.

Levinson, N. S. (2010). "Co-Creating Processes in Global Governance: The Case of the Internet Governance Forum," Fifth Annual Global Internet Governance Academic Network Conference, Vilnius, Lithuania. Available at <http://lawlibraryarchive.contentdm.oclc.org/cdm/singleitem/collection/p15430coll1/id/23>. Accessed September 23, 2011.

Malcolm, J. (2008). "Appraising the Success of the Internet Governance Forum," Internet Governance Project Paper IGP08-003. Available at <http://internetgovernance.org/pdf/MalcolmIGFReview.pdf>. Accessed July 20, 2010.

Mayer-Schönberger, V. and Ziewitz, M. (2009). "Jefferson Rebuffed—The United States and the Future of Internet Governance," John F. Kennedy School of Government Working Paper No. RWP06-018. Available at <http://ssrn.com/abstract=902374>. Accessed July 20, 2010.

Morris, J. and Davidson, A. (2003). "Policy Impact Assessments: Considering the Public Interest in Internet Standards Development," 31st Research Conference on Communication, Information and Internet Policy. Available at <http://www.cdt.org/publications/pia.pdf>. Accessed September 23, 2010.

Mueller, M. L. (2002). *Ruling the Root: Internet Governance and the Taming of Cyberspace*, Cambridge, MA: MIT Press.

—— (2010a). *Networks and States: The Global Politics of Internet Governance*, Cambridge, MA: MIT Press.

—— (2010b). "Internet Governance." Entry in the International Studies Association's *International Studies Compendium*.

—— and Kuerbis, B. (2010). "Building a New Governance Hierarchy: RPKI and the Future of Internet Routing and Addressing." Available at <http://www.internetgovernance.org/pdf/RPKI-VilniusIGPfinal.pdf>. Accessed September 23, 2010.

Paré, D. (2003). *Internet Governance in Transition: Who is the Master of This Domain?*, Oxford: Roman and Littlefield Publishers.

Pasquale, F. A. (2006). "Rankings, Reductionism, and Responsibility," Seton Hall Public Law Research Paper No. 888327. Available at <http://ssrn.com/abstract=888327>. Accessed August 24, 2010.

Wagner, B. (2008). "Deep Packet Inspection and Internet Censorship: International Convergence on an 'Integrated Technology of Control.'" Presented at the 3rd Annual Giganet Symposium in Hyderabad, India. Available at <http://advocacy.globalvoicesonline.org/2009/06/25/study-deep-packet-inspection-and-internet-censorship/>. Accessed September 23, 2010.

Weber, Rolf H. (2009). *Shaping Internet Governance: Regulatory Challenges*, Zurich: Springer.

Weiser, Philip (2001). "Internet Governance, Standards Setting, and Self-Regulation," *Northern Kentucky Law Review*, 28(4): 822–31.

—— (2009). "The Future of Internet Regulation." University of Colorado Law Legal Studies Research Paper No. 09–02. URL (last consulted July 2010): <http://ssrn.com/abstract=1344757>.

Werbach, Kevin (2009). "The Centripetal Network: How the Internet Holds Itself Together and the Forces Tearing it Apart," University of California Davis Law Review, 42: 343–412.

Wu, Tim (2005). "Network Neutrality, Broadband Discrimination," Journal of Telecommunications and High Technology Law, 2: 141–180.

Wu, Tim, Dyson, Esther, Froomkin, A. Michael, and Gross, David A. (2007). "On the Future of Internet Governance," American Society of International Law. Proceedings of the Annual Meeting. Vol. 101. URL (last consulted June 2010): <http://ssrn.com/abstract=992805>.

—— and Yoo, Christopher S. (2007). "Keeping the Internet Neutral?: Tim Wu and Christopher Yoo Debate," Federal Communications Law Journal, 59(3). URL (last consulted June 2010): <http://ssrn.com/abstract=953989>.

Yoo, Christopher S. (2004). "Would Mandating Broadband Network Neutrality Help or Hurt Competition? A Comment on the End-to-End Debate," Journal of Telecommunications and High Technology Law, 3: 23–68.

INDEX

Note: bold entries refer to figures and tables.

Abt, Clark 207
academic research, *see* e-research
access divide, *see* digital divide
access times, and online services 40
accountability:
  and e-government 295
  and industrial policy 519
Acquisti, A 494
addiction to the Internet 548
Advanced Research Projects Agency
      (ARPA) 28, 539
advertising:
  and free ad-supported services 249–50
  and online newspapers 380
  and online performance marketing 248
  and pay-per-action advertising 249
  and pay-per-click advertising 248–9
  and surveillance 491
Advertising Standards Authority (UK) 467
affiliate marketing 243, 249
Africa:
  and limited connectivity 533, 544
  and online learning 336–7
  and social network sites 544
African Charter on Human and People's
      Rights 442
Agarwala, A 475
age, and Internet use 134–5, 222
Alexander, Isabella 469
alienation 220, 549
Allagui, I 225–6, 229
Allen, I E 333
Al-Shakaa, R 229
Amazon 241–2
  and Mechanical Turk 256
American Recovery and Reinvestment Act
      (2009) 516

America's Army (game) 207–8
Amichai-Hamburger, Y 230
Anderson, C W 384
Andreessen, Marc 240
Annenberg School of Communication
      (University of Southern
      California) 12
anonymous posting, and Bulletin Board
      Systems (BBS) 34
AOL (America Online) 37
Apple:
  and control over apps 44
  and iTunes 242, 251, 258
application programming interfaces
      (APIs) 152
Arab Spring 62, 427, 431, 546
Araújo, V 221
ARPANET 27, 28, 29, 40–1, 448
Asia, and limited connectivity 533
Association for Progressive Communications
      (APC) 541
Association of Internet Researchers
      (AoIR) 10
astronomy, and e-research 310–11, 316
AT&T 30–1, 41
Atari 196, 197
Attewell, Paul 138
auction services 39, 242, 254
Australia, and Internet use 222–3
authoritarianism:
  and e-government 287, 291
  and the Internet 431
Autonomous System Numbers (ASNs), and
      Internet governance 561
autonomy, and freedom of
      expression 444
Autor, David H 139

Baer, Ralph 197
Baidu 545
Bailur, S 299
Bakardjieva, Maria 3n6
Baker, M A 11
Balfanz, D 494
banking, and development of electronic
        banking 33–4
Bannister, F 272, 274
Bargh, J 220
Barlow, John Perry 41
Baron, Naomi 13
Barr, K 412
Bateson, G 93
Battelle, John 161
Battle, Juan 138
Baym, Nancy 163, 366
BEA Systems 240
Beetham, David 422, 431
Be Free 243
Bell, Daniel 11, 124–5
    and post-industrialism 110, 111, 120, 124
Bendrath, R 491
Berkman Center for Internet and Society
        12, 516
    and Next Generation Connectivity 516, 519
Berners-Lee, Tim 9, 16, 28, 71, 239
    and Semantic Web 56
    and web addresses 99
Berne Treaty (1886) 473
Bertot, J C 292
Best, M 431, 543
Bildschirmtext 36
Bimber, B 366, 423
biometric database 547
Birnie, S 361
Blackberry, and encryption 456–7
blogpulse.com 80
blogs:
    and blogrolls 157–8
    and China 227
    and democracy 79
    and development of 54
    and link popularity 73
    and participation 360
    and public opinion research 80

Blue, Violet 87, 88, 89
Boczkowski, P J 379, 381, 382, 384, 387
Bokova, Irina 328, 336
Bonfadelli, Heinz 131–2
Bonikowski, Bart 139
bookselling, and the Internet 241–2
bootlegging, and distinction from
        piracy 468
Border Gateway Protocol (BGP) 561
boundary crossing 362–3
Bovens, M 290
Bowie, David 482
Bowker, G C 94
boyd, d 151, 168
Boyd, J 366
Boyera, Stephane 336
Brandtzæg, P B 134, 135
Brazil, and distance learning 332
Brenkert, G G 264, 265
Bresee, J 500
British National Party 413
broadband:
    and definition of 512
    and developing world 336
    and inequalities in access:
        global divide 133
        population segments 132
    and infrastructure development 511
    and network infrastructure
        policies 512–13
    and promotion of 513–17
        assessment of outcomes 523–4
        categories of policy 518
        demand considerations 522–3
        difficulty in foreseeing policy
            outcomes 520
        economic assessments of 520–2
        European Union 513–15
        evidence for policy 519–20, 523
        justification of 517–18, 524
        policy accountability 519
        South Korea 517
        United Kingdom 515
        United States 515–16
brochureware 39
Brock, A 361

Brown, Gordon 61, 336
Brown, T 337
browsers:
    and commercial implications of 240
    and development of 10, 240
Buckingham, D 222
Bulletin Board Systems (BBS) 34
Burgoon, J K 366
Burke, M 168
Burkell, J 495
Busch, L 98
Bushnell, Nolan 197
business models and strategy, and impact of
        the Internet:
    and affiliate marketing 243, 249
    and auctions 254
    and cloud computing infrastructure
        services 256–7
    and creation of new products and services
        in traditional businesses 241–2
    and creation of totally new
        businesses 242
    and crowdsourcing 255–6
    and difficulties in making money 242
    and distribution platforms 253
    and drivers of 243
        cost and speed of coordination 244
        marginal cost of distribution 243–4
        price discrimination 244–5
        versioning 244
    and enhancement of existing models and
        operations 241
    and free ad-supported services 249–50
    and freemium model 251–2
        digital media content 252–3
        market platforms and directories 253
        software products 252
    and group buying 255
    and integration of mobile devices 258
    and long-tail markets 253
    and market efficiency 259
    and multi-sided markets 247
    and music 242, 251
    and online performance marketing 248
    and pay-per-action advertising 249
    and pay-per-click advertising 248–9
    and platform-based competition 245–6
    and pricing strategies 258
    and scope for new software products and
        services 240–1
    and social network sites 243
    and strategies 258–9
    and subscriptions for digital goods and
        services 250
        cloud computing 250–1
        music 251
        software 250–1
        streaming digital data 251
    and trust 257, 262–3
    and viability of free and ad-based
        models 258
    and virtual goods 254–5
    and winner-takes-all dynamics 247
    see also e-commerce
Butler, Judith 101

Caiani, M 362
Calambokidis, J 315
Calenda, D 359
Cameron, David 56, 61, 432
Cammaerts, B 360
Canada:
    and development of online services
        31, 36
    and Internet use 224
Capgemini 286
capital-enhancing activities:
    and autonomy of Internet use 133
    and Internet use 130
    and socioeconomic status 135–6
capitalism:
    and the Internet 539
    and network capitalism 479
Cappella, J M 357
Captain videotex service 36
carbon emissions, and data warehouses 64
Cardoso, G 221
Carey, J 101
Carey, R 495
Caron, A 224
Caronia, L 224

Castells, Manuel 11, 95, 110, 464, 477, 538
  and mass self-communication 123
  and network capitalism 479
  and network society 112–13, 114, 115, 116,
      121, 124, 479
  and virtual reality 482
Castronova, E 202
censorship:
  and alternatives to filtering 451–2
  and child protection 457–8
  and deep packet inspection 569–70
  and filtering of content:
    critiques of 450–1
    how it works 449–50
    state-supported 449
  and international patterns of Internet
      freedom 452–4, 547
    democracies 453
    growth of government regulation 452–3
    regional variations 453–4
    types of material restricted 453
  and net neutrality 458–9
  and privacy vs national security 456–7
  and surveillance 491
  see also freedom of expression;
      surveillance
Centre for Embedded Network Sensing
    (CENS) 311–12
Cerf, Vinton Gray 'Vint' 9n8, 28
CERN (European Organization for Nuclear
    Research) 9, 28, 29, 307
  and GridPP 309
  and Large Hadron Collider 308–9
Cesca, J 500
Chadwick, A 415
Chai, L 274
Changchit, C 275
Chew, M 494
child protection, and freedom of
    expression 457–8
children, and video games 205–6
China:
  and blogs 227
  and censorship 452, 453
  and class and the Internet 121–2
  and Internet use 226–8
  and labor unrest 122–3

and microblogging 227
and number of Internet users 117
and re-envisioning of Cultural
    Revolution 114–15
and social network sites 121–2
Choi, A 226
Cisco 240, 542
citation analysis 77
  and hyperlinks 77–8
Citibank 34
civic engagement:
  and digital inequality 139–41
  and the Internet 411–12
    limited impact 413–14
  and online news consumption 387–8
  and social science research 358–9
class, and network society 120–4
  China 121–2
  immaterial labor 124
  India 122
  information have-less 121
  meritocracy 120–1
  network labor 123–4
  polarization of work 121
Clement, A 101
Clinton, Hilary 445
cloud computing:
  and business model 250–1
  and education 331
  and infrastructure services 256–7
Club Penguin 206
cognitive ability, and Internet use 134–5
Cohen, Stan 470
Coleman, Stephen 425
collective action 426
collective identity 403
collective memory:
  and Internet as channel for 116
  and user-created content 114–15
Comegys, C H 273
communication and the Internet, social
      science research on 370–1
  and changes in themes of 365
  and growth in coverage of 353, 354, 355
  and limitations 369–70
  and media attributes 356
    interactivity 356

and media implications, use and
    understanding 356–8
  credibility and trust 356–7
  diffusion of innovations 357
  harmful effects 358
  media effects 357
  media use/adaptation 357–8
  uses and gratifications 358
and meta-theory frameworks 365
  critiques 366
  integrated or new theoretical
    models 366
  reviews 366–7
and methodology of study 355
and participation 358–60
  civic engagement 358–9
  participatory media/users 359
  political participation 359
  public sphere 359–60
and relations among primary and global
    themes 367–9
  cluster analysis 368
and social relations 360–2
  community 360
  groups 360
  identity 360–1
  media use and sociality 361
  relational management 361
  social capital 362
  social networks 362
and societal 362–4
  boundary crossing 362–3
  cultural differences 363
  digital divide 363
  political economy 363
  privacy 364
and theory frameworks 364–5
  critiques 364
  integrated or new theoretical
    models 364–5
  reviews 365
communication rights, and Internet
    governance 568–70
  private industry 569–70
  role of government 568–9
community, and social science research 360
CompuServe 36

computer conferencing, and development
    of 32–3
Computer Emergency Response Team
    (CERT) 566
computer-mediated communication (CMC):
  and effectiveness of 163
  and first generation of virtual
    communities 162–3
  and genres of 162–4
  and one-to-many channels 162
  and one-to-one channels 162
  and origins of 162
  and relationship formation 185–6
  and social network sites 160, 163–4
  and trust 269–70
computer science (CS), and study of the
    Web 49
computer-supported cooperative work
    (CSCW) 91–2, 94
ComScore, and online dating 176
Confucianism 226
Connolly, R 272, 274
content analysis, and political campaigning
    on the Internet 405
Conway, D 539
Cook, S G 547
Cook, Thomas D 131
cookies 493
Copsey, N 413
copyright:
  and advantages over patenting 471
  and copying for personal use as civil
    offense 466
  and legal attempts to control file-
    sharing 474–7
  and maintenance of scarcity based
    exchange system 472
  see also file-sharing; intellectual property
    rights
Copyright Act (UK, 1906) 469
corporate social responsibility 569
Corritore, C L 269, 270
cosmopolitanism, and the Internet 423, 433
Council of Europe 497
country codes 87–8
Craigslist 253
Cranor, L F 500

credibility, and social science research 356–7
credit cards, and decline in use of 262
Critical Internet Resources (CIRs):
    and Autonomous System Numbers
        (ASNs) 561
    and Domain Name System 560–1
    and Internet addresses 559–60
    and Internet governance 558–61
    and meaning of 558–9
Crook, C K 330
crowds, and wisdom of 74
crowdsourcing 255–6, 545
culture:
    and Internet use 363
    and trust 273–5
cyber-crime 465
cyber-squatters 471
Cyprus 232
Cyr, D 274
Cyworld 151
Czech Republic 223
Czerniewicz, L 329
Czincz, J 548

Dahl, Robert 424, 428
Danay, Robert 476
Darfur is Dying (game) 208
Dasgupta, P 264
databases, online, and development of 32
data.gov 61
data.gov.uk 61–2
data protection 487
    and e-government 291
    and privacy protection 497
        legal instruments 498–9
        self-regulation 499–500
        technological instruments 500–1
        transnational instruments 497–8
    and Sweden 313
data retention 498
dating, see online dating
David, C 357
Dayan, D 115–16
Dean, Howard 401, 409
decentralization, and Web structure 51–2
deep packet inspection (DPI) 569–70

Deibert, R 431, 491
deliberation, political, and the Internet
        428–9
Delors, J 330
Delors Report (1996) 330
democracy, and the Internet 421
    and blogging 79
    and cosmopolitanism 423, 433
    and cross-national indicators of
        democracy 432
    and definition of democracy 422
    and deliberation 428–9
    and democratic citizenship 430
    and democratic institutions 424–7
    and elections 424
    and executive government 425–6
    and interest groups 426
    and Internet as 'Fifth Estate' 427, 428
    and legislatures 425
    and models of democracy 422–3
    and participation 429–30
    and pluralism 423, 432
    and political equality 432
    and political information
        acquisition of 427–8
        dissemination of 428
    and political parties 424–5
    and political science 421–2, 433
    and popular control 431–2
    and the public sphere 423, 433
    and referenda 424
    and republicanism 423, 433
    and voter turnout 429
    and voting mechanisms 424
Democratic Audit of the UK 422
democratization:
    and e-government 287
    and the Internet 431
    and the Web 71
denial of service attacks 451
de Pourbaix, R 335
dereferencing, and Uniform Resource
        Identifiers (URIs) 50
Dervin, B 131
De Sola Pool, Ithiel 4
Detica 491
Deutsch, M 265

Deutscher Commercial Internet Exchange (DE-CIX) 567
Deuze, M 380, 383, 390
developing countries:
    and access to the Internet 531-2
    and limited conceptions of the Internet 533
    and online learning 336-8
development, and the Internet 531, 535
    and access to 548
    and assumptions about 531
    and commercial interests 534, 542, 543
    and conception of Internet as inclusive development tool 536-7
    and conceptions of development 533-5
        capabilities 534-5
        corporate economic interests 534
        definitions of poverty 534
        poverty elimination 533, 534
    and defining objectives of development 548-9
    and dehumanizing and alienating effects 549
    and development as economic growth 542-3
    and development as equality 544-6
        net neutrality 544-5
    and development as freedom 546-8
    and future research on 549-50
    and information and communications technology (ICT) 535-6, **537**
    and Information and Communication Technologies and Development (ICTD) **537**, 538
    and Information and Communication Technologies for Development (ICT4D) 531, 536, **537**
    and multi-disciplinary approach to 538
    and private sector involvement 541-2
    and reasons for project failures 537
    and technology and development 538-40
    and World Summit on the Information Society (WSIS, 2003) 540-1
De Waal, E 380
Dhamija, R 60
Digg.com 74, 160
Digiplay Initiative 209
digital divide 129
    and access divide 531-2
        autonomy of use 133
        global divide 133
        population segments 132-3
    and differentiated skills and uses:
        age 134-5
        demographic groups 134-5
        gender 134
        global divide 136-7
        socioeconomic status 135-6
    and e-government 293
    and freedom of expression 447-8
    and implications of 137
        civic engagement 139-41
        educational outcomes 138
        financial capital 139
        human capital 137-8
        job-seeking 139
        labor market 139
        social capital 139-41
    and increase in 544
    and minority groups 115
    and national development levels 223
    and social exclusion 223
    and social inequality 141-2
    and social science research 363
    and socioeconomic status 131, 135-6, 223
    and theoretical approaches to digital inequality 130-2
        factors affecting 130
        knowledge gaps 131-2
        social stratification 130
        socioeconomic factors 131
        unequal distribution of resources 131
Digital Economy Act (UK, 2010) 469, 475-6, 515
digital inequality, *see* digital divide
Digital Millennium Copyright Act (USA, 1998) 474
digital rights management 478
Digital Youth Project 342, 343-4
digitization of research, *see* e-research
Dijkstra, Edsger 49
DiMaggio, Paul 130, 133, 139, 220
direct democracy 424

discourse analysis, and political campaigning
    on the Internet 405
distance learning, and the Internet 332
distributed computing 28
    and e-research 314
        Large Hadron Collider 309–10
distributed denial of service attacks
        (DDoS) 566
Dittmar, H 276
DNS (Domain Name System) 29
DoCoMo, and i-mode 45
Dodgeball 154
domain names 556–7
Domain Name System:
    and intellectual property rights
        563–4
    and Internet governance 560–1
Domingo, D 383
Douglas, A S 196
Downs, Anthony 429
Drew, D 429
Drezner, D 431
Dublin Core 60
Dunleavy, P 292, 295
Dutton, W H 272, 276, 384, 404, 427, 428
Duverger, M 425

Eastin, M 358
eBay 39, 242, 254
    and consumer trust in 263
e-campaigning, see political campaigning
        and the Internet
Eco, Umberto 218
ecology of games (EoG) 454–5
e-commerce:
    and growth in 263
    and impact of global economic
        crisis 262–3
    and trust 257, 262, 263, 269–71
        cultural influences 273–5
        future research on 275–6
        gender 272–3, 276
        online experience 271–2
        uncertainty 270–1
    see also business models and strategy, and
        impact of the Internet

Economic and Social Research Council
        (UK) 12
economic growth, and the Internet 542–3
    see also development, and the Internet
Economist Intelligence Unit 432
education:
    and digital inequality 138
    and the Internet 328–9
    and video games 206, 207
    see also learning, and the Internet
Education for All Fast Track Initiative 541
Edwards, P 90, 96
e-government 283–4
    as academic discipline 299–300
    and accountability 295
    and aims and objectives 288–9
    and authoritarianism 287, 291
    and barriers to 292
    and changes in government 294
    and data protection 291
    and definitional difficulties 284–5
    and democratization 287
    and de-skilling of staff 290
    and digital divide 293
    and e-consultation 297
    and enablers of 292
    and e-policy 297–8
    and e-public administration 295–6
    and e-services 296–7
        co-creation of 297
        personalization of 296–7
    and Gov 2.0 298–9
    and holistic government 296
    and (in)efficiency of government IT
        projects 291–2
    and international comparisons 286
        readiness rankings 288
        top 10 countries 286, 287
    and measurement of 287
    and methodological approaches to
        studying 299–300
    and organizational structure and
        power 290–1
    and pre-Internet computerization 285
    and privacy 291
    and public policy 297–8
    and public sector reform 295

and reduction in administrative
   discretion 290
and research focus 289
and social media 289, 298–9
and stages of 286–7
and surveillance 291
and transparency 295–6
and usability of 293–4
and usage of 293
Egypt 427, 431, 546
election campaigning, *see* political
   campaigning and the Internet
elections:
   and the Internet 424
   and voter turnout 429
   see also political campaigning and the
      Internet
Elesh, D 366
Ellison, N B 151
Elmer, G 366
email, and development of 33
Emergency Management Information
   Systems And Reference Index
   (EMISARI) 12
encryption:
   and file-sharing 478–9
   and freedom of expression 456–7
   and surveillance 478
Engelhard, Douglas 9
engineering:
   and misconceptions about 53
   and reflective practice 53
English Premier League 480
environmental concerns, and media
   studies 100
equality, and the Internet and
   development 544–6
e-research:
   and academic-business collaboration 314
      SwissBioGrid 314
   and access to 322
   and changes in everyday research
      practice 315–16
      VOSON 315–16
      whale research 315
   and changes in scholarly knowledge 308
   and complexities of data sharing 311–13

Centre for Embedded Network Sensing
   (CENS) 311–12
Genetic Association Information
   Network (GAIN) 312–13
Sweden 313
trust 313
and contribution to knowledge 319–20
and creation of a coherent network 323
and definition of 308
and disciplinary perspectives on 308
and distinctiveness of 323
and diversity of perspectives on 308
and engaging communities in
   humanities 316–17
   literary studies 316–17
   Pynchon Wiki 316
   specialisms 317
and physical core of research
   instruments 323
and physics:
   GridPP 309
   Large Hadron Collider 308–9
and role of research technologies in 319
and styles of science in 317–20
and transformation of academic
   research 308, 322–4
   disciplinary differences 320–1
and trust 313
and visibility of 321–2
and volunteer contributions:
   Galaxy Zoo 307, 310–11, 316
   humanities 316–17
Ericson, R 489
error handling, and Web architecture 51
Erstad, O 340
Estonia, and Internet voting 424
Ethiopia 533
ethnicity, and digital inequality 223
European Association of Public
   Administration 299
European Commission:
   and *Building the European Information
      Society* 519
   and Digital Agenda 514–15
   and eEurope initiative 514
   and e-government 292
   and Europe 2020 strategy 514–15

European Commission: (*cont.*)
  and European Digital Competitiveness
    Report 514
  and European Economic Recovery
    Plan 514
  and i2010 strategy for ICTs 514
  and promotion of broadband 513–15
European Convention on Human Rights
  (ECHR) 442
European Organization for Nuclear Research,
  see CERN
European Social Survey 430
European Union (EU):
  and digital inequality 136
  and e-government 62
  and Lisbon Strategy (2000) 514
  and privacy protection 497–8
  and promotion of broadband 513–15
Eurostat 136
evolutionary theory, and sexual-partner
  seeking 179, 184
Ewing, S 222–3
exchange, and trust 268–9
executive government, and the
  Internet 425–6
experts, and access to 74
ExpertsExchange.com 74
extranets, and development of 38–9

Facebook 10, 151
  and business model 249
  and personal information 75
  and political activism 426–7, 546
  and popularity of 79
  and privacy practices 167
  and unexpected success of 56
  and uses of 163
  and video games 200
fair information principles (FIPs) 498
Fairlie, Robert W 139
Falun Gong 62
Fanning, Shawn 242
Farrell, H 497
Federal Communications Commission (FCC,
  USA) 516, 545
  and *Connecting America* 516

Federation Against Copyright Theft
  (FACT) 466, 467, 468
file-sharing:
  and anti-piracy commercial 465
    parodies of 466
  and attempts to equate with piracy 467,
    468–9, 483
    term embraced by file-sharers 469, 470
  and decline in recorded music sales 469
  and deterritorialization 481
  and digital rights management 478
  and distinction from piracy 468
  and distributed networks 477–8
  and economic consequences of 464, 465–6
  and encryption 478–9
  and impact on demand for live
    performances 482
  and legal attempts to control 474–7
  and live-streaming 480
  and moral panic 470–1
  and music industry 465
  and The Pirate Bay 469–70
  and plagiarism 466
  and prosecution of individual
    uploaders 475
  and recording artists advocacy of 470
  and representation as theft 464, 465
  and surveillance 478, 479
  and torrent services 469, 475
  see also copyright; intellectual property
    rights
filtering of content:
  and critiques of 450–1
  and how it works 449–50
  and state's role in 449, 568
  and surveillance 491
  see also censorship; freedom of expression
financial capital, and digital inequality 139
Financial Times 252
Findahl, O 230
First Mile Solutions 544
Fischer-Hübner, S 500
Fishbein, N 357
Flanagin, A J 357, 366
Flash cookies 493
Flickr 61, 154
folksonomy, and tagging 74–5

Food and Agriculture Organization
        (FAO) 545
Foot, K A 404, 406
Football Association (FA) 480
Forman, Chris 139
formats, and Web architecture 50
Fortunati, L 124
Foucault, Michel 291, 489
Foursquare 154
Foxconn 120
France, and development of online
        services 31
    Minitel 35–6
free content, and hidden cost of 75–6
freedom, and development as 546–8
Freedom House 432, 449, 452
freedom of expression:
    and access to the Internet 445, 447–8
    and arguments for 444
        democracy 444
        knowledge and social progress 444
        personal autonomy 444
    and child protection 457–8
    and communication rights 568–70
    and control of online content, alternatives
            to filtering 451–2
    and digital inequality 447–8
    and domain names 561
    and ecology of freedom of expression
            framework 455–6
    and ecology of games (EoG)
            framework 454–5, 460
        implication of applying 459
    and exceptions to 442–3
    and filtering of content:
        critiques of 450–1
        how it works 449–50
        state-supported 449
    and freedom of information 443, 445
    and freedom to communicate 445–6
    as a fundamental right 442
        limitations on 442–3
    and international patterns of Internet
            freedom 452–4, 547
        democracies 453
        growth of government regulation 452–3
        regional variations 453–4

    types of material restricted 453
    and the Internet's contribution to
            446–7, 460
        concerns over 446
        expansion/limitation of 446–7
    and net neutrality 458–9
    in network society 444–6
    and privacy vs national security 456–7
    and surveillance 496
    and use of media 445
    and World Summit on the Information
            Society (WSIS, 2003) 444–5
        Declaration of Principles 445
    see also censorship; surveillance
freedom of information 443
    and freedom of expression 443, 445
freemium business model 251–2
    and digital media content 252–3
    and market platforms and directories 253
    and software products 252
Freese, Jeremy 135
Friedman, L M 501
'Friends' list, and social network sites 154,
        155–7
    context collapse 156
    distinguishing types of
            relationships 155–6
    management of 156
    purposes 155
    social graph 156–7
    uni-directional relationships 156
Friendster 151, 160
    and profiles 153–4
FTP (File Transfer Protocol) 50

Gadhafi, Moammar 88
Galácz, A 223
Galaxy Zoo 307, 310–11, 316
games, see video games
Gandy, O H, Jr 493
Garrett, R K 386
Gartner Group 286, 331
Gasser, U 496
Gates, Bill 41, 331
Gateway 36
gateways 98

Gefen, D 273–4, 275
Geldof, M 533
gender:
  and Internet use 132, 134
  and online dating 176, 178–9, 179–80, 184
  and trust 272–3, 276
General Purpose Technologies (GPTs) 517
Generation X 198
Genetic Association Information Network
      (GAIN) 312–13
Geographical Information Systems 298
GET method 86–7
Ghonim, Wael 546
Gibson, R 405, 425
GigaNet (Global Internet Governance
      Academic Network) 571
Gladwell, Malcolm 426–7
Global Alliance for ICTs and Development
      (GAID) 541
Global Fund to Fight AIDS, Tuberculosis and
      Malaria 541
Global Internet Governance Academic
      Network (GigaNet) 571
globalization, and surveillance 489
Godoy-Etcheverry, S 229
Goggin, A 117
Golembiewski, R T 265
Good, D 265
Goodwin, I 223
Google:
  and AdWords 245
  and data collected by 492
  and Google Plus 151, 156
  and net neutrality 544–5
  and PageRank 77
  and pay-per-click advertising 248–9
  and targeting of advertisements 79
Gotved, S 363
governance, see Internet governance
government:
  and development of online services 31
  and financial support of the Internet 42–3
  and the Internet 425–6, 547
  and open government data 61–2
  and surveillance by 490–1, 568
  see also e-government
Gowalla 154

Gower's Review of Intellectual Property (UK,
      2006) 469
Graber, D A 386
Grabner-Krauter, S 269
Graham, S 95
graphical user interface (GUI), and
      introduction of 29
Greenberg, B 131
GridPP 309, 310
Grokster 474, 475
Groshek, J 431
Grosslags, J 494
group buying business model 255
Groupon.com 255
groups, and social science research 360
Gunkel, D J 366
Gurevitch, M 383
Gurumurthy, A 541
Gutiérrez, F 224

Habermas, J 423, 539
hacker ethic 477
Hacking, I 317, 318, 319
Hagen, I 366
Haggerty, K D 489
Hameed, S S 359
Hamilton, J 381
Han Han 227
Hanyang Cyber University 333
Hara, N 334
Hardt, M 124
Hargittai, Eszter 133
Harvard University 12, 516
Harvey, D 538
Hawking, Stephen 93
Hayat, Z 230
Heart, T 273–4, 275
Hechanova, R M 548
Heeks, R 299, 536
Helsper, E J 134, 223, 229
Hermans, L 381
Hersman, E 546
Higginbotham, Wally 196
higher education, and online learning 332
  developed world 333–4
Himanen, P 477

Hindman, M 411
Hirsch, F 268
Hirshleifer, J 270
history:
    and infrastructure studies 94–5
    and media events 115–16
    and network society 113–16
Ho, S S 359
Holmes, Brian 474
Holmes, J 358
Hooper, Richard 42, 43–4
Horiuchi, Y 429
Horvath, P 361
Howard, P N 408, 431
HTTP (HyperText Transfer Protocol) 48,
    50, 57
Huduma 545
Hughes, Thomas Parke 94, 98
Hulu 251, 258
human capital, and digital inequality 137–8
human practices, and infrastructure 97–8
human rights, and freedom of
    expression 442–3
Hung, A Y H 361
Hungary 223
hyperlinks, see link popularity; link structure
hypermedia 28–9
hyperpersonal theory 185–6

IBM 240, 241
identity:
    and social science research 360–1
    and surveillance 501–2
identity politics 124
identity theft 466
ideology, and political campaigning on the
    Internet 413
Ilavarasan, P V 543
immaterial labor 124
i-mode 45
India:
    and biometric database 547
    and class and the Internet 122
    and online learning 337
individuality, and surveillance 501–2
industrial policy:

and accountability 519
and broadband infrastructure
    development 511
and infrastructure development 510–11
and market failure 510
and network infrastructure
    policies 511–13
and promotion of broadband 513–17
    assessment of outcomes 523–4
    categories of policy 518
    demand considerations 522–3
    difficulty in foreseeing policy
        outcomes 520
    economic assessments of 520–2
    European Union 513–15
    evidence for policy 519–20, 523
    justification of 517–18, 524
    policy accountability 519
    South Korea 517
    United Kingdom 515
    United States 515–16
inequality, see digital divide
InfoCom Corporation 88
information, and value of 58
information and communications technology
    (ICT):
    and assessing economic impact of
        520–2
    and development 535–6, 537
    and economic growth 542–3
    as general purpose technologies 517
    and Internet Studies 11–12
Information and Communication
    Technologies and Development
    (ICTD) 537, 538
Information and Communication
    Technologies for Development
    (ICT4D) 531, 536, 537
see also development, and the Internet
information resources, and Web
    architecture 50
information society 109
    and centrality of theoretical
        knowledge 111
    and ethnocentrism of concept 111–12
    and post-industrialism 110–11
    see also network society

infrastructure:
  and investment in 509–11
  and network infrastructure
      policies 511–13
infrastructure management, and Internet
      governance 566–8
infrastructure of the Internet 43
  and surveillance 490–2
    advertising 491
    censorship 491
    filtering of content 491
    government surveillance 490–1
    Internet Service Providers (ISPs) 490,
        491, 492
  and value of studying 86
infrastructure studies 89, 90, 102
  and attributes of infrastructure:
    dependence on human practices 97–8
    invisibility 96–7
    modularity 98
    momentum 98–9
    standardization 98
  and definition of 91
  and distinction from study of
      infrastructure 91
  and meaning of infrastructure 90
  and new materialist approach to
      99–102
    environmental concerns 100
  and relationist approach to 92
    applied nature of 93–4
    heuristics of infrastructure 96–9
    historical approach 94–5
    infinite series of infrastructure 93
    methods 96–9
    multiple perspectives 92–3
    origins of 91–2
    soft infrastructure 92
    urbanism 95
    use of infrastructure term 100
  and URL shortening services 87–8
Ingelstam, L 288
Innis, Harold 101
innovation, and diffusion of 357
Institute for Democracy and Electoral
      Assistance 422
Institute for the Future 12

Institute of Electrical and Electronics
      Engineers (IEEE) 562
institutional change, and infrastructure
      development 510
Integrated Services Digital Network
      (ISDN) 517
intellectual property rights 242
  and attempts to enforce formal regime
      on 464
  and copyright protection 471
  and digital rights management 478
  and domain names 561
  and global intellectual property
      regime 473–4
  and historical evolution of 472–3
  and Internet governance 563–5
    Domain Name System 563–4
    network operators 565
    royalty-bearing standards 564
    search engines 564–5
  and Internet's threat to 471
  and legal attempts to control
      file-sharing 474–7
  and limited duration of monopoly
      rights 472
  and live-streaming 480
  and romantic justifications for 472
  and surveillance 478, 479
  and trademarks 471
  and utilitarian justifications for 472
  and World Intellectual Property
      Organization 473–4
  see also copyright; file-sharing
interactivity:
  and social science research 356
  and Web 2.0 79
interest groups, and the Internet 426
International Communication Association
      (ICA) 355
International Criminal Court (ICC) 433
internationalized domain names (IDNs) 561
International Multilateral Partnership Against
      Cyber Threats (IMPACT) 548
International Organization for
      Standardization (ISO) 562
International Telecommunication Union
      (ITU) 133, 447, 540, 544, 557, 562

Internet:
    and addiction to 548
    and alienation 220, 549
    and American dominance 541, 545
    and capitalism 539
    and communication 221
    and definition of:
        broad conception 9, 532–3
        narrow conception 8–9
    and diffusion of 221, 441, 447
    and distinction from the Web 50
    and doubts over commercial use of 41
    and economic growth 542–3
    and economic impact of 539
    and foundational nature of 91
    and global significance of 15
    and governments' financial support
        for 42–3
    and harmful use 358
    and history of 9–10
    see also online services, and
        development of
    and lessons learned from earlier online
        activities 38–40
    and mobile access to 45
    as network of networks 9, 29
    and number of users 1
        global regional distribution 117
        top countries 118
    and offline consequences of 219–20
    and opened to commercial use 38, 41
    and origins of 28–9
    and predictive failures 41
    as a social fact 220
    and society 219–20
    and traditional media 224–5
    and transformative nature of 15, 151
    and usage patterns 221–2
    and user experiences 39–40
    and valence of 487, 502
    and value-system of 41
    see also infrastructure of the Internet
Internet Archive 75
Internet Assigned Numbers Authority
        (IANA) 560
Internet Corporation for Assigned Names
        and Numbers (ICANN) 541, 556–7

    and Uniform Domain-Name Dispute
        Resolution Policy 561
Internet Engineering Task Force (IETF) 240,
        557, 559, 562
Internet exchange points (IXPs) 567
Internet Explorer 10, 240
Internet governance:
    and communication rights 568–70
        private industry 569–70
        role of government 568–9
    as contested term 556
    and control of Critical Internet
        Resources 558–61
        Autonomous System Numbers 561
        Domain Name System 560–1
        Internet addresses 559–60
        meaning of 558–9
    and definition of 556–7
    and global nature of research 571
    and infrastructure management 566–8
    and intellectual property rights 563–5
        Domain Name System 563–4
        network operators 565
        royalty-bearing standards 564
        search engines 564–5
    as interdisciplinary field 571
    and internet protocol design 562–3
    and key topics of 558
    and misconceptions about 556–7
    and private industry's role 571
    and public interest issues 555–6
    and public invisibility of 570
    and research focus 555
    and security 565–6
    and technical architecture 555
    and tension between openness and
        enclosure 571–2
Internet Governance Forum 541, 542, 557, 571
Internet Science 14
Internet Service Providers (ISPs)
    and fiduciary relationship with
        customers 492
    and surveillance 490, 491, 492
Internet Studies:
    and broad scope of 2–3
    and central research challenge 4
    and defining the Internet:

Internet Studies: (*cont.*)
    broad conception 9
    narrow conception 8–9
  and driving force behind 15
  as emerging field 217
  and foundations in early research on
      ICTs 11–12
  and future of 13
    integration 14–15
    interdisciplinary status quo 13
    specialization and fragmentation 14
  and growth of 1–2
  and history of the Internet 9–10
  and increasing status of 2
  and interdisciplinary nature of 8
  and lack of consensus in field 8
  and multidisciplinary nature of 1, 8
  and origins of 10–11
  and particularistic conception of 10–11
  and policy as object of study 6
  and questions addressed by 3
  and scope of 218
  and stages in development of 218–19
  and synoptic conception of 10, 11
  and technology as object of study 3–4
  and transformative role of 13
  and use as object of study 4–5
    in everyday life 5
    media use 6
    in work and organizations 5–6
Internet Watch Foundation (IWF) 450
interpersonal communication, and the
     Internet 173, 174
intranets, and development of 38–9
invisibility:
  and infrastructure 96–7
  and Internet governance 570
IP Address:
  and Internet governance 559–60
  and surveillance 498–9
Iran 62
  and Green Revolution 546
Irvine Group 12
Islas, O 224
Ito, M 205–6, 342, 344
ITT Dialcom 33
iTunes 242, 251, 258

Jackson, S J 96
Jaeger, P T 292
Japan:
  and development of online services 31
  and Internet use 226
Java, and development of 240
JavaScript 240
Jenkins, Henry 205, 209, 344
Jenner, S 292
job-seeking, and Internet use 130, 139
Johansen, Jon 478
Johansen, Robert 12
Johnson, T 429
Joint Photographic Experts Group
    (JPEG) 562
journalists, *see* news production, online
Jowell, R 230
Justin.tv 480

Kahn, Robert 9n8, 28
Kaiser Family Foundation 205
Kaluscha, E A 269
Karlekar, K D 547
Karyda, M 495
Katz, E 115–16
Kaye, G 429
Kelley, P G 500
Kember, D 337
Kenny, C 543
Kenny, R 543
Kenya 535–6, 545
Kerr, Ian 492
Kiesler, Sara 12
Kim, E 381
Kim, K 274
Kim, S T 365, 369
Kim, Y 387
King, J L 294
Klinenberg, E 381
Kling, Rob 11, 12, 92, 97, 334
Klischewski, R 284
knowledge gaps, and digital inequality 131–2
Kohn, M 230, 231–2
Kokolakis, S 495
Kraemer, Kenneth 12, 294
Kreimer, S 496

Krueger, Alan 482
Kumar, Krishan 111

labor market, and digital inequality 139
labor unrest 122–3
Laguerre, M 366–7
Large Hadron Collider 309–10
large technical systems (LTS) research 94
LaRose, R 358
Lasswell, Harold 3n5
Laurie, B 494
Laurillard, D 338–9
law, and Internet Studies 6
Lawson-Borders, G 382
Lazzarato, M 124
learning, and the Internet:
    and cloud computing 331
    and commercial opportunities 331
    and critical approach to 345
    and democratization of educational
        access 331
    and formal learning 330
        blended learning 338
        blending with informal learning 344–5
        compulsory education 339–41
        contribution to 339, 344
        in developed world 333–6
        in developing world 336–8
        distance learning 332
        distinction from informal
            learning 330–1
        management systems 335–6, 338
        mobile learning 336–7
        post compulsory education 332
        reinforcement of existing practices 338
        role in 332–41
        students' difficulties 334–5
        teaching methods 335
    and informal learning 330, 341–4
        blending with formal learning 344–5
        categories of youth engagement 342–3
        distinction from formal learning 330–1
        nature of 342
        networked modes of 342
        solitary practices 342
        young people 343–4

and lack of research coherence 329
and multidisciplinary research 329
and relationship between academic work
    and practical implementation 329
Lee, B 360
legislatures, and the Internet 425
Lemley, Mark 564
Lessig, Lawrence 6, 52, 465, 479, 491
Levy, M R 543
Lewis, J 273
Libya 99
    and country code 87–8
Libyan Telecom and Technology (LTT) 87,
    88–9
Liebowitz, Stan 465
Lievrouw, L 218, 369
Light, P 330
Lilleker, D 414
Lim, J 386
linguistics, and analysis of Web content 80
Linked Data Web 56–7
    and how it works 57–8
    and open government data 61–2
    and trust 58–9
    and trusting data 60–1
        metadata 60–1
    and value of Linked Data 58
LinkedIn 151, 154
Linked Open Data project 58
linking, and the Web 51
link popularity:
    and power law 73
    and preferential attachment 72
    and search engine results 72, 77
link structure, and social science
    research 76–8
literary studies, and e-research 316–17
LiveJournal 154, 157–8
live-streaming 480
Livingstone, S 218, 220
Locke, John 472
long tail:
    and Internet retailing 253
    and niche sites 73
Lowrey, W 384
Lunn, R 225
Lyon, D 488, 489, 491

McAllister, D 265
MacArthur Foundation 342, 343
McBride report 446, 448
McCaw, Craig 41
McConkie, M 265
McCoy, M E 363
MCI Mail 33
McIntyre, D 341
McKelvey, F 491
McKenna, K 220
MacKenzie, D 220
McLelland, M 117
McLuhan, Marshall 218
McNeal, R 387, 429
McNeally, Scott 487
magazines, and adapting to the Web 39
Magnavox Odyssey 197
mailto 50, 51
Makutano Junction (tv series) 535–6
Malawi 533
Manell, R 366
Manovich, Lev 168
mapping the Web 55
Margetts, H 292, 297, 425, 427
market efficiency, and the Internet 259
market failure, and industrial policy 510
marketing:
    and affiliate marketing 243, 249
    and exploitation of personal
        information 79–80
    and online performance marketing 248
    and pay-per-action advertising 249
    and pay-per-click advertising 248–9
    see also advertising; business models and
        strategy, and impact of the Internet
Marshall, Lee 470
Martin, James 331
Marvin, S 95
Marwick, A 168
Marx, Karl 63
massively multi-player online games
        (MMOs) 199, 201–2
    and number of players 204–5
    and *World of Warcraft* 199, 202
    see also video games
mass participation:
    and tagging of web content 74–5

and wisdom of crowds 74
materialism, and infrastructure
        studies 99–102
Mauss, Marcel 220
May, Chris 472, 473, 479
Mayer, R C 267
Mayer-Schonberger, V 496
media attributes, and social science
        research 356
media effects, and social science
        research 357
media events 115–16
    and new media events 116
media use:
    and sociality 361
    and social science research 357–8
Meetup.com 409
Meijer, A 359
Melville, R 296
Mercer, C 536–7
meritocracy 120–1
Mesch, G S 361
metadata, and trusting data 60–1
Metcalfe, Ben 86n1
Metzger, A J 357, 364
Mexico, and Internet use 224
Michigan, University of 12
microblogging:
    and China 227
    and political uses of 62
Microsoft 331
    and Internet Explorer 10, 240
    and Xbox 199, 200
Middle East, and Internet use 225–6
Mikami, S 226
Mill, John Stuart 472
Millennium Development Goals (MDGs) 533
Minitel 35–6
minorities, and digital divide 115
MIT Mailbox 33
Mobile Internet, and Africa 544
mobile phones:
    and diffusion of 118
        countries by income levels **119**
        world regions **119**
    and economic impact of 543
    and educational use of 336–7

and Internet access 45
mobile technology, and Internet
    commerce 258
'modding' 124
modularity, and infrastructure 98
momentum, and infrastructure 98–9
moral panic 470–1
Morozov, Evgeny 62–3, 431
Morpheus 474, 475
Morris, Noel 33
Mosaic browser 10
  and creation of 29, 240
Mossberger, K 430
Motion Picture Association of America
    (MPAA) 467
Motion Picture Experts Group (MPEG) 562
Motlik, S 336–7
Mouzelis, N 218
MP3 242
Mueller, Milton 556, 560
multimedia consumption, and cross-national
    differences 136–7
Murdoch, Rupert 482
music, and Internet business models 242, 251
music industry:
  and decline in recorded music sales 469
  and file-sharing 465
  and increased demand for live
    performance 482
  and recording artists advocacy of
    file-sharing 470
  and royalties system 470
  see also file-sharing; piracy
Myanmar (Burma) 569
  and censorship 453
Myllyahti, M 380
MySpace 151, 154
  and development process 161
  and uses of 164

Napster 242, 258, 469, 474
National Center for Supercomputing
    Applications (University of
    Illinois-Urbana) 29, 240
National Communication Association 355
National Science Foundation (USA) 12n9

and NSFNET 29, 41
national security, and privacy 456–7
National Security Agency
    (NSA, USA) 491
National Telecommunication and
    Information Administration (NTIA,
    USA) 132
Neff, G 101
Negri, A 124
Nelson, Ted 9
neoliberalism, and elimination of traditional
    places 117
Neopets 206
Nepal 568–9
Netflix 251, 258
Net Mums 426
net neutrality 544–5
  and concerns over 44, 458–9
Netscape:
  and JavaScript 240
  and Netscape Navigator 10, 29, 240
network analysis 362
network corporations 481
network effects 246
network labor 123–4
network society 112–13
  and class 120–4
    China 121–2
    immaterial labor 124
    India 122
    information have-less 121
    meritocracy 120–1
    network labor 123–4
    polarization of work 121
  and freedom of expression in 444–6
  as fundamental mode of social
    organization 113
  and multiple network societies 109–10,
    124–5
  and plurality of 124–5
    trend towards 109–10
  and social exclusion 112–13
  and space 116–20
    diffusion of mobile communications
    118, **119**
    distribution of Internet users **117–18**
    spatial formation 119–20

network society (*cont.*)
 spatial transformation 116–17
 and time 113–16
  changed perceptions of 113–14
  collective memory 114–15
  historical rediscovery 115
  sequencing of events 116
  timeless time 114
Newell, J 385
Newman, A L 497–8
New Public Management 289, 295
news consumption, online 384–5, 388
 and audience fragmentation and
  homogenization 385–6
 and limitations of research on 388–90
 and political campaigning 402–3
 and political knowledge and
  participation 386–8
 and relationship with traditional media
  consumption 385
 and traditional and innovative
  practices 378–9
news media, and central role of 378
newspapers:
 and adapting to the Web 39
 and freemium business model 252–3
 and impact of Internet use 224–5
news production, online 379, 388
 and context of 379–80
  advertising revenue 380
  motivation 379
  profitability 379–80
 and innovation processes 380–1
 and journalists:
  challenge of user-generated content 383
  functions of 378
  professional identity 382
  self-perceptions of 383
 and limitations of research on 388–90
 and practices of 381–2
  increased speed 381–2
  news-gathering 381
  organizational integration 382
  workflow practices 381
 and users as co-authors of content 383–4
New York Times 253
New Zealand, and Internet use 223

Nguyen, A 379
niche sites 72
 and the long tail 73
 and viability of 73–4
Nieborg, D 359
Nielsen, and online dating 176
Nintendo Corporation 196, 198, 203
 and GameCube 200
 and Wii console 199, 200
Nisbet, M C 387
non-profit organizations, and development of
  online services 34
Nooteboom, B 267
Norris, Pippa 404, 407, 411, 430
Norway, and online learning 340
NSFNET 29, 41

Obama, Barack 56, 410–11, 412
Office of Emergency Preparedness 32
Ogburn, W F 98
Ogilvy and Mather (advertising agency) 36
online dating 173
 and age difference tolerance of users 178
 and characteristics of users of 176, **177**, 178
  in existing relationship 176–8
 and emergence of 174–5
 and format of sites 180
 and future research on 188–9
 and gender 176, 178–9, 179–80, 184
 and growth of 175, 187
 and growth of single population 174
 and market changes:
  free sites 187–8
  market fragmentation 188
  media companies 188
 and motivations of users of 178–9
 and online alternatives to 184–7
  deception 186
  relationship formation 185
  self-presentation 185–6
 and prevalence of 175
  corporate evidence 175
  online measurement 176
  self-report evidence 175–6
 and risks of 174–5
 and satisfaction with services 179–80

and self-disclosure 181–4
  deception 183–4
  differences from other online
    settings 181–2
  means of 181
  new identities 183
  use of emotional words 183
  warrants 183–4
and social acceptance of 176, 188
and social network sites 185–7
and success of 180
  establishment of relationships 181
  geographical proximity 180, 182
online services, and development of 45
  AOL (America Online) 37
  Bulletin Board Systems (BBS) 34
  CompuServe 36
  computer conferencing 32–3
  context for (1970s-80s) 30–1
  electronic banking 33–4
  email 33
  and fears over impact of 42
  government policies 31
  Internet and World Wide Web 28–9
  lessons from earlier online activities
    38–40
  Minitel 35–6
  non-profit organizations 34
  online databases 32
  Prestel 35
  Prodigy 37
  stand-alone services 31–4
  telephone companies 30–1, 41
  and user experiences 39–40
  videotex 31, 34–7
  Viewtron 36–7
Open Educational Resources (OER) 337, 545
Open Government Licence 62
openness, and the Web 44, 71
OpenNet Initiative 449, 452–3
open platforms, and videotex 43–4
open standards 562–3
Open University 333–4
O'Reilly, Tim 161
Organization for Asia-Pacific Economic
    Cooperation 497

Organization for Economic Cooperation
    and Development (OECD)
    497, 513
Orwell, George 291, 489
Oxford Internet Institute 12, 13
Oxford Internet Survey 271–2, 293, 427, 430

packet-switching 28
Palfrey, J 496
Palmlund, I 288
Papert, Seymour 12, 339
Paris Treaty (1883) 473
Parks, L 102
participation:
  and democracy 429–30
  and interest groups 426
  and social science research 358–60
    civic engagement 358–9
    participatory media/users 359
    political participation 359
    public sphere 359–60
Parton, N 298
patents, and copyright's advantages over 471
Patry, William 465
Paulussen, S 383
Pavlou, D 274
pay-per-action advertising 249
pay-per-click advertising 248–9
performance marketing 248
  and pay-per-action advertising 249
  and pay-per-click advertising 248–9
permanence of content 75
personal information:
  and commercial exploitation of 79–80
  and maintaining control over 493
  and motivations for revealing 495
  and permanence of content 75
  and protection on 486
  and risks of disclosure 493–4
    collective harms 496
    individual harms 494–6
  and surrendered for benefits 489
  and willingness to provide 495
  see also data protection
personally identifiable information
    (PII) 498–9

personal relationships:
  and computer-mediated
      communication 185–6
  and impact of online activities 140, 155–6
  and information about previous
      relationships on the Web 75
  and permanence of Web content 75
  see also online dating; social network sites
      (SNSs)
Pew Internet and American Life Project
      218–19, 343
Pew Research Center 404
pharmaceutical industry, and intellectual
      property rights 471
Phillips, D 101
physics, and e-research:
  GridPP 309
  Large Hadron Collider 308–9
Pickering, J 332n2
piracy:
  and anti-piracy commercial 465
      parodies of 466
  and attempts to equate file-sharing
      with 467, 468–9, 483
  and attempts to link with terrorism 467–8
  as commercial infringement 468
  and distinction from bootlegging 468
  and distinction from file-sharing 468
  as identity theft 466
  and legal definition of 468
  and moral panic 470–1
  and The Pirate Bay 469–70
  and positive connotations of term 470
  and term embraced by file-sharers
      469, 470
  and video games 201
  see also file-sharing; intellectual property
      rights
The Pirate Bay 469–70
pluralism, and the Internet 423, 432
policy research, and Internet Studies 6
political behavior, and the Internet:
  and deliberation 428–9
  and participation 429–30
  and political information:
    acquisition of 427–8
    dissemination of 428

and voter turnout 429
  see also civic engagement; participation
political campaigning and the Internet
      401–2
  and adaptation by political
      organizations 406–7
  and caution of political organizations 414
  and collective identity formation 403
  and communication 403–4
  and co-ordination of actions 403
  and debate and discussion 404
  and evolution of campaigning 407–8
  and future research on 415–16
  and hypermedia campaign 408–9
  and ideology 413
  and incentives for 413
  and information elite 409
  and information provision 402–3
  and interplay of online/offline
      environments 415
  and landmark campaigns:
    Barack Obama 410–11, 412
    Howard Dean 409
    Segolene Royal 410
  and methodological approaches to
      studying 404–6
    content analysis 405
    discourse analysis 405
    web sphere analysis 405–6
  and mobilization 403–4
  and national variations 402
  and network effects 408–9
  and political participation 411–12
    limited impact on 413–14
  and professionalization of
      campaigning 407
  and resources 413
  and targeting voters 408
    thin democracy 408
political knowledge, and online news
      consumption 386–7
political participation:
  and digital inequality 139–41
  and the Internet 411–12, 421
  and online news consumption 387–8
  and social science research 359
political parties, and the Internet 424–5

see also political campaigning and the
    Internet
politics, and Web Science 61–3
Pong (game) 197
pornography 358
positivism 539
Poster, Mark 466
post-industrialism:
    and ethnocentrism of concept 111–12
    and information society 110–11
    and internal contradictions 124
    and nature of 111
Post Office (UK), and videotex 34–5
poverty reduction, and development
    533, 534
power law, and link popularity 73
Prasad, A 475
preferential attachment, and link
    popularity 72
Prensky, M 222
Prestel 31, 33, 35
    and common carrier policy 43–4
pricing:
    and online services 39
    and subscription revenue 39
Prior, M 386
privacy:
    and commercial surveillance 75–6
    and data retention 498
    and e-government 291
    and governance of 486
    and inadequacy of concept 488
    and national security 456–7
    and permanence of content 75
    and prominence of issue 486–7
    and protection of 497
      legal instruments 498–9
      self-regulation 499–500
      technological instruments 500–1
      transnational instruments 497–8
    and risks of disclosure of
      information 493–4
      collective harms 496
      individual harms 494–6
    and significance of 487
    and social network sites 167
    and social science research 364

and technology 487
see also data protection; surveillance
Privacy Enhancing Technologies
    (PETs) 500–1
Problematic Internet Use (PIU) 189, 358
Prodigy 39
Prodigy videotex service 37
profiles, and social network sites 153–5, 164
    co-construction of 154
    dynamic nature of 155
    self-presentation 185–6
    updating 154–5
protocols:
    and internet protocol design 562–3
    and Web architecture 50
public administration, and
    e-government 295–6
public opinion, and using blogs to
    research 80
public policy:
    and accountability 519
    and broadband infrastructure
      development 511
    and difficulty in foreseeing outcomes 520
    and e-government 297–8
    and infrastructure development
      509–11
    and network infrastructure policies 511–13
    and promotion of broadband 513–17
      assessment of outcomes 523–4
      categories of policy 518
      demand considerations 522–3
      difficulty in foreseeing policy
        outcomes 520
      economic assessments of 520–2
      European Union 513–15
      evidence for policy 519–20, 523
      justification of 517–18, 524
      policy accountability 519
      South Korea 517
      United Kingdom 515
      United States 515–16
public sphere:
    and the Internet 404, 423, 433
      limited revitalization by 413–14
    and social science research 359–60

publishing industry, and apprehension over
        development of online services 31
Putnam, R D 204
Pynchon, Thomas 316
Pynchon Wiki 316

Qiu, J L 112
QQ 121–2, 226–7, 545
QWERTY keyboard 97

racial formation theory 361
Rainie, Lee 15
Ramirez, A 366
Razorfish 241
Recording Industry Association of
        America 466
Reddit 160
Reding, Viviane 443
referenda 424
reflective practice:
    and engineering 53
    and Web Science 53–4
Regional Internet Registries (RIRs) 557, 560
regulation of the Internet:
    and child protection 457–8
    and international patterns of Internet
        freedom 452–4
    and net neutrality 458–9
    and privacy vs national security 456–7
    see also Internet governance
Reidenberg, J 497
Reisdorf, B 222
relational management, and social science
        research 361
republicanism, and the Internet 423, 433
research, and impact of computerization 307
    see also communication and the Internet,
        social science research on; e-research
Research in Motion (RIM) 456–7
Resource Description Framework (RDF) 57
Rheingold, Howard 11, 163, 404
Rice, R E 366
Riley, J G 270
risk:
    and cyber-surveillance 493–4

collective harms 496
    individual harms 494–6
    and trust 267
Rohozinski, R 491
Rosenstiel, T 382
Royal, Segolene 410
Ruggiero, T E 366
Russia, and censorship 452

Sachs, Jeffrey 534
Safe Harbor 499
Salesforce.com 251, 252, 258
Sapient 241
Sarkozy, Nicolas 409–10
Sassen, Saskia 122
Sawhney, H 95
Sawyer, Ben 207
Scheb, J M 357
Scheufele, D A 387
Schneider, S M 404, 406
Schoenbach, K 380
scholarship, see e-research
Scholl, H 284
Schön, D A 54
schools, and online learning 339–41
Schudson, M 383
Schumpeter, Joseph 196
Schwartz, Paul 496
science, and styles of 317–18
    e-research 318–20
science and technology studies 92
scientometrics 77
Scolari, C A 364
Seaman, J 333
search engines:
    and Internet governance 564–5
    and surveillance 492–3
search results:
    and dominance of well-known sites 71, 72
    and link popularity 72, 73, 77
    and personalization of results 71
    and rich-get-richer effect 72
securitization, and surveillance 489
security, and Internet governance 565–6
Sega Dreamcast 200
self-presentation:

and computer-mediated settings 185–6
and online dating sites 181–4
and social network site profiles 153–5, 159,
        164, 185–6
self-regulation, and privacy
        protection 499–500
Sell, Susan 472
Selwyn, N 334, 345
Semantic Web 49
    and Berners-Lee 56
    see also Linked Data Web
Sen, A 534–5, 546
Serious Game Initiative 207
Setanta 480
Seymour-Ure, Colin 406
Shah, Dhavan V 140, 387
Sharia, and the Web 86, 87, 99
Shepherd, A 272, 276
Shrum, Wesley 11, 15
Silcock, R 284
Silver, D 90
Simmons, J L 496
Simon, L 426
Simpson, S 363
Singapore, and Internet use 226
Singer, J B 383
Smith, A 411
SMTP (Simple Mail Transfer Protocol):
    and development of 53
    and unintended consequences of 54
Snyder, David Pearce 233
social capital, and Internet use 139–41, 362
social exclusion:
    and digital inequality 223
    and network society 112–13
    see also digital divide
social graph, and 'Friends' list 156–7
social identity of deindividuation effects
        (SIDE) theory 185, 360
social inequality 130
    and Internet use 141–2
    see also digital divide
social informatics 14
social information processing theory 185
social media:
    and rise of 151
    and significance of 160

social mobility, and Internet use 130
social network sites (SNSs) 69, 169, 546
    as alternative to online dating sites 185–7
    and business model 243
    and challenge in studying 152
    and China 121–2
    and civic engagement 140
    as communication platform 159
    and computer-mediated
        communication 160, 163–4
    and conceptualizing community 164
    and definition of 151, 158–9, 200
        difficulties with 152
    as friendship-driven spaces 161
    and 'Friends' list 154, 155–7
        context collapse 156
        distinguishing types of
            relationships 155–6
        management of 156
        purposes 155
        social graph 156–7
        uni-directional relationships 156
    and geo-linguistic regions 119–20
    and media-centric sites 154, 159
    and media sharing 159
    and online communities 161
    and permanence of content 75
    and personal information, possible
        harms 494
    as platform 157
    and political activism 426–7, 546
    and popularity of 79, 343
    and primary driver of use of 159
    and primary features of 152
    and privacy practices 167
    and profile-centric sites 154
    and profiles 153–5, 164
        co-construction of 154
        dynamic nature of 155
        self-presentation 185–6
        updating 154–5
    and research challenges 165
        documenting socio-technical
            changes 165–7
        large datasets 167–9
        rapid innovation 165
    and rise of 151

social network sites (SNSs) (*cont.*)
  and social connectivity 140
  and traversing connections 157–8
  and uses of 163–4
  and video games 200
  and Web 2.0 160–2
social norms, and the Web 52
social presence theory 269–70
social relations, and social science
      research 360–2
  community 360
  groups 360
  identity 360–1
  media use and sociality 361
  relational management 361
  social capital 362
  social networks 362
social science research 70, 76, 219
  and link structure 76–8
  and Web 2.0 investigations 78–80, 81
  see also communication and the Internet,
      social science research on
social stratification, and Internet use 130
society, and the Internet 219–20
socioeconomic status:
  and access to resources 142
  and digital inequality 131, 135–6, 223
  and knowledge gaps 131–2
Software as a Service (SaaS), *see* cloud
      computing
Soghoian, C 492
Solove, D J 496
Solow, Robert 292n1
Sony 474–5
Sony PlayStation 198, 199–200
The Source 36, 38, 39
Sousa, H 382
Souter, D 542, 548
South Korea 42
  and online learning 333
  and promotion of broadband 517
space, and network society 116–20
  diffusion of mobile communications
      118, **119**
  distribution of Internet users **117–18**
  spatial formation 119–20
  spatial transformation 116–17

Spacewar! (game) 197
Spain, and Internet use 224
special interests, and viability of niche
      sites 73–4
Sprint Telemail 33
Sproull, Lee 12
standardization, and infrastructure 98
Standardization Administration of China
      (SAC) 562
Stanford Research Institute 9
Star, S L 90, 93, 97, 98, 100, 102
Starosielski, N 101
Sterne, J 101
Stohl, C 366
Stromer-Galley, J 414
Structure of Populations, Levels of
      Abundance and Status of Humpbacks
      (SPLASH) project 315
subscription revenue 39, 250–1
Sudulich, M L 413
Suman, M 225
Sun Microsystems 240
Sunnafrank, M 366
Sunstein, C 423
surveillance:
  and advertising 491
  and biometric database 547
  and data retention 498
  and deepening concern over 488
  and deep packet inspection 569–70
  and definition of 488
  and democratic consequences of 496
  and e-government 291
  and encryption 478
  and file-sharing 478, 479
  and Flash cookies 493
  and freedom of expression 496
  and global nature of 489
  and individuality 501–2
  and Internet as medium of 487, 489–90
  and Internet infrastructure 490–2
    advertisers 491
    censorship 491
    filtering of content 491
    government surveillance 490–1
    Internet Service Providers (ISPs) 490,
      491, 492

and mass surveillance 501
and nature of 488–9
and privacy protection 497
  legal instruments 498–9
  self-regulation 499–500
  technological instruments 500–1
  transnational instruments 497–8
and risks of 493–4
  collective harms 496
  individual harms 494–6
and search companies 492–3
and securitization 489
and social control 501
and trust 495
see also data protection; privacy
Suu Kyi, Auung San 453
Sweden:
  and data protection 313
  and e-research 313
  and Internet access 221
Swedish National Data Service (SND) 313
SwissBioGrid 314
Swiss Institute of Bioinformatics 314
Swiss National Grid Association (SwiNG) 314
Swiss National Supercomputing Centre 314
Syracuse University 12
systems analysis 91–2

tagging of web content 74–5
Tan, H P 358
Tanzania 536–7
technical change, and social network
  sites 165–7
technology:
  and consequences of 477
  and development 538–40
  and Internet Studies 3–4
  and privacy 487
Teledisc 41
Telenet 32
Telenor Group 542
telephone companies, and development of
  online services 30–1, 41
television:
  and development 535–6
  and impact of Internet use 224–5

and political campaigning 407
Telidon videotex system 36
terrorism, and attempts to link piracy
  with 467–8
Tewksbury, D 386
Text Encoding Initiative 60
38 Degrees (pressure group) 426
Thomas, J 222–3
Thurman, N 380
Tichenor, P J 131
time, and network society 113–16
  changed perceptions of 113–14
  collective memory 114–15
  historical rediscovery 115
  sequencing of events 116
  timeless time 114
TinyURL.com 87
Tolbert, C 387, 429
torrent services 469, 475
Touraine, A 111
trademarks 471
  and domain names 561
Trade-Related Aspects of Intellectual
  Property Rights (TRIPS) 468, 473
Transmission Control Protocol/Internet
  Protocol (TCP/IP) 9n8
  and development of 28
transparency, and e-government 295–6
Trippi, Joe 401
trust:
  and antecedents of 265–6
    ability 266
    benevolence 266
    integrity 266
  and attitudinal perspective
    on 264
  and categories of 265
  and computer-mediated
    communication 269–70
  and cultural influences 273–5
  and definition of 264–5
  and e-commerce 257, 262–3, 269–71
    cultural influences 273–5
    future research on 275–6
    gender 272–3, 276
    online experience 271–2
    uncertainty 270–1

trust: (cont.)
  and e-research 313
  and exchange 268–9
  and future research on 275–6
  and gender 272–3, 276
  and importance of 264
  and institutional trust production
      mechanisms 267–8
  and Linked Data Web 58–9
  and online trust 59–60
  and perceived risk 267
  and predictability view of 264
  and propensity to trust 266–7
  and research on 263
  and social science research 356–7
  and surveillance 495
  and trusting data 60–1
  and voluntarist view of 264–5
Tunisia 431, 546
  and censorship 452
Turkle, Sherry 11–12, 163
Turner, F 100
Turoff, Murray 12
Twitter 10, 156
  and success of 41–2
Tymnet 32

ubiquitous computing 82
Umesao, T 109
UNCTAD 542
UNESCO 328, 336
  and Delors Report (1996) 330
  and freedom of expression 443
  and McBride report 446, 448
Uniform Resource Identifiers (URIs):
  and changing 52
  and dereferencing 50, 61–2
  and Web architecture 50–1
unintended consequences of innovations 54,
    55–6
United Arab Emirates 225–6
United Kingdom:
  and development of online services 31
    videotex 34–5
  and Digital Britain (2009) 515
  and government surveillance 491

  and Internet use 222, 223
  and online learning 333–4
  and open government data 61–2
  and promotion of broadband 515
  and Vision for the Future of ICT in
      Schools 339
United Nations:
  and e-government 284, 286, 287
  and Universal Declaration of Human
      Rights (1948) 442
  and World Summit on the Information
      Society (WSIS, 2003) 123, 444–5,
      540–1, 557
United States:
  and development of online services 30–1
      videotex 36
  and dominance over the Internet 541, 545
  and financial support of the Internet 42–3
  and freedom of expression 443
  and government surveillance 490–1
  and intellectual property rights 472,
      473, 474
  and National Information
      Infrastructure 515
  and online learning 333
  and open government data 61
  and promotion of broadband 515–16
United States Constitution, and First
      Amendment 443
urbanism, and infrastructure studies 95
URL shortening services 87–9
US Defense Department 28, 539
Usenets 29
use of the Internet, and Internet Studies 4–5
  in everyday life 5
  media use 6
  in work and organizations 5–6
user-created content (UCC), and collective
      memory 114–15
Uses and Gratifications (U and G)
      approach 358
Ushahidi 545

Valenti, Jack 467
Vallee, Jacques 12
ValueClick 243

van Arkel, Hanny 311
Vanderbilt, T 90
Van Dijck, J 359
van Dijk, Jan A G M 131
Vanhanen, T 432
Van Reenen, J 521
Van Vleck, Tom 33
vb.ly (URL shortening service) 87
Vergeer, M 381
Verizon 545
video games 195, 209
  and casual games 203–5
    development costs 203
    number of players 205
  and children and young people 205
    Club Penguin 206
    genres of game play 205–6
    Neopets 206
    Whyville 206
  and development costs 203
  and education 206, 207
  and games consoles 199–200
    integrated Internet access 200
    number in the home **199**
  and history of:
    modern gaming (2004–) 198–201
    origins (1951–2003) 196–8
  and massively multi-player online games
      (MMO) 199, 201–2
    number of players 204–5
    World of Warcraft 199, 202
  and multi-user dungeons (MUDs) 201
  and networked gaming 200, 201
  and non-interoperability of systems 196
  and piracy 201
  and players of:
    adult audience for 203–4
    age 198
    characteristics of 202, 203
    gender 198
  and profitability of industry 195–6
  and research on 209
  and sales of 200–1
  and serious games 207–9
    America's Army 207–8
    classification of 207
    Darfur is Dying 208
  effectiveness of 208
  and social network sites 200
  and violence 205
  and virtual goods 254–5
  and virtual worlds 201–2
    Club Penguin 206
    Neopets 206
    Whyville 206
videotex:
  and attractiveness of 31
  and development of 31, 34–7
    AOL (America Online) 37
    CompuServe 36
    Minitel 35–6
    Prestel 35
    Prodigy 37
    Viewtron 36–7
  and lessons learned from 38–40
  and open systems 43–4
  and shortcomings of 40, 43
  and user context 44
Vietnam, and censorship 453
Viewdata 35
Viewtron 36
Vincents, Okechukwu Benjamin 475
violence, and video games 205
virtual communities:
  and development of 163
  and first generation of 162–3
  and social network sites 163–4
virtual goods 254–5
Virtual Observatory for the Study of Online
      Networks (VOSON) 315–16
virtual proxy networks/servers (VPNSs) 481
virtual worlds, and video games 201–2
  Club Penguin 206
  Neopets 206
  Whyville 206
Voice over Internet Protocol (VoIP) 542

Waage, J 539
Wade, K 431
Wagemann, C 362
wages, and digital inequality 139
Waipeng, L 359
Wajcman, J 220

Wallace, David Foster 316–17
Wall Street Journal 252–3
Walters, T 225–6
Walther, J B 366
Wannamaker, John 248
Ward, S 405, 425
warrants, and self-disclosure 183–4, 186
Waskul, D D 366
Weaver, D 365, 369, 429
Web 2.0 160–2
    and appeal to business 161
    and cultural shifts entailed by 161
    and e-government 289, 298–9
    as industry-driven phenomenon 161
    and interaction 79
    and meaning of 78
    and perpetual beta development 161
    and procedural basis of 161
    and public opinion research 80
    and significance of 160
    and social science research 78–80, 81
    and technical basis of 161
web addresses:
    and country codes 87–8
    and redundant prefixes 99
    and URL shortening services 87–9
Web of Science for Social Sciences 353–5, 421
webometrics, and hyperlink analysis 76–7
Web Science 14, 49
    and aim of 64
    and challenge for 63–4
    and dynamics of the Web 54–5
    and government 61–2
    and Linked Data Web 56–7
        how it works 57–8
        metadata 60–1
        open government data 61–2
        trust 58–9
        trusting data 60–1
        value of Linked Data 58
    and political effects of the Web 61–3
    as reflective practice 53–4
web sphere analysis, and political
        campaigning on the Internet 405–6
Webster, Frank 111
Weigert, A 273
Weiser, Phil 562–3

Weitzner, Daniel 499
Weizenbaum, Joseph 12
Wellman, Barry 11, 15, 218–19
West, D M 286, 292
Western Union Easy Link 33
Westin, A F 11
whales, and e-research 315
White, C 357
Whitty, M 182–3
Whyville 206
Wikipedia 72, 426
Williams, A 384
Williams, Raymond 101
Wilson, T 358
Winner, L 94, 570
Woodley, A 335
Wordsworth, William 472–3
working-class 120, 121, 122, 123
World Intellectual Property Organization
        (WIPO) 473–4
World Internet Project (WIP) 5, 15, 216, 447
    and differentiated Internet uses 136
    and diffusion of the Internet 222
    and future research 232–3
    and Internet usages patterns 221–2
        Australia 222–3
        Canada 224
        China 226–8
        Japan 226
        Mexico 224
        Middle East 225–6
        New Zealand 223
        Singapore 226
        Spain 224
        traditional media consumption 224–5
    and methodological challenges of
        cross-national studies 228–32
    and multiple levels of analysis 217–18
    and non-users of the Internet 228
    and origins of 216–17
    and pragmatic approach of 217
    and rationale of 217
World of Warcraft 199, 202
World Summit on Information Society
        (WSIS) 123, 444–5, 540–1, 557
World Trade Organization (WTO), and
        intellectual property rights 473–4

World Wide Web:
  and application development 54–5
  and architecture of 50–1
    error handling 51
    formats 50
    information resources 50
    protocols 50
    Uniform Resource Identifiers
      (URIs) 50–1
  and computer science research 49
  and creation of 9, 28–9
  as decentralized structure 51–2
  and development of 49
  and distinction from the Internet 50
  and interaction 51
  and lessons learned from earlier online
    activities 38–40
  and linking 51
  and mapping of 55
  and multidisciplinary approach to 48–9
  and openness of 44, 71
  and origins of 28–9
  see also online services, and development of
  and permanence of content 75
  and political effects of 61–3
  and social norms 52
  and social science 70, 76
  and transformative nature of 48
  and under-theorized nature of 48, 63
  and unintended consequences of
    innovations 54, 55–6
  see also Internet; Semantic Web
World Wide Web Consortium (WC3) 71,
  240, 562

Xanadu project 9
Xanga 157–8
XML (Extensible Markup Language) 240

Yahoo! 569
Yao Chen 227
young people:
  and informal learning on Internet 342–4
  and Internet use 135
  and political mobilization 412
  and video games 205–6
Youngs, G 367
YouTube 154

Zhao, S 366
Zillow.com 253
Zimic, Sheila 222
Zimmer, M 492
Zittrain, Jonathan 4, 42, 491
Zook, Matthew 118–19
Zooniverse 311
Zouridis, S 290
Zuckerberg, Mark 56, 243
Zynga 205

Printed and bound by CPI Group (UK) Ltd, Croydon, CR0 4YY